Cooking
Season by Season
1000 recipes to cook through the year

Cooking
Season by Season
1000 recipes to cook through the year

LONDON • NEW YORK
MELBOURNE • MUNICH • DELHI

Consultant Carolyn Humphries
Editors Emma Callery, Susannah Steel

DK UK AND US
Project Editor Shashwati Tia Sarkar
Senior Art Editor Sara Robin
US Consultant Kate Curnes Ramos
US Senior Editor Rebecca Warren
US Editors Christy Lusiak, Margaret Parrish
Editorial Assistant Christopher Mooney
Design Assistant Jade Wheaton
Managing Editor Dawn Henderson
Managing Art Editor Christine Keilty
Senior Jackets Creative Nicola Powling
Jackets Assistant Rosie Levine
Senior Production Editor Tony Phipps
Senior Production Controller Jen Lockwood
Creative Technical Support Sonia Charbonnier

DK INDIA
Senior Editor Chitra Subramanyam
Senior Art Editor Anchal Kaushal
Editors Ligi John, Janashree Singha
Art Editors Simran Kaur, Divya PR
Assistant Editor Priyanka Chatterjee
Assistant Art Editor Tanya Mehrotra
Managing Editor Glenda Fernandes
Managing Art Editor Navidita Thapa
DTP Designer Satish Chandra Gaur
CTS Manager Sunil Sharma
Picture Researcher Sumedha Chopra

First American Edition, 2012

Published in the United States by DK Publishing,
375 Hudson Street, New York, New York 10014

12 13 14 15   10 9 8 7 6 5 4 3 2 1

001—183117—Sept/2012

Published in Great Britain by Dorling Kindersley Limited.

A catalog record for this book is available
from the Library of Congress.

ISBN 978-0-7566-9819-5

DK books are available at special discounts when purchased in
bulk for sales promotions, premiums, fund-raising, or educational
use. For details, contact: DK Publishing Special Markets,
375 Hudson Street, New York, New York 10014
or SpecialSales@dk.com.

Color reproduction by Opus Multimedia Services, India

Printed and bound in China by Hung Hing

Discover more at
www.dk.com

contents

All-year **vegetables and fruit**

When thinking of seasonal foods, vegetables and fruit such as asparagus and strawberries are usually the first that come to mind. However, in addition to seasonal produce, there are some ingredients that are available all year and can be freely used. Some of these are best at certain times of year, but their availability does not wane. They include exotic ingredients, which can add color and interest to seasonal dishes.

vegetables cabbage (different varieties in their season) ▪ carrots ▪ cauliflower ▪ garlic ▪ lettuce (different varieties in their season) ▪ mushrooms (cultivated) ▪ onions ▪ parsnips ▪ potatoes ▪ spinach ▪ turnips ▪ watercress

fruit banana (imported) ▪ lemon ▪ lime ▪ mango (imported) ▪ papaya (imported) ▪ passion fruit (imported) ▪ pineapple (imported)

Lemons Extremely popular for flavoring, lemons can be found at all times of year, but are best in winter if you plan to use them as a star ingredient.

Mushrooms Due to their popularity, many mushroom varieties are cultivated throughout the year and their flavor is reliably consistent.

Passion fruit Grown in warm climates globally, exotic fruits such as passion fruit appear in stores all year and taste great combined with home-grown fruits.

Bananas The banana plant produces crops all year, making it a staple ingredient in many warmer countries and a ubiquitious imported ingredient.

Turnips Young turnips are available in spring but they grow throughout the year, peaking from fall to late winter.

Carrots Slender young carrots are superb in spring and early summer, but mature carrots are invaluable for hearty fall and winter dishes.

Cauliflower This vegetable is good at all times of year, making it useful for spring and winter, which are leaner months for produce.

Onion A kitchen essential, onions are never in short supply. In winter, when other vegetables are scarce, they can take a starring role in pastry and casserole dishes.

Potatoes Summer new potatoes are delicious, but the fully grown ones are stored throughout winter, making them useful all-year vegetables.

All-year **meat, poultry, and game**

Most meats are farmed and not affected by seasonal cycles. Lamb is now one of the only farmed animals whose meat can be considered seasonal: best-quality lamb is found in spring, early summer, and fall. Venison, too, is traditionally best in fall and winter, although it is farmed all year. Turkeys are often bred for the festive season, making them abundant in winter. For the best flavor and constant variety, cook meat with seasonal vegetables.

ingredients beef ▪ chicken ▪ cornish game hen ▪ duck ▪ lamb ▪ pork ▪ quail ▪ rabbit ▪ turkey ▪ veal ▪ venison ▪ wild boar

Beef roasts Hearty beef often works well with cold weather vegetables. Roasts are excellent in combination with seasonal squashes and roots.

Veal The delicate flavor of veal chops (above) or cubed (below) is excellent in spring and summer with spinach, sorrel, and herbs, although Osso Buco, using veal shanks, is a classic winter dish.

Beef steak Cuts that need light, quick cooking are best with a side of seasonal vegetables. Try them in summer with new potatoes, new carrots, beans, or peas.

Cubed veal

Chicken This universally farmed bird is justifiably popular as it works with all kinds of flavors in all seasons.

Pork The best flavor pairings for pork include pineapple, plums, eggplants, and tomatoes in spring and summer, and apples, cabbage, and leeks in fall and winter.

Cubed lamb

Lamb Whether you are cooking cubed lamb (above) or chops (below), lamb works beautifully with summer and fall produce such as beans, artichokes, and fruits.

Duck Although wild duck is found only in fall and winter, farmed birds are available all year. It is great teamed with fall and winter fare such as apples, turnips, and oranges.

All-year **fish and shellfish**

Fish and shellfish that are caught wild are subject to seasonal fluctuations in availability and, due to sustainability issues, there are sometimes fishing quotas imposed on them as well. However, many of the most popular fish and shellfish are now farmed and therefore easily obtainable all year round. Whether you choose wild fish or farmed fish, be sure that they come from sources that are both sustainable and environmentally sound.

ingredients halibut ▪ herring ▪ monkfish ▪ mussels ▪ Pacific or rock oysters ▪ salmon ▪ king scallops ▪ sea bass ▪ black rockfish ▪ brown trout ▪ rainbow trout ▪ sea trout ▪ turbot

Mussels Rope-grown mussels are an excellent sustainable seafood. Farming them in this way means that the traditional avoidance of the summer spawning season doesn't apply.

Scallops Farmed scallops are available all year, but are at their sweetest and best in the spring and summer months.

Salmon A popular fish worldwide, most Atlantic salmon now comes from fisheries. Farmed salmon can be of excellent quality and flavor, with a good balance of oil.

Halibut With its meaty, white flesh, farmed Atlantic halibut is a good fish to steam, pan-fry, grill, poach, and bake, making it suitable for use in all seasons.

▲ **Trout** Farmed trout, such as rainbow trout, are often bigger and have paler flesh than wild trout. The various wild species are best in spring and summer.

spring

at their best

vegetables broccoli rabe ▪ chicory ▪ green garlic ▪ nettles ▪ new carrots ▪ new potatoes ▪ pea shoots ▪ radishes ▪ sorrel ▪ spinach ▪ spring greens ▪ spring onions ▪ turnips ▪ watercress ▪ wild morel mushrooms ▪ wild garlic

fruit grapefruit ▪ hot house rhubarb ▪ limes ▪ meyer lemons ▪ oranges ▪ outdoor rhubarb ▪ pineapple

seafood clams ▪ cod ▪ crab (Dungeness, King, and blue) ▪ Dover sole ▪ Pacific Bay shrimp ▪ flounder ▪ haddock ▪ halibut ▪ oysters ▪ rainbow trout ▪ sea bass ▪ sea scallops ▪ shad ▪ striper ▪ wild King salmon

meat, poultry, game baby lamb ▪ Cornish game hens ▪ quail

also available

fruit apples ▪ pears **vegetables** asparagus ▪ broccoli ▪ cauliflower ▪ celery root ▪ Hass avocados ▪ kale ▪ leeks ▪ lettuce ▪ mushrooms (cultivated) ▪ onions ▪ potatoes (maincrop) ▪ rutabaga **seafood** blue shark ▪ farmed trout ▪ ling cod ▪ ocean perch ▪ rockfish ▪ snapper **meat, poultry, game** beef ▪ chicken ▪ duck (farmed) ▪ pork ▪ rabbit (farmed) ▪ turkey ▪ veal ▪ venison (farmed) ▪ wild boar (farmed)

spring recipe planner

ⓥ suitable for vegetarians

Vietnamese spring rolls p17

Pavlova with tropical fruit p62

Flemish vegetable tart p57

Marinated goat cheese salad p25

Spring rice salad p60

Rhubarb and ginger upside-down cake p65

Vegetables

Asparagus
Spring rice salad p60

Avocado
Avocado and spinach soup p16 ⓥ
Avocado and sorrel soup p16 ⓥ
Quesadilla with avocado, spring onion, and chile p59 ⓥ
Shrimp, avocado, and watercress sandwich p27
Shrimp and guacamole tortilla stacks p31

Broccoli
Asian chicken and shrimp broth with ginger and cilantro p28
Savory blue cheese and broccoli muffins p19 ⓥ
Spaghetti with chile flakes, broccoli, and spring onion p50 ⓥ

Carrot
Flemish vegetable tart p57 ⓥ
Malaysian chicken noodle and spring vegetable soup p28
Vietnamese spring rolls p17

Chicory
Chicken with chicory and bacon p55
Gratin of chicory and ham p60
Italian wedding soup p52
Marinated goat cheese salad p25 ⓥ
Marmalade-glazed ham with new potatoes and chicory p54
Turbot with cheese, ham, and chicory p55

Morel mushrooms
Morel and crimini mushroom barley p38 ⓥ

Nettles
Nettle and blue cheese frittata p52 ⓥ
Nettle soup p31 ⓥ

Pea shoots
Roasted quail and pea shoot salad p30

Radish
Blinis with smoked salmon p26

Sorrel
Avocado and sorrel soup p16 ⓥ
Sorrel and wild garlic with pine nuts and olives p61 ⓥ

Spinach
Avocado and spinach soup p16 ⓥ
Calzone with cheese, ham, and spinach p51
Cheese gougères and salmon p24
Creamy spinach tart p30 ⓥ
Filo pie with spinach, ricotta cheese, and pine nuts p26 ⓥ
Pizza with spinach and ricotta cheese p58 ⓥ
Sautéed scallops with pancetta and wilted spinach p18
Spinach and coconut shrimp curry p34
Spinach and goat cheese frittata p52 ⓥ
Spinach and goat cheese tart p18
Spinach sauce p61 ⓥ
Spinach-stuffed veal p55
Spinach with pine nuts and raisins p61 ⓥ

Spring greens
Chicken breasts with spring greens and hoisin p52
Italian wedding soup p52
Pork and spring greens p52

Spring onion
Blinis with red and black caviar p26
Cheesy bacon and spring onion muffins p19
Flemish vegetable tart p57 ⓥ
Lamb and potato pie p43
Malaysian chicken soup p28
Pad thai p36
Pork with spring onions, soy sauce, and cinnamon p47
Quesadilla with avocado, spring onion, and chile p59
Singapore noodles with shrimp and pork p36
Spaghetti with chile flakes, broccoli, and spring onion p50 ⓥ
Veggie pad thai p59 ⓥ
Vietnamese spring rolls p17

Turnip
Flemish vegetable tart p57 ⓥ
Lamb and potato pie p43
Malaysian chicken noodle and spring vegetable soup p28
Roast rack of lamb with harissa and baby turnips p46

Watercress
Shrimp, avocado, and watercress sandwich p27
Spicy watercress soup p16 ⓥ

Wild garlic
Sorrel and wild garlic with pine nuts and olives p61 ⓥ
Warm quail and pea shoot salad p30

Fruit

Kiwi
Asian fruit salad p64 ⓥ
Pavlova with tropical fruit p62 ⓥ

Mango
Asian fruit salad p64 ⓥ
Pavlova with tropical fruit p62 ⓥ
Tropical angel cake p65 ⓥ
Tropical trifle p64 ⓥ

Pear
Spicy watercress soup p16 ⓥ

Pineapple
Asian fruit salad p64 ⓥ
Fresh pineapple upside-down cake p62 ⓥ
Jerk chicken with roasted pineapple p56
Pan-fried ham with pineapple salsa p54
Pavlova with tropical fruit p62 ⓥ
Pineapple and kirsch floating islands p62 ⓥ
Pineapple broth with halibut p24
Pineapple broth with shrimp p24
Pineapple trifle p64 ⓥ
Tropical angel cake p65 ⓥ

Rhubarb
Rhubarb and custard ice cream p67 ⓥ
Rhubarb and ginger upside-down cake p65 ⓥ
Rhubarb and orange yogurt fool p67 ⓥ
Rhubarb brûlée flan p67

Seafood

Abalone
Abalone with oyster sauce p24

Clams
Pan-fried clams with chorizo p37
Pan-fried clams with parsley and garlic p37
Pasta with clams p38
Pork and clam cataplana p42
Shellfish soup p31

Crab
Crab and shrimp saffron tart p23
Minced crab balls p22
Pasta with crab and lemon p32
Seafood and tomato cioppino p32

Halibut
Pineapple broth with halibut p24
Seafood and tomato cioppino p32

Mussels
Pasta with mussels and saffron p38
Seafood and tomato cioppino p32
Shellfish soup p31

Oysters
Oysters skewered with pancetta p16

Salmon
Baked salmon p41
Blinis with smoked salmon p26
Cheese gougères and salmon p24

Gravalax p19
Salmon and shrimp fish pie p33
Salmon chowder p40
Salmon fish cakes p27
Salmon kedgeree p40
Spring rice salad p60

Scallops
Sautéed scallops with pancetta and wilted spinach p18
Scallops skewered with parma ham p16
Seafood and tomato cioppino p32
Shellfish soup p31

Shrimp
Asian chicken and shrimp broth with ginger and cilantro p28
Büsumer fish soup p20
Crab and shrimp saffron tart p23
Grilled shrimp with hot pepper sauce p30
Pad thai p36
Pan-fried shrimp with olives p38
Pineapple broth with shrimp p24
Salmon and shrimp fish pie p33
Sesame shrimp toasts p22
Shellfish soup p31
Shrimp and guacamole tortilla stacks p31
Shrimp, avocado, and watercress sandwich p27

Shrimp makhani p37
Shrimp risotto p34
Shrimp saganaki p34
Singapore noodles with shrimp and pork p36
Spinach and coconut shrimp curry p34
Thai fish cakes p23
Thai green curry p33
Vietnamese spring rolls p17

Sole
Lemon sole with herbs p41
Sole fillets in wine vinegar p39
Sole with butter sauce p51

Trout
Baked sea trout with dill p41
Büsumer fish soup p20
Creamy smoked trout soup p20
Instant smoked trout p42
Sautéed trout with hazelnuts p40
Scandinavian-style cured trout p19
Smoked trout and goat cheese bites p28
Smoked trout with chile and lime dressing p20
Trout in rice wine vinegar p39
Trout with herbs, caperberries, and olives p41

Meat

Cornish game hens
Cornish game hens glazed with honey and wrapped in bacon p58
Cornish game hens in vine leaves p56
Cornish game hens with mushrooms p56

Lamb
Flatbreads topped with lamb and hummus p47
Lamb and potato pie p43
Lamb filet basted with anchovy paste p48
Lamb with lemon and olives p50
Rack of lamb with flageolet beans and herbs p46
Rack of lamb with parsley crumb p49
Roast leg of spring lamb p48
Roast rack of lamb with harissa and baby turnips p46
Skewered lamb with crispy rosemary potatoes p43
Turkish-spiced lamb pizza with pine nuts p48

Quail
Roasted quail and pea shoot salad p30

Salmon and shrimp fish pie p33

Lamb filet basted with anchovy paste p48

Shrimp and guacamole tortilla stacks p31

Lemon sole with herbs p41

Flatbreads topped with lamb and hummus p47

Pork and spring greens p52

scallops skewered with parma ham

Fresh, juicy scallops can be served simply. For a meat-free dish, omit the Parma ham and roast for a few minutes less.

 10 MINS 8 MINS FREEZABLE

SPECIAL EQUIPMENT ▪ metal or wooden skewers

SERVES 4

8 scallops, halved

1 tbsp olive oil

juice of 1 lemon

salt and freshly ground black pepper

8 slices of Parma ham, halved

1 If using wooden skewers, soak them in cold water for 30 minutes. Preheat the oven to 375°F (190°C). Mix the scallops with the oil and lemon juice, and season with salt and pepper.

2 Wrap each scallop half in a piece of Parma ham, then thread onto metal or wooden skewers. You'll

probably need 2 scallop halves on each skewer, depending on how big they are.

3 Lay the skewers on a baking sheet, and roast in the oven for 5–8 minutes until the ham starts to crisp. Serve hot with a arugula leaf garnish.

variation

oysters skewered with pancetta

Prepare in the same way but use 16 shucked oysters instead of the scallops. Add a few drops of Tabasco to the oil and lemon juice, and wrap in thin strips of pancetta instead of Parma ham.

avocado and spinach soup

Creamy, slightly nutty avocados and iron-rich spinach blend beautifully for a soup that is great for lunch with some bread.

 15 MINS PLUS CHILLING ❄ FREEZABLE

SPECIAL EQUIPMENT ▪ blender or food processor

SERVES 4

3 large (or 4 medium) avocados

juice of 1 large lemon

5½oz (150g) baby spinach leaves

3 cups cold light chicken or vegetable stock

½ tsp harissa paste

2 tbsp chopped cilantro

salt and freshly ground black pepper

1 Peel the avocados and remove their pits, then chop the flesh and put it in a blender or food processor with the lemon juice. Coarsely chop the spinach and add to the avocados. Pour in the stock. Add the harissa

paste, cilantro, and seasoning, then pulse until smooth. Transfer to a bowl, cover, and chill in the fridge for at least 1 hour.

2 Pour into bowls or glasses, add an ice cube or two to each, and serve.

variation

avocado and sorrel soup

Prepare in the same way but use 2½oz (75g) sorrel and 2½oz (75g) butterhead lettuce leaves instead of spinach, and swap the cilantro for 1 tbsp flat-leaf parsley and 1 tbsp fresh thyme.

spicy watercress soup

Peppery watercress, curry leaf oil, and caramelized pear create a marvelous melange of flavors.

 20 MINS 30 MINS ❄ FREEZABLE

SPECIAL EQUIPMENT ▪ blender or food processor ▪ hand-held blender

SERVES 4–6

3 tbsp curry leaves

⅔ cup olive oil, plus 2 tbsp

1 onion, chopped

2 potatoes, chopped

3½ cups hot vegetable stock

9oz (250g) watercress

2 tbsp crème fraîche

salt and freshly ground black pepper

For the garnish

1 Bosc pear, peeled and finely diced

2 tbsp confectioner's sugar

pinch of coarsely ground black peppercorns

1 tbsp crème fraîche

1 First make the curry leaf oil. Drop the curry leaves into a pan of boiling water and cook for about 30 seconds. Remove and refresh with cold water. Pat dry with paper towels and transfer to a blender or food processor. Warm the ⅔ cup of olive oil and gradually pour into the blender as the leaves are being processed. Pulse to a smooth paste. Line a sieve

with paper towels and pour the curry leaf mixture into it—the oil will slowly drip through.

2 For the soup, heat the remaining 2 tbsp of oil in a large pan and add the onion and potatoes. Cover and cook over low heat, stirring frequently, until softened but not colored. Pour in the stock and simmer for another 10 minutes, until the potatoes are cooked. Add the watercress and cook for another minute. Season, and stir in 2–3 tsp of the curry leaf oil off the heat. Purée with a hand-held blender until smooth and sieve to remove any tough fibers.

3 For the garnish, toss the pear in confectioner's sugar seasoned with pepper. Place a frying pan over medium heat, add the diced pear, and cook until it has caramelized.

4 Reheat and re-season the soup and whisk in 2 tbsp of crème fraîche. Ladle the soup into bowls, and top with an extra dollop of crème fraîche. Scatter over the pears and finish with an extra drizzle of curry leaf oil.

vietnamese spring rolls

Spring rolls are a great way to celebrate young, new-season produce such as spring onions, carrots, and lettuce. These are wrapped in soft rice paper, unlike the crisp, fried version, and are served with a sweet and spicy dipping sauce.

 50-60 MINS **25 MINS**

SERVES 4

9oz (250g) boneless loin of pork

2 young carrots, scrubbed and cut in julienne strips

1 tsp sugar

2oz (60g) thin rice noodles

8 small lettuce leaves, plus more to serve

2½oz (75g) bean sprouts

12-15 sprigs of mint

15-20 sprigs of cilantro

8 round sheets of rice paper, 8½in (21cm) in diameter

4 spring onions or scallions, trimmed and cut in julienne strips

16 cooked, peeled shrimp

For the dipping sauce

2 garlic cloves, finely chopped

1 small red chile, finely chopped

2 tbsp sugar

4 tbsp rice vinegar

4 tbsp fish sauce (nam pla)

2 tbsp lime juice

1 For the dipping sauce, in a small bowl, combine the garlic, chile, sugar, rice vinegar, fish sauce, and ¼ cup water. Pour in the lime juice and whisk well until thoroughly mixed. Set aside for the flavors to meld together.

2 Half-fill a pan with water and bring to a boil. Add the pork, reduce the heat, cover, and simmer for 15–20 minutes, just until tender. Drain the pork, rinse with cold water and drain again. Cut it across the grain into ⅛in (3mm) slices.

3 In a bowl, toss the carrots with the sugar and set aside. Bring a large pan of water to a boil. Add the noodles and cook for 1–2 minutes, until tender but still slightly chewy. Drain and cut into 3in (7.5cm) lengths.

4 Wash the lettuce leaves. Dry, then tear large leaves into 2–3 pieces. Pick over the bean sprouts, discarding any that are discolored. Strip the mint and cilantro from the stalks, reserving a few sprigs for garnish.

5 Pour about ½in (1cm) of hot water into a shallow dish. Work with 1 sheet of rice paper at a time and keep the remaining sheets wrapped. Dip 1 sheet of rice paper into the hot water for 20–25 seconds, to soften. Remove and spread it out on a dry kitchen towel.

6 Place a lettuce leaf on the rice paper. Top with one-eighth of the noodles, carrot, spring onion or scallion, pork, bean sprouts, and mint and cilantro. Roll up the paper, halfway, into a cylinder. Fold both ends over the filling. Place a few more cilantro leaves on top, then 2 shrimp. Continue rolling the paper into a cylinder and press the end lightly to seal. Place the roll, shrimp-side up, on a tray or plate and cover with a dampened kitchen towel to keep the roll moist. Repeat with the remaining rice papers and filling. Serve with small bowls of the dipping sauce, and sprinkle with the reserved herbs and extra lettuce leaves.

sautéed scallops with pancetta and wilted spinach

This simple dish highlights the best of spring. Serve with some crusty bread or toss with pasta for a light dinner or lunch.

 5 MINS 15 MINS

SERVES 4

12 fresh sea scallops

salt and freshly ground black pepper

1–2 tbsp olive oil

4oz (115g) pancetta, diced

dash of good-quality thick balsamic vinegar

2 handfuls of spinach leaves, stems removed

juice of 1 lemon

1 Pat dry the scallops with paper towels, and season with salt and pepper. Heat the oil in a non-stick frying pan over medium-high heat. When hot, add the scallops, positioning them around the edge of the pan. Sear for 1–2 minutes on one side, then turn them over, starting with the first one you put in the pan. Once you have completed the circle, remove the scallops from the pan (again starting with the first one), and set aside to keep warm.

2 Add the pancetta to the same pan and cook for a couple of minutes until crispy. Add a generous amount of balsamic vinegar to the pan, increase the heat to high, and allow it to boil for a couple of minutes, stirring to deglaze the pan, then drizzle the sauce over the reserved scallops.

3 Still using the same pan, add in the spinach. Cook for 2–3 minutes, moving it around the pan, until it is just wilted. Squeeze the lemon juice over the spinach, and serve immediately with the scallops and pancetta sauce.

spinach and goat cheese tart

Fast becoming a modern classic, this dish can be adapted for vegetarians by substituting pancetta with toasted pine nuts.

 20 MINS 55–65 MINS ❄ FREEZABLE

SPECIAL EQUIPMENT ▪ 9in (23cm) tart pan with removable bottom ▪ ceramic baking beans

SERVES 6–8

5½oz (150g) store-bought pie dough, plus all-purpose flour for dusting

5½oz (150g) pancetta, diced

1 tbsp olive oil

5½oz (150g) baby spinach

3½oz (100g) goat cheese

sea salt and freshly ground black pepper

1¼ cups heavy cream

2 eggs

1 Roll the dough out on a floured work surface to a large circle, about ⅛in (3mm) thick, and use to line the tart pan, pressing it into the corners. Ensure it overlaps the sides by at least ¾in (2cm). Prick the bottom with a fork. Line with waxed paper and fill with ceramic baking beans. Place the tart pan on a baking sheet and bake for 20–25 minutes. Remove the beans and paper. Bake for another 5 minutes to crisp the bottom. Remove and leave to cool.

2 In a frying pan, cook the pancetta in the oil for 5 minutes until golden brown. Add the spinach and cook until it wilts. Drain off any water and allow to cool. Spread the spinach and pancetta mixture over the pastry, cube or crumble the goat cheese on top, and season.

3 Whisk the cream and eggs in a bowl. Place the tart pan on a baking sheet and, with the oven door open, rest it half on, half off the middle oven shelf. Hold the sheet with one hand, pour the cream and egg mix into the tart, and slide it into the oven. Bake for 30–35 minutes or until golden. Remove from the oven and leave for 10 minutes. Trim the overhanging pastry with a knife, remove the tart from the pan, and serve warm or cold.

gravalax

"Gravalax", a Scandinavian method of preserving salmon, makes a stunning starter. Salt draws moisture from the fish to flavor it and firm its texture. Allow 48 hours for curing.

 20 MINS PLUS CURING ❄ FREEZABLE

MAKES 2¼lb (1kg)

⅓ cup granulated sugar

1oz (30g) dill, chopped

1 tbsp lemon juice

¼ cup fine sea salt

1 tsp freshly ground black pepper

2 x 1lb 2oz (500g) thick fillets of very fresh salmon

1 To make the curing mix, put the sugar, dill, lemon juice, salt, and pepper in a small bowl and combine all the ingredients thoroughly.

2 Lay one fillet of salmon, skin-side down, in a large clean dish so it is completely flat. Spread all of the curing mixture evenly over the top of the salmon fillet.

3 Place the other piece of salmon, flesh-side down, on top of the covered fillet. Wrap the fillets tightly together in plastic wrap and weigh them down with a plate and 1–2 cans, or a similar weight. Refrigerate the fillets for 48 hours to cure.

4 Turn the salmon every 12 hours to compress each fillet, and drain off the fluid so the fillets firm up. After 48 hours, remove the fillets from the fridge, unwrap them, and pat them dry with paper towels. To serve, cut the salmon into thin diagonal slices with a sharp knife. Serve with brown bread and butter.

variation

scandinavian-style cured trout

For 4 people use 4 very fresh trout fillets and half the Gravalax cure ingredients. Prepare in pairs. Wrap the pairs separately, press and chill for 24 hours, turning once.

cheesy bacon and spring onion muffins

Spring onions have a milder taste than onion, so they are a perfect addition to these light savory muffins.

 15 MINS 25 MINS ❄ FREEZABLE

SPECIAL EQUIPMENT ▪ 4 x 5fl oz (150ml) ramekins or metal muffin tin

SERVES 4

5½oz (150g) thick-sliced bacon

7oz (200g) Cheddar cheese, cut into small pieces

1 cup fresh bread crumbs

4 spring onions or scallions, trimmed and finely chopped

3 large eggs

½ cup milk

handful of chives, chopped

salt and freshly ground black pepper

1 Preheat the oven to 375°F (190°C). Fry the bacon in a non-stick frying pan over medium-high heat until they are cooked but not too crispy. Then cut the bacon into bite-sized pieces with a pair of kitchen scissors.

2 Place the Cheddar cheese, bread crumbs, spring onions or scallions, eggs, and milk in a bowl and mix them together. Add the bacon and chives, stir them into the mixture, and season with salt and pepper.

3 Spoon the mixture into non-stick or greased muffin tins or ramekins and bake in the oven for about 25 minutes until risen and golden.

variation

savory blue cheese and broccoli muffins

Prepare these muffins in the same way, but use 5½oz (150g) cooked, well-drained, finely chopped broccoli rabe instead of bacon (don't use any tough stalks) and use 7oz (200g) mild blue cheese instead of Cheddar (or half and half). For extra flavor, add a few chopped sage leaves to the mixture in addition to the chopped chives.

büsumer fish soup

A delicious variation of this German soup, from a region on the North Sea coast. The original is made with white fish, but this one uses seasonal trout for an extra depth of flavor.

 15 MINS **20 MINS** **FREEZABLE**

SERVES 4

2 large carrots, chopped

1 large Russet potato, peeled and diced

1 large onion, diced

3½ cups hot vegetable stock

1 bay leaf

salt and freshly ground black pepper

juice of 1 lemon

1lb 2oz (500g) trout fillets, skinned, boned, and cut into bite-sized pieces

7oz (200g) button or crimini mushrooms, sliced

3½oz (100g) cooked, peeled cold water shrimp

½ cup heavy cream

small bunch of dill, chopped

1 Put the carrots, potato, and onion into a saucepan, add the hot stock and bay leaf, and bring to a boil. Reduce the heat, cover, and simmer for 10 minutes until just tender.

2 Sprinkle a little salt, pepper, and half the lemon juice over the fish pieces, then add these to the stock along with the mushrooms. Simmer for another 5 minutes over low heat.

3 Add the shrimp to the pan along with the remaining lemon juice, and simmer gently for 1 minute to just heat through the shrimp. Remove the bay leaf and season to taste with salt and pepper. Stir in the cream and half the dill and serve immediately, using the remaining dill to garnish.

creamy smoked trout soup

This comforting soup is based on a simple roux sauce, so it is vital to use very good stock to make it really sing. It makes an excellent light lunch.

 15 MINS **10 MINS** **FREEZABLE**

SERVES 6

3 tbsp butter

4 young carrots, very thinly sliced

1 small leek, very thinly sliced

3 tbsp all-purpose flour

2½ cups hot vegetable or fish stock

1 cup whipping cream

¼ cup white wine

2–3 tsp Worcestershire sauce

13oz (375g) hot-smoked trout fillets, skinned and flaked

2 tbsp chopped parsley

salt and freshly ground black pepper

squeeze of lemon juice

1 Melt the butter over low heat. Add the carrots and leek and stir well. Cover and cook very gently for 5 minutes until soft but not brown, stirring occasionally. Stir in the flour and cook for 1 minute, stirring. Remove from the heat and gradually stir in the stock until smooth. Return to the heat, bring to a boil, and cook for 2 minutes, stirring continuously.

2 Stir in the cream, white wine, Worcestershire sauce, flaked fish, and half the parsley, and heat for 2 minutes. Season to taste with salt, pepper, and the lemon juice. Ladle into soup bowls and garnish with the remaining parsley.

smoked trout with chile and lime dressing

In-season smoked trout has the fullest flavor. For extra texture, sprinkle over a pinch of toasted sesame seeds.

 10 MINS

SERVES 4

12oz (350g) hot- or cold-smoked trout fillets

large handful of seasonal salad leaves

bunch of spring onions or scallions, trimmed and finely sliced

4 radishes, finely sliced

For the chile and lime dressing

2 tbsp rice wine vinegar

2 tsp light soy sauce

splash of sesame oil

½–1 tsp granulated sugar

2 red chiles, seeded and finely chopped

juice of 1–2 limes

1 Whisk together the dressing ingredients, tasting as you go. Add all of the lime juice, if needed, or use less if the dressing is becoming too sour.

2 Divide the smoked trout among 4 serving plates, then toss together the salad leaves, spring onions or scallions, and radishes.

3 When ready to serve, lightly toss the salad with the some of the dressing, and drizzle the remainder over the trout. Serve immediately.

Season's best **trout**

Trout are elegant, oily fish, similar to salmon but with a sweeter, more delicate flavor. Some have pink flesh, others creamy white. They can be farmed all year, but if catching wild, are at their most delicious in spring, although still good through to fall. They are perfect pan-seared or grilled whole or, if very fresh, gently poached. Try with Hollandaise sauce or orange-flavored mayonnaise, almonds, watercress, herbs (dill, parsley, and chives), cucumber, and spring onions.

The rainbow trout has a bright, silvery skin with rainbow-hued speckles.

Rainbow trout The North American rainbow trout was introduced into Europe at the end of the 19th century. It grows quickly and is farmed extensively. In European waters, wild fish rarely grow bigger than 22lb (10kg); in the US they can be twice this size. It can be cooked whole or as fillets. Its very fine bones can be difficult to locate.

Trout fillets break into neat flakes when cooked and have a delicate, slightly earthy flavor.

essentials
varieties available

Farmed and wild rainbow trout, brown trout, and sea trout (brown trout that migrate to the sea). Hot- and cold-smoked; salted roe.

buy Whole, gutted, or fillets. Choose ones with slippery skin, bright prominent eyes, and red gills.

store Wrap well and store in the coldest part of the fridge. Eat within 24 hours.

cook Pan-fry, bake, grill, roast.

recipe ideas

Büsumer fish soup p20

Instant smoked trout p42

Sautéed trout with hazelnuts p40

Smoked trout with chile and lime dressing p20

how to gut fish through the gills

When you plan to poach fish whole (particularly useful with trout or salmon), it is best to gut it through the gills so the stomach is kept intact.

1 Hook your index finger under the gills to lift them from the base of the head. Using a fish knife, cut off the gills and discard. Through the hole so formed, pull out the guts and discard.

2 Make a small slit in the stomach at the ventral (anal) opening. Pull out any remaining guts. Rinse inside and out with cold, running water. Pat dry. Trim and scale as necessary.

sesame shrimp toasts

This is a delicious idea for cooking with shrimp while they are in season. If necessary, you can make the shrimp mix ahead of time, wrap it up, and leave in the fridge until needed.

 15 MINS **10 MINS**

SPECIAL EQUIPMENT ▪ blender or food processor

SERVES 4

10oz (300g) cooked, peeled cold water shrimp

2 garlic cloves, peeled but left whole

small handful of cilantro leaves

1 red chile, seeded and finely chopped

juice of 1 lime

salt and freshly ground black pepper

4 slices white bread

4½oz (125g) sesame seeds

1 Preheat the broiler to its highest setting. Pulse the shrimp, garlic, cilantro, chile, and lime juice to a paste in a blender or food processor. Season well with salt and pepper, and pulse again briefly.

2 Lightly toast the bread on both sides, then spoon the shrimp mixture onto one side of each piece of toast.

Spread the mixture evenly, covering the toast completely and pressing the mixture down firmly.

3 Lightly oil a baking sheet, pour the sesame seeds onto it, and spread them in an even layer. Place the toasts, shrimp-side down, on top of the seeds, and press them so that the seeds stick to the mixture and coat it. Carefully flip the toasts over on the baking sheet and cut them into triangles.

4 Slide the baking sheet under the hot broiler and cook the toasts for a few minutes until the sesame seeds begin to turn golden. Keep a careful eye on them, as they can burn very quickly. Serve immediately.

minced crab balls

When cooking a fresh crab, put it in the freezer 2 hours before boiling it in water. Cook for 15 minutes for the first 1lb 2oz (500g) and 2 minutes per 3½oz (100g) thereafter.

 10 MINS **15 MINS**

SPECIAL EQUIPMENT ▪ food processor

SERVES 4

9oz (250g) white crab meat

1 red chile, seeded

2 garlic cloves, peeled

handful of cilantro

grated zest and juice of 1 lemon

1 tsp fish sauce (nam pla)

2 large eggs, lightly beaten

salt and freshly ground black pepper

1 cup fine fresh bread crumbs

3 tbsp vegetable oil for shallow-frying

dark soy sauce, to serve

sweet chili sauce, to serve

1 Put the crab meat, chile, garlic, cilantro, lemon zest and juice, and fish sauce in a food processor. Pulse until a rough paste forms, then add the beaten egg and plenty of salt and pepper. Pulse again.

2 Place the bread crumbs onto a plate. Scoop the crab mixture up using your hands and roll into 1in (2.5cm) balls. Roll each crab ball in the bread crumbs until well covered.

3 Heat a little of the oil in a frying pan over medium heat. Add a few crab balls at a time to the pan and cook them in batches. Shallow-fry the crab balls for about 5 minutes until golden all over, moving them around the pan so that they brown evenly, and adding more oil as needed. Drain on paper towels and serve hot with soy sauce and sweet chili sauce for dipping.

crab and shrimp saffron tart

The delicate flavors of crab and shrimp balance wonderfully with the assertive pungency and musky taste of saffron.

 20 MINS   50-65 MINS   ❄ FREEZABLE

SPECIAL EQUIPMENT ▪ 6in (15cm) tart pan with removable bottom ▪ ceramic baking beans

SERVES 2-4

3½oz (100g) store-bought pie dough, plus all-purpose flour for dusting

pinch of saffron

4½oz (125g) white crab meat

3½oz (100g) cooked, peeled shrimp

¾ cup heavy cream

1 large egg

1 tbsp finely chopped tarragon or chervil

salt and freshly ground black pepper

1 Roll the dough out on a floured work surface to a large circle, about ⅛in (3mm) thick, and use to line the tart pan, pressing it into the corners. Ensure it overlaps the sides by at least ¾in (2cm). Prick the bottom with a fork. Line with waxed paper and fill with ceramic baking beans. Place the tart pan on a baking sheet and bake in the center of the oven for 20–25 minutes. Remove the beans and paper. Bake for 5 minutes to crisp the bottom. Leave to cool.

2 Splash 1 tbsp boiling water over the saffron in a small bowl to allow the color to develop. Put the crab meat and shrimp in a sieve over a sink and press down to remove any excess water. Toss together and scatter over the crust.

3 Whisk the heavy cream and egg in a bowl. Add the herbs, the saffron and its soaking water, and seasoning, and mix well. Put the tart pan on a baking sheet and, with the oven door open, rest it half on, half off the middle oven shelf. Hold the sheet with one hand, pour the cream and egg mix into the tart, and slide it into the oven. Bake for 30–35 minutes until golden. Remove from the oven and leave for 10 minutes. Trim off the overhanging crust with a knife, remove the tart from the pan, and serve warm or cold.

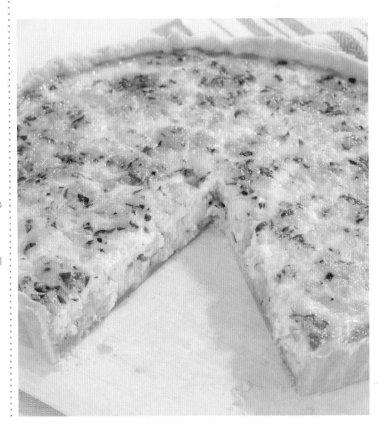

thai fish cakes

If you can find Thai basil, which has a spicy, delicate flavor, use it instead of regular basil. It also has a sweeter taste than regular basil, which marries well with fresh shrimp.

 15 MINS   15 MINS   ❄ FREEZABLE

SPECIAL EQUIPMENT ▪ food processor or blender

SERVES 4

10oz (300g) cooked, peeled cold water shrimp

3 garlic cloves, peeled but left whole

small handful of cilantro

2 red chiles, seeded

dash of fish sauce (nam pla)

dash of dark soy sauce

small handful of basil leaves

juice of 2 limes

1 large egg

salt and freshly ground black pepper

3-4 tbsp vegetable oil or sunflower oil

sweet chili sauce, to serve

1 Put all the ingredients except the egg and oil in a food processor or blender and process to a rough paste. Add the egg and plenty of salt and pepper, and pulse again.

2 Heat a little of the oil in a frying pan over medium-high heat. Scoop up a tablespoon of the mixture with a spoon, then carefully slide it into the pan and flatten slightly; it should be about ¾in (2cm) thick. Repeat until all the mixture has been used. Shallow-fry the fish cakes for a minute or two on each side until golden; you may need to cook them in batches, adding more oil as needed. Drain the fish cakes on a plate lined with paper towels.

3 Serve the fish cakes hot with a drizzle of sweet chili sauce and salad leaves, such as arugula.

cheese gougères and salmon

Smoked salmon and spinach give these puffs a luxurious edge.

 40-45 MINS 30-35 MINS

SERVES 8

For the choux pastry

3 tbsp unsalted butter cut into small pieces

¼ tsp salt

½ cup all-purpose flour, sifted

5-6 large eggs

4½oz (125g) Gruyère cheese, grated

For the filling

2¼lb (1kg) spinach, stems removed

1 tbsp butter

1 onion, finely chopped

4 garlic cloves, finely chopped

pinch of ground nutmeg

salt and freshly ground black pepper

9oz (250g) cream cheese

6oz (175g) smoked salmon, sliced into strips

¼ cup milk

1 Preheat the oven to 375°F (190°C) and grease 2 baking sheets. Melt the butter in a pan with 1 cup water and ¾ tsp salt. Bring to a boil. Remove from the heat, add the flour, and beat until smooth. Return the pan to the stove and beat over very low heat for 30 seconds to dry. Remove from the heat.

2 Add 4 eggs, one at a time, beating well after each. Beat the fifth egg; add it gradually until the pastry is shiny and soft. Stir in half the cheese. Using 2 spoons, drop eight 2½in (6cm) mounds of dough on to the baking sheets. Beat the last egg and ½ tsp salt and brush over the choux puffs. Sprinkle the remaining cheese over the puffs. Bake for 30-35 minutes until firm. Remove and transfer to a wire rack. Using a serrated knife, slice off the tops and leave to cool.

3 Bring a large pan of salted water to a boil. Add the spinach and wilt for 1-2 minutes. Drain and, when cool, squeeze it to remove the water, then chop finely. Melt the butter in a frying pan. Add the onion and cook until soft. Add the garlic, nutmeg, salt and pepper to taste, and the spinach. Cook, stirring, until any liquid has evaporated. Add the cream cheese and stir until the mix is thoroughly combined. Remove from the heat.

4 Add the smoked salmon, pour in the milk, and stir for 1-2 minutes until piping hot. Mound 2-3 spoonfuls of filling onto each cheese puff. Rest the lid against the side of each filled puff and serve at once, before the choux pastry becomes soft.

pineapple broth with halibut

The astringent quality of pineapple works well in savory dishes and is a marvelous match for fish and spices.

 30 MINS 40 MINS ❄ FREEZABLE

SPECIAL EQUIPMENT ▪ food processor ▪ blender or hand-held blender

SERVES 4

1 onion, diced

1¾oz (50g) raw peanuts, skinned, plus 2 tbsp toasted raw peanuts, roughly chopped, to garnish

2 tbsp unsweetened, shredded coconut

1¼in (3cm) piece ginger, chopped

1 tsp coriander seeds

2 tsp sesame seeds

1 tsp cumin seeds

1 tsp poppy seeds

¾ tsp chile powder

3 tbsp tamarind pulp

½ tsp turmeric

salt and freshly ground black pepper

2 tbsp vegetable oil

1 tsp light brown sugar

1¾ cups fish stock

¾ cup pineapple juice

1 x 14oz (400ml) can coconut milk

7oz (200g) halibut, chopped

juice of 1 lime

4½oz (125g) pineapple, chopped

2 tbsp mint leaves, roughly torn

1 Heat the onion, peanuts, coconut, ginger, and seeds in a cast-iron frying pan over low heat for 5 minutes so the coconut darkens and spices are aromatic. Allow to cool in a bowl, then pulse in a food processor. Add the chili powder, tamarind, and turmeric. Season and pulse to a smooth paste.

2 Heat the oil in a large saucepan. Cook the paste for 10 minutes over low heat. Add the sugar. As the paste begins to catch on the base of the pan, add the stock and juice. Simmer for 20 minutes, partially covered.

3 Take the pan off the heat. Purée with a blender or hand-held blender. Add the coconut milk, return to the heat, add the fish, simmer for 3 minutes, then add the lime juice, pineapple, and mint. Serve with the toasted peanuts scattered on top.

variation

pineapple broth with shrimp
Replace half the halibut in step 3 above with 7oz (200g) cooked, peeled shrimp.

abalone with oyster sauce

A type of sea snail with well-flavored flesh, abalone can be expensive so is often sold canned as well as on the shell.

 5 MINS 5 MINS ❄ FREEZABLE

SERVES 2

1 x 15oz (340g) can abalone, drained with the liquid retained

2 tbsp sunflower oil or vegetable oil

bunch of spring onions or scallions, trimmed and finely sliced

1 tsp finely grated fresh root ginger

2 tbsp oyster sauce

1 tbsp soy sauce

pinch of sugar

5 tbsp water

2 tsp cornstarch

1 Slice the abalone thinly. Heat the oil in a large frying pan, add in the sliced spring onions or scallions and grated ginger, and stir over low heat for 3-4 minutes. Add the abalone and toss together to heat through.

2 Mix together the oyster sauce, soy sauce, sugar, and water. Stir in the cornstarch and the retained abalone liquid. Add this sauce to the abalone and stir over medium heat until it just comes to a boil and the sauce has thickened. Serve immediately.

marinated goat cheese salad

In spring, both winter endives and summer lettuces are available; team them with these delightful goat cheeses marinated in herbs and golden oil. For an eye-catching salad, the goat cheese should be firm but not dry. For the best flavor, begin marinating it one week ahead of serving.

 20-25 MINS PLUS MARINATING

SERVES 4

8 slices of wholegrain bread

a variety of salad leaves, such as chicory, red oakleaf lettuce and butterhead lettuce

For the marinated goat cheeses

4 small round goat cheeses, each weighing about 2-3oz (60-90g), or 1 goat cheese log, weighing about 11oz (320g)

2 bay leaves

2-3 sprigs of thyme

2-3 sprigs of rosemary

2-3 sprigs of oregano

2 tsp black peppercorns

2 small dried red chiles

16fl oz (500ml) olive oil, plus more if needed

For the vinaigrette

2 tbsp red wine vinegar

1 tsp Dijon mustard

salt and freshly ground black pepper

leaves from 5-7 sprigs of thyme

1 Put the goat cheeses in a large glass jar with the bay leaves, thyme, rosemary, oregano, peppercorns, and chiles. Add enough oil to cover the ingredients generously. Cover and leave for at least 1 week before using. Alternatively, put a goat cheese log in a non-metallic bowl with the other ingredients, cover with plastic wrap, and marinate for 1-3 days.

2 Remove the cheeses from the marinade with a slotted spoon to drain off any excess oil. Strain the

marinading oil through a sieve into a bowl or wide-mouthed jar and reserve it. You will need about ⅓ cup of the reserved oil to make the vinaigrette, plus a little more for the wholegrain bread.

3 Pour the vinegar into a bowl and add the mustard, salt, and pepper. Whisk the ingredients together. Gradually whisk in the reserved oil so the vinaigrette emulsifies and thickens slightly. Stir in half the thyme and taste for seasoning.

4 Preheat the oven to 400°F (200°C). Cut each goat cheese in half horizontally. If you are using a goat cheese log instead, cut it into 8 equal slices. Using a pastry cutter, cut out a round from each slice of bread.

5 Set the bread rounds on a baking sheet and brush them with a little of the remaining strained olive oil. Bake in the oven for 3-5 minutes until lightly toasted. Heat the broiler, put a round of goat cheese on top of each toasted bread round, and broil for 2-3 minutes until the cheese is bubbling and golden.

6 Arrange the salad leaves on individual plates and drizzle with the vinaigrette. Place 2 cheese toasts on top of each salad, sprinkle with thyme leaves, and serve.

filo pie with spinach, ricotta cheese, and pine nuts

The freshest, tenderest spinach is most easily available in spring and is ideal for this subtly flavored pie.

 15 MINS   35 MINS

SPECIAL EQUIPMENT ▪ 8in (20cm) round or square spring-form cake pan

SERVES 4

1 tbsp olive oil

1 onion, finely chopped

salt and freshly ground black pepper

2 garlic cloves, grated or finely chopped

1¼lb (550g) fresh spinach leaves

handful of raisins

2½oz (75g) pine nuts, toasted

7oz (200g) ricotta cheese

1 large egg, lightly beaten

12 sheets filo pastry

2 tbsp butter, melted

1 Preheat the oven to 350°F (180°C). Heat the oil in a frying pan over low heat. Add the onion and a little salt, and sweat gently for about 5 minutes until soft and translucent. Add the garlic and cook for a few more seconds until the garlic turns white.

2 Add in the spinach and cook, stirring, for about 3 minutes until it wilts. Season well with salt and

pepper. Remove from the heat, stir through the raisins and pine nuts, and leave to cool. Add the ricotta and beaten egg, and stir well.

3 Lay 2 sheets of filo pastry, one on top of the other, in the cake pan, letting them hang over the edge on two sides. Next, lay 2 more sheets of filo at right angles to the first layer. Continue in this way until you have used 8 sheets for the base of the pie.

4 Spoon the spinach and ricotta mixture into the pie. Fold in the edges of the pastry and top the pie with the remaining 4 sheets of filo pastry, tucking them in neatly. Brush all over with the melted butter and bake in the oven for 20–30 minutes until golden and crisp. Serve warm.

blinis with smoked salmon

Spring radishes add a delightfully peppery punch to this dish, which can be tempered by the sour cream that is a mandatory and delicious traditional accompaniment to blinis.

 25-30 MINS   8-16 MINS

SERVES 8

2-3 tbsp capers, drained

1 small red onion, very finely diced

8 radishes, thinly sliced

6oz (175g) sliced smoked salmon

1 package store-bought blinis

¾ cup sour cream, to serve

8 tbsp butter, to serve (optional)

1 Coarsely chop the capers if they are large, place in a small bowl, and put the onion and radish in separate bowls. Place the slices of smoked salmon on a plate. Cover the plate and all the bowls, or place in the fridge, until needed.

2 Preheat the oven to 300°F (150°C). Arrange the blinis on a baking sheet and put them in the oven to warm through. Melt the butter for serving, if using. Arrange the blinis on a serving plate. Place a piece of folded smoked salmon on each blini, top with a couple of radish slices, and garnish with a few chopped capers and onions. Serve with a bowl of sour cream and a separate bowl of melted butter, if you like.

variation

blinis with red and black caviar

Choose lumpfish or beluga caviar, depending on your budget. Omit the capers, red onion, radishes, and smoked salmon accompaniments for this version of the dish. Hard-boil 2 eggs and leave to cool. Peel the eggs, then separate the yolks and whites and finely chop them both. Trim 2 spring onions and cut the green tops into thin diagonal slices. Warm the blinis as directed in step 2. Serve the blinis with 1oz (30g) each red and black caviar (or more to taste), egg yolks and whites, spring onion slices, and a spoonful of sour cream.

shrimp, avocado, and watercress sandwich

This winning combination of juicy and colorful spring fare is quick and easy to put together for a tasty instant lunch.

 30 MINS 5 MINS

SERVES 4

2oz (60g) cooked, peeled shrimp

1 tbsp fresh ginger, grated or finely chopped

1 small red chile, finely chopped

1 garlic clove, finely chopped

1 ripe avocado

¼ cucumber, thinly sliced

a few sprigs of mint, leaves picked and roughly torn

1 tbsp dill, finely chopped

1 tbsp capers, chopped, rinsed, and drained

½ small red onion, finely chopped

1 cup sour cream

juice of 1 lime

8 thick slices wholegrain bread

4 handfuls of watercress

1 Mix the shrimp with the ginger, chile, and garlic in a bowl. Set aside.

2 Halve, pit, and peel the avocado. Dice the flesh and put in another bowl. Add the cucumber, mint, dill, capers, onion, sour cream, and lime juice. Add in the shrimp and gently stir through, being careful not to mash the avocado.

3 Spread the mixture evenly over 4 slices of the bread. Arrange the watercress on top so that it will come out over the sides of the sandwich. Cover with the other slices of bread to make 4 sandwiches, cut in half diagonally if you like, and serve.

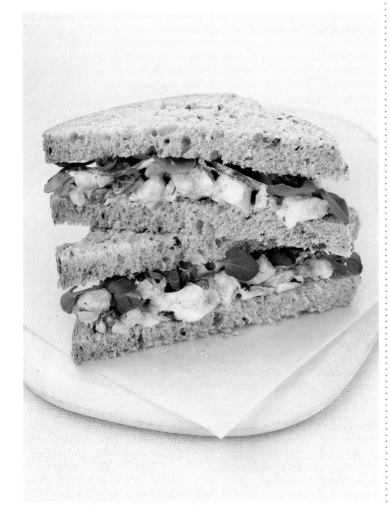

salmon fish cakes

These herby fish cakes are delicious served on a bed of tender young watercress and spinach leaves.

 15 MINS 30 MINS

SERVES 4

2lb (900g) potatoes, peeled and cut into chunks

2-3 tbsp of butter

2lb (900g) salmon, skinned

handful of curly leaf parsley, finely chopped

salt and freshly ground black pepper

a little vegetable oil, for frying

tartar sauce, to serve

lemon wedges, to serve

1 Boil the potatoes in a large saucepan of salted water for about 15 minutes until soft, then drain well and mash. Add the butter and mash again until smooth. Set aside.

2 Put the piece of salmon in a large frying pan and cover it with water. Bring the water just to a boil, turn the heat down, and simmer over low heat for 5–8 minutes until the salmon turns opaque. Remove with a fish spatula and put on a plate. Leave to cool for a minute or two. Using your fingers, flake the fish into pieces.

3 Gently mix the fish with the mashed potato. Add the parsley and season well with salt and pepper. Take a small handful of the mixture in your hands, roll it into a ball, and flatten into a cake. Continue the process until all the mixture has been used—there should be enough for 2 fish cakes per person. Dust the fish cakes with a little flour.

4 Heat just enough oil for shallow-frying in a non-stick frying pan over medium heat. Cook a few fish cakes at a time, frying them for about 5 minutes on each side until golden. Serve hot with tartar sauce and lemon wedges.

malaysian chicken soup

The poached chicken in this recipe has a silky texture; a generous handful of scallions adds flavor and crunch. Try adding seasonal greens, noodles, or shrimp at the end.

 15 MINS 40-50 MINS ❄ FREEZABLE

SERVES 4-6

3lb (1.35kg) chicken

1 onion, quartered

2in (5cm) piece of fresh ginger, peeled and sliced

6 garlic cloves, crushed

salt and freshly ground black pepper

splash of soy sauce

splash of fish sauce (nam pla)

1 cup hot vegetable stock (optional)

bunch of scallions, trimmed and finely sliced

1 Put the chicken, onion, ginger, and garlic in a large pan and cover with water. Season with salt and pepper and bring to a boil. Reduce to a simmer, cover, and cook over low heat for 30–40 minutes, or until the chicken is cooked and the juices flow clear when pierced with a sharp knife. Remove the chicken from the broth and set aside until it is cool enough to handle.

2 Remove the skin from the chicken and discard, then remove all the meat from the bones. Strain the broth from the pan into a clean heavy-bottomed pan, add the chicken meat, and stir in the soy sauce and fish sauce. Add more stock, if necessary, then simmer gently to warm through, taste, and season as required. Ladle into warmed soup bowls and top with the sliced scallions.

variation

malaysian chicken noodle and spring vegetable soup

For this main meal soup, prepare in the same way but add 2 baby carrots, thinly cut in diagonal slices, and 2 finely diced baby turnips to the stock at step 2. Simmer for a few minutes until the vegetables are just tender. Cook 7oz (200g) rice noodles, drain, and toss them in 2 tsp sesame oil. Divide the noodles between 4–6 large bowls and ladle in the soup.

asian chicken and shrimp broth with ginger and cilantro

Lots of complex flavors make up this warming broth. The shrimp and chicken add plenty of protein, making it a substantial dish.

 15 MINS 1 HR

SERVES 4-6

1 quart hot chicken stock

salt and freshly ground black pepper

1 tbsp dark soy sauce

3 tbsp fish sauce (nam pla)

3 tbsp mirin

1 tsp tahini

2 garlic cloves, finely chopped

2in (5cm) piece of fresh ginger, peeled and sliced into fine strips

½ tsp dried chile flakes

1 x 8oz (225g) can bamboo shoots, drained and rinsed

1 x 8oz (225g) can water chestnuts, drained and rinsed

4½oz (125g) button mushrooms, whole or larger ones halved

2 skinless chicken breasts, finely sliced

bunch of spring onions or scallions, trimmed and finely chopped

bunch of cilantro leaves

9oz (250g) cooked, peeled shrimp

1 Put the stock into a large heavy-bottomed pan, season with salt and pepper, and pour in another 2 cups of hot water. Add the soy sauce, fish sauce, mirin, and tahini, and bring to a boil.

2 Reduce to a simmer and add the garlic, ginger, and chile flakes together with the bamboo shoots, water chestnuts, and mushrooms. Stir, then add the chicken, cover with a lid, and cook gently for 40 minutes. Add more hot water if necessary.

3 Taste and adjust the seasoning as required, then stir in the spring onions or scallions and cilantro leaves, and simmer over low heat for another 10 minutes.

4 Finally, add the shrimp and simmer for 5 minutes. Ladle into warmed bowls and serve while piping hot.

smoked trout and goat cheese bites

A delicious blend of smoked trout and herbed goat cheese in a tortilla wrap.

 15 MINS

MAKES 28

6oz (165g) rindless soft goat cheese

2 tbsp chopped dill or chervil

grated zest of 1 lemon

salt and freshly ground black pepper

4 large flour tortillas

2 red bell peppers, roasted, peeled, and sliced into thin strips (p171)

1 cup flaked skinless smoked trout fillet

1 Mix the goat cheese, dill, and lemon zest together and season with salt and pepper.

2 Spread the tortillas with equal amounts of the cheese mixture. Arrange the peppers and smoked trout over the cheese. Roll up each tortilla as tightly as possible. Wrap each in plastic wrap and refrigerate at least 1 hour, until chilled. Cut each wrap diagonally into 7 pieces. Serve chilled.

variation

Smoked salmon and goat cheese bites

Substitute 4oz (115g) hot-smoked salmon for the smoked trout.

Season's best **scallions and spring onions**

Thin scallions and more bulbous spring onions are sold in bunches from spring through summer, usually untrimmed. They have a delicious, mild onion flavor and can be eaten raw or cooked, whole, chopped, or sliced. They enhance dairy-, egg-, and mayonnaise-based dishes and add color and flavor to rice, pasta, seafood, meat, poultry, beans, salads, and many Asian dishes.

Scallions and spring onions are grown extensively worldwide. They are simply young bulb onions, harvested early while the leaves are still green and the bulbs are not fully formed.

Spring onion More mature than scallions, they have a slightly stronger flavor but are delicious raw in salads. They can be trimmed and the bulbs cooked whole or pickled, and the greens used for garnish.

The bulbs are large enough to be sliced and separated into rings for salads. Chop the tops and add as well.

Scallions Also known as green onions, they just need to be trimmed and then the whole onion can be used to add flavor and color to dishes.

how to trim and chop scallions

Scallions are very simple to prepare in just two steps, but be sure you rinse them well, as dirt may be lodged in the green leaves.

1 Trim off the root ends and tips of the green tops (for the whole bunch, do this with them bound together). Peel off any damaged outer layers.

2 For stir-frying, starting at the white end, cut in diagonal slices, about 1in (2.5cm) long. Alternatively, chop into ¼in (5mm) slices.

essentials
varieties available

Thin scallions and larger, more bulbous spring onions.

buy They should be crisp with firm stalks, fresh green leaves, and no brown outer skin.

store Both scallion and varieties should be used as soon as possible, but can be stored in the fridge vegetable drawer, wrapped in a plastic bag, for up to 5 days.

cook Stir-fry, sauté; add to salads, soups, and sauces.

preserve Trimmed salad onion bulbs can be pickled.

recipe ideas

Cheesy bacon and spring onion muffins p19

Chicken stir-fried with scallion, basil, and lemongrass p175

Pork with spring onions, soy sauce, and cinnamon p47

Quesadilla with avocado, spring onion, and chile p59

creamy spinach tart

Spinach and watercress are a classic spring combination that is enriched here with heavy cream and a little nutmeg.

 15 MINS   **1 HR**

SPECIAL EQUIPMENT ▪ 8in (20cm) round loose-bottomed fluted tart pan ▪ ceramic baking beans ▪ food processor

SERVES 4-6

10oz (300g) store-bought pie crust

3 large eggs, 1 lightly beaten for egg wash

1 tbsp olive oil

1 onion, finely chopped

salt and freshly ground black pepper

2 garlic cloves, grated or finely chopped

1lb (450g) spinach leaves, stems removed

7oz (200g) watercress

¾ cup heavy cream

pinch of grated nutmeg

1 Preheat the oven to 400°F (200°C). Roll out the pie crust on a floured work surface until it is large enough to line the tart pan. Trim away the excess around the edges, line the pie crust with waxed paper, and fill with ceramic baking beans. Bake in the oven for 15–20 minutes until the edges are golden. Remove the beans and waxed paper, brush the bottom of the pie crust with a little of the egg wash, and return to the oven for 2–3 minutes to crisp.

Remove from the oven and set aside. Reduce the oven temperature to 350°F (180°C).

2 Heat the oil in a large frying pan over low heat. Add the onion and a pinch of salt, and cook gently for about 5 minutes until soft and translucent. Add the garlic and cook for a few more seconds until the garlic turns white. Spoon the mixture into the pie crust.

3 Put the spinach and watercress in a food processor and pulse a couple of times until broken up, but not mushy. Pour in the cream and the 2 eggs, and pulse again until everything is combined. Season well with salt and pepper, and pulse once more. Carefully pour the mixture into the pie crust, then sprinkle the nutmeg over the top, and bake in the oven for 20–30 minutes until set. Leave the tart to cool for 10 minutes before releasing it from the pan.

roasted quail and pea shoot salad

Dainty roast quail is perfect for an intimate dinner. Try to find quail that are tunnel boned, meaning the main body bones have been removed.

 25 MINS   **4 MINS PLUS RESTING**

SERVES 4

5 tbsp olive oil

salt and freshly ground black pepper

4 whole quail

For the salad

1 ripe avocado, pitted, peeled, and diced

1 tbsp lemon juice

4 spring onions or scallions, trimmed and cut into short diagonal lengths

4 young carrots, scrubbed and coarsely grated

8 radishes, sliced

2½oz (75g) pea shoots, or watercress and arugula

8 wild garlic leaves, shredded (optional)

For the dressing

2 tbsp white wine vinegar

2 tsp honey

½ tsp Dijon mustard

crusty bread, to serve

1 Preheat oven to 450°F (230°C). Heat 2 tbsp of the oil in a large oven-safe frying pan. Season the quail and cook for 2 minutes on each side or until lightly browned. Transfer the pan to the oven and roast for 10–12 minutes. Transfer to a plate and cover with foil. Reserve the frying pan for the dressing.

2 In a large bowl, toss the avocado in the lemon juice. Add the other salad ingredients and a grinding of black pepper, and toss gently. Pile the mixture on 4 plates.

3 Reheat the frying pan, add the remaining oil and vinegar, honey, and mustard. Heat, stirring constantly until blended. Season if needed.

4 Arrange quail on top of the salads. . Add any remaining juices in the foil to the frying pan. Pour the hot dressing over the salad and serve at once with the crusty bread.

grilled shrimp with hot pepper sauce

If you are lucky enough to find raw cold water shrimp, choose them. They take the same time to cook. Peeling hot shrimp can be messy, so place finger bowls on the table.

 10 MINS   **10 MINS**

SERVES 4

9oz (250g) raw or cooked, unpeeled shrimp

1 tbsp olive oil

1 red chile, seeded and finely chopped

For the hot pepper sauce

1 tbsp olive oil

1 garlic clove, grated or finely chopped

1 tsp hot chili powder

1 tsp paprika

pinch of ground cumin

juice of 1 lime

4-5 tbsp mayonnaise

salt and freshly ground black pepper

1 Put the shrimp in a medium-sized bowl and add the olive oil and the chile. Toss the shrimp well in the mixture and set aside to marinate for a few minutes.

2 To make the hot pepper sauce, use another bowl to combine the olive oil, garlic, chili powder, paprika, cumin, lime juice, and mayonnaise, stirring well. Taste and then season accordingly with salt and pepper.

3 Heat a large heavy-bottomed frying pan or ridged cast-iron grill pan over high heat. Add the shrimp and cook for 1–2 minutes on each side until piping hot. Serve the shrimp with the hot pepper sauce, a salad, and some crusty bread.

shellfish soup

Mix and match the shellfish to include whatever is seasonal in this delicious tomato-based soup. Add precooked lobster, and use fresh shellfish stock if you can find it.

 20 MINS 1 HR 15 MINS

SERVES 6

1 tbsp olive oil

2 celery stalks, finely chopped

2 carrots, peeled and finely diced

2 onions, finely diced

6oz (175g) thick-cut bacon, cut into bite-sized pieces

1 x 14oz (400g) can chopped tomatoes

1 star anise

2 cups hot fish stock

about 1¾lb (800g) shellfish, such as scallops, cooked and peeled shrimp, clams, and mussels (cleaned; discard any that do not close when tapped) (p364)

bunch of flat-leaf parsley, finely chopped

1 Heat the oil in a large flameproof casserole, add the celery, carrots, and onion, and cook for about 10 minutes, or until soft. Add the bacon and cook for about 5 minutes, then stir in the tomatoes and add the star anise. Pour in the stock and bring to a boil. Reduce the heat and simmer gently for about 45 minutes, adding more stock with a little hot water if it starts to reduce too much.

2 Add the shellfish and cook for 5–10 minutes, or until the clams and mussels have opened (discard any with shells that do not open once cooked). Sprinkle over the parsley and stir it in. Ladle into warmed bowls and serve with crusty bread and some spicy mayonnaise.

nettle soup

This simple soup is a fantastic way to use a much maligned fragrant weed. Choose young, tender nettles or pick nettle tips, and wear a double layer of latex gloves to gather them.

 10 MINS 20 MINS FREEZABLE

SPECIAL EQUIPMENT ▪ hand-held blender

SERVES 4

2 tbsp grapeseed or olive oil

4 spring onions or scallions, or 1 bunch, trimmed and sliced

3 leeks, coarsely chopped

1lb 7oz (650g) potatoes, washed but not peeled, cut into ¾in (2cm) cubes

salt and freshly ground black pepper

3½ cups vegetable stock

3½oz (100g) young nettles or nettle tips, washed

juice of ½ lemon

natural thick yogurt, to serve

1 Heat the grapeseed or olive oil in a large soup pan over medium heat. Add the spring onions or scallions, leeks, and potatoes, along with a little sea salt. Stir, cover with a lid, and cook for 5 minutes, stirring frequently.

2 Add the stock and bring to a boil. Add the nettles, stir, and simmer for 10 minutes, or until the potato is soft. Allow to cool briefly, then purée the soup with a hand-held blender until it is completely smooth. Taste for seasoning, then squeeze in the lemon juice, grind in some black pepper, and give the soup another stir. To serve, pour the soup into bowls, add a dollop of yogurt to each bowl, grind a little more black pepper on top, and serve immediately.

shrimp and guacamole tortilla stacks

These tasty Mexican-style canapés are simple to make. Assemble the stacks just before serving to keep them fresh.

 15 MINS 10-15 MINS

SPECIAL EQUIPMENT ▪ 1¼in (3cm) pastry cutter ▪ piping bag with small plain nozzle

MAKES 50

5 wheat or corn tortillas

3½ cups vegetable oil

2 ripe avocados, pitted and peeled

juice of 1 lime

Tabasco sauce

4 tbsp cilantro, finely chopped, plus extra as a garnish

4 spring onions or scallions, trimmed and finely chopped

salt and freshly ground black pepper

50 large cooked, peeled shrimp

1 Cut at least 100 discs out of the tortillas with a pastry cutter. Heat the oil in a medium-sized saucepan. Drop the tortillas into the oil, a handful at a time, and deep-fry until golden. Do not overcrowd the pan, or the tortillas will not crisp up properly.

Remove them with a slotted spoon, drain on paper towels, put aside, and allow to cool.

2 In a bowl, mash the avocados with half the lime juice, a dash of Tabasco, 3 tbsp of the chopped cilantro, the chopped onions, and salt and pepper to taste.

3 When there are about 30 minutes left before serving, marinate the shrimp with the remaining lime juice and the remaining 1 tbsp chopped cilantro in a small bowl.

4 To serve, pipe a little guacamole on to a tortilla using a piping bag, top it with another tortilla, pipe more guacamole on top, and finish with a shrimp and a little of the remaining cilantro as a garnish.

pasta with crab and lemon

There are many ways to cook versatile crab while it is in season; one of the simplest is to stir it through hot pasta together with a few other flavorful ingredients.

 5 MINS 10 MINS

SERVES 4

1 tbsp olive oil

1 large onion, cut into quarters, then finely sliced

salt and freshly ground black pepper

2 garlic cloves, finely sliced

grated zest and juice of 1 lemon

handful of flat-leaf parsley, finely chopped

7oz (200g) white crab meat, or canned crab meat, drained

12oz (350g) linguine or spaghetti

chile oil, to serve (optional)

1 Heat the oil in a large frying pan, add the onion and a little salt, and cook over low heat for 5 minutes or until the onion is soft and translucent. Stir in the garlic and lemon zest and cook for a few seconds more until the garlic is white.

2 Add the parsley and crab meat to the frying pan and stir, then season well with salt and lots of pepper. Add the lemon juice to taste.

3 Meanwhile, cook the pasta in a large pan of boiling salted water for 6–8 minutes, or until it is tender but still al dente. Drain, keeping back a tiny amount of the cooking water. Return the pasta to the pan and toss together with the reserved cooking water. Add the crab sauce, toss again, drizzle with chile oil, if using, and serve.

seafood and tomato cioppino

A classic seafood dish from San Francisco.

 45–50 MINS 20–25 MINS

SERVES 4–6

¼ cup olive oil

2 large onions, diced

3 garlic cloves, finely chopped

1 tbsp tomato paste

3 x 14oz (400g) can chopped Italian plum tomatoes

pinch of cayenne pepper

salt and freshly ground black pepper

1 bouquet garni of 5–6 parsley stalks, 2–3 thyme sprigs, and 1 bay leaf

2 cups dry white wine

1lb 2oz (500g) skinned halibut fillets, or other meaty white fish, rinsed

9oz (250g) bay scallops

4oz (115g) crab meat and 4–6 large crab claws

1lb 10oz (750g) mussels, scrubbed and debearded (discard any that do not close when tapped) (p364)

leaves from a small bunch of flat-leaf parsley, finely chopped

1 Heat the oil in a saucepan over low heat, add the onions, and cook for 3–5 minutes until soft. Add the garlic, tomato paste, tomatoes, cayenne, salt, pepper, and bouquet garni. Pour in the white wine. Cover the pan and simmer gently, stirring occasionally, for about 20 minutes.

2 Cut the fish into chunky 2in (5cm) pieces. Discard the tough crescent-shaped membrane at the side of each scallop, if not already removed. Make sure the scallops have no black or brownish intestinal vein around the edge; if they do, pull it off and discard.

3 Discard the bouquet garni. Pack the fish into the bottom of a casserole in an even layer, then add the scallops. Arrange the crab and mussels on top. Ladle the hot tomato broth over the seafood and add water, if necessary, so the seafood is just covered. Cover the casserole with the lid and bring to a boil. Simmer for 3–5 minutes, until the mussels have opened and the white fish flakes easily when tested with a fork.

4 Discard any mussels that have not opened. Taste for seasoning. Serve the cioppino immediately in warmed bowls with a crab claw in each bowl and chopped parsley on top. Serve with slices of sourdough bread.

salmon and shrimp fish pie

Shrimp and salmon are in plentiful supply in spring, so it makes sense to combine them in a tasty dish like this.

 15 MINS 35 MINS

SPECIAL EQUIPMENT ■ 1.2-liter (2-pint) ovenproof dish

SERVES 4

1½lb (675g) potatoes, peeled and quartered

salt and freshly ground black pepper

1⅓ cups milk

12oz (350g) salmon fillet

7oz (200g) cooked, peeled shrimp

2-3 tbsp butter, plus extra for topping

2 tbsp all-purpose flour

1 tbsp wholegrain mustard

1 Preheat the oven to 400°F (200°C). Cook the potatoes in a pan of boiling salted water for about 15 minutes until soft, then drain them. Mash well with 2 tbsp of the milk and set aside.

2 Poach the salmon in the remaining milk in a covered shallow pan over low heat for 3-5 minutes until just cooked. Drain, reserving the milk.

Flake the fish into chunks, discarding any skin and bones. Place in the ovenproof dish and add the shrimp.

3 Rinse out the fish cooking pan and melt the butter in it over low heat. Remove from the heat and blend in the flour with a balloon whisk or wooden spoon. Gradually blend in the fish cooking milk. Return the pan to the heat, bring to a boil, and cook for 2 minutes, whisking or stirring all the time, until the sauce is thickened and smooth. Stir in the mustard and season to taste.

4 Pour the sauce over the shrimp and salmon in the dish and combine. Cover with the mashed potato to make a topping and dot with the extra butter. Bake in the oven for 15-20 minutes until heated through and the topping is crisp and golden.

thai green curry

Succulent, slightly sweet shrimp taste divine in this light, fragrantly spiced coconut curry with a kick.

 10 MINS 30 MINS

SERVES 4

1 tbsp sunflower oil or vegetable oil

1 onion, finely diced

1-2 tbsp Thai green curry paste (depending on how hot you like it)

1 x 14oz (400ml) can coconut milk

2 tbsp fish sauce (nam pla)

1-2 tsp palm sugar or brown sugar

2-3 kaffir lime leaves (optional)

salt and freshly ground black pepper

1 x 7oz (220g) can bamboo shoots, drained

7oz (200g) cooked, peeled shrimp

1 Heat the oil in a large, deep frying pan or wok over low-medium heat. Add the diced onion and sauté it for about 5 minutes until it is soft and translucent. Add the green curry paste, stir it around, and cook for another 2-3 minutes until it gives a fragrant aroma.

2 Pour in the coconut milk, then fill the can with water and add this to the pan or wok. Bring to a boil, reduce the heat slightly, and add the fish sauce, sugar, and lime leaves, if using. Season the sauce with salt and pepper.

3 Simmer over low heat for about 15 minutes, then stir in the bamboo shoots and shrimp. Cook for about 10 minutes, or until the shrimp are warmed through. Taste and adjust the seasoning if needed. Serve while still hot.

shrimp risotto

Risotto with shrimp is perfect food for a cool spring night.

 15–20 MINS   25–30 MINS

SERVES 6

4 tbsp olive oil

2 garlic cloves, finely chopped

leaves from a small bunch of flat-leaf parsley, chopped

salt and freshly ground black pepper

¼ cup dry white wine

3¼ cups fish or chicken stock

1 onion, finely chopped

15oz (420g) arborio rice

1lb 2oz (500g) cooked, peeled shrimp

1 Heat a third of the oil in a saucepan and add the garlic, parsley, salt, and pepper. Cook for 1–2 minutes, stirring frequently. Pour in the wine and stir thoroughly. Simmer the liquid in the pan for 2–3 minutes, until reduced by three-quarters. Add the stock and 1 cup water, and bring to a boil. Keep the liquid simmering.

2 Heat half the remaining oil in a large saucepan. Add the onion and cook, stirring, for 2–3 minutes until it is soft and translucent. Add the rice and stir until it is shiny and coated with oil. Ladle in just enough of the simmering liquid to cover the rice.

3 Stir the rice constantly until all the liquid is absorbed. Add more liquid to just cover the rice and simmer, stirring, until completely absorbed. Continue adding liquid to the rice in this way. Stop when the rice is al dente: just tender, but firm to the bite; it should take 25–30 minutes.

4 Stir in the shrimp and the remaining oil, allow the shrimp to heat until warmed through, and then season to taste with salt and pepper (you may not need much salt). Spoon the risotto into warmed bowls and serve immediately.

shrimp saganaki

Try this quick, delicious, and popular Greek one-pot recipe for a simple way to cook with fresh shrimp.

 10 MINS   45 MINS

SERVES 4

1 tbsp olive oil

1 onion, finely chopped

2 garlic cloves, crushed or finely chopped

1 x 14oz (400g) can chopped tomatoes

2 tbsp tomato paste

1 cup dry white wine

½ tsp sugar

salt and freshly ground black pepper

12oz (350g) large cooked, peeled shrimp

4½oz (125g) feta cheese

small handful of thyme leaves

1 Heat half the oil in a large frying pan, add the onion, and cook over low heat for 8 minutes, or until soft and translucent. Stir through the garlic and cook for a few more seconds, then add the tomatoes, ⅔ cup water, tomato paste, wine, sugar, and a little salt and pepper. Bring to a boil, reduce the heat, and simmer gently, stirring occasionally for 20–30 minutes until thick and pulpy.

2 Stir the shrimp into the sauce, remove from the heat, and crumble over the feta cheese. Pop under the broiler until the cheese melts and turns golden brown, then sprinkle over the thyme leaves. Serve with a crisp salad and fresh crusty bread.

spinach and coconut shrimp curry

This mild, creamy curry flavored with coconut is ideal if you have a quantity of spinach to use up. It makes a light and fragrant supper that needs just simple accompaniments.

 15 MINS   20 MINS

SERVES 4

2 tbsp sunflower or vegetable oil

2 red onions, finely chopped

4 garlic cloves, finely chopped

large thumb-sized knob of fresh ginger, grated

¼–½ tsp chili powder

½ tsp turmeric

2 tsp ground cumin

1 tsp ground coriander

4 large tomatoes, peeled (p197) and finely chopped

1 x 14oz (400ml) coconut milk

10 fresh or dried curry leaves (optional)

5½oz (150g) spinach, stems removed and leaves finely shredded

14oz (400g) large cooked, peeled shrimp

½ tsp granulates sugar

sea salt

1 Heat the sunflower oil in a large, deep frying pan or wok. Add the onions, garlic, and ginger, and cook for 2–3 minutes over low heat until soft and translucent. Add the spices and cook for another 1–2 minutes to release their flavors.

2 Add the tomatoes and continue to cook over low heat for another 2 minutes until their flesh starts to break down. Add the coconut milk and curry leaves (if using), and bring to a boil. Mix in the spinach and lower the heat, continuing to cook until the spinach has wilted. Baby spinach will take 1–2 minutes, bigger leaves up to 4 minutes.

3 Add the shrimp, sugar, and a pinch of sea salt, and cook for another 2–3 minutes until the shrimp are heated through. Serve with basmati rice, naan bread, and a couple of lime wedges on the side.

Season's best **shrimp**

Northern (cold water) shrimp are native to Britain and Europe, and the US. They have sweet, succulent flesh, while the large, warm water shrimp are meatier and more robust. In season spring and winter, they are a classic for shrimp cocktail. They toughen quickly and so are often added toward the end of cooking. They are excellent with mayonnaise, citrus, asparagus, avocados, artichokes, other seafood, and chicken.

Cooked Northern (cold water) shrimp You will find them fresh or frozen, precooked, whole, or peeled. They are graded by size.

Raw Northern (cold water) shrimp These are small, pinkish-gray, and translucent. They turn bright pink and opaque when cooked.

Buy them shell on, then peel yourself, for the best flavor.

Unpeeled shrimp have the most succulent flesh, if you can find them.

essentials
varieties available

Northern (cold water) shrimp, occasionally raw whole, but mostly cooked, whole, or peeled. Available frozen and canned.

buy Buy from fisheries using sorting grids to reduce by-catch. They should be fresh-smelling and undamaged.

store Eat on day of purchase.

cook Grill, fry, steam, or add to soups, stews, sauces, rice, and pasta dishes. Use cold in salads and sandwiches.

recipe ideas

Asian chicken and shrimp broth with ginger and cilantro p28

Grilled shrimp with hot pepper sauce p30

Shrimp and guacamole tortilla stacks p31

Shrimp, avocado, and watercress sandwich p27

Salmon and shrimp fish pie p33

how to peel shrimp

Peeling cooked shrimp is a useful skill. It can be tedious, but worth it as cold water shrimp have the sweetest meat of all shrimp. If serving whole and unshelled, give your diners finger bowls or damp cloths to wipe their hands on.

1 Hold the shrimp firmly in the middle. With the other hand, pinch the head gently and pull it off. Repeat with the tail unless the recipe says otherwise.

2 Turn it upside-down and peel away the back legs and body shell. It will slide off over the back of the shrimp. Use the shells for fish stock.

singapore noodles with shrimp and pork

Loaded with shrimp and scallions, as well as pork, mushrooms, and fragrant spices, this is a dish for sharing.

 15 MINS PLUS MARINATING   🍲 30 MINS

SERVES 4

1lb (450g) pork tenderloin, cut into 1in (2.5cm) strips

3 tbsp fish sauce (nam pla)

2 tbsp dark soy sauce

2 tbsp rice wine vinegar

2 tsp five-spice powder

8oz (225g) thin rice vermicelli

1½ tsp sunflower or vegetable oil

1 large garlic clove, finely chopped

½ tsp ground coriander

9oz (250g) crimini mushrooms, sliced

7oz (200g) large cooked, peeled shrimp

1 large onion, finely chopped

2 red or jalapeño chiles, seeded and finely sliced

salt and freshly ground black pepper

5½oz (150g) bean sprouts

4 scallions, trimmed and finely chopped

small handful of cilantro, chopped

1 Put the pork in a mixing bowl, add the fish sauce, soy sauce, rice wine vinegar, and five-spice powder, and leave to marinate for at least 30 minutes. Meanwhile, put the vermicelli in a bowl, cover with boiling water, and leave for 6 minutes, or until soft. Drain, rinse, and set aside.

2 Put 1 tbsp of the oil in a large wok over high heat and swirl around the pan. Add the pork and, stirring continuously, cook for 6–8 minutes, or until beginning to turn golden and crisp. Remove with a slotted spoon and set aside. Heat another 1 tbsp of the oil in the wok, then add the garlic and ground coriander and stir. Add the mushrooms and cook for a couple of minutes, then add the shrimp and stir-fry over high heat for 5–8 minutes, or until pink. Remove with a slotted spoon and set aside.

3 Heat the remaining oil in the wok, then add the onions and chiles and stir-fry for 1 minute. Add the vermicelli, season with salt and pepper, then stir in the bean sprouts. Return the pork and shrimp mixture to the wok and stir well. Remove from the heat, top with the scallions and cilantro, and serve.

pad thai

There are numerous variations of this classic Thai dish. This version has lovely pieces of omelet, shrimp, and chicken.

 15 MINS   15 MINS

SERVES 4

9oz (250g) medium or thick rice noodles

1½ tbsp sunflower or vegetable oil

2 large eggs, lightly beaten

½ tsp shrimp paste (optional)

2 red or jalapeño chiles, seeded and finely chopped

3 skinless chicken breasts, cut into ¼in (5mm) slices

1 bunch of scallions, trimmed and finely chopped

splash of fish sauce (nam pla)

juice of 1 lime, plus lime wedges, to serve

1 tbsp light brown sugar

salt and freshly ground black pepper

4oz (115g) cooked, peeled shrimp

5½oz (150g) unsalted peanuts

small handful of cilantro, finely chopped

1 Put the noodles in a large bowl, cover with boiling water, and leave for 8 minutes, or until soft. Drain and put to one side. Meanwhile, put ½ tbsp of the oil in a large wok over high heat and swirl around the pan. Add the beaten egg and whisk it around the wok for about a minute, or until it begins to set—don't let it set completely—then spoon it out and set aside.

2 Add the remaining oil to the pan, then add the shrimp paste (if using) and chiles and stir. With the heat still high, add the chicken and stir vigorously for 5 minutes, or until it is no longer pink. Stir in the scallions, fish sauce, lime juice, and sugar and toss together well. Cook for a few minutes until the sugar has dissolved, then season well with salt and pepper. Add the shrimp and toss for a minute or two to heat through. Return the egg to the pan.

3 Add the noodles to the pan and toss together to coat with the sauce, then add half the peanuts and half the cilantro and toss again. Transfer to a large shallow serving bowl and scatter over the rest of the peanuts and cilantro. Garnish with lime wedges and serve.

shrimp makhani

Shrimp are mostly available cooked, so they can simply be stirred in at the end to heat through.

 20 MIN   40 MINS

SERVES 4

12oz (350g) large, cooked, peeled shrimp

salt and freshly ground black pepper

3 garlic cloves, crushed or finely chopped

3in (7.5cm) piece fresh ginger, peeled and grated or finely chopped

1½ tbsp vegetable oil

1 tsp chili powder

1 piece of cinnamon stick

2 red chiles, seeded and finely chopped

3 cardamom pods, crushed

1 x 14oz (400g) can chopped tomatoes

½ cup thick natural yogurt

2oz (60g) cashew nuts, ground, plus a handful, coarsely chopped, to garnish

1 tsp ground fenugreek

½ cup heavy cream

1 Season the shrimp with salt and pepper and toss with half the garlic, half the ginger, 1 tsp of the oil, and the chili powder. Set aside.

2 Heat the remaining oil in a large deep frying pan. Add the rest of the garlic and ginger, the cinnamon, chiles, and cardamom pods, and cook over low heat, stirring occasionally, for 2 minutes. Add the tomatoes and yogurt, bring to a boil, reduce the heat, and simmer gently for 10 minutes, or until pulpy (the mixture will curdle at first).

3 Push the tomato mixture through a sieve. Return to the pan, then stir in the ground cashew nuts and fenugreek and simmer for 10 minutes, adding a little hot water if the sauce starts to look too thick. Add the shrimp along with the cream, stir, taste, and season, if needed. Cook gently for 5 minutes, then garnish with the chopped cashew nuts and serve with rice.

pan-fried clams with parsley and garlic

Throughout the Mediterranean, garlic and wine are classic partners for the fresh, briny flavor of clams.

 10 MINS   20 MINS

SERVES 4

1 tbsp olive oil

1 onion, finely chopped

salt

2 garlic cloves, grated or finely chopped

1 green bell pepper, seeded and finely chopped (optional)

1 cup dry white wine

1lb (450g) clams (discard any with broken shells and any that do not close when tapped)

handful of flat-leaf parsley, finely chopped

1 Heat the oil in a large frying pan over medium heat. Add the onion and a pinch of salt, and cook for about 5 minutes until soft and translucent. Add the garlic and pepper, if using, and gently cook until they begin to soften. Increase the heat to high, and add the wine. Cook for a couple of minutes until the wine begins to evaporate.

2 Add the clams, shaking the pan occasionally, and cook for 5–6 minutes until the clams open (discard any that do not). Add the parsley, and stir to combine.

3 Serve the clams piping hot with a squeeze of lemon and fresh crusty bread to mop up the juices.

variation

pan-fried clams with chorizo

Prepare in the same way, but substitute 1 small leek, quartered lengthwise and chopped, for the pepper. Add 2¼oz (70g) Spanish-style chorizo cubes to the pan in Step 1 after the leek has softened. Cook for 2 minutes, stirring, then add the wine and continue with the recipe.

pasta with clams

Fresh seafood can speak for itself. Clams only require the simplest of serving suggestions to delight the palate.

 10 MINS   15 MINS

SERVES 4

1 tbsp olive oil, plus extra to serve

1 onion, finely diced

3 garlic cloves, finely diced

small handful of flat-leaf parsley, finely chopped

½ cup dry white wine

1lb (450g) clams (discard any with broken shells and any that do not close when tapped)

12oz (350g) dried linguine or spaghetti

salt and freshly ground black pepper

1 Heat the oil in a large frying pan and cook the onion over low heat for 2 minutes, or until the onion begins to soften. Add the garlic and parsley and stir for a few seconds.

2 Add the wine, increase the heat, then add the clams and stir. Allow to boil for 5 minutes, or until the shells start to open, and shake the pan from time to time. Then turn the heat off and put a lid on the pan.

3 Meanwhile, cook the pasta in a large pan of boiling salted water for about 6 minutes, or until it is tender, but still al dente. Drain, keeping back a tiny amount of the cooking water. Return the pasta to the pan and toss it in the reserved cooking water. Add a drizzle of oil and season with salt and pepper. Discard any clams that have not opened, then toss the pasta with the clams and serve.

variation

pasta with mussels and saffron

Add 4 young carrots and ¼ small celery root, finely chopped, with the onion. Cover and cook gently for 5 minutes until soft, stirring occasionally. Add a good pinch of saffron strands with the wine and use mussels instead of clams.

morel and crimini mushroom barley

If you can't find any fresh morels at your local supermarket, use 2 dried ones, soaked according to package directions, and use the soaking water as part of the stock.

 10 MINS   45 MINS

SERVES 4

1 tbsp butter

1 onion, chopped

1 garlic clove, crushed

2 large morel mushrooms, cleaned and sliced

8oz (225g) crimini mushrooms, cleaned and sliced

⅔ cup dry white wine

7oz (200g) pearl barley

2 tsp chopped thyme, plus a few leaves for garnish

2½ cups chicken or vegetable stock

salt and freshly ground black pepper

2-3 tbsp half-and-half

Parmesan cheese, grated

1 Melt the butter in a large saucepan over medium heat, then add the onion and garlic and let them soften for about 2 minutes, stirring often. Add the sliced morels and crimini mushrooms and the wine, and simmer for 2 minutes. Then stir in the pearl barley and thyme. Add the stock and season well. Bring to a boil, reduce the heat, and simmer for 40 minutes or so, stirring twice. The barley is ready when it is tender, but still has some bite and the liquid is almost absorbed.

2 Stir in the half-and-half, and taste and re-season if necessary. Serve topped with a little grated Parmesan cheese and a garnish of thyme leaves.

pan-fried shrimp with olives

This Spanish-influenced shrimp dish makes a quick and easy weeknight supper.

 5 MINS   15 MINS

SERVES 4

1 tbsp olive oil

1 onion, finely chopped

2 garlic cloves, grated or finely chopped

dash of dry sherry

1 x 14oz (400g) can chopped tomatoes

large handful of mixed olives, pitted

14oz (400g) large cooked, peeled shrimp

salt and freshly ground black pepper

small handful of basil, chopped

small handful of flat-leaf parsley, chopped

1 Heat the oil in a large frying pan over medium heat. Add the onion and sauté for about 5 minutes until it is soft and translucent. Add the garlic and cook for a few seconds.

2 Add the sherry and continue cooking for 5 minutes, stirring until the alcohol has evaporated. Add the tomatoes and olives, and simmer for 5 minutes until the sauce has thickened slightly. Add the shrimp and simmer for another few minutes to heat through. Stir in the herbs and season to taste. Serve immediately with some crusty bread.

sole fillets in wine vinegar

This is an old Italian dish. Marinate the fish the night before you want to eat it; if you would prefer a milder marinade, use just half the quantity of vinegar and an equal amount of white wine.

 30–35 MINS PLUS MARINATING   2–4 MINS

SERVES 4–6

⅓ cup olive oil

1 large onion, thinly sliced

salt and freshly ground black pepper

1 cup red wine vinegar

1½oz (45g) raisins

1lb 2oz (500g) sole fillets

1 tbsp all-purpose flour

1oz (30g) pine nuts

For the salad

juice of ½ orange

3 tbsp olive oil

9oz (250g) salad leaves, such as arugula

1 Heat a third of the oil in a saucepan over low heat. Add the onion and season. Cover and cook the onion for 15 minutes until soft. Lift the lid, increase the heat, and cook the onion until it has caramelized. Add the vinegar and raisins and boil for 2 minutes. Set aside.

2 Rinse the fish and pat dry with paper towels. Cut each fillet across into 2in (5cm) pieces with a sharp knife. Spread the flour on a large plate and season. Coat the fish pieces in flour.

3 Heat the remaining oil in a frying pan over medium-high heat. Add the fish fillets and cook for 1–2 minutes,

until browned on one side. Then turn over and cook for another 1–2 minutes, until the flesh just flakes when tested with a fork. Drain the fillets on paper towels and allow to cool completely.

4 Place the fish in the bottom of a baking dish and cover with the onion and vinegar mixture. Sprinkle the pine nuts over the top, then cover the dish tightly and leave to marinate in the fridge for 12 hours, or even up to 24 hours if you have time. Remove it from the fridge 1 hour before serving.

5 Pour the orange juice into a bowl. Gradually whisk in the oil, so the

vinaigrette emulsifies and thickens slightly. Taste and season. Add the salad leaves and toss. Serve with the sole, with a little marinade spooned over the top.

variation

trout in rice wine vinegar

Use 1lb 2oz (500g) trout fillets instead of the sole. Prepare in the same way, but use 4 large spring onions instead of the ordinary one. Slice the green tops and add to the salad; slice the bulbs and use as the onion. Use rice wine vinegar instead of red wine vinegar.

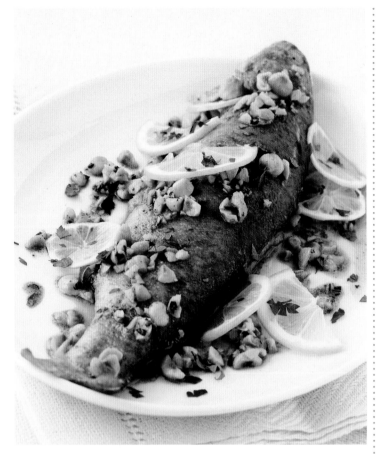

sautéed trout with hazelnuts

This recipe is about as quick as cooking gets, and produces a fresh, satisfying, and wholesome family dish. Serve with a rice pilaf for a heartier meal.

 20-25 MINS   10-15 MINS

SERVES 4

4 whole trout, about 10oz (300g) each, cleaned and scaled

2oz (60g) hazelnuts

2 lemons

1 tbsp all-purpose flour

salt and freshly ground black pepper

8 tbsp butter

2 tbsp chopped flat-leaf parsley

1 Cut the fins from the trout and trim the tails. Rinse inside and out, and pat dry with paper towels.

2 Preheat the oven to 350°F (180°C). Spread the hazelnuts on a baking sheet and toast them in the oven for 8-10 minutes until browned. While still hot, rub them in a kitchen towel to remove the skins, then set aside.

3 Trim the ends from a lemon, halve it lengthwise, and cut into thin semi-circles. Peel the second lemon, removing all the white pith, and cut into thin rounds. Remove any seeds.

4 Put the flour on a large plate and season with salt and pepper. Coat each trout in flour, patting to coat evenly. Heat half the butter in a large frying pan until foaming. Add two of the trout to the pan and brown over medium heat for 2-3 minutes. Turn the fish over and continue cooking over low heat for 3-5 minutes. When ready, the trout will be browned and the flesh will flake easily when tested with a fork. Keep the cooked trout warm while you cook the remaining two fish in the rest of the butter.

5 Add the hazelnuts to the pan and sauté them over medium heat for 3-4 minutes until golden brown, stirring frequently. Then stir in most of the parsley. Serve the fish on warmed plates with the hazelnuts spooned over the top. Decorate each trout with the lemon semi-circles and rounds, and sprinkle with the remaining parsley.

salmon chowder

Chowder makes a warming lunchtime soup on chilly spring days. Buying wild salmon is always best. If you buy farmed salmon, make sure it comes from a sustainable source.

 15 MINS   25 MINS PLUS RESTING

SERVES 4

2 tbsp olive oil

4 slices bacon, chopped

6 spring onions or scallions, trimmed and cut into 1in (2.5cm) slices

3 sprigs thyme

2 bay leaves

1lb 5oz (600g) baby new potatoes, thickly sliced

1 tbsp butter

1 tbsp all-purpose flour

2½ cups fish or chicken stock

14oz (400g) salmon fillets, skinned and cut into chunks

⅔ cup half-and-half

2-3 tbsp dill, chopped

grated zest of ½ lemon

salt and freshly ground black pepper

1 Heat 1 tbsp of the oil in a wide, deep sauté pan. Add the bacon and fry until crisp. Drain on paper towels and set aside. Pour the remaining oil into the pan, add the spring onions or scallions, thyme, and bay leaves, and stir-fry for 1 minute. Then add the potatoes and cook them for 2-3 minutes.

2 In another saucepan, melt the butter and beat in the flour. Cook for 1-2 minutes and then gradually add the stock. Bring to a boil and then simmer gently for 3-4 minutes or until thickened slightly. Add the thickened stock to the potatoes and bring it back to a boil. Cook the potatoes for 10 minutes, without stirring, until they are just tender.

3 Reduce the heat and submerge the salmon chunks into the stock. Simmer them very gently for 3-5 minutes, just until the fish is cooked. Don't stir the chowder, or the fish will break up.

4 Remove the pan from the heat. Without stirring, add in the half-and-half and scatter over the dill and lemon zest. Allow the soup to stand for 5-10 minutes for all the flavors to blend. When ready to serve, warm it through gently and briefly, discard the thyme and bay leaves, and add any seasoning if needed. Ladle into bowls and serve scattered with black pepper and the crispy bacon.

salmon kedgeree

Replacing robust smoked haddock with the gentle flavor of salmon turns a traditional rice dish into a light yet filling meal.

 10 MINS   20 MINS

SERVES 4

3 tbsp butter

1 onion, finely chopped

1 tsp mild curry powder

1 tsp cayenne pepper

12oz (350g) long-grain rice, such as basmati

2½ cups hot vegetable stock

salt and freshly ground black pepper

1lb 2oz (500g) salmon fillet, skinned

fresh mango, sliced, to garnish

1 Melt the butter in a saucepan over low heat. Add the chopped onion and cook gently for a few minutes until soft.

2 Add the curry powder, cayenne, and the long-grain rice and stir until the grains are well coated in the butter. Gradually add the hot vegetable stock, season, cover the pan (tilt the lid slightly so that steam can escape), and simmer gently for 10 minutes. Lay the salmon on top of the rice, re-cover, and cook gently for another 10 minutes until all the liquid has been absorbed and the salmon and rice are cooked.

3 Gently break up the salmon into large flakes. Lightly fold the fish through the rice and taste and re-season, if necessary. Serve hot with fresh mango slices.

baked salmon

It's vital that the fish you buy is always 100 percent fresh and never smells "fishy." Use any leftover salmon for a salad or sandwiches.

 15 MINS   40-45 MINS

SERVES 6

4lb (1.8kg) whole salmon, head removed, or a piece cut from a larger fish

4½oz (125g) butter

salt and freshly ground black pepper

handful of flat-leaf parsley, plus extra to garnish (or use watercress)

lemon wedges, to serve

1 Preheat the oven to 350°F (180°C). Lay a large piece of foil (enough to pull up and cover the salmon) over a large baking tray. Sit the salmon on the foil and dot the butter all over it. Season well, then scatter the parsley over the fish, stuffing a little in the cavity, too.

2 Loosely fold the foil over the salmon and seal. Bake in the oven on the baking tray for about 40–45 minutes, calculating the cooking time at 10 minutes per 1lb (450g) of fish. The salmon is cooked when it looks opaque and the flesh flakes easily when tested with a fork.

3 Unwrap the foil, remove any straggly bits of parsley, and carefully transfer the salmon to a warm plate. Garnish with fresh parsley or watercress and the lemon wedges. Serve with sautéed potatoes and salad or grilled asparagus.

variation

baked sea trout with dill

Prepare a large sea trout instead of the salmon, and use dill instead of parsley. Leave the head on or remove as you wish. Cook for 10 minutes per 1lb (450g). You can use small trout and bake in the same way; simply cook for 15–20 minutes instead.

lemon sole with herbs

The white flesh of flat fish is lean, textured, and flavorful, and should be firm or rigid to the touch when you buy it (if it is soft, it will be past its best).

 10 MINS   20 MINS

SERVES 4

3 tbsp extra virgin olive oil

1 tbsp white wine vinegar

1 tsp Dijon mustard

small handful of fresh mixed herbs such as parsley, thyme, and dill

salt and freshly ground black pepper

4 lemon sole fillets, about 6oz (175g) each, or other flat fish fillets, such as plaice or brill

1 Preheat the oven to 400°F (200°C). Make the herb dressing first: whisk together the oil and vinegar in a bowl. Add the mustard and herbs and mix well. Season well with salt and pepper and whisk once again.

2 Lay out the fish in a roasting pan and cover them with about ¼in (5mm) water. Season well with salt and pepper. Bake in the oven for 15–20 minutes, until the fish is cooked through and the water has almost evaporated. To check whether the lemon sole is cooked, see if the flesh lifts away from the bone easily. The flesh should also be opaque with no traces of pink.

3 Using a fish spatula, carefully lift the fish onto a serving dish or individual plates. Spoon over some of the herb dressing. Serve hot with sautéed potatoes and broccoli rabe.

variation

trout with herbs, caperberries, and olives

Use whole, cleaned trout instead of the sole fillets. For the dressing, omit the mustard and add a pinch of sugar, 1oz (30g) pickled capers, and 1oz (30g) sliced green olives, stuffed with pimiento, with the herbs.

pork and clam cataplana

This combination of rich pork and salty clams has been enjoyed for centuries in Portugal.

 20 MINS PLUS MARINATING   30 MINS   ❄ FREEZABLE

SERVES 4

1lb (450g) lean pork (leg or tenderloin), cut into bite-sized pieces

2 tbsp dry sherry

2 garlic cloves, finely chopped

1 tsp paprika

1 tsp dried chile flakes

salt and freshly ground black pepper

3 tbsp olive oil

5½oz (150g) chorizo, diced

1 tbsp tomato paste

1 onion, grated

1 bay leaf

⅔ cup white wine

2¼lb (1kg) clams (discard any with broken shells and any that do not close when tapped)

small handful of flat-leaf parsley, chopped

1 Put the pork in a bowl with the sherry, half the garlic, paprika, and chiles. Season with salt and pepper and set aside to marinate for 30 minutes, or overnight in the fridge.

2 Heat 1 tbsp of the oil in a large frying pan, add the chorizo, and cook over medium heat, stirring often, for 5 minutes, or until starting to crisp. Remove with a slotted spoon and set aside. Heat another 1 tbsp of the oil in the pan, add the pork and marinade, and cook for 8–10 minutes, or until the meat is golden all over. Remove with a slotted spoon and set aside.

3 Heat the remaining oil in the pan, add the tomato paste, remaining garlic, onion, and bay leaf and stir well. Leave to simmer over very low heat for 10 minutes, or until the onion is soft and translucent. Season well.

4 Add the wine, increase the heat, and allow to boil for a few minutes until the alcohol evaporates. Add the clams and cook for 4–5 minutes until the shells open. Discard any that do not. Return the pork and chorizo to the pan, warm through, then transfer to a large serving dish. Sprinkle with the parsley and serve.

instant smoked trout

A wok with a lid makes a great instant smoker. It must be well sealed to keep smoke from escaping and used over low heat. Fish and shellfish are perfect for instant smoking.

 15-20 MINS   25-30 MINS   ❄ FREEZABLE

SPECIAL EQUIPMENT ■ wok with a lid and rack

MAKES 2

1 tbsp light wood chips, such as apple

2 whole trout, gutted and cleaned with heads on

4 fennel fronds or 6–8 sprigs of tarragon (optional)

1 Line the inside of the wok with a double sheet of foil. Place the wood chips in the center of the foil (so it will smoke evenly) and place the wok rack inside the wok.

2 Wipe the insides of the trout and make 2 or 3 slashes on each side of the fish. Stuff the insides of the fish with the herbs, if you are using them.

3 Place the fish on the rack and put the lid on. Put a foil collar around the edge of the lid to keep the smoke in. Cook over low heat for 10–15 minutes. Then turn off the heat and leave the sealed wok for 15 minutes to allow the flavors to infuse the fish.

lamb and potato pie

For some great comfort food on cool spring evenings, this is a great way to use up leftover roast lamb.

 20 MINS   **50 MINS**

SPECIAL EQUIPMENT ▪ 9in (23cm) round pie dish

SERVES 4

1lb (450g) potatoes, peeled and quartered

1 tbsp olive oil

1 onion, finely chopped

1 leek, trimmed and sliced

4 baby turnips, peeled and quartered

handful of rosemary sprigs, leaves picked and chopped

7oz (200g) leftover roast lamb, roughly shredded or sliced

salt and freshly ground black pepper

1 tbsp all-purpose flour

1¼ cups hot vegetable stock

2-3 tsp mint sauce

9oz (250g) pie dough

1 large egg, lightly beaten, for egg wash

1 Preheat the oven to 400°F (200°C). Cook the potatoes in a pan of boiling salted water for about 15 minutes until soft; drain and set aside. Heat the oil in a large pan over low heat. Add the onion, leek, and turnips, and cook gently for about 5 minutes until soft and translucent. Stir through the rosemary and add the lamb. Season with salt and pepper.

2 Add in the flour and stir through, then pour in the stock. Keep stirring for about 10 minutes until the liquid begins to thicken, then add the reserved potatoes and stir in the mint sauce. Simmer for another 10 minutes. Allow to cool slightly.

3 Divide the dough into 2 pieces, one a little larger than the other. Roll out the larger piece into a large circle on a floured work surface. Use to line the pie dish, letting the dough hang over the edges. Roll out the other piece to make the lid for the top of the pie.

4 Spoon the lamb mixture into the crust, then sit the pastry lid on top. Pinch together the edges of the pastry to seal. Trim away the excess. Brush with a little egg wash and bake for 40–50 minutes until the pastry is golden. Leave to cool in the dish for at least 15 minutes before serving. Cut into slices and serve.

skewered lamb with crispy rosemary potatoes

Lamb is at its most succulent and its flavor most subtle at this season, as spring lambs are only aged between 3 and 5 months old.

 15 MINS   **30 MINS**

SPECIAL EQUIPMENT ▪ wooden skewers

SERVES 4

1½lb (675g) potatoes, peeled and diced

1-2 tbsp olive oil, plus extra for coating the lamb

handful of rosemary stalks

salt and freshly ground black pepper

2lb (900g) lean lamb steak or neck filet, cut into bite-sized pieces

juice of 1 lemon

2 tsp paprika

1 Preheat the oven to 400°F (200°C). Soak 8–10 wooden skewers in cold water for at least 30 minutes before using. Put the potatoes, ½ tbsp of the olive oil, rosemary, and some salt in a roasting pan. Using your hands, mix everything together so that the potatoes are evenly coated. Roast toward the top of the oven for 20–25 minutes until golden and crispy.

2 Meanwhile, put the lamb in a bowl and toss with the remaining olive oil, the lemon juice, paprika, some salt, and plenty of pepper. Thread the pieces of lamb onto the skewers until they are tightly packed.

3 Put the lamb skewers in a single layer in a separate roasting pan and roast below the potatoes for 10–15 minutes until cooked to your liking. Serve the skewers with the potatoes and a green salad.

Season's best **lamb**

Lamb comes from sheep less than 1 year old; when aged from 3 to 5 months old, it is called spring lamb. The meat of small spring lambs is pale pink, mild, and highly prized. The meat from older autumn lamb is darker and stronger. Lamb is versatile, and marries well with rosemary, mint, and most herbs, sweet spices, such as cumin and cinnamon, dried fruits, and fresh spring vegetables. Older lamb is good with apricots, berries, squashes, and eggplant.

Rack An elegant dinner party roast, this should have the backbone chined (removed) to allow slices to be cut between the ribs. Allow 2–3 ribs per person.

When the ends of the rib bones are scraped clean and exposed, this is called a French rack.

▼ **Cutlets** These are cut from the best end of the neck (rack) to the fore end of the loin. The eye of the meat is the tender, succulent neck fillet, which is also sold as a separate cut.

Chump chops These meaty chops are best grilled or fried.

Loin chops Because they are quite thick, loin chops can either be roasted or grilled. Double loin chops have fillet on one side of the bone and loin on the other.

Leg steaks These are cut from the top of the leg of a lamb. Grill or fry.

Lamb shanks very often have the bone end neatly trimmed.

Leg This top-quality joint can be fast- or slow-roasted.

Shanks Slow, moist cooking is required to turn the sinews in the shank to a succulent jelly. Allow one shank per person. Fore-leg shanks are slimmer than those from the back leg.

how to butterfly a leg of lamb

Boning and opening out the lamb is necessary if you wish to stuff and then tie it for roasting, or to marinate it, or to enable it to cook evenly when barbecuing (on a covered grill). The leg has 3 bones: the pelvis (the broadest), then the thigh, and the shank. They are cut away systematically, then the boned meat is opened out flat.

1 Place the fleshiest side down on a cutting board. Locate the pelvis at the widest end. Hold it firmly. Use a sharp, boning knife to cut around and expose the leg bone.

2 Cut through the flesh to the bone from the pelvis to the bottom of the leg. Using short, sweeping strokes, work your knife closely around the leg bone, releasing it.

3 When you reach the leg end, cut through the sinew and tendons to release the bone completely. Lift all 3 bones (the pelvis, thigh, and shank) away in one piece.

4 Open out the leg so that the meat lies flat on the cutting board. With short strokes, make cuts downward through the thick meaty pieces on either side.

essentials
cuts available

Leg, leg steaks, shanks, saddle (double loin roast), loin joint, loin chops, rack, cutlets, neck fillets, scrag end of neck, breast, diced meat, ground, and offal. Also available smoked.

buy All lamb should have just a thin covering of white fat. When becoming more mature it can have quite a lot of intramuscular and external fat.

store Keep wrapped, in the bottom of the fridge, for up to 4 days.

cook Roast, grill, fry, stew, or casserole (depending on the cut).

recipe ideas

Lamb with lemon and olives p50

Rack of lamb with flageolet beans and herbs p46

Skewered lamb with crispy rosemary potatoes p43

rack of lamb with flageolet beans and herbs

Flageolet beans are young white beans that have been harvested early in the season before they are fully ripe and then dried for preservation. They are small and cream-colored with a delicate flavor and form the ideal accompaniment to lamb.

 15 MINS 40 MINS

SERVES 4

1 rack of lamb (8 cutlets)

½ tbsp olive oil

a few sprigs of rosemary leaves, finely chopped

salt and freshly ground black pepper

⅔ cup hot vegetable stock

1 tsp redcurrant jelly

15oz can flageolet beans, drained

handful of mint leaves, finely chopped

1 Preheat the oven to 400°F (200°C). Smother the lamb with the oil, sprinkle over the rosemary, and season well with salt and pepper. Sit the rack in a roasting pan and put in the oven to roast for 40 minutes, or longer if you like your meat well done.

2 Remove the lamb from the pan and keep warm (covered with foil) while you prepare the beans. Sit the roasting pan on the stove top over medium to high heat, add the stock, and bring to the boil. Reduce to a simmer, stir in the redcurrant jelly until dissolved, then stir in the flageolet beans and simmer gently for 5 minutes. Remove from the heat and stir through the mint.

3 Slice the rack into 8 cutlets and serve on warmed plates with the beans and some potatoes.

variation

roast rack of lamb with harissa and baby turnips

Prepare in exactly the same way but before roasting, smear the lamb skin with 1 tbsp harissa paste and omit the rosemary. Boil 6 quartered baby turnips and add to the pan with the flageolet. Stir in 2 tsp tomato paste and a pinch of sugar instead of the redcurrant jelly. Stir in a handful of thyme leaves instead of mint.

pork with spring onions, soy sauce, and cinnamon

Asian flavors successfully perk up pork. Five-spice powder is a favorite Asian ingredient and is made from Szechuan pepper, star anise, fennel seeds, cloves, and cinnamon.

 15 MINS   **2 HRS 15 MINS – 2 HRS 30 MINS**

SERVES 4–6

2½lb (1.1kg) pork shoulder or leg, cut into bite-sized pieces

2 tsp five-spice powder

2–3 tbsp olive oil

2 bunches of spring onions or scallions, trimmed, white and green parts separated and finely chopped

3 garlic cloves, sliced

2in (5cm) piece of fresh ginger, peeled and sliced

½ cup dark soy sauce

2 cinnamon sticks, broken in half

9oz (250g) small button mushrooms, any large ones halved

about 3 cups hot chicken stock

freshly ground black pepper

1 Preheat the oven to 325°F (160°C) and toss the pork in the five-spice powder. Heat half the oil in a large flameproof casserole over medium-high heat, and cook the pork in batches for 5–6 minutes until it turns golden. Remove and set aside.

2 Heat the remaining oil in the casserole over medium heat. Add the spring onion or scallion whites and cook for a minute, then stir in the garlic and ginger until coated. Stir in the soy sauce, add the cinnamon and mushrooms, and return the pork to the casserole. Finally, add the stock, bring to a boil, then reduce to a simmer and season with black pepper. Cover with the lid and put in the oven for 2 hours.

3 If the sauce is too thin, remove the meat with a slotted spoon and set aside, then sit the casserole on the stove top and let it simmer for about 10 minutes, to reduce a little and intensify the flavors. Return the meat, remove the cinnamon sticks, and top with the spring onion or scallion greens. Ladle into warmed bowls and serve with noodles or rice.

shallow-fried red mullet

Pan-frying, a simple method of cooking, makes the most of the delicate sweetness of red mullet.

 15 MINS   **5 MINS**

SERVES 4

4 red mullet, gutted, scaled, trimmed, and heads removed

sea salt and freshly ground black pepper

cornmeal or polenta, for coating

grapeseed oil, for frying

lemon juice, to serve

1 Season the fish with sea salt and pepper, then coat them on both sides with cornmeal or polenta, shaking off any excess. Set a non-stick frying pan over medium heat and add enough oil to coat the bottom of the pan.

2 Put the prepared fish into the hot oil, presentation-side (the side that will be uppermost when serving) down. Shallow-fry for 2 minutes, or until the fish is golden brown.

3 Turn the fish using tongs and cook for 2–3 minutes, or until the other side is golden brown. To test for doneness, insert a thin-bladed knife into the center of the fish, then touch the tip of the knife to your thumb. If the knife is warm, the fish is ready. Drain briefly on paper towels and serve with a squeeze of lemon juice together with some boiled potatoes and steamed spring greens.

flatbreads topped with lamb and hummus

Lamb is so popular at this time of year, and this tasty Middle Eastern-style recipe is the perfect use for any leftovers from a roast joint.

 10 MINS   **20 MINS**

SERVES 2

1 tbsp olive oil, plus extra for drizzling

1 onion, finely chopped

3 garlic cloves, grated or finely chopped

7oz (200g) leftover roast lamb, shredded

pinch of ground allspice

pinch of ground cinnamon

salt and freshly ground black pepper

2 flatbreads or plain naan

handful of pine nuts, toasted

handful of mint leaves, coarsely chopped

hummus, to serve

1 Preheat the oven to 400°F (200°C). Heat the oil in a frying pan over medium heat, add the onion, and cook for about 5 minutes until the onion is soft and translucent.

2 Stir in the garlic and cook for a few more seconds. Now add the leftover lamb and stir through. Sprinkle over the allspice and cinnamon and cook for a few minutes, stirring occasionally. Season with salt and pepper.

3 Lay the flatbreads or naan on a baking sheet and drizzle with a little oil. Spoon over the lamb mixture and cook in the oven for about 10 minutes until the lamb is heated through. Scatter over the pine nuts and mint leaves, and top each flatbread or naan with a dollop of hummus. Serve immediately.

roast leg of spring lamb

A classic spring dish, roast lamb served with roast potatoes, mint sauce, and seasonal vegetables. Perfection on a plate.

 15 MINS   1 HR 45 MINS

SERVES 6–8

4½lb (2kg) leg of lamb

4 garlic cloves, peeled but left whole

handful of rosemary sprigs

salt and freshly ground black pepper

2 cups hot vegetable stock

1 tsp redcurrant jelly

1 Preheat the oven to 400°F (200°C). Spike the leg of lamb evenly all over with the point of a sharp knife, then stuff the garlic cloves and small sprigs of rosemary into the holes. Season the lamb with salt and pepper.

2 Sit the leg of lamb in a roasting pan and roast in the oven for about 15 minutes, until it begins to brown. Reduce the oven temperature to 350°F (180°C), and continue to roast for another 1 hour (for rare), basting it with its juices halfway through the cooking time; allow 1½ hours for well done. Transfer the lamb to a large plate, cover with foil, and leave to rest in a warm place for 15 minutes while you make the gravy.

3 To make the gravy, tilt the roasting pan at a slight angle and skim off any fat. Sit the pan over high heat on the stove top. Add the stock and redcurrant jelly and bring to a boil, scraping up any bits from the bottom of the pan with a wooden spoon. Reduce the heat slightly and simmer, stirring all the time, for 5–8 minutes. Taste, and season if needed. Carve at the table and serve with roast or creamy mashed potatoes, fresh mint sauce, and seasonal vegetables.

lamb filet basted with anchovy paste

Anchovies give new-season lamb a punchy flavor. You can buy store-bought anchovy paste, but it's not difficult to make, as shown here.

 15 MINS PLUS MARINATING   40 MINS

SPECIAL EQUIPMENT ▪ blender or food processor

SERVES 4

1 whole lamb neck filet, about 1½lb (675g)

2 salad onions, trimmed and coarsely chopped

5oz (150g) jar salted anchovies in oil, drained

2 tbsp capers in vinegar, drained

3 tbsp olive oil

1 Score the lamb filet in a crisscross pattern about ½in (1cm) deep. Put the remaining ingredients in a blender or food processor and process to a fine paste. Liberally spread the paste all over the lamb, making sure that it makes its way into the scores. Allow to marinate in the fridge for about 30 minutes.

2 Preheat a broiler to medium and sit the lamb filet on the broiler pan. Cook in the lower part of the broiler for 15–20 minutes, turning occasionally, until browned and cooked to your liking. Transfer the lamb to a plate and leave it to rest in a warm place for 10 minutes.

3 Cut into ½in (1cm) slices and serve with warm pita bread, hummus, and seasonal salad leaves.

turkish-spiced lamb pizza with pine nuts

Pine nuts and paprika introduce Turkish flavors that meld perfectly with garlicky lamb on an unusual flatbread base.

 5 MINS   20 MINS

SERVES 4

1 tbsp olive oil

1 onion, finely chopped

2 garlic cloves, finely chopped

1lb (450g) ground lamb

pinch of chili powder

juice of 1 lemon

salt and freshly ground black pepper

4 flatbreads, such as pita or naan

handful of pine nuts

sprinkling of mild paprika

small handful of cilantro, to garnish

hummus, to serve

1 Preheat the oven to 400°F (200°C). Heat the oil in a large frying pan over medium heat, add the onion, and cook for 3–4 minutes until the onion is soft. Then add the garlic and lamb and cook, stirring to break up lumps, until the meat is browned.

2 Add the chili powder and lemon juice. Season with salt and pepper and stir through. Spoon the lamb mixture onto the flatbreads, scatter over the pine nuts, and sprinkle on the paprika.

3 Place on a baking sheet and cook in the oven for 5–10 minutes until golden. Garnish with the cilantro and serve with hummus.

rack of lamb with parsley crumb

A rack of lamb is among the more expensive cuts, so be sure to cook it correctly. Medium is really the best way, to keep the meat at its most succulent. The bread crumbs mixed with finely chopped parsley give a crisp finish to this dish.

 35-40 MINS 25-30 MINS

SPECIAL EQUIPMENT ▪ blender or food processor

SERVES 4

2 racks of lamb, weighing 1lb 10oz–2¼lb (750g–1kg) each, chine bones removed

2 garlic cloves, cut into slivers

2 tbsp olive oil

salt and freshly ground black pepper

4 slices of white bread, crusts cut off

3 tbsp butter

leaves from a small bunch of flat-leaf parsley, finely chopped

For the gravy

½ cup white wine

1 cup lamb, beef, or chicken stock

1 Set a rack of lamb on a cutting board, ribs upward, and with a sharp knife, cut out any sinew lying under the ribs. Turn the rack over. Cut away the small crescent of cartilage at one end.

2 Make a small incision under the thin layer of skin covering the fat. Using your fingers, pull off the skin. If you can't get a good grip, use a clean kitchen towel to help. Score through the fat and meat down to the rib bones, about 2in (5cm) from the ends of the bones.

3 Turn the rack over. Place it over the edge of the board and score down to the bone, about 2in (5cm) from the ends of the bones. Cut out the meat between the bones, using the point of a knife. Scrape the bones clean, being sure to scrape away all skin. Repeat for the second piece of meat.

4 Preheat the oven to 450°F (230°C). Make several incisions in the lamb with the point of a knife and push in the garlic slivers. Transfer the racks to a roasting pan, ribs downward. Wrap the bones in foil to prevent them from burning. Spoon the oil over the lamb and sprinkle with salt and

pepper. Roast in the oven for 25–30 minutes, basting once or twice with the juices in the roasting pan. The meat will shrink away from the bones a little.

5 Test the lamb with a metal skewer: when inserted for 30 seconds, it will feel warm to the touch when withdrawn. A meat thermometer should register 140°F (60°C). This will give medium meat.

6 For the parsley crumb, put the bread in a blender or food processor and pulse to form crumbs. Melt the butter in a frying pan, add the bread crumbs, and cook for 2–3 minutes, stirring, until just golden. Stir in the parsley and season.

7 When the lamb is cooked to your taste, transfer the racks to a cutting board. Discard the foil used to cover the bones. Insulate the racks with more foil

and set aside to rest. This allows all the juices to flow back evenly through the meat, giving juicier lamb. Heat the broiler.

8 To make the gravy, discard the fat from the roasting pan. Add the wine and boil until reduced by half, stirring to dissolve the roasting juices from the bottom of the pan. Add the stock and boil for 5–7 minutes, until the gravy is well flavored. Season to taste. Strain and keep warm until ready to serve. You can stir in 1–2 tsp cornstarch, mixed with cold water until smooth, if you want a thicker gravy.

9 Press the bread crumbs on to the top surface of the lamb and baste with the roasting juices. Broil, bread crumb-side up, for 1–2 minutes until lightly browned. Watch that the bread crumb coating does not scorch. Carve and serve on warmed plates with the gravy on the side.

spaghetti with chile flakes, broccoli, and spring onion

This is a simple way to enjoy fresh greens at their best. You can use other pasta instead if you prefer—try the sauce with bucatini or the large, flat pappardelle for a change.

 10 MINS   12 MINS

SERVES 4

12oz (350g) dried spaghetti

salt and freshly ground black pepper

7oz (200g) sprouting broccoli or broccoli rabe

5 tbsp olive oil

bunch of spring onions or scallions, trimmed and chopped

1 tsp dried chile flakes

1 tbsp lime juice

Parmesan cheese, grated, to serve

1 Cook the spaghetti in boiling salted water according to package instructions. Drain and return to the pan.

2 Meanwhile, trim the broccoli, cut the heads into small florets, and chop the stalks.

3 Heat the oil in a large frying pan or wok. Add the broccoli and spring onions or scallions and stir-fry for about 4 minutes until just tender.

4 Pour the contents of the pan into the spaghetti. Add the flakes, lime juice, and seasoning to taste. Toss gently, pile onto plates, and serve with plenty of Parmesan cheese.

lamb with lemon and olives

Using whole lemons, rather than simply the juice, adds a sharpness of flavor to this dish. The addition of olives successfully elaborates on the Mediterranean theme.

 25 MINS   35 MINS

SERVES 4

3 tbsp olive oil

bunch of spring onions or scallions, trimmed and finely chopped

1lb 2oz (500g) lean lamb, cut into bite-sized pieces

6 garlic cloves, finely sliced

1 lemon, cut into eighths

1 tsp chopped rosemary leaves

handful of flat-leaf parsley, chopped

1 tsp paprika

3 tbsp green olives

salt and freshly ground black pepper

1 Preheat the oven to 400°F (200°C). Heat the oil in a frying pan, add the spring onions or scallions, and cook over medium heat for 5 minutes, or until they are beginning to soften. Add the lamb and cook, stirring occasionally, for 5 minutes, or until no longer pink. Add the garlic and lemon and cook for 1 minute, then add the rest of the ingredients and cook for another 2 minutes, stirring well.

2 Transfer the mixture to a small baking dish, packing it in tightly. Add 2 tbsp water, mix well, and then bake for 20 minutes.

3 Remove from the oven and allow to rest for 10 minutes before serving with fresh crusty bread and a crisp green salad.

calzone with cheese, ham, and spinach

Calzone is a folded Italian pizza. For a crispy finish, sprinkle the top of the dough with some water before baking.

 15 MINS 20 MINS

MAKES 1

For the dough

1 cup bread flour

pinch of salt

pinch of granulated sugar

¾ tsp dried yeast

1 tbsp olive oil

⅓ cup warm water

For the filling

7oz (200g) spinach leaves, wilted and drained

4½oz (125g) cooked ham, chopped

4½oz (125g) mozzarella, torn into pieces

handful of torn basil leaves

1 Sift the flour, salt, and sugar into a bowl. Add the yeast. Stir in the oil and enough warm water to form a soft but not sticky dough. Knead gently on a lightly floured surface for several minutes until smooth and elastic. Return to the bowl, cover with oiled plastic wrap, and leave in a warm place for about 40 minutes until the dough has doubled in bulk.

2 Preheat the oven to its highest setting. Very lightly oil a baking sheet and put it in the oven to get hot. Turn out the dough on a floured surface and knock it back by re-kneading briefly. Roll out thinly to a round, about 10in (25cm) diameter, and transfer to the hot baking sheet, spreading it out firmly again.

3 Squeeze any remaining liquid from the spinach and spread it over half the pizza base, leaving about ½in (1cm) around the edge. Top with the ham, mozzarella, and basil, then dampen all around the edge of the pizza with water. Fold one half of the pizza over the other, seal the edges together with your fingers, then sprinkle the top with a little water. Bake for 15–20 minutes, or until golden and crispy.

sole with butter sauce

This sauce is perfect with any flat fish, such as the sole suggested here. Alternatively, use tarragon (sparingly!) or dill instead of some or all of the parsley.

 15 MINS 10 MINS FREEZABLE

SERVES 4

4 small whole sole, fins and tail trimmed

8 tbsp butter, diced, plus 2 tbsp butter, melted

salt and freshly ground black pepper

1 small onion, finely chopped

2 tbsp cider vinegar

2 tbsp chopped parsley

1 Preheat the broiler. Lay the fish on the broiler rack and brush all over with the melted butter. Season lightly with salt and pepper and broil for about 5 minutes on each side until lightly golden and cooked through.

2 Meanwhile, put the onion in a small pan with 2 tbsp water and the cider vinegar. Bring to a boil, reduce the heat, and simmer until the onion is soft and the liquid is reduced by half.

3 Whisk in the diced butter, a piece at a time, until the sauce has thickened. Then stir in the parsley and season with more salt and pepper to taste.

4 Transfer the fish to warmed plates, spoon over the sauce, and serve with baby carrots and plain potatoes.

spinach and goat cheese frittata

This makes a delicious light lunch or supper dish, served hot or cold. You can use dollops of soft, creamy goat cheese in place of the cubed pieces if you prefer.

 8 MINS   12 MINS

SERVES 4

2 tbsp olive oil

pat of butter

4 spring onions, trimmed and chopped

2 large handfuls of baby spinach

6 eggs, beaten

salt and freshly ground black pepper

3½oz (100g) goat cheese, cut into cubes

6-8 basil leaves, chopped

1 Heat the oil and butter in a large non-stick frying pan. Add the spring onions and cook, stirring, for 2 minutes until soft. Add the spinach and stir for another 1–2 minutes until wilted. Simmer for a minute or two more to evaporate any juice. Spread the spinach out evenly in the pan.

2 Season the eggs with salt and pepper and pour into the pan. Scatter the goat cheese and then the basil over. Cook over low heat, lifting and stirring the mixture gently and tilting the pan to allow the uncooked egg to run underneath. Meanwhile, preheat the broiler to medium.

3 Lift the edges of the frittata with a palette knife to check the bottom. After about 5 minutes, when the bottom is golden and set but the top is still slightly runny, set the pan under the hot broiler for 2–3 minutes to brown. Cut into wedges and serve with fresh crusty bread.

variation

nettle and blue cheese frittata

Prepare in the same way, but use 2 large handfuls of young nettle tops instead of the spinach (use gloves when picking and washing them). Add 2 tbsp water when wilting them in the pan, then evaporate the juice, as before. Substitute 3½oz (100g) soft, creamy blue cheese, such as Dolcelatte, for the goat cheese and 6-8 chopped sage leaves instead of the basil. Cook and broil as before.

pork and spring greens

Choose your greens with the seasons—this quick stir-fry makes the most of the leafy seasonal produce available.

 10 MINS   10 MINS

SERVES 4

1 tbsp olive oil

12oz (350g) pork filet, cut into thin strips

4 garlic cloves, sliced

2 heads of spring greens, shredded

2 tsp nigella seeds

salt and freshly ground black pepper

1 Heat the oil in a wok over medium-high heat. When the oil is hot, add the pork. Stir-fry the pork for about 5 minutes, moving it around the wok as it heats up.

2 Add the garlic and greens. Continue to stir-fry over medium-high heat for 1 minute, or until the greens have just wilted. Add the nigella seeds and stir to combine, then season with salt and pepper. Serve immediately with fluffy rice.

variation

chicken breasts with spring greens and hoisin

Prepare in the same way but use 8 boneless, skinless chicken breasts, cut into thin strips, instead of the pork. Use sunflower oil instead of olive. Stir-fry for 2 minutes, then add 2 tbsp hoisin sauce and stir-fry for 1 minute more. When cooked, add a dash of soy sauce, to taste.

italian wedding soup

The Italian name for this robust, rustic soup is *minestra maritata*, which simply means the flavors marry well together. All this soup needs with it is some crusty bread.

 10 MINS   1 HR 40 MINS   ❄ FREEZABLE

SERVES 4-5

5½oz (150g) beef stew meat, diced

1 ham hock

4oz (115g) piece of salami, diced

1 bone-in, skin-on chicken breast

1 large onion, chopped

3½ cups beef stock

sprig of rosemary

1 bay leaf

salt and freshly ground black pepper

¼ head spring greens, shredded

1 head of green or red chicory

2oz (60g) soup pasta shapes

Parmesan cheese, grated

crusty bread, to serve

1 Put all the meats in a large pan with the onion, stock, rosemary, and bay leaf, and season well with salt and pepper. Bring to a boil, skim the surface, reduce the heat, cover, and simmer very gently for 1½ hours until the meat is meltingly tender.

2 Discard the herbs. Lift out the chicken and ham hock, discard the skin from both, remove all flesh from the bones, cut into neat pieces, and return all meat to the pot. Add the greens, chicory, and pasta. Bring back to a boil, reduce the heat, and simmer for 10 minutes. Taste and adjust the seasoning, if necessary. Ladle into large open soup plates, sprinkle with grated Parmesan cheese, and serve with the bread.

Season's best **spring leafy greens**

All varieties of leafy greens have a sweet flavor with an appealing hint of bitterness. Spinach varieties are delicate, with the new season's large leaves having the best flavor. They add a beautiful green color to dishes. Spring greens (available late winter through spring) have squeaky leaves and are more robust. Try both with ginger, chile, garlic, and soy sauce, and also with the more subtle flavors of cream, nuts, and eggs.

True spinach (and baby leaves) needs frequent sowings to provide a sustainable crop. Perpetual varieties re-grow once cut. Spring greens are a hardy crop that can survive harsh winters to become available in spring.

Large leaf spinach Spinach has juicy, tender leaves with a distinctly earthy, acidic flavor. As they are composed mostly of water, they greatly reduce in bulk once cooked.

Spring greens The leaves appear tough, but cook quickly to be sweet and tender, yet retain a pleasing texture.

Tear coarse midribs and stems from large spinach leaves before cooking.

The stems and midribs are undeveloped, so the leaves do not need trimming.

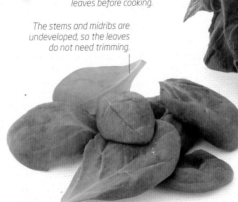

essentials
varieties available

Spring greens, baby spinach, large leaf spinach (true and perpetual varieties).

buy Look for glossy leaves with freshly cut stem ends. Avoid broken or slimy leaves.

store Keep in the fridge in an open plastic bag for 3–4 days.

cook Boil, steam, sauté, stir-fry, or braise all. Wilt any spinach in hot butter or dressing. Eat baby spinach raw in salads.

preserve Blanch and freeze.

recipe ideas

Filo pie with spinach, ricotta cheese, and pine nuts p26

Italian wedding soup p52

Pork and spring greens p52

Baby spinach The mildly flavored leaves are brittle but soft. They are good in a salad with bacon and avocado, or wilted in an omelette or frittata.

how to trim greens

Spring (and winter) greens need trimming and shredding before cooking. Cut out the thick stems of large-leaf spinach (or Swiss chard), as in Step 1, then cook and eat with melted butter and Hollandaise sauce, like asparagus.

1 Discard all limp and discolored leaves. Slice each leaf along both sides of the center rib, then remove it and discard.

2 Working with a few leaves at a time, roll them loosely into a bunch. Cut across the roll to the desired width, making strips.

marmalade-glazed ham with new potatoes and chicory

The marmalade gives a wonderfully sticky-sweet finish to this ham, which is roasted with seasonal chicory.

 15 MINS   **1 HR 45 MINS**

SERVES 4–6

4lb (1.8kg) boneless ham

2 cups dry hard cider

2 bay leaves

3 tbsp marmalade

1 tbsp brown sugar

2½lb (1.1kg) small salad potatoes

1 tbsp olive oil

zest of 1 orange

salt and freshly ground black pepper

4 heads chicory, trimmed and quartered lengthwise

1 Sit the ham in a large pan, add the cider and bay leaves, then add enough hot water to cover, if needed. Cover with the lid, bring to a boil, then reduce to a simmer and cook for 40 minutes. Preheat the oven to 350°F (180°C).

2 Remove the ham from the pan and score it on all sides in a diamond pattern. Put the marmalade in a pan and heat gently over low heat until runny. Brush the ham liberally with the marmalade, then sprinkle over the sugar.

3 Sit the ham in a roasting pan. Toss the potatoes with the oil and orange zest, season well with salt and pepper, then add to the pan. Put in the oven to roast for 50 minutes to 1 hour. Add the chicory heads for the last 20 minutes of cooking, tossing them in some of the juices.

4 Remove the ham from the pan and keep warm while it rests for at least 15 minutes. Slice and serve with the potatoes and chicory.

pan-fried ham with pineapple salsa

A contemporary take on a traditional classic. Rather than leaving as whole rings, here the pineapple is chopped very finely for a salsa to serve with the ham.

 5 MINS   **20 MINS**

SERVES 4

1 tbsp olive oil

4 ham steaks

9oz (250g) peeled pineapple, cored and thinly sliced

1 tbsp honey

2-3 tbsp butter

3 tomatoes, peeled (p197) and chopped

½ red onion, finely diced

1 Heat the oil in a large non-stick frying pan over high heat. Add the pieces of ham and cook for about 3–4 minutes on each side, depending on their thickness, until golden and cooked through. Remove from the pan and set aside to keep warm.

2 Smother the pineapple rings in honey. Melt the butter in the same frying pan. Add the pineapple and cook for a couple of minutes until golden and lightly charred. Remove from the pan, cool slightly, and chop into small pieces.

3 To make the salsa, put the pineapple, tomatoes, and red onion in a bowl, and mix until combined.

4 To serve, transfer the ham steaks onto warmed plates and serve with the salsa and perhaps some thick-cut fries or a salad.

chicken with chicory and bacon

Chicory has a bitter taste, but once roasted it is much more mellow. For added flavor, sprinkle Parmesan cheese over the chicory once it is in the roasting pan, if you like.

 5 MINS   40 MINS

SERVES 4

2-3 tbsp butter

pinch of brown sugar

3 large heads chicory, trimmed and halved lengthwise

1 tbsp olive oil

4 large chicken breasts with skin on

12 thick-cut bacon slices

1 Preheat the oven to 400°F (200°C). Put the butter and the sugar in a large frying pan over low heat. Cook until the sugar has dissolved and the butter melted. Add the chicory and cook for 5–8 minutes until golden, then set aside.

2 Increase the heat to medium-high and add the oil to the same pan. When hot, add the chicken, skin-side down, and brown for 3–5 minutes on each side until golden all over. Transfer the chicken to a roasting pan.

3 Wrap the bacon around the reserved chicory and tuck it into the roasting pan, so that it all sits snugly. You want everything tightly packed, so that the dish will produce plenty of juice. Roast in the oven for about 25 minutes until golden. Serve hot with baby roast potatoes.

variation

turbot with cheese, ham, and chicory
Prepare in the same way but use 4 turbot fillets (about 5oz/150g each) instead of the chicken breasts. Bake in the oven for 10 minutes, then top the fish with slices of Gruyère or Cheddar cheese and return to the oven for another 10 minutes, or until the fish is cooked through and the cheese is golden and bubbling.

spinach-stuffed veal

The rolls can be cooked up to 2 days ahead, covered, and refrigerated. Their flavor will mellow.

 45-50 MINS   30-40 MINS

SERVES 4

1lb 2oz (500g) spinach leaves, trimmed

4 tbsp olive oil, plus more if needed

8 garlic cloves, finely chopped

1½oz (45g) walnuts, chopped

1oz (30g) Parmesan cheese, grated

grated nutmeg

salt and freshly ground black pepper

8 veal escalopes, total weight about 1lb 6oz (625g), pounded between two sheets of parchment paper

1 onion, thinly sliced

1 carrot, thinly sliced

2 celery ribs, thinly sliced

1 cup dry white wine

1 cup chicken stock

1 Bring a saucepan of water to a boil, add the spinach, and simmer for 1–2 minutes, then drain. Squeeze to remove excess water, then chop. Heat 2 tbsp of the oil in a frying pan and add the spinach. Stir until any moisture has evaporated. Remove from the heat and add half the garlic, the walnuts, Parmesan, and nutmeg. Stir and taste for seasoning.

2 Lay one escalope on a work surface and season. Spread an eighth of the spinach stuffing on top. Roll up the meat, tucking in the ends. Repeat with the remaining escalopes and stuffing. Tie up the rolls.

3 Heat the remaining oil in a sauté pan and add the veal rolls. Cook over high heat for 2–3 minutes, turning occasionally, until browned all over. Transfer to a plate and set aside.

4 Stir the onion and remaining garlic into the pan and cook until softened. Add the carrot and celery. Reduce the heat and cook for 8–10 minutes, until tender. Pour in the wine, bring to a boil, and simmer to reduce by half.

5 Return the veal to the pan and add the stock. Cover and simmer for 30–40 minutes, until tender. Strain the liquid into a saucepan, reserving the vegetables, and boil until reduced to ¾ cup. Slice the veal rolls and serve with the sauce.

cornish game hens with mushrooms

For the best result, use the melted butter for frequent basting.

 30-40 MINS **35-40 MINS**

SERVES 2

6 tbsp butter

2 Cornish game hens, backbone removed (ask your butcher to do this)

salt and freshly ground black pepper

2½ tbsp Dijon mustard, or to taste

2 tbsp dried bread crumbs

2 tbsp all-purpose flour

5½oz (150g) mushrooms, sliced

2 shallots, finely chopped

1 garlic clove, finely chopped

¼ cup medium dry white wine

¼ cup white wine vinegar

1½ cups chicken stock

bunch of watercress, to garnish

1 Heat the broiler. Brush the broiler pan with oil. Melt 2 tbsp of the butter in a small saucepan for basting. Brush the hens with half the melted butter and sprinkle with salt and pepper.

2 Broil the hens in the broiler pan, skin-side up, about 3in (7.5cm) from the heat. Cook for about 15 minutes, basting once with the butter. Turn,

brush the underside of the birds with the remaining melted butter, and broil for another 10 minutes. Turn again so the birds are breast-side up once more. Brush the skin with 1 tbsp of the mustard, then sprinkle evenly with the bread crumbs. Broil, skin-side up, for about 10 minutes until tender.

3 In a shallow dish, mash 2 tbsp of the remaining butter with the flour. Set aside. Melt 1 tbsp of the butter in a pan, add the mushrooms, and cook, stirring, for 3–5 minutes, until tender and lightly browned.

4 Melt the remaining butter in another pan, add the shallots and garlic, and cook until soft. Add the wine and vinegar and reduce to about 2 tbsp. Stir in the remaining mustard and stock, and then the mushrooms. Simmer for 5 minutes. Whisk in the flour paste a small piece at a time, to slightly thicken the sauce. Season and arrange the birds on warmed plates and serve with the sauce, garnished with watercress.

jerk chicken with roasted pineapple

A store-bought jerk marinade would work just as well here.

 10 MINS PLUS MARINATING **40 MINS** **FREEZABLE**

SPECIAL EQUIPMENT ▪ blender or food processor

SERVES 4

For the jerk marinade

1-2 red chiles, seeded

1-2 green chiles, seeded

pinch of ground cinnamon

pinch of grated nutmeg

pinch of salt and 1 tsp black pepper

grated zest and juice of 2 limes

3 tbsp brown sugar

2 tbsp vegetable oil

handful of flat-leaf parsley

handful of cilantro

a few sprigs of thyme, leaves picked

For the chicken

1 whole chicken, cut into 8 pieces (ask your butcher to do this)

1 small pineapple, peeled, cored, thickly sliced, and cut into chunks

1 To make the marinade, put all the ingredients in a blender or food processor. Pulse to a paste and add a little more oil if needed.

2 Deeply slash all the chicken pieces, then put in a large plastic freezer bag. Add the jerk marinade and squish everything together until the chicken is well coated. Leave to marinate in the fridge for at least 30 minutes, or preferably overnight.

3 Preheat the oven to 400°F (200°C). Arrange the chicken pieces in a large roasting pan, making sure that there is plenty of room. Roast in the oven for 35–40 minutes until golden and crisp. Add the pineapple pieces for the last 10 minutes of cooking time. Serve hot with fluffy rice.

cornish game hens in vine leaves

Each bird makes a generous portion; perfect for a dinner party.

 45-50 MINS **1 HR - 1 HR 10 MINS**

SERVES 4

6 strips thick-cut bacon, sliced

1 shallot, finely chopped

1 chicken liver, coarsely chopped

handful of tarragon leaves, chopped

handful of parsley leaves, chopped

pinch of ground allspice

¼ cup white bread crumbs

salt and freshly ground black pepper

4 Cornish game hens, seasoned inside and out

8-12 preserved vine leaves, rinsed, drained, and dried in paper towels

2 tbsp vegetable oil

1 cup dry white wine

1 cup chicken stock

1 For the stuffing, fry 2 of the bacon strips in a pan, turning, for 3–5 minutes until crisp. Set aside. Cook the shallot for 2–3 minutes until soft. Add the liver and cook, stirring, for 1–2

minutes, until brown. Combine with the bacon, herbs, allspice, and bread crumbs, and season with black pepper.

2 For each hen, spoon one-quarter of the stuffing into the cavity, wrap 2 or 3 vine leaves over the breast, top with bacon, and tie with string like a parcel to hold it all together.

3 Preheat the oven to 350°F (180°C). Heat the oil in a roasting pan on the stove top, and brown the hens all over. Cover and bake for 45–55 minutes, until the juices run clear when a metal skewer is inserted.

4 Transfer the hens to warm plates. Discard the strings and cover with foil. Spoon the fat from the pan, then add the white wine. Bring to a boil, then simmer, stirring, until reduced by half. Add the stock and reduce again by half. Strain, season to taste and serve the sauce with the game hen.

flemish vegetable tart

A quick brioche dough makes a sumptuous crust for this unusual vegetable tart. You can choose to cook the tart in a frying pan, if you like, for a more rustic effect. Don't be worried about making brioche: this version is very easy indeed, and has the advantage that it can be made the day ahead and refrigerated, wrapped in plastic wrap, overnight.

 50-55 MINS PLUS RISING   **40-50 MINS**

SPECIAL EQUIPMENT ▪ 12in (30cm) flan dish or tart pan

SERVES 8

1½ tsp dried yeast

2 cups bread flour, more if needed

salt and freshly ground black pepper

7 large eggs

15 tbsp unsalted butter, softened

4 carrots, cut in julienne strips

1lb 2oz (500g) mushrooms, stems removed and caps thinly sliced

2 turnips, cut in julienne strips

8-10 spring onions or scallions, trimmed and finely sliced

1 cup heavy cream

¼ tsp grated nutmeg

1 For the dough, sprinkle the yeast over 2 tbsp lukewarm water in a bowl and let stand for 5 minutes. Oil a medium bowl. Sift the flour on to a work surface with 1 tsp salt. Make a well in the center and add the yeast and 3 eggs. Work the ingredients until thoroughly mixed. Draw in the flour and work into the other ingredients with your fingertips to form a smooth dough; add more flour if it is sticky.

2 Place the dough on a floured surface and knead for about 10 minutes, lifting it up and throwing it down until it is very elastic. Work in more flour as necessary, so it is slightly sticky but peels easily from the work surface. Add 5 tbsp of the butter, and pinch and squeeze to mix it into the dough. Knead for 3–5 minutes, until smooth again. Shape into a ball and put into the oiled bowl. Cover with plastic wrap and chill for about 1 hour.

3 Melt the remaining butter in a pan. Add the carrots and cook gently for about 5 minutes, stirring occasionally. Add the mushrooms and turnips, and season with salt and pepper. Press buttered foil over the vegetables, cover with a lid, and cook for about 10 minutes until tender, stirring occasionally. Remove from the heat, add the spring onions or scallions, and season.

4 Heat the oven to 400°F (200°C) and butter the flan dish. Place the dough on a floured surface and lightly knead it to knock out the air. Roll out to a round 3in (7.5cm) larger than the dish. Line the dish and spread the vegetable mixture in the crust. Whisk together the cream, salt, pepper, and nutmeg with the remaining eggs, and pour over the vegetables.

5 Fold the top edge of the dough rim over the filling to form a border. Let rise in a warm place for 20–30 minutes until puffed up. Bake for 40–50 minutes until the brioche crust is very brown and the custard is set but retaining a slight wobble. Serve hot or at room temperature.

game hens glazed with honey and wrapped in bacon

Cornish game hens are young chickens and the best season for them is spring. Wrapping them in bacon keeps them moist.

  20 MINS   1 HR

SERVES 4

4 cornish game hens

2 onions, coarsely chopped

2 tbsp honey

12 bacon or pancetta slices

6 leeks, trimmed and chopped into 2in (5cm) pieces

1 tbsp olive oil

salt and freshly ground black pepper

1 Preheat the oven to 400°F (200°C). Wipe the game hens thoroughly with paper towels, then stuff with the onions. Brush all over with the honey, then cover the breast of each game hen with 3 slices of the bacon or pancetta. Sit in a large roasting pan.

2 Toss the leeks with the oil, then add to the pan, tucking them in around the birds. Season with salt and pepper, then put in the oven to roast for 45 minutes to 1 hour, or until the game hens are cooked. To test, pierce them with the tip of a sharp knife—if the juices run clear, they are ready. If the bacon begins to blacken, cover the game hens with foil.

3 Remove the birds from the pan and keep warm. Using a slotted spoon, transfer the leeks to a serving dish and keep warm. Place the pan on the unlit stove top and tilt to one side. Skim away any fat, then pour in a little hot water and set over high heat. Bring to a boil, scraping up any crispy bits from the bottom of the pan, then simmer for a few minutes. Pour into a gravy boat or pitcher and serve with the game hen, leeks, and some creamy mashed potatoes.

pizza with spinach and ricotta cheese

It is important to squeeze excess liquid from the spinach to prevent the pizza base from becoming soggy.

 15 MINS PLUS RISING   10 MINS

MAKES 1

¾ cup bread flour

pinch of salt

pinch of granulated sugar

¾ tsp dried yeast

1 tbsp olive oil

⅓ cup warm water

a little semolina, for sprinkling

2-3 tbsp tomato paste

7oz (200g) spinach leaves, wilted and drained

2-3 tbsp ricotta cheese

1 Sift the flour, salt, and sugar into a bowl. Add the yeast. Stir in the oil and enough warm water to form a soft but not sticky dough.

2 Place the dough on a slightly floured surface, and knead gently for several minutes until smooth and elastic. Return to the bowl, cover with oiled plastic wrap, and leave for about 40 minutes, until the dough has doubled in size.

3 Preheat the oven to its highest setting. Place a lightly oiled baking sheet in the oven to get hot. Turn out the dough onto a floured surface and briefly re-knead to knock out the air. Roll out thinly into a round, about 10in (25cm) diameter. Sprinkle the hot baking sheet with semolina and transfer the pizza base onto it, spreading it out firmly again.

4 Spoon and smooth the tomato paste onto the pizza base, using the back of the spoon. Squeeze any liquid from the spinach, then spread it on the tomato paste. Dot with spoonfuls of ricotta cheese, season with black pepper, and bake for 10 minutes, or until the crust is golden and crispy.

quesadilla with avocado, spring onion, and chile

These wonderfully simple-to-make stuffed tortillas are a useful speedy standby to have ready at hand for a lunch or light supper.

 10 MINS 5 MINS

MAKES 1

4 spring onions or scallions, trimmed and finely chopped

1–2 red chiles, seeded and finely chopped

juice of ½ lime

salt and freshly ground black pepper

1½ tbsp olive oil

2 wheat tortillas or corn tortillas

½ avocado, pitted, peeled, and sliced

1¾oz (50g) Cheddar cheese, grated

1 Place the spring onions or scallions, chiles, and lime juice in a bowl, season well with salt and pepper, and mix together. Leave to sit for a couple of minutes to let the flavors develop.

2 Heat the olive oil in a non-stick frying pan, then cook one tortilla for about 1 minute, or until lightly golden. Scatter the avocado slices over the top, leaving a little space around the edge, spoon on the spring onion mixture, and sprinkle with the cheese.

3 Top with the other tortilla, pressing it down with the back of a spatula to sandwich the two together. Scoop up the quesadilla, carefully turn it over, and cook the other side for another minute, or until golden. Slice in half or quarters, and serve.

veggie pad thai

Scallions are the classic topping for an Asian noodle dish. Make sure they are finely chopped into strips.

 15 MINS 15 MINS

SERVES 4

9oz (250g) wide or medium rice noodles

3–4 tbsp vegetable oil

7oz (200g) firm tofu, cut into cubes

2 garlic cloves, grated or finely chopped

1 large egg, lightly beaten

⅔ cup hot vegetable stock

juice of 1 lime

1 tsp fish sauce (nam pla), (optional)

2 tsp tamarind paste

2 tsp brown sugar

1 tbsp dark soy sauce

1 red or jalapeño chile, seeded and finely chopped

2½oz (75g) dry-roasted peanuts, coarsely chopped

1 bunch of scallions, trimmed and finely chopped

2½oz (75g) bean sprouts (optional)

small handful of cilantro

1 Soak the noodles in boiling water for 10 minutes, then drain. Meanwhile, heat 1 tbsp of the oil in a wok over medium-high heat, and swirl it around the pan. Add the tofu and cook for about 10 minutes until golden (you may need to use more oil). Remove with a slotted spoon and set aside.

2 Add another 1 tbsp of oil to the pan. When hot, add the garlic and cook for 10 seconds, then add in the egg and cook, stirring and breaking it up with a wooden spoon, until scrambled. Remove from the pan and set aside.

3 Add another 1 tbsp of the oil. When hot, add the noodles and stir gently to coat with the oil. Pour over the stock, lime juice, fish sauce, tamarind paste, sugar, and soy sauce; toss to combine. Let it simmer for a few minutes, then stir in the chile.

4 Add half of the peanuts with the scallions and the bean sprouts, if using, and stir-fry for a minute. Now add the reserved scrambled egg, stir to combine, and transfer to a serving plate. Scatter over the remaining peanuts and a sprinkling of cilantro to serve.

spring rice salad

Asparagus spears appear in late spring. The spears are young and slender and don't need peeling.

 20–25 MINS PLUS CHILLING 15–20 MINS

SERVES 4-6

For the salad

salt and freshly ground black pepper

1 lemon, cut in half

7oz (200g) long-grain rice

9oz (250g) asparagus spears

3 celery stalks, peeled and diced

9oz (250g) smoked salmon, cut into strips

For the vinaigrette

3 tbsp tarragon vinegar

2 tsp Dijon mustard

⅔ cup vegetable oil

1 Bring a large saucepan of salted water to a boil. Squeeze the juice from one half of the lemon into the water, then drop in the lemon half as well. Add the rice, stir, and bring back to a boil. Simmer for 10–12 minutes until the rice is tender, stirring occasionally.

2 Meanwhile, make the vinaigrette. Put the vinegar and mustard in a small bowl, add seasoning, and whisk

together well. Gradually whisk in the oil in a thin stream so the vinaigrette emulsifies and thickens slightly.

3 Drain the rice, discard the lemon half, then place in a sieve and rinse with cold water to wash away the starch. Drain again thoroughly. Repeat a couple of times more. Transfer to a large bowl.

4 Bring a large saucepan of salted water to a boil, add the asparagus, and simmer for 5–7 minutes until tender when pierced with the tip of a knife. Drain and cut the stalks into chunky pieces.

5 Briskly whisk the vinaigrette again and pour it over the rice. Stir the rice well and add the asparagus, celery, smoked salmon, and lemon juice from the reserved half. Toss all the ingredients together and taste for seasoning. Cover and chill for at least 1 hour to allow the flavors to mingle together. Serve at room temperature.

gratin of chicory and ham

Chicory gratin is a marvelous accompaniment to meat and game dishes. This indulgent version includes ham, so you could even serve it as an appetizer, if you wish.

 15–20 MINS 1 HR – 1 HR 15 MINS

SERVES 4

8 heads of chicory, trimmed

1 tsp granulated sugar

salt and freshly ground black pepper

2 cups milk

1 slice of onion

1 bay leaf

6 peppercorns

¼ cup all-purpose flour

4 tbsp butter

pinch of grated nutmeg

8 thin slices of cooked ham

1½oz (45g) Gruyère cheese, grated

1 Preheat the oven to 350°F (180°C). Brush a shallow baking dish with butter. Arrange the chicory in the dish and sprinkle with the sugar, salt, and pepper. Press a piece of buttered foil on top. Bake for 45–55 minutes, until tender and slightly caramelized. Transfer to a plate and let cool slightly. Wipe the baking dish.

2 Heat the milk in a saucepan with the onion, bay leaf, and peppercorns to just short of boiling. Cover the pan

and set it aside in a warm place off the heat for 10 minutes. Melt the butter in another saucepan over medium heat. Whisk in the flour and cook for 30–60 seconds, whisking all the time, until foaming.

3 Remove the pan from the heat, then strain in the hot milk and whisk. Return to the heat, whisking constantly, until the sauce boils and begins to thicken. Add seasoning and nutmeg, and simmer for 2 minutes more, stirring continuously, to cook out the raw taste of the flour.

4 Increase the oven temperature to 400°F (200°C). Butter the baking dish again. Lay a slice of ham on a work surface. Set a head of chicory on top and roll the ham around to form a cylinder. Repeat with the remaining ham and chicory, arranging them in the dish, seam-side down. Ladle over the béchamel sauce, sprinkle with the cheese, and bake for 20–25 minutes, until bubbling and browned.

spinach sauce

This quick and easy sauce is a perfect accompaniment for chicken, fish, or new potatoes, or stir in a handful of grated Cheddar cheese and serve the sauce stirred into some pasta.

 15 MINS   **20 MINS**   ❄ **FREEZABLE**

SERVES 8

¼ cup olive oil

2 large onions, finely diced

4 garlic cloves, finely sliced

2 red chiles, seeded and finely chopped

1¼lb (550g) baby spinach leaves, rinsed and coarsely chopped

1¼ cups dry white wine

2 tbsp all-purpose flour

3 cups milk

salt and freshly ground black pepper

1 Heat the oil in a large heavy-bottomed pan over medium heat, add the onions, and cook for about 5 minutes, until the onions are soft and translucent. Stir in the garlic and chiles and cook for 2 minutes. Add the spinach and cook for 3 minutes, or until wilted.

2 Add the wine and simmer for 5 minutes, or until reduced by half. Add the flour and combine well. Stir in half the milk, and then add the rest of the milk a little at a time, stirring constantly, and cook for 5 minutes, or until you have a creamy sauce. Season well with salt and pepper.

spinach with pine nuts and raisins

This dish can be served hot or cold and adds a piquant flavor to roast chicken alongside a baked potato.

 5 MINS   **10 MINS**

SERVES 4

1 tbsp olive oil

3 tbsp raisins

3 tbsp pine nuts

3 tbsp dry sherry

7oz (200g) spinach leaves, roughly chopped

1 tsp paprika

salt and freshly ground black pepper

1 Put the oil, raisins, and pine nuts in a shallow frying pan over medium heat. When the raisins and pine nuts start to sizzle, cook for 2 minutes, moving them all the time. Carefully add the sherry and cook until the liquid has reduced by half.

2 Add the spinach and paprika and cook, stirring constantly, for 5 minutes, or until the spinach has wilted. Season with salt and pepper.

variation

sorrel and wild garlic with pine nuts and olives

Prepare in the same way but omit the raisins. Use half sorrel and half wild garlic in place of the spinach (or spinach and 1 small garlic clove, crushed). Add a handful of olives with the leaves. To turn it into a light meal, spoon into bowls, top with poached eggs, and serve with crusty bread.

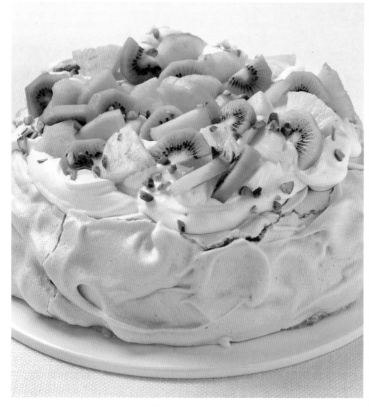

pavlova with tropical fruit

You'll find that many tropical fruits are good in spring. They add a luscious sweetness to this light, chewy meringue.

 25-30 MINS 2 HRS - 2 HRS 30 MINS ❄ FREEZABLE

SPECIAL EQUIPMENT ▪ electric hand whisk or mixer

SERVES 6-8

For the meringue

6 large egg whites

salt

1½ cups granulated sugar

1 tbsp cornstarch

1 tsp distilled malt vinegar

1⅔ cups heavy cream

2 tbsp chopped pistachios, to serve

For the fruit

3 mangoes, total weight about 2¼lb (1kg), cut in half to remove the pit, and the flesh sliced into cubes and then cut away from the skin

5 kiwi fruit, peeled, sliced, and with the slices cut in half

1 pineapple, weighing about 1lb 10oz (750g), peeled, core removed, thinly sliced, and cut into chunks

2 tbsp granulated sugar

2 tbsp kirsch

1 Preheat the oven to 350°F (180°C). Line a baking sheet with waxed paper. Put the egg whites in a large, clean mixing bowl with a little salt.

Whisk with an electric hand whisk or mixer until stiff. Whisk in the sugar, 1 tbsp at a time, until the egg whites are stiff and shiny, then whisk in the cornstarch and the vinegar.

2 Spoon the meringue onto the baking sheet and spread to form an 8in (20cm) circle. Bake for 5 minutes, then reduce the oven temperature to 275°F (140°C) and cook for another 1 hour and 15 minutes, or until the outside is crisp. Allow it to cool completely before transferring to a serving plate.

3 Whip the cream in a large, clean bowl until it holds its shape, then spoon it onto the meringue base.

4 Put the fruit in a large bowl. Sprinkle over the sugar and kirsch. Stir the fruit gently with a clean, wooden spoon to distribute the flavorings evenly. Arrange the fruit neatly on top of the cream, sprinkle with the chopped pistachios, and serve immediately. Do not leave it to stand, or the cream will make it soggy.

fresh pineapple upside-down cake

The sweet acidity of fresh pineapple makes this simple cake taste amazing. It is good enough to eat either straight out of the oven and piping hot, or cold.

 10 MINS 50 MINS ❄ FREEZABLE

SPECIAL EQUIPMENT ▪ electric hand whisk or mixer
▪ 1-quart (1-liter) ovenproof dish

SERVES 4-6

2-3 tbsp corn syrup

1 small pineapple, peeled, core removed, and cut into 6 slices

11 tbsp butter

½ cup granulated sugar

2 large eggs

1½ cups all-purpose flour, sifted

1-2 tbsp milk

half-and-half, to serve

1 Preheat the oven to 350°F (180°C). Grease the ovenproof dish. Drizzle in the corn syrup to cover the base, then top with the pineapple rings, and put to one side.

2 Put the butter and sugar in a mixing bowl and whisk with an electric hand whisk or mixer until pale and creamy. Mix in the eggs, one at a time, adding a little of the flour after each egg. Fold in the remaining flour, then add the milk a little at a time until the mixture drops easily off the beaters. Pour the mixture over the pineapple and spread it out evenly. Bake in the oven for 40-50 minutes, or until the cake is golden brown and springy to the touch.

3 Loosen the edge all round with a butter knife, then carefully turn out, upside-down, onto a serving plate. Serve with half-and-half.

pineapple and kirsch floating islands

Soft meringue islands float on top of pineapple bathed in a creamy, buttery custard laced with kirsch. Replace the kirsch with white rum if you like—or omit it altogether.

 25 MINS 30 MINS PLUS COOLING

SPECIAL EQUIPMENT ▪ 1-quart (1-liter) ovenproof dish ▪ food processor
▪ electric hand whisk or mixer

SERVES 4

1 small pineapple, peeled with the core removed

4 tbsp butter

½ cup granulated sugar

2 large eggs, separated

¼ cup cornstarch

1 tbsp kirsch

¾ cup milk

1 cup half-and-half

1 Preheat the oven to 300°F (150°C). Chop the pineapple in a food processor, but don't allow it to become puréed. Strain the chopped pineapple through a fine sieve over a bowl. Reserve the juice and spread the fruit across the base of the dish.

2 Beat the butter and half the sugar together until light and fluffy. Beat in the egg yolks, cornstarch, reserved pineapple juice, and the kirsch.

3 Warm the milk and cream until hot but not boiling. Gradually whisk into the egg yolk mixture. Rinse the pan, pour the custard back in, and cook gently, stirring until thickened and smooth. Do not allow it to boil. Pour over the pineapple.

4 Whisk the egg whites until stiff. Add the rest of the sugar and whisk until glossy and peaking. Drop 4 large spoonfuls of meringue over the custard. Bake for 30 minutes, or until the meringues are a pale biscuit color. Leave to cool, chill, then serve.

Season's best **pineapples**

The rough, knobby skin of a pineapple is divided into dozens of lozenges, which makes it resemble an enlarged pinecone topped with a gray-green plume of spiky leaves. The firm, rich yellow to pale cream flesh is juicy and sweet with an astringent finish. They are imported all year, but are particularly good in spring. Use in salsas, fruit salads, desserts, smoothies, and preserves. Good flavor pairings include pork, chicken, fish, cottage cheese, ginger, Cointreau, and rum.

Pineapples grow on spiky cactus-like plants. When pollinated, a cluster of flowers fuse to make one fruit. They can be grown in a pot from a cut-off pineapple top.

Pineapple Varieties of pineapple differ slightly in size, shape, and color—some have a golden shell when ripe, others are dark green or reddish—as well as in their degree of sweetness. All can be eaten fresh or used in salads and desserts.

If you can easily pull out one of the inner leaves, the pineapple is ripe and ready for eating.

how to prepare pineapples

Pineapples have sharp, spiky skin, so handle with care. Use a large, sharp knife for slicing as the central core can be really tough.

1 Trim both ends of the pineapple. Stand it on its base and slice the skin from the top down, all the way around.

2 Quarter it lengthwise, cut away the core, then dice; or cut in slices, then cut out the central core, making rings.

essentials
varieties available

Differing sizes from miniature to the size of a torpedo!

buy Pineapples are picked ripe, but color does not indicate ripeness—some are green, some gold. They should smell sweet but feel firm. Avoid if soft, bruised, or withered.

store Eat soon after purchase, or prepare then store in an airtight container in the fridge for up to 3 days.

cook Prepare and use raw for fruit salads, cold desserts, and smoothies; grill, fry, or bake.

preserve Dry, candy as a dried fruit, bottle in syrup.

recipe ideas

Fresh pineapple upside-down cake p62

Jerk chicken with roasted pineapple p56

Pineapple and kirsch floating islands p62

Pineapple broth with halibut p24

asian fruit salad

Although this dessert is quick and simple to prepare, the sharp sweetness of pineapple and kiwi mixed with mango create a stunning and complex explosion of flavors.

 15 MINS

SERVES 4

1 mango, peeled and sliced

1 pineapple, peeled, core removed, sliced thinly, and cut into chunks

1 kiwi fruit, peeled and sliced

juice of 1 orange

juice of 1 lime

1 passion fruit, halved

small handful of mint leaves, finely chopped

1 Arrange the mango, pineapple, and kiwi fruit pieces in a shallow serving bowl or platter. Pour in the orange juice and lime juice.

2 Scoop out the flesh and seeds from the passion fruit and spoon over the fruit. Sprinkle with mint leaves and serve.

pineapple trifle

Refreshing pineapple and spicy ginger are a winning combination, and as pineapple is in abundance in spring, make the most of it with this dessert.

 15 MINS PLUS CHILLING

SPECIAL EQUIPMENT ▪ electric hand whisk

SERVES 6

9oz (250g) store-bought ginger cake, sliced

½ cup pineapple juice

9oz (250g) pineapple, finely chopped

1¼ cups heavy or whipping cream

2-3 tbsp syrup from a jar of stem ginger or more pineapple juice

2 balls stem ginger in syrup, finely chopped or ¼ cup chopped crystallized ginger

1 Line the bottom of a serving bowl with the slices of ginger cake, then pour in the pineapple juice and scatter with the pineapple.

2 Put the cream and ginger syrup in a mixing bowl and whisk with an electric hand whisk until soft peaks form. Spoon the cream mixture over the pineapple, then scatter with the chopped stem ginger. Chill in the fridge for 30 minutes or more, and then serve.

variation

tropical trifle

Use cubed mango or chopped banana instead of the pineapple in step 1, or use a mixture of all three. To prepare the mango, cut it in half to remove the pit, slice the flesh into cubes with a sharp knife, then cut the cubes away from the mango skin.

tropical angel cake

Pineapple and mango crown a deliciously tasty coconut cake.

 15 MINS   **30 MINS**

SPECIAL EQUIPMENT ▪ electric hand whisk or mixer
▪ 10in (25cm) tube pan

SERVES 6-8

For the cake

4 large egg whites

½ tsp cream of tartar

¾ cup granulated sugar

¼ cup all-purpose flour

1 tbsp cornstarch

1oz (25g) unsweetened flaked coconut

For the topping

7oz (200g) Greek-style yogurt

7oz (200g) mixed peeled and chopped tropical fruit, such as pineapple and mango

seeds and pulp from 2 passion fruits

lime zest, to decorate

1 Preheat the oven to 375°F (190°C). Put the egg whites, cream of tartar, and 1 tbsp cold water in a large mixing bowl and whisk with an electric whisk or mixer until stiff peaks form. Whisk in 1 tbsp sugar at a time until the mix is stiff and shiny.

2 Sift in the flour and cornstarch and gently fold them in together with the coconut until well combined. Carefully spoon the mixture into the pan and smooth the top, pressing down gently so there are no air pockets left. Bake in the oven for 15 minutes, then reduce the oven temperature to 350°F (180°C) and bake for another 15 minutes until the cake is firm to the touch and golden brown.

3 Place the pan upside-down on a wire rack and leave until completely cold, then carefully ease the cake out of the pan with a butter knife or small metal spatula and place on a serving plate.

4 To make the topping, beat the yogurt lightly so it is smooth and creamy, then spoon it into the center of the cake. Top it with the tropical fruit, then drizzle the passion fruit seeds and pulp over the top. Finish by scattering over the lime zest.

rhubarb and ginger upside-down cake

Young rhubarb is cooked into a simple upside-down cake to give a modern twist on a classic dessert.

 40 MINS   **40-45 MINS**

SPECIAL EQUIPMENT ▪ 9in (23cm) round springform cake pan
▪ electric hand whisk or mixer

SERVES 6-8

11 tbsp unsalted butter, softened

¾ cup dark brown sugar

4 tbsp finely chopped, preserved stem ginger or chopped crystallized ginger

1lb 2oz (500g) young, pink rhubarb, chopped into ¾in (2cm) lengths

3 large eggs

1 cup self-rising flour

2 tsp ground ginger

1 tsp baking powder

heavy cream, whipped, or crème fraîche, to serve (optional)

1 Preheat the oven to 350°F (180°C). Melt a little butter and use to grease the pan with a brush. Line the bottom and sides of the cake pan with parchment paper.

2 Scatter a little of the sugar evenly over the bottom of the cake pan. Scatter half of the chopped stem ginger evenly over the sugar. Lay the rhubarb over the sugar and ginger so it is tightly packed and completely covers the bottom of the cake pan.

3 Place the butter and remaining sugar in a large mixing bowl and whisk with an electric hand whisk or mixer until pale and creamy. Beat in the eggs, one at a time, whisking as much air as possible into the mixture. Gently fold the remaining chopped stem ginger into the batter.

4 In a separate bowl, sift together the flour, ground ginger, and baking powder. Add the sifted ingredients to the bowl containing the cake batter. Gently fold in the dry ingredients, keeping volume in the batter as you do so. Spoon the cake batter into the cake pan, taking care not to disturb the arranged rhubarb, and spread it evenly with a palette knife.

5 Bake the cake in the center of the oven for 45 minutes until springy to the touch. Remove from the oven and leave to cool for 20-30 minutes before carefully turning the cake out of the pan and onto a serving plate. Serve warm with whipped heavy cream or crème fraîche.

Season's best **rhubarb**

Rhubarb is technically a vegetable, but is treated like a fruit for the most part. Different varieties offer a range of sizes and colors, but all have a sharp, tangy flavor. Forced in winter to spring, then grown outdoors from late spring through summer, it is popular in pies, crumbles, for ice cream, fools, and mousses. It also makes a delicious sauce to serve with oily fish, particularly mackerel. Ideal flavor pairings include orange, cinnamon, ginger, lavender, and vanilla.

Grown from crowns, rhubarb is planted outdoors in temperate climates, producing thick green and red stalks, but is also forced indoors in the dark to produce tender, pink thinner sticks.

The green leaves are poisonous. Their only use is to boil them in aluminum pans to remove stains.

Forced rhubarb It has slim, pink stalks with a delicious acidic flavor that needs less sugar than outdoor varieties.

Adding a pinch of baking soda during cooking reduces the amount of sugar needed to sweeten.

Outdoor rhubarb It has long stalks with a coarse texture. They are best puréed for sauces and desserts. Add a few drops of pink food coloring to the cooked pulp for a pleasing color.

essentials
varieties available

Coarser red and green outdoor, and thinner, uniformly pink forced rhubarb.

buy Choose firm straight stems that snap easily. Avoid if the stems are very pliable.

store Wrap in moist paper towels and store in a plastic bag in the fridge for up to a week.

cook Stew, bake, or roast. Use in pies and jams, and in sauces to accompany oily fish or pork.

preserve Freeze; make into jams, chutneys, or relishes; make wine or cordial.

recipe ideas

Rhubarb and custard ice cream p67

Rhubarb and ginger upside-down cake p65

Rhubarb brûlée flan p67

rhubarb and orange yogurt fool

A quick dessert that takes very little work. You could try using strawberry yogurt instead of plain and, for a special occasion, use half whipped cream and half yogurt.

 5 MINS PLUS CHILLING **10 MINS**

SPECIAL EQUIPMENT ▪ blender or hand-held blender

SERVES 4

1lb (450g) rhubarb, trimmed and cut in short lengths

¼ cup granulated sugar

grated zest and juice of 1 orange

1 cup Greek-style yogurt

4 tsp honey, to serve,

1 Put the rhubarb in a pan with the sugar and orange zest and juice. Cook gently, stirring until the juice runs, then cover and continue to simmer for about 10 minutes, stirring occasionally until pulpy.

2 Cool slightly, then purée in a blender (or use a hand-held blender in the pan). Set aside to cool. When completely cold, fold in the yogurt, taste, and add more sugar, if necessary. Spoon into glasses and chill until ready to serve. Drizzle each with a teaspoon of honey just before serving.

rhubarb brûlée flan

A delicious make-ahead dessert. Use vanilla wafers if you prefer and add a couple of pieces of stem ginger in syrup (if available), finely chopped, to the rhubarb pulp for added zest.

 20 MINS PLUS CHILLING **8 MINS**

SPECIAL EQUIPMENT ▪ 8in (20cm) tart pan with removable bottom or flan dish ▪ electric hand whisk or mixer

SERVES 6

1lb (450g) rhubarb, chopped

⅓ cup granulated sugar

2 tsp powdered gelatin

4oz (115g) gingersnaps, crushed

4 tbsp butter, melted

1¼ cups heavy cream, whipped

3-4 tbsp brown sugar

1 Put the rhubarb in a saucepan with 2 tbsp water and ¼ cup of the granulated sugar. Bring to a boil, stir, cover, reduce the heat, and cook gently for 5 minutes. Remove the lid and boil rapidly for about 3 minutes, stirring occasionally, until the juice has evaporated and the rhubarb is pulpy.

2 Stir in the gelatin until dissolved and set aside to cool.

3 Mix the crushed gingersnaps with the melted butter and the remaining granulated sugar. Press into the base and sides of an 8in (20cm) flan dish. Chill to firm.

4 When the rhubarb is cold but not set, fold in half the whipped cream and transfer to the flan crust. Smooth the surface and chill until set.

5 Just before serving, preheat the broiler. Spread the remaining whipped cream over the rhubarb. Sprinkle liberally with the brown sugar and broil until the sugar melts and bubbles. Serve immediately. Alternatively, use a blow torch to caramelize the sugar.

rhubarb and custard ice cream

If you have an abundance of rhubarb, try this ice cream; it gives a new twist to the traditional rhubarb and custard.

 30 MINS PLUS CHILLING AND FREEZING **20 MINS** ❄ **FREEZABLE**

SPECIAL EQUIPMENT ▪ blender or food processor ▪ electric hand whisk or balloon whisk

SERVES 4-6

1lb (450g) rhubarb, cut into chunks

1⅔ cups granulated sugar

5 egg yolks

salt

1¾ cups milk

⅔ cup half-and-half

1 tsp pure vanilla extract

1 Gently stew the rhubarb with ¼ cup of the sugar and 2 tbsp water for 10 minutes, or until tender, in a covered pan, stirring occasionally. Purée in a blender or food processor. Leave to cool.

2 Put the egg yolks, the remaining sugar, and a little salt in a large heatproof bowl and whisk with an electric hand whisk or balloon whisk, until pale, thick, and creamy. Gently heat the milk and cream in a pan until steaming and stir into the egg mix with the vanilla. Put the bowl over a pan of gently simmering water and stir until the custard just coats the back of a wooden spoon. Remove the bowl from the pan and leave to cool.

3 When the custard is completely cold, mix it with the rhubarb purée and freeze in an ice cream maker, following the manufacturer's directions. Alternatively, pour into a shallow, freezerproof container with a lid and freeze for about 2 hours until frozen around the edges. Beat well with a fork to break up the ice crystals, freeze for another 2 hours, beat again, then freeze until firm.

early summer

at their best

vegetables artichokes ▪ arugula ▪ asparagus ▪ cucumber ▪ dandelion greens ▪ fava beans ▪ fennel ▪ fiddlehead ferns ▪ kholrabi ▪ leeks ▪ lettuce ▪ nettles ▪ new potatoes ▪ peas ▪ pea shoots ▪ radishes ▪ ramps ▪ scallions ▪ sea bean ▪ sorrel ▪ spinach ▪ snow peas ▪ sugarsnap peas ▪ Swiss chard ▪ watercress ▪ waxy potatoes ▪ white asparagus ▪ wild morel mushrooms

fruit apricots ▪ cherries ▪ kiwi ▪ raspberries ▪ outdoor rhubarb ▪ strawberries ▪ wild strawberries

seafood bonito shark ▪ cod ▪ flounder ▪ haddock ▪ hake ▪ mackerel ▪ mako shark ▪ mussels ▪ oysters ▪ pollock ▪ rainbow trout ▪ salmon (chum, coho, King, sockeye) ▪ sea scallops ▪ squid ▪ swordfish

meat, poultry, game spring lamb

also available

fruit blueberries ▪ lemons ▪ limes ▪ mango **vegetables** baby beets ▪ broccoli ▪ carrots ▪ cauliflower ▪ celery ▪ mushrooms (cultivated) ▪ onions ▪ radishes **seafood** clams ▪ halibut ▪ ocean perch ▪ rockfish ▪ sea scallops
meat, poultry, game beef ▪ chicken ▪ Cornish game hens ▪ duck (farmed) ▪ pork ▪ quail (farmed) ▪ rabbit (farmed) ▪ turkey ▪ veal ▪ venison (farmed) ▪ wild boar (farmed)

early summer recipe planner

Ⓥ suitable for vegetarians

Asparagus frittata on crostini p81

Sliced beef and arugula salad with green olive and raisin salsa p72

Grated zucchini and goat cheese omelet p101

Vegetables

Artichokes
Artichokes, butter beans, and peas p112 Ⓥ
Grilled sea bass with roast artichokes and fennel p92
Herb and garlic artichokes p76 Ⓥ
Lamb with artichokes, fava beans, and dill p113
Lentils with artichokes and bell peppers p99
Pepper and artichoke salad p91 Ⓥ

Arugula
Fava bean and feta panzanella p116 Ⓥ
Pasta with pancetta and arugula p90
Quesadilla with Cheddar cheese, arugula, and sun-dried tomatoes p94 Ⓥ
Salami and arugula salad with black olives and sun-dried tomato salsa p72
Sliced beef and arugula salad with green olive and raisin salsa p72

Asparagus
Asparagus and herb tart p92 Ⓥ
Asparagus and taleggio risotto p92 Ⓥ
Asparagus, broccoli, ginger, and mint stir-fry p95 Ⓥ
Asparagus frittata on crostini p81 Ⓥ
Asparagus in oil p135 Ⓥ
Asparagus with lemon dressing p73 Ⓥ
Cream of asparagus soup p82 Ⓥ
Crepes with asparagus, feta cheese, and dill p80 Ⓥ
Fresh pea and mint dip with seasonal crudités p84 Ⓥ
Grilled asparagus and pancetta p86
Grilled asparagus with Gorgonzola cheese p73 Ⓥ
Penne with asparagus and zucchini p112 Ⓥ
Risotto primavera p105 Ⓥ
Warm pea pancakes with grilled asparagus p111 Ⓥ
White asparagus with herb mayonnaise p88 Ⓥ

Beets
Grilled sea bass with roasted baby beets and dill p92

Broccoli
Asparagus, broccoli, ginger, and mint stir-fry p95 Ⓥ
Zucchini, herb, and lemon tagine p110 Ⓥ

Cabbage
Ham, cabbage, and potato soup p77

Carrot
Curried vegetable pies p83 Ⓥ
Fresh pea and mint dip with seasonal crudités p84 Ⓥ
Mediterranean vegetable pies p83 Ⓥ
Spaghetti primavera p104 Ⓥ

Cucumber
Baked salmon with salsa verde and cucumber p90
Creamy cucumber and scallion dip p80 Ⓥ
Crudités with tapenade p80
Mini chicken tortillas topped with yogurt, cucumber, and mint dip p82
Mini pea tortillas with yogurt, cucumber, and mint dip p82 Ⓥ
Raita p117 Ⓥ
Salmon salad with mint yogurt dressing p107

Fava beans
Baby fava bean, bacon, and goat cheese omelet p101
Baby fava bean soup p84 Ⓥ
Chicken and chorizo paella p100
Chicken with fava beans p100
Dill and fava bean dip p84 Ⓥ
Fava bean and feta panzanella p116 Ⓥ
Ham with minted peas and fava beans p116
Hot and spicy lamb with fava beans p96
Lamb with artichokes, fava beans, and dill p113
Lentil, fava bean, and feta salad p114 Ⓥ
Niçoise-style salad p81
Pea shoot, ham, fava bean, and Cheddar cheese salad p117
Pork chops with tomato and fava bean sauce p101
Risotto primavera p105 Ⓥ
Sausages with fava beans p100

Fennel
Grilled sea bass with roast artichokes and fennel p92
Lamb chops in paper with fennel p110

Fresh garlic
Simple garlic confit p135 Ⓥ

Lettuce
Caesar salad with poached eggs p97
Chicken caesar salad p97
Lettuce soup with peas p76 Ⓥ

Niçoise-style salad p81
Pepper and artichoke salad p91 Ⓥ
Potage Saint Germain p82 Ⓥ

New potatoes
Chicken and pea filo pie p106
Deviled lamb cutlets with crushed potato and mustard seed salad p104
German potato salad p114
Papas arrugadas p115 Ⓥ
Roasted new potatoes and sardines p113
Roasted new potatoes and sausages with rosemary and chile p113
Salmon with new potatoes, flageolet beans, and parsley sauce p96
Stuffed sardines with crushed new potatoes p108

Peas and pea shoots
Artichokes, butter beans, and peas p112 Ⓥ
Chicken and pea filo pie p106
Dressed pea salad p115 Ⓥ
Feta and pea salad with watercress mayonnaise p115 Ⓥ
Fresh pea and mint dip with seasonal crudités p84 Ⓥ
Ham with minted peas and fava beans p116
Lettuce soup with peas p76 Ⓥ
Mini pea tortillas with yogurt, cucumber, and mint dip p82 Ⓥ
Pasta with pecorino and peas p91 Ⓥ
Pea, ham, and potato soup p77
Pea shoot, ham, fava bean, and Cheddar cheese salad p117
Potage Saint Germain p82 Ⓥ
Spaghetti primavera p104 Ⓥ
Warm pea pancakes with grilled asparagus p111 Ⓥ
Zucchini and pea mini tortillas p86 Ⓥ

Peppers
Asparagus, broccoli, ginger, and mint stir-fry p95 Ⓥ
Chicken and chorizo paella p100
Chicken fajitas with tomato and avocado salsa p99
Crab, radish, and pepper salad p73

Crudités with tapenade p80
Lamb with chickpeas, green bell peppers, and couscous p111
Lentils with artichokes and bell peppers p99
Crepes with bell peppers and basil p88 Ⓥ
Papas arrugadas p115 Ⓥ
Pepper and artichoke salad p91 Ⓥ
Quesadilla with peppers, green olives, and feta cheese p94 Ⓥ
Smoked salmon with radishes and spiced yogurt dressing p73
Veal scallops with bell peppers p98

Potato
Curried vegetable pies p83 Ⓥ
Ham, cabbage, and potato soup p77
Mediterranean vegetable pies p83 Ⓥ
Pea, ham, and potato soup p77

Radish
Crab, radish, and pepper salad p73
Crudités with tapenade p80
Fresh pea and mint dip with seasonal crudités p84 Ⓥ
Smoked salmon with radishes and spiced yogurt dressing p73

Scallions
Asian noodle salad p106
Asparagus, broccoli, ginger, and mint stir-fry p95 Ⓥ
Cashew and zucchini rice p117 Ⓥ
Chicken fajitas with tomato and avocado salsa p99
Creamy cucumber and scallion dip p80 Ⓥ
Crudités with tapenade p80
Curried vegetable pies p83 Ⓥ
Fava bean and feta panzanella p116 Ⓥ
Fresh pea and mint dip with seasonal crudités p84 Ⓥ
Lentil, fava bean, and feta salad p114 Ⓥ
Mediterranean vegetable pies p83 Ⓥ
Potage Saint Germain p82 Ⓥ
Watercress, flageolet bean, and smoked cheese salad p117 Ⓥ
Zucchini stuffed with pickled lemon, raisins, and scallions p89 Ⓥ

Hazelnut torte with berries p122   **Cherry jam** p132

Stuffed sardines with crushed new potatoes p108

scallops with lemon-herb potatoes

Scallops need to be cooked carefully. If overcooked, they will be dry and rubbery, rather than juicy and silky in texture.

 45–50 MINS 20 MINS

SPECIAL EQUIPMENT ▪ blender or food processor

SERVES 6

1lb 2oz (500g) potatoes, peeled and cut into pieces

6 tbsp butter

4–6 sprigs of parsley, leaves removed

4–6 sprigs of tarragon, leaves removed

grated zest and juice of 1 lemon

salt and freshly ground black pepper

⅓ cup milk, plus more if needed

¼ cup all-purpose flour

1lb 2oz (500g) large scallops (with or without coral, depending on preference), cleaned

2 tbsp olive oil

lemon wedges and arugula leaves

1 Put the potatoes in a saucepan of cold water, cover, and bring to a boil. Simmer for 15–20 minutes, until tender. Meanwhile, put 4 tbsp of the butter, herb leaves, and lemon zest in a blender or food processor. Pulse to chop the herbs. Drain the potatoes and mash in the pan. Beat in the herb purée until smooth. Season, cover with the milk, and keep warm.

2 Put the flour on a plate and season. Roll the scallops in the flour and pat off the excess. Heat the remaining butter and oil in a frying pan. Sauté the scallops for 2–3 minutes, turning once, until just crisp and brown.

3 Stir the milk into the potatoes, adding 2–3 tsp more if needed. Remove the scallops from the pan and add the lemon juice to taste. Arrange the mashed potatoes and scallops on warmed plates and spoon over the pan juices. Serve with the lemon wedges and arugula leaves.

variation

scallops poached in cider

Put 2 diced shallots and the juice of 2 lemons in a saucepan with ½ cup each hard cider and white wine and 1 cup water. Add the scallops, heat to simmering, and poach for 30 seconds. Remove from the heat. Reduce the scallop liquid to 1 cup and whisk in 2 tbsp all-purpose flour, then 2 egg yolks beaten with ½ cup heavy cream. Serve with the lemon-herb potatoes.

sliced beef and arugula salad with green olive and raisin salsa

Arugula leaves start coming into their own in early summer. Their sharp, peppery taste and pretty leaves make them the ideal base for many a fresh salad in the coming months.

 15 MINS

SERVES 4

16–20 green olives, pitted and sliced

large handful of plump raisins

4 tsp capers, rinsed and gently squeezed dry

drizzle of olive oil

handful of flat-leaf parsley, finely chopped

salt and freshly ground black pepper

handful of arugula leaves

12oz (350g) sliced pastrami or other sliced cooked beef

1 For the salsa, mix together the olives, raisins, capers, oil, and parsley in a bowl. Taste and season with a pinch of salt and some black pepper.

2 Arrange the arugula and pastrami or other sliced beef in a shallow serving bowl. Spoon the salsa over and serve at room temperature.

variation

salami and arugula salad with black olives and sun-dried tomato salsa

Prepare the salsa by mixing together 8–10 pitted, sliced black olives, 6 chopped sun-dried tomatoes, 2 tbsp chopped gherkins, a drizzle of olive oil, a small handful of chopped fresh thyme, and a little seasoning. Arrange 24 thin slices of salami on 4 serving plates with a handful of arugula. Spoon the salsa over and serve.

asparagus with lemon dressing

Asparagus needs very little to accompany it since the spears are so particularly flavorful. For a starter like this, some sharp lemon brings out the best of this popular summer vegetable.

🥄 5 MINS   🍲 6 MINS

SERVES 4

6 tbsp olive oil

2–3 tbsp lemon juice

pinch of granulated sugar

1 tsp mayonnaise

salt and freshly ground black pepper

12oz (350g) asparagus spears, trimmed

handful of arugula leaves

1 To make the dressing, put the oil and lemon juice in a small bowl and whisk until combined. Add the sugar and mayonnaise and whisk well. Season with salt and pepper.

2 Cook the asparagus spears in boiling salted water for 2–4 minutes, or until soft. To serve, sit the asparagus on the arugula leaves and dress liberally with the dressing.

variation

grilled asparagus with gorgonzola cheese

Cook the asparagus as in step 2, drain, and transfer to a barbecue or grill pan. Cook over medium heat for about 5 minutes, brushing the spears with extra virgin olive oil and turning them as they grill. Serve hot with 5½oz (150g) Gorgonzola cheese crumbled over, a drizzle of extra virgin olive oil, and a good grinding of black pepper.

smoked salmon with radishes and spiced yogurt dressing

Peppery radishes are a brilliant match with the rich flavor of smoked salmon in this fabulously colorful summer dish.

🥄 15 MINS

SERVES 4

3 tomatoes, peeled, seeded (p197), and cubed

1 tbsp capers, rinsed, gently squeezed dry, and chopped

handful of radishes, cubed

1 orange bell pepper, seeded and cubed

4 scallions, trimmed and finely chopped

1 red or jalapeño chile, seeded and finely chopped

juice of 1 large orange

juice of 1 lime

salt and freshly ground black pepper

9oz (250g) smoked salmon, chopped into bite-sized pieces

For the spiced yogurt dressing

4–6 tbsp Greek-style yogurt

juice of 1 lemon

pinch of five-spice powder

1 In a bowl, mix together the tomatoes, capers, radishes, bell pepper, scallions, and chile. Add the orange and lime juice, and season with salt and pepper. Toss together and let stand for about 10 minutes, to allow the flavors to develop.

2 To make the spiced yogurt dressing, mix together the yogurt, lemon juice, and five-spice powder in a small bowl. Season to taste.

3 When ready to serve, add the smoked salmon pieces to the salad mixture and combine well. Serve with the yogurt dip on the side.

variation

crab, radish, and pepper salad

For a less rich version of this dish, use 9oz (250g) white cooked crab meat instead of the smoked salmon.

battered haddock with lemon mayonnaise

The secret behind a successful mayonnaise is having all your ingredients at room temperature and adding the oil as slowly as you possibly can to prevent the sauce from curdling.

 20 MINS   **10 MINS**

SPECIAL EQUIPMENT ▪ blender or food processor

SERVES 4

1 large egg, plus 1 large egg yolk

grated zest and juice of 1 lemon

1 cup olive oil

salt and freshly ground black pepper

1 cup all-purpose flour

1 tsp baking soda

1 tsp paprika

⅔ cup cold sparkling water

1 cup olive oil, for frying

10oz (300g) haddock fillets, skinned (p75) and cut into ½in (1cm) strips

1 To make the mayonnaise, put the egg, egg yolk, lemon zest and juice in a blender or food processor and pulse for 1–2 minutes, or until a light yellow color. Reduce the speed and slowly add the oil, a little at a time, until you have a smooth, creamy emulsion. Season with salt and pepper, transfer to a serving dish, and place in the fridge to chill.

2 For the batter, put the flour, baking soda, paprika, and sparkling water in a mixing bowl, season with salt and pepper, then whisk until smooth. Put the oil in a deep frying pan and set over a high heat until it reaches 400°F (200°C). To test the heat, pop a cube of bread in the fat. If it sizzles it is ready.

3 Put the fish in the batter one piece at a time and coat. Carefully place in the hot oil. Cook, turning occasionally, for 2–3 minutes, or until the fish pieces are golden. Make sure they don't stick together. Remove with a slotted spoon and place on sheets of paper towel to drain. Sprinkle with a little salt and serve hot with the lemon mayonnaise.

variation

haddock in beer batter
Use beer instead of sparkling water in the batter. It will give a rich, dark batter.

skewered lemon and herb haddock

This is a lovely barbecue dish. The freshest haddock will be firm and thread onto skewers easily.

 10 MINS PLUS MARINATING   **4–6 MINS**

SPECIAL EQUIPMENT ▪ 12 bamboo or wooden skewers

SERVES 4

1lb 2oz (500g) thick haddock fillets, skinned (p75) and cut into chunks

1 garlic clove, crushed or finely chopped

1 tbsp fresh ginger, peeled and finely chopped

1 small red or jalapeño chile, seeded and finely chopped

1 tsp finely chopped rosemary, plus extra to garnish

4 sprigs of thyme, leaves picked and finely chopped, plus extra to garnish

grated zest and juice of 1 lemon

4 tbsp olive oil

salt and freshly ground black pepper

2 large mangoes, cut in half to remove the pit, and the flesh sliced lengthwise and then cut away from the skin

juice of 1 lime

1 Soak 12 bamboo or wooden skewers in cold water for 30 minutes. Put the haddock, garlic, ginger, chile, rosemary, thyme, lemon zest and juice, and oil in a bowl. Season with salt and pepper, and leave to marinate in the fridge for 20–30 minutes.

2 Put the mango slices in a bowl, add the lime juice, and season with salt and pepper. Stir gently to mix well, and set aside.

3 Preheat a broiler or barbecue until medium-hot, and brush the barbecue with oil. Thread the fish onto the skewers. Grill for 2–3 minutes on each side, brushing lightly with the marinade, until the fish is golden and cooked through. Serve the skewers with the mango piled on top, and a scattering of rosemary and thyme.

crab bisque

This creamy soup makes the most of seasonal crab with the addition of some crab butter for extra flavor when serving.

 30 MINS   **50–55 MINS**

SPECIAL EQUIPMENT ▪ blender or food processor

SERVES 4–6

1 large fresh cooked crab

3½ cups fish or chicken stock

5 tbsp butter, softened

1 tbsp chopped flat-leaf parsley

bunch of scallions, trimmed and chopped

5 tbsp dry vermouth

2 tbsp brandy

3 tbsp all-purpose flour

5 tbsp milk

⅔ cup half-and-half

salt and freshly ground black pepper

1 Remove all the meat from the crab; keep the dark and light meat separate. Put the crab shell in a pan with the stock and half the dark crab meat. Bring to a boil, reduce the heat, cover, and simmer gently for 45 minutes. Strain, and reserve the stock.

2 Make the crab butter by mashing the remaining dark meat with 3 tbsp of the butter and the parsley. Spoon the butter onto a piece of wax paper, then roll into a log shape. Twist the edges of the paper, and put the roll in the fridge.

3 Fry the scallions gently in the remaining butter until soft. Add the vermouth and simmer for 5 minutes. Flame the brandy and stir in. Mix the flour with the milk and stir in. Add half the strained stock, bring to a boil, and cook for 2 minutes, stirring. Pour into a blender or food processor and purée with the white crab meat. Return to the pan, stir in the remaining stock and the half-and-half. Season to taste with salt and pepper and heat through. Ladle into warm bowls and top each with a slice of the crab butter. Serve immediately.

Season's best **haddock**

Haddock is found on both sides of the North Atlantic and has a brownish-gray, flecked body. In season from early summer through to winter, it is smaller and sweeter than cod, with delicious, chunky flesh. Cheese and bacon go particularly well with it, as do tomatoes, garlic, white wine, and cider. Smoked haddock is an extremely popular delicacy.

Haddock It has a black lateral line on a gray back and a silver flank. Traditionally used for fish and chips, and preferred in this dish in Scotland, but also commonly used poached, for fish pie. It has a delicate, creamy, and sweet flavor.

The black spot on its shoulder is known as St Peter's mark or thumbprint.

The thick, scaly skin is easy to remove, but can be left on if poaching and removed afterward.

Haddock fillet Its meaty texture and good, thick flakes make haddock a favorite for frying, grilling, and baking. The fillets are also popular smoked, both dyed and undyed.

Quality haddock will have milky-white flesh.

essentials

cuts available

Loins or fillets, also hot smoked (Arborath smokies) or cold smoked (undyed and dyed fillet and whole Finnan haddock).

buy Firm, moist flesh, must smell pleasantly fishy.

store Best eaten on the day of purchase, or keep wrapped, in the coldest part of the fridge, for up to 24 hours.

cook Fry, grill, bake, steam, poach.

recipe ideas

Baked haddock in white wine with parsley p107

Battered haddock with lemon mayonnaise p74

Portuguese haddock soup p363

Skewered lemon and herb haddock p74

Spiced haddock with coconut, chile, and lime p176

how to skin a fillet

When skinning, keep the knife in contact with the board, or you will leave too much flesh behind. Dip your fingers in salt for a better grip on the slippery skin.

1 With a flexible boning knife, make a cut between the skin and the flesh at the tail end (the thinnest part), keeping the knife close to the skin.

2 With your free hand, grip the flap of skin. Keeping it taut, and the knife at a 30° angle, saw and push along the fillet, separating flesh from skin.

lettuce soup with peas

For the best flavor choose very fresh, crisp lettuce for this refreshing chilled soup. The ginger adds a surprising zing to what might otherwise look like straightforward fare.

 20 MINS PLUS CHILLING

SPECIAL EQUIPMENT ▪ blender or food processor

SERVES 4

4½oz (125g) peas (shelled weight)

1 small garlic clove

sea salt and freshly ground black pepper

2 round heads of lettuce, torn into pieces and solid cores discarded

1 cup natural yogurt

¾in(2cm) piece fresh ginger, peeled and finely grated

handful of mint leaves

juice of ½ lemon

1 Bring a small amount of water to a boil in a pan, add the peas, and cook for 1 minute. Drain (reserving the cooking water), cool under cold running water, and chill in the fridge.

2 Halve the garlic clove and crush the halves with a pinch of coarse salt. Combine the garlic with all the other ingredients (except the peas) in a blender or food processor, adding just enough of the reserved cooking water to get the blades moving or until the desired consistency is achieved—it is best if you can get it fairly smooth, with a bit of texture.

3 Transfer the soup to a large bowl and chill for 30 minutes. When ready to serve, stir in the cooked peas, leaving a few to garnish.

herb and garlic artichokes

Baby globe artichokes with tender stems are best for this delicious appetizer. Serve warm or at room temperature.

 25-30 MINS   🍲 25-40 MINS

SERVES 6

6 baby globe artichokes, stem trimmed to 1½in (4cm)

2 lemons, halved, plus 1 to garnish

6 garlic cloves, finely chopped

small bunch of flat-leaf parsley, leaves finely chopped

8-10 sprigs of mint, leaves finely chopped, plus more to garnish

salt and freshly ground black pepper

½ cup olive oil

1 Snap the large bottom leaves off the artichokes. Continue to remove the leaves, tearing off about three-quarters of each one so the edible white part remains attached to the heart. Continue until you reach the cone of soft, small leaves in the center. Trim the cone with a sharp knife and rub the cut edges of the artichoke with a lemon half to prevent discoloration.

2 Peel the stems, cutting away the tough, fibrous exterior. Trim the green parts of the base to remove any tough, fibrous leaves. Scoop out the hairy choke with a teaspoon and squeeze lemon juice into the hollowed-out center. Rub the juice around the inside with your finger.

3 Combine the garlic, herbs, and a little salt in a bowl. Put 2-3 spoonfuls in the center of each artichoke and press it down well against the bottom and sides so they are as full as possible. Keep back 2-3 tbsp to sprinkle on top.

4 Set the artichokes, tops down and stems up, in a single, tight layer in a large pan. Sprinkle the remaining stuffing over and pour on the oil. Sprinkle with salt and pepper and add enough water to come halfway up the sides, not including the stems. Bring to a boil, cover, and simmer for 25-45 minutes, until tender. Add more water if necessary, so the artichokes are always half covered. To test if they are cooked, pierce them with the point of a knife; they should be tender.

5 Transfer the artichokes to a large, warmed serving dish with a slotted spoon, arranging them in a single layer, still with their stems upward. Take as little as possible of the cooking liquid and then boil it until it is reduced to about 1 cup.

6 Squeeze the juice from a lemon half, discard seeds, and add to the cooking liquid. Taste for seasoning. Pour the cooking liquid over the artichokes and leave to cool to room temperature. Serve decorated with lemon wedges and mint sprigs.

broiled sardines on toast

To fillet a sardine, cut off its head, slice along its belly with a knife, and gently flatten it out. Run your fingers along the backbone and then gently lift out the bones.

 10 MINS PLUS MARINATING   🍲 6 MINS

SERVES 4

8 sardines, cleaned, gutted, and filleted

4 tbsp olive oil

3 garlic cloves, finely sliced

1 jalapeño chile, seeded and finely chopped

juice of 1 lemon

1 tsp fennel seeds, crushed

2 tbsp flat-leaf parsley, finely chopped

salt and freshly ground black pepper

ciabatta, sliced and toasted, to serve

1 Brush the sardines with a little of the oil and cook under a medium broiler for 3 minutes on each side. Remove and allow to cool.

2 Meanwhile, put all the remaining ingredients (except for the ciabatta) in a mixing bowl and combine well. Add the sardines, then leave to marinate for 20 minutes, if you have time. Serve on the warm toasted ciabatta.

pea, ham, and potato soup

A firm and traditional favorite with everyone, this soup tastes even better if prepared in advance and reheated to serve the next day. Go easy on the salt when adding seasoning, since the ham may be salty enough for most people's taste.

 15 MINS **2 HRS** ❄ **FREEZABLE**

SPECIAL EQUIPMENT ▪ handheld blender

SERVES 4–6

2½ lb (1.1kg) unsmoked or smoked ham

1 bay leaf

1 tbsp olive oil

1 onion, finely chopped

salt and freshly ground black pepper

1 tbsp Dijon mustard

3 garlic cloves, finely chopped

2 sprigs of rosemary

handful of thyme, leaves only

4 cups hot vegetable or chicken stock

1lb (450g) peas (shelled weight)

3 potatoes, peeled and chopped into bite-sized pieces

1 Put the ham and bay leaf in a large pan, cover with 4 cups of water, and bring to a boil. Partially cover, reduce the heat, and simmer for about 1 hour, or until the ham is cooked. Skim away any scum that comes to the surface. Discard the ham stock, or strain and reserve a little to add to the soup. Set the ham aside until cool enough to handle.

2 Heat the oil in a large heavy-bottomed pan over medium heat, add the onion, and cook for 3–4 minutes until the onions are soft. Season with salt and pepper, then stir in the mustard, garlic, and herbs (reserve some thyme leaves for garnish). Add a little stock and bring to a boil, then add in the peas and remaining stock. Bring to a boil, reduce to simmer, and cook for 45 minutes, adding hot water as needed.

3 About 20 minutes before the end of the cooking time, bring a separate pan of water to a boil. Add the potatoes, bring back up to a boil, and then simmer for 12–15 minutes until soft. Drain and set aside. Remove the rosemary from the soup, then use a handheld blender to gently purée the peas. Return them to the pan and stir in the potatoes.

4 Remove any fat from the ham, chop into bite-sized pieces, and stir into the soup. Taste and season as needed. Garnish with the reserved thyme leaves and serve with whole-wheat bread.

variation

ham, cabbage, and potato soup

Prepare in exactly the same way but use half a head of cabbage, shredded, instead of the peas. Cook the potatoes in the soup for the last 20 minutes and do not purée any of it.

Season's best **lettuce**

A delicate vegetable with crunchy leaves, crisp texture, and mild flavor, lettuce is an ideal choice for salads, wraps, and sandwiches. It is a good source of vitamins A and C. Lettuce is available in different shapes, sizes, textures, and colors, in tight heads or with looser leaves. Essentially summer crops, some are grown all year. Ideal flavor pairings include specialty oils and vinegars, with fresh torn herbs and other salad vegetables.

An annual or biennial herbaceous plant, cultivated for centuries and grown in moderate climates worldwide, lettuce thrives in moist, mild weather.

Don't discard the flavorful outer leaves. Tear them into bite-sized pieces and mix with the heart.

Oakleaf An attractive loose-leaf lettuce with a well-rounded sweet, earthy flavor, this variety has thin, soft leaves and crunchy stalks.

The tender, flavorful leaves are often used in a typical mesclun mix of young leaves and shoots.

Butterleaf (Round) Probably the most popular of all lettuce types, butterleaf has thick, soft, tender leaves with a mild, sweet flavor.

Cut away the thick stalks from outer leaves as they can be bitter and slightly fibrous.

Romaine (Cos) One of the best tasting varieties of all, Romaine is valued for its crunch and full-bodied flavor. The succulent leaves are ideal for burgers, salads, sandwiches, and wraps.

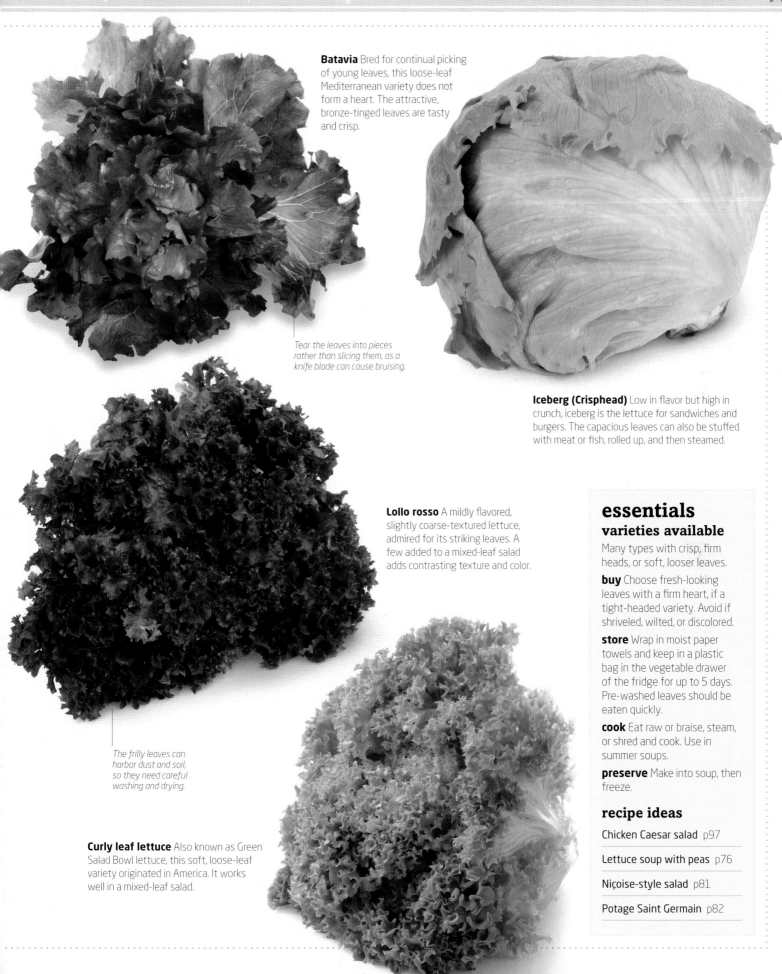

Batavia Bred for continual picking of young leaves, this loose-leaf Mediterranean variety does not form a heart. The attractive, bronze-tinged leaves are tasty and crisp.

Tear the leaves into pieces rather than slicing them, as a knife blade can cause bruising.

Iceberg (Crisphead) Low in flavor but high in crunch, iceberg is the lettuce for sandwiches and burgers. The capacious leaves can also be stuffed with meat or fish, rolled up, and then steamed.

Lollo rosso A mildly flavored, slightly coarse-textured lettuce, admired for its striking leaves. A few added to a mixed-leaf salad adds contrasting texture and color.

The frilly leaves can harbor dust and soil, so they need careful washing and drying.

Curly leaf lettuce Also known as Green Salad Bowl lettuce, this soft, loose-leaf variety originated in America. It works well in a mixed-leaf salad.

essentials
varieties available
Many types with crisp, firm heads, or soft, looser leaves.

buy Choose fresh-looking leaves with a firm heart, if a tight-headed variety. Avoid if shriveled, wilted, or discolored.

store Wrap in moist paper towels and keep in a plastic bag in the vegetable drawer of the fridge for up to 5 days. Pre-washed leaves should be eaten quickly.

cook Eat raw or braise, steam, or shred and cook. Use in summer soups.

preserve Make into soup, then freeze.

recipe ideas
Chicken Caesar salad p97

Lettuce soup with peas p76

Niçoise-style salad p81

Potage Saint Germain p82

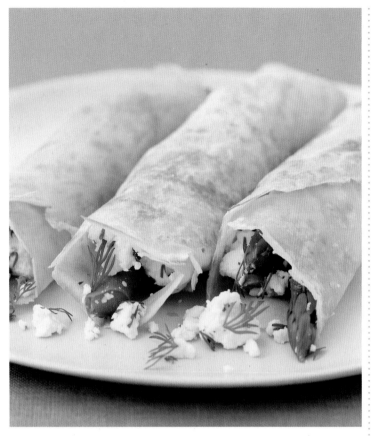

crepes with asparagus, feta cheese, and dill

A crepe is a most versatile carrier for fillings of all descriptions. Here they are folded around feta cheese and dill, adding salty and sweet flavors to in-season asparagus.

 5 MINS PLUS STANDING   **15 MINS**

MAKES 8

1 cup all-purpose flour

salt and freshly ground black pepper

1 egg

1¼ cup milk

8-12 fine asparagus spears, trimmed and cut into 3 pieces

handful of dill, finely chopped

9oz (250g) feta cheese, crumbled

drizzle of olive oil, for frying

1 Put the flour in a mixing bowl with a pinch of salt, stir, then make a well in the center. Crack the egg into the well and add a tiny amount of the milk. Using a wooden spoon, stir the egg and milk, letting the flour gradually tumble in. Add the rest of the milk, little by little, stirring continuously, until all the flour has been incorporated and the mixture is lump-free. Put it in the fridge to stand for 30 minutes, if you have time.

2 Cook the asparagus in boiling salted water for 2–4 minutes, or until soft. Drain, refresh in cold water, and drain again. Transfer to a bowl and mix with the dill, feta cheese, and some black pepper.

3 In a small, flat frying pan or crepe pan, heat a drizzle of olive oil over high heat, swirling it around the pan, then tipping it out again. Stir the batter mix, then spoon 2 tbsp of it into the pan, swirling it around so it reaches the edges. Cook for a couple of minutes, until a light golden color, then pull up the edges with a palette knife. Turn the crepe over and cook the other side for 1 minute. Slide it out onto a plate. Repeat with the remaining batter.

4 Spoon the filling onto the crepes and either roll or fold them up.

crudités with tapenade

Keep the tapenade for up to 1 week in the fridge by topping it with a thin layer of olive oil and covering.

 30-35 MINS   **10-15 MINS**

SPECIAL EQUIPMENT ▪ blender or food processor

SERVES 6-8

6 slices of white bread, crusts cut off

4 garlic cloves, peeled

7oz (200g) pitted black olives

1oz (30g) capers, drained

6 canned anchovy fillets

½ cup olive oil

lemon juice, to taste

freshly ground black pepper

1 baguette, cut into ¼in (5mm) diagonal slices

For the crudités

bunch of scallions, trimmed and cut into 2in (5cm) pieces

1 cucumber, peeled, quartered, seeded, and cut into strips

1 red bell pepper, seeded and cut into strips

1 green bell pepper, seeded and cut into strips

bunch of radishes, trimmed

9oz (250g) cherry tomatoes

1 Tear the bread into pieces and cover with cold water in a bowl. Soak for 5 minutes, squeeze dry, and put into a blender or food processor.

2 Add the garlic, olives, capers, and anchovies and pulse coarsely. With the blades turning, gradually add the oil. Add lemon juice and black pepper to taste and pulse again. It can be a coarse or fairly smooth paste. Transfer to a bowl, cover, and set aside.

3 Preheat the oven to 375°F (190°C). Bake the baguette on a baking sheet for 10–15 minutes, until crisp. Serve the tapenade with the crudités and toasted bread.

variation

creamy cucumber and scallion dip

Beat ⅔ cup thick natural yogurt with 4oz (115g) cream cheese. Stir in 2 finely chopped scallions and ¼ cucumber, peeled and finely chopped. Add a few drops of Tabasco and season to taste. Serve with the crudités.

niçoise-style salad

This dish is an international classic. In its heyday, it included raw red bell peppers and shallots with artichoke hearts instead of potatoes. Try these seasonal ingredients for variety.

 15 MINS

SERVES 4

2 x 7oz cans tuna in olive oil, drained

10 cherry tomatoes, halved

handful of flat-leaf parsley, finely chopped

bunch of chives, finely snipped

salt and freshly ground black pepper

4½oz (125g) fava beans (shelled weight), skinned (p85, optional)

12 black olives, pitted

12 salted anchovies

1 crisp lettuce such as Romaine, leaves separated

2-3 scallions, trimmed and finely sliced

For the dressing

6 tbsp extra virgin olive oil

2 tbsp white wine vinegar

2 garlic cloves, grated or finely chopped

1-2 tsp Dijon mustard

salt and freshly ground black pepper

1 To make the dressing, put all the dressing ingredients in a screw-top jar, season well with salt and pepper, cover with the lid, and shake to combine.

2 Put the tuna and tomatoes in a bowl and drizzle half of the dressing over the top. Sprinkle in half of the fresh herbs and season generously with salt and pepper. Toss together. Add the fava beans, olives, and anchovies and mix gently.

3 Line a shallow serving bowl with the lettuce leaves and arrange the tuna mixture on top. Drizzle with the remaining dressing and sprinkle the remaining herbs over the top. Top with the scallions and serve.

asparagus frittata on crostini

Two Italian mainstays—crunchy crostini and the frittata—are combined for a lunchtime snack or evening appetizer. Thin asparagus would be best to ensure they cook successfully.

 20 MINS   20 MINS

SERVES 4

¼ cup olive oil

4 thick slices crusty sourdough bread

salt and freshly ground black pepper

1 garlic clove, peeled but left whole

8 asparagus spears, trimmed

2 tbsp finely chopped onion

4 large eggs

½ cup heavy cream

2oz (60g) Parmesan cheese, grated

handful of flat-leaf parsley, to garnish

1 Preheat the oven to 400°F (200°C). Pour 2 tbsp of the oil onto a baking sheet, then gently press the bread into the oil on both sides. Season with salt and pepper. Bake in the oven for 12–15 minutes until golden brown. Remove from the oven and lightly rub each slice of bread with the garlic. Set aside on a wire rack to keep the crostini crisp.

2 Meanwhile, cook the asparagus spears in boiling salted water for 2–4 minutes, or until soft. Drain, refresh in cold water, and drain again. Place on a cutting board and cut each spear in half. Heat the remaining oil in a heavy-bottomed frying pan over medium heat, add the onion, and cook for 3–4 minutes until the onion is soft and translucent. Add the halved asparagus spears and cook for another 2 minutes. Preheat the broiler to its highest setting.

3 In a bowl, whisk together the eggs, cream, and Parmesan cheese. Season with salt and pepper, and pour the mixture over the asparagus and onion mixture in the pan. As the bottom is cooking, tilt the pan so the uncooked egg mixture from the top runs under the frittata. Continue cooking for 3–5 minutes until almost set.

4 To finish off, place the pan under the broiler and cook until the top of the frittata is golden brown. To serve, tear the frittata into 4 rough pieces and sit on top of the crostini. Cut each piece in half, scatter with parsley, and serve immediately.

mini chicken tortillas topped with yogurt, cucumber, and mint dip

Tiny morsels to pop into your mouth on a summer evening with a cool, refreshing drink. The fresh flavors of cucumber, mint, and cilantro round off the spicy chicken perfectly.

 20 MINS

MAKES 8–10

¾ cup Greek-style yogurt

½ cucumber

bunch of mint, leaves picked

salt and freshly ground black pepper

9oz package plain-flavored corn chips

½–1 cup mango chutney

12oz (350g) cooked chicken tikka pieces, chopped into small pieces

small handful of cilantro, to garnish

1 To make the dip, pour the yogurt into a bowl. Trim the ends from the cucumber, peel, cut in half lengthwise, and scoop out the seeds with a teaspoon. Finely cube and add to the yogurt with the mint leaves. Season well with salt and pepper. Taste, and season more if needed.

2 Pour the corn chips onto a clean surface and spread out in a single layer. Add 1 tsp of mango chutney to each one.

3 Add some chicken pieces to each corn chip. Spoon on about 1 tsp of the dip and garnish with cilantro. Serve immediately.

variation

mini pea tortillas with yogurt, cucumber, and mint dip

Instead of chicken, purée 8oz (225g) cooked shelled peas with 2oz (60g) cream cheese, a pinch of grated nutmeg, and some salt and pepper. Use tomato chutney instead of mango. Assemble with the dip as before.

cream of asparagus soup

If you are a fan of puréed soups, pulse the mixture in a blender at the end of cooking, then pass it through a sieve and reheat.

 10 MINS   **40 MINS**   ❄ **FREEZABLE**

SERVES 4

salt and freshly ground black pepper

4 tbsp butter

1lb 2oz (500g) asparagus spears, trimmed, peeled (reserve the trimmings), and cut into 1in (2.5cm) lengths

1¼ cups milk

¼ cup all-purpose flour

pinch of granulated sugar

pinch of grated nutmeg

2 egg yolks

2 tbsp heavy cream

1½ tbsp chopped flat-leaf parsley

1 Put 3½ cups water into a pan with 1 tsp salt and 2 tbsp of the butter. Add the asparagus trimmings. Bring to a boil, cover, reduce the heat, and simmer for 15 minutes. Strain through a sieve (reserving the cooking liquid) and discard the trimmings.

2 Cook the asparagus spears in boiling salted water for 2–4 minutes, or until soft, then drain, reserving the cooking liquid. Add enough of the milk to the cooking liquid to make 3½ cups.

3 Melt the remaining butter in a pan, add the flour, and cook over low heat, stirring, for 2–3 minutes, or until smooth. Gradually add the milk mixture, stirring vigorously with a whisk to make sure there are no lumps. Bring to a boil and cook, uncovered, over low heat for 5 minutes, stirring occasionally. Add the sugar and nutmeg and season with salt and pepper.

4 Stir the egg yolks into the cream and slowly add the mixture to the soup, stirring to get a smooth texture. Add the asparagus and reheat gently. Do not let the soup boil. Serve garnished with the parsley.

potage saint germain

Scallions, peas, and lettuce form the basis for this summery soup; so it is perfect for using up any excess.

 15 MINS   **1 HR**   ❄ **FREEZABLE**

SPECIAL EQUIPMENT ▪ blender or food processor

SERVES 4

1 tbsp olive oil

1 tbsp butter, plus 2 tbsp chilled butter, cubed

4 large scallions (white parts only), trimmed and chopped

5½ cups hot vegetable stock

5½oz (150g) green split peas, rinsed and drained

salt and freshly ground black pepper

1lb 2oz (500g) peas (shelled weight)

1 head of soft lettuce, leaves snipped

1 large egg yolk

3 tbsp crème fraîche

1–2 tbsp Madeira or port

1 tbsp snipped chervil, to garnish

1 Put a large sauté pan over medium heat. Add the oil and 1 tbsp butter. Add in the scallions. Reduce the heat and sweat for 5 minutes, stirring frequently. Pour the stock into the pan and then add the split peas. Season it lightly and bring back to simmer. Reduce the heat a little, cover, and cook for another 20 minutes, stirring occasionally.

2 Add the peas and lettuce, stir, and cook for 5 minutes. Leave to cool, then pour into a blender or food processor and pulse until smooth. Push the soup back into the pan through a fine sieve, mashing the vegetables with the back of a spoon. Pour ½ cup water through the sieve to thin the soup, then gently reheat.

3 In a cup or small bowl combine the egg yolk and the crème fraîche with 2–3 tbsp of the hot soup. Whisk this into the pan a little at a time. Continue cooking until the soup is piping hot. Adjust the seasoning. Just before serving, stir in the Madeira or port, whisk in the cubed butter, and garnish with the chervil.

curried vegetable pies

A summer vegetable medley of young carrots, zucchini, and scallions is combined with potatoes in these pies. Their handy size makes them easy to take on a picnic or for a lunchtime snack. Depending on how hot you like your curry, you can buy curry pastes ranging from mild to extra hot. The pastes are a mixture of ground herbs and spices pounded into a vegetable oil.

 15 MINS 45 MINS FREEZABLE

SPECIAL EQUIPMENT ▪ 6in (15cm) round cookie cutter

MAKES 4

1 carrot, cubed

2 potatoes, peeled and finely cubed

salt and freshly ground black pepper

1lb (450g) ready-made
  pie dough

1 egg, lightly beaten, for egg wash

1 tbsp curry paste

2 tbsp Greek-style yogurt

1 garlic clove, grated or finely chopped

1in (2.5cm) piece of fresh ginger,
  peeled and finely chopped

1 zucchini, cubed

2 scallions, trimmed and
  finely sliced

handful of cilantro, finely chopped

juice of ½ lemon

1 Preheat the oven to 400°F (200°C). Cook the carrot and potatoes in a pan of salted water for about 15 minutes until soft; drain well.

2 Roll out the pie dough on a floured work surface, then cut out 4 circles using the cookie cutter. Put the pie dough rounds on a baking sheet and brush the edges with a little of the egg wash.

3 Put the carrot and potatoes in a bowl and gently mix with the curry paste and yogurt. Add the garlic, ginger, zucchini, scallions, cilantro, and lemon juice, and season well with salt and pepper. Stir in gently until well mixed.

4 Divide the vegetable mixture evenly among the pie dough circles, spooning it into the center of each one. Fold over the pie dough to make a half-moon shape, and pinch the edges together to seal. Transfer to a baking sheet. Using a sharp knife, make 2 or 3 slashes in the top of each pie, then brush all over with the remaining egg wash. Bake in the oven for 20–30 minutes until golden. Serve hot or cold.

variation

mediterranean vegetable pies

Prepare in the same way, but substitute 1 tbsp tomato paste and a pinch of sugar for the curry paste. Use a handful of chopped fresh basil instead of the cilantro. When the pies are on the baking sheet, brush with egg wash, then sprinkle with a handful of grated Cheddar cheese before baking.

baby fava bean soup

This soup is a perfect summery starter since it makes good use of that early summer vegetable, the fava bean.

 20 MINS **1 HR** ❄ **FREEZABLE**

SPECIAL EQUIPMENT ▪ blender or food processor

SERVES 4–6

3 slices toasting bread, for croutons

6 tbsp olive oil

3 large mild onions, sliced

4 scallions, trimmed and chopped

3lb 3oz (1.5kg) fava beans (shelled weight), skinned (p85, optional)

4 garlic cloves, crushed

small handful of chives, snipped

4 new potatoes, peeled and chopped

salt and freshly ground black pepper

leaves from a bunch of radishes

drizzle of extra virgin olive oil

1 To make the croutons, cut the bread into ½in (1cm) cubes. Heat 3 tbsp of the oil in a large frying pan over medium-high heat. Add the bread cubes and spread them out. Fry for a minute, then stir and turn them over. Fry for another minute. Spread them on a plate lined with paper towels. Pat with more paper towels to absorb excess oil. Set aside.

2 Heat the remaining oil in a large heavy-bottomed flameproof casserole dish over medium heat. Add the onions and scallions and cook for 5–7 minutes until they are soft.

3 Add the fava beans with the garlic, chives, and potatoes. Stir, then pour in about 10½ cups water. Season lightly with salt and pepper and stir in the radish leaves. Increase the heat a little and bring to a boil, then leave to simmer gently for 15–20 minutes.

4 Allow to cool a little, then pour the soup into a blender or food processor and process until smooth. Strain back into the pan. (If you prefer, you can omit the straining, in which case the soup will serve 6–8 people.) Reheat until piping hot before serving. Top with the croutons and a drizzle of extra virgin olive oil.

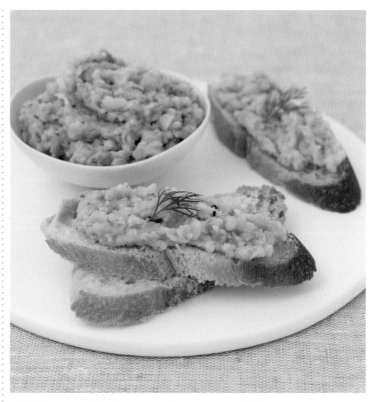

dill and fava bean dip

In addition to the in-season fava bean, this dip makes use of Italian large white cannellini beans. Similar in shape and size to navy beans, they are readily available in cans.

 30 MINS **45 MINS**

SPECIAL EQUIPMENT ▪ blender or food processor

SERVES 8

3 tbsp olive oil

1 small onion, finely chopped

1lb 10oz (750g) fava beans (shelled weight), skinned (p85, optional)

salt and freshly ground black pepper

14oz (400g) can cannellini beans, drained

1 tbsp chopped dill

2 scallions, trimmed and thinly sliced on the diagonal

1 Heat the oil in a heavy-bottomed pan over medium heat, add the onion, and cook for 3–4 minutes until the onion is soft and translucent.

2 Add in the fava beans and cook for 10–15 minutes, stirring occasionally. Add 2 cups water, season with salt and pepper, and partially cover the pan with a lid. Reduce the heat and simmer for 25 minutes, mashing the beans a little during this time. Drain and allow to cool.

3 Put the cooled fava bean mixture in a blender or food processor. Add the cannellini beans, dill, and scallions, and pulse to a chunky purée. Season with salt and pepper. Transfer to a serving bowl and serve with fresh crusty bread.

variation

fresh pea and mint dip with seasonal crudités

Prepare in the same way but use 1lb 10oz (750g) peas in their pods. Shell them but leave the skins. Cook, then blend as before but add 1 tbsp chopped fresh mint instead of dill and serve with snow peas, thin asparagus tips, scrubbed baby carrots (or young carrot sticks), and radishes.

Season's best **fava beans**

Before the discovery of the New World, fava beans were the only beans available, and they are still enjoyed worldwide, fresh and dried. In season in spring and early summer, they have a unique meaty, slightly herbaceous flavor, are succulent and sweet when young, becoming floury and more strongly flavored with age. They are delicious with bacon and cured meats, lamb, meaty white fish, beans, spices (particularly harissa), potatoes, and spinach.

The first early fava beans are usually prolific, depending on the harshness of the winter, and they are particularly delicious. The later sowing is harvested in high summer.

Fava bean A delicious and nutritious bean at its best when young and tender, but still edible puréed or in soup when old and floury.

Brown speckling on older pods is quite normal and is not a sign of poor quality.

Young beans can be eaten raw, drizzled with olive oil, with Pecorino cheese (Italian-style).

essentials
varieties available

Finger-length immature pods, mature pods; also dried.

buy Choose bright green and firm bean pods, evenly filled but not too swollen.

store Keep unshelled in the vegetable drawer of the fridge for up to 2 weeks (don't worry if the pods go limp).

cook Usually boil or steam; serve hot or cold in salads or in béchamel or parsley sauce. Add to soups, stews, and casseroles. Use the pods for stock.

preserve Blanch and freeze.

recipe ideas

Baby fava bean soup p84

Chicken with fava beans p100

Ham with minted peas and fava beans p116

Hot and spicy lamb with fava beans p96

Lamb with artichokes, fava beans, and dill p113

Pork chops with tomato and fava bean sauce p101

how to shell and skin fava beans

If pods are smaller than your middle finger, trim and eat whole, pod and all. Fava beans usually need shelling, except for the tiny beans eaten in their pod. For best results, remove the outer skins of the beans after cooking.

1 Snap the stalk end and pull off the string all down the edge. Slit open with your thumbs and slip out the beans.

2 When cooked, drain the beans in a colander. When cool enough to handle, gently pop the beans out of their skins.

zucchini and pea mini tortillas

Bursting with fresh green summer vegetables, these mini tortillas make a great appetizer. Alternatively, for a tasty packed lunch, simply wrap them in foil to transport.

 20 MINS 5 MINS

MAKES 20

3 zucchini, grated

2oz (50g) baby spinach leaves

grated zest and juice of 1 lemon

9oz (250g) peas (shelled weight)

2oz (50g) pine nuts, toasted

salt and freshly ground black pepper

10 flour tortillas, halved

2 tbsp reduced-fat mayonnaise

large handful of snow peas

large handful of pea shoots

1 In a large bowl, mix the zucchini, spinach, lemon zest and juice, peas, and pine nuts together. Season well.

2 Heat a frying pan over high heat. Place 2 tortilla halves in the pan at a time and heat for 15 seconds on each side. Cover the heated tortillas with a kitchen towel to keep warm.

3 Brush one of the tortilla halves with mayonnaise. Place a little of the filling in the center. Arrange some snow peas and pea shoots on top, so that they stick out at one end, then roll up the tortilla. Repeat to make 20 mini tortillas.

grilled asparagus and pancetta

Ideal for party food, this simple recipe cleverly combines the sweetness of the new season's asparagus and the salty richness of the pancetta with a zesty dressing.

 15 MINS 5 MINS

SERVES 4

12 asparagus spears, trimmed

salt and freshly ground black pepper

24 thin slices of pancetta

1 garlic clove, crushed

¼ cup olive oil

1 tbsp balsamic vinegar

1 tbsp freshly squeezed orange juice

1 tsp Dijon mustard

1 small head of radicchio, torn into bite-sized pieces

1 head of butterhead lettuce, torn into bite-sized pieces

3½oz (100g) arugula leaves

7oz (200g) cherry tomatoes

3½oz (100g) Parmesan cheese, shaved

1 Blanch the asparagus spears in boiling salted water for 2–4 minutes, or until soft. Drain, immediately refresh in a bowl of cold water, and drain again.

2 Heat a ridged cast-iron grill pan until hot. Wrap 2 slices of the pancetta around each asparagus spear. Grill the asparagus spears for about 3–4 minutes until beginning to char, turning once halfway during the cooking time. Set aside.

3 To make the dressing, whisk together the garlic, oil, balsamic vinegar, orange juice, and mustard in a small bowl. Season with salt and pepper and whisk again.

4 Toss the salad leaves, tomatoes, and dressing together in a bowl and divide among 4 serving plates or bowls. Top each serving with 3 of the asparagus and pancetta spears, and sprinkle the Parmesan shavings over the top. Serve immediately.

cheddar and zucchini soufflés

The zucchini mixture for these soufflés can be prepared up to 3 hours ahead, up to the end of step 4. Then, just whisk the egg whites and finish the recipe just before baking.

30-35 MINS   30-35 MINS

SPECIAL EQUIPMENT ▪ 6 x 12fl oz (350ml) ramekins

SERVES 6

4 tbsp unsalted butter

2 shallots, finely chopped

1lb 2oz (500g) zucchini, coarsely grated

salt and freshly ground black pepper

⅔ cup milk

3 tbsp all-purpose flour

½ cup heavy cream

pinch of ground nutmeg

4 eggs, separated, plus 2 egg whites

3oz (85g) Cheddar cheese, grated

1 Melt half the butter in a frying pan. Add the shallots and cook until soft. Then add the zucchini, season, and cook for 3–5 minutes until tender. Transfer to a sieve set over a bowl and leave to drain.

2 Scald the milk in a small pan. Melt the remaining butter in a medium pan. Over the heat, add the flour all at once and whisk briskly for 30–60 seconds, until the mixture starts to foam. Remove from the heat, slowly pour in the milk, whisking until mixed.

3 Return to the heat and whisk. When the sauce boils, pour in the cream and whisk again. Season with salt, pepper, and nutmeg. Simmer for 2 minutes. Whisk the egg yolks into the sauce, one at a time, return the pan to the heat, and bring to a boil. Keep whisking, and simmer for 1 minute.

4 Remove the pan from the heat and stir in the Cheddar and zucchini. Preheat the oven to 375°F (190°C). Brush the ramekins with a little melted butter. Reheat the zucchini mixture until hot.

5 Beat the egg whites with a pinch of salt in a metal bowl for 3–5 minutes until stiff peaks form. Add one-quarter to the warm mixture and stir. Add the mixture to the remaining egg whites in the bowl. Fold together until the egg whites are thoroughly incorporated. Spoon into the prepared dishes. Bake for 10–15 minutes until puffed and brown.

6 Serve immediately: the soufflés will lose much of their volume within minutes as they cool.

zucchini fritters with dill tzatziki

Zucchini is lovely when picked young, but, a member of the concurbit family, it can become watery if left to grow too large. To offset any wateriness, salt larger zucchini before use.

20 MINS PLUS DRAINING   10 MINS

SERVES 4

7oz (200g) zucchini, coarsely grated

sea salt and freshly ground black pepper

3½oz (100g) ricotta cheese

1 large egg

2 tbsp all-purpose flour

3 garlic cloves, crushed

small handful of basil, chopped

small handful of flat-leaf parsley, chopped

light olive oil, for frying

2 tbsp finely chopped dill

7oz (200g) Greek-style yogurt

juice of ½ lemon

1 Sprinkle the zucchini with 1 tsp sea salt and leave to drain in a sieve for 1 hour. Rinse and squeeze dry in a clean kitchen towel.

2 In a bowl, whisk together the ricotta cheese, egg, and flour. Add 2 of the crushed garlic cloves, the basil, and parsley, and season well. Mix in the zucchini.

3 Fill a frying pan with olive oil to a depth of ½in (1cm) and fry 2 tbsp of the zucchini and cheese batter over medium heat for 2–3 minutes on each side, until golden brown. Drain on paper towels.

4 To make the tzatziki, mix the last clove of garlic with the dill, some sea salt and pepper, and the yogurt. Add a squeeze of lemon juice and serve immediately with the hot fritters.

crepes with bell peppers and basil

It is worth leaving the crepe batter to stand for a while as it makes the end result that little bit lighter. For a nutty-tasting version, try buckwheat flour instead of the all-purpose flour.

 10 MINS PLUS STANDING **20 MINS**

MAKES 8

1 cup all-purpose flour

salt

1 large egg

1¼ cups milk

2 tbsp olive oil, plus a little extra for frying

4 red bell peppers, seeded and cut into strips

½ tsp granulated sugar

large handful of fresh basil leaves, torn

1 Put the flour in a mixing bowl with a pinch of salt, stir, and make a well in the center. Crack the egg into the well and add a tiny amount of the milk. Using a wooden spoon, stir the egg and milk, letting the flour gradually tumble in. Add the rest of the milk, little by little, stirring continuously until all the flour has been incorporated and the mixture is lump-free. Put it in the fridge to stand for 30 minutes, if you have time.

2 Heat 1 tbsp of the olive oil in a frying pan, add the bell peppers, the sugar, and a pinch of salt, and cook over low heat for 10–15 minutes, or until soft. Stir in the basil.

3 In a small, flat frying pan or crepe pan, heat a drizzle of olive oil over high heat, swirling it around the pan, then tipping it out again. Stir the batter mix, then spoon 2 tbsp of it into the pan, swirling it around so it reaches the edges. Cook for a couple of minutes until a light golden color, then pull up the edges with a palette knife. Turn the crepe over and cook the other side for 1 minute. Slide it out onto a plate.

4 Spoon the filling onto the crepes, then fold them up.

white asparagus with herb mayonnaise

The delicate color of white asparagus is produced by growing it in the dark, a method known as forcing.

🥄 **5 MINS** 🍲 **10 MINS**

SPECIAL EQUIPMENT ▪ blender or food processor

SERVES 4

1lb 2oz (500g) white or thick green asparagus spears, trimmed

2 large egg yolks

2 tbsp white wine vinegar

1 tsp Dijon mustard

1¼ cups light olive oil

juice of ½ lemon

sea salt and freshly ground black pepper

1 garlic clove, crushed

1 tbsp chopped flat-leaf parsley

1 tbsp chopped tarragon

1 Cook the asparagus spears in boiling salted water for 2–4 minutes, or until soft. Drain, refresh in cold water, and drain again.

2 To make the mayonnaise, put the egg yolks, vinegar, and mustard in a blender or food processor and pulse for 1–2 minutes, or until a light yellow color. Reduce the speed and slowly add the oil, a little at a time, until you have a smooth creamy emulsion.

3 Spoon the mayonnaise into a bowl and stir in the lemon juice. Season to taste with salt and pepper, and stir in the garlic, parsley, and tarragon. Serve as a dip for the cooked asparagus spears.

creamy scallop bisque

A rich broth sets off the sweetness of the scallops perfectly.

  20 MINS 🍲 **40 MINS**

SPECIAL EQUIPMENT ▪ blender or food processor

SERVES 4

1¼ cups dry white wine

1 tbsp butter

1 small onion, finely chopped

1 small shallot, very finely chopped

1 ripe tomato, chopped

10oz (300g) white fish, such as pollock or cod, skinned and cut into chunks

1 tsp anchovy paste (optional)

2 tbsp chopped flat-leaf parsley

2 tsp dill seeds

3 tbsp brandy

salt and freshly ground black pepper

½ cup half-and-half

3oz (75g) dried Spanish chorizo, cubed

12 small scallops (white part only)

1 tbsp finely snipped chives, to garnish

1 Boil 2½ cups water with the wine. Heat the butter in a frying pan over medium heat, add the onion and shallot, and cook for 3–4 minutes, until they are soft and translucent. Stir in the tomato, fish, anchovy paste, if using, parsley, and dill seeds, and cook for 5 minutes. Stir in the brandy and cook for a minute. Pour in the boiling wine mixture and season lightly with salt and pepper. Reduce the heat and simmer for 10 minutes. Take off the heat and let cool. Stir and mash down the soup with the back of a spoon. Gently heat the half-and-half in another pan until hot.

2 Transfer the soup to a blender or food processor and pulse until creamy. Strain through a sieve into the pan and stir in the half-and-half. Return to simmer, then remove from the heat and adjust the seasoning. Cover and keep warm.

3 Put a nonstick frying pan over medium heat. Add the chorizo and fry for 3–5 minutes until cooked through and crispy. Set aside on a plate lined with paper towels and keep warm.

4 Add the scallops to the pan. Cook for 2 minutes on each side. Remove from the heat. Ladle the soup into 4 bowls and add the scallops. Scatter over the chorizo and snipped chives and serve.

zucchini stuffed with golden raisins, red onion, and pine nuts

Pine nuts are most frequently used as the basis for pesto sauce as well as scattered over salads. Here they are warmed through with golden raisins and topped with feta to add a hint of Middle Eastern flavor to the ever-versatile zucchini.

 10 MINS 20 MINS

SERVES 4

8 zucchini

1 tbsp olive oil

1 red onion, finely chopped

pinch of dried chile flakes

salt

handful of golden raisins

handful of pine nuts, toasted

2½oz (75g) feta cheese, crumbled

1 Preheat the oven to 400°F (200°C). First, prepare the zucchini. Cut in half lengthwise. Scoop out the flesh, coarsely chop, and set aside with the zucchini shells.

2 Heat the oil in a large frying pan over medium heat, add the onion, and cook for 3–4 minutes until the onion is soft and translucent. Stir in the zucchini flesh, chile flakes, and a pinch of salt, and cook for a couple more minutes.

3 Stir in the golden raisins and half of the pine nuts, then remove from the heat. Spoon the mixture into the zucchini shells and top with the feta. Sit on a baking sheet and roast in the oven for 10–15 minutes until golden.

4 Sprinkle over the remaining pine nuts and serve hot with a simple salad of mixed leaves and tomatoes.

variation

zucchini stuffed with preserved lemon, raisins, and scallions

At step 2, fry 2 chopped scallions instead of the red onion. At step 3, stir in a finely chopped preserved lemon and a handful of raisins. Use a handful of pumpkin seeds instead of pine nuts, adding half now and the rest for garnish. Continue as at step 3.

poached salmon with salsa verde and cucumber

Here is a superfresh cold dish, just right for a light summer's day meal. The salsa verde combines herbs with a caper and anchovy dressing to give some added zing to the meal.

 15 MINS   5–6 MINS PLUS COOLING

SERVES 4

1lb (450g) salmon fillet

1 bay leaf

½ cup white wine

salt and freshly ground black pepper

handful of basil leaves, finely chopped

handful of mint leaves, finely chopped

handful of flat-leaf parsley, finely chopped

2 tbsp white wine vinegar

2 tsp capers, rinsed, gently squeezed dry, and finely chopped

2 garlic cloves, grated or finely chopped

8 anchovies in oil, drained and finely chopped

2 tsp whole-grain mustard

6 tbsp extra virgin olive oil

1 cucumber

1 Put the salmon in a frying pan. Add the bay leaf, wine, and just enough water to cover the fish. Season lightly with salt and pepper. Bring to a boil, reduce the heat, cover, and poach for 4–5 minutes until just cooked through. Remove from the heat and leave to cool in the liquid. Lift out of the poaching liquid and break into bite-sized pieces.

2 To make the salsa verde, put the herbs in a bowl. Drizzle in the vinegar and stir through. Add the capers, garlic, and anchovies, and stir again. Then add the mustard and season well with salt and pepper. Slowly stir in the olive oil. Taste and adjust the seasoning if needed, adding a little more vinegar or oil as required. Transfer to a serving bowl.

3 Trim the ends from the cucumber, peel, cut in half lengthwise, and scoop out the seeds with a teaspoon. Cube the flesh and put in a serving bowl.

4 Arrange the cooked salmon on a platter or individual plates. Spoon the salsa verde over the fish, place the cucumber on the side, and serve.

pasta with pancetta and arugula

Arugula leaves have a particularly strong peppery flavor so won't be subsumed by the spicy pancetta. A grating of Parmesan cheese is the essential finishing touch.

 5 MINS   15 MINS

SERVES 4

1 tbsp olive oil

1 onion, finely chopped

1 red or jalapeño chile, seeded and finely chopped

9oz (250g) pancetta, diced

2 garlic cloves, grated or finely chopped

12oz (350g) spaghetti

7oz (200g) arugula leaves

salt and freshly ground black pepper

Parmesan cheese, grated, to serve

1 Heat the oil in a large frying pan over medium heat, add the onion, and cook for 3–4 minutes until the onion is soft. Add the chile and cook for a few minutes more. Add the pancetta and cook for 5 minutes, or until crisp and golden, then stir in the garlic and cook for a few more seconds.

2 Meanwhile, cook the pasta in a large pan of boiling salted water for about 12 minutes, or until it is tender but still firm to the bite. Drain, keeping back a tiny amount of the cooking water. Return the pasta to the pan and toss with the pancetta mixture. Add the arugula, season with salt and pepper, and toss gently. Sprinkle with the Parmesan cheese and serve immediately.

pepper and artichoke salad

Artichoke hearts and roasted red peppers are served in this hearty salad with tasty blue cheese wafers.

 40–45 MINS PLUS CHILLING   **25–35 MINS**

SERVES 4

2½oz (75g) Stilton cheese, cut into chunks

2½oz (75g) Cambozola or Bavarian blue cheese, cut into chunks

5 tbsp butter, softened

¾ cup all-purpose flour

2 tbsp balsamic vinegar

1 tbsp Dijon mustard

salt and freshly ground black pepper

6 tbsp olive oil

leaves from ½ head of lollo rosso

leaves from ½ head of round lettuce

4½oz (125g) spinach leaves

2 red bell peppers, roasted, peeled, and cut into strips (p171) (or from a jar)

1oz (30g) pine nuts, toasted

2 cooked artichoke hearts, quartered (p309) (or from a jar)

1 Beat the cheese into the butter with a wooden spoon until the mixture is creamy and smooth. Stir in the flour until the dough comes together.

2 Shape the dough into a 1½in (4cm) diameter log. Wrap tightly in parchment paper. Twist the ends of

the paper to seal and freeze for 1–2 hours until firm.

3 Whisk the vinegar, mustard, and salt and pepper in a small bowl. Slowly whisk in the oil so the vinaigrette emulsifies and thickens slightly.

4 Preheat the oven to 350°F (180°C). Cut half the cheese wafer dough in ¼in (5mm) thick slices using a thin-bladed knife dipped in hot water. Space out on a baking sheet. Rewrap the remaining dough and return to the freezer.

5 Bake the wafers for 6–8 minutes until golden. Allow to cool slightly, then transfer to a wire rack lined with paper towels. Allow the baking sheet to cool, slice the remaining dough, and bake as before.

6 Put the leaves in a bowl and add the peppers. Toss with the vinaigrette and sprinkle with the pine nuts. Top with the artichoke hearts, add some wafers, and serve the rest separately.

pasta with pecorino and peas

Pecorino is a hard Italian cheese made from sheep's milk. In some Italian regions it is used in place of Parmesan cheese. Think of Sicily and sunshine when enjoying this dish.

 10 MINS   **20 MINS**

SERVES 4

1 tbsp olive oil

1 onion, finely chopped

1 garlic clove, grated or finely chopped

1 red or jalapeño chile, seeded and finely chopped

salt and freshly ground black pepper

2 tsp all-purpose flour

¼ cup dry white wine

⅔ cup milk

5½oz (150g) peas (shelled weight)

4½oz (125g) pecorino cheese, grated, plus extra to serve

12oz (350g) farfalle

1 Heat the oil in a large frying pan over medium heat, add the onion, and cook for 3–4 minutes until the onion is soft and translucent. Stir in the garlic and chile, add some salt, and cook for a few seconds more. Stir in the flour, then add the wine and simmer for a couple of minutes. Add the milk and stir.

2 Stir in the peas, then add the pecorino and cook on low simmer—do not allow to boil—for about 10 minutes, or until the sauce has thickened slightly. Season well with salt and pepper.

3 Meanwhile, cook the pasta in a large pan of boiling salted water for about 12 minutes, or until it is tender but still firm to the bite. Drain, keeping back a tiny amount of the cooking water. Return the pasta to the pan and toss with the sauce. Top with extra pecorino and serve.

asparagus and taleggio risotto

Taleggio is a mellow, creamy Italian cheese that melts into the rice and complements the asparagus.

 10 MINS   30–40 MINS

SERVES 4

1 tbsp olive oil

2 tbsp butter

1 onion, finely chopped

3 garlic cloves, finely chopped

salt and freshly ground black pepper

10oz (300g) arborio rice or carnaroli rice

1 cup white wine

3 cups hot chicken or vegetable stock

bunch of asparagus spears, trimmed

2½oz (75g) Taleggio cheese, coarsely sliced

1 Heat the oil and butter in a large heavy-bottomed pan over medium heat, add the onion, and cook for 3–4 minutes until the onion is soft. Stir in the garlic and cook for another minute. Season with salt and pepper.

2 Stir in the rice and turn it in the oily butter so all the grains are coated. Cook for a few seconds. Increase the heat, add the wine, and let it bubble for 1–2 minutes, or until it has been absorbed. In a separate saucepan, simmer the stock. Add a ladleful to the rice and stir until absorbed. Continue doing this for 20–30 minutes until the rice is cooked but still firm to the bite and is creamy. You may not need all the stock or you may need a little more.

3 Meanwhile, cook the asparagus spears in boiling salted water for 2–4 minutes, or until soft. Drain, refresh in cold water, and drain again. Slice each spear into three and add to the rice along with the Taleggio cheese. Taste and season, if needed.

asparagus and herb tart

The asparagus laid in neat rows in this rectangular tart makes for a fun and unusual piece of presentation.

 15 MINS   1 HR

SPECIAL EQUIPMENT ▪ 7 x 12in (18 x 30cm) fluted rectangular tart pan with removable bottom ▪ ceramic baking beans

SERVES 6-8

9oz (250g) store-bought pie dough

3 large eggs, 1 lightly beaten, for egg wash

12oz (350g) asparagus spears, trimmed

1 tbsp olive oil

bunch of scallions, trimmed and finely chopped

handful of mint leaves, finely chopped

salt and freshly ground black pepper

4½oz (125g) Cheddar cheese, grated

¾ cup heavy cream

pinch of grated nutmeg

1 Preheat the oven to 400°F (200°C). Roll out the pie dough on a floured work surface, and use to line the tart pan. Trim the excess, line the tart crust with wax paper, and fill with ceramic baking beans. Bake for 15–20 minutes until the edges are golden. Remove the beans and paper, and brush egg wash over the bottom of the crust. Return to the oven for 2–3 minutes to crisp. Remove from the oven and set aside. Reduce the oven temperature to 350°F (180°C).

2 Cook the asparagus spears in boiling salted water for 2–4 minutes, or until soft. Drain, refresh in cold water, and drain again. Heat the oil in a pan over low heat. Add the scallions, and sweat for 2 minutes. Remove from the pan with a slotted spoon, and scatter over the bottom of the tart crust. Arrange the asparagus on top. Scatter over the mint, add seasoning, and sprinkle over the cheese. Mix the cream, 2 eggs, and the nutmeg. Pour the mixture over the tart, and bake for 30–40 minutes until set and golden. Leave in the pan for 10 minutes before serving with a tomato salad.

grilled sea bass with roast artichokes and fennel

Welcome early summer artichokes by pairing them with sea bass. A hot grill pan ensures that the fish skin crisps nicely.

 45 MINS   25 MINS

SERVES 4

6 tbsp extra virgin olive oil

4 sea bass fillets, scaled and pinboned

salt and freshly ground black pepper

8 small or 3–4 large artichoke bottoms

squeeze of lemon juice

1 large fennel bulb, finely sliced

3 garlic cloves, finely sliced

large handful of basil, shredded

1 Preheat the oven to 400°F (200°C). Brush a grill pan with 2 tbsp of the oil. Slash the skin of each fillet 3 times, and season. Set aside.

2 Cut the artichoke bottoms into quarters and blanch in boiling water with the lemon juice for 3–4 minutes. Drain and put into a large roasting pan with the fennel and garlic. Toss with the remaining olive oil. Season generously and roast in the oven for 15–18 minutes, or until the fennel is roasted and the artichokes are soft.

3 Heat the grill pan until just smoking, add the fish, skin-side down, and cook for 2–3 minutes on each side: the skin will be charred and the flesh white and firm. Scatter the basil over and serve immediately.

variation

grilled sea bass with roasted baby beets and dill

Peel and halve 8 baby beets. Put in the roasting pan with the olive oil and garlic instead of the artichokes and fennel. Scatter 1 tbsp chopped dill over. Roast as before. Mix ½ cup crème fraîche with 2 tbsp chopped dill and 1 finely chopped scallion. Grill the fish. Serve with the beets and the dill cream.

Season's best **asparagus**

The succulent stems of green (and purple) asparagus have a flavor reminiscent of fragrant, freshly cut grass. The fat, white asparagus, prized in Europe, is simply green asparagus blanched by growing under the soil. It has a more delicate taste and creamier texture. All are delicious served with melted butter or Hollandaise sauce, but also go well with olive oil, balsamic vinegar, Parmesan cheese, sun-dried tomatoes, pine nuts, prosciutto, and eggs.

Asparagus grows in temperate zones worldwide where there is regular summer water from either rain or irrigation. Spears can range in thickness from pencil-thin to the size of your thumb.

Green asparagus Of all the asparagus types, green asparagus has the most pronounced flavor. Slender spears are best briefly steamed; fatter ones can be brushed with oil and grilled or roasted.

Spears should be straight and crisp.

essentials
varieties available

Green, purple, and white. Thin asparagus spears and short, ready-trimmed tips are also sold.

buy Avoid any with woody, dirty stems. The growing tips should be tightly closed.

store Best eaten fresh, or store for up to 3 days wrapped in damp paper towels in the vegetable drawer of the fridge.

cook Steam, boil, stir-fry, roast, grill, or broil.

preserve Freeze, or preserve in oil.

recipe ideas

Asparagus and herb tart p92

Asparagus and taleggio risotto p92

Asparagus in oil p135

Cream of asparagus soup p82

Penne with asparagus and zucchini p112

White asparagus with herb mayonnaise p88

White asparagus The fat white spears are milder in flavor than the green type. They are deprived of light as they emerge from the ground, which prevents them from becoming green.

The skin of white asparagus can be tough, so it should be peeled off before cooking.

how to trim asparagus

The tough stalk bases should always be removed. For thicker spears, it is best to peel off the outer, fibrous sheath to ensure each stem is perfectly tender.

1 With a sharp knife, cut the hard ends from the spears. Alternatively, snap the bottoms off the asparagus spears.

2 Rotating the spear, use a vegetable peeler to remove a thin layer of skin from all sides.

teriyaki fish with noodles

Teriyaki is a Japanese technique for cooking food that has first been marinated in a sweetened soy sauce. Here the sauce is added to cod and then baked until tender.

 10 MINS PLUS MARINATING **15 MINS**

SERVES 4

- 1-2 tbsp dark soy sauce
- 1 tbsp honey
- 1in (2.5cm) piece of fresh ginger, peeled and grated
- pinch of sugar
- 1 tbsp mirin or dry sherry
- 4 thick cod fillets, about 5½oz (150g) each
- 9oz (250g) thick or medium udon noodles
- 4 scallions, trimmed and sliced
- handful of cilantro, leaves only
- lime quarters, to serve

1 Preheat the oven to 400°F (200°C). To make the teriyaki sauce, put the soy sauce, honey, ginger, sugar, and mirin or sherry in a bowl, and mix well. Pour this over the fish and leave to marinate for about 10 minutes.

2 Sit the fish pieces with the sauce in a roasting pan and bake in the oven for about 15 minutes until the fish is cooked through.

3 Meanwhile, put the noodles in a bowl and pour boiling water over the top. Leave for a few minutes, then drain and toss with the scallions and cilantro. Serve with the fish and wedges of lime to squeeze over.

variation

teriyaki chicken with noodles

Prepare in exactly the same way but marinate the chicken for at least 1 hour and bake for about 25 minutes, or until the juices run clear when the chicken is pierced with the tip of a knife. Add a handful of shredded snow peas, steamed for 1 minute, to the noodles and scallions.

quesadilla with peppers, green olives, and feta cheese

The quesadilla originated from Mexico and is a flour or corn tortilla filled with cheese and other toppings. As the summer progresses, look for the first peppers to use in this dish.

 5 MINS **15 MINS**

MAKES 1

- 2 tbsp olive oil
- 2 red peppers, seeded and coarsely chopped
- salt and freshly ground black pepper
- 2 flour tortillas or corn tortillas
- handful of pitted green olives, sliced
- 4½oz (125g) feta cheese, crumbled

1 Heat 1 tbsp of the oil in a frying pan over a low heat, add the peppers, and cook for 10 minutes until the peppers are soft. Season with salt and pepper.

2 Heat the remaining oil in a nonstick frying pan, then fry one tortilla for 1 minute, or until golden. Spoon the peppers onto it, leaving a little room around the edge. Scatter with the olives and feta cheese.

3 Top with the other tortilla, pressing it down with the back of a fish spatula to sandwich the two together. Scoop up the quesadilla, carefully turn it over, and cook the other side for another minute, or until golden. Slice in halves or quarters, and serve.

variation

quesadilla with cheddar cheese, arugula, and sun-dried tomatoes

Fry the first tortilla in 1 tbsp olive oil as before. Add a handful of grated Cheddar cheese and spread it out, not quite to the edges. Top with a handful of arugula. Scatter 2–3 chopped sun-dried tomatoes and 3–4 chopped fresh basil leaves over the top. Continue at step 3.

roasted salmon with swiss chard and herb butter

Swiss chard is a versatile vegetable that can be boiled, steamed, stir-fried, and roasted. Prepare it lots of different ways when it is growing in abundance in the summer.

  10 MINS   30 MINS

SERVES 4

4 salmon fillets, about 5½oz (150g) each

1 tbsp olive oil

salt and freshly ground black pepper

2 handfuls of Swiss chard, trimmed

juice of 1 lemon

pinch of dried chile flakes

For the herb butter

8 tbsp butter, softened

handful of curly parsley, finely chopped

handful of dill, finely chopped

1 For the herb butter, put the butter and herbs in a mixing bowl and beat well until everything is combined. Spoon the butter onto a piece of wax paper, then roll into a log shape. Twist the edges of the paper and put the roll in the fridge.

2 Preheat the oven to 400°F (200°C). Sit the salmon fillets in a nonstick roasting pan, drizzle with the oil, and season with salt and pepper. Bake in the oven for 15–20 minutes until the salmon is cooked through.

3 Meanwhile, cook the Swiss chard in a large pan of boiling salted water for 5–8 minutes until it still has a bite to it. Drain well and transfer to a serving dish. Squeeze over the lemon juice and add a pinch of chile flakes.

4 Divide the Swiss chard between 4 warmed plates. Add a salmon fillet and a slice of the herb butter, and serve immediately.

asparagus, broccoli, ginger, and mint stir-fry

Here is a speedy stir-fry, perfect for using up excess fresh produce. In place of red bell pepper, consider using snow peas or finely shredded white cabbage leaves.

  15 MINS   15 MINS

SERVES 4

1 tbsp sesame oil or vegetable oil

2 red or jalapeño chiles, seeded and finely chopped

2in (5cm) piece of fresh ginger, peeled and sliced into thin strips

bunch of scallions, trimmed and cut into 2in (5cm) lengths

2 garlic cloves, grated or finely chopped

1 red bell pepper, seeded and cut into thin strips

10oz (300g) broccoli, cut into florets

bunch of fine asparagus spears, trimmed and halved

1 tbsp granulated sugar

salt and freshly ground black pepper

handful of mint leaves

1 Heat the oil in a wok over medium-high heat and swirl to coat the surface. Add the chiles and ginger, and toss for a few seconds, then add the scallions, and a few seconds later add the garlic. Stir-fry for 5 minutes until soft.

2 Add the pepper and stir-fry for a few minutes. Add the broccoli and stir-fry for a few minutes more, before adding the asparagus. Continue stir-frying for another minute or two.

3 Sprinkle the sugar over the top and season well with salt and pepper. Stir-fry for a few seconds until the sugar has dissolved. Remove from the heat and stir in the mint leaves. Serve immediately either on its own, or with some fluffy rice.

salmon with new potatoes, flageolet beans, and parsley sauce

Succulent summer salmon is paired here with a creamy sauce and in-season new potatoes. When serving this dish, you can leave the pieces of salmon whole, if you prefer.

 15 MINS **30 MINS**

SERVES 4

1½lb (675g) new potatoes

salt and freshly ground black pepper

1lb (450g) salmon fillets, skinned

1¼ cups milk

pat of butter

1 tbsp plain flour

⅔ cup heavy cream

handful of curly parsley, finely chopped

14oz (400g) can flageolet or navy beans, drained and rinsed

handful of dill, finely chopped

1 Cook the potatoes in a pan of boiling salted water for 15–20 minutes until soft. Drain and set aside to keep warm.

2 Meanwhile, put the salmon in a saucepan with the milk. Bring to a boil, reduce the heat, and poach gently for 3–4 minutes until just cooked. Remove from the pan with a slotted spoon and keep warm.

3 Melt the butter in a clean pan over low heat. Remove from the heat and stir in the flour with a whisk. Add a little of the salmon milk and whisk until smooth. Gradually whisk in the remaining milk and then the cream. Return the pan to the heat, bring to a boil, whisking constantly, then reduce the heat and simmer for 5–8 minutes, whisking all the time. Remove from the heat, season well with salt and pepper, and stir in the parsley.

4 Put the beans in a pan and gently heat through. Season, if you like, and stir in the dill. Break the salmon into neat pieces, if preferred. Place on a platter or individual plates with the flageolet beans and new potatoes on the side and the parsley sauce spooned over the salmon and potatoes.

hot and spicy lamb with fava beans

Fava beans are at their best in early summer and offer a soft, creamy contrast to the spicy lamb in this one-pot dish.

 30 MINS PLUS MARINATING **2 HRS 10 MINS**

SERVES 4

2½lb (1.1kg) lamb (from the leg), cut into bite-sized pieces

2 tbsp olive oil

4 garlic cloves, grated or finely chopped

1–2 tbsp harissa (according to taste)

1 tbsp finely chopped rosemary leaves

6 salted anchovy fillets, finely chopped

3 tbsp Worcestershire sauce

1 tbsp finely chopped thyme leaves, plus a few extra to garnish

juice of 1 lemon

salt and freshly ground black pepper

2 onions, finely chopped

1lb (450g) fava beans (shelled weight), skinned (p85, optional)

2lb (900g) potatoes, peeled and cut into bite-sized pieces

4 cups hot vegetable stock

1 Put the lamb in a bowl, add the oil, garlic, harissa, rosemary, anchovies, Worcestershire sauce, thyme, and lemon juice, and mix. Season with salt and pepper, then transfer to a plastic bag and leave to marinate for 30 minutes (or overnight in the fridge).

2 Preheat the oven to 400°F (200°C). Transfer the mixture to a large cast-iron pan and cook over medium-high heat, turning occasionally, for 10 minutes, or until the lamb is browned. Add the onions and cook for 5 minutes.

3 Add the fava beans and potatoes, pour in the stock, and bring to a boil. Cover and put in the oven for 2 hours, or until tender. If it starts to dry out, add more hot water. Season with salt and pepper, and serve garnished with a few thyme leaves.

baked salmon in wine with cilantro and lime

Sharp lime and fragrant cilantro cut through the richness of the salmon in this quick and simple recipe. Cooking the fish in a foil package perfectly seals in all the flavor and succulence.

 5 MINS **25 MINS**

SERVES 4

1lb 5oz (600g) side of salmon, descaled and cleaned, but not skinned

handful of cilantro sprigs

2 limes, peeled, segmented, and coarsely chopped

salt and freshly ground black pepper

¼ cup dry white wine

1 Cut the side of salmon in half lengthwise so that it opens up, but take care not to slice all the way through the skin.

2 Preheat the oven to 400°F (200°C). Coarsely chop a large handful of fresh cilantro and mix with the peeled, segmented, and coarsely chopped limes. Season with salt and pepper. Spread the herb and lime mixture on the opened salmon, season well once again, then fold over to close.

3 Place the salmon on a large sheet of foil and pour over ¼ cup of dry white wine. Loosely seal the foil to make a package. Place on a baking sheet and bake in the oven for 25 minutes. Serve hot with boiled new potatoes.

chicken caesar salad

This restaurant classic makes a perfect lunch dish. Although anchovies did not feature in chef Caesar Cardini's original recipe, they add a salty tang and work really well with the sweet young lettuce leaves and the rich Parmesan and chicken. The dressing can be prepared in advance and stored in an airtight container in the fridge overnight.

 15 MINS

SERVES 4

2 handfuls of crisp lettuce leaves, such as romaine

5½oz (150g) store-bought croutons

1¾oz (50g) Parmesan cheese, grated

12oz (350g) cooked chicken, sliced

10 salted brown anchovy fillets

For the dressing

2 egg yolks

2 tbsp lemon juice

pinch of dry mustard

½ tbsp Worcestershire sauce

½ tbsp Tabasco sauce

⅔ cup sunflower oil

¼ cup olive oil

1 First, make the dressing. In a bowl, whisk together the egg yolks, lemon juice, dry mustard, Worcestershire sauce, and Tabasco sauce. As you are whisking, add a tiny amount of the sunflower oil; keep whisking and adding the sunflower oil, then the olive oil, a little at a time, until the dressing emulsifies. If it is too thick, add a little cold water.

2 Put a little of the dressing in a bowl, then add the lettuce leaves, croutons, and half of the Parmesan. Toss together gently, making sure the leaves are coated. Lay out the leaves on 4 individual serving plates or a serving dish, and top with the chicken and anchovies. Sprinkle with the remaining Parmesan, drizzle over some more dressing, and serve.

variation

caesar salad with poached eggs

Prepare in exactly the same way but omit the chicken. Poach 4 eggs in gently simmering water with 1 tbsp lemon juice for about 3 minutes. Remove with a slotted spoon and place an egg on top of each salad.

chicken stuffed with spinach and gruyère cheese

The mild, clean taste of fresh spinach complements pan-fried chicken perfectly. For an extra depth of flavor, add a splash of balsamic vinegar to the cherry tomatoes as they cook.

 10 MINS   25 MINS

SERVES 4

7oz (200g) spinach leaves, stems removed

2½oz (75g) Gruyère cheese, grated

pinch of ground nutmeg

salt and freshly ground black pepper

4 large skinless, boneless chicken breasts or chicken thighs

1 tbsp olive oil

8-12 cherry tomatoes

1 Put the spinach in a saucepan with a sprinkling of water, and cook for a few minutes until just wilted. Alternatively, put in a microwave-proof bowl, cover loosely, and wilt in the microwave on medium for about 2 minutes. Drain, and squeeze out any excess water. Mix the spinach with the Gruyère cheese and nutmeg in a mixing bowl, and season well with salt and pepper.

2 Slice each of the chicken breasts lengthwise to form a pocket—be careful not to cut all the way through.

Stuff each pocket with some of the spinach and cheese mixture, then fold the top of the breast back over the mixture to seal it.

3 Heat the oil in a large frying pan over medium-high heat. Add the chicken breasts carefully to the pan, pocket-side down, and leave to cook undisturbed for 6–8 minutes. Gently turn the chicken over, and cook the other side for about the same amount of time until golden and cooked all the way through and the juices run clear when pierced with a sharp knife.

4 Meanwhile, add the tomatoes to the frying pan toward the end of the cooking time. Leave them to cook undisturbed for 5 minutes until they begin to split. Remove the chicken from the pan when it is cooked, and set aside to keep warm. Stir the tomatoes around for a couple of minutes to break them up a little, then serve with the warm chicken.

veal scallops with bell peppers

A northern Italian classic. Give the scallops enough room in the pan, or they will steam instead of developing a crisp crust.

 20-25 MINS   9-12 MINS

SERVES 6

¼ cup all-purpose flour

salt and freshly ground black pepper

2 large eggs

½ cup dried bread crumbs

2oz (60g) Parmesan cheese, grated

6 veal scallops, about 13oz (375g) in total, and each ⅛in (3mm) thick (place between 2 large pieces of parchment paper and flatten with a mallet or rolling pin, if needed)

4 tbsp olive oil, plus more if needed

1 garlic clove, finely chopped

2 small green bell peppers, seeded and cut into strips

2 small red bell peppers, seeded and cut into strips

7-10 sprigs of oregano, leaves picked and finely chopped, plus more to serve

2 tbsp butter

1 lemon, sliced, to serve

1 Season the flour with salt and pepper and sift onto a sheet of parchment paper. Lightly beat the eggs in a shallow dish. Mix the bread crumbs and Parmesan cheese in a small bowl and spread on another sheet of parchment paper. Coat each side of the veal in the seasoned flour, dip in the egg mix using a fork, then press each side into the bread crumb and cheese mixture. Put the slices on a plate and refrigerate, uncovered.

2 Heat 2 tbsp of the oil in a frying pan. Add the garlic and bell peppers, season, and sauté until soft, stirring occasionally. Remove from the heat, add the oregano, and keep warm.

3 Heat the butter and rest of the oil in a large frying pan. Add 2 scallops and fry over medium-high heat until golden brown, 1–2 minutes on each side, until no longer pink in the center. Reduce the heat if the crumbs threaten to burn. Transfer to a plate lined with paper towels and keep warm. Fry the remaining veal, adding more oil if necessary; don't add too much, or the veal will be soggy. Serve with the bell peppers, lemon slices, and a sprig of oregano.

chicken fajitas with tomato and avocado salsa

This is ideal as an easy lunch or for al fresco dining. The punchy salsa is a quicker alternative to guacamole.

 15 MINS   15 MINS

SERVES 4

1 tbsp olive oil

2 onions, sliced into strips

2 red bell peppers, seeded and cut into strips

2 green bell peppers, seeded and cut into strips

2 red or jalapeño chiles, seeded and finely chopped

2 garlic cloves, sliced

4 skinless, boneless chicken breasts, cut into strips

½ cup dry white wine

handful of cilantro, finely chopped

12 soft corn tortillas

For the salsa

1 ripe avocado

handful of cherry tomatoes, chopped

bunch of scallions, trimmed and finely chopped

handful of flat-leaf parsley, finely chopped

1 tbsp olive oil

1 tbsp white wine vinegar

salt and freshly ground black pepper

1 For the salsa, halve, pit, peel, and chop the avocado. Put in a bowl with the tomatoes, scallions, and parsley. Drizzle over the oil and vinegar, season with salt and pepper, combine gently, and set aside.

2 Heat the oil in a large frying pan over low heat. Add the onions and red and green bell peppers, and sauté for 5 minutes until starting to soften. Stir through the chile and garlic, and cook for a few seconds.

3 Increase the heat to medium-high, and add the chicken. Keep the mixture moving around the pan so it doesn't burn and the chicken is evenly cooked. Stir-fry for 3–5 minutes until the chicken is no longer pink. Pour in the wine and cook fiercely for 5 minutes. Stir in the cilantro.

4 To serve, spoon the chicken mixture onto the tortillas. Top with the salsa, and roll into wraps. Serve with any extra mixture on the side.

lentils with artichokes and bell peppers

This is a satisfying and filling salad, with artichoke hearts adding a creamy, almost buttery, texture to sweet red bell peppers and nutty Puy lentils.

 15 MINS

SERVES 4

4–6 cooked artichoke hearts (p309)

4 red bell peppers, roasted and peeled (p171)

14oz (400g) can Puy lentils, drained and rinsed

1–2 sprigs of fresh thyme, leaves only

handful of flat-leaf parsley, finely chopped

4 scallions, trimmed and finely chopped

2–3 tbsp walnut oil

1 tbsp cider vinegar

salt and freshly ground black pepper

4–5 slices of prosciutto, chopped

handful of arugula leaves

1 Halve the artichoke hearts and place in a large bowl. Deseed and cut the roasted bell peppers into strips. Add to the bowl with the lentils, herbs, and scallions. Drizzle over the oil and vinegar, season with salt and pepper, and toss gently to combine.

2 Add the prosciutto and arugula, and toss gently once more. Transfer to a serving dish, and serve with a green salad on the side.

chicken with fava beans

Use the freshest baby fava beans you can find to give this dish the maximum amount of flavor.

 10 MINS **1 HR**

SERVES 4

8 chicken thighs with skin on

salt and freshly ground black pepper

2 tbsp olive oil

1 onion, finely chopped

2 celery sticks, finely chopped

2 garlic cloves, crushed or finely chopped

a few sprigs of rosemary, leaves picked and finely chopped

¾ cup dry white wine

7oz (200g) shelled baby broad beans (shelled weight)

2 cups hot chicken stock

1 Preheat the oven to 400°F (200°C). Season the chicken pieces well with salt and pepper. Heat 1 tbsp of the oil in a large flameproof casserole dish over medium-high heat. Add the chicken thighs, skin-side down, and brown for 5–6 minutes on each side until golden all over. Remove from the pan and set aside.

2 Reduce the heat to low and add the remaining oil to the casserole dish. Add the onion and a little salt, and cook for 5 minutes until soft and translucent. Add the celery, garlic, and rosemary, and cook for another 5 minutes. Increase the heat, pour in the wine, and simmer the ingredients for about 5 minutes.

3 Stir in the fava beans and return the chicken to the pan, tucking the pieces in and around the beans. Pour over the stock, cover, and cook in the oven for 45–60 minutes. Check halfway through the cooking time, adding a little hot water if too dry. Serve with oven-roasted tomatoes and fresh crusty bread.

variation

sausages with fava beans

You could make this dish using 8–12 thick pork sausages instead of the chicken. Add 1 tbsp chopped fresh sage in step 2 instead of the rosemary.

seafood risotto

Squid, sea bass, and scallops make for an impressive rice dish.

 20 MINS **30 MINS**

SERVES 4

2–3 tbsp olive oil

1lb (450g) baby squid, gutted and cleaned, cut into rings, and tentacles chopped (p263)

salt and freshly ground black pepper

1lb (450g) mixed white fish, such as sea bass, monkfish, and haddock, cut into bite-sized pieces

16 scallops (with or without coral, depending on preference), cleaned

2 pats of butter

2 onions, finely chopped

4 garlic cloves, grated or finely chopped

1½lb (675g) risotto rice

1½ cups white wine

7 cups hot vegetable stock, or light fish stock

6 tomatoes, skinned (p197) and finely chopped

large handful of flat-leaf parsley, finely chopped

handful of dill, finely chopped

lemon wedges, to serve

1 Heat 1 tbsp of the oil in a frying pan. Add the squid and seasoning, and stir-fry for 1 minute over medium heat. Remove with a slotted spoon and set aside. Repeat with the fish, adding more oil, if needed. Cook for 2 minutes or until opaque and cooked. Repeat with the scallops.

2 Melt a pat of butter in the pan, add the onion, and cook until soft and translucent. Add the garlic and cook for a few seconds. Add the rice to the frying pan and stir to coat. Season, add the wine, raise the heat a little, and boil for a few seconds. In a separate saucepan, simmer the stock. Add a ladleful to the rice and stir until absorbed. Repeat until the rice is firm to the bite and creamy.

3 Add the tomatoes, return the seafood and fish to the pan, then stir in the herbs and remaining butter. Taste and season if needed, and serve with the lemon wedges.

chicken and chorizo paella

A saffron-flavored rice dish with baby fava beans, named after the Spanish paellera in which it is traditionally cooked.

 25 MINS **40–45 MINS PLUS STANDING**

SERVES 4–6

a large pinch of saffron threads

2 tbsp olive oil

8 chicken thighs, on the bone if preferred, cut into neat chunks

salt and freshly ground black pepper

6oz (175g) chorizo sausage, cut in ½in(1cm) slices

1 large onion, diced

1 red bell pepper, seeded and sliced

1 green bell pepper, seeded and sliced

13oz (375g) paella rice or other short-grain rice

2 garlic cloves, finely chopped

14oz (400g) can chopped tomatoes

7oz (200g) baby fava beans (shelled weight)

1–2 tbsp chopped flat-leaf parsley

1 Put 3–4 tbsp boiling water in a small bowl and add the saffron. Leave to soak for at least 15 minutes.

2 Heat the oil in a large frying pan. Season the chicken and sauté it, turning, for 10–12 minutes, until brown. Transfer to a plate. Sauté the chorizo for 1–2 minutes on each side, until brown. Transfer to the plate with a slotted spoon. Add the onion and peppers to the pan; cook, stirring occasionally, for 5–7 minutes until soft. Add the rice and cook, stirring, for 2–3 minutes. Add the garlic, the saffron with its soaking liquid, and 2½ cups water. Season, then add the chicken, chorizo, tomatoes, and beans. Bring to a boil.

3 Cover, reduce the heat to low, and simmer very gently for 25 minutes until the liquid has almost evaporated and the rice is tender and firm to the bite. Do not stir or the rice will become sticky. If the rice is undercooked, add a little more water and simmer for a few more minutes. Remove from the heat and stand, covered, for 5 minutes. Sprinkle with parsley and serve.

pork chops with tomato and fava bean sauce

This dish of tender pork chops is a delicious way of making the most of the season's crop of fava beans.

 5 MINS   45 MINS   ✳ FREEZABLE

SERVES 4

4 pork chops, about 5½oz (150g) each, trimmed

2 tbsp olive oil

pinch of dried oregano

salt and freshly ground black pepper

1 onion, finely chopped

2 garlic cloves, grated or finely chopped

14oz (400g) can whole plum tomatoes, chopped

4½oz (125g) fava beans (shelled weight)

handful of flat-leaf parsley, very finely chopped

1 Preheat the oven to 400°F (200°C). Brush the chops with 1 tbsp of the oil and sprinkle the oregano over the top. Season well with salt and pepper. Sit the chops in a roasting pan and roast in the oven for 15 minutes until golden. Cut into one of the chops with a sharp knife to check they are cooked through.

2 Meanwhile, heat the remaining oil in a frying pan over low heat, and add the onion and a little salt. Cook for 5 minutes until soft and translucent, then add the garlic and stir for a couple of seconds.

3 Add the tomatoes, including any juices, and bring to a boil. Reduce the heat slightly and simmer for about 15 minutes. Add the fava beans to the pan and cook for another 10 minutes, adding a little water if the mixture dries out.

4 Taste the sauce and add more seasoning if needed. Stir in the parsley, sit the chops on the sauce, and serve hot.

variation

pork chops with peas and tomato sauce

Add 4½oz (125g) shelled peas instead of fava beans in step 3.

grated zucchini and goat cheese omelet

A combination of light, delicate zucchini, aromatic thyme, and tangy goat cheese turns this easy dish into a wonderfully moist, fresh-tasting brunch, lunch, or dinner.

 10 MINS   15 MINS

MAKES 1

3 large eggs, lightly beaten

1 small zucchini, grated

salt and freshly ground black pepper

pat of butter

1¾oz (50g) soft goat cheese, crumbled

small handful of thyme, leaves picked, to garnish (optional)

1 Put the beaten eggs and grated zucchini in a bowl. Season with salt and pepper and combine.

2 Melt the butter in a small nonstick frying pan over medium-high heat until foaming. Pour in the egg mixture, swirling it around the pan to cover the base. Lift the edge gently with a palette knife and tilt the pan to allow the raw egg to run underneath.

3 When the omelet is partially set, scatter over the goat cheese and half of the thyme leaves so that it covers the omelet evenly. Continue cooking

until the center is almost cooked, but still just a little wet. Remove from the heat, and leave for a couple of minutes to set—the retained heat will continue to cook the omelet a little more.

4 Sprinkle over a little black pepper, and garnish with the remaining thyme leaves (if using). Carefully slide out of the pan and serve immediately.

variation

baby fava bean, bacon, and goat cheese omelet

Prepare in the same way but use a handful of cooked baby fava beans, popped out of their skins instead of the grated zucchini, and scatter a chopped, cooked strip of bacon over with the goat cheese.

Season's best **summer squashes**

Summer squashes are harvested young through summer, before their skins harden and the seeds mature. They have a moist, delicate texture and mild flavor. They can absorb different flavorings, from garlic and butter or olive oil to chile and any other spices or fragrant herbs you can think of. They mix beautifully with other summer vegetables, such as tomatoes, peppers, fennel, and asparagus. The flowers are also edible.

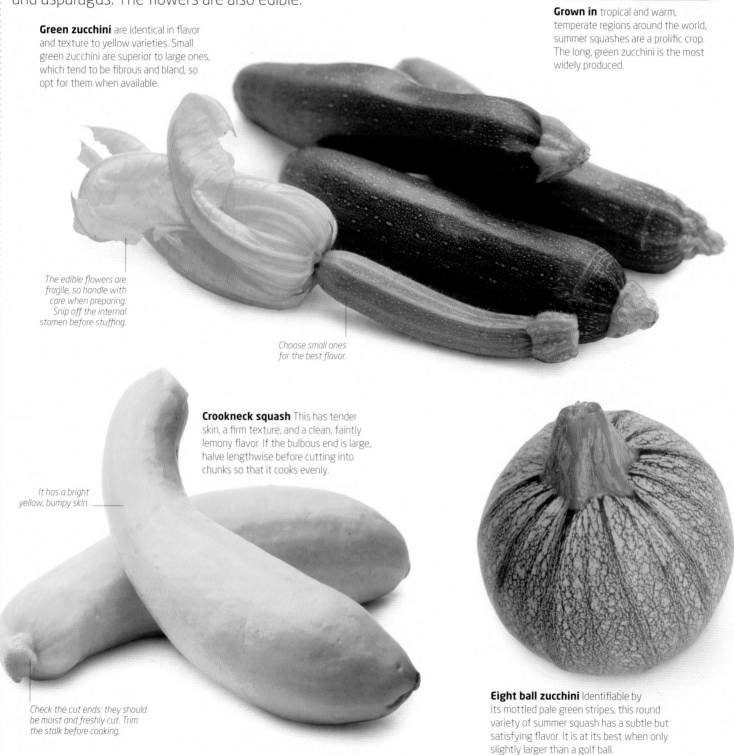

Grown in tropical and warm, temperate regions around the world, summer squashes are a prolific crop. The long, green zucchini is the most widely produced.

Green zucchini are identical in flavor and texture to yellow varieties. Small green zucchini are superior to large ones, which tend to be fibrous and bland, so opt for them when available.

The edible flowers are fragile, so handle with care when preparing. Snip off the internal stamen before stuffing.

Choose small ones for the best flavor.

Crookneck squash This has tender skin, a firm texture, and a clean, faintly lemony flavor. If the bulbous end is large, halve lengthwise before cutting into chunks so that it cooks evenly.

It has a bright yellow, bumpy skin.

Check the cut ends: they should be moist and freshly cut. Trim the stalk before cooking.

Eight ball zucchini Identifiable by its mottled pale green stripes, this round variety of summer squash has a subtle but satisfying flavor. It is at its best when only slightly larger than a golf ball.

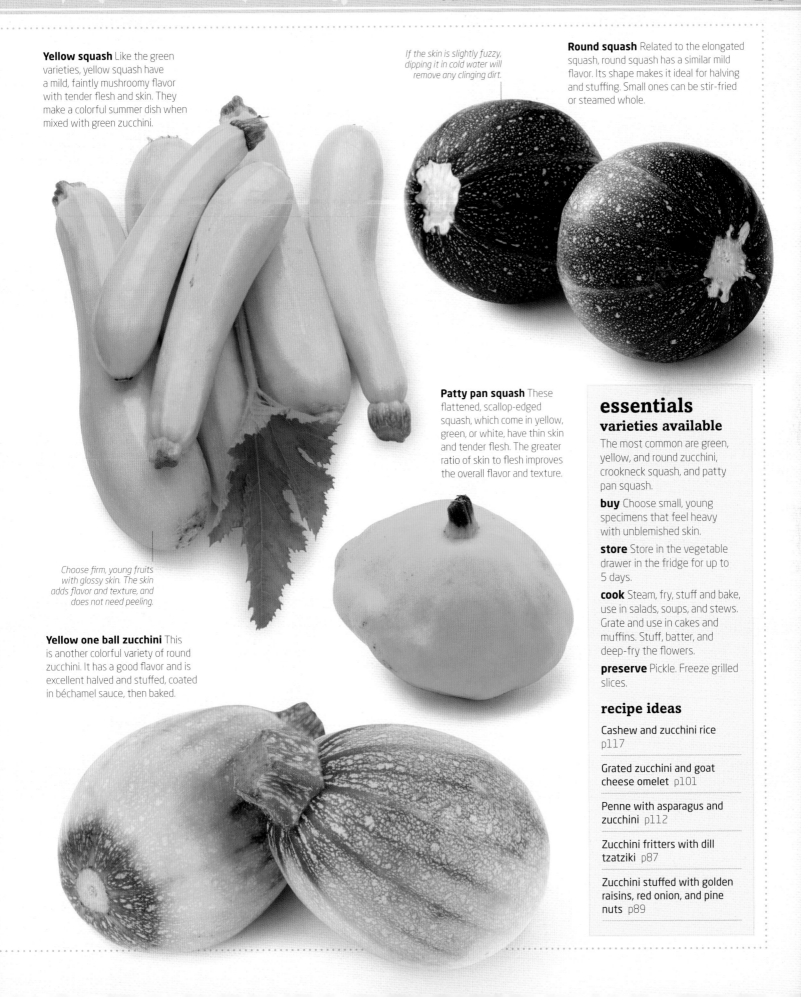

Yellow squash Like the green varieties, yellow squash have a mild, faintly mushroomy flavor with tender flesh and skin. They make a colorful summer dish when mixed with green zucchini.

If the skin is slightly fuzzy, dipping it in cold water will remove any clinging dirt.

Round squash Related to the elongated squash, round squash has a similar mild flavor. Its shape makes it ideal for halving and stuffing. Small ones can be stir-fried or steamed whole.

Patty pan squash These flattened, scallop-edged squash, which come in yellow, green, or white, have thin skin and tender flesh. The greater ratio of skin to flesh improves the overall flavor and texture.

Choose firm, young fruits with glossy skin. The skin adds flavor and texture, and does not need peeling.

Yellow one ball zucchini This is another colorful variety of round zucchini. It has a good flavor and is excellent halved and stuffed, coated in béchamel sauce, then baked.

essentials
varieties available

The most common are green, yellow, and round zucchini, crookneck squash, and patty pan squash.

buy Choose small, young specimens that feel heavy with unblemished skin.

store Store in the vegetable drawer in the fridge for up to 5 days.

cook Steam, fry, stuff and bake, use in salads, soups, and stews. Grate and use in cakes and muffins. Stuff, batter, and deep-fry the flowers.

preserve Pickle. Freeze grilled slices.

recipe ideas

Cashew and zucchini rice p117

Grated zucchini and goat cheese omelet p101

Penne with asparagus and zucchini p112

Zucchini fritters with dill tzatziki p87

Zucchini stuffed with golden raisins, red onion, and pine nuts p89

spaghetti primavera

The younger the zucchini, carrots, and peas, the tastier and sweeter this dish will be. Their beautiful pale greens and orange epitomize the colors of early summer.

  45–50 MINS   15–25 MINS

SERVES 4

2 zucchini, cubed

salt and freshly ground black pepper

2 carrots, cubed

7oz (200g) peas (shelled weight)

1lb 2oz (500g) spaghetti

3 tbsp butter

¾ cup heavy cream

1oz (30g) Parmesan cheese, grated

1 Bring a saucepan of water to a boil. Add the zucchini and some salt and cook for 2–3 minutes, until barely tender to the tip of a knife. Drain well, then blot dry on paper towels. Set aside on some fresh paper towels to ensure the blanched zucchini are not at all soggy.

2 Put the carrots in a saucepan, cover with cold water, add salt, and bring to a boil. Simmer for about 5 minutes or until just tender, then drain, rinse with cold water, drain again, and set aside. Bring a clean saucepan of salted water to the boil. Add the peas and simmer for

3–8 minutes, depending on their size, until tender. Drain, rinse with cold water, and set aside. It is necessary to blanch the vegetables separately because each must be cooked to be at the peak of their sweetness, and they all cook at a different rate.

3 Cook the spaghetti in a large pan of boiling salted water for about 12 minutes, or until it is tender but still firm to the bite. Drain well.

4 Meanwhile, heat the butter in a large saucepan over low heat, add the zucchini, carrot, and peas, and sauté for 1 minute.

5 Add the cream to the pan of vegetables, stir well, and bring to a simmer. Take the pan from the heat, add the spaghetti, and toss well in the mixture. Add the Parmesan and toss again. Serve on warmed plates, with a good grinding of black pepper.

deviled lamb cutlets with crushed potato and mustard seed salad

New-season lamb, accompanied by sweet, waxy new potatoes, is coated in a tangy marinade and oven-baked.

 10 MINS   35–45 MINS

SERVES 4

9oz (250g) new potatoes

salt and freshly ground black pepper

8 lamb cutlets

1 tbsp olive oil

1 tbsp mustard seeds

bunch of scallions, trimmed and finely chopped

For the coating

2 tbsp English mustard

2 tbsp ketchup

1 tbsp cayenne pepper

2 tbsp finely chopped onion

1 tbsp olive oil

1 Preheat the oven to 400°F (200°C). Cook the potatoes in a large pan of boiling salted water for about 15 minutes until soft, then drain.

2 While the potatoes are cooking, mix together all the ingredients for the coating, and season well with salt and pepper. Coat the lamb cutlets evenly in the mixture and place in a roasting pan. Roast in the oven for 20–30 minutes, or until cooked through to your liking.

3 Add the olive oil to the drained potatoes and then crush them gently with a fork. Mix gently with the mustard seeds and scallions, and season with salt and pepper. Serve the potato salad with the lamb cutlets.

turkish lamb kebabs

Succulent, broiled ground lamb skewers can be easily whipped up for a relaxed lunch or evening meal.

 30-35 MINS PLUS DRAINING   **10-15 MINS**

SPECIAL EQUIPMENT ▪ 6 wooden or metal skewers ▪ food processor

SERVES 6

1 large onion, cut into chunks

2¼lb (1kg) ground lamb

2 tsp ground cumin

salt and freshly ground black pepper

3 garlic cloves, finely chopped

3–5 sprigs of mint, leaves picked, finely chopped, plus more leaves for garnish

3–5 sprigs of flat-leaf parsley, leaves picked and finely chopped

olive oil

For the yogurt

1 large cucumber, trimmed and grated

1 tsp salt

2 cups Greek-style yogurt

1 garlic clove, finely chopped

1 Soak wooden skewers in cold water for 30 minutes. For the yogurt, mix the cucumber with the salt, and put in a colander. Leave to drain for 10 minutes. Squeeze the excess water from the cucumber. Put the yogurt in a bowl and mix with the cucumber, garlic, and salt to taste. Cover and chill.

2 Put the onion in a food processor and pulse until finely chopped. In a large bowl, mix the lamb, onion, cumin, salt and pepper, garlic, and herbs together. To test for seasoning, fry a spoonful of meat until browned on both sides. Taste, and add more salt and pepper to the raw mix if needed.

3 Heat the broiler and set the rack 2in (5cm) from the heat. Wet your hands to make the lamb mixture easier to work with, and divide it into 12. Roll into cylinders about 1in (2.5cm) in diameter.

4 Brush the metal skewers (if using) and the broiler rack with oil. Thread the meat cylinders onto the skewers, pressing them into shape, and place on the broiler rack. Brush with oil and broil for 5–7 minutes, or until brown.

5 Turn the skewers and broil the other side. The meat should remain juicy in the center. Serve on a bed of herb bulgur wheat salad, with extra mint leaves and the yogurt sauce.

risotto primavera

This risotto is bursting with the verdant early summer flavors of asparagus, peas, and zucchini.

 15 MINS   **1 HR**

SERVES 4-6

2 tbsp olive oil

4 tbsp butter

1 onion, finely chopped

salt and freshly ground black pepper

3 garlic cloves, finely chopped

10oz (300g) arborio rice or carnaroli rice

1 cup white wine

2 cups hot vegetable stock

4½oz (125g) fava beans (shelled weight), skinned (p85, optional)

bunch of asparagus spears, trimmed and chopped into bite-sized pieces

2 small zucchini, cubed

1oz (30g) Parmesan cheese, grated, plus extra to serve

1 Heat 1 tbsp of the oil and half of the butter in a large heavy-bottomed saucepan over medium heat. Add the onion and cook for 3–4 minutes until soft and translucent. Season with salt and pepper, then add the garlic and cook for a minute. Add the rice and stir in the oily butter so that all the grains are coated. Cook for a few seconds. Then increase the heat, add the wine, and boil it for 1–2 minutes until it has been absorbed.

2 In a separate saucepan, simmer the stock. Add a ladleful to the rice and stir. Repeat for 30–40 minutes, or until the rice is cooked and is firm to the bite and creamy. You may not use all the stock, or you may need a little more.

3 While the rice is cooking, add the fava beans to a large pan of boiling salted water. Cook for 3–4 minutes, then drain well and set aside. Heat the remaining oil in another frying pan over medium heat, add the asparagus and zucchini, and cook for a few minutes until they just begin to color. When the rice is cooked, stir all the vegetables into the risotto, dot the remaining butter all over, and stir it in. Then stir in the Parmesan cheese, taste, and season, if needed. Serve with more Parmesan and a lightly dressed arugula and tomato salad on the side.

chicken and pea filo pie

This impressive-looking pie of baby new potatoes, peas, and chicken is actually simple and quick to make. Use leftover roast chicken pieces instead of fresh if they need to be eaten.

 20 MINS 30 MINS FREEZABLE

SPECIAL EQUIPMENT ▪ 7in (18cm) square pie or cake pan

SERVES 6

12oz (350g) skinless, boneless chicken breasts

9oz (250g) baby new potatoes, quartered

¾ cup chicken stock

4½oz (125g) peas (shelled weight)

12 sheets filo pastry

4 tbsp butter, melted, plus extra if needed

1–2 tbsp mild curry powder

salt and freshly ground black pepper

1 Cook the chicken and the potatoes in the stock in a medium-sized saucepan for about 10 minutes, or until both are tender, adding the peas for the last 5 minutes of cooking time. Drain, reserving the stock. Leave to cool, then cut the chicken into neat pieces.

2 Preheat the oven to 400°F (200°C). Lightly brush 6 sheets of filo pastry with the melted butter. Use them to line the bottom of the pie or cake pan, allowing them to overlap the sides.

3 Put the chicken, potatoes, peas, and curry powder in a mixing bowl. Moisten with 3–4 tbsp of the reserved chicken stock, using just enough to wet the mixture and produce a little gravy, but without adding so much that it soaks the pastry. Toss the ingredients together and season well with salt and pepper.

4 Spoon the chicken filling into the filo pastry crust. Fold the pastry edges in towards the middle, and top the pie with the remaining 6 filo sheets, each brushed with a little melted butter. Tuck the edges of the pastry down neatly at the sides, and make sure that the top is well glazed with melted butter. Bake in the oven for 20–30 minutes until the pastry is cooked and golden. Serve hot.

asian noodle salad

A fantastic spicy dressing really lifts this satisfying dish of chicken noodles with snow peas and scallions.

 30–35 MINS PLUS MARINATING 6–9 MINS

SERVES 6

¾in (2cm) piece of fresh ginger, peeled and finely chopped

2 jalapeño chiles, seeded and diced

2 garlic cloves, finely chopped

2 tsp granulated sugar

salt and freshly ground black pepper

4 tbsp rice wine vinegar

½ cup soy sauce

¼ cup sunflower oil

2 tbsp sesame oil

9oz (250g) thin egg noodles

6oz (175g) snow peas, trimmed

4 scallions, trimmed and cut into diagonal slices

2½oz (75g) roasted unsalted peanuts, coarsely chopped

small bunch of cilantro, chopped

13oz (375g) cooked chicken, cut in neat pieces

1 Put the ginger, chiles, garlic, sugar, pepper, vinegar, and soy sauce in a bowl. Whisk in the oils gradually until the sauce thickens slightly.

2 Cook the noodles in a large pan of boiling salted water for about 4–6 minutes, or until tender but still firm to the bite. Stir occasionally to prevent sticking. Drain, rinse with hot water, and drain again thoroughly. Transfer to a large bowl. Briskly whisk the dressing, pour it over the noodles, and toss until well coated. Set aside for at least 1 hour to marinate.

3 Cook the snow peas in boiling salted water for 2–3 minutes until tender but still crisp. Drain, rinse with hot water, and drain again thoroughly. Cut each diagonally into 2–3 slices. Then add the snow peas, scallions, two-thirds of the peanuts and the cilantro, and all the chicken to the noodles. Toss the ingredients well and taste for seasoning.

4 Mound the noodle salad onto a serving plate, scatter the remaining chopped peanuts and cilantro over the top, and serve.

spiced seafood salad

A tangy Thai dish of scallops, squid, and haddock has a delicate and refreshing flavor, just perfect for early summer.

 30–40 MINS 12–15 MINS

SERVES 4

salt

9oz (250g) small squid, gutted and cleaned and cut into ½in (1cm) wide rings (p263)

9oz (250g) large scallops, trimmed and cut in half horizontally

9oz (250g) thick haddock fillet

9oz (250g) thick salmon fillet

4 kaffir lime leaves, deveined and finely diced, or grated zest of 1 lime

2 garlic cloves, finely chopped

1 jalapeño chile, seeded and finely chopped

1 stalk of lemongrass, peeled, crushed, and thinly sliced

juice of 3 large limes, plus more if needed

¼ cup fish sauce (nam pla), plus more if needed

2 tbsp sugar

small lettuce leaves, to serve

1 Fill a large saucepan with 2in (5cm) of water, add salt, and bring to a boil. Reduce the heat, add the squid, and simmer for 2 minutes until opaque and starting to curl. Remove with a fish spatula and drain on paper towels. Repeat with the scallops and fish.

2 Put the lime leaves, garlic, chile, lemongrass, lime juice, fish sauce, and sugar in a small bowl. Stir until the sugar dissolves. Put the squid and scallops in a large bowl. Pour the dressing over the seafood and toss. Remove any skin from the haddock and salmon, break into large pieces, then add it, tossing gently to mix. Taste for seasoning, adding more lime juice or fish sauce if needed.

3 Arrange the lettuce on plates, pile some dressed seafood on top, and place a crab claw to one side, if using.

baked haddock in white wine with parsley

Firm-fleshed haddock is at its best at this time of year. It is a versatile fish to cook, and retains its flavor and texture well when baked with white wine and tomatoes.

 5 MINS   20 MINS

SERVES 4

1½lb (675g) haddock, skinned and cut into 4 pieces

salt

¾ cup white wine

12 cherry tomatoes

handful of flat-leaf parsley, finely chopped

1 Preheat the oven to 375°F (190°C). Sprinkle the fish with salt, then lay in an ovenproof dish. Pour over the wine, then add the tomatoes and the parsley.

2 Cover the dish tightly with foil and bake in the oven for 15–20 minutes, until the fish is cooked through and the alcohol has evaporated. Serve with salad and fresh crusty bread or new potatoes.

variation

baked salmon in rosé wine with dill

Use a flameproof dish. Substitute four 6oz (175g) salmon fillets for the haddock, rosé wine for white wine, ½ large cucumber, peeled, seeded, and cut into chunks for the tomatoes, and a handful of chopped dill for the parsley. Once cooked, transfer the salmon to plates. Stir 1–2 tbsp crème fraîche into the cooking juices in the dish, place over medium heat to warm through, season to taste, then spoon over the fish.

salmon salad with mint yogurt dressing

This is an ideal way to serve succulent salmon on a warm day. Prepare the dressing and cook the salmon in advance, if needed, and then plate up at the last minute.

 15 MINS   25 MINS

SERVES 4

2 tbsp red wine vinegar

2 tbsp finely chopped mint, plus extra mint leaves, to garnish

4 tbsp Greek-style yogurt

salt and freshly ground black pepper

1¼lb (550g) side of salmon

handful of dill, chopped

1 lemon, sliced

1 cucumber, trimmed and cut into ribbons, to serve

1 Put the red wine vinegar, chopped mint, and Greek-style yogurt in a bowl, season, and whisk together. Set aside.

2 Lay the side of salmon on a large piece of foil. Sprinkle over the handful of chopped dill and overlap a few slices of lemon on top. Season and loosely seal the foil to make a package. Place on a baking sheet and bake in a preheated 400°F (200°C) oven for 20–25 minutes. Allow to cool.

3 Transfer the cool salmon to a plate, drizzle over the dressing, and scatter a few fresh mint leaves over the top. Serve with a cucumber salad and a slice of lemon on the side.

stuffed sardines with crushed new potatoes

Sardines are best cooked simply to bring out their full flavor. Grill them lightly—on a barbecue or charcoal grill if you have one—and serve them with new potatoes and a plain salad.

 15 MINS   25 MINS

SERVES 4

1lb 5oz (600g) new potatoes

¼ cup extra virgin olive oil

salt and freshly ground black pepper

2 tbsp finely chopped flat-leaf parsley

16 fresh sardine fillets

For the hazelnut stuffing

3 tbsp olive oil

1 garlic clove, crushed

1¾oz (50g) hazelnuts, finely chopped

½ cup fresh white bread crumbs

2 tbsp finely chopped flat-leaf parsley

1 Put the potatoes in a large saucepan and cover with cold water. Bring to a boil and cook for 15–20 minutes until tender. Drain, arrange on a flat baking sheet, and crush slightly with the flat side of a potato masher. Drizzle with the olive oil, season, sprinkle with the parsley, set aside, and keep warm.

2 For the stuffing, heat the oil in a frying pan over low heat. Add the garlic and cook for 30 seconds. Add the hazelnuts, bread crumbs, and parsley, and cook for 5 minutes until the bread crumbs are golden brown. Season with salt and pepper.

3 Heat a barbecue, charcoal grill, or a broiler until hot and brush with oil. Rinse the sardines, pat them dry with paper towels, and season. Grill half the sardines skin-side down over high heat for about 1 minute on each side. Remove to a plate and keep warm while you grill the remaining fillets.

4 To serve, divide half the sardine fillets among 4 serving plates. Spoon a little of the hazelnut stuffing on top of each fillet, then cover with the remaining fillets. Put the potatoes into a serving bowl for guests to help themselves. Serve immediately with crisp, fresh salad leaves on the side.

mixed fish stew with toasted croutons

This is an easy-to-cook stew for relaxed dining. Choose fish and shellfish in season for the best flavor, and serve with a garlic mayonnaise sauce (rouille), if you like.

 15 MINS   30 MINS

SERVES 4

2½lb (1.1kg) mixed seasonal fish such as pollock, whiting or cod, sea bass, smoked haddock, salmon, and squid

1½ tbsp olive oil

2 garlic cloves, crushed or finely chopped

1 tbsp tomato paste

1 small onion, finely chopped

4 tomatoes, peeled (p197) and chopped

½ tsp fennel seeds

a few strands of saffron

pinch of paprika

2 cups light fish stock

salt and freshly ground black pepper

½ baguette

2½oz (75g) Gruyère cheese, grated

handful of flat-leaf parsley, finely chopped, to garnish

1 Wash the fish, then cut it into chunky bite-sized pieces and set aside. Put the oil in a large wide pan, add the garlic, tomato paste, and onion, and cook over very low heat for 5–8 minutes, or until the onion is soft and translucent.

2 Add the tomatoes, fennel seeds, saffron, and paprika, pour in the stock, and season with salt and pepper. Bring to a boil, then reduce to a simmer and cook for 10 minutes. Add all the fish and simmer for another 5–8 minutes, or until the fish is cooked.

3 Slice the bread diagonally and toast. Serve the stew in shallow bowls with the toasted croutons and a sprinkle of cheese on top, and finish with a garnish of parsley.

grilled herring with mustard butter

Many breakfast herring recipes use bacon and oatmeal, but the mustard here makes this recipe a special way to start the day. Enjoy this with hot buttered toast.

 10 MINS   4–6 MINS

SERVES 4

8 herrings, scaled, gutted, and trimmed; heads removed

1 tbsp vegetable oil

salt and freshly ground black pepper

4oz (115g) watercress, to garnish

lemon wedges, to garnish

For the mustard butter

2½oz (75g) butter, softened

1 tbsp whole-grain mustard

1 tsp thyme leaves

squeeze of lemon juice

1 Preheat the broiler. Pat the herrings dry with paper towels, brush with oil, and season lightly. Place on a large sheet of lightly buttered foil on a baking sheet.

2 Mix the butter, mustard, and thyme together. Add a little lemon juice and season. Broil the herrings for 2–3 minutes on each side, or until cooked: it will be firm to the touch.

3 Lift the herrings onto a large, warmed serving dish and dot with the mustard butter to melt over the fish. Garnish with watercress and lemon wedges.

Season's best **herrings and sardines**

Members of the same family, herrings and sardines are both sustainable, oily fish, making them excellent choices for both health and ethical reasons. Sardines are at their best in summer, but herrings can be fished all year. They move in huge shoals to warmer waters through the summer months, so are a fine catch then. Delicious simply with lemon or fresh herbs, they are also good with stronger Mediterranean flavors, too.

Atlantic herring Also known as sea herrings, these are found on both sides of the Atlantic. They can grow up to 18in (46cm) long, but most are caught much smaller. They have a lot of fine bones but, when fresh, the flavor is good and sweet and not too oily.

Sardine This fast-growing fish is rounded, oil-rich, and high in omega-3 essential fatty acids. It has a greeny-blue back, bright silvery sides and belly, and loose scales. It has a lot of bones, a coarse texture, and is meaty with a robust flavor. Large sardines are called pilchards.

how to bone a herring

Herrings are full of tiny bones and the majority can be removed with the backbone using this method. You will need to feel over the flesh and pull out any remaining bones with tweezers, too. The butterflied fillets can be egged, then crumb- or oat-coated and fried, or they can be stuffed and re-shaped, then baked, or rolled and pickled. Sardines and pilchards are usually cooked whole and eaten straight off the bone, but can be filleted first (though it is a bit difficult).

1 Lay the fish on a board and cut off the head with a sharp knife; also cut off the tail.

2 Clean the fish, if not already gutted, then open the fish out and lay it, skin-side up, on the board.

3 Hold the fish and firmly run your thumb up and down the backbone several times to loosen the bones.

4 Turn the fish over and gently lift the backbone and attached bones away. Remove any loose bones, too.

essentials
varieties available

Atlantic herring (whole or fillets), sardine, pilchard (Cornish sardine). Herrings are also sold pickled, cold smoked as kippers (split) and bloaters (whole), and hot smoked as buckling. Sardines and pilchards are also popular canned (in olive oil or tomato sauce).

buy Choose shiny, firm fish with a fresh smell of the sea and, if whole, with bright eyes.

store Best eaten fresh. Wrap and store in the coldest part of the fridge for up to 24 hours.

cook Pan-fry, broil, or barbecue. Herrings are also good roasted and pickled.

recipe ideas

Broiled sardines on toast p76

Rollmops p135

Stuffed sardines with crushed new potatoes p108

lamb chops in paper with fennel

Chops enclosed in parchment paper steam in their own juices, using minimum fat for maximum flavor. The paper packages puff up and turn golden brown in the oven and, when opened, release wafts of delicious, gentle aniseed aroma.

 25-30 MINS   35-40 MINS

SERVES 4

2¼lb (1kg) fennel bulbs

4 tbsp olive oil

2 garlic cloves, finely chopped

14oz (400g) can chopped tomatoes

3 tbsp pastis

salt and freshly ground black pepper

4 lamb loin chops, each 1in (2.5cm) thick, about 1lb 6oz (625g) total weight

melted butter, to brush

1 large egg

1 Trim off and discard the fennel stems and root, along with any tough outer layers from the bulb. Reserve some green fronds for garnish. Thinly slice each fennel bulb.

2 Heat half the oil in a frying pan over medium heat, add the fennel and garlic, and cook for 6–8 minutes until the fennel begins to soften.

3 Add three-quarters of the tomatoes, the pastis, and salt and pepper to the pan and cook, stirring occasionally, for 20–25 minutes until the mixture is thick and most of the moisture has evaporated. Taste for seasoning.

4 Meanwhile, cut the "tail" from each chop and season. Heat the remaining oil in another frying pan over a high heat, add the chops and tails, and cook for 1–2 minutes until well browned. Turn and brown the other side.

5 Fold a large sheet of parchment paper measuring about 12 x 15in (30 x 37.5cm) in half, and draw a curve to make a heart shape when unfolded, large enough to leave a 3in (7.5cm) border around a chop. Cut out the heart shape with scissors. Repeat to make 4 paper hearts. Open out and brush each one with melted butter, leaving a border of about 1in (2.5cm) unbuttered.

6 Beat the egg with ½ tsp salt. Brush the egg glaze on the unbuttered border of each paper heart.

7 Preheat the oven to 375°F (190°C). Spoon a bed of the fennel mixture on 1 half of a paper heart. Set a lamb chop and tail on top of the

fennel mixture. Spoon a little of the reserved tomato over and lay a fennel frond on top. Fold the paper over the filling and run your fingers along the edge to stick the 2 sides of the heart together. Make small pleats to seal the edges of the paper package.

8 Twist the ends of the paper package to finish. Repeat the process with the remaining ingredients to make 4 paper packages. Place on a baking sheet and bake for 10–14 minutes until puffed and brown. Serve at once with steamed asparagus or other seasonal vegetables, allowing each diner to open their own package.

zucchini, herb, and lemon tagine

If you have an earthenware tagine dish then do use it; if not, a large heavy-bottomed pan does the job just as well.

 25 MINS   40 MINS

SERVES 4

2 tbsp olive oil

1 red onion, finely chopped

salt and freshly ground black pepper

2 garlic cloves, grated or finely chopped

pinch of fennel seeds

pinch of ground cinnamon

1–2 tsp harissa paste

2 preserved lemons, halved, pith removed, and halved again

14oz can plum tomatoes, chopped

1 head of broccoli, broken into florets

3 zucchini, sliced

juice of 1 lemon

handful of dill, finely chopped

handful of flat-leaf parsley, chopped

1 Heat half the oil in a large heavy-bottomed pan over medium heat, add the onions, and cook for 3–4 minutes until soft. Season well with salt and pepper. Stir through the garlic, fennel seeds, cinnamon, harissa, and preserved lemons. Add the tomatoes and crush them with the back of a wooden spoon. Bring to a boil, then reduce the heat and simmer for 30–40 minutes. If the sauce starts to dry out, add a little hot water.

2 Cook the broccoli in a pan of boiling salted water for 3–5 minutes or until tender, then drain and refresh in cold water. Drain again and set aside. Heat the remaining oil in a frying pan over low heat, add the zucchini, and cook over low heat, stirring, for 5 minutes until they start to color. Add the lemon juice, some seasoning, and stir in the dill.

3 Add the broccoli and zucchini to the sauce and stir in the parsley. Serve hot with some fluffy couscous and lemon wedges to squeeze over.

lamb with chickpeas, green bell peppers, and couscous

Lamb and cousous: quintessential north African food.

 10 MINS   30 MINS

SERVES 4

1 tbsp olive oil

1 onion, finely chopped

2 garlic cloves, grated or finely chopped

2lb (900g) lean lamb, cut into bite-sized pieces

1 tsp ground cinnamon

1 tsp paprika

salt and freshly ground black pepper

2–3 green bell peppers, seeded and coarsely chopped

14oz can chickpeas, drained and rinsed

3 cups hot vegetable stock

6oz (175g) couscous

1¾oz (50g) pine nuts, toasted

handful of flat-leaf parsley, chopped

1 Heat the oil in a large frying pan over medium heat, add the onion, and cook for 3–4 minutes until the onion is soft. Add the garlic, lamb, cinnamon, and paprika, and season with salt and pepper.

2 Add the bell peppers and chickpeas, and cook, stirring occasionally, until the meat is browned on all sides. Pour in 2 cups of the hot stock, cover the pan, and simmer gently for 20 minutes. Add a little hot water if the mixture starts to dry out.

3 Meanwhile, pour the couscous into a bowl and pour in enough of the remaining stock just to cover. Leave for about 5 minutes, then fluff up with a fork and season with salt and pepper. To serve, sprinkle the lamb mixture with the pine nuts and parsley, and serve immediately with the couscous.

warm pea pancakes with grilled asparagus

A deceptively simple dish to prepare, this recipe showcases early summer produce. The bright colors of the peas and asparagus contrast beautifully with the golden yolk of the egg.

 10 MINS   30 MINS

SPECIAL EQUIPMENT ▪ food processor

SERVES 4

14oz (400g) fresh peas (shelled weight)

large handful of mint leaves, chopped

4 tbsp melted butter, plus extra for frying

¼ cup all-purpose flour

¼ cup heavy cream

2 tbsp Parmesan cheese, grated

6 large eggs

salt and freshly ground black pepper

1 large bunch of asparagus spears, trimmed

1 tsp extra virgin olive oil

1 Put the peas in a pan and blanch in boiling water for 1–2 minutes, then drain and leave to cool.

2 Put the peas and mint into a food processor and pulse together to get a rough texture. Add the melted butter, flour, cream, Parmesan, and 2 eggs, and season. Process the mixture to a stiff paste.

3 Heat some butter or oil in a large frying pan and add 1 or 2 tbsp of the mixture for each pancake. Cook on medium heat and use the back of a spoon to smooth the top of the mixture. After 3–4 minutes, the edges of the pancakes will change color. Carefully turn them over and cook for another 1–2 minutes.

4 Meanwhile, bring a large pan of water to a boil and lightly poach the remaining eggs until just set. Remove them with a slotted spoon.

5 Meanwhile, grill the asparagus in a hot grill pan with a little olive oil, seasoning while cooking, until golden. Serve on the side with an egg on top of the pancakes.

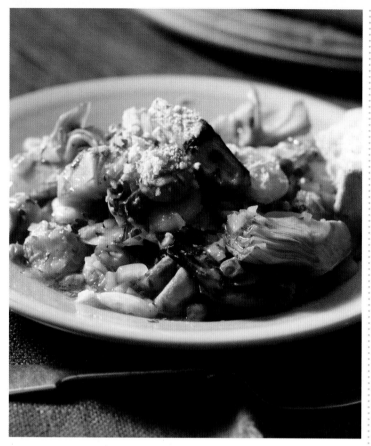

artichokes, butter beans, and peas

This is a substantial vegetarian dish. The artichokes and butter beans give it a wonderful creamy finish, and bread crumbs are stirred in at the last minute to add some texture.

 15 MINS   1 HR 30 MINS

SERVES 4–6

1 tbsp olive oil

1 onion, finely chopped

3 garlic cloves, finely chopped

9oz (250g) small button mushrooms, larger ones halved

2 x 14oz cans butter beans, drained

pinch of ground nutmeg

juice of ½ lemon

salt and freshly ground black pepper

2 cups hot vegetable stock

4½oz (125g) peas (shelled weight)

8 cooked artichoke hearts (p309), halved or quartered (or a large jar, drained)

½ cup bread crumbs, toasted

a few sprigs of flat-leaf parsley, finely chopped, to serve

1 Heat the oil in a large heavy-bottomed pan over medium heat, add the onion, and cook for 3–4 minutes until soft and translucent. Then stir in the garlic and mushrooms and cook for about 5 minutes until the mushrooms are tender.

2 Stir in the butter beans, add the nutmeg and lemon juice, and season with salt and pepper. Pour in the stock and bring to a boil. Boil for about 10 minutes, then reduce to simmer, partially cover with a lid, and cook for 45 minutes. Check occasionally that there is enough stock in the pan and it's not drying out, and add a little hot water if necessary.

3 Stir in the peas and artichokes and cook on low heat for another 15–20 minutes, or until the butter beans are completely soft. Spoon the bread crumbs over the top and carefully fold some in, then top with parsley. Serve with freshly baked crusty bread.

penne with asparagus and zucchini

Choose smaller zucchini for better flavor and young asparagus with tender stems for this quick, lemony pasta.

 10 MINS   20 MINS

SERVES 4

1 tbsp olive oil

1 onion, finely chopped

salt

4 small zucchini, 2 cubed and 2 grated

3 garlic cloves, grated or finely chopped

bunch of fine asparagus spears, trimmed and stems cut into 3 pieces

½ cup white wine

1–2 tsp capers, rinsed and chopped

zest of 1 lemon

12oz (350g) penne

handful of flat-leaf parsley, finely chopped

Parmesan cheese, grated, to serve

1 Heat the oil in a large frying pan, add the onion and salt, and cook over low heat for 5 minutes, or until soft and translucent. Add all the zucchini and cook for 10 minutes, or until they have softened. Don't allow them to brown.

2 Stir in the garlic and asparagus. Add the wine, raise the heat, and allow to boil for 2–3 minutes, then return to simmer. Cook for another 2–3 minutes, or until the asparagus has softened, then stir in the capers and lemon zest.

3 Meanwhile, cook the pasta in a large pan of boiling salted water for about 10 minutes, or until it is tender but still firm to the bite. Drain, keeping back a tiny amount of the cooking water. Return the pasta to the pan and toss with the cooking water. Add the zucchini mixture and parsley, then toss again. Sprinkle with Parmesan cheese and serve.

lamb with artichokes, fava beans, and dill

This is a light stew that is full of early summer flavors.

 15 MINS   **1 HR 45 MINS**   ❄ **FREEZABLE**

SERVES 4-6

2¾lb (1.25kg) lamb shoulder, with bones, trimmed and cut into bite-sized pieces
salt and freshly ground black pepper
2 tbsp olive oil
2 onions, coarsely chopped
3 carrots, peeled and coarsely chopped
1 tbsp all-purpose flour
½ cup dry white wine
3 cups hot vegetable stock
a few sprigs of rosemary
grated zest of ½ lemon and juice of 1 lemon
4 large cooked artichoke hearts (p309), quartered
12oz (350g) fava beans (shelled weight), skinned (p85, optional)
bunch of dill, finely chopped

1 Preheat the oven to 350°F (180°C). Season the meat with salt and pepper. Heat half the oil in a large flameproof casserole dish over high heat, add the lamb (in batches, if necessary), and cook for 6–8 minutes until no longer pink. Remove from the casserole dish and set aside.

2 Heat the remaining oil in the casserole dish over medium heat, add the onions, and cook for 3–4 minutes until soft. Season with salt and pepper, add the carrots, and cook for another 5 minutes. Sprinkle over the flour, stir, and cook for a couple of minutes. Add the wine, increase the heat, and cook the sauce for a minute.

3 Add the stock, rosemary, lemon juice and zest, and lamb. Bring to a boil, cover, and put in the oven for 1 hour. Check occasionally that it's not drying out and add a little hot water if needed. Stir in the artichokes and fava beans and cook for another 30 minutes, or until the vegetables are tender. Taste and season as required and add the dill to taste. Serve with crusty bread.

roasted new potatoes and sausages with rosemary and chile

Flavorsome new potatoes roasted in their skins with sprigs of rosemary taste simply delicious. Choose sausages that have a high percentage of meat and low percentage of fat.

 15 MINS   **40 MINS**

SERVES 4

8-12 pork sausages
2 red onions, peeled and cut into eighths
pinch of chile flakes
handful of rosemary sprigs
2½lb (1.1kg) new potatoes, large ones halved
salt and freshly ground black pepper
1 tbsp olive oil

1 Preheat the oven to 400°F (200°C). Put the sausages in a roasting pan with the onion, sprinkle over the chile flakes and rosemary, then add the new potatoes. Season well with salt and pepper, drizzle the oil over the top, and combine together well.

2 Put the pan in the oven to roast for 30–40 minutes, turning the sausages and potatoes halfway through cooking. When the sausages are golden all over and cooked through, remove from the oven and serve on warmed plates.

variation

roasted new potatoes and sardines

Prepare the potatoes and onions in the same way, place in the roasting pan with a handful of thyme leaves instead of rosemary and seasoning as before. Drizzle with olive oil and toss. Roast for 30 minutes, turning once. Lay 8 cleaned and descaled sardines on top, drizzle with a little more olive oil, season and roast for another 10 minutes or until the fish and vegetables are cooked.

german potato salad

The piquant caraway dressing on this salad is inspired by recipes that came from the Black Forest in Germany, where few dishes are complete without ham or sausage, or both.

🥣 25–30 MINS PLUS CHILLING   🍲 15–20 MINS

SERVES 6–8

3lb (1.35kg) red-skinned new potatoes

salt and freshly ground black pepper

1 small red onion, very finely chopped

3 tbsp red wine vinegar

3 tbsp sour cream

2 tbsp hot mustard

2 tsp caraway seeds

1 cup vegetable oil

5½oz (150g) thinly sliced smoked ham

7-10 sprigs of parsley, leaves picked and chopped

1 Scrub the potatoes under cold, running water but do not peel. Cut any larger potatoes into 2–4 pieces. Put in a large saucepan with plenty of cold, salted water, cover, and bring to a boil. Simmer for 15–20 minutes, just until tender, then drain.

2 Put the onion in a bowl with the vinegar, sour cream, mustard, and salt and pepper. Sprinkle in the caraway seeds. Whisk together just until mixed, then gradually whisk in the oil so the dressing emulsifies and thickens slightly. Taste for seasoning and set aside.

3 While still warm, cut the potatoes into ½in (1cm) slices. Transfer to a large bowl. Briskly whisk the dressing, then pour it over the warm potatoes. Stir gently to thoroughly coat and leave to cool.

4 Trim the fat from the ham, then cut into ½in (1cm) strips. Add the ham to the potatoes. Sprinkle three-quarters of the parsley over the top. Stir, taste for seasoning, cover, and place in the fridge for at least 1 hour.

5 Transfer the salad to a large platter, or individual plates or shallow bowls, and sprinkle evenly with the remaining chopped parsley. Serve at room temperature.

lentil, fava bean, and feta salad

The lentils in this salad can be whatever color you happen to have on hand: green, brown, or anything else. The fava beans and feta cheese add further color to the finished dish.

🥣 15 MINS

SERVES 4

3oz (85g) baby fava beans (shelled weight), skinned (p85, optional)

14oz (400g) can lentils in water, drained and rinsed

salt and freshly ground black pepper

bunch of scallions, trimmed and finely chopped

1 jalapeño chile, seeded and finely chopped

6oz (175g) feta cheese, cut into cubes

handful of flat-leaf parsley, finely chopped

For the dressing

3 tbsp olive oil

1 tbsp white wine vinegar

1in (2.5cm) piece of fresh ginger, peeled and grated

pinch of granulated sugar (optional)

1 Cook the fava beans in boiling, lightly salted water for 4–5 minutes until just tender. Drain, rinse with cold water, and drain again.

2 Put the lentils in a serving bowl and season with salt and pepper. Add the scallions, chile, and drained fava beans and stir well.

3 To make the dressing, put the oil, vinegar, and ginger in a small bowl. Season with salt and pepper and a pinch of sugar, if using, and whisk until well combined. Drizzle over the salad and leave to stand for 10 minutes, to allow the flavors to develop. When ready to serve, stir in the feta cheese and parsley.

papas arrugadas

Going by the delightful name of "wrinkly potatoes," this dish originates in the Canary Islands. Serve as tapas with other dishes, or as a light lunch with a crisp green salad.

 15 MINS 45 MINS

SPECIAL EQUIPMENT ▪ blender or food processor

SERVES 4-6

2¼lb (1kg) new potatoes, scrubbed

sea salt and freshly ground black pepper

½ cup extra virgin olive oil

1 red bell pepper

juice of 1 lemon

2 heaped tbsp tomato paste

1 tsp smoked paprika

½ tsp ground cumin

pinch of chile powder, or to taste

1 garlic clove, crushed

2 tbsp chopped flat-leaf parsley or cilantro (optional)

1 Preheat the oven to 400°F (200°C). Place the potatoes on a baking sheet, toss in some sea salt and 1 tbsp of the oil, and roast whole for about 45 minutes or until golden brown, turning occasionally.

2 Meanwhile, rub the pepper in olive oil and roast in the same oven for around 30 minutes, turning occasionally, until tender and soft. Remove the bell pepper from the oven, place it in a plastic bag for 2–3 minutes to loosen the skin, then cool, peel, and seed. Coarsely chop the cooked bell pepper.

3 Put the bell pepper, lemon juice, tomato paste, spices, and garlic in a blender or food processor, together with the remaining oil. Pulse to form a thick dipping sauce, adding a little more oil if needed. Check the seasoning, add the parsley or cilantro, if using, and serve with the potatoes.

feta and pea salad with watercress mayonnaise

This recipe features a mayonnaise with a difference: puréeing watercress with some horseradish into the sauce introduces quite a kick to the usual creamy condiment.

 15 MINS

SPECIAL EQUIPMENT ▪ blender or food processor

SERVES 4

handful of watercress, coarsely chopped

3–4 tbsp mayonnaise

1 tsp creamed horseradish

salt and freshly ground black pepper

6oz (175g) feta cheese, cut into cubes

4½oz (125g) peas (shelled weight)

2 handfuls of baby spinach leaves

small handful of mint leaves

lemon wedges, to serve

1 Put the watercress, mayonnaise, and horseradish sauce into a blender or food processor and pulse until well combined. Taste and season with salt and pepper.

2 Put the feta, peas, spinach, and mint leaves in a bowl and gently mix together. Season with a little black pepper if you wish. Transfer to a serving bowl and serve with the mayonnaise and lemon wedges on the side.

variation

dressed pea salad

For a less elaborate side dish, omit the watercress, mayonnaise, and feta. Simply assemble the peas, spinach, and mint, and drizzle with olive oil and white balsamic vinegar. Season and toss gently. Divide between 4 bowls and serve.

ham with minted peas and fava beans

This easy dish is big on summer produce and makes a quick, tasty meal. Serve it with chunks of good bread, or include it as one of a selection of warm and cold salads at a meal.

 10 MINS 20 MINS

SERVES 4

1 tbsp olive oil

1 onion, finely chopped

2 garlic cloves, finely chopped

5½oz (150g) fava beans (shelled weight), skinned (p85, optional)

2½oz (75g) peas (shelled weight)

⅔ cup hot chicken stock

handful of mint leaves, chopped

6oz (175g) cooked ham, cut into cubes

1 Heat the oil in a large frying pan over medium heat, add the onion, and cook for 3–4 minutes until the onion is soft. Add the garlic cloves and stir in the fava beans and peas.

2 Pour in the hot chicken stock and bring to a boil. Reduce the heat slightly and simmer for 15 minutes. Add the mint leaves and ham and stir well. Serve immediately.

fava bean and feta panzanella

Inspired by the classic Italian bread salad, panzanella, this unusual green version is redolent of the fresh colors and flavors of summer, cut with the salty tang of crumbled feta.

 25 MINS PLUS STANDING 10 MINS

SERVES 4

5½oz (150g) ciabatta, chopped into ¾in (2cm) cubes

⅔ cup extra virgin olive oil

sea salt and freshly ground black pepper

2 tbsp white wine vinegar

1 large garlic clove, crushed

14oz (400g) fava beans (shelled weight), skinned (p85, optional)

4 scallions, green parts removed, and finely chopped

7oz (200g) feta cheese, chopped into ½in (1cm) cubes or coarsely crumbled

handful of mint, chopped

2 tbsp chopped dill (optional)

4 handfuls of arugula leaves, watercress, or baby lettuce leaves

juice of 1 lemon

1 Preheat the oven to 425°F (220°C). Toss the cubed bread in ¼ cup of the oil, sprinkle with a little sea salt and pepper, and cook at the top of the hot oven for about 8 minutes, turning once, until the bread is golden brown and crispy.

2 In a large serving bowl, whisk together the remaining oil with the vinegar and garlic, then season with plenty of black pepper and just a little sea salt (the feta is salty). Add the fava beans, toasted bread, chopped scallions, feta, and herbs, and toss well to coat everything.

3 Leave the salad for 30 minutes to develop the flavors and soften the bread. To serve, add the salad leaves, pour the lemon over the top, and check again for seasoning.

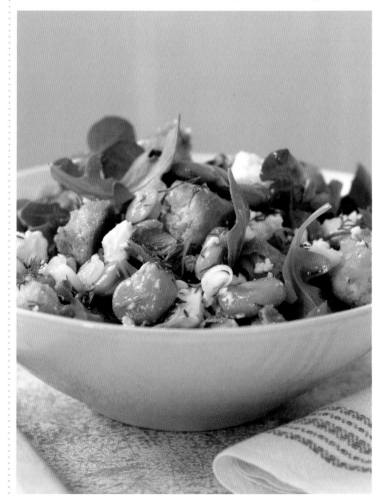

raita

A cooling, yogurt-based dipping sauce that makes use of the cucumbers that are coming into their own early in the summer. It is traditionally served with most Indian meals.

 10 MINS PLUS STANDING

MAKES 1¼ cups

1 cucumber, peeled

½ tsp salt

½ tsp cumin seeds, dry-roasted

½ natural full-fat yogurt

½ tsp granulated sugar

1 garlic clove, crushed

1 tbsp chopped mint

1 tbsp chopped cilantro

1 Finely grate the cucumber. Toss with the salt and leave for 1 hour.

2 Squeeze out as much liquid from the cucumber as you can.

3 Crush the cumin seeds to a fine powder in a mortar with a pestle. Add to the cucumber with the remaining ingredients, mix, and chill before serving.

watercress, flageolet bean, and smoked cheese salad

Don't feel that you have to use the Applewood smoked cheese listed in the ingredients; you can experiment with, say, a smoked Gruyère or Gouda for a different flavor.

 15 MINS

SERVES 4

14oz (400g) can of flageolet beans, drained and rinsed

1 tsp Dijon mustard

handful of flat-leaf parsley, finely chopped

salt and freshly ground black pepper

½ red onion, finely chopped

2 large handfuls of watercress, trimmed, and coarsely chopped

juice of 1 lemon

4½oz (125g) lightly smoked cheese, such as Applewood, cubed

1 Put the beans in a large bowl. Add the mustard and parsley, and stir together. Season with salt and pepper. Add half of the chopped onion and stir well.

2 Arrange the watercress on a large platter or individual plates. Drizzle the lemon juice over the greens and sprinkle with a pinch of salt. Spoon the bean mixture on top, then scatter the remaining onions and the smoked cheese over the beans and serve.

variation

pea shoot, ham, fava bean, and cheddar cheese salad

Cook 8oz (225g) shelled fava beans and removed them from their skins (p85). Mix with 2 chopped scallions instead of the red onion. Omit the mustard. Drizzle the beans with a little olive oil and the lemon juice. Add the chopped parsley and season to taste. Pile onto pea shoots instead of watercress and scatter 2 slices of cooked ham, cubed, and some cubed Cheddar cheese instead of Applewood over the top.

cashew and zucchini rice

You can serve this nutty, gingery pilaf on its own or with grilled lamb or fish. Grated ginger freezes well, so wrap small quantities in plastic wrap and you'll always have some on hand.

 15 MINS **40 MINS**

SERVES 4

1–2 tbsp olive oil

1 onion, finely chopped

salt and freshly ground black pepper

4in (10cm) piece of fresh ginger, peeled and grated

4 zucchini, sliced into quarters lengthwise and chopped into bite-sized pieces

3 garlic cloves, finely chopped

1 tbsp cider vinegar

pinch of cayenne pepper

7oz (200g) basmati rice

3 cups hot vegetable stock

2½oz (75g) cashew nuts, coarsely chopped

bunch of scallions, green parts only, thinly sliced

bunch of cilantro, leaves only, chopped

1 Heat 1 tbsp of the oil in a large heavy-bottomed pan over medium heat, add the onion, and cook for 3–4 minutes until soft. Season with salt and pepper, increase the heat, and stir in the ginger and zucchini. Cook for 2–5 minutes until the zucchini is lightly golden (adding more oil, if necessary), then add the garlic and cook for another 3 minutes.

2 Increase the heat, add the vinegar, and let it cook for a minute, then stir in the cayenne pepper and rice. Add a little stock and turn it so all the grains are coated. Bring to a boil, add enough stock to cover, cover with a lid, and simmer gently for about 20 minutes, or until the rice is tender. Add more stock when needed.

3 Stir through the cashew nuts, scallions, and half the cilantro. Taste and season as needed. Sprinkle with the remaining cilantro to serve.

strawberry and raspberry granita

Lemon juice really brings out the vivid flavors of the early summer berries in this refreshing frozen dessert.

 10 MINS PLUS FREEZING ❄ FREEZABLE

SPECIAL EQUIPMENT ▪ blender or food processor

SERVES 6

1 cup confectioners' sugar

1 tbsp lemon juice

⅔ cup boiling water

9oz (250g) raspberries

9oz (250g) strawberries, hulled

half-and-half, to serve (optional)

1 Put the confectioners' sugar and lemon juice in a blender or food processor with the boiling water and pulse until the sugar has completely dissolved. Add the raspberries and strawberries, and pulse to a purée.

2 Transfer the mixture to a shallow freezerproof plastic container, cover, and place in the freezer for 4 hours.

3 Remove from the freezer every 2 hours and stir with a fork, breaking the mixture up into small pieces.

When the mixture has completely broken up into frozen, gravelly pieces, leave in the freezer until ready to serve. It will keep for up to 1 month. Serve straight from the freezer on its own, or with a drizzle of half-and-half.

variation

strawberry and watermelon granita

Prepare the syrup in the same way but use the grated zest and juice of 1 lime instead of the lemon juice. Add 9oz (250g) strawberries and 9oz (250g) peeled, cubed, and seeded watermelon instead of raspberries. Freeze as before.

raspberry soufflés with kirsch custard

For the very best flavor, choose freshly picked, sweet and juicy raspberries for these pretty pink soufflés.

 15 MINS 20-22 MINS

SPECIAL EQUIPMENT ▪ food processor

SERVES 6

1⅓ cups milk

¾ cup granulated sugar

5 large eggs, separated

1 tbsp cornstarch

2-3 tbsp kirsch

1lb 2oz (500g) raspberries

confectioners' sugar, sifted, to serve

1 For the custard, pour the milk into a heavy-bottomed saucepan and bring to a boil. Set aside ⅓ cup milk. Add ¼ cup of the sugar to the remaining milk, stirring until dissolved. In a bowl, whisk the egg yolks and cornstarch until smooth. Add the sweetened milk to the egg yolks, whisking until smooth. Cook the custard over medium heat, stirring constantly, until it comes to a boil and thickens enough to coat the back of

a spoon. Remove from the heat and stir in the reserved milk. Strain and cool. Stir in the kirsch, cover, and chill.

2 Brush 6 ramekins with melted butter, coat evenly with a little sugar, and place on a baking sheet. Preheat the oven to 375°F (190°C).

3 Purée the raspberries with half the remaining sugar in a blender or food processor. Sieve the purée into a large bowl. Whisk the egg whites until stiff. Add the remaining sugar and whisk until glossy. Add one-quarter of the meringue to the purée and stir. Return this to the remaining meringue; fold together. Spoon the mixture into the ramekins. Bake for 10-12 minutes, until puffed. Dust with confectioners' sugar and serve immediately with the custard.

cherry strudel

Walnuts add extra crunch to luscious ripe cherries in this quick-to-make version of the Viennese classic.

 15 MINS 30-40 MINS

SERVES 6-8

1lb 2oz (500g) cherries

1 lemon

2½oz (75g) walnuts

6 large sheets filo pastry

4 tbsp butter, melted

½ cup light brown sugar

1 tsp ground cinnamon

confectioners' sugar, for dusting

1 Pit all the cherries. Grate the zest from the lemon onto a plate. Coarsely chop the walnuts; nuts are best chopped by hand to control the finished texture, although this will always be uneven.

2 Preheat the oven to 375°F (190°C). Place 3 sheets of filo pastry overlapping by about 2in (5cm), side

by side on a clean cloth. Brush with melted butter, then lay the last three sheets on top in the same way. Brush with more butter.

3 Sprinkle the buttered strudel dough with the pitted cherries, chopped walnuts, brown sugar, lemon zest, and cinnamon. Using the cloth to help, roll up from a long side to form a long, filled roll. Carefully lift onto a buttered baking sheet in a horseshoe shape. Brush all over with the remaining butter.

4 Bake for 30–40 minutes until crisp and golden brown. Dust with confectioners' sugar and serve hot or cold, with cream or crème fraîche.

bavarian raspberry gâteau

Tart, fresh raspberries are enlivened with the kirsch in the rich custard cream filling of this elegant dessert.

 55-60 MINS   20-25 MINS

SPECIAL EQUIPMENT ▪ 9in (23cm) round springform cake pan ▪ electric hand mixer ▪ blender or food processor

SERVES 8

4 tbsp unsalted butter

1 cup all-purpose flour

pinch of salt

4 eggs, beaten

⅔ cup granulated sugar

2 tbsp kirsch

For the Bavarian raspberry cream

1lb 2oz (500g) raspberries

3 tbsp kirsch

¾ cup granulated sugar

1 cup heavy cream

3½ cups milk

1 vanilla bean, split,
   or 2 tsp pure vanilla extract

10 large egg yolks

3 tbsp cornstarch

1 tbsp powdered gelatin

1 Preheat the oven to 425°F (220°C). Grease the cake pan with a little butter and line the bottom with buttered parchment. Sprinkle in 2–3 tbsp flour to prevent the cake from sticking. Melt the butter in a pan and set aside to cool. Sift the flour and salt into a bowl. In a separate bowl, beat the eggs and sugar, using an electric hand mixer for 5 minutes. Sift one-third of the flour over the egg mixture and fold. Add the remaining flour in 2 batches, then the melted butter and fold. Pour into the pan and bake for 20–25 minutes until risen.

2 Turn the cake onto a wire rack to cool. Remove the parchment. Trim the top and bottom so that they are flat. Cut the cake horizontally in half. Clean, dry, and regrease the pan. Put a cake round in the pan and sprinkle with 1 tbsp of kirsch.

3 Purée three-quarters of the berries in a blender or food processor, then work through a sieve to remove the pits. Stir in 1 tbsp of kirsch with ½ cup of the sugar. Whip the cream until it forms soft peaks.

4 Pour the milk in a pan. Add the vanilla bean or extract and bring to a boil. Remove the pan from the heat, cover, and set aside for 10–15 minutes. Remove the bean. Set aside one-quarter of the milk, then stir the remaining sugar into the milk in the pan. Beat the egg yolks and cornstarch in a bowl. Add the hot milk and whisk until smooth. Pour the yolk mixture back into the pan and cook over medium heat, stirring, until the custard boils. Stir in the reserved milk.

5 Strain the custard equally into 2 bowls. Stir 2 tbsp of kirsch into one bowl and set aside to serve with the

finished dessert. Sprinkle the powdered gelatin over ¼ cup of water in a small pan and leave for 5 minutes. Heat until melted. Stir into the bowl of unflavored custard, along with the raspberry purée. Set the bowl in a pan of iced water and stir the mixture until thickened, then remove the bowl. Fold the raspberry custard into the whipped cream. Pour half into the cake pan and sprinkle a few reserved raspberries over the top. Pour the remaining Bavarian cream on the berries. Sprinkle 1 tbsp of kirsch over the second cake round.

6 Lightly press the cake round, kirsch-side down, on the cream. Cover with plastic wrap and refrigerate for 4 hours until firm. To serve, remove the side of the pan, decorate the top of the cake with the reserved raspberries, and serve with the kirsch custard sauce.

Season's best **strawberries**

Plump and juicy, the many hybrids of this gorgeous fruit vary in color from scarlet to pinkish-orange, and can be conical, globular, oval, or heart-shaped. The aroma and flavor of the first summer outdoor berries are delightful, but they are available from late spring right through to autumn. Fragrant wild strawberries are also cultivated. All taste heavenly with chocolate, cream, and other fruits, and chile or black pepper enhances their flavor.

Strawberries are grown in all temperate regions. Their season is extended by growing in hothouses in cooler regions. Wild strawberries are found in woods and shady pastures.

Chandler This large, firm variety has a typically flat, wedge shape. It is a good all-purpose strawberry with a brilliant, glossy color and excellent berry flavor.

Elsanta One of the most popular commercial varieties in the UK, Elsanta has glossy good looks, but muted flavor. It is a useful berry for cold desserts, such as fools and mousses.

how to hull strawberries

Hull strawberries before adding to desserts, but if serving with melted chocolate or cream to dip, leave the stem on as a natural handle, then bite the fruit off.

1 Wash the fruit and drain well. If ripe, hold the fruit in one hand and twist off the green calyx between your thumb and forefinger.

2 If the fruit is not very ripe, cut off the stem end with a small, sharp knife, but don't take too much fruit.

Driscoll These berries were developed in 1904 in California. They are now internationally renowned for their excellent shape, color, and flavor. The Kent Driscoll Jubilee is shown here.

Wild strawberry Also known as *fraises des bois*, these are found in the wild as well as cultivated (when they are often called Alpine strawberries). The tiny, fragile red or white fruit has an exquisite, fragrant taste. Use in tarts or as a special dessert.

The wild strawberry is small in size, but big in flavor.

Albion A modern Californian variety with a long growing season, Albion is an extra-large, dark red conical berry with a lush, very sweet taste. It makes quite an impact in desserts and cakes.

The flesh is red throughout.

The berries look like red spinning tops with a bright green hull.

Mieze Schindler A classic German variety, the berries are plump and heart-shaped, and have a delicious, full-fruit flavor. Enjoy them fresh or make into excellent jam.

Evie These strawberries are dark red and full-flavored and can crop three times in a season, making them very productive.

Sonata This is a mid-season fruit with large uniform berries, sweet, firm flesh, and a stunning aroma. It is a cross between the popular Elsanta and Polka.

The fruit keeps well without darkening in color.

essentials
varieties available
Hundreds of cultivated strawberry varieties of varying shape, color, and size, plus wild ones that are now also grown commercially.

buy Choose firm, fragrant berries. Avoid if bruised or the juice is running. The calyces should be fresh and green.

store Use as soon as possible. Discard moldy or squashed berries, then cover loosely and keep at the bottom of the fridge.

cook Eat unadorned or dipped in chocolate. Top cheesecakes and tarts. Purée for coulis, cold and iced desserts, and milkshakes. Use in pie fillings.

preserve Bottle in syrup; make jam or flavored vinegar.

recipe ideas
Strawberry baked Alaska p123

Hazelnut torte with berries p122

Strawberry and cream Victoria sandwich p131

Strawberries and cream whoopie pies p126

Strawberry conserve p133

summer fruit millefeuilles

This beautiful, appetizing dessert with soft berries suits any occasion, from a dinner party to a buffet or garden party.

 2 HRS PLUS CHILLING 25–30 MINS

SPECIAL EQUIPMENT ▪ electric hand mixer

SERVES 8

1lb 5oz (600g) store-bought puff pastry

1 cup heavy cream

1 quantity crème pâtissière (p229)

14oz (400g) mixed summer fruits, such as strawberries (hulled and cubed) and raspberries

confectioners' sugar, for dusting

1 Preheat the oven to 400°F (200°C). Sprinkle a baking sheet evenly with cold water. Roll out the pastry on a floured work surface to a rectangle larger than the baking sheet and about ⅛in (3mm) thick. Roll around the rolling pin and unroll onto the baking sheet so the edges overhang. Chill for 15 minutes.

2 Prick the pastry all over with a fork. Cover with parchment paper, then set a wire rack on top of it. Bake for 15–20 minutes until it just begins to brown. Gripping the sheet and rack, invert the pastry. Slide the baking sheet back under and continue baking for 10 minutes until both sides are browned. Remove from the oven and slide the pastry onto a cutting board. While still warm, trim the edges, then cut lengthwise into 3 equal strips. Allow to cool.

3 Whip the heavy cream in a mixing bowl with an electric hand mixer until stiff peaks form. Fold into the pastry cream. Spread half the pastry cream filling over 1 pastry strip. Sprinkle with half the fruit. Repeat with another pastry strip to make 2 layers. Put the last pastry strip on top and press down gently. Sift the confectioners' sugar thickly over the top of the millefeuilles and serve.

hazelnut torte with berries

A layered cream tower with strawberries and raspberry coulis.

 40–45 MINS PLUS CHILLING 15–18 MINS

SPECIAL EQUIPMENT ▪ food processor ▪ electric hand mixer

SERVES 8

9oz (250g) hazelnuts

⅔ cup granulated sugar plus 1½ tbsp for the cream

1 cup all-purpose flour

½ tsp salt

11 tbsp unsalted butter

1 large egg yolk

1lb 2oz (500g) raspberries

2–3 tbsp confectioners' sugar

1–2 tbsp kirsch (optional)

1lb 10oz (750g) strawberries, hulled

1⅔ cups heavy cream

1 tsp pure vanilla extract

1 Preheat the oven to 350°F (180°C). Spread the nuts on a baking sheet. Toast for 8–10 minutes, until lightly browned. Rub in a clean kitchen towel to remove the skins. Leave to cool, then pulse with the sugar to a fine powder in a food processor. Put the mix on a work surface and sift the flour and salt on top. Make a well in the center, add the butter and egg yolk, and with your fingers work the ingredients together in the well until a soft dough ball forms. Knead until smooth on a floured work surface. Wrap in plastic wrap. Chill for 30 minutes.

2 Preheat the oven to 400°F (200°C). Divide the dough ball into 3. Press each into an 8in (20cm) round on a baking sheet and set 1in (2.5cm) apart. Bake for 15–18 minutes until the edges are brown. While still warm, trim into neat rounds with a knife and cut 1 of the layers into 8 equal wedges. Then transfer to wire racks to cool completely.

3 Pulse the raspberries in the food processor. Stir in confectioners' sugar to taste, and the kirsch, if using, then work the purée through a sieve to remove the pits. Set aside 8 small strawberries for decoration, and halve or quarter the rest. Pour the cream into a chilled mixing bowl. Whip with an electric hand mixer until soft peaks form. Then add the sugar and vanilla, and whip again until stiff peaks form.

4 Set a pastry round on a serving plate, cover with a quarter of the cream, and put half the strawberries on top. Repeat with the second pastry round, half the remaining cream, the rest of the strawberries, and more cream. Top with the pastry wedges arranged at an angle and the whole strawberries on top. Serve in wedges, drizzled with the coulis.

strawberry baked alaska

This clever dessert is a festive way to conclude a celebration.

 45-50 MINS   30-40 MINS

SPECIAL EQUIPMENT ▪ electric hand mixer ▪ blender or food processor ▪ 8in (20cm) square cake pan

SERVES 8-10

4 large eggs, beaten

⅔ cup granulated sugar

1 tsp pure vanilla extract

salt

1 cup all-purpose flour, sifted

4 tbsp unsalted butter, melted

10oz (300g) strawberries, hulled

2-3 tbsp confectioners' sugar, to taste

2 cups granulated sugar

9 large egg whites

2¾ pints (1.5 liters) vanilla ice cream

1 Preheat the oven to 350°F (180°C). Butter the pan and line the bottom with buttered parchment paper. Coat the bottom and sides in 2 tbsp flour and tap out the excess. Put the eggs and sugar in a large bowl. Beat until pale, thick, and creamy. Beat in the vanilla. Add salt to the flour, add a third of the flour to the bowl, and fold in. Fold in another third, then the remaining flour and butter, and pour into the pan. Bake for 30–40 minutes until just firm to the touch. Transfer to a wire rack, peel off the paper, and allow to cool.

2 Purée the strawberries in a food processor and pour into a bowl. Add the confectioners' sugar to taste. Dissolve the sugar in a pan with 1 cup water and boil without stirring until a sugar thermometer registers 248°F (120°C), or test if the syrup forms a pliable ball in your finger and thumb. Meanwhile, whip the egg whites into stiff peaks. Gradually pour in the hot syrup, beating constantly until the egg whites are cool and stiff.

3 Trim the cake to 6in (15cm) square, split horizontally into 2 layers, and arrange to form a rectangle on a greased heatproof serving plate. Pulse the cake trimmings in a processor. Add 1 cup of the strawberry coulis, and pulse. Spread the rest of the coulis over the cake. Arrange two layers of scooped ice cream balls over the cake and smooth with a palette knife. Cover with strawberry crumbs, then spoon the meringue over the top and sides. Freeze for 2 hours. Preheat the oven to 425°F (220°C). Sprinkle the alaska with sugar and let stand for 1 minute. Bake for just 3–5 minutes. Serve at once.

gooseberry tart

Tangy gooseberries quiver in smooth, just-set custard, in a light sweet pastry crust for a sublime seasonal treat.

 30 MINS PLUS CHILLING   1 HR

SPECIAL EQUIPMENT ▪ electric hand mixer ▪ 10in (25cm) round fluted tart pan with removable bottom ▪ ceramic baking beans

SERVES 6-8

1½ cups all-purpose flour

5 tbsp butter

⅓ cup granulated sugar

2 large egg yolks, plus 2 large eggs

1 cup heavy cream

14oz (400g) gooseberries, hulled

thick cream, to serve (optional)

1 In a large bowl, rub together the flour and butter until they resemble crumbs. Stir in 2 tbsp of the sugar, add the egg yolks, then bring the ingredients together to form a dough. Wrap in plastic wrap and chill for 30 minutes.

2 Preheat the oven to 350°F (180°C). To make the custard, put the heavy cream, eggs, and the remaining sugar in a mixing bowl and beat together with an electric hand mixer. Then leave to chill in the fridge.

3 Roll out the pastry on a floured work surface to a circle a little larger than the pan. Line the pan with the pastry, pressing it into the corners. Prick the bottom with a fork. Line the pastry crust with wax paper and fill with baking beans. Bake in the oven for 20 minutes. Remove the beans and paper and return to the oven for 5 minutes more to crisp. Remove from the oven and set aside.

4 Arrange a layer of gooseberries over the bottom of the pastry crust. Pour the custard over and bake for 35 minutes until set and golden. Allow to cool slightly before removing from the pan and serving with thick cream, if you like.

raspberry tart with chocolate cream

A chocolate-lined tart is a perfect partner for raspberries.

 40 MINS PLUS CHILLING   20-25 MINS

SPECIAL EQUIPMENT ▪ 9in (23cm) round fluted tart pan with a removable bottom ▪ ceramic baking beans

SERVES 6–8

1 cup all-purpose flour

¼ cup cocoa powder

7 tbsp unsalted butter, cubed

⅔ cup granulated sugar

1 large egg yolk, plus 2 large eggs

1½ tsp pure vanilla extract

½ cup cornstarch, sifted

1¾ cup whole milk

6oz (175g) dark chocolate, in pieces

14oz (400g) raspberries

1 Rub together the flour, cocoa, and butter to resemble bread crumbs. Stir in ¼ cup of the sugar. Beat the egg yolk with ½ tsp of the vanilla and add to the flour mixture, bringing it together to form a soft dough. Add a little extra water if it seems too dry. Wrap in plastic wrap and chill for 1 hour.

2 Preheat the oven to 350°F (180°C). Roll the dough out on a floured surface to ⅛in (3mm) thick and use to line the pan, pressing it into the corners and overlapping the edges by ¾in (2cm). Prick the bottom with a fork. Line the dough with wax paper and fill with baking beans. Place on a baking sheet and bake for 20 minutes. Remove the beans and paper, and return to the oven for 5 minutes. Then trim the overlapping crust.

3 Beat ½ cup of the sugar, the eggs, cornstarch, and 1 tsp of the vanilla in a bowl. In a pan, bring the milk and 3½oz (100g) of the chocolate to a boil, whisking all the time. Take off the heat as it starts to bubble. Pour onto the egg mixture, whisking. Return to the cleaned-out pan and bring to a boil over medium heat, whisking. Reduce the heat to its lowest when it thickens and cook for 2–3 minutes, whisking. Pour into a bowl, cover with plastic wrap, and cool.

4 Melt the remaining chocolate in a bowl set over a pan of simmering water, and brush around the inside of the tart crust. Leave to set. Beat the chocolate cream with a wooden spoon and pour into the crust. Arrange the raspberries on top, remove from the pan, and serve dusted with confectioners' sugar.

chocolate decadence with raspberry coulis

A tart raspberry coulis cuts through this deliciously rich cake.

 30-40 MINS PLUS CHILLING   20 MINS

SPECIAL EQUIPMENT ▪ food processor ▪ electric hand mixer ▪ 9in (23cm) round springform pan

SERVES 8

1lb 2oz (500g) dark chocolate

11 tbsp unsalted butter

6 large eggs, separated

2 tbsp granulated sugar

1 tbsp all-purpose flour

1lb 10oz (750g) raspberries, plus more to serve

2-3 tbsp confectioners' sugar

crème fraîche or whipped heavy cream, to serve

1 Preheat the oven to 400°F (200°C). Butter the pan and line with wax paper. Coat the bottom and sides in 2 tbsp flour and tap out the excess. Pulse the chocolate coarsely into pieces in a food processor. Cut the butter into pieces and put in a heatproof bowl with the chocolate. Set over a pan of hot, but not simmering, water. Stir until melted and smooth. Let cool, stirring occasionally.

2 Beat the egg yolks into the cooled chocolate with a wooden spoon. Put the egg whites in a clean bowl and whip until stiff peaks form. Add the sugar and continue beating for about 20 seconds until glossy. Stir the flour into the chocolate mix, then fold in one-third of the egg whites to lighten it. Fold in the rest of the beaten egg whites in 2 batches, then transfer to the pan.

3 Bake for about 20 minutes until crusty on top. Let cool completely in the pan, then set on a wire rack. When cold, chill for 2 hours. Then remove from the pan and peel off the paper.

4 Pulse the raspberries in a food processor. Add confectioners' sugar to taste, pulse briefly, then work the puréed raspberries through a sieve into a bowl to remove all the seeds.

5 Using a serrated knife, cut the cake into 8 wedges. Set 1 wedge in the center of each plate. Ladle a small pool of raspberry coulis onto each plate near the tip of the wedge of cake. Decorate each plate with a few whole raspberries and serve with crème fraîche or whipped heavy cream.

strawberries and cream macarons

This delectable dessert is a creative twist on the traditional English combination of strawberries and cream. The art of macaron making may seem complex, but these little almond-flavored meringues are in fact easy to make, and this recipe is ideal to try at home. Unfilled macaron shells can be stored for up to 3 days.

  30 MINS **18–20 MINS**

SPECIAL EQUIPMENT ▪ food processor with blade attachment ▪ electric hand mixer ▪ piping bag with small, plain nozzle

MAKES 20

2½oz (75g) ground almonds

¾ cup confectioners' sugar

2 large egg whites, at room temperature

⅓ cup granulated sugar

For the filling

¾ cup heavy cream

5–10 very large strawberries, preferably the same diameter as the macarons

1 Preheat the oven to 300°F (150°C). Line 2 baking sheets with parchment paper. Trace 20 x 1¼in (3cm) circles with a pencil onto the paper, allowing 1¼in (3cm) between the circles. Then invert the paper.

2 Pulse the almonds and confectioners' sugar in a food processor. Then put the egg whites in a mixing bowl and beat with an electric hand mixer until stiff peaks form. Add the granulated sugar to the egg whites, a little at a time, beating as you do so and beating well between each addition. At this point the meringue mixture should be very stiff (more so than for a regular meringue). Gently fold in the almond mixture, a spoonful at a time, until just incorporated into the meringue.

3 Transfer the macaron mixture to the piping bag, placing the bag into a bowl to aid you. Using the pencil guidelines, pipe the mix into the center of each circle, holding the bag vertically. Try to keep the disks equal in size and volume; the mix will spread only very slightly. Bang the baking sheets down a few times if there are any peaks left in the center. Bake in the middle of the oven for 18–20 minutes until the surface is set firm. Test one macaron shell: if you prod it with a finger, the top of the macaron should crack. Leave for 15–20 minutes, then transfer to a wire rack and allow to cool completely.

4 Pour the cream into a large mixing bowl and beat with the electric hand mixer until stiff peaks form; a soft whip would ooze out of the sides of the macarons and soften the shells. Transfer the cream into the (cleaned) piping bag used earlier, with the same nozzle. Pipe a blob of the whipped cream onto the flat surfaces of half the macarons.

5 Slice the strawberries widthwise into thin slices so they are the same diameter as the macarons. Put a slice of strawberry on top of the cream filling of each macaron, put the remaining macaron shells on top, and sandwich together gently. The fillings should peek out at the sides. Arrange on a serving plate or cake dish and serve immediately.

tiramisu cherry bombe

It's best to make this decadent treat a day in advance, since a well-chilled bombe is easiest to unmold without breaking.

20 MINS PLUS CHILLING

SPECIAL EQUIPMENT ▪ 1 quart soufflé dish ▪ electric hand mixer

SERVES 8

6oz package sponge fingers

2-3 tbsp brandy

¼ cup of strong coffee, cooled

2 cups heavy cream

2 tbsp cocoa powder, plus more to dust

2 tbsp confectioners' sugar, plus more to dust

10oz (300g) cherries, pitted and halved

3 whole cherries, to decorate

4½oz (125g) dark chocolate, grated

1 Lightly grease the dish and line the bottom with a circle of wax paper. Dip all but 5 sponge fingers in the brandy and then the coffee. Line the base with halved sponge fingers (sugar-side out), then line the sides with whole ones.

2 Put the cream in a bowl and beat with an electric hand mixer until soft peaks form. Transfer half of the cream to another bowl. Stir the cocoa powder and confectioners' sugar into one bowl. Add the pitted cherries to the other.

3 Spoon the separate mixtures into the dish in alternate layers, and top with the remaining sponge fingers, pressing them down well. Chill in the fridge for at least 2 hours.

4 To serve, place a plate on top of the dish and turn the tiramisu upside down. Remove the dish, then dust with cocoa powder and confectioners' sugar, and top with the whole cherries and grated chocolate.

strawberries and cream whoopie pies

Best served immediately, these strawberry-layered whoopie pies make a lovely addition to a traditional afternoon tea.

40 MINS **12 MINS**

SPECIAL EQUIPMENT ▪ electric hand mixer

MAKES 10 PIES

12 tbsp unsalted butter, softened

¾ cup light brown sugar

1 large egg

1 tsp pure vanilla extract

2 cups self-rising flour

⅔ cup cocoa powder

1 tsp baking powder

⅔ cup whole milk

2 tbsp Greek-style yogurt or thick natural yogurt

⅔ cup heavy cream, whipped

9oz (250g) strawberries, hulled and thinly sliced

1 Preheat the oven to 350°F (180°C). Line several baking sheets with wax paper. Put the butter and sugar in a mixing bowl and beat with an electric hand mixer until pale and creamy. Beat in the egg and vanilla. Sift the flour, cocoa, and baking powder into another bowl. Mix these dry ingredients and the milk, alternately, into the creamed mixture, a spoonful at a time. Then fold in the yogurt. Place heaped tablespoons of the batter onto the baking sheets, leaving space for the mix to spread. Dip a spoon in warm water and use the back to smooth over the surface of the pies. Bake for 12 minutes until well risen. Leave for a few minutes, then turn onto a wire rack to cool.

2 Spread the cream onto half the cakes. Top with a layer of strawberries and a second cake. Dust with confectioners' sugar and serve.

variation

black forest whoopie pies

Substitute the strawberries for 8oz (225g) black cherries. Chop half the cherries and fold into the cake batter and bake as normal. To make the filling, purée the remaining cherries and mix with 2 tbsp granulated sugar and 9oz (250g) mascarpone.

raspberry cream meringues

These mini meringues are filled with fresh raspberries and whipped cream; perfect for a summer buffet.

 20 MINS 1 HR

SPECIAL EQUIPMENT ▪ piping bag with plain nozzle ▪ electric hand mixer

MAKES 8-10

4 egg whites, at room temperature

about 1 cup granulated sugar

3½oz (100g) raspberries

1¼ cup heavy cream

1 tbsp confectioners' sugar, sifted

1 Preheat the oven to around 250°F (130°C). Line a baking sheet with wax paper. Weigh the egg whites, then measure out exactly double the weight of sugar to egg whites.

2 Put the egg whites in a mixing bowl and beat with an electric hand mixer until stiff peaks form. Slowly add half the sugar, a couple of tablespoons at a time, beating the mixture in between. Then gently fold in the remaining sugar.

3 Pipe the meringue mixture onto the baking sheet using a plain nozzle (or spoon the mixture onto the sheet) leaving 2in (5cm) gaps in between each. Bake for 1 hour. The meringues are ready when they lift easily from the wax paper and sound hollow when tapped.

4 Put the raspberries in a bowl and crush them with the back of a fork. Pour the heavy cream into a separate bowl and beat with the electric hand mixer until stiff peaks form. Gently fold together the cream, raspberries, and confectioners' sugar. Spread the raspberry mixture onto half the meringues. Top with the remaining meringue halves, gently press together to form meringue sandwiches, and serve.

strawberry-raspberry tart

This heavenly summer tart is nothing more than fresh fruits, whipped cream, and hazelnuts on a pie crust.

 35-40 MINS PLUS CHILLING 30-35 MINS

SPECIAL EQUIPMENT ▪ 9-10in (23-25cm) round springform fluted tart pan ▪ electric hand mixer ▪ food processor

SERVES 6-8

5oz (140g) hazelnuts

melted butter, for brushing

1lb 2oz (500g) store-bought pie dough

1 cup heavy cream

3-4 tbsp confectioners' sugar, plus more to dust

2 tbsp Marsala wine

4½oz (125g) raspberries

(10oz (300g) strawberries, hulled and cut in half or into quarters if large

1 Preheat the oven to 350°F (180°C). Spread the nuts on a baking sheet. Toast for 8-10 minutes until lightly browned. Rub in a clean kitchen towel to remove the skins. Leave to cool, coarsely chop 2oz (60g) of the nuts and reserve, and grind the rest to a powder in a food processor.

2 Brush the tart pan with melted butter. Roll out the dough on a floured work surface to a circle larger than the pan and about ⅛in (3mm)

thick, and use it to line the pan, pressing it into the corners. Chill for at least 15 minutes in the fridge until firm. Preheat the oven to 350°F (180°C) and bake for 30-35 minutes until golden brown and shrinking slightly from the pan. Cool, then remove the sides of the pan.

3 Pour the cream into a mixing bowl and beat with an electric hand mixer until soft peaks form. Add the ground hazelnuts, confectioners' sugar, and Marsala wine. Continue beating until stiff peaks form.

4 Ensuring the crust is cold, spread two-thirds of the Marsala and hazelnut whipped cream evenly over the pie crust, just to the edge. Arrange most of the fruit evenly over the cream. Top with the remaining Marsala cream, then scatter with the remaining fruits and the reserved chopped nuts. Chill in the fridge, then sift over a little confectioners' sugar before serving.

cherry clafoutis

Tart cherries give the most flavor, and contrast very successfully with the sweet batter they are cooked in.

 20–25 MINS 30–35 MINS

SPECIAL EQUIPMENT ▪ 2-quart round baking dish

SERVES 6–8

melted butter, for brushing

1lb 6oz (625g) cherries

⅔ cup all-purpose flour

salt

⅔ cup milk

⅓ cup heavy cream

4 large eggs, plus 2 large egg yolks

½ cup granulated sugar

3 tbsp kirsch

2 tbsp confectioners' sugar

1 Brush the baking dish with melted butter. Sprinkle some granulated sugar into the dish. Turn the dish around and shake it, to coat the bottom and side evenly. Turn the dish upside down and tap the bottom with your knuckles to remove any excess sugar. Spread the cherries in an even layer over the bottom of the dish.

2 Sift the flour and a pinch of salt into a bowl. Make a well in the center with your fingers. Pour the milk and cream into the well at the same time and stir with a whisk, gradually drawing in the flour and whisking constantly, to make a smooth paste and work out any lumps. Add the eggs, egg yolks to add richness, and granulated sugar, and continue whisking to make a smooth batter.

3 Preheat the oven to 350°F (180°C). Just before baking, ladle the batter evenly over the cherries—it should partially cover them—then drizzle the kirsch over the top.

4 Bake the clafoutis in the heated oven for 30–35 minutes, until puffed up and beginning to turn golden brown. If it threatens to scorch before it is cooked, cover with foil. When cooked, the clafoutis will begin to pull away slightly from the sides of the baking dish. Just before serving, sift confectioners' sugar over the top. Serve warm or at room temperature, with a serving of crème fraîche or whipped cream, if desired.

cherry pie

Cherry pie is an all-American favorite that can be made with sweet or sour cherries, or hybrids; whichever you prefer.

 20 MINS PLUS CHILLING 35–45 MINS

SPECIAL EQUIPMENT ▪ shallow 9in (23cm) round pie dish

SERVES 6

7 tbsp butter

⅔ cup lard

1¾ cups all-purpose flour

salt

3 tbsp brown sugar

1lb 10oz (750g) cherries, pitted

1 tbsp cornstarch

½ tsp ground cinnamon

2 drops of almond extract

1 tbsp lemon juice

1 egg white, beaten with 1 tbsp water

milk and granulated sugar, to glaze

1 Preheat the oven to 400°F (200°C) and grease the pie dish. To make the pie dough, rub 5 tbsp of the butter with the lard into the flour with a pinch of salt until the mixture resembles crumbs. Bind the dough with 2–3 tbsp water. Chill in the fridge for 30 minutes.

2 For the filling, dissolve the brown sugar in 1¼ cups water in a heavy-bottomed saucepan, then boil rapidly for 3–4 minutes. Add the cherries to the syrup and bring back to a boil. Drain the cherries and allow to cool.

3 Gently mix together the cherries, cornstarch, cinnamon, almond extract, and lemon juice. Roll out two-thirds of the pie dough on a floured work surface and use it to line the pie dish. Brush the pie dough with the egg white to prevent sogginess. Spoon in the cherry mixture and dot with the remaining butter.

4 Roll out the remaining dough and lay it over the pie. Trim the overhang to about ¾in (2cm). Moisten the edges where they meet, then press together lightly and turn under. Crimp the edge decoratively and make small snips in the top crust so steam can escape. Brush with milk and dust with granulated sugar.

5 Place the pie dish on a baking sheet and bake for 30–40 minutes, or until the crust is golden brown. Cool on a wire rack before serving warm or at room temperature.

summer fruit meringue roulade

Stuffed with seasonal fruits, this delicious roulade makes an ideal dessert for a summer buffet.

 25 MINS 15 MINS ❄ FREEZABLE

SPECIAL EQUIPMENT ▪ 10 x 14in (25 x 35cm) jelly roll pan ▪ electric hand mixer

SERVES 8

5 egg whites

1 cup granulated sugar

½ tsp white wine vinegar

1 tsp cornstarch

½ tsp pure vanilla extract

1 cup heavy cream, whipped

confectioners' sugar, for dusting

9oz (250g) mixed berry fruit, such as strawberries, raspberries, and blueberries, any large fruit chopped

1 Preheat the oven to 350°F (180°C) and line the pan with parchment paper. Beat the egg whites with an electric hand mixer until stiff peaks form, then gradually beat in the granulated sugar. Fold in the vinegar, cornstarch, and vanilla extract. Spread the mixture into the pan and bake for 15 minutes. Remove from the oven and cool.

2 Place the roulade on a piece of parchment paper dusted with confectioners' sugar. Spread the cream over the roulade and then the fruits. Roll the meringue up around the cream filling. Place seam-side down on a serving plate, cover, and chill. Sift confectioners' sugar over the top to serve.

Season's best **cherries**

There are two kinds of cherries ripening now through summer: plump, sweet ones that are either firm and crisp or soft and juicy, delicious raw; and the usually smaller, sour ones, which range from almost sweet to bitter, but taste great when cooked. They vary in color from pale creamy-yellow with a pink blush, to deep red, or purple-black. They are delicious in sauces with duck and game, and are wonderful with chocolate, almonds, brandy, and amaretto.

Native to western Asia, cherries are now cultivated in many countries. The trees are often trained along walls to protect the fruit from birds.

essentials

varieties available

Several varieties of red/black, yellow, or sour ones. Look out for wild, too. Available dried and candied.

buy Best bought with the stem, they should be plump, firm, and shiny with pliant green stems. Avoid if too soft, split, or shriveled.

store Keep (unwashed and on the stem) in an open paper bag in the fridge for a few days.

cook Use in cakes, pies, compôtes, soups, salads, and sweet or savory sauces.

preserve Make jam; preserve in brandy or syrup; pickle or crystallize; freeze.

recipe ideas

Cherry and cassis conserve p132

Cherry clafoutis p128

Cherry pie p128

Cherry strudel p118

Tiramisu cherry bombe p126

Red cherries There are several popular varieties—all sweet, round, and different shades of reddish-purple with a slightly crisp texture. Delicious raw or cooked.

Sour cherries Sour cherries such as Morello have a very short midsummer season. They have clear juice and a fresh, tart flavor. Unpalatable raw, but when cooked and sweetened they taste outstanding.

Sour cherries are bright to dark red in color.

how to pit cherries

Eating raw cherries is a pleasure and no one minds spitting out the pits. However, when cooking for desserts, the flavor and texture is ruined if they are left inside.

1 Wash the cherries and remove the stems. Place a cherry, stem end up, in a pitter chamber and hold over a bowl (to catch the pits and juice).

2 Press the handle down so the blunt spike goes through the cherry, forcing the pit out. Repeat until all the cherries are pitted.

Yellow cherries Golden-skinned, often with a pink blush, there are several varieties, including Rainier, pictured here. They are rich and juicy but bruise easily, so tend to be expensive.

chocolate strawberry shortcakes

These delightful little treats are perfect served with afternoon tea. For a party canapé, cut smaller versions, sandwich with a single slice of strawberry, and serve to your guests.

 15 MINS   10 MINS

SPECIAL EQUIPMENT ▪ 3in (7.5cm) round cookie cutter

SERVES 6

1½ cups all-purpose flour

¼ cup cocoa powder

2 tsp baking powder

4 tbsp butter, softened

¼ cup granulated sugar, plus extra for sweetening

1 large egg

1 tsp pure vanilla extract

6 tbsp milk

8oz (225g) strawberries

⅔ cup heavy cream, whipped

1 Preheat the oven to 450°F (230°C). Sift the flour, cocoa, and baking powder into a bowl. Add the butter and rub in with fingertips. Stir in the sugar. Beat the egg with the vanilla and stir in. Add enough milk to form a soft, but not sticky, dough. Knead gently until smooth.

2 Pat out the dough to about ½in (1cm) thick. Cut into 6 rounds using a 3in (7.5cm) cookie cutter. Place on a lightly greased baking sheet. Bake in the oven for about 10 minutes until risen and the bases sound hollow when tapped. Transfer to a wire rack to cool for 5-10 minutes.

3 Halve 3 strawberries for decoration, leaving the calyces intact, and reserve. Hull and slice the remaining strawberries in half, and sweeten with a little granulated sugar, if necessary.

4 Split the shortcakes and sandwich with the sliced strawberries and some of the cream. Top with the remaining cream and decorate with the reserved, halved strawberries.

zucchini cake

This intriguing alternative to carrot cake makes an unusual use of zucchini when they are at their most plentiful.

 20 MINS   45 MINS   ❄ FREEZABLE

SPECIAL EQUIPMENT ▪ 9in (23cm) round springform cake pan

SERVES 8-10

3½oz (100g) hazelnuts

1 cup sunflower or vegetable oil

3 large eggs

1 tsp pure vanilla extract

1 cup granulated sugar

7oz (200g) zucchini, grated

½ cup self-rising flour

½ cup whole-wheat self-rising flour

pinch of salt

1 tsp cinnamon

grated zest of 1 lemon

1 Preheat the oven to 350°F (180°C). Oil the bottom and sides of the pan and line the bottom with baking parchment. Spread the hazelnuts on a baking tray and cook for 5 minutes until lightly browned. Put the nuts on a clean kitchen towel and rub them to get rid of any excess skin. Roughly chop and set aside.

2 Pour the oil and eggs into a bowl, then add the vanilla and sugar. Whisk the oil mixture until lighter in color and thickened. Squeeze moisture from the zucchini and fold in with the nuts. Sift the flour over the top. Add the salt, cinnamon, and lemon zest, and fold.

3 Pour the batter into the pan. Bake for 45 minutes, or until springy to the touch. Turn out onto a wire rack to cool completely.

rhubarb and strawberry pie

Tart rhubarb and sweet strawberries go into this wonderful pie, which is delicious served warm with ice cream.

 20 MINS PLUS CHILLING   50-55 MINS

SPECIAL EQUIPMENT ▪ 9in (23cm) pie dish

SERVES 6-8

melted butter, for brushing

1lb 2oz (500g) store-bought pie dough

2¼lb (1kg) rhubarb, sliced

grated zest of 1 orange

1 cup granulated sugar

¼ tsp salt

¼ cup all-purpose flour

13oz (375g) strawberries, hulled

1 tbsp unsalted butter, cubed

1 tbsp milk

1 tbsp granulated sugar

1 Brush the pie dish with melted butter. On a lightly floured surface roll out two-thirds of the pie dough into a round, 2in (5cm) larger than the dish. Using the rolling pin, drape the pie dough over the dish and press it into the bottom and sides.

2 Lift the dish and trim the dough at the outer edge, using a table knife. Reserve the trimmings. Chill the pie crust for about 15 minutes until firm.

3 In a bowl, combine the rhubarb, orange zest, sugar, salt, and flour, and stir to mix. Add the strawberries and toss gently. Spoon the fruit into the lined pie dish and dot with butter.

4 Brush the edge of the dough with cold water. Roll out the remaining dough into an 11in (28cm) round and drape over the filling. Trim the top crust to be even with the bottom. Press the edges together to seal.

5 Cut steam vents around the top crust of the pie. Brush with milk and sprinkle with sugar. Chill for about 15 minutes. Preheat the oven to 425°F (220°C). Put a baking sheet in the center of the oven to heat.

6 Bake the pie on the baking sheet for 20 minutes. Reduce the oven temperature to 350°F (180°C). and bake for 30–35 minutes longer, or until the rhubarb is tender.

cherry crumble

Ground almonds in the topping are a classic combination with the cherries in the filling of this crumble. They grow on related species of tree, so perhaps this isn't surprising.

 15 MINS 40 MINS ❄ FREEZABLE

SPECIAL EQUIPMENT ▪ 2-quart baking dish

SERVES 6

9 tbsp butter, cubed

1 cup all-purpose flour

4½oz (125g) ground almonds

¼ cup granulated sugar

For the filling

1¼lb (550g) cherries, pitted (p129)

2 tbsp granulated sugar

2 tbsp apple juice

1 Preheat the oven to 350°F (180°C). In a bowl, rub the butter into the flour and ground almonds with your fingertips until the mixture resembles rough bread crumbs. Stir in the granulated sugar.

2 Place the cherries in the baking dish and scatter on the sugar and apple juice. Sprinkle the crumble mixture over the cherries and bake for 35–40 minutes, or until the crumble is golden brown.

variation

raspberry and peach oat crumble

Prepare in the same way, but for the crumble use ½ cup rolled oats and ½ cup all-purpose flour, instead of all flour. For the filling, use 3 peaches, peeled, pitted, and sliced, and 12oz (350g) raspberries.

cherry and chocolate brownies

Dense chocolate brownies become luxuriously rich with the addition of sweet, ripe cherries. Use a cherry pitter to remove the cherry pits.

 15 MINS 30-35 MINS

SPECIAL EQUIPMENT ▪ 8 x 10in (20 x 25cm) brownie pan

MAKES 16

11 tbsp unsalted butter, cubed

5½oz (150g) dark chocolate, broken into pieces

1 cup light brown muscovado sugar

3 large eggs

1 tsp pure vanilla extract

1¼ cups self-rising flour, sifted

4oz (115g) cherries, pitted

3½oz (100g) dark chocolate chunks

1 Preheat the oven to 350°F (180°C). Grease a brownie pan and line with wax paper. Melt the butter and chocolate in a heatproof bowl over a pan with a small amount of simmering water. Remove from the heat, add the sugar, and stir well to combine thoroughly. Let cool slightly.

2 Mix the eggs and vanilla extract into the melted chocolate mixture. Pour the wet mixture into the sifted flour and fold together, being careful not to overmix. Fold in the cherries and chocolate chunks.

3 Pour the brownie mixture into the pan and bake in the center of the oven for 20–25 minutes. The brownies are ready when the edges are firm, but the middle is still soft to the touch.

4 Let the brownies cool in the pan for 5 minutes. Then turn out, cut into squares, and place on a wire rack to cool completely.

strawberry and cream victoria sandwich

A traditional afternoon tea favorite, instead of buttercream and jam, this version makes the most of luscious strawberries when they are at their juicy peak.

 20 MINS 25 MINS ❄ FREEZABLE

SPECIAL EQUIPMENT ▪ 2 x 8in (20cm) round cake pans ▪ electric hand mixer

SERVES 8

16 tbsp butter, softened

1 cup granulated sugar

4 large eggs, lightly beaten

2 cups self-rising flour

For the strawberry and cream filling

½ cup heavy cream

6oz (175g) strawberries, hulled and sliced

1 Preheat the oven to 350°F (180°C). Line the bottoms of the cake pans with parchment paper. In a bowl, mix the butter and sugar with an electric hand mixer until light and creamy. beat in the eggs a little at a time, adding in a little of the flour if the mixture looks as if it is going to curdle. Sift in the remaining flour and fold in gently with a large plastic spatula. Divide the mixture between the pans and bake for 25 minutes, or until risen and firm to the touch. Leave to cool in the pans for 5 minutes, then transfer to a wire rack to cool completely.

2 To make the filling, place the cream in a bowl and beat with an electric hand mixer until soft peaks form. Spread over one of the cakes, then top with the strawberries. Place the other cake on top, then dust thickly with confectioners' sugar.

cherry jam

This jam has just a hint of brandy to help cut through the sweetness of the cherries.

 15 MINUTES **30-35 MINUTES**

SPECIAL EQUIPMENT ▪ preserving pan ▪ muslin

MAKES APPROX 2¼lb (1kg)

1lb 2oz (500g) dark cherries, pitted, with the pits reserved

juice of 2 lemons

2¼ cups granulated granulated sugar

2 tbsp brandy or cherry brandy

1 Place the cherry pits in a small square of muslin, gather into a small bag, and tie with string. Put the cherries in a preserving pan or a large heavy-bottomed saucepan and pour in 1¼ cups of water. Bring to a boil and simmer for 10–15 minutes, or until the cherries are tender and begin to soften. Discard the pits. Pour in the lemon juice and add the sugar. Heat gently, stirring until the sugar has all dissolved. Bring to a boil and keep at a rolling boil, stirring occasionally, for 10 minutes or until it reaches the setting point.

2 Remove from the heat. Test for a set with a sugar thermometer or a wrinkle test (chill a plate in the fridge before cooking). If you use a thermometer, the temperature must reach 220°F (105°C); the mixture will also thicken around the sides of the pan, boil sluggishly, and the bubbles "plop" rather than froth. Or put 1 tsp jam on the chilled plate, allow to cool for a moment, then push it with a finger. If it leaves a trail and wrinkles slightly, it is set.

3 Stir in the brandy, then ladle into warm sterilized jars, cover with disks of waxed paper, seal, and label. Store in a cool, dark place for up to nine months and refrigerate after opening.

gooseberry and raspberry jam

The flavor of ripe gooseberries and raspberries comes through distinctly in this jam.

 10 MINS **45-50 MINS**

SPECIAL EQUIPMENT ▪ preserving pan

MAKES APPROX 2½lb (1.1kg)

1lb (450g) gooseberries, hulled

grated zest of ½ lemon

8oz (225g) raspberries

3 cups granulated sugar

small pat of butter

1 Put the gooseberries in a preserving pan or a heavy-bottomed saucepan with ⅔ cup of water and the lemon zest. Bring to a boil, reduce the heat, cover, and cook for 30 minutes until soft and pulpy. Add the raspberries and cook just until their juices run.

2 Add the sugar and stir over low heat until it has dissolved. Bring to a boil and boil rapidly for about 15 minutes, or until the setting point is reached. Remove from the heat and test for a set with a sugar thermometer or a wrinkle test (chill a plate in the fridge before cooking). If you use a thermometer, the temperature must reach 220°F (105°C); the mixture will also thicken around the sides of the pan, boil sluggishly, and the bubbles "plop" rather than froth. Or put 1 tsp jam on the chilled plate, allow to cool for a moment, then push it with a finger. If it leaves a trail and wrinkles slightly, it is set.

3 Use a skimmer to skim off the surface scum, then stir in the butter to disperse any residual scum. Ladle into warm sterilized jars, cover with disks of waxed paper, seal, and label. Store in a cool, dark place and refrigerate after opening.

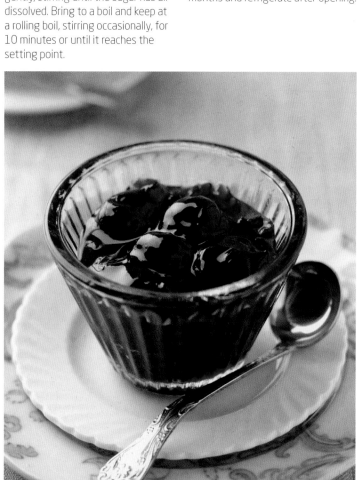

cherry and cassis conserve

It's worth preparing a rich cherry conserve such as this to make the most of the short cherry season. It should be a soft-set texture, so don't overcook it or it will become sticky.

 20 MINS PLUS STANDING **30 MINS**

SPECIAL EQUIPMENT ▪ preserving pan

MAKES APPROX 2½lb (1.1kg)

1lb 5oz (600g) cherries, pitted

1¼ cups granulated sugar

1 tsp pure vanilla extract

juice of 2 lemons

4 tbsp cassis

1 Layer the fruit and sugar in a large bowl, cover, and leave for several hours or overnight at room temperature.

2 Put the fruit, sugar, vanilla, and lemon juice in a preserving pan or a large heavy-bottomed saucepan and cook on low heat for 15 minutes, or until the cherries are soft.

3 Turn up the heat until the conserve reaches a rolling boil and cook for 5–8 minutes, or until it reaches the setting point. Remove from the heat and test for a set with a sugar thermometer or a wrinkle test (chill a plate in the fridge before cooking). If you use a thermometer, the temperature must reach 220°F (105°C); the mixture will also thicken around the sides of the pan, boil sluggishly, and the bubbles "plop" rather than froth. Or put 1 tsp jam on the chilled plate, allow to cool for a moment, then push it with a finger. If it leaves a trail and wrinkles slightly, it is set.

4 Stir in the cassis, ladle into warm sterilized jars, cover with waxed paper disks, seal, and label. Store in a cool, dark place. Refrigerate after opening.

strawberry conserve

This ever-popular soft-set conserve is best made with freshly picked juicy strawberries. Serve with thick cream and scones for a classic summer afternoon tea.

 20 MINUTES PLUS STANDING   20-25 MINUTES

SPECIAL EQUIPMENT ▪ preserving pan ▪ muslin

MAKES APPROX 2¼lb (1kg)

2lb (900g) juicy strawberries, hulled

4 cups granulated sugar

juice of 1 lemon

juice of 1 lime

1 Layer the strawberries and sugar in a large bowl, cover, and leave for several hours or overnight.

2 Pour the fruit and sugar into a preserving pan or a large heavy-bottomed saucepan, and cook over low heat, stirring continuously, until the sugar has dissolved. Then boil gently

for about 5 minutes, just enough for the fruit to soften but not break up. Remove the pan from the heat, cover it loosely with some muslin, and leave the cooked fruit overnight.

3 Remove the muslin, put the pan back on the heat, stir in the lemon and lime juice, and bring to a boil. Boil gently for 5–10 minutes, or until thickened and the setting point is reached, skimming any scum off the surface as needed. Remove from the heat and test for a set with a sugar thermometer or a wrinkle test (chill a plate in the fridge before cooking).

If you use a thermometer, the temperature must reach 220°F (105°C); the mixture will also thicken around the sides of the pan, boil sluggishly, and the bubbles "plop" rather than froth. Or put 1 tsp jam on the chilled plate, allow to cool for a moment, then push it with a finger. If it leaves a trail and wrinkles, it is set.

4 Ladle into warm sterilized jars, cover with disks of waxed paper, seal, and label. Store in a cool, dark place for up to six months. Refrigerate after opening.

variation

three-fruit conserve

Prepare in exactly the same way but use 10oz (300g) strawberries, hulled; 10oz (300g) raspberries, picked over and any calyces removed; and 10oz (300g) red cherries, pitted. Cook and can as before.

rhubarb and rose petal syrup

The rose gives this syrup an aromatic kick. Dilute to taste with still or sparkling water, or drizzle over ice cream.

 20 MINUTES 25-35 MINUTES

SPECIAL EQUIPMENT ▪ jelly bag or muslin-lined sieve

MAKES APPROX 2 CUPS

1lb (450g) pink or red-stemmed rhubarb, cut into short lengths

1½ cups granulated sugar

8 scented pink rose petals

2 tbsp rosewater

1 tsp citric acid

1 Put enough water in a heavy-bottomed saucepan to just cover the base. Add the rhubarb, sugar, and rose petals. Bring to a boil, stir gently, cover, reduce the heat, and simmer for 20–30 minutes until really pulpy, stirring once or twice.

2 Strain the pulp in a jelly bag or a muslin-lined sieve set over a measuring cup or bowl. Press the pulp to extract maximum juice. Return the juice to the pan and bring back to a boil.

3 Remove from the heat and stir the rosewater and citric acid into the strained juice. Pour immediately into warm sterilized bottles using a sterilized funnel. Seal, label, and leave to cool, then store in the fridge for up to 1 month. Shake before use.

bottled watermelon in ginger syrup

Watermelon needs lemon juice added to it to make it suitable for bottling, so don't omit it.

 20 MINS 10 MINS

SPECIAL EQUIPMENT ▪ melon baller ▪ mandoline

MAKES 2 CUPS

1 small watermelon

1in (2.5cm) piece fresh ginger

⅔ cup granulated sugar

2 tbsp lemon juice

1 Cut the melon in half, remove the seeds, and either scoop the flesh into balls using a melon baller, or remove the skin and cut the flesh into bite-sized cubes.

2 Peel the ginger and cut into wafer-thin slices using either a mandoline, the slicer blade on a grater, or a sharp knife.

3 Make the syrup using 1¼ cups water and the ginger, sugar, and lemon juice. Add the melon and boil for 2 minutes. Place the warm sterilized jars on a wooden board or cloth. Using a slotted spoon, pack the fruit tightly into the jars without squashing it, leaving ½in(1cm) of space at the top. Fill the jars to the brim with the hot syrup, then tap the jars lightly on a board to remove air bubbles. Add extra syrup if needed to cover the fruit completely. Fit the rubber band or metal lid seal and clamp on the lid. If using screw-band jars, loosen by a quarter of a turn.

4 Preheat the oven to 300°F (150°C), place the jars on a baking sheet lined with newspaper, and heat-process in the center of the oven for 40–50 minutes. Tighten the lids or put on the screw-band, leave for 24 hours, then test for a seal. (If using preserving jars with metal lids, you will know immediately or soon after processing if you have a seal, since the lid becomes slightly concave and is firm with no "give" when pressed. You may even hear a "pop" as the seal forms.) Store in a cool, dark place, and then refrigerate after opening.

raspberry and vanilla syrup

Combine this syrup with milk, stir well, and top with raspberry ice cream for a delicious milkshake.

 15 MINUTES 20 MINUTES

SPECIAL EQUIPMENT ▪ muslin-lined sieve

MAKES APPROX 2 CUPS

1lb (450g) ripe raspberries

1 vanilla bean, split

1 cup granulated sugar

1 tsp citric acid

1 Put the raspberries and ¾ cup water in a saucepan. Heat over low heat until the juices run. Crush the fruit with a potato masher or the back of a large spoon.

2 When the fruit is really soft, strain through a muslin-lined sieve (or use a new clean disposable kitchen towel) into a clean bowl. Squeeze or press to extract the maximum juice. Return the juice to the rinsed-out pan. Add the vanilla bean to the pan with the sugar. Stir, then heat gently, without stirring, until the sugar dissolves. Bring to a boil and boil for 5 minutes, or until syrupy. Remove from the heat, discard the vanilla bean, and stir in the citric acid.

3 Pour immediately into warm sterilized bottles using a sterilized funnel. Seal, label, and leave to cool, then store in the fridge for up to two months. Shake before use.

simple garlic confit

This is a heavenly way to eat and preserve newly harvested garlic. Simply squeeze the cloves from their skins and use for garlic toast, in mashed potato, roast meats, and other dishes.

 1 MIN   45 MINS–1 HOUR

MAKES APPROX 8oz (225g)

2 large plump garlic bulbs, with the cloves separated

⅓–⅔ cup extra virgin olive oil, plus extra as needed

1 sprig of thyme

1 bay leaf

sea salt

2 tbsp balsamic or sherry vinegar

1 Pack the unpeeled cloves of garlic into a small snug-fitting ovenproof dish, pour in enough olive oil to cover the garlic, tuck in the thyme and bay leaf, and sprinkle with salt.

2 Cook in a low oven at 300°F (150°C) for 45–60 minutes or until the garlic cloves are soft (this will depend on the size of the cloves).

3 To store, allow to cool, transfer the cooked cloves to a sterilized jar, and add the vinegar, stirring to ensure all the cloves are well coated. Fill the jar with the garlic-infused oil they were cooked in, adding extra fresh oil if needed. Store in the fridge, ensuring that the cloves are always completely covered in oil, and use within 1 month.

asparagus in oil

Since the season for asparagus is so short, it makes sense to preserve them in oil for a little longer. Asparagus has a unique flavor that is greatly intensified when grilled.

 15 MINS   15 MINS

MAKES APPROX 2 CUPS

12oz (350g) medium asparagus spears, trimmed to the height of your jar

¼ cup extra virgin olive oil, plus extra if needed for coating and topping

sea salt and freshly ground black pepper

juice of 2 lemons in a small bowl

1 Smother the asparagus in 3 tbsp olive oil, using your hands to coat them, and season them well with salt and pepper.

2 Heat a grill pan until hot, then add the asparagus spears in batches and turn occasionally. Cook each batch for about 5 minutes, or until they begin to char slightly and soften but are not limp.

3 Toss the asparagus spears in the lemon juice and let cool in the juice. Then stand them upright in a sterilized jar, tips upright. Pack them in tightly and add oil to cover them completely. Seal, label, and store in the fridge. Once opened, keep refrigerated, add oil if necessary so the asparagus spears are always covered, and use within 3 weeks.

variation

grilled zucchini in oil

Replace the asparagus spears with 1lb (450g) baby zucchini, sliced thinly lengthwise. Put the slices in a large bowl with the olive oil and seasoning and toss them together with your hands until the slices are evenly covered. Then follow step 2, cooking the zucchini for about 3 minutes on each side, or until golden. Layer the slices in a sterilized jar in step 3 and press them down lightly to remove any air bubbles once you have covered them in oil.

rollmops

Pickling herrings in vinegar in effect "cooks" the fish and dissolves tiny bones. Make the flavorings as mild or sharp as you want (for a mild pickle, use half the quantity of vinegar).

 20–25 MINS PLUS SALTING AND MATURING

SPECIAL EQUIPMENT ▪ preserving jar or crock ▪ toothpicks

MAKES APPROX 2½ CUPS

6–8 very fresh herring fillets, with any visible bones removed

¼ cup sea salt per 2 cups cold water

2 cups hard cider or white wine vinegar

1 tbsp light brown sugar

6 black peppercorns

6 allspice berries

1 mace blade

3 bay leaves

1 dried chilli

1 red onion, peeled, halved, and finely sliced

6–8 pickled gherkins

1 Put the fillets in a glass dish. Dissolve the sea salt in the water, pour the brine over the fish, and leave to soak for 2–3 hours. Then drain and pat dry with paper towels.

2 Put the vinegar, sugar, and spices into a stainless-steel saucepan, bring slowly to a boil, simmer for 1–2 minutes, and then set the mixture aside to cool.

3 Lay the fillets skin-side down on a clean cutting board. Place a slice of onion and gherkin at the tail end of each and roll them up. Secure each rollmop with a toothpick. Pack into a snug-fitting sterilized preserving jar or crock. Pour the cold, spiced vinegar and its spices over the rollmops so they are completely submerged.

4 Add vinegar if needed. Seal and store in the fridge for 3–4 days to mature. Always keep the fish submerged in vinegar.

high summer

at their best

vegetables arugula ▪ chiles ▪ cucumbers ▪ eggplant ▪ fennel ▪ green beans ▪ kohlrabi ▪ lettuce ▪ lima beans ▪ okra ▪ peas ▪ peppers ▪ radishes ▪ romano beans ▪ snow peas ▪ squash blossoms ▪ sugarsnap peas ▪ summer squash ▪ sweet corn ▪ tomatoes ▪ yellow wax beans ▪ zucchini

fruit apricots ▪ apriums ▪ blackberries ▪ blueberries ▪ cantaloupe melons ▪ charentais melons ▪ cherries ▪ damson plums ▪ fresh figs ▪ galia melons ▪ gooseberries ▪ greengage plums ▪ honeydew melons ▪ huckleberries ▪ nectarines ▪ peaches ▪ pluots ▪ raspberries ▪ rhubarb ▪ strawberries ▪ watermelon

seafood Albacore tuna ▪ brown trout ▪ cod ▪ flounder ▪ gulf shrimp ▪ haddock ▪ hake ▪ halibut ▪ King salmon ▪ lobster ▪ mackerel ▪ mussels ▪ ocean perch ▪ Pacific smelt ▪ rockfish ▪ rock shrimp ▪ salmon (chum, coho, sockeye) ▪ sea scallops ▪ shark (blue, bonito, mako, thresher) ▪ snapper ▪ squid ▪ swordfish ▪ rainbow trout ▪ walleye

meat, poultry, game beef ▪ chicken ▪ duck (farmed) ▪ pork ▪ quail (farmed) ▪ rabbit (wild and farmed) ▪ turkey ▪ veal ▪ venison (farmed) ▪ wild boar (farmed)

also available

vegetables beets ▪ cabbages ▪ broccoli ▪ carrots ▪ cauliflower ▪ celery ▪ garlic ▪ mushrooms (cultivated) ▪ new potatoes ▪ onions ▪ scallions ▪ spinach ▪ swiss chard **fruit** apples **seafood** clams ▪ crawfish ▪ octopus

high summer recipe planner

Ⓥ suitable for vegetarians

Spicy chicken balls with chile and ginger sauce p143

Roasted red bell pepper tart p153

Tomato and harissa tart p145

Egg and fennel potato salad p200

Vegetables

Arugula

Arugula, almond, and blue cheese pesto
p200 Ⓥ
Arugula and Parmesan soup p156 Ⓥ
Arugula and tomato pasta salad p204 Ⓥ
Arugula, green bean, and pesto salad
p204 Ⓥ
Arugula pesto p200 Ⓥ
Arugula, ricotta cheese, and black olive
dip p158 Ⓥ
Goat cheese, beets, and pistachios
p151 Ⓥ
Green bean, red onion, and Camembert
salad p151 Ⓥ
Spaghetti with cherry tomato, arugula,
and black olive sauce p158 Ⓥ
Summer vegetable bread salad p195 Ⓥ
Tomato, red onion, and mozzarella salad
p151 Ⓥ

Beets

Goat cheese, beets, and pistachios
p151 Ⓥ
Spiced beet pickle p245 Ⓥ
Tomato borscht p159 Ⓥ

Carrot

Gado gado p181 Ⓥ
Malaysian-style pickled vegetables
p205 Ⓥ
Mixed vegetable pickle p237 Ⓥ

Cauliflower

Malaysian-style pickled vegetables
p205 Ⓥ
Mixed vegetable pickle p237 Ⓥ

Chile

Baked eggs with tomatoes and bell
peppers p170 Ⓥ
Caribbean stew with allspice and ginger
p173
Chicken, eggplant, and tomato tagine
p184
Chicken stir-fried with scallion, basil, and
lemongrass p175
Chile beef and bean soup p142
Chile cornbread p203 Ⓥ
Chipotle chicken p184
Crispy beef and vegetables p182
Cucumber-chile salad p201 Ⓥ

Cucumber, chile, and roasted pepper
salad p201 Ⓥ
Escabeche p152
Fish tagine p191
Fiery pepper noodles p173 Ⓥ
Gado gado p181 Ⓥ
Greek stuffed tomatoes p173
Hot chile sauce p198 Ⓥ
Lemongrass chicken p180
Malaysian-style pickled vegetables
p205 Ⓥ
Mini chicken burgers with tomato and
chile sauce p142
Mixed vegetable pickle p237 Ⓥ
Paneer and sweet pepper curry p181 Ⓥ
Pan-fried salmon with coconut, chile,
and lime p176
Pan-fried scallops with chile, ginger, and
an anchovy dressing p165
Potato and pea curry p187 Ⓥ
Salmon jungle curry p191
Sardines with sweet chile and chive
sauce p160
Scallops with sweet chile sauce p160
Spiced haddock with coconut, chile,
and lime p176
Spicy chicken balls with chile and
ginger sauce p143
Spicy stuffed eggplants with feta cheese
p187 Ⓥ
Tomato and chile jam p232 Ⓥ
Tortilla bean salad p202 Ⓥ
Whipped yogurt soup with sautéed
zucchini p146 Ⓥ
Vietnamese beef soup p174

Cucumber

Cucumber-chile salad p201 Ⓥ
Cucumber, chile, and roasted bell
pepper salad p201 Ⓥ
Cucumber and dill soup p148 Ⓥ
Cucumber pickle p244 Ⓥ
Gado gado p181 Ⓥ
Greek salad p195 Ⓥ
Hot cucumber and tarragon soup p162 Ⓥ
Lemongrass chicken p180
Malaysian-style pickled vegetables
p205 Ⓥ
Marinated cucumber and dill salad
p201 Ⓥ

Pickled gherkins p236 Ⓥ
Pickled gherkins with spring onions
p236 Ⓥ
Smoked chicken with basil mayonnaise
on cucumber rounds p162
Smoked trout with horseradish
mayonnaise on cucumber rounds p162
Summer vegetable bread salad
p195 Ⓥ
Tabbouleh with cacik p199 Ⓥ
Tabbouleh with grilled eggplant dip
p199 Ⓥ
Tomato and cucumber pilaf p205 Ⓥ

Eggplant

Eggplant and chickpea pâté p164 Ⓥ
Eggplant, potato, and feta cheese frittata
p185 Ⓥ
Eggplants stuffed with tomato rice
p187 Ⓥ
Baba ganoush p164 Ⓥ
Chicken, eggplant, and tomato tagine
p184
Chorizo with eggplant and zucchini
p160
Fish with zucchini, eggplants, and
tomatoes p168
Grilled eggplant with spiced tomato
sauce p194 Ⓥ
Grilled Mediterranean vegetables
p202 Ⓥ
Hot-spiced eggplant chutney p244 Ⓥ
Moroccan-style crepes p164 Ⓥ
Pasta with eggplant sauce p187 Ⓥ

Roasted tomato and eggplant soup
p148 Ⓥ
Roasted sardines with vegetable medley
p168
Spicy stuffed eggplants with feta cheese
p187 Ⓥ
Stuffed eggplant rolls with salsa p165 Ⓥ
Summer frittata with ratatouille p185 Ⓥ
Tabbouleh with grilled eggplant dip
p199 Ⓥ

Fennel

Chicken roasted with fennel and lemon
p183
Egg and fennel potato salad p200 Ⓥ
Smoked trout, fennel, and mascarpone
crostini p158

Green beans

Arugula, green bean, and pesto salad
p204 Ⓥ
Gado gado p181 Ⓥ
German chicken broth p154
Green bean and zucchini chutney
p245 Ⓥ
Green bean, red onion, and Camembert
salad p151 Ⓥ
Malaysian-style pickled vegetables
p205 Ⓥ
Spiced haddock with coconut, chile,
and lime p176

Kohlrabi

German chicken broth p154
Kohlrabi soup with pesto p152 Ⓥ

Scallop and sweet corn chowder p157

Baked eggs with tomatoes and bell peppers p170

Gado gado p181

Mediterranean burgers p189

Paneer and sweet pepper curry p181

high summer recipe planner continued

ⓥ suitable for vegetarians

Génoise cake with raspberries and cream p231

Blueberry-ripple cheesecake p226

Figs with cassis mascarpone p220

Apricots with amaretti cookies and mascarpone p210

Cold raspberry soufflés p210

Raspberry and almond bake p213

Pizza with tomatoes, olives, and capers **p193** ⓥ
Pork and fennel sausages with fresh tomato salsa **p144**
Roast lamb with cherry tomatoes and new potatoes **p188**
Roasted sardines with vegetable medley **p168**
Roasted tomato and eggplant soup **p148** ⓥ
Roasted tomato soup **p148** ⓥ
Sausage and tomato pie **p192**
Salted cod and red pepper dip **p146**
Spaghetti with cherry tomato, arugula, and black olive sauce **p158** ⓥ
Spanish bell pepper and tomato soup **p166** ⓥ
Spiced pork, apricot, and tomato skewers **p145**
Spicy sausage and tomato skewers **p145**
Stuffed eggplant rolls with salsa **p165** ⓥ
Stuffed lamb, Greek style **p182**
Summer frittata with ratatouille **p185** ⓥ
Summer vegetable bread salad **p195** ⓥ
Sweet corn fritters with tomato salsa **p167** ⓥ
Tabbouleh with cacik **p199** ⓥ
Tabbouleh with grilled eggplant dip **p199** ⓥ
Tomato and chile jam **p232** ⓥ
Tomato and cucumber pilaf **p205** ⓥ
Tomato and harissa tart **p145** ⓥ
Tomato and roasted bell pepper chutney **p233** ⓥ

Tomato and tarragon pilaf **p205** ⓥ
Tomato borscht **p159** ⓥ
Tomato, red onion, and mozzarella salad **p151** ⓥ
Tomato salad with butter beans and lime **p198** ⓥ
White fish with Swiss chard, harissa, tomatoes, and pumpkin seeds **p169**

Zucchini
Chicken and zucchini mousse **p163**
Chorizo with eggplant and zucchini **p160**
Crepes with zucchini and Emmental **p147** ⓥ
Crepes with zucchini, tomatoes, and mozzarella **p147** ⓥ
Fiery pepper noodles **p173** ⓥ
Fish with zucchini, eggplants, and tomatoes **p168**
Green bean and zucchini chutney **p245** ⓥ
Grilled Mediterranean vegetables **p202** ⓥ
Mediterranean sweet corn soup **p154** ⓥ
Roasted sardines with vegetable medley **p168**
Summer frittata with ratatouille **p185** ⓥ
Whipped yogurt soup with sautéed zucchini **p146** ⓥ
Zucchini and hazelnut bread **p202** ⓥ
Zucchini and potato soup **p146** ⓥ
Zucchini tian **p204** ⓥ

Fruit

Apricot
Apricots and almonds in amaretto **p237** ⓥ
Apricot and champagne conserve **p237** ⓥ
Apricot clafoutis **p224** ⓥ
Apricot conserve **p238** ⓥ
Apricot crumble shortbread **p230** ⓥ
Apricot friands **p218** ⓥ
Apricot meringue roulade **p208** ⓥ
Apricot pastries **p208** ⓥ
Apricots with amaretti cookies and mascarpone **p210** ⓥ
Rumtopf **p242** ⓥ
Spiced pork, apricot, and tomato skewers **p145**

Blackberries
Berry syrup **p234** ⓥ
Boozy berries with mint and elderflower cream **p220** ⓥ
Chilled rice pudding with warm berry sauce **p227** ⓥ
Gratin of fresh berries with sabayon **p230** ⓥ
Mixed berries with white chocolate sauce **p226** ⓥ
Mixed berry ice cream cake **p228** ⓥ
Mixed berries with white chocolate sauce **p226** ⓥ

Black currants
Black currant and rosemary cheesecake **p212** ⓥ
Chilled rice pudding with warm berry sauce **p227** ⓥ

Blueberries
Berry friands **p218** ⓥ
Blueberry and almond bake **p213** ⓥ
Blueberry and raspberry freezer jam **p243** ⓥ
Blueberry muffins **p218** ⓥ
Blueberry pancakes **p211** ⓥ
Blueberry-ripple cheesecake **p226** ⓥ
Blueberry upside-down cake **p206** ⓥ
Boozy berries with mint and elderflower cream **p220** ⓥ
Chilled rice pudding with warm berry sauce **p227** ⓥ
Gratin of fresh berries with sabayon **p230** ⓥ
Mixed berries with white chocolate sauce **p226** ⓥ
Mixed berry crepes with white chocolate sauce **p226** ⓥ
Mixed berry jam **p239** ⓥ

Currants
Boozy berries with mint and elderflower cream **p220** ⓥ
Rumtopf **p242** ⓥ

Cherries
Cherries in brandy **p242** ⓥ
Cherry and almond cake **p213** ⓥ
Cherry and white chocolate trifle **p212** ⓥ
Cherry cheesecake **p231**
Rumtopf **p242** ⓥ
Sweet and sour duck with cherries **p190**
Sweet and sour nectarine and cherry relish **p242** ⓥ

Damson plums
Damson cheese **p232** ⓥ

Figs
Figs with cassis mascarpone **p220** ⓥ
Figs and raspberries with framboise **p220** ⓥ
Fresh figs in honey syrup **p244** ⓥ

Gooseberries
Gooseberry and strawberry summer fool **p228** ⓥ
Gooseberry fool with elderflower **p228** ⓥ

Grapes
Chilled melon and ginger soup **p143** ⓥ
Rumtopf **p242** ⓥ

Greengage plums
Greengage wine **p243** ⓥ

Melon
Chilled melon and ginger soup **p143** ⓥ
Melon and raspberry baskets with ginger Chantilly **p224** ⓥ
Melon and tomato salad **p194** ⓥ
Minted melon with vodka **p221** ⓥ
Triple melon cocktail **p221** ⓥ

Nectarine
Peach and nectarine puff pastry tart **p215** ⓥ
Nectarine meringue melba **p218** ⓥ
Sweet and sour nectarine and cherry relish **p242** ⓥ

Peach
Amaretti, peaches, and mascarpone **p210** ⓥ
Baked peaches with amaretti **p214** ⓥ
Creamy rice pudding with peaches **p215** ⓥ
Peach and nectarine puff pastry tart **p215** ⓥ
Peach and raspberry conserve **p243** ⓥ
Peach crème brûlée **p206** ⓥ
Peaches in syrup **p238** ⓥ
Peaches with meringue and raspberry sauce **p218** ⓥ
Peach melba ice cream **p221** ⓥ
Peach pie **p214** ⓥ
Peach tarte tatin **p219** ⓥ
Rumtopf **p242** ⓥ

Plums
Bavarian plum tart **p225** ⓥ
Plum and marzipan clafoutis **p212** ⓥ
Plum and rum jam **p234** ⓥ
Plum crumble shortbread **p230** ⓥ
Plum wine **p243** ⓥ
Plums in brandy **p234** ⓥ
Rumtopf **p242** ⓥ

Raspberries
Almond and raspberry lattice tart **p207** ⓥ
Berry friands **p218** ⓥ
Blueberry and raspberry freezer jam **p243** ⓥ
Boozy berries with mint and elderflower cream **p220** ⓥ
Chilled rice pudding with warm berry sauce **p227** ⓥ
Cold raspberry soufflés **p210** ⓥ
Double chocolate raspberry tart **p206** ⓥ
Figs and raspberries with framboise **p220** ⓥ
Génoise cake with raspberries and cream **p231** ⓥ
Gratin of fresh berries with sabayon **p230** ⓥ
Melon and raspberry baskets with ginger Chantilly **p224** ⓥ
Mixed berries with white chocolate sauce **p226** ⓥ
Mixed berry crepes with white chocolate sauce **p226** ⓥ
Mixed berry ice cream cake **p228** ⓥ
Mixed berry jam **p239** ⓥ
Peach and raspberry conserve **p243** ⓥ
Peaches with meringue and raspberry sauce **p218** ⓥ
Peach melba ice cream **p221** ⓥ
Raspberry and almond bake **p213** ⓥ
Raspberry and mint conserve **p242** ⓥ
Raspberry and white chocolate trifle **p212** ⓥ
Raspberry crème brûlée **p206** ⓥ
Raspberry jam **p239** ⓥ
Raspberry muffins **p218** ⓥ
Rumtopf **p242** ⓥ
Swedish crepe stack cake **p227** ⓥ

Strawberries
Boozy berries with mint and elderflower cream **p220** ⓥ
Boozy wild strawberries with elderflower cream **p220** ⓥ
Gooseberry and strawberry summer fool **p228** ⓥ
Gratin of fresh berries with sabayon **p230** ⓥ
Knickerbocker glory **p228** ⓥ
Strawberry shortcakes **p211** ⓥ
Strawberry tart **p229** ⓥ
Mixed berries with white chocolate sauce **p226** ⓥ
Mixed berry ice cream cake **p228** ⓥ
Mixed berry jam **p239** ⓥ

Mixed berry pancakes with white chocolate sauce **p226** ⓥ
Rumtopf **p242** ⓥ

Watermelon
Watermelon salad with feta and pumpkin seeds **p159** ⓥ
Minted melon with vodka **p221** ⓥ
Watermelon and lime sorbet **p224** ⓥ
Triple melon cocktail **p221** ⓥ

Seafood

Cod
Escabeche **p152**
White fish with spinach and pine nuts **p169**
White fish with Swiss chard, harissa, tomatoes, and pumpkin seeds **p169**

Dover sole
Sole bonne femme **p193**

Haddock
Fish with tomatoes, potatoes, and onions **p176**
Fish with zucchini, eggplants, and tomatoes **p168**
Spiced haddock with coconut, chile, and lime **p176**
White fish with spinach and pine nuts **p169**
White fish with Swiss chard, harissa, tomatoes, and pumpkin seeds **p169**

Halibut
Oriental halibut en papillote **p189**

Herring
Quick salted herrings **p245**

Lobster
Brandied lobster chowder **p156**

Pollock
Fish with zucchini, eggplants, and tomatoes **p168**
White fish with spinach and pine nuts **p169**
White fish with Swiss chard, harissa, tomatoes, and pumpkin seeds **p169**

Salmon
Pan-fried salmon with coconut, chile, and lime **p176**
Salmon jungle curry **p191**

Sardines
Butterflied sardines stuffed with tomatoes and capers **p168**
Roasted sardines with vegetable medley **p168**
Sardines with sweet chile and chive sauce **p160**

Scallops
Pan-fried scallops with chile, ginger, and an anchovy dressing **p165**
Scallop and sweet corn chowder **p157**
Scallops with sweet chile sauce **p160**

Sea bass
Fish tagine **p191**
Fish with tomatoes, potatoes, and onions **p176**
Sea bass in a salt crust **p192**
Sea bass with herb butter sauce **p175**

Sole bonne femme p193

Strawberry shortcakes p211

Peach and nectarine puff pastry tart p215

Fish with zucchini, eggplants, and tomatoes p168

Scallops with sweet chile sauce p160

chile beef and bean soup

Ideal for bringing a little heat to a cooler summer evening, this hearty soup makes the most of bell peppers, spicy chiles, and fragrant summer parsley.

 20 MINS   **2 HRS**   ❄ **FREEZABLE**

SERVES 8

2 tbsp olive oil

2 onions, finely chopped

salt and freshly ground black pepper

2 red bell peppers, seeded and finely chopped

2–3 red or jalapeño chiles, seeded and finely chopped

1¼lb (550g) beef stew meat, cut into 2.5cm (1in) cubes

1 tbsp all-purpose flour

8 cups hot beef stock

2 x 14oz (400g) cans kidney beans, drained, rinsed, and drained again

handful of flat-leaf parsley, finely chopped, to serve

1 Heat the oil in a large heavy-bottomed pan, add the onions, and cook over low heat for 6–8 minutes, or until soft and translucent. Season with salt and pepper, then stir in the bell peppers and chiles and cook for 5 minutes. Add the meat and cook, stirring frequently, for 5–10 minutes, or until beginning to brown all over.

2 Sprinkle in the flour, stir well, and cook for 2 minutes. Add the stock, bring to a boil, then cover with a lid and reduce to simmer. Cook for 1½ hours, or until the meat is tender. Add the kidney beans and cook for 10 minutes more, then season to taste with salt and pepper. Stir in the parsley and serve.

mini chicken burgers with tomato and chile sauce

These mini chicken patties are infused with fragrant Middle Eastern spices and are served elegantly on a bed of bell peppers. They are complemented by a refreshing tomato sauce.

 30 MINS PLUS CHILLING   **30 MINS**

SPECIAL EQUIPMENT ■ food processor

SERVES 12

1¾lb (800g) skinless, boneless chicken breast, chopped into pieces

1 tbsp finely chopped flat-leaf parsley

1 tsp finely sliced sage leaves

2 garlic cloves, 1 finely chopped, 1 peeled but left whole

3½oz (100g) dates, chopped

1¾oz (50g) hazelnuts, coarsely chopped

2 tsp Middle Eastern spice mix (dukkah)

2 large eggs

2 tbsp olive oil, plus extra for brushing

¾ cup fresh bread crumbs

salt and freshly ground black pepper

14oz (400g) jar tomato sauce

1 red or jalapeño chile, finely chopped (optional)

handful of basil leaves, torn

baguette, cut into 12 thick slices

2 yellow bell peppers, grilled, seeded, and sliced

2 red bell peppers, grilled, seeded, and sliced

1 Grind the chicken in a food processor for 10–15 seconds; be careful not to blend into a paste. Transfer to a bowl and add the herbs, chopped garlic, dates, hazelnuts, dukkah, eggs, olive oil, and bread crumbs. Mix thoroughly and season with salt and pepper. Cover with plastic wrap and chill for about 1 hour.

2 Preheat the broiler. Shape the chilled chicken mixture into 12 burger-style portions, then brush with a little oil. Broil the chicken burgers for 6–8 minutes on each side until cooked through. Set aside for 15 minutes in a warm place.

3 Warm the tomato sauce, adding the chile and basil. Brush the baguette slices with some oil and toast on both sides under the broiler. Rub each slice with the whole garlic clove. To serve, layer the broiled yellow and red bell peppers on each bread slice, then top with a burger and spoon over a little sauce.

chilled melon and ginger soup

This is a soup to make in a hurry. All that's needed to bring out its fruity flavor is a seriously good chill—and a perfectly ripe melon.

 15 MINS PLUS CHILLING   ❄ **FREEZABLE**

SPECIAL EQUIPMENT ■ blender or food processor

SERVES 4

1 ripe Galia melon, peeled and seeded

1in (2.5cm) piece of fresh ginger, peeled

1 tsp fennel seeds

7oz (200g) white seedless grapes

grated zest and juice of 1 lime

1 tsp dried mint

¼ cup Greek-style yogurt, beaten

salt and freshly ground black pepper

For the garnish

2 tbsp mint leaves

pinch of sugar

1oz (25g) crystallized ginger, finely chopped

1 Coarsely chop three-quarters of the melon flesh into bite-sized chunks. Finely chop the remainder and set aside. Grate the ginger and squeeze any juice over the melon chunks. Discard the leftover ginger.

2 Heat a heavy-bottomed frying pan over low heat and lightly toast the fennel seeds for about 30 seconds, until you smell an aniseedlike aroma. Grind the seeds to a coarse powder using a mortar and pestle.

3 Put the ground fennel seeds into a blender or food processor with the coarsely chopped melon and ginger juice. Add the grapes, lime juice and zest, and dried mint. Pulse until smooth and push through a sieve to remove the skins.

4 Stir in the yogurt, season, and chill thoroughly—it's best to half-freeze this soup, then blend it well just before serving. Spoon into bowls, adding a small pile of the reserved melon to each one. Shred the fresh mint, mix with the sugar and crystallized ginger, and scatter over the soup. Serve immediately.

spicy chicken balls with chile and ginger sauce

Crisp, spicy chicken enriched with honey, dried apricots, and macadamia nuts is well-matched with a zesty sauce in which the chile is given an extra kick by the addition of fresh lime.

🥢 **20 MINS**   🍲 **30 MINS**

SPECIAL EQUIPMENT ■ food processor

SERVES 8

1¾oz (50g) dried apricots

1 tbsp honey

3 tbsp brandy

4 skinless, boneless chicken breasts, 7oz (200g) each, coarsely chopped

1¾oz (50g) macadamia nuts, chopped

2oz (60g) cooked and cooled rice

2 garlic cloves, grated or finely chopped

2 tbsp finely chopped sage leaves

1 tbsp finely chopped basil leaves

1 tbsp finely chopped flat-leaf parsley

2 small red or jalapeño chiles, seeded and chopped

1 large egg

salt and freshly ground black pepper

light olive oil, for deep-frying

cress, to serve

For the sauce

juice of 4 limes

2 small red or jalapeño chiles, seeded and chopped

2 tbsp olive oil

1 tbsp finely chopped fresh ginger

1 scallion, finely sliced

1 Put the apricots, honey, and brandy in a small pan. Simmer for about 15 minutes until the apricots soften and the liquid has been absorbed. Leave to cool.

2 Grind the chicken in a food processor for 15–20 seconds; be careful not to turn it into a paste. Transfer to a bowl and add the cooled apricots, nuts, rice, garlic, herbs, chiles, and egg. Season with salt and pepper and mix well. Using wet hands, shape the mixture into walnut-sized balls; you should end up with 36–40.

3 Heat enough oil for deep-frying over medium-high heat. Cooking in batches, deep-fry the balls for about 15 minutes, or until golden brown. Drain on paper towels and keep warm.

4 To make the sauce, put all the sauce ingredients in a bowl and mix well. Arrange the spicy chicken balls on a platter, pour over the sauce, and scatter some cress over the top. Serve immediately.

chilled tomato and red bell pepper soup

A variation on the Spanish classic gazpacho, this nutritious soup retains all the vitamins and vivid color from the raw vegetables. Chopped boiled egg is also good as a topping.

 15 MINS

SPECIAL EQUIPMENT • blender or food processor

SERVES 4

3 slices white bread, crusts removed

1 garlic clove, coarsely chopped

1 tbsp sherry vinegar or red wine vinegar

1 tbsp olive oil

6 very ripe tomatoes, coarsely chopped

2 red bell peppers, halved, seeded, and coarsely chopped

1 red chile, seeded and coarsely chopped

salt and freshly ground black pepper

For the garnish

1 tomato, finely cubed

¼ cucumber, finely cubed

1 scallion, finely chopped

1 Using the blender or food processor, purée the bread, garlic, and vinegar until smooth. With the motor running, gradually pour in the oil and continue to purée until incorporated. Add the tomatoes, bell peppers, and chile, and blend until well combined.

2 Keep the motor running and slowly add about 2 cups ice water, checking the consistency of the soup as you go—it should be like a gazpacho. Taste and season with a pinch of salt and some pepper. Add a dash of vinegar if the soup needs it. Chill until required.

3 Make the garnish just before serving. Put the tomato, cucumber, and scallion in a small bowl and stir to combine. Serve the soup well chilled, topped with the garnish.

pork and fennel sausages with fresh tomato salsa

If you feel like having a barbecue, then this is the recipe to use. The salsa is a summery mix of tomatoes and olives and is a refreshing sauce to serve alongside the herb sausages.

 10 MINS PLUS MARINATING   15 MINS

SERVES 4

4 Italian-style pork and fennel sausages

3 tbsp olive oil

2 garlic cloves, grated or finely chopped

4 sprigs of dill

salt and freshly ground black pepper

4 thick slices of Italian-style crusty ciabatta, toasted to serve

For the tomato salsa

4 ripe tomatoes, seeded and cubed

4oz (115g) kalamata olives, pitted and cubed

large handful of basil leaves, torn

2 tbsp extra virgin olive oil

1 Put the sausages in a shallow glass or ceramic dish. Add the oil, garlic, and dill, and season with a little salt and pepper. Stir the sausages around so that they are well coated. Cover with plastic wrap and leave to marinate in the fridge for at least 1 hour.

2 Meanwhile, to make the salsa, combine all the ingredients in a bowl and mix well. Season with salt and pepper.

3 Heat a broiler, barbecue, or heavy-bottomed frying pan until hot. Grill the sausages for 10–15 minutes until cooked through, turning halfway during cooking to brown both sides.

4 Divide the sausages between 4 warmed plates, and serve immediately on a piece of toasted ciabatta, with the tomato salsa spooned over the top.

spicy sausage and tomato skewers

Cherry tomatoes are ideal for skewers, as they hold their shape far more successfully than quartered or halved larger tomatoes. Team them with chile or paprika flavored sausages.

 15 MINS   **20 MINS**

SPECIAL EQUIPMENT ▪ wooden or bamboo skewers

SERVES 4

12 spicy sausages, cut into large pieces

12 cherry tomatoes

a few bay leaves

a little olive oil

large sprig of rosemary, leaves picked and finely chopped

sea salt and freshly ground black pepper

1 If you are using wooden or bamboo skewers, soak them in cold water for 30 minutes.

2 Thread the spicy sausages and cherry tomatoes alternately onto the skewers, interspersing them with a few bay leaves. Brush each sausage and tomato skewer with oil, sprinkle the chopped rosemary leaves over the top, and season.

3 Heat a barbecue or ridged cast-iron grill pan until hot. Add the skewers and grill for 5–8 minutes on each side until the sausages are well cooked and lightly charred.

variation

spiced pork, apricot, and tomato skewers
Cut 12oz (350g) pork tenderloin in 1in (2.5cm) chunks. Add 8 cherry tomatoes and 4 halved and pitted apricots. Toss in 2 tbsp olive oil mixed with 1 crushed garlic clove, 1 tsp smoked paprika, 1 tsp ground cinnamon, and some salt and pepper. Marinate for 2 hours. Thread alternately on skewers with a few bay leaves. Grill as before, brushing with any remaining marinade.

tomato and harissa tart

Harissa paste is a thick chile sauce that includes chile peppers as well as garlic, cilantro, chile powder, and caraway blended with olive oil. Use as much of the paste as suits your taste.

 10 MINS   **15 MINS**

SERVES 6

14oz (400g) store-bought puff pastry

2 tbsp red bell pepper pesto

6 tomatoes, halved

2–3 tbsp harissa paste

1 tbsp olive oil

a few sprigs of thyme, leaves picked

1 Preheat the oven to 400°F (200°C). Roll out the pastry on a floured work surface into a large rectangle or square. Lay on a baking sheet, then use a sharp knife to score a border about 2in (5cm) in from the edges all the way around, being careful not to cut all the way through the pastry. Next, using the back of the knife, score the pastry around the outer edges—this will help it to puff up.

2 Working inside the border, smother the pastry with the pesto. Arrange the tomatoes on top, cut-side up. Mix the harissa paste with the oil and drizzle it over the tomatoes. Scatter the thyme leaves on top.

3 Bake in the oven for about 15 minutes until the pastry is cooked and golden. Serve hot.

salt cod and red pepper dip

Salt cod used to be dried outdoors in the sun and wind, but now it is usually dried with electric heaters.

 25 MINS   **1 HR**   ❄ **FREEZABLE**

SPECIAL EQUIPMENT ▪ blender or food processor

SERVES 12

2 red bell peppers

2 garlic cloves, peeled

1 small red onion, finely chopped

4 tbsp olive oil

salt and freshly ground black pepper

2 tbsp finely chopped Spanish onion

1lb (450g) plum tomatoes, skinned (p197) and chopped (or a 14oz can whole plum tomatoes)

1lb 2oz (500g) salt cod

2 tbsp finely chopped marjoram

2 tbsp finely chopped dill

handful of basil leaves, finely chopped

handful of flat-leaf parsley, finely chopped

juice of 1 lemon

Turkish bread or crostini, grilled to serve

1 Preheat the oven to 400°F (200°C) and line a baking sheet with parchment paper. Slice the tops off the bell peppers and remove the seeds and membrane. Put a garlic clove and half of the chopped red onion in the cavity of each bell pepper. Sit the bell peppers on the baking tray.

Drizzle with 1 tbsp of the oil and season with salt and pepper. Roast in the oven for about 1 hour. Remove from the oven and set aside to cool.

2 While the bell peppers are roasting, heat the remaining oil in a heavy-bottomed frying pan over medium heat. Add the Spanish onion and sweat for 3–4 minutes until soft. Add the chopped tomatoes, including any juices, and cook for another 10 minutes, stirring from time to time. Season with salt and pepper.

3 Meanwhile, slice the skin off the salt cod and flake the flesh into chunks. Add to the tomato sauce after the 10 minutes' cooking time and cook on low heat for another 10 minutes. Set aside to cool.

4 Put the cooled, roasted peppers in a blender or food processor with the cooled tomato and cod mixture. Pulse until smooth, then transfer to a serving bowl, and season with salt and pepper. Add the herbs and lemon juice, and stir to mix well. Serve with grilled Turkish bread or crostini.

zucchini and potato soup

A very simple soup that is easy to make and with very few ingredients. The zucchini and potatoes are lifted out of the ordinary by the gentle aniseed tang of dill.

 10 MINS   **15 MINS**   ❄ **FREEZABLE**

SPECIAL EQUIPMENT ▪ food processor or handheld blender

SERVES 4

2 large potatoes, peeled and cubed

2 cups hot chicken stock

salt and freshly ground white pepper

1 tbsp olive oil

3 zucchini, peeled and finely cubed or grated

1 onion, finely cubed or grated

½ cup heavy cream

1¼ cup milk

small bunch of dill, chopped

1 Put the potatoes in a pan with the hot stock and 1 tsp salt, bring to a boil, and simmer for about

5 minutes, or until tender. Remove the pan from the heat and using a food processor or handheld blender, purée until smooth. Return to the pan.

2 In another saucepan, heat the oil, add the zucchini and onion, and cook over low heat for 2–3 minutes, or until slightly softened but not colored. Stir in a dash of the white pepper, the cream, milk, and puréed potato broth, and simmer gently for 5 minutes, or until the zucchini have softened. Add the dill and season to taste. Serve hot.

whipped yogurt soup with sautéed zucchini

This spin on a popular Indian curry makes an innovative first course. The crackling curry leaves, toasted spices, and tangy tamarind work well with the yogurt base.

 30 MINS PLUS STANDING   **25 MINS**

SERVES 4

3 tbsp vegetable oil

2 dried red chiles

1 tsp mustard seeds

¼ tsp fenugreek seeds

1 tsp cumin seeds

12 curry leaves

3 tbsp gram flour

½ tsp turmeric

1¾ cups Greek-style yogurt

salt

2 tbsp tamarind pulp

2 tbsp chopped cilantro leaves, to garnish

For the sautéed zucchini topping

2 tbsp vegetable oil

1 small red onion, cubed

1 zucchini, finely cubed

1 jalapeño chile, seeded and finely chopped

sea salt

1 Heat the oil in a wok over medium heat. Toss in the chiles and mustard seeds and swirl around for a few

seconds before adding the fenugreek, cumin, and curry leaves. Reduce the heat and stir-fry for a few seconds. Sprinkle in half the flour and stir-fry for 2–3 minutes, or until lightly toasted. Remove from the heat, add the turmeric, and leave to cool slightly.

2 Whisk the remaining flour with the yogurt and 1¾ cups water and add to the wok. Return to the heat and, whisking all the time, bring to simmer and cook for 3–4 minutes. Add more water, if needed, to loosen the consistency. If you wish, you can sieve the soup at this stage. Season with salt and tamarind to sharpen.

3 For the sautéed zucchini topping, heat the oil in a frying pan over medium heat. Add the onion and cook for 3–4 minutes until the onion is soft. Add the zucchini and green chille and continue cooking for another minute. Season with sea salt and add to the hot soup. Garnish with the chopped cilantro.

crepes with zucchini and emmental

If you can't get hold of Emmental (also known as Swiss cheese), there are other cheeses that you can use here in its place. Try the Dutch Leerdammer or Norwegian Jarlsberg, which are also hard cheeses with a similar mild and slightly sweet flavor that don't overwhelm the delicate flavor of the zucchini in these light stuffed crepes.

 10 MINS PLUS RESTING 15 MINS FREEZABLE

MAKES 8

1 cup all-purpose flour

salt and freshly ground black pepper

1 large egg

1¼ cups milk

1 tbsp olive oil, plus a little extra
  for cooking

2 small zucchini, grated

4½oz (125g) Emmental cheese, grated

1 Put the flour in a mixing bowl with a pinch of salt, stir, and make a well in the center. Crack the egg into the well and add a tiny amount of the milk. Using a wooden spoon, stir the egg and milk, letting the flour gradually tumble in. Add the rest of the milk, little by little, stirring continuously until all the flour has been incorporated and the mixture is lump-free. Put it in the fridge to rest for 30 minutes, if you have time.

2 Heat 1 tbsp of the oil in a frying pan over medium heat, add the zucchini, and cook for 5–8 minutes, or until golden. Season well with salt and pepper, then remove from the heat and stir in the Emmental.

3 In a small flat frying pan or crepe pan, heat a drizzle of oil on high heat, swirling it around the pan, then pouring it out again. Stir the batter mix, then spoon in 2 tbsp of it, swirling it around the pan so it reaches the edges. Cook for a couple of minutes, then pull up the edges with a palette knife. Turn the crepe over and cook the other side for 1 minute. Slide it out onto a plate.

4 Spoon the filling onto the crepes, sprinkle with black pepper, then either roll or fold them up.

variation

crepes with zucchini, tomatoes, and mozzarella

Prepare in the same way, but use 1 zucchini and 2 chopped, ripe tomatoes. Stir-fry for 5 minutes. Add 1 tbsp tomato purée, a pinch of sugar, and 6 chopped, fresh basil leaves. Season to taste. Substitute mozzarella for Emmental. Don't mix in, but sprinkle over the filling before rolling.

cucumber and dill soup

This refreshing soup makes an elegant starter. For a lunch or dinner party, try serving it with smoked salmon.

 30 MINS PLUS CHILLING

SPECIAL EQUIPMENT ▪ blender or food processor

SERVES 4

2 medium cucumbers

salt and freshly ground black pepper

3½ cups whole or 2% milk

small bunch of dill

⅔ cup natural yogurt

1 Peel the cucumbers, leaving one or two strips of skin on for color. Slice, put into a colander, and sprinkle with a teaspoon of salt. Toss and leave to stand over a bowl for one hour. Meanwhile, pour the milk into another bowl, add a few whole dill fronds, stir, and chill in the fridge for 1 hour to allow the flavors to infuse slightly.

2 Rinse the cucumber slices under cold water, then press down on them with your hand to extract as much moisture as possible. Remove the dill fronds from the milk. Put the milk and cucumber in a blender or food processor. Add a few more fronds of dill and some black pepper and blend well. Pour into a bowl and chill in the fridge for 3 hours.

3 Place a sieve over a second bowl, pour the chilled soup through the sieve and push the pulp through with the back of a wooden spoon. Add ⅓–⅔ cup chilled water to the soup and return to the fridge until ready to serve.

4 Stir in the yogurt, taste, and adjust the seasoning if necessary. Whisk until frothy with a handheld blender or whisk, then pour into cups, bowls, or glasses. Decorate with a little more dill and serve.

minted pea and ham soup

If you have a glut of fresh peas, this is a delicious soup to make with them. If they are not cooked soon after picking, you may need to add a little sugar.

 15 MINS **20-25 MINS** ❋ **FREEZABLE**

SPECIAL EQUIPMENT ▪ blender or handheld blender

SERVES 4-6

3 tbsp butter

2 shallots, finely chopped

1 potato, peeled and chopped

1¼ cup hot vegetable stock

1lb 2oz (500g) peas (shelled weight)

2 handfuls of mint leaves

5½oz (150g) cooked ham, cubed

salt and freshly ground black pepper

⅔ cup crème fraîche, to serve

1 Melt the butter in a saucepan over low heat, add the shallots, and cook for 2-3 minutes until soft. Add the potato and continue cooking, covered, for another 7-10 minutes, or until the potato is tender. Pour in the hot stock and simmer for 10-15 minutes.

2 In a separate pan, boil 1¾ cups water and cook the peas for 4-5 minutes, or until tender. Add the mint leaves for the last 20 seconds of cooking. Pour the peas and mint into a sieve over a bowl, reserving the cooking liquid in the bowl. Add the peas and mint to the potato and onion stock. Purée the soup until smooth in a blender, or in the pan using a handheld blender, pouring in enough reserved cooking liquid from the peas to loosen the consistency. Stir in the cubed ham.

3 Reheat the soup and season with salt and pepper, to taste. Serve in bowls with a dollop of crème fraîche in the center.

roasted tomato soup

For homemade food in a jiffy, roast the plum tomatoes up to 3 days in advance and store them in the fridge.

 10 MINS **30 MINS** ❋ **FREEZABLE**

SPECIAL EQUIPMENT ▪ blender or handheld blender

SERVES 4

8 plum tomatoes, about 1½lb (675g) in total, quartered

1 red onion, cut into 8 wedges

2 garlic cloves, unpeeled

3 tbsp olive oil

sea salt and freshly ground black pepper

3½ cups hot vegetable stock

3 tbsp sun-dried tomato paste

1 Preheat the oven to 375°F (190°C). Put the tomatoes, onion, and garlic on separate baking sheets lined with wax paper. Drizzle with the oil and season well with sea salt and pepper. Roast until they are soft, caramelized, and slightly browned—allow 10-15 minutes for the garlic, 15-20 minutes for the onion, and about 25 minutes for the tomatoes. Squeeze the garlic cloves from their skins once they have cooled slightly.

2 Transfer to a blender, or to a pan if you are using a handheld blender, add the stock and tomato paste, and purée until smooth but still slightly chunky. Season to taste, reheat gently, and serve hot in bowls.

variation

roasted tomato and eggplant soup

Prepare in exactly the same way, but substitute 4 of the tomatoes with a small eggplant. Roast the eggplant for about 40 minutes until really soft; the other vegetables as before. Halve the eggplant and scoop out the flesh. Put all the vegetables in the blender as before, and add ½ tsp dried oregano. Blend until smooth. Season and serve in bowls and drizzle with a little chile oil before serving.

Season's best **peas**

Peas start to appear in spring months in warmer climates and can be continuously harvested through the summer months. Freshly picked English peas, snow peas, and sugarsnaps are wonderfully sweet. They pair perfectly with mint, chile, garlic, and ginger and complement ham, bacon, duck, and seafood.

Originally from the Middle East, peas are now grown in warm climates worldwide. One of the most difficult tasks for the farmers is to protect the plants from birds.

English peas Plump, juicy English peas have a uniquely sweet, grassy flavor and a tender-crisp texture. They should be lightly cooked to prevent them from becoming starchy.

The tiny peas need only a minute or two in boiling water.

▲ **Petits pois** A naturally small-seeded variety, petits pois are the sweetest of all peas. They are delicious eaten raw or lightly cooked.

essentials
varieties available

Essentially two varieties: peas for shelling and those eaten pod and all.

buy Pods should be evenly green, with no brown, yellow, or decay spots. Look for plump English peas that are not quite touching in the pod; avoid fat pods with oversized peas. Snow peas and sugarsnap peas should be crisp and moist.

store Eat as soon as possible to preserve their sweetness. Keep them in a closed plastic bag in the fridge for no more than 1–2 days.

cook Boil or steam until just tender. Also stir-fry or tempura-fry snow peas and sugarsnap peas.

preserve Blanch and freeze.

recipe ideas

Minted pea and ham soup p148

Pea and mint risotto p184

Pea and pancetta tart p183

▶ **Snow peas** The flat, edible pods and minuscule seeds have a sweet, herbaceous flavor. They add crisp texture and brilliant color to stir-frys.

Sugarsnap peas Rounder and fatter than snow peas, the edible, fleshy pods and seeds are crunchy and wonderfully sweet. Eat them whole or thickly sliced.

pea soup with mint gremolata

Growing peas is one of the greatest pleasures, but discarding the pods can seem like such a waste. Here, the pods as well as the peas are used to make a vibrant summer soup.

 10 MINS   35 MINS

SPECIAL EQUIPMENT ▪ food processor or handheld blender

SERVES 6

2 tbsp butter

1 onion, finely chopped

1 potato, peeled and coarsely chopped

1¼lb (550g) peas in their pods, coarsely cut up

4 cups hot chicken or vegetable stock

1 tsp granulated sugar

sprig of mint

sea salt and freshly ground black pepper

half-and-half, to serve

For the gremolata

2 tbsp finely chopped flat-leaf parsley

2 tbsp finely chopped mint

2 tsp grated lemon zest

1 garlic clove, finely chopped

1 Melt the butter in a pan over low heat, add the onion, and cook for 7–10 minutes until the onion is soft. Add the remaining soup ingredients, except for the half-and-half. Bring to a boil, reduce the heat, partly cover, and simmer for 20 minutes until the peas and potato are soft. Discard the mint.

2 Remove the soup from the heat and using a food processor or handheld blender, purée until smooth. Pass through a sieve to remove any tough bits of pod and pea skins. Taste and season again, if necessary. Reheat to serve.

3 To make the gremolata, mix together all the ingredients. Ladle the soup into bowls. Add a swirl of half-and-half and sprinkle with gremolata.

roasted red bell pepper soup

Sweet red bell peppers spiced up with some dried chile flakes and served with summery basil leaves is a delicious soup to be making and eating at this time of year.

 15 MINS   1 HR   ❄ FREEZABLE

SPECIAL EQUIPMENT ▪ food processor or handheld blender

SERVES 8

2 tbsp olive oil

2 onions, finely chopped

3 garlic cloves, grated or finely chopped

pinch of dried chile flakes

salt and freshly ground black pepper

10 red bell peppers, roasted, peeled (p171), and seeded

8 cups hot vegetable stock

large handful of basil leaves, torn, to serve

drizzle of extra virgin olive oil, to serve

1 Heat the oil in a large heavy-bottomed pan over medium heat, add the onions, and cook for 3–4 minutes until the onion is soft. Stir in the garlic and chile flakes and season with salt and pepper. Add the roasted bell peppers and juices, pour in the stock, and bring to a boil. Reduce the heat and simmer for 15 minutes.

2 Remove the soup from the heat and using a processor or handheld blender, purée until smooth. Season to taste with salt and pepper. Stir in the basil, drizzle with oil, and serve with fresh crusty bread.

tomato, red onion, and mozzarella salad

Packed wth strong Mediterranean flavors, this colorful salad combines peppery arugula and sweet, spicy basil to bring out the juiciness of the ripe tomatoes.

 10 MINS

SERVES 4

8 ripe plum tomatoes, sliced

6 cherry tomatoes, halved

1 small red onion, peeled and sliced

handful of basil leaves, torn

extra virgin olive oil, for drizzling

salt and freshly ground black pepper

2 handfuls of arugula leaves

balsamic vinegar, for drizzling

2 balls of mozzarella, torn

1 Put the tomatoes, red onion, and half of the basil leaves in a bowl. Drizzle plenty of the oil over the top, season well with salt and pepper, and toss until well mixed.

2 Arrange the arugula leaves on a serving platter and drizzle on a little oil and some balsamic vinegar.

Season with salt and pepper, and spoon the tomato and basil mixture over the top. Add the torn mozzarella. Scatter the remaining basil leaves over the top and drizzle again with a little oil and balsamic vinegar. Serve immediately.

variation

green bean, red onion, and camembert salad

Substitute the plum tomatoes with 6oz (175g) lightly cooked green beans, trimmed and cut in thirds. Place in a bowl with the cherry tomatoes. Chop the onion instead of slicing and dress in the same way, but add a squeeze of lemon juice with the oil. Place on the arugula and top with 4oz (115g) Camembert, cut in thin wedges, instead of mozzarella.

goat cheese, beets, and pistachios

Beets starts fattening up well at this time of the year. It introduces a burst of purple-red color and brings a smooth texture and flavor to a dish.

 15 MINS PLUS STANDING

SERVES 4

For the salad

2 handfuls of arugula leaves

4–6 large beets, cooked, peeled (p255), and coarsely chopped

6oz (175g) goat cheese, sliced

handful of shelled pistachio nuts, coarsely chopped

For the dressing

3 tbsp extra virgin olive oil

1 tbsp white wine vinegar

2 shallots, finely chopped

1 tsp grainy mustard

pinch of sugar

salt and freshly ground black pepper

1 To make the dressing, put the oil, vinegar, and shallots in a small bowl, and whisk together thoroughly. Add the mustard and sugar, and season well with salt and pepper. Whisk again, then taste. Season again as needed, then let the dressing stand for a while, to allow the flavors to develop.

2 Arrange the arugula leaves on a large platter or 4 individual plates, then top with the beets and goat cheese. Drizzle a little of the dressing over the top, then sprinkle on the pistachio nuts. Add more dressing, if you wish. Serve with crusty bread.

fresh tomatoes stuffed with fruity couscous

Large but firm summer tomatoes are ideal for this easy-to-make starter. Alternatively, for a light lunch, serve the tomatoes on top of any extra couscous.

 30 MINS PLUS STANDING

SERVES 4

4 large beef tomatoes

⅔ cup tomato juice

4½oz (125g) couscous

1¾oz (50g) golden raisins

handful of basil leaves, chopped

handful of flat-leaf parsley, chopped

salt and freshly ground black pepper

1 Slice the tops off the tomatoes and reserve. Scoop out the seeds and flesh from the tomatoes, so that you are left with a "shell," and put in a large bowl with the tomato juice. Set the tomato shells aside.

2 Put the couscous in a separate bowl, pour in ⅔ cup hot water so that it just covers the couscous, and let stand for 10 minutes. Use a fork to fluff up the grains, then add the tomato seeds and flesh. Mix together and let stand for another 10 minutes.

3 Stir the couscous well, breaking up any chunks of tomato. Add the golden raisins, basil, and parsley, and mix again. Taste and season with salt and pepper as needed. Spoon the mixture into the reserved tomato shells and put the tops on to serve.

escabeche

 Escabeche means "pickled" in Spanish, and oily fish are often prepared this way. Try using white, meaty fish, since the result has a cleaner, less rich flavor.

 30 MINS PLUS MARINATING **15 MINS**

MAKES 4-6 SERVINGS

1½lb (675g) thick cod fillet, skinned

3 tbsp all-purpose flour

salt and freshly ground black pepper

2 tsp chopped thyme, plus a few leaves for garnishing (or 1 tsp dried thyme, and garnish with a little chopped parsley)

6 tbsp olive oil, plus extra for drizzling

1 onion, thinly sliced into rings

1 large garlic clove, crushed

1 large carrot, cut into thin matchsticks

1 red bell pepper, halved, seeded, and cut into thin strips

1 celery stick, cut into thin matchsticks

1in (2.5cm) piece fresh ginger, peeled and grated

2-4 large jalapeño chiles, seeded and sliced

1 cup white wine vinegar

¼ tsp sea salt

½ tsp granulated sugar

1 Cut the cod into 2in (5cm) pieces. Mix the flour with a little salt and pepper and the herbs. Use this mixture to coat the fish.

2 Heat half the oil in a frying pan and fry the fish quickly on all sides until brown and just cooked—about 4 minutes. Place in a large, shallow serving dish.

3 Wipe out the pan, heat the remaining oil, and fry the onion, garlic, carrot, bell pepper, and celery on low heat for 5 minutes, stirring until just tender, but still with some "bite." Remove from the pan with a slotted spoon and set aside.

4 Add the remaining ingredients to the pan, bring to a boil, reduce the heat, and simmer for 5 minutes. Stir in the vegetables, then spoon the mixture over the fish. Allow to cool slightly, then cover and leave to marinate overnight.

5 Serve the same day at room temperature, drizzled with oil and sprinkled with a few fresh thyme or parsley leaves. It can also be stored in the fridge for up to 3 days (bring back to room temperature before garnishing and serving).

kohlrabi soup with pesto

If you are a fan of smooth soups, you can pulse this recipe in a blender at the end of step 1, and then swirl the pesto through the resulting delicate, light green purée.

 5 MINS **15 MINS** **FREEZABLE**

SERVES 6

2 tbsp butter

3-4 kohlrabi, cut into bite-sized cubes

3½ cups hot vegetable stock

2 tbsp crème fraîche

salt and freshly ground black pepper

6 tsp pesto, to garnish

1 Melt the butter in a frying pan, add the kohlrabi, and cook for 5 minutes, or until light golden brown. Pour in the stock and bring to a boil. Add the crème fraîche and season with salt and pepper. Cook for 8–10 minutes, or until the kohlrabi is tender, but not mushy.

2 Taste and adjust the seasoning, then ladle the soup into warm bowls and garnish each with a teaspoon of pesto.

roasted red bell pepper tart

Red pesto and mascarpone add depth to this sweet bell pepper filling. Preheat a baking sheet in the oven and place the tart pan on top to achieve a really crisp pie crust.

  15 MINS **1 HR** **FREEZABLE**

SPECIAL EQUIPMENT ▪ 9in (23cm) square fluted tart pan with removable bottom ▪ ceramic baking beans ▪ food processor

SERVES 6-8

4 large red bell peppers

1 tbsp olive oil

10oz (300g) store-bought pie dough

3 large eggs, 1 lightly beaten for egg wash

1 tbsp mascarpone

handful of basil leaves, plus extra to garnish

salt and freshly ground black pepper

1 tsp red pesto

1 Preheat the oven to 400°F (200°C). Put the peppers in a roasting pan. Using your hands, smear each one with the oil. Roast in the oven for about 20 minutes until lightly charred. Transfer to a plastic bag and leave until cool enough to handle, before skinning and seeding.

2 Meanwhile, roll out the dough on a floured work surface and use to line a tart pan. Trim away the excess, line the pie dough with wax paper, and fill with ceramic baking beans. Bake in the oven for 15–20 minutes until the edges are golden. Remove the beans and paper, brush the bottom of the crust with the extra egg wash, and return to the oven for 2–3 minutes to crisp. Remove from the oven and set aside. Reduce the oven temperature to 350°F (180°C).

3 Put the roasted bell peppers, the 2 eggs, mascarpone, and the basil leaves in a food processor and pulse until combined. Season well with salt and pepper. Spread the pesto evenly over the bottom of the pie dough, then carefully pour in the pepper mixture. Bake in the oven for 25–35 minutes until set. Leave to cool for 10 minutes before releasing from the pan. Garnish with extra basil leaves and serve with a wild arugula and fennel salad.

german chicken broth

Based on a Thuringian vegetable soup, this recipe uses kohlrabi, beans, and snow peas. It benefits from a flavorful chicken stock, so prepare your own, if you prefer.

 10 MINS **25 MINS** ❄ **FREEZABLE**

SERVES 4-6

4 cups chicken stock

5½oz (150g) green beans, trimmed and strings removed

2 large carrots, sliced

7oz (200g) kohlrabi, cubed

5½oz (150g) snow peas or sugar snap peas, trimmed

salt and freshly ground black pepper

half-and-half or heavy cream, to serve

1 bunch of chervil, finely chopped

1 Bring the stock to a boil in a medium-sized saucepan, add the green beans, and simmer for 5 minutes. Add the carrots and kohlrabi and cook for 5 minutes, then add the snow peas or sugar snap peas and cook for another 5 minutes—be careful not to overcook these or they will lose their delightful crunchiness.

2 Season with salt and pepper and remove the pan from the heat. Ladle into serving bowls, add a swirl of cream to each, and sprinkle with chervil before serving.

sweet corn and bell pepper filo triangles

Canned or frozen corn doesn't quite compare to the crisp, succulent kernels from a fresh corncob. Combined with red bell peppers, they make these pastries crunchy and sweet.

 20 MINS **20 MINS** ❄ **FREEZABLE**

SERVES 2

1 tbsp olive oil

1 onion, finely chopped

salt and freshly ground black pepper

3 red bell peppers, seeded and cubed

4 sweet corncobs, kernels removed (about 1lb/450g kernels, p155)

6oz (175g) feta cheese, cut into small cubes

7oz (200g) filo pastry

a little butter, melted, plus extra for glazing

1 Preheat the oven to 400°F (200°C). Heat the oil in a large frying pan over low heat. Add the onion and a little salt, and cook on low heat for about 5 minutes until soft and translucent. Add the bell peppers and corn, cover, and continue cooking on low heat for another 10 minutes until the bell peppers are soft and the corn is tender, stirring occasionally. Stir in the feta and season well with black pepper.

2 Lay out the filo sheets into four piles of 3 or 4 layers about 12 x 4in (30 x 10cm), brushing each pile with a little melted butter. Divide the bell pepper mixture between each pile of pastry, spooning it onto the bottom right-hand corner of every one. Fold this corner so that it makes a triangle, then fold the top right-hand corner down. Repeat until you have made 5 folds in all for each one and you end up with 4 large triangles.

3 Brush the triangles all over with a little melted butter and put them on an oiled baking sheet. Bake in the oven for about 20 minutes until crisp and golden. Serve hot.

mexican sweet corn soup

A flavorful soup of sweet corn and red bell pepper. If you don't have chile-flavored olive oil, stir a little piquant pimentón, harissa, or smoked paprika into fruity olive oil.

 15 MINS **20 MINS** ❄ **FREEZABLE**

SPECIAL EQUIPMENT ▪ blender or handheld blender

SERVES 4

3 tbsp olive oil

1 Spanish onion, finely chopped

1 red bell pepper, seeded and finely chopped

1 garlic clove, crushed

1 tsp fennel seeds

1 tsp fresh thyme leaves

3-4 sweet corncobs, kernels removed (about 14oz/400g kernels, p155)

salt and freshly ground black pepper

½ cup half-and-half

1½ tbsp chile-flavored olive oil, to serve

1 Heat the oil in a large sauté pan over moderate heat, add the onion, red bell pepper (reserving a tablespoon of the pepper as a garnish), garlic, fennel seeds, and thyme, and stir-fry for 3 minutes. Add the sweet corn and season lightly. Continue stirring and cooking for 2 minutes, then pour in 2 cups hot water, stir, and bring to low heat. Lower the heat, cover, and simmer for 15 minutes, or until the vegetables are tender and cooked through. Stir in the half-and-half and let cool for a few minutes.

2 Purée the soup until smooth in a blender (you may need to do this in batches), or in the pan using a handheld blender. Return to the pan and reheat the soup gently, stirring occasionally. Taste and adjust the seasoning if necessary. Ladle into warmed bowls and add the reserved red bell pepper as a garnish. Drizzle a little chile-flavored olive oil over the top and serve immediately.

variation

mediterranean sweet corn soup

Use the kernels from 2 corncobs. Add 4 peeled and chopped tomatoes, and a finely chopped zucchini with the bell pepper. Add 2½ cups chicken or vegetable stock instead of water. Do not purée. Omit the cream, and stir in 1 tbsp chopped, fresh basil when adjusting the seasoning. Serve topped with grated Parmesan instead of drizzling with chile oil.

Season's best **sweet corn**

True to its name, sweet corn is a type of maize with the sweet, golden, or white kernels set in rows along the central cob. The kernels can be eaten on the cob or cut off before cooking. Harvested in high summer through to early autumn, they have a short season. Best paired with melted butter or bacon, they also taste amazing with Cheddar cheese, fish, chicken, chiles, and peppers.

Native to Mexico and Guatemala, but grown all over the world from the tropics to any northern region with a sufficient growing season, sweet corn is an important staple crop.

essentials

varieties available

Whole cobs; baby cobs; kernels; fresh, frozen, or canned. Other products include cornstarch, cornmeal, polenta, and popcorn.

buy The cut end of the cob should not be dry and the leaves should be fresh and bright. Choose well-filled cobs; if you puncture a kernel with the thumbnail, the fluid should be milky, not clear or paste-like.

store Best eaten on day of purchase or store, wrapped in damp paper towels, in the fridge for 1–2 days at most.

cook Roast whole in the husk, or shuck (remove husk and silk) and then boil, roast, or grill. Boil, braise, bake, or sauté kernels.

preserve Kernels and shucked cobs can be frozen.

recipe ideas

Mexican sweet corn soup p154

Scallop and sweet corn chowder p157

Sweet corn and bell pepper filo triangles p154

The tiny cobs are no more than 4in (10cm) long.

Baby corn Unlike full-grown ears, baby corn is completely edible, including the central cob. With its mild flavor and crunchy texture, it is a useful ingredient in stir-fry meals, as a colorful vegetable crudité, and cut in pieces in soups, stews, and salads.

Deep yellow kernels will not be sweet. Choose pale, creamy-yellow ones.

Yellow sweet corn Classic corn varieties have differing sugar contents: "normal", "sugar enhanced", and "super sweet".

how to remove sweet corn kernels

One of the sweetest vegetables, the flavor of fresh sweet corn easily beats that of canned or frozen ones. Preparing the cobs to eat whole or removing the kernels is very straightforward.

1 Remove the husks and all the silk threads from the corn-on-the-cob. Rinse the husked corn under cold running water.

2 Place the blunt end on the cutting board. Use a sharp chef's knife and slice straight down the cob. Rotate the cob and repeat.

White sweet corn The flavor is not as sweet as yellow corn but is still delicious. It is a popular vegetable in farmers' markets. Look for mixed white and yellow cobs.

chicken and sweet corn soup

Sweet corn comes into its own in high summer, as it ripens on the cob. Its sweet flavor complements the chicken in this soup deliciously.

 10 MINS   30 MINS

SPECIAL EQUIPMENT ▪ blender or food processor

SERVES 4

1 tbsp olive oil

2 tbsp butter

1 onion, finely chopped

2 garlic cloves, crushed

1 large potato, peeled and sliced

4 cups hot chicken stock

4 sweet corncobs, kernels removed (about 1lb/450g kernels, p155)

2 skinless, boneless chicken breasts, cut into thin strips

salt and freshly ground black pepper

handful of flat-leaf parsley, finely chopped

1 Heat the oil and butter in a large pan over medium heat, add the onion, and cook for 3–4 minutes until the onion is soft. Add the garlic and potato and cook, stirring, for 1 minute.

2 Add the stock and corncobs. Bring to a boil, lower the heat, and simmer for 15 minutes until the vegetables are really tender. Remove the corncobs, then pour the soup into a blender or food processor and purée until smooth. Return to the pan.

3 Add the chicken and corn kernels. Bring to a boil, reduce the heat, and simmer for 10 minutes until the chicken is cooked and the corn is tender. Taste and season if needed. Stir in the flat-leaf parsley just before serving.

brandied lobster chowder

Serve this delightful soup with some nutty rye bread and chilled unsalted butter. If you like, you can use crab as a less expensive alternative to the lobster.

 20 MINS   1 HR

SERVES 4

1 small cooked lobster

⅔ cup dry white wine

1 bay leaf

pat of unsalted butter

2 shallots, finely chopped

4 tbsp brandy

1 large tomato, peeled (p197) and cubed

2 tsp anchovy paste

4 large new potatoes, peeled and cubed

8 baby corn, cut in short lengths

salt and freshly ground black pepper

2oz (60g) snow peas, cut in short lengths

5 tbsp half-and-half

4 thick slices of lemon

4 sprigs of parsley

1 Twist the legs and claws off the lobster. Cut the body in half lengthwise and remove the dark vein that runs along it. Lift out the tail meat and cut in small pieces. Crack the large claws, remove the meat, and cube. Set all the meat aside. Leave the remaining bits of meat in the shell. Roughly chop it up and put it in a saucepan with the claws and legs. Add 3 cups water with the wine and bay leaf. Bring to a boil, reduce the heat, cover, and simmer for 30 minutes. Strain and reserve the stock.

2 Melt the butter in another large saucepan over low heat. Add the shallots and cook gently, stirring, for 1 minute. Add the brandy, ignite, and shake the pan until the flames subside. Add the tomato, anchovy paste, potatoes, and corn. Return the stock to the pan. Season and bring to a boil. Reduce the heat, cover, and simmer for 20 minutes until the potatoes are tender.

3 Meanwhile, blanch the snow peas in a little boiling water for 2 minutes until just tender. Drain, rinse with cold water, and drain again. Then add to the soup along with the cream and lobster meat. Taste and season again. Reheat the soup but do not boil it. Ladle into warmed bowls. Serve with a slice of lemon and a small sprig of parsley in each bowl.

arugula and parmesan soup

This makes good use of peppery late-season arugula that may have become a bit leathery.

 10 MINS   30 MINS   ❄ FREEZABLE

SPECIAL EQUIPMENT ▪ food processor or handheld blender

SERVES 4

2 tbsp olive oil

2 onions, chopped

1lb 7oz (650g) potatoes, washed but not peeled, cut into ¾in(2cm) cubes

sea salt and freshly ground black pepper

4 small or 2 large garlic cloves, crushed

3½ cups hot vegetable stock

1 Parmesan rind, about 1¼ x 3½in (3 x 9cm), cut into tiny cubes

4½oz (125g) arugula leaves, chopped

Parmesan cheese, grated to serve

1 Heat the oil in a pan over medium heat, add the onion, and cook for 3–4 minutes until the onion is soft. Stir in the potatoes with a little sea salt, cover, and cook for 5 minutes, stirring.

2 Add the garlic and stir for a few seconds until fragrant, then pour in the stock. Bring to a boil, add the Parmesan rind, then reduce the heat and simmer for about 10 minutes, stirring occasionally, until the potato is soft. Add the arugula, stir, and cook for 3–5 minutes until tender but still bright green.

3 Remove the soup from the heat and using a food processor or handheld blender, purée until smooth. Taste for seasoning. Serve each bowl with grated Parmesan.

scallop and sweet corn chowder

This is a luxurious American classic. A wonderful dish for a special occasion that marries the sweetness of both the shellfish and sweet corn with salty bacon. Oyster crackers are the traditional accompaniment. Serve on the side so diners can crumble them over their own bowl.

 25-30 MINS   15-20 MINS

SERVES 4

2 sweet corncobs, about 8oz (225g) kernels

13oz (375g) small scallops, cleaned

4½oz (125g) bacon, cut into strips

1 onion, thinly sliced

9oz (250g) new potatoes, scraped and cubed

1 bay leaf

salt and freshly ground black pepper

1⅔ cups hot fish stock

½ cup heavy cream

1 cup milk

paprika, for sprinkling

1 Hold each sweet corncob vertically on a cutting board and cut from the tip down to remove the kernels. Put them in a small bowl. Working over the bowl, with the back of the knife, scrape the pulp and milk from each cob.

2 If necessary, discard the tough, crescent-shaped membrane at the side of each scallop. Make sure there is no black intestinal vein running around the edge of the shellfish. If you find one, peel it off and discard.

3 Heat a large saucepan, add the bacon, and fry for 3–5 minutes, stirring until the fat has rendered. With a slotted spoon, transfer the bacon to a plate lined with paper towels.

4 Reduce the heat, then add the onions and cook, stirring frequently, for 3–4 minutes until soft and translucent. With a slotted spoon, transfer the onions to the lined plate. Discard any remaining fat from the pan.

5 Add the potatoes to the pan with the bay leaf, salt, and pepper. Pour in the stock. Bring to a boil, then reduce the heat and simmer gently for 7–10 minutes, until the potatoes are slightly soft.

6 Return most of the bacon and onions to the pan with the sweet corn kernels and pulp, cream, and milk. Bring to a boil, then reduce the heat and simmer for 7–10 minutes until the potatoes are tender. Add the scallops. Bring back to a boil to cook the scallops. Taste and reseason if necessary. Discard the bay leaf, ladle into warmed bowls, and sprinkle with paprika and the reserved onion and bacon.

arugula, ricotta cheese, and black olive dip

A member of the mustard family, arugula leaves are abundant at this time. They add an extra peppery dimension to this quick-to-make dip and pep up the mild ricotta and rich olives.

 15 MINS

SPECIAL EQUIPMENT ▪ blender or food processor

SERVES 4

3½oz (100g) arugula leaves

2 garlic cloves, grated or finely chopped

3½oz (100g) black olives, pitted

grated zest and juice of 1 lemon

⅓ cup olive oil

9oz (250g) ricotta cheese

freshly ground black pepper

1 Put the arugula leaves, garlic, olives, lemon zest and juice, and oil in a blender or food processor, and pulse or blend until smooth.

2 Transfer the arugula and olive mixture to a bowl, add the ricotta cheese, and season with black pepper. Mix well.

3 Serve with torn chunks of warm sourdough bread, thick toasted slices of baguette, or grilled flatbread.

variation

spaghetti with cherry tomato, arugula, and black olive sauce

This makes a great pasta sauce, but you only need half the ingredients for four people. Simply cook 12oz (350g) spaghetti according to the package directions. Drain and return to the pan. Add 12 halved cherry tomatoes and then half the arugula dip. Toss over low heat until the dip has melted and coats the spaghetti. The tomatoes should have softened just slightly, but retained their shape. Pile into bowls and serve hot with some freshly grated Parmesan sprinkled over the top. Store the rest of the dip in the fridge in an airtight container and use within 3 days.

smoked trout, fennel, and mascarpone crostini

In this easy appetizer, the richness of the trout and mascarpone is nicely balanced by the fresh, light flavor and crunch of the summer fennel.

 25 MINS 15 MINS

SERVES 4

2 tbsp olive oil

4 thick slices of crusty sourdough bread

salt and freshly ground black pepper

1 garlic clove, peeled but left whole

2 smoked trout, about 10oz (300g) each

5½oz (150g) fennel bulb, trimmed, halved, and thinly sliced

½ cup mascarpone

1oz (30g) flaked almonds, toasted

juice of ½ lemon

sprigs of chervil, to garnish

1 lemon, cut into wedges, to serve

1 Preheat the oven to 400°F (200°C). Pour the oil onto a baking sheet, then gently press the bread into the oil on both sides. Season with salt and pepper. Bake in the oven for 12–15 minutes until golden brown. Remove from the oven and lightly rub each slice with the garlic. Set aside on a wire rack to keep the crostini crisp.

2 Meanwhile, remove the skin from the smoked trout and gently remove the flesh from the bones in big chunks.

3 Put the trout, fennel, mascarpone, flaked almonds, and lemon juice in a bowl. Season with black pepper and gently mix together.

4 To serve, arrange the trout mixture over the crostini, season with some more pepper, and garnish with the chervil. Serve immediately with lemon wedges, which can be squeezed over the appetizer.

tomato borscht

In Russia and Ukraine, borscht often includes tomatoes as well as beets. This version may seem unusual, but you will love its rich color and fantastic taste.

 25 MINS 25 MINS ❄ FREEZABLE

SPECIAL EQUIPMENT ▪ food processor or handheld blender

SERVES 4

2 tbsp olive oil

1 small onion, finely chopped

1 garlic clove, chopped

8oz (225g) raw beets, peeled and finely grated

1 tsp freshly ground toasted cumin seeds, plus unground to serve

¼ tsp ground cinnamon

8oz (225g) ripe tomatoes, skinned (p197) and coarsely chopped

1 cup tomato juice

1 tbsp sun-dried tomatoes, very finely chopped

2 cups vegetable stock

1 tbsp light soy sauce

salt and freshly ground black pepper

sour cream or crème fraîche, to serve

1 Heat the oil in a heavy-bottomed pan over medium heat, add the onion and garlic, and cook for 3–4 minutes until the onion is soft. Then add the beets and sweat gently for another 10 minutes, stirring occasionally, until softened.

2 Add the ground spices, tomatoes, tomato juice, and sun-dried tomatoes, then pour in the stock. Bring to a boil. Reduce the heat slightly, cover, and simmer very gently for 15 minutes, or until all the vegetables are soft. Remove the soup from the heat and using a processor or handheld blender, purée until smooth. Check the seasoning, adding the soy sauce, salt, and pepper to taste.

3 Serve chilled, at room temperature, or slightly warm. If you reheat the soup, do so gently over low heat. To serve, spoon into serving bowls and garnish with toasted cumin seeds and a spoonful of sour cream or crème fraîche.

watermelon salad with feta and pumpkin seeds

This salad is fast becoming a modern classic. The sweetness of the ripe melon contrasts wonderfully with the salty feta and the nuttiness of the pumpkin seeds.

 10 MINS 5 MINS

SERVES 4

2oz (60g) pumpkin seeds

sea salt and freshly ground black pepper

¼ tsp chile powder

¼ cup light olive oil

juice of 1 lemon

1lb 2oz (500g) watermelon, peeled, seeded if preferred, and cut into ¾in (2cm) squares

½ red onion, finely sliced

4 large handfuls of mixed salad leaves, such as watercress, arugula, or baby spinach

10oz (300g) feta cheese, cut into ½in (1cm) squares

1 Dry-fry the pumpkin seeds for 2–3 minutes until they start to pop. Add a pinch of sea salt and the chile powder, stir, and cook for another minute. Set aside to cool.

2 In a large bowl, whisk together the oil, lemon juice, and sea salt and pepper to taste. Add the watermelon, red onion, and salad leaves, and toss well to coat with the dressing.

3 Scatter the feta cheese and the seeds over the top of the salad and serve immediately.

scallops with sweet chile sauce

Red chiles are relatively high in capsaicin, the chemical that creates a fiery sensation in the mouth, and this chile sauce is designed to give sweet-flavored scallops a little bit of a kick.

 10 MINS PLUS MARINATING   5 MINS

SERVES 4

4 garlic cloves, grated or finely chopped

3 red chiles, seeded and finely chopped

3 tbsp dry sherry

1 tsp granulated sugar

2 tbsp olive oil, plus a little extra for cooking

12 large scallops

1 Put the garlic, chiles, sherry, and sugar in a bowl and mix well until the sugar dissolves. Add the oil and scallops, toss together, then leave to marinate for at least 30 minutes.

2 Transfer the scallops to a plate, using a slotted spoon. Reserve the marinade. Heat a little oil in a nonstick frying pan and cook the scallops over high heat for 1 minute on each side. Remove from the pan and pour in the marinade. Bring to a boil, stirring all the while, then pour on the scallops. Serve with a crisp green salad.

variation

sardines with sweet chile and chive sauce

Substitute 12 cleaned sardines for the scallops and prepare in exactly the same way. Add 2 tbsp snipped chives to the marinade when heating, and serve with lemon wedges.

chorizo with bell peppers

Spicy chorizo sausage needs just the addition of some chunky mixed bell peppers and seasonings to turn it into a tasty tapas dish or starter. Serve with crusty bread.

 10 MINS   10 MINS

SERVES 4

2 tbsp olive oil

2 red bell peppers, seeded and cut into ¾in (2cm) squares

2 green bell peppers, seeded and cut into ¾in (2cm) squares

3 garlic cloves, crushed

10oz (300g) chorizo cut into ¾in (2cm) cubes

2 tbsp dry sherry

1 tbsp chopped oregano

salt and freshly ground black pepper

1 Heat the oil in a frying pan, add the bell peppers, and cook over medium heat, stirring occasionally, for 5 minutes. Add the garlic, chorizo, and sherry and cook for 5 more minutes.

2 Sprinkle on the oregano, season with salt and pepper, and serve.

variation

chorizo with eggplant and zucchini

Substitute 1 cubed eggplant and 2 cubed zucchini for the bell peppers, then prepare in exactly the same way. Add 2 tbsp chopped parsley along with the oregano, and crumble 3oz (85g) feta cheese over the top just before serving.

feta-stuffed peppers

A specialty in northern Spain, these piquant little peppers take on a smoky-sweet flavor once roasted, and taste divine stuffed with tangy feta cheese.

 15 MINS 20 MINS

SERVES 4

5½oz (150g) feta cheese

3 garlic cloves, crushed

1 tbsp finely chopped flat-leaf parsley

1 tsp freshly ground black pepper

12 piquillo peppers

4 tbsp olive oil

1 Preheat the oven to 400°F (200°C). Put the feta, garlic, parsley, and black pepper in a mixing bowl and mash them with the back of a fork to form a smooth paste.

2 Cut the stalk end off each pepper and discard. Carefully seed them (p171), then stuff with the feta cheese mixture. Brush with oil, then pack tightly into a small baking dish. Spoon the remaining oil over the top and bake in the oven for 20 minutes, or until the peppers are soft. Serve hot with fresh crusty bread.

variation

cream cheese and sweet corn stuffed peppers
Prepare and cook the peppers in the same way, and replace the feta cheese filling with 4oz (115g) cream cheese mixed with the kernels of 1 corncob (p155), 1 crushed garlic clove, 1 tbsp chopped thyme, and seasoning to taste.

bruschetta with tomato and basil

These tasty appetizers of toasted ciabatta topped with juicy tomatoes and fragrant basil are ideal for serving with a drink outdoors, or before an evening meal.

 10 MINS 4-5 MINS

MAKES 8

6 ripe tomatoes, coarsely cubed

handful of basil leaves, coarsely torn

4 tbsp extra virgin olive oil

salt and freshly ground black pepper

1 loaf ciabatta

3 garlic cloves, peeled but left whole

1 Put the tomatoes, basil, and oil in a bowl. Season really well with salt and pepper. Set aside to allow the flavors to develop.

2 Preheat the broiler. Slice the ciabatta horizontally lengthwise, then cut each piece into quarters so that you have 8 pieces of bread in total. Toast both sides of the ciabatta until golden.

3 Immediately rub each piece of toasted bread with the garlic. Spoon on the tomato and basil mixture, and serve immediately.

variation

bruschetta with roasted bell peppers and olives
Substitute 1 small roasted red bell pepper and 1 small roasted green bell pepper, peeled, seeded, and cubed (p171), and 2 tbsp pitted, sliced black olives for 4 of the tomatoes.

hot cucumber and tarragon soup

Cooked cucumber has a subtle flavor that combines well with the more assertive but still delicate tarragon.

 15 MINS   **20 MINS**

SPECIAL EQUIPMENT ▪ blender or food processor

SERVES 4

2 medium-large or 3 small cucumbers

1 tbsp sunflower or canola oil

4 tbsp chilled butter, cubed

2 tbsp chopped tarragon

3½ cups light vegetable or chicken stock

salt and freshly ground black pepper

2 tbsp cornstarch

4 heaping tsp cream cheese (optional)

1 Peel the cucumbers, cut crosswise in half, then cut each half lengthwise. With a pointed teaspoon, scoop out and discard all the seeds and chop the flesh coarsely.

2 Place a sauté pan over moderate heat. Add the oil and 1½ tbsp of the butter. Once the butter has melted, add the cucumber and half the tarragon. Stir for 2 minutes, then pour in the stock and season lightly.

3 Bring to simmer, reduce the heat a little, then cover and simmer gently for 10–15 minutes. Stir in the cornstarch and cook for another 2 minutes. Take off the heat and let cool a little.

4 Transfer to a blender or food processor and pulse until smooth. Return to the pan and whisk in the remaining butter. Taste and adjust the seasoning, stir in the rest of the tarragon, and serve hot. If you like, add a dollop of cream cheese (if using) to each bowl when serving.

smoked chicken with basil mayonnaise on cucumber rounds

A slice of succulent cucumber is the perfect size for eating in a single bite, and so is the ideal base for an *hors d'oeuvre*. Serve these tasty appetizers before dinner or at a party.

 20 MINS

SERVES 6-8

approx 9oz (250g) smoked chicken breast

3 tbsp mayonnaise

1 tbsp store-bought pesto

freshly ground black pepper

approx 10oz (300g) cucumber, cut into ¼in(5mm) thick slices

1 Remove the skin from the chicken. Slice across the breast into thin slices and finely chop into small cubes. Put the chicken, mayonnaise, and pesto in a mixing bowl. Season with black pepper and mix well.

2 Spoon 1 heaping teaspoon of the smoked chicken mixture onto a slice of cucumber and arrange on a platter. Repeat with the remaining mixture and cucumber slices.

variation

smoked trout with horseradish mayonnaise on cucumber rounds

Prepare in the same way, but use smoked trout fillets, skinned and flaked (but not too finely) instead of chicken, and horseradish sauce instead of the pesto. Garnish each with a slice of cherry tomato and a tiny sprig of parsley.

sea bean soup with poached eggs

For absolute decadence, top each bowl with a little chopped hard-boiled egg, instead of poached, and a shucked oyster.

 10 MINS   **30 MINS**   **FREEZABLE**

SPECIAL EQUIPMENT ▪ blender or food processor

SERVES 4

7oz (200g) young sea bean, washed

pat of unsalted butter

1 large leek, sliced

1 large potato, peeled and cubed

1 thick slice of lemon

small handful of parsley

3 cups light vegetable or chicken stock

freshly ground black pepper

a little milk (optional)

1 tbsp white wine vinegar

4 large eggs

1 Boil the sea bean in a little water for 3–5 minutes, or until tender. Drain, rinse in cold water, and drain again.

2 Melt the butter in a large saucepan. Add the leek and potato and cook gently, stirring, for 2 minutes, or until soft but not browned. Add the lemon, parsley, stock, and black pepper. Bring to a boil, reduce the heat, cover, and simmer gently for 20 minutes, or until soft. Discard the lemon and pulse in a blender with the sea bean flesh. Return to the pan, taste, and add more black pepper if necessary. If freezing, cool and freeze at this point, then defrost and continue. Thin with a little milk, if desired, then reheat gently.

3 Meanwhile, bring a large pan of water to a boil and add the vinegar. Swirl around to make an eddy and break in the eggs one at a time. Poach until cooked to your liking, then remove with a slotted spoon. Ladle the soup into wide, shallow soup plates, then rest a poached egg in the center of each one to serve.

chicken and zucchini mousse

This smooth, creamy mousse wrapped in fine slices of zucchini makes an impressive hot first course. The trick to success is to butter the ramekin dishes well to make sure that the prettily arranged zucchini slices do not stick when unmolding.

 25-35 MINS PLUS CHILLING   **20-30 MINS**

SPECIAL EQUIPMENT ▪ meat grinder or food processor ▪ 6 x 12fl oz (350ml) ramekins

SERVES 4

1lb 2oz (500g) skinless, boneless chicken breasts

2 large egg whites

salt and freshly ground black pepper

pinch of grated nutmeg

⅔ cup heavy cream

2 zucchini

melted butter, for brushing

For the sauce

8 tbsp butter

2 garlic cloves, finely chopped

2 shallots, finely chopped

¼ cup Madeira

1 tbsp heavy cream

1 Cut the chicken into chunks and work it through the fine blade of a meat grinder, or process in a food processor until ground. It should not be too fine but remain a coarsely ground mixture. Whisk the egg whites until frothy. Gradually add them to the chicken, beating with a wooden spoon until smooth and firm after each addition. Season with salt, pepper, and nutmeg. Beat in the cream, a little at a time. Chill the mixture for about 15 minutes, or until firm. It should hold its shape. To test for seasoning, fry a little piece in a frying pan and taste. Adjust the seasoning if necessary.

2 Cut the zucchini into very thin slices. Bring a saucepan of salted water to a boil. Add the zucchini and simmer for 1–2 minutes until softened. Drain in a colander, rinse under cold water to stop the cooking, then drain on paper towels.

3 Using a ramekin as a guide, cut out 6 circles of parchment paper. Butter the ramekins. Lay a parchment paper circle in the bottom of each and brush it, too, with butter. Be sure to cover all the paper to prevent the zucchini slices from sticking. Meanwhile, preheat the oven to 350°F (180°C). Line the bottoms and sides of the ramekins with overlapping slices of zucchini.

4 Spoon the chicken mousse mixture into the ramekins, smoothing the top, then put in a baking dish. Pour in boiling water to come more than halfway up the sides. Cover the dish with parchment paper and bake for 20–30 minutes, or until a skewer inserted in the center is hot to the touch. During baking, do not let the water boil or the mousse will separate.

5 For the sauce, heat about 2 tbsp of the butter in a small saucepan, add the garlic and shallots, and cook, stirring, for 2–3 minutes. Make sure the garlic does not brown, or the sauce will taste bitter. Add the Madeira and bring to a boil, stirring to dissolve the pan juices, for 2–3 minutes, or until it has reduced to a syrupy glaze. Add the cream and boil again until reduced to a glaze. Remove from the heat and add the remaining butter, a few pieces at a time, whisking constantly and moving the pan on and off the heat to make sure the sauce does not become too hot (or it will separate).

6 Run a fine, sharp knife around the edge of each ramekin. Unmold the chicken mousses onto warm plates, carefully rearranging any slices of zucchini that have become displaced. Spoon the warm Madeira sauce around each mousse.

variation

chicken mousse with tomato and mint coulis

Prepare and cook the mousse as directed in the main recipe. Leave to cool. Omit the butter sauce and make a tomato coulis instead: skin, seed, and roughly chop 9oz (250g) fresh tomatoes (p197), then purée in a food processor until very smooth. With the motor running, gradually add 1 tbsp of olive oil to make an emulsion. Serve the mousses with the tomato coulis spooned around them and sprinkle evenly with chopped fresh mint.

baba ganoush

Thought to originate from India, eggplant has long been popular in Western dishes, too. Smoky baba ganoush, with its garlicky overtones, is one of the most inviting ways to eat it.

 15 MINS   45 MINS

SPECIAL EQUIPMENT ▪ blender or food processor

SERVES 6

2 large eggplants

4 garlic cloves, crushed

small handful of oregano, leaves picked (optional)

grated zest and juice of 1 lemon

⅓ cup olive oil

5½oz (150g) pine nuts, toasted and chopped

½ cup Greek-style yogurt

salt and freshly ground black pepper

1 Heat the grill of a barbecue or a ridged cast-iron grill pan until very hot. Add the whole eggplants and grill, turning every so often, for 30–45 minutes until their skin is charred and blistered all over; it will become quite black. Remove from the heat and let cool a little before peeling away the skin and coarsely chopping the flesh.

2 Put the chopped eggplant, garlic, oregano (if using), lemon zest and juice, and oil in a blender or food processor, and blend to a chunky spread. Transfer to a bowl and add the pine nuts and yogurt. Season with salt and pepper and mix the ingredients well.

3 Serve with torn chunks of sourdough bread, or toasted slices of baguette.

variation

eggplant and chickpea pâté
Prepare in the same way, but use 1 eggplant instead of 2, substitute a drained 14oz (400g) can of chickpeas for the pine nuts, and add a pinch of dried chile flakes with the other ingredients. Blend until chunky, stopping and scraping down the sizes as necessary. Serve in chunks of cucumber, halved, and the seeds scooped out, topped with dried mint.

moroccan-style crepes

Modern eggplants are less bitter than in the past, and rarely need to be salted. But if first salted, left in a colander for half an hour, washed, then dried, they absorb less oil during cooking.

 5 MINS   25 MINS

MAKES 2–4

1 cup all-purpose flour

salt and freshly ground black pepper

1 large egg

1¼ cup milk

1 tbsp olive oil, plus a little extra for frying

1 eggplant, cubed

2 tomatoes, finely chopped

pinch of ground cinnamon

small handful of mint leaves, finely chopped

lemon wedges, to serve

1 Put the flour in a mixing bowl with a little salt, stir, and make a well in the center. Crack the egg into the well and add a tiny amount of the milk. Using a wooden spoon, stir the egg and milk, adding the flour gradually. Add the rest of the milk, little by little, stirring continuously until all the flour is incorporated and the mixture is lump-free. Put in the fridge to rest for 30 minutes, if you have time.

2 Heat the oil in a frying pan, add the eggplant, and cook over medium heat for 5–8 minutes, or until golden. Add the tomatoes and cook for another 5 minutes, or until they start to break down a little. Season well with salt and pepper, then add the cinnamon and mint and stir well.

3 In a small, flat frying pan or crepe pan, heat a drizzle of oil over high heat, swirl it around the pan, then pour it out. Stir the batter, then spoon 2 tbsp of the mixture into the frying pan, swirling it around so it reaches the edges. Cook for a couple of minutes, then pull up the edges with a palette knife. Turn the crepe over and cook the other side for 1 minute. Slide the crepe out onto a plate and keep warm. Repeat with the rest of the batter.

4 Spoon the filling onto the crepes and either roll or fold them up, or simply place the eggplant mixture on top. Serve with lemon wedges.

pan-fried scallops with chile, ginger, and an anchovy dressing

In general, the smaller the chile, the hotter its flavor. If you enjoy something truly hot, look for habañero chiles.

 10 MINS 30 MINS

SERVES 4

For the scallops

2–3 tbsp olive oil

1½lb (675g) waxy potatoes, peeled and thinly sliced

12 scallops (with or without coral, depending on preference), cleaned

salt and freshly ground black pepper

1 red chile, seeded and finely chopped

1in (2.5cm) piece of fresh ginger, peeled and grated

1 lemon, halved

handful of flat-leaf parsley, finely chopped

For the anchovy dressing

3 tbsp extra virgin olive oil

1 tbsp white wine vinegar

8 anchovies in oil, drained and finely chopped

pinch of sugar (optional)

1 Heat 1–2 tbsp of the oil in a large nonstick frying pan over medium-high heat. Add the potatoes and sauté for 15–20 minutes until the potatoes are golden and cooked through. Drain on paper towels and set aside to keep warm.

2 Meanwhile, make the anchovy dressing. In a bowl, whisk together the oil, vinegar, and anchovies until well combined. Taste and add a pinch of sugar if it needs it. Season with black pepper.

3 Pat dry the scallops with paper towels and season with salt and pepper. Put the remaining oil in the frying pan over high heat. When hot, add the scallops. Sear for about 1 minute on one side, then turn them over. Add the chile and ginger, and squeeze in the lemon juice, being careful, since it may spit. Remove the pan from the heat and sprinkle the parsley over the top.

4 Serve immediately with the sautéed potatoes and a drizzle of the anchovy dressing.

stuffed eggplant rolls with salsa

Fried eggplant slices cleverly become wraps, with creamy ricotta cheese and pesto centers and a tangy tomato salsa.

 20 MINS 20 MINS

SPECIAL EQUIPMENT ▪ toothpicks

SERVES 4

1 large eggplant, cut lengthwise into eight ¼in (5mm) thick slices

1 cup fresh toasted bread crumbs

1 tbsp chopped flat-leaf parsley

1 garlic clove, crushed

2 tbsp grated Parmesan cheese

salt and freshly ground black pepper

2 eggs, lightly beaten

½ cup all-purpose flour

½ cup olive oil

9oz (250g) ricotta cheese

1 tbsp store-bought pesto

For the salsa

3 tomatoes, finely chopped

small handful of flat-leaf parsley, finely chopped

1 tbsp olive oil

1 Put the eggplant slices in a colander, rinse well, and drain. Pat dry with paper towels. Put the bread crumbs, parsley, garlic, and Parmesan cheese in a large flat dish. Season, and mix thoroughly until well combined. Put the beaten eggs in another flat dish and the flour in a third. Dip the eggplant slices first in the flour, then in the beaten egg, and finally in the bread crumbs, coating evenly.

2 Heat the oil in 2 large heavy-bottomed frying pans over medium heat, using half of the oil in each one. Divide the eggplant slices among the 2 pans and shallow-fry for 2–4 minutes on each side until golden. Alternatively, cook in 2 batches. Drain on a baking sheet lined with paper towels and keep warm.

3 Meanwhile, put the ricotta cheese and pesto in a bowl and lightly mix together with a fork. To make the tomato salsa, put the tomato, parsley, and oil in a separate bowl. Season with salt and pepper and stir in gently.

4 To serve, put 1 tbsp of the ricotta mixture toward the end of each of the eggplant slices. Roll and secure with a toothpick. Place 2 rolls in the center of each of 4 serving plates and pile the tomato salsa on top.

salade lyonnaise

A dressing of red wine vinegar and bacon peps up this warm spinach salad. For a more sizable dish, top with a warm poached egg, breaking the yolk into the dressing as you eat.

 30-35 MINS   20-25 MINS

SERVES 6

½ baguette

3 tbsp olive oil

1 garlic clove

2 large eggs

1lb 2oz (500g) spinach leaves

9oz (250g) thick-cut bacon, chopped

¼ cup red wine vinegar

1 Preheat the oven to 400°F (200°C). Cut the baguette into ¼in(5mm) slices. Brush both sides of each slice with oil and set on a baking sheet. Bake for 7–10 minutes, until toasted and golden brown, turning once. Cut the garlic clove in half. Rub one side of each slice of toasted bread with the cut side of the garlic. Set the croûtes aside.

2 Hard-boil and shell the eggs. Tear the spinach leaves into large pieces and put in a bowl. Separate the egg yolks from the whites by gently pulling the whites apart. Chop the whites. Put the yolks in a sieve set over a bowl and work them through with the back of a metal spoon.

3 Heat a frying pan, add the bacon, and cook, stirring, for 3–5 minutes, until it is crisp and the fat is rendered. Add to the spinach and toss vigorously for 30 seconds, until the spinach is slightly wilted.

4 Pour the vinegar into the frying pan. Bring it to a boil, stirring, and boil it for about 1 minute, until reduced by one-third. Pour the vinegar over the spinach and bacon and toss together well.

5 Pile the salad onto 6 individual plates. Sprinkle each serving evenly with the chopped egg whites and sieved yolks, and serve immediately, with a pile of the croûtes on the side.

chinese egg drop soup

This can be a simple chicken broth with just the drizzled egg, but it's more tasty and filling with the addition of summery sweet corn and baby spinach, and Chinese seasonings.

 5 MINS   25 MINS

SERVES 4

3½ cups hot chicken stock

1 garlic clove, grated or finely chopped

½ tsp grated fresh ginger

2 scallions, trimmed and chopped

2 tbsp soy sauce

½ tsp Chinese five-spice powder

2 sweet corncobs, kernels removed (about 8oz/225g kernels, p155)

2 large handfuls of baby spinach

2 tbsp cornstarch

2 large eggs, beaten

1 Put the stock in a pan with the garlic, ginger, scallions, soy sauce, and five-spice powder. Add the sweet corn kernels and bring to a boil. Reduce the heat, cover, and simmer gently for 20 minutes.

2 Add the spinach, bring back to a boil, reduce the heat, and simmer for 1 minute or until the spinach has just wilted. Taste and add more soy sauce if necessary.

3 Mix the cornstarch with 4 tbsp water and stir into the soup. Bring back to a boil and simmer, stirring, for 1 minute to thicken slightly. Gradually trickle in the beaten eggs, stirring gently, so that it forms thin strands. Serve in warmed soup bowls.

spanish bell pepper and tomato soup

Just a touch of chile and paprika enlivens this soup and the slow cooking of the peppers enhances their sweet flavor. You could add canned chickpeas for a more substantial soup.

 20 MINS   1 HR 15 MINS–1 HR 30 MINS   FREEZABLE

SPECIAL EQUIPMENT ▪ food processor or handheld blender

SERVES 4-6

1 tbsp olive oil

1 onion, finely chopped

salt and freshly ground black pepper

2 celery stalks, coarsely chopped

3 garlic cloves, finely chopped

1 large carrot, chopped

pinch of dried chile flakes

pinch of paprika

6 red bell peppers, seeded and coarsely chopped

3 tomatoes, coarsely chopped

5 cups hot vegetable stock

3oz (85g) feta cheese, crumbled, to serve (optional)

1 Heat the oil in a large heavy-bottomed pan over medium heat, add the onion, and cook for 3–4 minutes until soft. Season with salt and pepper, add the celery, garlic, and carrot, and cook for 5–10 minutes until soft, stirring occasionally.

2 Stir in the chile flakes and paprika and cook for a minute, then add the peppers and tomatoes. Cook on very low heat for about 20 minutes, stirring so they don't stick. Pour in half of the stock and bring to a boil, then reduce to simmer and partially cover with the lid. Cook on low heat for 45–60 minutes, adding the reserved stock as the cooking liquid reduces.

3 Remove the soup from the heat and, using a food processor or handheld blender, puree until smooth. Add a ladleful of hot water if it is too thick. Pour the soup into a clean pan, taste, season as needed, and heat through. Serve with a little feta cheese on top, if using, together with some crusty bread.

sweet corn fritters with tomato salsa

Homegrown sweet corn is so tender that there is no need to cook it before making these fritters. The generous flavors used here will turn your cobs into something the whole family will enjoy. A fresh tomato salsa is the perfect partner.

 20 MINS **10 MINS**

SPECIAL EQUIPMENT ▪ blender or food processor

MAKES 14-16

1 cup self-rising flour

1 tsp baking powder

2 large eggs

4 tbsp milk

2 sweet corncobs, kernels removed (about 8oz/225g kernels, p155)

1 tsp smoked paprika

2 scallions, trimmed, finely chopped, and green and white parts separated

¼ cup chopped cilantro

1 red or jalapeño chile, seeded and finely chopped (optional)

salt and freshly ground black pepper

2 tbsp sunflower or vegetable oil

2 ripe tomatoes, peeled (p197) and coarsely chopped

2 tbsp extra virgin olive oil

dash of Tabasco or chile sauce

1 Sift the flour and baking powder into a bowl. Mix the eggs and milk together in a bowl, then gradually whisk them into the flour to make a thick batter.

2 Add the sweet corn kernels, paprika, the white parts of the scallions, 2 tbsp of the cilantro, and the chile, if using. Mix well and season with salt and pepper.

3 Heat the sunflower oil in a large frying pan and add the batter mixture in tablespoons. Use the back of the spoon to spread the fritters out slightly, and fry for 2–3 minutes on each side until puffed up and golden brown. Batch-fry until all the mixture is cooked, adding a little more sunflower oil as necessary.

4 For the salsa, put the tomatoes, the remaining cilantro and scallions, olive oil, and Tabasco or chile sauce into a blender or food processor, and pulse until blended but still quite chunky. Check the salsa for seasoning and serve the hot fritters with the salsa on the side.

butterflied sardines stuffed with tomatoes and capers

If you would rather barbecue these sardines, first bake the tomato mix, then lightly oil the grill, and barbecue the fish until golden and cooked through. Combine to serve.

 15 MINS　 10 MINS

SERVES 4

4–6 tomatoes, peeled (p197) and finely chopped

2 tsp capers, rinsed and gently squeezed dry

handful of flat-leaf parsley, finely chopped, plus extra to garnish (optional)

2 garlic cloves, grated or finely chopped

salt and freshly ground black pepper

12 sardines, butterflied

a little olive oil

juice of 1 lemon

1 Preheat the oven to 400°F (200°C). Put the tomatoes, capers, parsley, and garlic in a bowl. Season with salt and pepper and stir well to combine.

2 Lay the sardines out flat, skin-side down, and spoon on the tomato mixture. Either roll up the sardines lengthwise or just fold them over, then sit them all in a baking sheet. Drizzle the sardines with the oil and lemon juice.

3 Bake in the oven for 10–15 minutes until the sardines are cooked through. Garnish with extra parsley, if you wish, and serve with a crisp green salad.

fish with zucchini, eggplants, and tomatoes

Roasted eggplant marries well with full-bodied ingredients like tomatoes and lemon. Either haddock or pollack (a sustainable choice) are good seasonal options for this dish.

 15 MINS　 35 MINS

SERVES 4

1½lb (675g) white fish loins, such as haddock or pollock, peeled and cut into chunky pieces

2 tbsp olive oil

1 tsp fennel seeds, crushed

grated zest of 1 lemon

salt and freshly ground black pepper

4 small to medium zucchini, sliced

2 eggplants, cut into bite-sized pieces

12 cherry tomatoes

handful of dill, finely chopped

lemon wedges, to serve

1 Preheat the oven to 400°F (200°C). Toss the fish pieces with half the oil, half the fennel seeds, and half the lemon zest. Season well with salt and pepper, then cover and set aside.

2 Meanwhile, put the zucchini and eggplants in a roasting pan with the remaining oil, fennel seeds, and lemon zest and toss together well.

Season with salt and pepper, then put the vegetables in the oven to roast for 20 minutes, or until they begin to soften.

3 Stir and turn the vegetables well. Add the fish and the tomatoes and cook for another 15 minutes, or until the fish is cooked through. Sprinkle the dill over the top and serve with the lemon wedges and some fresh crusty bread.

variation

roasted sardines with vegetable medley

Prepare in a similar way, but use 8 cleaned, large sardines (pilchards) instead of the white fish. Stuff them with some sprigs of thyme and omit the fennel seeds. Drizzle the fish with olive oil before baking. When cooked, scatter a few fresh thyme leaves on top instead of the dill.

white fish with spinach and pine nuts

Haddock, flounder, and pollock are all excellent, flaky white fish substitutes for cod, and are full of flavor.

 10 MINS 15 MINS

SERVES 4

4 haddock fillets or other white fish, such as flounder, pollock, or cod, about 5½oz (150g) each

salt and freshly ground black pepper

2 tbsp olive oil

1 onion, finely chopped

handful of plump raisins

handful of pine nuts, toasted

1-2 tsp capers, rinsed and gently squeezed dry

2 large handfuls of spinach, rinsed and drained

1 Season the fish with salt and pepper. Heat 1 tbsp of the oil in a large nonstick frying pan over medium heat. Add the fish and cook gently for 5–6 minutes on one side. Turn over and cook on the other side until cooked through—this will depend on the thickness of the fish, but be careful not to overcook. Remove from the pan and set aside to keep warm.

2 Carefully wipe out the pan with paper towels, then add the remaining oil. Sauté the onion for about 5 minutes until soft and translucent. Add the raisins, pine nuts, and capers and cook for a few minutes more, breaking up the capers with the back of a fork. Add the spinach and cook until just wilted. Taste and season if needed. Serve the fish on a bed of the wilted spinach mixture.

variation

white fish with swiss chard, harissa, tomatoes, and pumpkin seeds

Prepare in the same way, but use 6 sun-dried tomatoes in oil, drained and chopped, instead of the raisins, pumpkin seeds instead of the pine nuts, and add 1 tbsp harissa paste. Use 12oz (350g) Swiss chard leaves instead of the spinach, thickly shredded. Add 12 halved cherry tomatoes along with the Swiss chard.

chicken jambalaya

Jambalaya, a traditional Southern dish from Louisiana, combines the summer flavors of bell peppers, peas, and herbs and adds a little heat with some cayenne pepper.

 15-20 MINS 1 HR 30 MINS

SERVES 4-6

2 tbsp olive oil

6 boneless chicken pieces (thigh and breast), cut into large chunky pieces

salt and freshly ground black pepper

2 tbsp chopped oregano

2 tsp cayenne pepper

1 red onion, finely chopped

3 garlic cloves, finely chopped

1 green bell pepper, seeded and finely chopped

1 red bell pepper, seeded and finely chopped

7oz (200g) thick slices cooked ham, coarsely chopped

3 cups hot chicken stock

6oz (175g) long-grain rice

5oz (140g) peas (shelled weight)

small handful of cilantro, finely chopped (optional)

1 Heat half the oil in a large flameproof casserole dish over medium-high heat. Season the chicken pieces with salt and pepper, toss in the oregano and cayenne pepper, then add to the casserole dish (in batches, if necessary) and cook for 6–10 minutes until golden brown. Remove and set aside.

2 Heat the remaining oil in the casserole dish over medium heat, add the onion, garlic, and bell peppers and cook for 5–8 minutes, stirring, until soft. Return the chicken to the casserole dish and stir in the ham. Pour in the stock and bring to a boil, then reduce to simmer, season well, partially cover with the lid, and cook gently for about 40 minutes. Check occasionally that it's not drying out and add a little hot water if needed. Stir in the rice, turning it so it absorbs all the stock, and cook for about 15 minutes or until the rice is cooked, adding more stock if necessary. Add the peas for the last 5 minutes.

3 Taste and add seasoning, if needed, and stir in the cilantro, if using. Serve with a green salad, green beans, plain yogurt or sour cream, and some crusty bread.

baked eggs with tomatoes and bell peppers

This dish is instantly enlivened by colorful peppers, tomatoes, and chiles. Omit or reduce the quantity of chiles slightly if you don't like too much heat in your food.

 10 MINS 20 MINS

SERVES 4

1 tbsp olive oil

1 red onion, sliced

salt and freshly ground black pepper

2 red peppers, seeded and sliced

2 yellow bell peppers or orange bell peppers, seeded and sliced

2 red chiles, seeded and finely chopped

3 tomatoes, peeled (p197) and coarsely chopped

2 handfuls of spinach leaves

pinch of paprika

4 eggs

1 Preheat the oven to 400°F (200°C). Heat the oil in a large ovenproof frying pan over low heat. Add the onion and a little salt. Cook for 5 minutes until the onion is soft, then add the peppers and chiles. Cook for another 5 minutes until the peppers soften.

2 Stir in the tomatoes and cook, stirring well until they begin to soften. Add the spinach and paprika and cook for a few minutes more until the spinach begins to wilt.

3 Make a little pocket in the mixture for each of the eggs, then carefully break an egg into each pocket. Slide the pan into the oven and cook for about 5 minutes until the eggs are baked. Be careful not to let them overcook—the residual heat will keep cooking them after you have removed them from the oven. Sprinkle with black pepper and serve immediately.

calzone with bell peppers, capers, and olives

A family crowd-pleaser with sweet bell peppers and salty capers. All you need to accompany this is a fresh, seasonal salad.

  15 MINS 20 MINS ❋ FREEZABLE

MAKES 1

1 cup bread flour

salt and freshly ground black pepper

pinch of sugar

¾ tsp dried yeast

1 tbsp olive oil

4 red bell peppers, roasted, peeled, and chopped (p171)

handful of pitted black olives, coarsely chopped

1-2 tsp capers, rinsed

2-3 tbsp ricotta cheese or mozzarella, torn into pieces

1 Sift the flour, a pinch of salt, and the sugar into a bowl and add the yeast. Stir in the oil and add up to ⅓ cup warm water to form a soft, but not sticky, dough. Knead gently on a floured work surface for several minutes until smooth and elastic. Return to the bowl, cover with oiled plastic wrap, and leave in a warm place (you can preheat the oven and leave the bowl on the stovetop) for 30-40 minutes, or until doubled in size.

2 Turn the dough onto a floured work surface again and punch it down by rekneading briefly. Preheat the oven to its highest setting and heat a lightly oiled baking sheet. Roll out the dough thinly to a round, about 10in (25cm) in diameter. Transfer the pizza crust to the baking sheet, spreading it out firmly again.

3 Spoon the peppers, olives, capers, and ricotta cheese or mozzarella onto half the pizza crust, leaving about ½in(1cm) around the edge. Season well with salt and pepper. Dampen the edges of the pizza with a little water, then fold one half of the pizza over the other and seal together with your fingers. Sprinkle the top with a little water and bake in the oven for 15-20 minutes, or until golden and crispy. Serve while hot.

Season's best **peppers**

Members of the capsicum family, sweet peppers are usually bell-shaped or long and flat. They range in color from green when unripe to yellow, orange, or red, getting sweeter as they change color. You may also find purple, brown, or near black ripe varieties. At their best in high summer and autumn, they are particularly delicious with garlic, onions, tomatoes, and other Mediterranean vegetables and fragrant rosemary, basil, and oregano.

Peppers are native to the tropical Americas, but are now grown worldwide. They need heat and light so, in cooler climates, are grown under glass or in polytunnels.

essentials
varieties available

Bell-shaped or long and pointed, there are many varieties ranging in color from green through red to almost black.

buy Choose fruits that are glossy and firm, with no soft spots or mold. They should have some heft to them, rather than feel light.

store Keep in paper bags or open-topped plastic bags in the fridge for up to 2 weeks. Once cut, use within 24 hours.

cook Stuff and bake, roast, grill, or barbecue. Stew, sauté, stir-fry, or use raw as crudités or in salads.

preserve Pickle in vinegar or in oil.

recipe ideas

Chilled tomato and red bell pepper soup p144

Mixed bell peppers in oil p232

Three-pepper pizza with cheese p172

Red bell pepper As they ripen, bell peppers turn from green to red, and become sweeter and fleshier. With their boxy shape, they are ideal for stuffing or roasting whole.

Green bell pepper Unripe green bell peppers have thinner walls than ripe bell peppers, and a distinct herbaceous flavor that mellows as they mature.

Romano (Ramiro) pepper The Italian heirloom variety Nardello has a mild flavor when green, becoming intensely sweet when red. It is ideal stuffed, or fried with slices of Italian sausage.

how to roast and peel peppers

Bell peppers can have thick skins, which are easiest to remove by char-roasting. The technique also imparts a delicious, slightly smoky taste and enhances the sweetness of the pepper flesh. The same roasting and peeling method can be used for chile peppers as well as for tomatoes and even garlic.

1 Using long-handled tongs, hold each pepper over an open flame, rotating slowly to char the skin on all sides until black all over.

2 While they are still hot, place the charred peppers into a plastic bag and seal tightly. Set aside to allow steam to loosen the skin.

3 After about 10 minutes, and once cooled, peel away the charred skin from each pepper with your fingers. Slice or chop the flesh as needed.

three-pepper pizza with cheese

Choose brightly colored, firm bell peppers with no soft spots, and add finely sliced chiles instead of cayenne, if you prefer.

 1 HR 15 MINS PLUS STANDING 20-25 MINS

SERVES 4-6

1 cup bread flour

salt and freshly ground black pepper

pinch of sugar

¾ tsp dried yeast

5 tbsp olive oil

2 onions, thinly sliced

2 red bell peppers, seeded and cut into strips

1 green bell pepper, seeded and cut into strips

1 yellow bell pepper, seeded and cut into strips

3 garlic cloves, finely chopped

small bunch of any herb, such as rosemary, thyme, basil, or parsley, or a mixture, leaves finely chopped

cayenne, to taste

6oz (175g) mozzarella cheese, sliced

1 Sift the flour, a pinch of salt, and the sugar into a bowl and add the yeast. Stir in 1 tbsp of the oil and add up to ⅓ cup warm water to form a soft, but not sticky, dough. Knead gently on a floured work surface for several minutes until smooth and elastic. Return to the bowl, cover with oiled plastic wrap, and leave in a warm place (you can preheat the oven and leave the bowl on the stovetop) for 30–40 minutes, or until doubled in size.

2 Heat 1 tbsp of the oil in a frying pan, add the onions, and stir for 2–3 minutes until soft. Transfer to a bowl and set aside. Add the remaining oil to the pan, then add the bell peppers, garlic, and half the herbs. Season with salt and cayenne. Sauté, stirring, for 7–10 minutes until soft. Taste for seasoning; it should be quite spicy.

3 Preheat the oven to 450°F (230°C). Put a baking sheet near the bottom of the oven to heat up and generously flour a second baking sheet. Turn the dough onto a floured work surface again and punch it down by rekneading briefly. Roll out the dough thinly to a round, about 10in (25cm) in diameter. Transfer the pizza crust to the floured baking sheet and press up the edge to form a shallow rim, if you like.

4 Spread the onions and then the bell peppers evenly over the pizza crust, leaving a ³⁄₄in (2cm) border all around the edge (if you haven't made a shallow rim), so it can become golden in the oven. Spoon any remaining oil from the frying pan over the bell peppers and top them evenly with the slices of mozzarella. Let the assembled pizza stand in a warm place for 10–15 minutes, until the dough has puffed up well around the edges. Don't leave it for any longer, since it should be baked as soon as possible to retain maximum flavor.

5 With a sharp, jerking movement, slide the pizza onto the heated baking sheet at the bottom of the oven. Bake for about 20–25 minutes, or until brown all over and the cheese has melted. If you are using finely sliced chile instead of cayenne, add it 5 minutes before the end of the cooking time. Remove from the oven, scatter the reserved herbs over the top of the pizza, and serve.

caribbean stew with allspice and ginger

Fiery Scotch Bonnets are the quintessential Caribbean chile.

 30 MINS PLUS MARINATING   **30 MINS**   **FREEZABLE**

SPECIAL EQUIPMENT ▪ blender or food processor

SERVES 8

1–2 Scotch Bonnet chiles (according to taste), seeded

2 tsp ground allspice

handful of thyme leaves

2 tsp tamarind paste

2in (5cm) piece of fresh ginger, peeled and coarsely chopped

salt and freshly ground black pepper

3 tbsp olive oil

4 large boneless, skinless chicken breasts, peeled and cut into bite-sized pieces

1 tbsp all-purpose flour

5 cups hot chicken stock

4 mixed bell peppers, seeded and coarsely chopped

5 tomatoes, peeled (p197) and chopped

1 Put the chiles, allspice, thyme, tamarind, ginger, and seasoning in a food processor and pulse to a paste.

Add a little of the oil and pulse again. Pour into a plastic bag, add the chicken, and marinate for 30 minutes, or overnight in the fridge.

2 Heat the remaining oil in a large cast-iron pan or flameproof casserole dish, add the chicken and marinade, and cook, stirring often, over medium heat for 10 minutes, or until the chicken is golden. Stir in the flour, add a little stock, and stir to scrape up any crispy pieces from the bottom of the pan. Pour in the rest of the stock and stir until the flour has blended in.

3 Stir in the bell peppers and tomatoes and season well with salt and pepper. Bring to a boil, then reduce to simmer and cook over low heat for 30 minutes, or until the sauce has begun to thicken slightly. Taste and season again if needed. Serve piping hot with baked or mashed sweet potatoes.

fiery pepper noodles

A wonderfully spicy vegetarian dish, where lime and chile work extremely well with bell peppers, scallions, and peanuts.

 30 MINS   **4–5 MINS**

SERVES 4

1 red bell pepper

1 green bell pepper

1 tbsp sunflower or vegetable oil

4 scallions, chopped

1 garlic clove, finely chopped

1 zucchini, finely chopped

1 or 2 jalapeño or poblano chiles, seeded and chopped

1 tsp grated fresh ginger

1 tbsp chopped flat-leaf parsley

1 tbsp chopped cilantro, plus a few torn leaves, to serve

grated zest and juice of 1 lime

¼ cup crunchy peanut butter

3 tbsp soy sauce

1 tbsp dry sherry

1lb 2oz (500g) fresh egg noodles

2oz (60g) chopped roasted peanuts, to serve

1 Preheat the oven to 400°F (200°C). Put the bell peppers in a roasting pan and cook for 25–30 minutes until they begin to char. Remove from the oven, put in a plastic bag, and leave to cool before removing the stems and skin, seeding, and coarsely chopping.

2 Heat the oil in a wok or large frying pan. Add the scallions, garlic, and zucchini and stir-fry for 1 minute. Add the bell peppers, chiles, ginger, herbs, lime zest and juice, peanut butter, soy sauce, sherry, and 9 tbsp water. Stir the ingredients until the peanut butter melts.

3 Add the noodles and toss for 2 minutes until piping hot. Pile into warm bowls and sprinkle with peanuts and a few torn cilantro leaves.

greek stuffed tomatoes

With their thick, plump flesh, large beefsteak tomatoes make ideal "containers" within which to bake other ingredients. This recipe also includes medium-hot chiles for added flavor.

 10 MINS   **1 HR 30 MINS**

SERVES 4

4 large beefsteak tomatoes

½ tbsp olive oil

14oz (400g) ground lamb

pinch of paprika

pinch of ground cumin

pinch of ground cinnamon

2 jalapeño chiles, seeded and finely chopped

1 tbsp tomato paste

1 tbsp harissa paste

handful of mint leaves, chopped

⅔ cup hot vegetable stock

sea salt and freshly ground black pepper

1 Slice the tops off the tomatoes and scoop out the flesh. Reserve the shells and "lids," and coarsely chop and reserve the scooped-out flesh (including juices and seeds). Preheat the oven to 400°F (200°C).

2 Heat the oil in a large frying pan over medium heat. Add the ground lamb and cook, stirring to break up any lumps, until the meat is browned and no longer pink.

3 Add the reserved chopped tomato flesh and the paprika, ground cumin, and ground cinnamon. Cook, stirring, for a couple of minutes.

4 Add the chiles, tomato paste, harissa, and mint leaves, and stir. Pour in the hot vegetable stock and bring to a boil. Simmer for 15 minutes until the mixture has thickened, then season with sea salt and pepper.

5 Spoon the mixture into the reserved tomato shells, put their lids on, and sit the stuffed tomatoes on a roasting pan. Cover with foil and bake in the oven for 1 hour, then serve.

vietnamese beef soup

It's the slow-cooked beef stock, flavored with gentle spices that really makes this dish. Add extra scallions, chiles, or julienned carrots and bean sprouts, if you wish.

 15 MINS   1 HR 15 MINS

SERVES 4–6

about 1½lb (675g) beef bones, rinsed and dried

1 tbsp dark soy sauce

1 tbsp olive oil

1 star anise

1 tsp black peppercorns

1 cinnamon stick

½ tbsp fish sauce (nam pla)

1 onion, finely chopped

3 garlic cloves, finely chopped

1 chile, seeded and finely chopped

1 lemongrass stalk, trimmed, tough outer leaves removed, and finely chopped

1in (2.5cm) piece of fresh ginger, peeled and finely sliced

salt and freshly ground black pepper

12oz (350g) beef tenderloin, very finely sliced across the grain

2oz (60g) vermicelli noodles, soaked in hot water for 5 minutes (or as per package instructions) and drained

bunch of green scallions, trimmed and finely sliced

1 First, make the beef stock. In a bowl, toss the beef bones with the soy sauce. Heat a little of the oil in a large heavy-bottomed pan over medium-high heat, add the bones, and cook, stirring, for about 15 minutes until the meat is no longer pink.

2 Transfer them to a large stock pan, pour in 5 cups water, and add the star anise, peppercorns, cinnamon stick, and fish sauce. Bring to a boil, then partially cover with the lid, reduce to simmer, and cook for 1 hour. Strain the stock through a sieve into a clean pan, adding water to 3 cups, if necessary, and reserve.

3 Heat the remaining oil in a large heavy-bottomed pan, add the onion, and cook for 3–4 minutes until soft. Do not brown. Stir in the garlic, chile, and lemongrass and cook for a minute. Then pour in the beef stock, add the ginger, and taste, adding seasoning if needed. Gently simmer for a few minutes, then add the sliced steak to the stock and cook for 2–3 minutes. Stir in the noodles and scallions and ladle into warmed bowls.

lacquered chicken salad

A chicken salad with crunchy lettuce and baby sweet corn.

 25–30 MINS PLUS MARINATING   10–15 MINS

SERVES 4

4 boneless, skinless chicken breasts, total weight about 1lb 10oz (750g)

½in (1cm) piece of fresh ginger, peeled and finely chopped

1 garlic clove, finely chopped

¼ cup brown sugar

2 tbsp Dijon mustard

3 tbsp rice wine

3 tbsp sesame oil

salt and freshly ground black pepper

¼ cup soy sauce

½ cup vegetable oil

4½oz (125g) bean sprouts

leaves from 1 head of Romaine lettuce, shredded

3oz (85g) baby sweet corn, halved lengthwise

1 Lightly score the top of each chicken breast and set them in a shallow, nonmetallic dish.

2 Combine the ginger, garlic, brown sugar, mustard, 1 tbsp each of the rice wine and sesame oil, and black pepper in a bowl. Pour in the soy sauce and stir. Remove and reserve ¼ cup of the marinade, then pour the rest over the chicken, cover, and chill in the fridge for 1–2 hours, turning 3–4 times.

3 Add the remaining rice wine and sesame oil to the reserved marinade and mix. Gradually whisk in the vegetable oil until the dressing emulsifies and thickens slightly. Taste for seasoning and set aside, or chill in the fridge, tightly sealed, for up to 12 hours if you have time. Put the bean sprouts in a bowl. Cover generously with boiling water and leave to stand for 1 minute. Drain, rinse with cold, running water, and drain again.

4 Preheat the broiler and oil the broiler rack. Put the chicken on the rack and brush with the marinade. Broil about 3in (7.5cm) from the heat, brushing often with the marinade, for 5–7 minutes on each side until well browned and glossy, but still tender. Put chicken on a cutting board and cut diagonally into slices.

5 Put the shredded lettuce in a mixing bowl and add the bean sprouts and sweet corn. Briskly whisk the dressing again and pour it over the salad. Toss and taste for seasoning. Arrange the salad on a serving plate, top with the chicken, and serve while still warm.

sea bass with herb butter sauce

An impressive dish of superbly flavored sea bass to share.

 40–45 MINS 30–40 MINS

SPECIAL EQUIPMENT ▪ food processor

SERVES 4

bunch of watercress, half reserved as a garnish

8 spinach leaves

10–12 sprigs of parsley, leaves picked

10–12 sprigs of chervil, leaves picked

1 garlic clove, peeled

2 anchovy fillets

2 tsp capers, drained

1 small gherkin

5 tbsp butter

3 tbsp olive oil

1 lemon, cut in half lengthwise, one half cut crosswise into thin slices, and the other half squeezed

1 tsp Dijon mustard

salt and freshly ground black pepper

1 whole sea bass, about 4½lb (2kg)

3–5 sprigs of thyme

2 tbsp butter

½ cup dry white wine

1 Bring a pan of well-salted water to a boil. Add half the watercress, spinach, parsley, and chervil, and simmer for 1–2 minutes until tender. Drain, rinse with cold water, and drain again. Squeeze the leaves with your hands to remove all excess water.

2 Preheat the oven to 375°F (190°C). Pulse the garlic, anchovies, capers, and gherkin in a food processor. Add the butter, piece by piece, and pulse to a purée. Add the greens and pulse again. With the blade turning, slowly pour in the oil. Add the lemon juice, mustard, and seasoning, and pulse briefly. Transfer to a serving dish.

3 Slash the fish, about ½in (1cm) deep, diagonally 3–4 times on each side. Set in a roasting pan and tuck a sprig of thyme and a slice of lemon into each slash. Dot with the butter and sprinkle with white wine, salt, and pepper. Roast, basting occasionally, for about 30 minutes, until it just flakes easily when tested with a fork and is no longer translucent in the center. Be careful not to overcook. Serve with the sauce and reserved watercress.

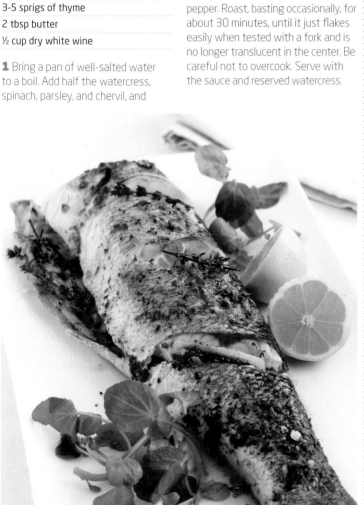

chicken stir-fried with scallion, basil, and lemongrass

Stir-frying is such a quick way to cook food that it's best to chop and prepare all your ingredients first.

 10 MINS 15 MINS

SERVES 4

2–3 skinless chicken breasts, sliced into strips

salt and freshly ground black pepper

1 tbsp cornstarch

2 tbsp sesame oil or vegetable oil

bunch of scallions, trimmed and sliced diagonally

3 garlic cloves, sliced

1 lemongrass stalk, trimmed, tough outer leaves removed, and chopped

2 red chiles, seeded and sliced

1 tbsp Chinese rice wine

handful of basil leaves

1 Season the chicken with salt and pepper. Put the cornstarch on a plate and toss the chicken strips in it until very well coated.

2 Heat 1 tbsp of the oil in a wok over high heat. Swirl it around the wok, then add the chicken and stir-fry quickly, moving the chicken around for 3–5 minutes until golden and cooked through. Remove with a slotted spoon and keep warm.

3 Carefully wipe out the wok with paper towels, reduce the heat to medium-high, and add the remaining oil. When hot, add the scallions, garlic, lemongrass, and chiles. Stir-fry for a couple of minutes, then increase the heat to high once again, add the rice wine, and boil for a few minutes.

4 Return the chicken to the wok to just heat through, then stir in the basil and serve immediately with some fluffy rice.

spiced haddock with coconut, chile, and lime

Chopped red chile and lime juice add intensity and heat to this Thai-inspired dish of mild, creamy coconut and white fish.

 10 MINS   20 MINS

SERVES 4

4 haddock fillets, about 1½lb (675g) in total

salt and freshly ground black pepper

14oz (400ml) can coconut milk

1 red chile, seeded and finely chopped

juice of 1 lime

splash of fish sauce (nam pla)

pinch of sugar (optional)

5½oz (150g) fresh green beans, trimmed

1 tbsp vegetable or sunflower oil

For the spice mixture

1–2 tsp cayenne pepper, to taste

1 tsp paprika

1 tsp ground cinnamon

1 tsp ground coriander

1 tbsp cornstarch

1 To make the spice mixture, combine the spices and the cornstarch in a bowl. Season the haddock, then coat well with the spice mixture. Set aside.

2 Pour the coconut milk into a wide pan, add the chile, and bring to a boil. Reduce the heat to simmer and add the lime juice, fish sauce, and a pinch of sugar (if using). Throw in the green beans and simmer for about 5 minutes.

3 Meanwhile, heat the oil in a nonstick frying pan over high heat. Add the fish and fry for about 5 minutes on each side until golden. To serve, add the fish to the sauce and serve hot. Alternatively, serve the sauce on the side.

variation

pan-fried salmon with coconut, chile, and lime
Replace the haddock with 4 salmon fillets, about 1½lb (675g) in total, in step 1.

sausage and chicken jambalaya

This is a highly flavored, gutsy dish with okra and mixed peppers. Serve with a salad and crusty bread.

 15 MINS   2 HRS 15 MINS   FREEZABLE

SERVES 6

1–2 tbsp olive oil

4 chicken thighs, chopped in half

9oz (250g) smoked sausage, cut into bite-sized pieces

9oz (250g) dry Spanish chorizo, chopped into thick slices

2 onions, cubed

1 green bell pepper, seeded and cubed

1 red bell pepper, seeded and cubed

salt and freshly ground black pepper

3 garlic cloves, finely chopped

2 tsp Cajun seasoning

1 tbsp all-purpose flour

3 cups hot chicken stock

2 tbsp Worcestershire sauce

10oz (300g) white rice

2 bay leaves

9oz (250g) okra, sliced

handful of flat-leaf parsley, chopped

1 Preheat the oven to 300°F (150°C). Heat the oil in a large flameproof casserole dish over medium-high heat, add the chicken, and fry quickly, turning, until browned all over. Remove with a slotted spoon and set aside. Add the sausages and cook for 5–8 minutes until golden. Remove and set aside.

2 Reduce the heat to medium, add the onions, and cook for 3–4 minutes until soft. Add the peppers and cook for a few minutes. Season, add the garlic and Cajun seasoning, and cook for 1 minute. Stir in the flour, ladle in a little stock, and stir well. Return the chicken and sausages to the pan and add the Worcestershire sauce.

3 Stir in the rice and bay leaves, then pour over the remaining stock. Mix well, cover, and put in the oven for 1½ hours. Occasionally check that it's not drying out and add a little hot water if needed. Stir in the okra, re-cover, and cook for another 30 minutes. Remove the bay leaves, taste and season if needed, then stir in the parsley and serve.

fish with tomatoes, potatoes, and onions

Use a combination of fish in this summery all-in-one meal. Flaky, sweet haddock and sea bass are both good choices.

 30 MINS   15 MINS

SERVES 8

3 tbsp olive oil

5 large potatoes, cut into bite-sized pieces

salt and freshly ground black pepper

4 garlic cloves, grated or finely chopped

handful of flat-leaf parsley, finely chopped

1¼lb (550g) cherry tomatoes, halved

1½ cup dry white wine

1½lb (675g) mixed firm-flesh fish, such as haddock and sea bass, cut into bite-sized pieces

16 anchovy fillets in oil, drained

1 Heat the oil in a large, shallow heavy-bottomed pan, add the potatoes, and season well with salt and pepper. Cook over medium heat, stirring frequently, for 10–15 minutes, or until beginning to turn golden brown. Lower the heat, then stir in the garlic and parsley, and cook for a few seconds before adding the tomatoes.

2 Cook for 6–8 minutes, or until the tomatoes begin to split, then raise the heat, add the wine, and allow to boil for a couple of minutes while the alcohol evaporates. Turn the heat to low, add the fish and the anchovies, cover, and cook for 10–15 minutes, or until the fish is tender. Transfer to a large, shallow serving dish and serve with a crisp, dressed salad and some fresh crusty bread.

cobb salad

This California classic is a wonderful main course salad. With its smooth textures of avocado and Roquefort cheese mixed with crispy bacon bits, cooked chicken, and crunchy lettuce leaves, it is bound to satisfy. A tarragon vinaigrette helps to bring the whole dish together.

 20-25 MINS   5 MINS

SERVES 4-6

4lb (1.8kg) whole cooked chicken or 1lb 2oz (500g) cooked skinless, boneless chicken

6 slices bacon, chopped

2 avocados

juice of 1 lemon

1 shallot, finely chopped

1lb 2lb (500g) large head of Romaine lettuce or Little Gem lettuces, leaves sliced into strips

2 large tomatoes, cored and sliced

3oz (85g) Roquefort or other blue cheese, crumbled

For the vinaigrette

4 tbsp red wine vinegar

2 tsp Dijon mustard

½ tsp salt

¼ tsp pepper

¾ cup vegetable oil

3 sprigs of tarragon, leaves picked and finely chopped

1 If using a whole cooked chicken, remove the meat from the bones, discarding all skin and any gristle, and cut into thin slices.

2 To make the vinaigrette, put the vinegar, mustard, salt, and pepper in a small bowl and whisk together. Add the oil in a steady stream, whisking constantly. The dressing will emulsify and thicken slightly. Stir the chopped tarragon into the dressing and taste for seasoning, adjusting it if needed.

3 Heat a small frying pan over medium heat and cook the bacon strips until golden and crispy and the fat has rendered. Remove with a slotted spoon and drain on paper towels to blot off any excess fat.

5 Cut lengthwise around the avocados, remove the pit, peel, and thinly slice. Toss the avocado slices gently in the lemon juice to prevent any discoloration.

6 Toss the chicken, shallot, and lettuce with a little of the dressing. Arrange in bowls with all the other ingredients added, and drizzle more vinaigrette on top before serving.

variation

sweet corn, avocado, and bacon salad

Omit the chicken. Blanch 4 shucked corncobs in boiling, lightly salted water for 3–4 minutes. Drain, cool, then cut off the kernels (p155). Make the rest of the salad in the same way, adding the corn at step 6 instead of the chicken.

Season's best **chiles**

Chiles come in hundreds of varieties, colors, shapes, and sizes, and ripen in high summer. They can add a tingle or an explosive fieriness. Chile lovers don't just taste heat, but can detect the complex flavors of each variety. Chiles go wonderfully with cheeses, seafood, meats, poultry, and game. Add them to pasta and beans, or to enhance many fruit and vegetable dishes.

Native to tropical regions, chiles are in such huge demand worldwide, they are now also grown in temperate areas, in greenhouses to protect them from the elements.

Jalapeño These are green, some with dark patches, torpedo-shaped, and quite fat with crisp, thick flesh. Sometimes roasted and peeled, they have a light flavor and are medium-hot. They are sweeter and less hot when red and fully ripe. Also sold *en escabeche* (pickled), they are widely used as a table condiment.

Piri piri This fiery chile is used in Portuguese piri piri sauce, made with lemon, spices, and herbs.

Scotch bonnet Yellow-green to orange-red, with a wrinkled top and flattened base, the Scotch bonnet chile is very hot and has a deep, fruity, smoky flavor, similar to the habanero. It is used in many Caribbean hot sauces and in jerk seasoning.

how to seed and cut chiles

Choose a type of chile to suit your recipe, but if you are not a fan of heat, removing the seeds and membranes may reduce some potency. Although some chiles are added whole, they are usually shredded or chopped before use.

1 Cut the chile lengthwise in half. Using the tip of your knife, scrape out the seeds and remove the membrane and stem.

2 Flatten each chile half with your hand and slice lengthwise into thin strips. Use like this, or chop.

3 To chop, hold the strips firmly together and slice crosswise to make equal-sized pieces. The hotter the chile, the finer it is chopped.

Aji Limon This chile is yellow and crinkly with a hot and distinctive herby, citrus flavor. It is good with white meats and fish.

Serrano has a distinctive bullet shape.

Serrano This Mexican chile is mid-green, cylindrical, and crisp-textured, with a concentrated, fresh, grassy flavor and very pungent seeds and veins. It ripens to bright red, and is commonly used in sauces.

Thai Used fresh and dried, this slender chile is bright red or green, with a lingering heat. Add whole to curries and stir-fries or chop for pastes and dips.

In Thailand, these are offered chopped in fish sauce instead of salt and pepper.

Poblano This chile is delicious roasted and peeled, then stuffed or fried. It pairs well with corn and tomatoes, and has a rich flavor. The dried form is the ancho, which is the most popular dried chile in Mexico and the US.

Poblanos are large, green, and triangular, with a ridge around the base of the stem.

essentials
varieties available
Hundreds of varieties, from fairly mild poblanos and moderately hot jalapeños to extremely hot Scotch Bonnets. Also available dried (whole, flakes, or powder).

buy They should be shiny, smooth-skinned, and firm.

store They can be refrigerated for a week or two.

cook In curries, stews, casseroles, salsas, rubs, marinades, and sauces. Stuff and roast or grill large ones. Good in chocolate desserts, and also in some fruit ones.

preserve Freeze, dry, or preserve in oil.

recipe ideas

Chipotle chicken p184

Cucumber-chile salad p201

Hot chile sauce p198

Scallops with sweet chile sauce p160

Spicy chicken balls with chile and ginger sauce p143

Tomato and chile jam p232

chicken with pancetta, peas, and mint

Fresh peas and mint are a perfect match, and epitomize the flavors and aromas of summer. Here they are incorporated into a tasty chicken stew that requires minimal effort.

 15 MINS   **1 HR 45 MINS**

SERVES 4

2 tbsp olive oil

4 large or 8 smaller chicken pieces, such as thighs and breasts, skin on

2 onions, finely chopped

7oz (200g) pancetta, diced, or bacon lardons

2 garlic cloves, grated or finely chopped

1½ cups dry white wine

2 cups hot chicken stock

salt and freshly ground black pepper

8oz (225g) peas (shelled weight)

handful of flat-leaf parsley, finely chopped

handful of mint leaves, finely chopped

1 Preheat the oven to 300°F (150°C). Heat 1 tbsp of the oil in a large flameproof casserole dish (preferably cast-iron) over medium heat. Add the chicken pieces and cook for about 8 minutes until golden all over. Remove from the casserole dish and set aside.

2 Reduce the heat to low and add the remaining oil and onions to the casserole dish. Cook gently for about 5 minutes until soft and translucent, then add the pancetta or bacon. Increase the heat a little and cook for another 5 minutes until the pancetta or bacon is golden. Stir in the garlic, then pour in the wine. Increase the heat to high and simmer for a few minutes until the alcohol has evaporated.

3 Add the stock and bring to a boil once again. Season with salt and pepper, add the peas, and stir in. Return the chicken pieces to the casserole dish. Stir in the parsley and mint, cover with a lid, and transfer to the oven to cook for 1½ hours. Check the level of liquid occasionally while cooking—it needs to be fairly dry, but if it is too dry, just add a little hot water. Serve hot with fresh crusty bread or sautéed potatoes.

lemongrass chicken

A delicious, warm Southeast Asian salad with chiles, scallions, and cucumber. Since chiles can vary wildly in strength, choose ones as mild or as fiery as you dare for this dish.

 45–55 MINS PLUS MARINATING   **10 MINS**

SERVES 4

2 lemongrass stalks, trimmed, tough outer leaves removed, and finely chopped

2 garlic cloves, finely chopped

3 tbsp fish sauce (nam pla), more if needed

¼ tsp freshly ground black pepper

8 large skinless, boneless chicken thighs, about 2½lb (1.1kg) total weight, cut into 1in (2.5cm) cubes

1 small cucumber

leaves from ½ head of round lettuce

4½oz (125g) bean sprouts

leaves from 1 small bunch of basil, preferably Asian basil

2 tbsp oil

2 red chiles, finely sliced

1 tsp sugar

3 scallions, trimmed and finely sliced

1oz (30g) roasted unsalted peanuts

1 Combine the lemongrass, garlic, 2 tbsp of the fish sauce, and the black pepper in a large bowl and mix well. Add the chicken and toss until well coated. Cover the bowl tightly and chill in the fridge for at least 1 hour and up to 24 hours.

2 Trim the cucumber and, with a vegetable peeler, remove strips of skin to create a striped effect. Slice the cucumber in half lengthwise, then slice each half finely. Arrange the lettuce, bean sprouts, half the basil, and the cucumber in piles on plates. Cover tightly and chill.

3 Heat a wok over high heat until hot. Drizzle in the oil to coat the bottom and sides. Continue heating until the oil is hot. Add the chicken and marinade and stir-fry, stirring and tossing frequently, for 8–10 minutes, until the chicken is golden.

4 Add the remaining fish sauce, the chiles, sugar, and scallions. Stir-fry for about 1 minute. Add the remaining basil and toss quickly to mix. Taste for seasoning, adding more fish sauce, if necessary. Serve the chicken on the salads and scatter a few peanuts over each serving.

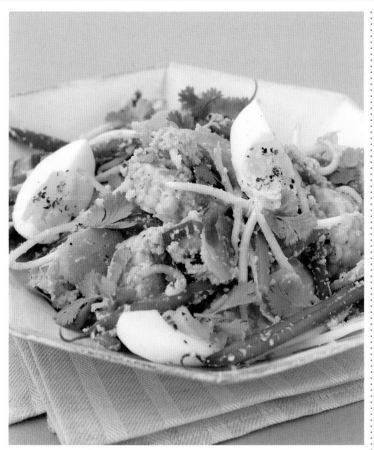

paneer and sweet pepper curry

Paneer is a very mild, unsalted cheese with a dense, crumbly texture and fresh flavor that benefits from the stronger flavors of pepper, chile, tomato, and spices in this curry.

 15 MINS   40 MINS

SERVES 8

4 tbsp ghee or vegetable oil

2 x 9oz packages paneer, cubed

4in (10cm) piece of fresh ginger, peeled and sliced

3 red or jalapeño chiles, seeded and finely chopped

2 tbsp dried curry leaves, crushed

2 tsp cumin seeds

4 tsp garam masala

2 tsp ground turmeric

8 red bell peppers, seeded and sliced

8 tomatoes, peeled (p197) and coarsely chopped

salt and freshly ground black pepper

bunch of cilantro, finely chopped

1 Heat half of the ghee or oil in a large wide pan over medium-high heat, add the paneer, and cook for 5–8 minutes, or until golden all over. Keep turning the pieces so they don't turn too brown. Remove with a slotted spoon and set aside.

2 Heat the remaining oil or ghee in the pan. Add the ginger, chiles, curry leaves, cumin, garam masala, and turmeric, and stir well to coat with the oil or ghee. Add the bell peppers and cook over low heat for 10 minutes, or until they begin to soften.

3 Add the tomatoes and cook for 10 minutes. Return the paneer to the pan, season with salt and pepper, then simmer gently for 10–15 minutes. Stir in the cilantro and serve with rice, chapati, or naan bread.

gado gado

This tasty Indonesian dish is a combination of both cooked and uncooked ingredients—including chile, sweet corn, green beans, and cucumber—and literally means "mix mix."

 20 MINS   20 MINS

SPECIAL EQUIPMENT ▪ food processor

SERVES 8

4 corn on the cob

12oz (350g) green beans, trimmed

1¼lb (550g) potatoes, unpeeled

1lb (450g) roasted peanuts

4 garlic cloves

3 red chiles, seeded

salt and freshly ground black pepper

2 tsp brown sugar

juice of 1 lime

4 carrots, finely sliced

7oz (200g) bean sprouts

half a cucumber, chopped into bite-sized pieces

6 eggs, hard-boiled, shelled, and quartered

handful of cilantro, chopped

1 Cook the corn on the cob in a pan of boiling salted water for 6–8 minutes, or until soft. Add the green beans for the last 5 minutes of cooking time. Drain, slice the corn on the cob into chunky rings, and place them and the green beans in a large, shallow serving bowl. Meanwhile, cook the potatoes in a pan of boiling salted water for about 15 minutes, or until just beginning to soften. Drain and set aside to cool, then slice and add to the sweet corn and beans.

2 Put the peanuts, garlic, and chiles in a food processor and pulse until finely ground. Season with salt and pepper. Add a little water and pulse again to make a paste. Add the sugar and lime juice and pulse again, adding more water if needed—the paste should be smooth, but not too runny.

3 Add the carrots, bean sprouts, and cucumber to the cooked vegetables, then pour over the sauce and toss together. Top with the hard-boiled eggs and cilantro, and serve.

crispy beef and vegetables

Use fat red chiles, which are relatively mild, for this dish—it's their color and gentle heat you want, so they won't mask the flavors of the scallions, sugar snap peas, and Swiss chard.

 15 MINS   30 MINS

SERVES 4

1½ tbsp cornstarch

1 large egg

salt and freshly ground black pepper

2 tbsp vegetable oil

1¼lb (550g) flank steak, cut into thin strips

4 scallions, trimmed and sliced in four lengthwise

1-2 red chiles, finely shredded

1 large garlic clove, finely sliced

7oz (200g) sugar snap peas, shredded

4-6 Swiss chard leaves, shredded

1½ tbsp dark soy sauce

1½ tbsp rice wine or dry sherry

2 tsp sugar

1 Put the cornstarch and egg in a mixing bowl, season with salt and pepper, and mix together well. Heat 1 tbsp of the oil in a wok, dip the beef into the cornstarch mixture, coat well, and add a few pieces at a time to the wok. Add more oil, if you need to. Cook for 2 minutes, or until crispy and golden. Remove with a slotted spoon and set aside.

2 Wipe out the wok with paper towels and heat the remaining oil. Add the scallions, chiles, and garlic and cook for a few seconds, stirring all the time. Add the sugar snap peas and Swiss chard and stir-fry for 2-3 minutes. Add the soy sauce, rice wine or sherry, and sugar, and cook until the sugar has dissolved and the alcohol has evaporated. Return the meat to the pan, toss together well, and serve with rice.

stuffed lamb, greek style

Olives, feta cheese, and thyme are all synonymous with Greek cuisine. Here they are combined with a succulent leg of lamb stuffed with red bell peppers and served with roasted tomatoes.

 30 MINS   2 HRS 15 MINS—2 HRS 45 MINS

SERVES 4-6

1 leg of lamb, boned and butterflied (about 4lb/1.8kg after boning) (p45); ask your butcher to do this, or use a boneless shoulder

salt and freshly ground black pepper

2 tbsp olive oil

1 tbsp dried oregano

2 red bell peppers, seeded and finely chopped

2oz (60g) pitted black olives, finely chopped

6oz (175g) feta cheese, finely chopped

3 red onions, roughly chopped

4-6 tomatoes, roughly chopped

1¾ cups red wine

a few sprigs of thyme

1 Preheat the oven to 325°F (160°C). Lay the lamb out flat and season well. Rub both sides all over with the oil and oregano. Cover one side of the lamb with the red peppers, then the olives, and then the feta. Starting from one end, roll up the lamb, tucking in any loose pieces to neaten it. Tie it up with butcher's twine, so it is secure.

2 Heat a large flameproof casserole dish over medium heat, add the lamb, and cook for 4-6 minutes on each side until it begins to color. Add the red onions and tomatoes to the pan, and cook for a minute more, then pour in the wine. Bring to a boil, then reduce to simmer and add some seasoning and the thyme. Cover with the lid and put in the oven for 2-2½ hours, or until cooked to your liking. Check occasionally that it's not drying out, and add a little hot water, if needed.

3 Remove from the oven, cover the meat loosely with foil, and let rest for 15 minutes. Remove the twine and carve into slices. Serve with some of the sauce, together with baby roast potatoes with rosemary and wilted spinach.

pea and pancetta tart

The delicate aroma and crisp texture of freshly shelled peas translates into a sweet burst of flavor in this creamy tart.

🥣 **10 MINS**   🍲 **1 HR 15 MINS**   ❄ **FREEZABLE**

SPECIAL EQUIPMENT ▪ 7in (18cm) round straight-sided tart pan with a removable bottom ▪ ceramic baking beans

SERVES 4–6

10oz (300g) store-bought pie dough

3 large eggs, 1 lightly beaten, for egg wash

1 tbsp olive oil

1 onion, finely chopped

salt and freshly ground black pepper

4½oz (125g) pancetta, diced

6 sage leaves, roughly chopped

8oz (225g) peas (shelled weight)

⅔ cup heavy cream

1 Preheat the oven to 400°F (200°C). Roll out the dough on a floured work surface to a large circle about ⅛in (3mm) thick and use to line a tart pan, pressing it into the corners. Trim away the excess and prick the bottom with a fork. Line the dough with wax paper and fill with ceramic baking beans. Bake in the oven for 15–20 minutes until the edges are golden. Remove the beans and paper, brush the bottom of the crust with a little of the egg wash, and return to the oven for 2–3 minutes to crisp. Remove from the oven and set aside. Reduce the oven temperature to 350°F (180°C).

2 Meanwhile, heat the oil in a large frying pan over low heat. Add the onion and a pinch of salt, and cook gently for about 5 minutes until soft and translucent. Add the pancetta and sage, increase the heat a little, and cook for 6–8 minutes until the pancetta is golden and crispy. Stir in the peas, and then season well with salt and pepper.

3 Spoon the onion and pancetta mixture into the crust and level the top. Mix together the cream and eggs, season, and carefully pour the mixture over the filling to cover. Bake in the oven for 20–30 minutes until set and golden. Let cool for 10 minutes before releasing from the pan. Serve warm with a tomato salad.

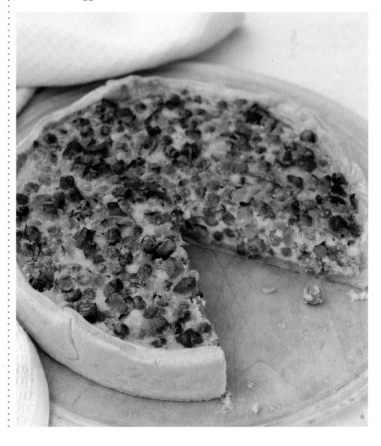

chicken roasted with fennel and lemon

If you want to cook something easy, then one-pot recipes such as this are perfect. Creamy mashed potatoes are all that's needed to complement these sharp, tangy flavors.

🥣 **15 MINS PLUS MARINATING**   🍲 **1 HR**

SERVES 4

4 large chicken thighs, with skin on

sea salt and freshly ground black pepper

drizzle of extra virgin olive oil

juice of 1 lemon, and 2 small lemons, quartered

a few sprigs of thyme, leaves picked

1 large fennel bulb, roughly chopped

handful of green olives, pitted

¾ cup dry white wine

1 Season the chicken thighs generously with salt and pepper. Drizzle the oil and lemon juice over the top, scatter on the thyme leaves, then transfer to a large bowl or plastic bag and leave to marinate for 30 minutes. Preheat the oven to 400°F (200°C).

2 Using a slotted spoon, transfer the chicken to a small roasting pan and add the fennel and lemon quarters. Season well and bake for 20 minutes.

3 Remove the roasting pan from the oven and add the olives and wine. Return to the oven and cook for another 20 minutes, then turn the heat down to 350°F (180°C), cover the pan with foil, and cook for another 20 minutes, so the alcohol evaporates but the chicken remains moist. Check if the chicken is ready to eat by piercing the plumpest thigh with the tip of a sharp knife; if the juices run clear, it is cooked. Allow the chicken to rest for 5 minutes, then serve.

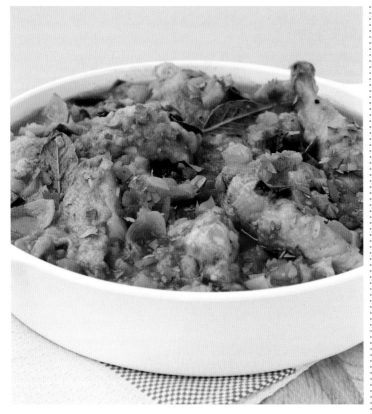

chicken, eggplant, and tomato tagine

Originally from North Africa, a tagine is a wonderfully aromatic stew that is cooked slowly and gently so that the meat and vegetables are richly flavored and tender.

 30 MINS   25 MINS

SERVES 8

3–4 tbsp olive oil

8 chicken pieces (thighs and breasts)

salt and freshly ground black pepper

2 eggplants, cut into bite-sized cubes

1 tsp ground cinnamon

2 onions, grated

3 red chiles, seeded and finely chopped

2 tsp ground cumin

2 bay leaves

4lb (1.8kg) tomatoes

1 tbsp tomato paste

4 preserved lemons, halved and pith discarded

handful of cilantro, finely chopped

1 Heat 1 tbsp of the oil in a large, wide heavy-bottomed pan, season the chicken with salt and pepper, and add to the pan. Cook for 8 minutes, or until golden, stirring occasionally, then remove and set aside. Toss the eggplants in the cinnamon and add to the pan with 1 tbsp of the oil. Cook over medium heat, stirring occasionally, for 10 minutes, or until golden. Add more oil if needed. Remove and set aside.

2 Add 1 tbsp of the oil to the pan, then add the onions, chiles, cumin, and bay leaves. Season well with salt and pepper and cook over low heat for 5 minutes. Return the chicken and eggplant to the pan along with the tomatoes and tomato paste. Cover with a lid and simmer over low heat for 25 minutes, adding hot water if it begins to look too dry.

3 Stir in the preserved lemon halves and cilantro, and serve with plenty of fluffy couscous and some harissa on the side.

chipotle chicken

Hot and spicy, with the flavors of Mexico; add some seeded and finely chopped chipotle chiles if you like it really hot. Serve with plain boiled rice, some sour cream, and tortillas.

 15 MINS   1 HR 45 MINS   ❄ FREEZABLE

SERVES 4–6

1 tbsp olive oil

8 chicken thighs, with skin on

salt and freshly ground black pepper

1 onion, finely chopped

3 garlic cloves, finely chopped

½ tsp cumin seeds

2 red bell peppers, seeded and coarsely chopped

¼ cup finely chopped chipotles in adobo

grated zest of ½ lime and juice of 1 lime

1 tbsp white wine vinegar

2 x 14oz (400g) cans whole tomatoes

2 cups hot chicken stock

14oz (400g) can black beans, drained and rinsed

1 cinnamon stick

handful of cilantro, leaves coarsely chopped

1 avocado, pitted, peeled, and chopped into bite-sized pieces (optional)

1 Preheat the oven to 350°F (180°C). Heat the oil in a large flameproof casserole dish over medium to high heat. Season the chicken with salt and pepper and cook for 6–8 minutes until golden. Remove and set aside. Lower the heat, add the onion, garlic, and cumin seeds, and cook for 1 minute. Add the peppers and cook for 5 minutes. Return the chicken to the casserole dish and stir in the chipotles. Add the lime zest, juice, and vinegar, increase the heat, and let the sauce bubble for a few minutes.

2 Add the tomatoes and a little stock and bring to a boil. Pour in the remaining stock and add the beans. Boil for 2–3 minutes then reduce to simmer. Add the cinnamon stick and some pepper, cover with a lid, and put in the oven for 1½ hours. Add water occasionally if needed. Remove the cinnamon stick, stir in most of the cilantro, and top with avocado, if using. Sprinkle the remaining cilantro leaves on top, and serve.

pea and mint risotto

Risotto is the perfect foil for delicate flavors and this one is beautifully scented with summer herbs.

 10 MINS   25 MINS   ❄ FREEZABLE

SERVES 4

4 cups light vegetable stock

1 tbsp olive oil

pat of butter

1 onion, finely chopped

salt and freshly ground black pepper

12oz (350g) risotto rice, such as Arborio

¾ cup dry white wine

5½oz (150g) peas (shelled weight)

1¾oz (50g) Parmesan cheese, grated

handful of mint leaves

handful of basil leaves

1 First, pour the stock into a large pan and heat to simmer.

2 Heat the oil and butter in a large nonstick frying pan over low heat. Add the onion and a pinch of salt.

Sweat for 5 minutes until soft and translucent, then stir in the rice, making sure that the grains are completely coated. Increase the heat to medium-high, pour in the wine, and let it simmer for a couple of minutes until the alcohol has evaporated.

3 Reduce the heat slightly and add the simmering stock a ladleful or two at a time, stirring frequently with a wooden spoon; when each addition of stock has been absorbed, add some more. Continue like this for about 20 minutes until the rice is cooked; it should be slightly firm so that it still has a bite to it.

4 Stir in the peas, Parmesan, mint, and basil. Season well with salt and pepper and serve hot.

summer frittata with ratatouille

While the eggs cook slowly in this Italian-style omelet, you can sit back and enjoy a glass of wine. Use any vegetables you have on hand to make the filling, which can be prepared up to 24 hours in advance and kept, tightly covered, in the fridge. Cook the frittata just before serving.

 20-25 MINS 20-25 MINS

SERVES 3-4

1 small eggplant

1 zucchini

salt and freshly ground black pepper

¼ cup olive oil, plus more if needed

1 green bell pepper, sliced into strips

1 onion, thinly sliced

9oz (250g) tomatoes, peeled, seeded (p197), and chopped, or 7oz (200g) can chopped tomatoes

2 garlic cloves, finely chopped

5-7 thyme sprigs, leaves picked, plus a few sprigs to decorate

½ tsp ground coriander

1 large bouquet garni (10-12 sprigs of parsley, 4-5 sprigs of thyme, and 2 bay leaves)

6 large eggs

1-2 tbsp butter

1 Trim the eggplant and cut into ½in (1cm) chunks. Cut the zucchini into ½in (1cm) slices. Put the eggplant and zucchini on a baking sheet and sprinkle generously with salt. Leave for 30 minutes, then place in a colander, rinse, and pat dry with paper towels.

2 To make the ratatouille, heat about half the oil in a frying pan. Add the eggplant to the pan and stir-fry for 3-5 minutes, until browned. Transfer to a bowl with a slotted spoon. Repeat with the zucchini slices.

3 Add the green bell pepper to the pan with a little more oil and stir-fry until it is softened; remove to the bowl. Heat about 1 tbsp more oil in the pan, add the onion, and sauté for 2-3 minutes, until soft and slightly translucent.

4 Return the eggplant, zucchini, and bell pepper to the pan, and add the tomatoes, garlic, salt, pepper, thyme, coriander, and the bouquet garni. Stir until well mixed. Cover and cook for 10-15 minutes, until tender. Remove and discard the bouquet garni. Let cool.

5 Whisk the eggs in a bowl until completely mixed. Stir in the ratatouille mixture thoroughly and season well with salt and pepper.

6 Wipe the frying pan; melt the butter over medium heat until foaming, then add the egg mixture. Reduce the heat, cover, and cook very gently for 20-25 minutes, until the center is set and the bottom is cooked and lightly browned when you lift the edge with a palette knife. Invert the frittata onto a large warmed plate and decorate with the reserved thyme sprigs. Cut the frittata into wedges and serve.

variation

eggplant, potato, and feta cheese frittata

Omit the zucchini, pepper, and tomatoes. Fry 1 large, cubed eggplant with 1 finely sliced onion in 6 tbsp olive oil for 5 minutes, stirring until soft. Add 12oz (350g) cooked, sliced new potatoes. Cook, stirring gently, for 2 minutes, season with ½ tsp ground cinnamon and the thyme leaves, then pour into a bowl. Continue at step 5 but scatter 4oz (115g) crumbled feta cheese over the egg mix before covering and cooking. Slide out onto a plate, but don't invert.

Season's best **eggplant**

Eggplant is also known as aubergine, eggfruit, and brinjal. It was named *mala insana* (apple of insanity) by the Ancient Romans, who thought it was poisonous. It has slightly bitter, tender flesh. It is at its best in high summer, but is in season throughout summer and fall. Its flesh acts like a sponge, soaking up flavors and liquid, and works well with sweet spices, oregano, ham, lamb, mushrooms, cheeses, peppers, olives, and tomatoes.

Eggplant is grown all over the world in many shapes and sizes. Native to tropical Asia, it needs plenty of warmth so, in some areas, is grown in greenhouses and polytunnels.

Baby eggplant Perfect for curries and Southeast Asian dishes, they have thinner skins than their larger relative and have a sweet, delicate flavor.

Oval deep purple eggplant
The familiar, fat, elongated eggplant develops a complex flavor and silky texture when cooked. It is good thickly sliced and grilled, or roasted whole and then puréed with spices.

The skin keeps its attractive mottled stripes · even when cooked.

Italian striped eggplant
Rosa Bianca, an heirloom variety, has firm, creamy flesh, which makes it a choice ingredient for melanzane alla parmigiana.

essentials
varieties available
Oval deep purple, baby purple, and Italian striped (round and long white ones).

buy Look for relatively small, firm eggplant with glossy skin and bright green cap and stalk.

store Use it on the day of purchase, or at least by the next day. Keep in a cool spot until needed.

cook Bake or roast, braise, grill, barbecue, broil, stir-fry, sauté, coat in batter and deep-fry, curry, or stew.

preserve Grill slices, then freeze.

recipe ideas
Eggplant massaman curry p289

Eggplant stuffed with tomato rice p187

Baba ganoush p164

Hot-spiced eggplant chutney p244

Melanzane alla parmigiana p304

potato and pea curry

Here is a vegetarian curry that puts summer vegetables to good use; spicing up peas, tomatoes, and new potatoes. It doesn't take long to make either.

 10 MINS 30 MINS

SERVES 4

1 tbsp sunflower or vegetable oil

1in (2.5cm) piece of fresh ginger, peeled and finely chopped

2–3 green jalapeño chiles, seeded and finely chopped

1 tsp cumin seeds

1 tsp mustard seeds

small handful of curry leaves

6 tomatoes, peeled (p197) and chopped

1½lb (675g) new potatoes, peeled and cubed

1 tsp ground turmeric

1¼ cups hot vegetable stock

2½oz (75g) peas (shelled weight)

salt and freshly ground black pepper

handful of cilantro, finely chopped

1 Heat the oil in a large frying pan over medium heat. Add the ginger, chiles, cumin seeds, and mustard seeds, and crumble in the curry leaves. Cook for a couple of minutes until the mustard seeds start to pop. Add the tomatoes, stir in, and cook for a few more minutes.

2 Add the potatoes and turmeric, and pour in the stock. Bring to a boil, reduce the heat slightly, cover, and simmer for about 15 minutes.

3 Add the peas, stir in, and cook for another 5–10 minutes. Season well with salt and pepper, and stir in the cilantro. Serve hot with rice or naan bread.

pasta with eggplant sauce

Eggplants have a mild smoky flavor and spongy flesh that softens when cooked. This recipe calls for a bulbous, deep purple variety to accompany tomatoes and pesto sauce.

 10 MINS 25 MINS

SERVES 4

1 large eggplant, cut into cubes

salt and freshly ground black pepper

2–3 tbsp olive oil

¼ cup red wine

1 onion, finely diced

2 garlic cloves, grated or finely chopped

6 ripe tomatoes, peeled (p197) and chopped

pinch of dried oregano

1 tsp sun-dried tomato pesto

12oz (350g) large pasta shells

Parmesan cheese, grated, to serve (optional)

1 Place the eggplant cubes in a colander and sprinkle well with salt. Cover with a plate, then place a heavy weight on top for 10 minutes to extract the bitter juices.

2 Heat the oil in a large frying pan over medium heat, add the eggplant cubes, and cook for 4–6 minutes, or until they turn golden. Add the wine, increase the heat, and allow to boil

for a couple of minutes. Stir in the onion and garlic and cook for a few seconds, then add the tomatoes and stir. Add the oregano and pesto, part-cover and simmer very gently for 10–15 minutes, stirring occasionally.

3 Meanwhile, cook the pasta in a large pan of boiling salted water for about 12 minutes, or until it is tender but still firm to the bite. Drain, keeping back a tiny amount of the cooking water. Return the pasta to the pan. Thin the sauce with a little of the pasta water if necessary. Taste the sauce and season with salt and pepper. Toss with the pasta, sprinkle with grated Parmesan cheese, if using, and serve.

variation

pasta with yellow bell pepper sauce

Prepare in the same way, but substitute 2 large yellow bell peppers for the eggplant. Omit step 1.

eggplants stuffed with tomato rice

Stuffed eggplants are popular in the Middle East. Use a larger variety so that when you scoop out the center flesh there is enough left around the edge to keep its shape.

 10 MINS 30 MINS

SERVES 4

4 eggplants, halved lengthwise

2 tbsp olive oil, plus extra for brushing

7oz (200g) long-grain rice, rinsed

1¼ cups tomato juice

1 tsp sugar

salt and freshly ground black pepper

1 onion, finely chopped

small handful of dill, finely chopped

1 Preheat the oven to 400°F (200°C). Scoop out the flesh from the eggplants, chop the flesh into bite-sized chunks, and set aside. Sit the shells in a roasting pan and brush with olive oil. Cover with foil and roast in the oven for 10–15 minutes while you cook the rice.

2 Cook the rice in a pan of boiling salted water for about 10 minutes, or until it is tender. Drain if needed, then pour in the tomato juice. Sprinkle in the sugar and season well with salt and pepper. Stir the rice until the tomato juice is absorbed.

3 Heat 1 tbsp of the oil in a large frying pan over medium heat, add the onion, dill, and a pinch of salt, and cook for 3–4 minutes until the onion is soft and translucent. Then add the reserved eggplant flesh and cook for another 5 minutes. Season with black pepper, add the tomato rice mixture, and stir well.

4 Remove the eggplant shells from the oven and carefully spoon the mixture into them. Drizzle in the remaining oil and return to the oven for another 5 minutes. Serve hot with a crisp green salad.

variation

spicy stuffed eggplants with feta cheese

Prepare in the same way, but add 2 seeded, chopped red chiles to the tomato rice and crumble over 7oz (200g) feta cheese before drizzling with oil at step 4.

roast lamb with cherry tomatoes and new potatoes

A little red currant jelly brings out the sweetness of these summer tomatoes roasted on the vine. Cooking the baby potatoes in their skins helps to retain all their flavor, too.

 15 MINS   1 HR 30 MINS

SERVES 4

1 tbsp olive oil

2lb (900g) butterflied leg of lamb (p45)

2½lb (1.1kg) baby new potatoes

salt and freshly ground black pepper

handful of thyme sprigs

12–16 cherry tomatoes on the vine

1–2 tsp red currant jelly

1 Preheat the oven to 375°F (190°C). Pour half the oil into a large roasting pan and set over high heat. When very hot, add the lamb and cook for 4–6 minutes, or until browned, then turn and brown the other side for 4–6 minutes.

2 Toss the new potatoes with the remaining oil and add to the pan. Season well with salt and pepper, and add the thyme. Put into the oven to cook for 45 minutes, if you like your lamb rare, 1 hour for medium, and 1¼ hours for well done. Add the tomatoes for the last 15 minutes

of cooking. Remove the lamb and cover with foil to keep warm while it rests.

3 Meanwhile, make the gravy. Using a slotted spoon, transfer the potatoes and tomatoes to a serving dish and keep warm. Place the pan on the unlit stovetop and tilt to one side. Skim away any fat, then add the red currant jelly and set over high heat. Stir well, adding a little boiling water until the gravy reaches the required consistency. Allow to boil, then reduce to simmer and cook for a couple of minutes. Slice the lamb and serve with the potatoes, tomatoes, gravy, and some mint sauce or jelly on the side.

swiss chard and gruyère cheese tart

Select young, tender stems of Swiss chard with unblemished dark green leaves. Its slightly bitter, assertive flavor works well with the rich cheese filling of this tart.

 15 MINS   1 HR   ❄ FREEZABLE

SPECIAL EQUIPMENT ▪ 9in (23cm) round, fluted tart pan with removable bottom ▪ ceramic baking beans

SERVES 6

10oz (300g) store-bought pie dough

3 large eggs, 1 lightly beaten for egg wash

1 tbsp olive oil

1 onion, finely chopped

salt and freshly ground black pepper

2 garlic cloves, grated or finely chopped

a few sprigs of rosemary, leaves picked and finely chopped

9oz (250g) Swiss chard, stems trimmed

4½oz (125g) Gruyère cheese, grated

4½oz (125g) feta cheese, cubed

¾ cup heavy cream

1 Preheat the oven to 400°F (200°C). Roll out the dough on a floured work surface and use to line a tart pan. Trim away the excess, line the pie dough with wax paper, and fill with ceramic baking beans. Bake in the oven for 15–30 minutes until the edges are golden. Remove the beans and paper, and brush the bottom of the shell with a little of the egg wash. Return to the oven for 1–2 minutes to crisp. Remove from the oven and set aside. Reduce the oven temperature to 350°F (180°C).

2 Heat the oil in a pan over low heat. Add the onion and salt and sweat gently for about 5 minutes until soft and translucent. Add the garlic and rosemary and cook for a few seconds, then coarsely chop the Swiss chard and add to the pan. Stir for about 5 minutes until it wilts.

3 Spoon the onion and chard mixture into the pie crust. Scatter evenly with the Gruyère and feta cheeses, and season. Mix together the cream and the 2 eggs until well combined, then carefully pour the mixture over the tart filling. Bake in the oven for 30–40 minutes until set and golden. Let cool for 10 minutes before releasing from the pan. Serve warm.

variation

spinach and gruyère tart

Substitute 9oz (250g) spinach for the Swiss chard, cooking until just wilted in step 2. Continue with the recipe.

mediterranean burgers

The chopped red bell peppers in these well-seasoned gourmet burgers give a delicious crunch and hint of sweetness. You could also barbecue the burgers for extra flavor.

 10 MINS   15 MINS

SERVES 4

1lb 2oz (500g) ground beef

1 onion, finely chopped

2 garlic cloves, finely chopped

1 tbsp dried oregano

2 red bell peppers, seeded and finely chopped

handful of basil leaves, finely chopped

handful of flat-leaf parsley, finely chopped

sea salt and freshly ground black pepper

splash of red wine

pat of butter

1 In a large bowl, combine the ground beef, onion, garlic, dried oregano, red bell peppers, basil leaves, and parsley. Season and add a splash of red wine.

2 Using your hands, mix the ingredients together until well combined. Divide the mixture into 4 large balls and flatten into burgers.

3 Melt the butter in a frying pan over medium-high heat, and fry the burgers for 3–5 minutes on each side until browned and cooked through. Serve sandwiched in a fresh bun or roll, with fresh lettuce leaves and tomato.

oriental halibut en papillote

Noodles and stir-fried crisp vegetables would be excellent alongside this fragrant dish.

 15-20 MINS   10-12 MINS

SERVES 4

4½oz (125g) snow peas, trimmed

4 garlic cloves, finely chopped

1in (2.5cm) piece of fresh ginger, peeled and finely chopped

2 tbsp black bean sauce

3 tbsp light soy sauce

2 tbsp dry sherry

½ tsp granulated sugar

1 tbsp sesame oil

2 tbsp vegetable oil, for brushing

1 egg

salt

4 x 6oz (175g) skinned halibut fillets or steaks

4 scallions, trimmed and thinly sliced

1 Bring a pan of salted water to a boil. Add the snow peas and simmer for 1–2 minutes. Combine the garlic, ginger, black bean sauce, soy sauce, sherry, sugar, and sesame oil in a bowl. Set aside.

2 Fold a sheet of parchment paper (about 12 x 15in/30 x 34.5cm) in half and draw a curve with a pencil to make a heart shape when unfolded. It should be large enough to leave a 3in (7.5cm) border around a fish fillet.

Cut out the heart shape with scissors. Repeat to make 4 paper hearts. Open each out and brush with the vegetable oil, leaving a border about 1in (2.5cm) wide at the edges.

3 Put the egg and ½ tsp salt in a small bowl and beat together. Brush this egg glaze evenly on the border of each of the paper hearts.

4 Preheat the oven to 400°F (200°C). Rinse the fish fillets and pat dry with paper towels. Arrange a quarter of the snow peas on one side of each paper heart and set a halibut fillet on top.

5 Spoon a quarter of the seasoning on top of each fillet and sprinkle with a quarter of the scallions. Fold the paper over the fish and run your finger along the edge to stick the 2 sides of paper together. Make small pleats to seal the edges.

6 Twist the "tails" of each paper package to seal them, so that the filling does not ooze out during baking. Lay the packages on a baking sheet and bake for 10–12 minutes, until puffed and brown. Transfer to warmed plates, allowing each guest to open their own aromatic fish package.

sweet and sour duck with cherries

Really tart cherries are key to this dish from Limousin, central France, where cherries grow wild in the hedgerows.

 30-35 MINS **1 HR 15 MINS - 1 HR 30 MINS**

SPECIAL EQUIPMENT ▪ trussing needle and string

SERVES 2-3

1 duck, weighing about 4lb (1.8kg)

salt and freshly ground black pepper

1 tbsp vegetable oil

¼ cup granulated sugar

¼ cup red wine vinegar

1⅔ cup rich chicken stock

13oz (375g) tart cherries, pitted

sprigs of flat-leaf parsley, to serve (optional)

1 Wipe the inside of the duck with paper towels and season inside and out. Pull off and discard any loose bits of fat. With a small knife, remove the wishbone to make the duck easier to carve later. Set the duck breast-side up. Push the legs back and down. Push a trussing needle into the flesh at the knee joint, through the bird and out, through the other knee joint. Turn the duck over. Pull the neck skin over the neck cavity and tuck the wing tips over it. Push the needle through one of the wings into the neck skin. Continue under the backbone of the duck to the other side. Repeat with the second wing.

2 Preheat the oven to 425°F (220°C). Turn the duck onto its side. Pull the ends of the string firmly together, and tie them together securely. Turn the duck breast-side up. Tuck the tail into the cavity of the bird and fold over the top skin. Push the needle through the skin. Loop the string around one of the drumsticks, under the breastbone, and over the other drumstick. Tie the ends of the string together.

3 Heat the oil in a roasting pan. Set the duck on its side and roast in the oven for 15 minutes. Turn the duck over and roast for another 15 minutes. Spoon the fat from the roasting pan and discard. Prick the skin all over to release the fat. Reduce the temperature to 375°F (190°C). Turn the duck on to its breast and roast for another 15 minutes. Discard any melted fat. Finally, set the duck on its back and continue roasting for another 15–20 minutes, until the juices run clear. Transfer to a warmed platter and cover with foil to rest and keep warm.

4 Put ¼ cup water and the sugar into a small heavy-bottomed saucepan and heat gently, until the sugar is dissolved, stirring occasionally. Increase the heat and boil, without stirring, until the syrup starts to turn golden. Reduce the heat and cook to a deep golden caramel. Remove from the heat and let the bubbles subside. Pour in the vinegar. Simmer, stirring occasionally, for 3–5 minutes, until the caramel is dissolved and the mixture is reduced by half. Remove from the heat and set aside.

5 In a medium saucepan, combine the caramel vinegar and the stock. Add the cherries to the pan and simmer for 3–5 minutes, until just tender. Transfer the cherries to a bowl with a slotted spoon. Discard any remaining fat from the duck roasting pan. Add the caramel sauce and bring to a boil, stirring to dissolve the pan juices. Simmer until this sweet-sour sauce is reduced by half.

6 Discard the trussing string and carve the duck. Arrange the meat on warmed plates and spoon over some of the cherry sauce. Decorate with parsley sprigs, if you like, and serve at once. Serve the remaining cherry sauce separately.

fish tagine

This light dish of potatoes, red bell peppers, and sea bass has a lively mix of herbs and spices.

 20 MINS PLUS MARINATING   1 HR 30 MINS

SPECIAL EQUIPMENT ▪ food processor

SERVES 4-6

1-2 tbsp olive oil

2 onions, sliced into rings

2 celery sticks, finely chopped

salt and freshly ground black pepper

3 garlic cloves, chopped

1 tsp ground ginger

1 tsp ground cumin

1 tsp sweet paprika

1 red or jalapeño chile, seeded and coarsely chopped

1 preserved lemon, flesh only, finely chopped, or use grated zest of ½ lemon

2 carrots, sliced

2 red bell peppers, seeded and coarsely chopped

6 new potatoes, halved

about 2 cups hot fish stock

2lb (900g) sea bass, cut into chunky pieces

3 tomatoes, seeded and chopped into thin slices

squeeze of lemon juice

cilantro leaves, to serve (optional)

1 Heat the oil in a large flameproof casserole dish or tagine over medium heat, add the onions and celery, season, and cook for 5–6 minutes until soft. Stir in the garlic, ginger, cumin, paprika, chile, lemon flesh or zest and cook for a few minutes. Then add the carrots and bell peppers and cook for 5 more minutes.

2 Add the potatoes and stock, bring to a boil, cover with the lid, and cook on very low simmer for about 45 minutes, adding a little hot water if needed. Then add the fish and layer the tomatoes over the top, re-cover, and bring up to simmer once again. Cook for another 15–30 minutes until the fish is opaque and cooked through. Taste and season, if needed, add a squeeze of lemon juice, and stir in the cilantro leaves, if using. Serve with fluffy couscous and lemon wedges to squeeze over.

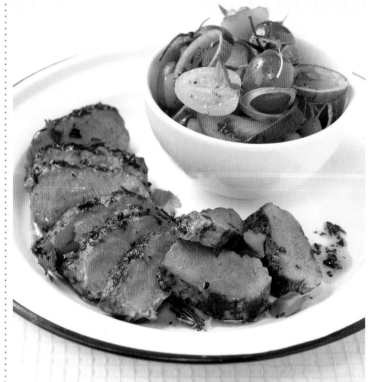

salmon jungle curry

This is a hot fish curry with baby sweet corn. Small green pea eggplants are a classic Thai ingredient that are each about the size of a grape and give a slightly bitter burst of flavor.

 10 MINS   20 MINS

SERVES 4

2 tbsp vegetable oil

2 tbsp Thai green curry paste

3 garlic cloves, crushed

2in (5cm) piece fresh ginger

2 red chiles, seeded and cut into fine strips

14oz (400ml) can coconut milk

splash of fish sauce (nam pla)

7oz (200g) can bamboo shoots, drained

2 heaping tbsp pea eggplants (optional)

3½oz (100g) baby sweet corn, halved diagonally

14oz (400g) skinned salmon, cut into 1½in (4cm) chunks

small handful of Thai basil leaves

1 Heat the oil in a large frying pan until hot. Add the Thai green curry paste and stir it around the pan to combine it with the oil.

2 Throw in the garlic, ginger, and chiles. Stir constantly for 2–3 minutes. Pour in the coconut milk, bring to a boil, then add a generous splash of fish sauce, the bamboo shoots, pea eggplants (if using), and baby corn. Reduce the heat slightly and simmer for 5 minutes.

4 Add the salmon chunks and Thai basil leaves. Simmer for another 5–10 minutes until the salmon is opaque and cooked through when tested with a fork. Season and serve hot with sticky Thai jasmine rice.

lamb loin with tomato and basil salad

Garlic, chile, rosemary, and parsley combine to add piquancy to this flash-grilled marinated lamb.

 15 MINS PLUS MARINATING   20 MINS

SPECIAL EQUIPMENT ▪ barbecue or charcoal grill

SERVES 4

1½lb (165g) lamb loin

3 tbsp olive oil

1 large garlic clove, crushed

1½ tbsp finely chopped flat-leaf parsley, plus extra to garnish

sprig of rosemary, leaves picked

small pinch of dried chile flakes

salt and freshly ground black pepper

drizzle of extra virgin olive oil

For the tomato and basil salad

2 ripe plum tomatoes, cut into quarters lengthwise

9oz (250g) cherry tomatoes on the vine, separated but still with their stems

4½oz (125g) yellow bell or cherry tomatoes, halved

small handful of basil leaves

1 small garlic clove, crushed

½ small red onion, thinly sliced into rings

1½ tbsp extra virgin olive oil

1 Trim the lamb of any fat. Mix together the olive oil, garlic, parsley, rosemary, and chile flakes in a large bowl and season with salt and pepper. Add the lamb, massaging the marinade into the meat. Allow to marinate in the refrigerator for at least 1 hour.

2 Heat the barbecue or charcoal grill until hot. Grill the lamb over medium heat for 8–10 minutes on each side for medium-rare, or until cooked to your liking. Remove to a plate, cover with foil, and leave to rest in a warm place for 20 minutes.

3 To make the salad, put all the ingredients in a bowl, season with salt and pepper, and toss gently. When ready to serve, slice the lamb diagonally and arrange on a serving platter. Scatter with the parsley leaves and a drizzle of extra virgin olive oil and serve accompanied by the salad.

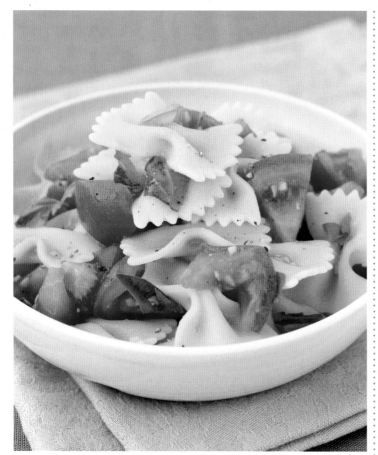

pasta with no-cook tomato sauce

For a sauce that is this simple, you should select really ripe, plump tomatoes and pungent basil. Prepare it before you cook the pasta and the flavors will have time to develop.

 5 MINS 10 MINS

SERVES 4

6 tomatoes, seeded and roughly chopped

2 garlic gloves, grated or finely chopped

handful of basil leaves, torn

pinch of dried chile flakes

3 tbsp extra virgin olive oil

salt and freshly ground black pepper

12oz (350g) farfalle

1 Put the tomatoes, garlic, basil, chile flakes, and oil in a large bowl and season well with salt and pepper. Stir well to combine, then set aside while you cook the pasta—the flavors will develop.

2 Cook the pasta in a large pan of boiling salted water for 10 minutes, or until it is cooked but is still firm to the bite. Drain well, then toss with the tomato sauce and serve.

sausage and tomato pie

Complemented by the oregano, sweet, plump tomatoes release their juices into this pie as it cooks, keeping the lightly spiced sausage wonderfully moist.

 15 MINS 40 MINS ❄ FREEZABLE

SPECIAL EQUIPMENT ▪ 8in (20cm) square pie dish or fluted tart pan
▪ ceramic baking beans

SERVES 4

8oz (225g) store-bought pie dough

1 large egg, lightly beaten

½ tbsp olive oil

1 onion, finely chopped

salt and freshly ground black pepper

14oz (400g) good-quality pork sausages, skinned

1 tsp dried oregano

4 tomatoes, sliced

1 Preheat the oven to 400°F (200°C). Roll out the pastry on a floured work surface and use to line a pie dish or tart pan. Trim away any excess, line the dough with wax paper, and fill with ceramic baking beans. Bake in the oven for 15–20 minutes until the edges are golden. Remove the beans and paper, brush the bottom of the dough with a little of the beaten egg, and return to the oven for 2–3 minutes to crisp. Remove from the oven and set aside. Reduce the oven temperature to 350°F (180°C).

2 Meanwhile, heat the oil in a large frying pan over low heat. Add the onion and a pinch of salt and sweat gently for about 5 minutes until soft and translucent. Add the sausage, breaking it up with a fork or the back of a spatula. Season well with salt and pepper and sprinkle in the oregano. Cook, stirring regularly, over low-medium heat for about 10 minutes until no longer pink. Leave to cool, then mix in the remaining egg.

3 Spoon the sausage mixture into the pie crust, then layer the tomatoes over the top. Bake in the oven for about 20 minutes until lightly golden. Leave to cool for about 10 minutes, then slice in the dish or pan. Serve with a crisp green salad.

sea bass in a salt crust

This classic dish from northern Italy is traditionally made using sea bass (known locally as branzino) but you could also use sea bream as an excellent alternative.

 15 MINS 22-25 MINS

SERVES 4

1 whole sea bass (3-4½lb/1.35-2kg) trimmed and gutted, but not scaled

2¼lb (1kg) sea salt

1-2 large egg whites

1 Preheat the oven to 425°F (220°C). Gut the fish, making the smallest incision possible. Clean well and rinse—do not scale.

2 Spread a layer of salt over a large piece of foil on a baking sheet. Arrange the fish on top. Moisten the remaining salt with the egg whites and a splash of water, if necessary. Pack this mixture on the fish to encase it completely.

3 Bake in the oven for 22–25 minutes. Lift the fish onto a serving dish. Take to the table and carefully chip off any remaining salt crust. Carefully peel away the skin and serve the fish straight from the bone. Accompany the fish with some aioli or mayonnaise and a green salad.

pizza with tomatoes, olives, and capers

This thin-based Italian-style pizza is ideal for using up a glut of homegrown summer tomatoes.

 10 MINS PLUS RISING 15 MINS FREEZABLE

MAKES 1

2–3 tbsp tomato sauce

3 tomatoes, sliced

handful of pitted black olives

1–2 tsp capers, rinsed

pinch of freshly ground black pepper

For the pizza dough

1 cup bread flour

pinch of salt

pinch of granulated sugar

¾ tsp dried yeast

1 tbsp olive oil

a little semolina, for sprinkling

1 Sift the flour, salt, and sugar into a bowl. Add the yeast. Stir in the oil and enough warm water to form a soft but not sticky dough ⅓ cup.

2 Place the dough on a slightly floured surface and knead gently for several minutes until smooth and elastic. Return to the bowl, cover with oiled plastic wrap, and leave in a warm place for about 40 minutes, until the dough has doubled in size.

3 Preheat the oven to its highest setting. Very lightly oil a baking sheet and put it in the oven to get hot. The baking sheet and the oil both need to be really hot before cooking the pizza.

4 Place the dough on a floured surface and roll it out as thinly as you can; about 10–12in (25–30cm) in diameter. Sprinkle the hot baking sheet with a little semolina and transfer the pizza dough onto it.

5 Spoon the tomato paste onto the pizza crust, using the back of the spoon to smooth it out evenly. Top with the tomato slices, then arrange the olives and capers on top. Bake for 10–15 minutes, or until the crust is crisp and golden. Season with black pepper and serve.

sole bonne femme

The bones from the filleted sole are used to make the stock, which itself is the basis for this recipe's creamy sauce.

 30–35 MINS 25–30 MINS

SPECIAL EQUIPMENT ▪ 8in (20cm) square baking dish

SERVES 4

1 tbsp butter

9oz (250g) mushrooms, sliced

salt and freshly ground black pepper

2 shallots, finely chopped

2 Dover sole, 2¼lb (1kg) each, filleted, heads and bones reserved for the stock

For the fish stock

heads and bones from 2 Dover sole

1 onion, sliced

1 tsp peppercorns

3–5 sprigs of parsley

1 cup white wine or juice of 1 lemon

For the velouté sauce

2 tbsp butter

2 tbsp all-purpose flour

3 tbsp heavy cream

3 large egg yolks

juice of ½ lemon, or to taste

1 Cut the washed fish heads and bones into 4–5 pieces. Put in a pan with the onion, 2 cups water, peppercorns, and parsley. Add the wine. Boil, then simmer for 20 minutes. Pour through a sieve into a second pan.

2 Preheat the oven to 350°F (180°C). Melt the butter in a frying pan and add the mushrooms, salt, pepper, and 3–4 tbsp water. Cover with buttered foil and cook for 5 minutes.

3 Butter a baking dish and add the shallots. Fold each fillet in half, skin-side inward, and place on the shallots. Season and half cover with stock. Top with buttered foil and cook in the oven for 15–18 minutes. Reserve the liquid.

4 Add the liquid and shallots to the stock and boil until reduced to 1½ cups. For the sauce, melt the butter in another pan and whisk in the flour. Cook for 1–2 minutes. Remove from the heat and cool. Strain the stock into the butter and flour, and boil, whisking until thickened, then simmer for 5 minutes. Remove from the heat and add the mushrooms and liquid.

5 Whisk the cream and egg yolks in a bowl, add a little hot sauce, and whisk to mix. Stir the cream mixture into the sauce in the pan. Return to the heat and cook gently for 2–3 minutes. Remove from the heat. Add lemon juice, salt, and pepper. Heat the broiler. Arrange the fillets on flameproof plates, ladle the sauce over, and broil for 1–2 minutes. Serve at once.

grilled eggplant with spiced tomato sauce

Paprika, a spice made from dried sweet pepper pods, adds a lively flavor to this tomato sauce and complements the creamy flesh of the plump, ripe eggplants.

 15 MINS   20 MINS

SERVES 4

2 large eggplants, cut into slices ½in (1cm) thick

salt and freshly ground black pepper

4 tbsp olive oil

2 garlic cloves, sliced

½ tsp paprika

4 large, ripe tomatoes, peeled (p197) and chopped

1 tbsp tomato paste

good pinch of sugar

1 Put the eggplants in a colander, sprinkle with salt, and weigh down with a plate. Let drain for 15 minutes, rinse, and pat dry with paper towels.

2 Meanwhile, heat 1 tbsp of the oil in a pan over low heat. Add the garlic and paprika and cook gently for a few seconds. Stir in the tomatoes, tomato paste, and sugar and cook fairly gently, stirring frequently, for about 10 minutes until pulpy. Season with salt and pepper.

3 Place a ridged cast-iron grill pan over medium-high heat until hot. Brush the eggplant slices with the remaining oil, then grill for 3 minutes on each side until golden. Serve immediately with the sauce drizzled over, or in a bowl on the side.

melon and tomato salad

This refreshing salad, with its sweet and savory dressing, can be made up to 6 hours ahead and kept, covered and without the dressing, in the fridge.

 15–20 MINS PLUS CHILLING

SERVES 6

2 small orange- or yellow-fleshed melons, such as cantaloupe, about 3lb (1.35kg) total weight

1 medium green-fleshed melon, such as galia, about 3lb (1.35kg)

13oz (375g) cherry tomatoes

handful of mint

For the dressing

¼ cup port

juice of 2 lemons

2 tbsp honey

salt and freshly ground black pepper

1 Halve the melons, scoop out the seeds with a spoon, and discard.

2 Using a melon baller, cut balls from the flesh of each melon and place into a large bowl.

3 Remove the stalks from the cherry tomatoes. Immerse in a saucepan of boiling water very briefly, just until

the skins start to split, then plunge into a bowl of cold water. When cold, peel off the skins. Add the tomatoes to the melon.

4 Strip the mint leaves from the stalks, reserving some sprigs for garnish. Pile the mint leaves on a board and coarsely chop. Add the mint to the melon and tomatoes.

5 For the dressing, put the port in a bowl. Add the lemon juice, honey, salt, and pepper and whisk. Taste for seasoning. Pour the dressing over the melon, tomatoes, and mint. Stir gently and taste for seasoning, adding more of the dressing ingredients, if you like. Cover the bowl and refrigerate for about 1 hour, so the flavors mellow. Serve decorated with the reserved mint sprigs. It complements cold or cured meats especially well.

bread salad

This traditional Italian recipe (known as panzanella) is not only a great way to use up any leftover bread, but also adds another dimension to the classic combination of tomatoes and basil.

 15 MINS

SERVES 4

3 slices ciabatta or other rustic country-style bread, toasted and cut into chunky bite-sized cubes

2–3 tbsp olive oil

handful of basil leaves, torn

salt and freshly ground black pepper

2 red peppers, roasted, peeled (p171), and sliced

4 tomatoes, coarsely chopped

handful of toasted pine nuts

4½oz (125g) Dolcelatte or other mild blue cheese, cut into bite-sized cubes

1 Put the bread cubes in a large bowl and drizzle the oil over the top. Add the basil and season with salt and pepper. Toss together and let stand for about 10 minutes, to allow the flavors to develop.

2 Add the peppers, tomatoes, pine nuts, and cheese and toss gently until everything is evenly mixed. Serve with cold cooked meats.

variation

summer vegetable bread salad

Prepare and dress the bread in the same way but with a small handful of fresh mint leaves instead of basil. Add 1 avocado, pitted, peeled, and cubed, and tossed in lemon juice instead of the peppers. Add the tomatoes, coarsely chopped, a large handful of raw, shelled peas, ¼ cubed cucumber, and a handful of arugula. Season and toss gently. Serve with poached eggs or grilled ham.

greek salad

A classic, deeply refreshing combination that needs very ripe, flavorful tomatoes. Make sure you use very tasty, pungent black olives, and an aromatic, strong extra virgin olive oil.

 25–30 MINS PLUS STANDING

SERVES 6–8

2 small cucumbers

2¼lb (1kg) tomatoes

1 red onion

2 green bell peppers, cored, seeded, and cubed

4½oz (125g) Kalamata or other Greek olives

6oz (175g) feta cheese, cubed

For the herb vinaigrette

3 tbsp red wine vinegar

salt and freshly ground black pepper

½ cup extra virgin olive oil

3–5 sprigs of mint, leaves picked and finely chopped

3–5 sprigs of oregano, leaves picked and finely chopped

7–10 sprigs of parsley, leaves picked and finely chopped

1 To make the vinaigrette, whisk together the vinegar, salt, and pepper. Gradually whisk in the oil, so the vinaigrette emulsifies and thickens slightly. Add the herbs, then whisk again and taste for seasoning.

2 Peel the cucumbers and cut each in half lengthwise. Scoop out the seeds with a teaspoon. Discard the seeds. Cut the cucumbers lengthwise into 2–3 strips, then into ½in(1cm) slices.

3 With the tip of a small knife, core the tomatoes. Cut each one into 8 wedges, then cut each wedge in half. Peel and trim the red onion and cut into very thin rings. Gently separate the concentric circles within each ring with your fingers.

4 Put the cucumbers, tomatoes, onion rings, and peppers in a large bowl. Briskly whisk the dressing, pour it over, and toss thoroughly. Add the olives (they may be either left whole or pitted) and feta and gently toss again. Taste for seasoning. Allow the flavors to mellow for about 30 minutes before serving.

Season's best **tomatoes**

The myriad varieties of this quintessential ingredient range in color from near black through red, yellow, to almost white; in size from that of a pea to a huge sphere; and in taste from sweet to spritely acidic. Best in high summer and fall, they suit all cheeses. Good flavorings are garlic, herbs (basil, cilantro, oregano, or thyme), orange, vodka, or chile. Onions, peppers, meat, fish, or eggs are also perfect partners.

Tomatoes grow in almost all temperate climates, even Siberia. They are grown either outdoors, or in polytunnels or hothouses, but when ripened in the sun in summer, they have the scent and flavor everyone desires.

Red Cherry These small-fruited varieties are usually more flavorful than larger ones. Handy to eat whole as a snack, or when lightly crushed and warmed in oil, they make a colorful pizza topping.

Uniform bright red, glossy skin and sweet, juicy flesh.

Brandywine A gourmet-quality tomato, Brandywine is highly praised for its distinctive, well-balanced acidity and sweetness.

Moneymaker A prolific cropper with a rich tomato flavor. It is a popular used in salads, broiling or frying in halves, or for sauces.

The yellow pear tapers at the top, making it stand out from other cherry varieties.

With its generous diameter, Brandywine is ideal for slicing, to use in salads and sandwiches.

Beam's yellow pear An attractive little yellow tomato with a distinctive shape. It looks great halved in salads.

Most of the flavor is in the jelly surrounding the seeds, so do not discard them.

San Marzano With its superior, rich tomato flavor and meaty interior, this is the classic variety for canning and paste-making. Many consider it to be the best sauce tomato in the world.

Green Zebra A good-sized tomato with greenish-gold stripes and spots, this variety has an excellent, tangy flavor. It is good used raw in salads and salsas.

Gardener's delight A very popular cherry tomato with a bright red color and a sweet flavor.

If the fruit turns too yellow, it is overripe.

White beauty This is a rarer tomato, with creamy white flesh all the way through. It has a delicate flavor and is very sweet.

essentials
varieties available
Tomberries, cherry, cocktail (larger than cherry), baby plum, plum, standard, beefsteak.

buy Choose ones that smell of the vine, not too soft, with fresh, bright green calyces.

store Keep at room temperature, not in the fridge, unless they are very ripe. Arrange so tomatoes don't touch each other.

cook Bake whole, roast, broil, fry, sauté, or stew. Make into sauce or soup. Add to casseroles and stews.

preserve Oven-dry and pack in olive oil; make ketchup or chutney; pickle green (unripe) tomatoes.

recipe ideas
Fresh tomatoes stuffed with fruity couscous p152

Roasted tomato soup p148

Sausage and tomato pie p192

how to peel and seed tomatoes
Tomatoes are best peeled and seeded if you plan to use them for sauces or soups. When using cold for salads or for stuffing, this isn't necessary.

1 Remove the green stem, score an "X" in the skin of each tomato, at the base, then immerse it in a pan of boiling water for 20 seconds, or until the skin loosens.

2 With a slotted spoon, remove the tomato from the boiling water and place it immediately into a bowl of iced water to cool quickly.

3 Lift out of the water and, using a paring knife, peel away the loosened skin. To seed, halve the tomato, then gently squeeze out the seeds over a bowl to catch them.

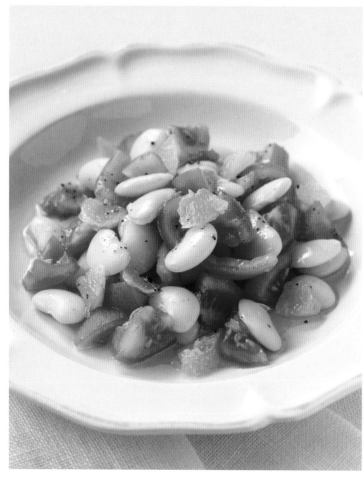

tomato salad with butter beans and lime

If it's a light lunch that you're after, then this fresh, zingy salad is just the thing to accompany whatever else you have in the fridge, whether cold meats, cheese, or bread.

 20 MINS

SERVES 4

14oz (400g) can butter beans, drained and rinsed

8 tomatoes, peeled (p197) and coarsely chopped

2 limes, peeled, segmented, and chopped

salt and freshly ground black pepper

drizzle of extra virgin olive oil

1 Put the beans, tomatoes, and lime segments in a bowl and gently toss together. Season well with salt and pepper.

2 Drizzle the oil over the top. Serve with crusty bread and a selection of sliced cooked meats.

concentrated tomato sauce

Sauces and purees are the ideal use for a glut of tomatoes, especially if they are overripe. This thick version is great for pizzas and in other savory dishes.

 15 MINS   **1 HR** 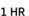 **FREEZABLE**

MAKES ABOUT 4 CUPS

5½–6½lb (2.5–3kg) very ripe tomatoes, coarsely chopped

1 large onion, sliced

1 large sprig of parsley, basil, and/or celery leaves

1 bay leaf

1 large garlic clove

1 Put all the ingredients into a large heavy-bottomed saucepan and bring to a boil. Reduce the heat to very low and simmer for about 1 hour, or until the mixture becomes

thick and concentrated. Stir frequently. The sauce is ready when there is no discernible liquid left.

2 Remove and discard the bay leaf and garlic and sieve the sauce through a metal sieve into a bowl, pressing hard to extract as much of the sauce as possible. Leave the sauce to cool.

3 Pour the concentrated tomato sauce into small, clean freezer pots, then seal, label, and freeze. Thaw before using.

hot chile sauce

This blend of ingredients gives an extra kick to everything from cold meat to kebabs, scrambled eggs to cheese on toast. The tamarind paste adds sharpness to the sauce, but it's optional.

 15-20 MINS   **45-60 MINS**   **FREEZABLE**

SPECIAL EQUIPMENT ▪ preserving pan (optional) ▪ blender or food processor

MAKES 600ml (1 PINT)

4 red bird's eye (thin) chiles, stems removed

1 dried chipotle chile

4 ripe tomatoes, quartered

1 carrot, chopped

1 small onion, chopped

1 celery stalk, chopped

2 tbsp agave syrup or honey

1 tbsp tomato paste

2 tbsp red wine vinegar

1 tsp tamarind paste (optional)

⅔ cup apple juice

salt and freshly ground black pepper

1 Put all the ingredients except the salt and pepper (and the tamarind paste if you aren't using it) in a large heavy-bottomed, stainless-steel saucepan or a preserving pan. Bring to a boil, reduce the heat, cover, and simmer gently, stirring occasionally, for 45 minutes or until pulpy.

2 Pour the sauce into a blender or food processor with 5 tbsp water and pulse until smooth, stopping and scraping down the sides as necessary. Then run through a sieve into a bowl. Season to taste with salt and pepper.

3 Pour the sauce into warm sterilized jars with nonmetallic or vinegar-proof lids, top with waxed paper disks, seal, label, and refrigerate for up to 1 month after opening.

tabbouleh and cacik

Warmed pita bread makes a fitting and delicious accompaniment to these mezze salads. Mezze are little dishes of vegetables, salads, olives, and such like that are standard features for meals all over the Middle East.

 35–40 MINS PLUS SOAKING AND CHILLING

SERVES 4

- 3½oz (100g) bulgur wheat
- 1 small cucumber
- salt and freshly ground black pepper
- 9oz (250g) tomatoes, peeled (p197), seeded, and chopped
- 2 scallions, trimmed and chopped
- small bunch of flat-leaf parsley, leaves chopped
- 3 tbsp lemon juice
- ¼ cup olive oil
- 1 bunch of mint, leaves chopped
- 1 large garlic clove, finely chopped
- ¼ tsp ground coriander
- ¼ tsp ground cumin
- 1 cup natural yogurt
- 3–4 pita breads

1 Put the bulgur wheat in a large bowl and pour in enough cold water to cover generously. Let it soak for 30 minutes, then drain through a sieve and squeeze out any remaining water with your fist.

2 Trim the ends from the cucumber, cut in half lengthwise, and scoop out the seeds with a teaspoon. Cube the cucumber halves, put in a colander, sprinkle with salt, and stir to mix. Leave for 15–20 minutes, to draw out the bitter juices, then rinse under cold, running water and drain.

3 For the tabbouleh, in a large bowl, combine the bulgur, tomatoes, scallions, parsley, lemon juice, oil, two-thirds of the mint, and plenty of salt and pepper. Mix and taste for seasoning, then cover and chill in the fridge for at least 2 hours.

4 To make the cacik, put the cucumber in a bowl and add the garlic, remaining mint, ground coriander, ground cumin, and salt and pepper. Pour in the yogurt. Stir to combine and taste for seasoning. Chill in the fridge for at least 2 hours, to allow the flavors to blend.

5 Warm the pita breads in a low oven for 3–5 minutes, then remove and cut into strips. Take the salads from the fridge and allow to come to room temperature, then arrange them in separate bowls with the warm pita bread fingers alongside.

variation

tabbouleh with grilled eggplant dip

Make the tabbouleh the same way, but substitute chopped cilantro for the flat-leaf parsley. For the dip, trim and slice an eggplant, brush with olive oil, and grill the slices for 2–3 minutes on each side until soft and striped brown. Cool, finely chop, and mix with the 1 cup yogurt and the spices as before. Serve with individual Little Gem lettuce leaves to use as receptacles for the tabbouleh and dip as well as the pita breads.

arugula pesto

Arugula is one of the fastest growing salad crops. To use up the glut, make batches of this pesto sauce and freeze it in ice cube trays to be used as and when you need it.

🥣 10 MINS 🍲 2-3 MINS ❄ FREEZABLE

SPECIAL EQUIPMENT▪ blender or food processor

MAKES ABOUT I CUP

1¾oz (50g) pine nuts

1¾oz (50g) arugula leaves

¼oz (10g) basil leaves (optional)

1oz (30g) Parmesan cheese, grated

1 small garlic clove, crushed

salt and freshly ground black pepper

½ cup extra virgin olive oil

1 In a dry frying pan, over low heat, gently toast the pine nuts for 2–3 minutes, moving them all the time, until they are golden brown all over. Set aside to cool.

2 Put the arugula and basil leaves, if using, with the cooled pine nuts, Parmesan, garlic, salt, and a generous grinding of pepper into a blender or food processor. Add 2–3 tbsp of the oil and process to a thick paste. If you are serving it with pasta, you can add a little more garlic and Parmesan, but use less if you are using it as an accompaniment to grilled chicken or fish.

3 Reduce the speed and continue to add the oil, in a thin stream, until the pesto becomes a thin paste. Taste and adjust the seasoning if needed. If you prefer a coarser texture, pulse in the food processor until you reach the desired consistency. Serve on warmed plates mixed into cooked pasta, such as pappardelle.

variation

arugula, almond, and blue cheese pesto

In place of the pine nuts, use blanched almonds and replace the Parmesan cheese with an equal quantity of blue cheese, crumbled or cubed. Omit the basil leaves. Follow the recipe as written.

egg and fennel potato salad

The mild aniseed flavor of fennel gently enlivens this potato salad. Look for a small, blemish-free, pale-green bulb that is firm and tightly packed to ensure you buy the freshest fennel.

🥣 10 MINS 🍲 15 MINS

SERVES 4

4 large eggs

9oz (250g) new potatoes, scrubbed and cut into bite-sized pieces

drizzle of olive oil

sea salt and freshly ground black pepper

handful of flat-leaf parsley, finely chopped

1 fennel bulb, trimmed and finely chopped

1 Boil the eggs in a small saucepan of water for 6 minutes; less if you prefer a runnier yolk.

2 Cook the new potatoes in lightly salted boiling water in a large pan for 15–20 minutes until soft, then drain. Drizzle some olive oil over the potatoes while they are still hot and season with sea salt and pepper.

3 Mix in the parsley and the fennel bulb. Then pour the potato mixture into a serving bowl.

4 Shell and quarter the hard-boiled eggs and add them to the potato salad. Serve immediately.

variation

egg, pea, and potato salad

Cook the eggs as before. At step 2, add 6oz (175g) shelled peas and a sprig of mint to the potatoes after 10 minutes of cooking. Discard the mint after cooking. Add a splash of white balsamic vinegar with the olive oil. Mix in the parsley but omit the fennel.

marinated cucumber and dill salad

This beautifully simple Scandinavian dish is an elegant accompaniment to a piece of grilled or cold poached salmon. The cooling cucumber adds color as well as crunch.

 10 MINS PLUS STANDING   ❄ **FREEZABLE**

SPECIAL EQUIPMENT ▪ mandoline or food processor

SERVES 4–6

2 cucumbers, thinly sliced using a mandoline or food processor

2 tbsp coarse sea salt

2 tbsp granulated sugar

4 tbsp rice wine vinegar, or white wine vinegar

freshly ground black pepper

handful of dill, finely chopped

juice of ½ lemon (optional)

1 Put the sliced cucumber in a colander and toss in the sea salt. Place a slightly smaller bowl on top of the cucumber and weigh down with weights, or a few unopened cans of food. Set over a sink for 1 hour to allow the cucumber to lose any excess water.

2 Remove the weighted bowl, wrap the cucumber carefully in a clean kitchen towel, and squeeze out the excess water. Transfer to a bowl, cover, and leave in the fridge for at least 1 hour, until completely chilled.

3 Meanwhile, put 2 tbsp boiling water into a bowl and stir in the sugar to dissolve. Add the vinegar, a generous grinding of black pepper, and the dill, then place the bowl in the fridge to cool. Once the dressing and cucumber are completely cold, mix the two together. Adjust the seasoning to taste before serving. If using rice wine vinegar, add the lemon juice.

cucumber-chile salad

Delicious with grilled or barbecued dishes, the longer this salad is left to marinate, the spicier it will be. Even if you like a milder dish, give it at least 1 hour for the flavors to meld.

 15–20 MINS PLUS MARINATING

SERVES 4

½ cup granulated sugar, plus extra to taste

salt

½ cup rice vinegar, plus extra to taste

1 cucumber

1 red or jalapeño chile, seeded and cut into very thin strips

1 Pour ½ cup water into a small pan and pour in the sugar and ½ tsp salt. Place over medium heat and stir until the sugar has dissolved, then bring to a boil. Remove from the heat, stir in the vinegar, and set aside to cool.

2 Trim the ends from the cucumber, peel, cut in half lengthwise, and scoop out the seeds with a teaspoon. Cut the halves lengthwise into long thin slices.

3 Combine the cucumber, chile, and vinegar mixture in a bowl. Cover and marinate in the fridge for at least 1 hour and up to 4 hours. Taste just before serving, adding more salt, sugar, or vinegar to taste.

variation

cucumber, chile, and roasted bell pepper salad

Roast 1 red, 1 yellow, and 1 green bell pepper, seed, and slice (p171). Use only ½ cucumber but prepare in the same way as before. Use 1 green (preferably jalapeño) chile instead of the red one.

tortilla bean salad

For an even more dramatic-looking bowlful, you could use black beans. Don't be timid with the chiles, since beans can take a lot of seasoning and will soak up much of the heat.

 25-30 MINS PLUS CHILLING   1 HR-1 HR 30 MINS

SERVES 6-8

- 2 x 14oz cans red kidney beans, rinsed
- 4 sweet corncobs, kernels removed (about 1lb/450g kernels, p155)
- 1lb 10oz (750g) tomatoes, peeled (p197) and coarsely chopped
- 1 red bell pepper, seeded and cubed
- 1 green bell pepper, seeded and cubed
- 1 yellow bell pepper, seeded and cubed
- 6 corn tortillas
- ¼ tsp cayenne pepper

For the dressing

- ½ cup cider vinegar
- ½ tsp ground cumin
- salt and freshly ground black pepper
- 3 jalapeño chiles, seeded and finely cubed
- ½ cup vegetable oil, plus more for tortillas and baking sheet
- small bunch of cilantro, leaves finely chopped

1 For the dressing, whisk together the vinegar and cumin, and season with salt and pepper. Add the chiles, then gradually whisk in the oil, so the vinaigrette emulsifies and thickens slightly. Stir in the cilantro, reserving a little for garnish. Taste for seasoning.

2 In a large bowl, combine the kidney beans, sweet corn, tomatoes, bell peppers, and dressing. Gently toss the salad and taste for seasoning. Cover and chill in the fridge for at least 1 hour.

3 Just before serving, preheat the broiler and oil a baking sheet. Brush the tortillas with oil and season with salt and cayenne pepper, then slice them into triangles.

4 Spread the tortilla triangles on the baking sheet. Broil, 4in (10cm) from the heat, for 4–6 minutes, until golden brown and crisp, stirring occasionally so they color evenly.

5 Divide the salad among 6–8 deep plates and top with the tortilla triangles. Sprinkle the reserved chopped cilantro over the top. Serve chilled or at room temperature.

zucchini and hazelnut bread

Hazelnuts add taste and texture to this quick and easy bread.

 20 MINS   50 MINS PLUS RESTING   FREEZABLE

MAKES 1 LOAF

- 1¾ cups all-purpose flour
- 1 cup whole-wheat flour, plus 1 tsp baking powder
- 1 tsp baking soda
- salt
- 1¾oz (50g) hazelnuts, coarsely chopped
- 5½oz (150g) zucchini, coarsely grated
- 1 cup buttermilk

1 Preheat the oven to 425°F (220°C). Line a baking sheet with parchment paper. In a bowl, mix the all-purpose, flour, the whole-wheat flour, baking powder, baking soda, ½ tsp salt, and hazelnuts. Add the grated zucchini, mixing it in well.

2 Make a well in the center of the dry ingredients and stir in the buttermilk, bringing the mixture together to form a loose dough. Use your hands to bring the mixture together into a ball, then turn it onto a floured surface and knead for 2 minutes, until it forms a smooth dough. You may need to add a little extra flour at this stage.

3 Shape the dough into a round about 6in (15cm) in diameter. With a sharp knife, slash a cross in the top of the dough to help it to rise easily when baking.

4 Place the dough on the baking sheet and cook in the middle of the oven for 30 minutes. Reduce the temperature to 400°F (200°C) and bake for 20 minutes until well risen, golden brown, and a skewer inserted into the middle emerges clean. Transfer to a wire rack and allow it to rest for at least 20 minutes before serving.

grilled mediterranean vegetables

These vegetables are a perfect side dish. You can also chop them up and layer them between sheets of lasagne and top them with a cheese sauce for something more substantial.

 15 MINS   10-15 MINS   FREEZABLE

SPECIAL EQUIPMENT ▪ grill pan or electric grill

MAKES ABOUT 3lb (1.35kg)

- 2 small eggplants, trimmed and cut into strips lengthwise, about ¼in (5mm) thick
- 4 zucchini, trimmed and cut into strips lengthwise, about ¼in (5mm) thick
- a drizzle of olive oil, plus extra for brushing
- 4 red bell peppers, seeded and cut into 6-8 strips

1 Preheat a grill pan. Prepare 3–4 baking sheets with a layer of wax paper or parchment paper.

2 Brush the eggplants and zucchini with oil on both sides. Put the bell peppers in a shallow dish, drizzle with a little oil, and toss with your hands to coat them completely.

3 When the grill pan is very hot, but not smoking, add a single layer of vegetables (don't overcrowd them). Press them down firmly with a fish spatula, until the undersides are nicely striped. Turn the vegetables over and cook for another 2–3 minutes, until just cooked and striped. Don't overcook them, or they will become too soft. Transfer to the prepared baking sheets to cool.

4 Repeat for the remaining vegetables, reheating the grill between each batch. Serve with grilled fish or chicken, or mix in with flageolet beans, navy beans, or chickpeas, and dress with pesto.

cornbread

Cornbread is a traditional American loaf that makes a quick and easy accompaniment to soups and stews. The name is given to any bread that is made with corn rather than wheat and leavened with baking powder, instead of yeast. For a non-vegetarian cornbread, add finely chopped cooked bacon with the corn.

 15–20 MINS   20–25 MINS

SPECIAL EQUIPMENT ▪ 9in (23cm) flameproof cast-iron frying pan or similar-sized round springform cake pan

SERVES 8

1 cup fine yellow cornmeal
  or polenta

1 cup bread flour

¼ cup granulated sugar

1 tbsp baking powder

1 tsp salt

2 sweet corncobs, kernels removed
  (about 8oz/225g kernels, p155)

2 large eggs

4 tbsp unsalted butter or bacon
  drippings, melted and cooled

1 cup milk

1 Preheat the oven to 425°F (220°C). Grease the frying pan or round cake pan with butter or drippings. Place in the oven.

2 Sift the cornmeal or polenta, flour, sugar, baking powder, and 1 tsp salt into a bowl. Add the kernels.

3 In a bowl, whisk together the eggs, melted butter or bacon drippings, and milk. Pour three-quarters of the milk mixture into the flour mixture and stir. Draw in the dry ingredients, adding the remaining milk mixture. Stir just until smooth.

4 Carefully take the hot pan or cake pan out of the oven and pour in the batter; it should sizzle. Quickly brush the top with butter or bacon drippings, return the pan or cake pan to the oven, and bake for 20–25 minutes. The bread should shrink away from the sides of the pan and a skewer inserted into the middle should come out clean.

5 Let the cornbread cool slightly on a wire rack. Serve warm, with soup, chile con carne, or fried chicken. The cornbread does not keep well, but leftovers can be used as a stuffing for roast poultry.

variation

chile cornbread

Prepare in exactly the same way but add 2 red chiles, seeded and finely chopped to the mixture. For extra kick, sprinkle the surface with 1 tsp dried chile flakes after brushing with butter or bacon drippings before baking at step 4.

zucchini tian

This is an excellent side dish for roast lamb or chicken or good on its own as a vegetarian dish. Try to use small zucchini, since they have a more concentrated flavor than larger varieties.

 30–35 MINS   20–30 MINS

SPECIAL EQUIPMENT ▪ 1 quart baking dish

SERVES 6

¼ cup olive oil

2¼lb (1kg) small zucchini, cut into ¼in(5mm) thick slices

salt and freshly ground black pepper

2¼oz (65g) long-grain rice

2 onions, thinly sliced

3 garlic cloves, finely chopped

5–7 sprigs of flat-leaf parsley, leaves picked and finely chopped

2oz (60g) Parmesan cheese, grated

3 large eggs

1 Heat one-third of the oil in a large frying pan over medium heat. Add the zucchini and salt and pepper, and cook, stirring occasionally, for 10–15 minutes, until tender and evenly browned. Spread the slices out over a large plate to cool.

2 Cook the rice in a pan of boiling salted water for about 10 minutes, or until it is tender. Drain the rice in a colander, rinse with cold water to remove some of the starch, and drain again thoroughly. Let the rice cool for 8–10 minutes, then stir with a fork.

3 Heat half the remaining oil in the frying pan over medium heat, add the onions and garlic, and cook, stirring occasionally, for 3–5 minutes until soft but not colored.

4 Preheat the oven to 350°F (180°C). Brush the baking dish with oil. Coarsely chop the cooled zucchini.

5 In a large bowl, combine the zucchini, onion mixture, parsley, rice, and Parmesan. Stir to mix, then taste for seasoning. Crack the eggs into a bowl and beat to mix. Stir them into the vegetable mixture with the wooden spoon.

6 Spread the mixture in the baking dish and sprinkle with the remaining oil. Bake the tian for 10–15 minutes, until set. Increase the temperature to 400°F (200°C) and bake for a further 10–15 minutes, until brown. Serve hot, or at room temperature, from the baking dish.

arugula and tomato pasta salad

Arugula leaves and tomatoes are a classic combination. Tossed together with pasta and mayonnaise, the end result is a creamy dish, perfect for a light summer's day lunch.

 15 MINS   10 MINS

SERVES 4

8oz (225g) pasta, such as penne, fusilli, or farfalle

2 tbsp mayonnaise

handful of arugula leaves

4½oz (125g) fresh or cooked garden peas (shelled weight)

6 cherry tomatoes, finely chopped

salt and freshly ground black pepper

1 Cook the pasta in a large pan of boiling salted water for about 12 minutes, or until it is tender but still firm to the bite. Drain, keeping back a tiny amount of the cooking water, then return the pasta to the pan.

2 Mix the pasta with the mayonnaise, arugula leaves, peas, and tomatoes. Season well with salt and pepper. When cool, cover with plastic wrap, and keep in the fridge. Serve at room temperature.

variation

arugula, green bean, and pesto salad

Use 4½oz (125g) green beans, cut in short lengths instead of the peas and cook them with the pasta for the last 4–5 minutes. Flavor the mayonnaise with green pesto to taste. Garnish with some black olives.

malaysian-style pickled vegetables

This assortment of vegetables tossed in a golden turmeric sauce will enliven any stir-fry, curry, or Asian noodle dish.

 35-45 MINS 10 MINS PLUS STANDING

SPECIAL EQUIPMENT ▪ blender or food processor (optional)

SERVES 4

½ cucumber

2 carrots

florets from ¼ small cauliflower

15 green beans, trimmed

4½ oz (125g) wedge of green cabbage, cored and finely shredded

1oz (30g) roasted unsalted peanuts

For the pickling sauce

3 roasted unsalted macadamia nuts

1 garlic clove, finely chopped

3 shallots, cubed

¾in (2cm) piece of fresh galangal or ginger, peeled and finely chopped

1 tsp ground turmeric

1 red or jalapeño chile, seeded and finely chopped

2 tbsp vegetable oil

¼ cup granulated sugar

salt

¼ cup rice vinegar

1 Trim the ends from the cucumber, peel, cut in half lengthwise, and scoop out the seeds with a teaspoon. Cut lengthwise into ¼in (5mm) strips, then into 2in (5cm) sticks. Cut the carrots into sticks as well. Cut any large cauliflower florets in half.

2 Fill a wok 2in (5cm) deep with water and bring to a boil. Add the carrots, cauliflower, and beans. Simmer for 2–3 minutes, until tender but still crisp, then add the cucumber and cabbage for 1 minute. Drain well.

3 For the pickling sauce, finely chop the macadamia nuts. Then pound the nuts, garlic, shallots, galangal, turmeric, and chile in a mortar and pestle, adding one ingredient at a time and pounding well after each addition. Alternatively, work the ingredients to a paste in a blender or food processor.

4 Heat a wok over medium heat until hot. Drizzle in the oil to coat the sides and bottom. When the oil is hot, add the chile-nut paste and stir for 3–5 minutes, until slightly thickened and the spices are fragrant.

5 Stir in the sugar, a pinch of salt, and vinegar and bring to a boil. Remove the wok from the heat and add the vegetables, tossing to coat. Transfer to a bowl and cover. Let stand for about 1 hour at room temperature, or at least 2 hours in the fridge. To serve, coarsely chop the peanuts and sprinkle on top.

tomato and tarragon pilaf

A pilaf is a Turkish dish with rice cooked in a seasoned stock. It is made in one pot so saves on clean-up, as well as being a quick and easy dish to cook for a midweek supper.

 10 MINS 25 MINS

SERVES 4

1 tbsp olive oil

pat of butter

1 onion, finely chopped

salt and freshly ground black pepper

2 garlic cloves, grated or finely chopped

9oz (250g) basmati rice

2 cups hot vegetable stock

1lb (450g) tomatoes, quartered

2 or 3 sprigs of tarragon, leaves picked and torn

1 Heat the oil and butter in a large frying pan over medium heat, add the onion, and cook for 3–4 minutes until soft and translucent. Add some salt and stir in the garlic and rice, making sure the rice is well coated and soaks up the butter.

2 Pour in the hot stock, stir, reduce the heat to as low as possible, cover, and cook for 15 minutes or until the rice is cooked and has absorbed the stock. If the pilaf starts to dry out, add a little more hot water.

3 Remove the lid, let stand for a few minutes, season well with salt and pepper, then stir in the tomatoes and tarragon. Serve the pilaf hot with a crisp green salad.

variation

tomato and cucumber pilaf

Substitute a peeled, seeded, and cubed cucumber for half the tomatoes and add a handful each of toasted pine nuts and currants.

blueberry upside-down cake

This is an unusual yet delicious way of turning a container of blueberries and a few pantry essentials into a quick and delicious dessert for a crowd.

 15 MINS 40 MINS

SPECIAL EQUIPMENT ▪ 9in (23cm) round springform cake pan ▪ electric hand mixer

SERVES 8-10

11 tbsp unsalted butter, softened

⅔ cup granulated sugar

3 large eggs

1 tsp pure vanilla extract

1 cup self-rising flour

1 tsp baking powder

1¾oz (50g) ground almonds

9oz (250g) blueberries

1 Preheat the oven to 350°F (180°C) and place a baking sheet inside to heat up. Grease the cake pan and line the bottom with parchment paper.

2 Cream together the butter and sugar using an electric hand mixer, until light and fluffy. Gradually beat in the eggs and vanilla extract, whisking well between each addition, until well combined. Sift together the flour and baking powder, add the ground almonds, and fold into the batter.

3 Pour the blueberries into the pan and spread the batter gently over them. Bake the cake on the baking sheet in the center of the oven for 35–40 minutes until golden brown and springy to the touch; a skewer should come out clean when inserted in the center. Leave the cake to cool for a few minutes, before removing from the pan.

4 Place the cake on a serving plate. Serve warm as a dessert, topped with cream or light vanilla custard; or serve cold, dusted with confectioners' sugar.

double chocolate raspberry tart

This impressive dessert uses the classic combination of raspberries and chocolate, but is quick and simple to make with a good quality store-bought pie crust.

 40 MINS PLUS COOLING

SERVES 6-8

3½oz (100g) white chocolate, broken into pieces

2½oz (75g) dark chocolate, broken into pieces

1 store-bought chocolate pie dough

1 cup heavy cream

14oz (400g) raspberries

confectioners' sugar, for dusting

1 Melt the white chocolate in a heatproof bowl by setting over a pan of barely simmering water. Let cool.

2 Melt the dark chocolate in a separate bowl in the same way, and use a pastry brush to paint the inside of the pie crust with a layer of chocolate. This will keep the pie crust from becoming soggy once it is filled with the raspberry and chocolate cream. Let it set.

3 Whip the cream until it forms stiff peaks. Fold the cooled white chocolate into the whipped cream. Crush half the raspberries and gently fold them through the cream mixture. Pile the filling into the crust evenly. Decorate the top with the remaining raspberries, dust with confectioners' sugar, and serve.

raspberry crème brûlée

This dessert looks so attractive served in little individual dishes. The raspberries add some sharpness.

 10 MINS PLUS SETTING 30 MINS ❄ FREEZABLE

SPECIAL EQUIPMENT ▪ 6 x 6fl oz (160ml) ramekins ▪ electric hand mixer ▪ grill or cook's blowtorch

MAKES 6

7oz (200g) raspberries

4 large egg yolks

½ cup granulated sugar

2¼ cups heavy cream

1 tsp pure vanilla extract

1 Divide the raspberries among the ramekins. Put the egg yolks and 2 tbsp of the sugar in a large bowl and beat with an electric hand mixer until the mixture begins to thicken and becomes pale and creamy.

2 Heat the cream gently in a pan for 5 minutes. Do not let it boil. Remove from the heat, stir in the vanilla extract, and allow to cool for 5 minutes.

3 Slowly add the warm cream to the egg mixture a little at a time, beating constantly. Pour the mixture back into the pan and cook over low heat for a few minutes, stirring all the time with a wooden spoon until thick. Do not allow to boil. Pour the custard into the ramekins and allow to cool completely. Transfer to the fridge to set for a couple of hours or overnight.

4 When ready to serve, preheat the broiler. Sprinkle the tops of the custards evenly with the remaining sugar and place under the broiler until the sugar bubbles and turns golden brown. Alternatively, use a cook's blowtorch, making sweeping movements with the flame until the sugar starts to caramelize. Allow the topping to harden for 20 minutes before serving.

variation

peach crème brûlée

Use 7oz (200g) ripe peaches, peeled, pitted, and chopped, instead of the raspberries.

almond and raspberry lattice tart

This is the Viennese specialty Linzertorte made with almond lattice pastry.

 30-35 MINS PLUS CHILLING 40-45 MINS

SPECIAL EQUIPMENT ▪ 9in (23cm) round fluted tart pan with removable botom ▪ food processor ▪ fluted pastry wheel (optional)

SERVES 6-8

1 cup all-purpose flour

pinch of ground cloves

½ tsp ground cinnamon

1½ cups ground almonds

8 tbsp unsalted butter, softened and cubed

1 large egg yok

½ cup granulated sugar

salt

grated zest of 1 lemon, and juice of ½ lemon

For the filling

½ cup granulated sugar

13oz (375g) raspberries

1-2 tbsp confectioners' sugar, for dusting

1 Sift the flour into a bowl. Mix in the cloves, cinnamon, and almonds, and make a well in the center.

2 In a separate bowl and using your fingers, mix together the butter, yolk, sugar, ¼ tsp salt, and lemon zest and juice. Place in the well. Then draw in the flour and work it until coarse crumbs form. Mix the dough into a ball. Knead the dough for 1–2 minutes until smooth, then wrap in plastic wrap and chill in the fridge for 1–2 hours.

3 For the filling, put the sugar and raspberries in a pan over low heat and gently cook for 10–12 minutes until thick. Let cool, then with the back of a wooden spoon, press half of the fruit pulp through a sieve. Stir in the remaining pulp.

4 Preheat the oven to 375°F (190°C) and butter a tart pan. Flour the work surface and roll out two-thirds of the dough into an 11in (28cm) round. Use the dough to line the pan and cut off any excess overhanging the sides. Spread the filling in the crust.

5 Roll the rest of the dough to a 6 x 12in (15 x 30cm) rectangle. Using a fluted wheel, for a decorative edge (if you have one, or a sharp knife if you don't), cut the dough into 5 x ½in (12 x 1cm) wide strips. Arrange half the strips from left to right over the tart, ¾in (2cm) apart. Turn the tart through 45 degrees. Lay the other strips diagonally over the top. Trim the overhang, roll out the trimmings, and cut 4 more strips.

6 Brush the edge of the tart with water and attach the edge strips. Let chill in the fridge for 15 minutes. Bake for 15 minutes. Reduce the temperature to 350°F (180°C) and bake for another 25–30 minutes. Take the tart out of the oven, let it cool, then remove from the pan. About 30 minutes before serving, lightly dust the top with confectioners' sugar.

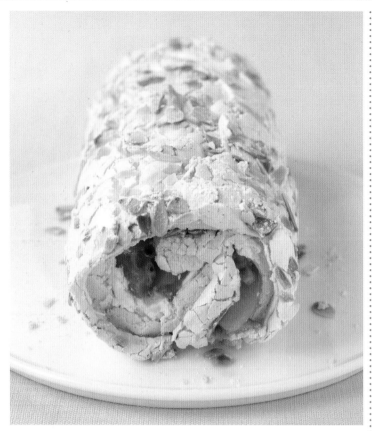

apricot meringue roulade

Don't be put off by the thought of rolling the meringue base to make the roulade. Using the parchment paper that it is cooked on helps prevent your fingers from getting sticky.

 30 MINS   **15–20 MINS**   ❄ **FREEZABLE**

SPECIAL EQUIPMENT ▪ 13 x 9in (32.5 x 23cm) jelly roll pan
▪ electric hand mixer

SERVES 8

4 large egg whites

salt

1 cup granulated sugar

1oz (25g) sliced almonds

confectioners' sugar, for dusting

4 apricots, halved and pitted

⅔ cup apple juice

1¼ cups heavy cream

seeds and pulp from 2 passion fruits

1 Preheat the oven to 375°F (190°C). Line a jelly roll pan with parchment paper. Place the egg whites in a bowl with a pinch of salt and beat with an electric hand mixer until soft peaks form. Beat in the sugar 1 tbsp at a time until the mixture is stiff and shiny. Spoon into the jelly roll pan and smooth into the corners. Scatter the sliced almonds over the top, then bake for 15–20 minutes, or until just firm to the touch and golden. Turn the meringue onto a sheet of parchment paper dusted with confectioners' sugar, and let cool.

2 Meanwhile, poach the apricots gently in the apple juice in a covered pan for about 5 minutes until tender. Set aside to cool. Drain the fruit halves on paper towels, then cut into neat pieces.

3 Place the cream in a bowl and beat with an electric hand mixer until soft peaks form. Spread the cream over the meringue, then scatter the apricots and passion fruit seeds over the top. Roll up the meringue, starting from one short end and using the parchment paper to help you. Wrap tightly in the parchment paper and chill until ready to serve.

4 To serve the roulade, unwrap it and place on a serving plate. Dust with a little more confectioners' sugar and serve cut in thick slices.

apricot pastries

What better than a fresh pastry with a steaming cup of coffee?

🥣 **30 MINS PLUS CHILLING AND RISING**   🍲 **15–20 MINS**

MAKES 8

¼ cup warm milk

1 tsp dried yeast

2 tbsp granulated sugar

1 large egg, plus 1 large egg for glazing

2 cups bread flour

salt

8 tbsp chilled butter, cut into 4 slices

3½oz (100g) apricot jam

8 apricots, halved and pitted

1 Mix the milk, yeast, and 1 tbsp of the sugar in a bowl. Cover for 20 minutes, then beat in the egg. Sift the flour into a bowl and add a pinch of salt and the remaining sugar. Make a well and pour in the yeast mix. Mix into a soft dough. Knead for 15 minutes until soft. Place in an oiled bowl, cover with plastic wrap, and chill for 15 minutes. On a floured surface, roll the dough into a square ½in (1cm) thick. Lay the butter slices on one-half, leaving a border all around. Fold the other half over the top, pressing the edges with a rolling pin to seal.

2 Generously flour and roll it into a rectangle 3 times as long as it is wide and ½in (1cm) thick. Fold the top third into the middle, then the bottom third back over it. Wrap; chill for 15 minutes. Repeat Step 2 twice.

3 Roll the dough on a well-floured work surface to a 12in (30cm) square. Trim the edges and cut out eight 4in (10cm) squares.

4 Spread 1 tbsp of the jam over each square using the back of a spoon and leaving a border of about ½in (1cm). Place an apricot half in 2 opposite corners of each square. Take the 2 corners without apricots and fold them into the middle. Place on lined baking sheets, cover, and leave in a warm place for 30 minutes to rise. Preheat the oven to 400°F (200°C). Brush the pastries with egg and bake for 15–20 minutes until golden. Melt the remaining jam and brush over the pastries, to glaze. Transfer to a wire rack.

Season's best **apricots**

Apricots are small and sweet but with a hint of tartness. They are in season throughout the summer, but best in early summer. With golden-orange, velvety skin often flushed with red, they exude a delicious fragrance when ripe. They are not as juicy as other stone fruits, but blossom when cooked. Apricots are delicious poached in amaretto, and with almonds or coconut. Team them with lamb, ham, poultry, or venison, too.

Apricots need well-drained soil and sun but don't require much attention. They are often picked unripe, but since they don't ripen any further, it may result in disappointing fruit.

Royal Blenheim This is a delicate, exquisite heritage variety with a musky perfume and soft, downy skin, which resembles golden suede lightly speckled with pink. It is a rare find, so if you are lucky, savor it fresh.

Goldstrike This large, meaty apricot has an attractive orange color with a red blush. You can eat these fresh or make into delicious jam.

Patterson A popular, widely grown variety, Patterson scores highly in terms of durability and shelf life. It is plump, well shaped, and soft to the touch when ripe. It is an excellent choice for baking and cooking.

essentials
varieties available
Numerous varieties: either pure orange, green-tinged, or with pink specks or a red blush.

buy Select plump, smooth, slightly soft apricots with a rich color. Reject pale, dull, or hard fruit.

store Can be kept at room temperature (for a few days) or in an open paper bag at the bottom of the fridge.

cook Bake stuffed or in tarts and pastries, poach, purée for desserts and sauces.

preserve Bottle in liqueur or syrup; make jam or chutney.

recipe ideas
Apricots and almonds in amaretto p237

Apricot clafoutis p224

Apricot conserve p238

Apricot crumble shortbread p230

Apricot meringue roulade p208

how to pit apricots
Apricots are very easy to prepare if ripe, so always check before buying and cutting. Unlike peaches, their skin is seldom removed before cooking.

1 Choose ripe apricots. To test, place in the palm of the hand and squeeze gently. It should give slightly. Wash and dry with paper towels before cutting.

2 Cut in halves and the pits will come away easily with the point of a knife. If they don't, the fruit is not ripe.

cold raspberry soufflés

An elegant recipe like this shows raspberries at their best. This fragrant dessert is a perfect finale to a summer meal.

30 MINS

SPECIAL EQUIPMENT ▪ ramekins ▪ food processor

SERVES 4

2 tbsp rosewater

1 tbsp powdered gelatin

12oz (350g) raspberries

1 tbsp lemon juice

⅔ cup confectioners' sugar, sifted

1¾ cup heavy cream

4 large egg whites

mint leaves, to garnish (optional)

1 Wrap double-layered bands of wax paper around the outsides of 4 ramekins, so they sit 2in (5cm) above the rim. Secure with adhesive tape. Brush the inside rim of the paper lightly with oil.

2 Place the rosewater in a small bowl, sprinkle with the gelatin, and let soak for 2 minutes, or until it becomes spongy. Set the bowl in a larger bowl, half filled with boiling water, and stir to dissolve the gelatin. Remove from the heat and allow to cool slightly.

3 Place all but 8 of the raspberries in a food processor and blend to a puree. Sieve, discarding any pits. Stir in the lemon juice and sugar, then stir in the gelatin mixture. Leave in a cool place until just beginning to set.

4 Whip the cream to soft peaks and fold into the raspberry mixture. In a separate bowl, whisk the egg whites until stiff and fold into the raspberry mixture. Pour into the ramekins and chill in the fridge until set.

5 Remove from the fridge, peel off the wax paper from each ramekin, and decorate with the reserved whole raspberries and mint leaves (if using).

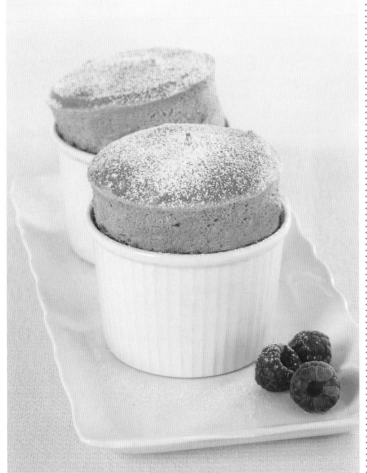

apricots with amaretti cookies and mascarpone

Apricots and amaretti are a food pairing made in heaven, but as amaretti is made from almonds (a close relation to the apricot) or ground apricot kernels, it's not really surprising.

15 MINS

SERVES 4

8 amaretti cookies

7oz tub mascarpone cheese

16 ripe apricots, halved and pitted

handful of blanched almonds, halved

1 Lightly crush the amaretti cookies with a rolling pin, then divide among 4 individual glass dishes. Lightly beat the mascarpone with a wooden spoon until thickened.

2 Layer the apricots and mascarpone on top of the amaretti cookies, finishing with a layer of mascarpone. Sprinkle with the almonds and serve.

variation

amaretti, peaches, and mascarpone

Use 8 ripe, peeled peaches instead of the apricots and follow the recipe exactly as above.

strawberry shortcakes

Made with a sconelike dough and filled with strawberries and a tangy coulis, the shortcakes are perfection.

🥄 **15–20 MINS** 🍲 **12–15 MINS**

SPECIAL EQUIPMENT ▪ 3in (7.5cm) cookie cutter ▪ blender or food processor

SERVES 6

2 cups all-purpose flour, sifted

1 tbsp baking powder

½ tsp salt

⅓ granulated sugar, plus 2–3 tbsp

4 tbsp unsalted butter, cubed

1¾ cup heavy cream

2¼lb (1kg) strawberries, hulled

2–3 tbsp confectioners' sugar

1 tsp pure vanilla extract

1 Preheat the oven to 425°F (220°C). Butter a baking sheet. In a bowl, mix the flour, baking powder, salt, and granulated sugar. Rub in the butter with your fingertips to form fine crumbs. Add ⅔ cup of the cream and toss to form larger crumbs; add a little more cream if dry. Lightly press the crumbs together to form a ball of dough.

2 On a floured surface, lightly knead the dough for a few seconds. Pat out to ½in (1cm) thick and cut out

6 rounds with the cookie cutter. Transfer to the baking sheet. Bake for 12–15 minutes until lightly browned, then transfer to a wire rack to cool.

3 Pure half the strawberries in a blender or food processor. Transfer to a bowl and stir in the confectioners' sugar. It should be thick enough to coat the back of a spoon. Slice the remaining strawberries, reserving some for decoration. Sprinkle the sliced berries with the 2–3 tbsp granulated sugar and let stand for 5–10 minutes.

4 Whip the remaining cream until soft peaks form. Add 2–3 tbsp granulated sugar and the vanilla extract. Whip until stiff. Cut the cakes in half with a serrated knife. Spoon the strawberries on the bottom halves. Pile on the cream and top each with its lid and the reserved sliced strawberries. Serve with the coulis.

blueberry pancakes

Dropping the blueberries on top of the half-cooked pancakes stops the juice from leaking out into the pan and burning.

🥄 **10 MINS** 🍲 **15–20 MINS**

MAKES 30

1½ cups self-rising flour

1 tsp baking powder

¼ cup granulated sugar

1 cup milk

2 large eggs

1 tsp pure vanilla extract

2 tbsp unsalted butter, melted, plus extra for frying and to serve

5½oz (150g) blueberries

maple syrup, to serve

1 Sift the flour and baking powder into a bowl, then stir in the sugar until evenly mixed with the flour. Form a well in the center with a spoon.

2 In a bowl, lightly beat together the milk, eggs, and vanilla extract until well blended. Pour a little of the egg mixture into the well and start to whisk it in. Wait until each addition of the egg mixture has been incorporated before whisking in more. Then whisk in the melted butter until the mixture is entirely smooth.

3 Melt a pat of butter in a large nonstick frying pan over medium heat. Pour 1 tbsp of the batter into

the pan to form a round pancake. Continue to add tablespoons of batter, leaving space in between for them to spread.

4 As they begin to cook, sprinkle a few blueberries over the uncooked surface. They are ready to turn when small bubbles appear and pop, leaving little holes. Turn the pancakes over carefully with a palette knife and continue to cook for 1–2 minutes until golden brown on both sides.

5 Remove the pancakes from the pan and drain briefly on paper towels. Then place them on a plate and transfer to a warm oven. Wipe out the frying pan with paper towels and add another pat of butter. Repeat for all the batter and wipe between batches. The pan should not get too hot.

6 Remove the pancakes from the oven and serve warm in piles, with butter and maple syrup.

raspberry and white chocolate trifle

Make the most of the raspberries in this trifle by squashing them lightly so they release some of their juices.

 25 MINS PLUS CHILLING ✳ FREEZABLE

SERVES 6-8

10oz (300g) Madeira cake or plain sponge cake, cut into ¾in (2cm) slices

1½lb (700g) raspberries

2 x 7oz tubs mascarpone

1¼ cups heavy cream

7oz (200g) white chocolate

1 Line the base and sides of the glass bowl or individual glass dishes with the cake. Spoon half the raspberries over and place in the fridge for at least 15 minutes while the cake soaks up the juices.

2 Meanwhile, put the mascarpone and cream in a bowl and beat with a wooden spoon. Break three-quarters of the chocolate into pieces and place in a small heatproof bowl. Sit the bowl over a pan of barely simmering water and stir occasionally until the chocolate has melted. Remove from the heat. Spoon half over the raspberries and mix half with the mascarpone and cream.

3 Add the cream mixture and the remaining raspberries to the trifle(s) in layers, ending with a cream topping. Grate over the remaining chocolate. Chill in the fridge for 15–30 minutes, then serve.

variation

cherry and white chocolate trifle

Replace the raspberries with 1lb 9oz (700g) ripe cherries. Pit and halve the cherries and place them in a bowl. Squash slightly to release some of their juices. Add 2 tbsp kirsch to the cherries and set aside while you prepare the cake in step 1. Continue with the recipe, layering the trifle with the cherries and kirsch, instead of the raspberries.

black currant and rosemary cheesecake

Summer black currants are always a treat. Here, the delicate fragrance of rosemary enhances this sweet, sharp, and creamy dessert that is simple to put together.

 20 MINS PLUS CHILLING 1 HR–1 HR 15 MINS

SPECIAL EQUIPMENT ▪ 8in (20cm) round pan with removable bottom

SERVES 8-10

7oz (200g) vanilla wafers

6 tbsp butter

1 tbsp chopped rosemary

1½lb (675g) cream cheese

1 cup granulated sugar

2 large eggs

1 tsp pure vanilla extract

For the topping

8oz (225g) black currants

granulated sugar, to taste

1 tsp arrowroot

1 Preheat the oven to 300°F (150°C). Grease the cake pan. Put the wafers in a plastic bag and crush with a rolling pin. Melt the butter in a pan, then add the wafer crumbs and rosemary, and stir until coated. Press the crumbs into the bottom of the pan.

2 Beat the cream cheese with the sugar, eggs, and vanilla extract. Spoon into the prepared pan, level the surface, and bake for up to 1¼ hours, until set. Turn off the oven and leave the cheesecake there until cold. Transfer to the fridge to chill.

3 Meanwhile, stew the black currants in ¼ cup water until the juices run but the currants still hold their shape. Sweeten to taste. Blend the arrowroot with 1 tsp water and stir in. Cook, stirring, until thickened and clear. Leave to cool.

4 Remove the cheesecake from the pan and place on a serving plate. Spoon the black currant topping over so that the fruits trickle down the sides a little and serve.

plum and marzipan clafoutis

This stunning version of a clafoutis is equally good made with damson plums or cherries, but instead of putting the marzipan in the fruit cavities, dot pieces between each fruit.

 30 MINS 50 MINS ✳ FREEZABLE

SPECIAL EQUIPMENT ▪ 2-quart shallow baking dish

SERVES 6

1½lb (675g) plums, halved and pitted

4 large eggs, plus 1 large egg yolk

½ cup granulated sugar

4 tbsp butter, melted

½ cup all-purpose flour, sifted

1¾ cups milk

⅔ cup half-and-half

For the marzipan

4oz (115g) ground almonds

½ cup granulated sugar

½ cup confectioners' sugar, plus extra for dusting

dash of almond extract

½ tsp lemon juice

1 large egg white, lightly beaten

1 Preheat the oven to 375°F (190°C). Mix the marzipan ingredients with enough of the egg white to form a stiff paste. Push a tiny piece into each plum half.

2 Grease the baking dish and arrange the plums cut-side down in a single layer in the dish, with the marzipan pieces underneath.

3 Add any leftover egg white from the marzipan to the eggs and egg yolk. Add the sugar and whisk until thick and pale. Whisk in the melted butter, flour, milk, and cream to form a batter. Pour over the plums and bake in the oven for about 50 minutes until golden and just set. Serve warm, dusted with confectioners' sugar.

cherry and almond cake

A classic combination of flavors and a traditional cake that is always popular with guests.

 20 MINS   **1 HR 30 MINS—1 HR 45 MINS**   ❄ **FREEZABLE**

SPECIAL EQUIPMENT ▪ 8in (20cm) round deep springform cake pan
▪ electric hand mixer or stand mixer

SERVES 8-10

11 tbsp unsalted butter, softened

¾ granulated sugar

2 large eggs, lightly beaten

2 cups self-rising flour, sifted

1 tsp baking powder

1⅓ cups ground almonds

1 tsp pure vanilla extract

¼ cup whole milk

14oz (400g) cherries, pitted

1oz (25g) blanched almonds, chopped

1 Preheat the oven to 350°F (180°C). Grease the pan and line the base with parchment paper. Put the butter and sugar in a mixing bowl and beat with an electric hand mixer or stand mixer until pale and creamy. Beat in the eggs one at a time, adding 1 tbsp of flour to the mixture before adding the second egg.

2 Mix in the remaining flour, baking powder, ground almonds, vanilla extract, and milk. Mix in half the cherries, then spoon the mixture into the pan and smooth the top. Scatter the remaining cherries and all the almonds over the surface.

3 Bake for 1½–1¾ hours, or until golden brown and firm to the touch. A skewer inserted into the center should come out clean. If the surface of the cake starts to brown before it is fully cooked, cover with foil. When cooked, let cool in the pan for a few minutes, then remove the foil and parchment, and transfer to a wire rack to cool completely before serving.

raspberry and almond bake

This fruity cake is enhanced by lemon to bring out the raspberry taste. The ground almonds help to keep the cake moist as well as adding some contrasting flavor.

 20 MINS   **40 MINS**   ❄ **FREEZABLE**

SPECIAL EQUIPMENT ▪ 8in (20cm) square cake pan with removable bottom

SERVES 8

1 cup all-purpose flour

1 tsp baking powder

¾ cup ground almonds

11 tbsp butter, cubed

7oz (200g) granulated sugar

juice of 1 lemon

1 tsp pure vanilla extract

2 large eggs

7oz (200g) raspberries

confectioners' sugar, for dusting (optional)

1 Preheat the oven to 350°F (180°C). Grease the pan and line the base and sides with parchment paper. Sift the flour into a bowl, add the baking powder and ground almonds, and mix well. In a pan, melt the butter, then add granulated sugar and lemon juice, stirring until well combined.

2 Stir this syrupy mixture into the dry ingredients, then mix in the vanilla extract and the eggs, one at a time, until the mixture is smooth and well combined. Pour into the pan, then scatter the raspberries over the top. Bake for 35–40 minutes, or until golden and a skewer inserted into the center comes out clean.

3 Cool in the pan for 10 minutes, then turn out and cool completely on a wire rack. Dust with confectioners' sugar before serving, if using. To serve, cut into rectangles.

variation

blueberry and almond bake

This cake also works well with blueberries, or a mix of soft berries, instead of the raspberries. Swap the raspberries for an equal quantity of blueberries or a mixture of soft berries and bake as instructed.

baked peaches with amaretti

A classic from northern Italy, as delicious as it is easy to prepare, this can be served hot or cold. Choose fruits that feel heavy for their size, showing they contain lots of juice.

 15–20 MINS 1 HR–1 HR 15 MINS

SPECIAL EQUIPMENT ▪ blender or food processor

SERVES 6

7 large peaches, about 2¼lb (1kg) total weight

8–10 amaretti cookies

¼ cup granulated sugar, plus 1–2 tbsp

1 large egg yolk

½ cup heavy cream

1–2 tbsp amaretto liqueur

1 Immerse 1 peach in boiling water for 10 seconds, then plunge into ice water. Cut the peach in half, using the indentation on one side of the peach as a guide. Using both hands, sharply twist each half to loosen it from the pit. Scoop out the pit with a small knife. Peel the skin from the peach halves. Discard the pit and skin.

2 Preheat the oven to 350°F (180°C). Crush the amaretti cookies in a plastic bag with a rolling pin and pour them into a bowl. Put the 2 peeled peach halves in a blender or food processor, and pulse to a thick, smooth puree.

3 Transfer the peach puree to a large bowl, scraping it from the food processor with a spatula. Add the sugar, egg yolk, and amaretti crumbs to the peach puree and mix well.

4 Butter a baking dish. Halve and remove the pit from the remaining peaches, without peeling them. If necessary, spoon out a little of the flesh from the center of each, so the cavity is large enough for the filling.

5 Set the peach halves, cut-side up, in the baking dish. Spoon some filling into each. Bake for 1–1¼ hours, until tender. Meanwhile, whip the cream with the 1–2 tbsp sugar and liqueur until stiff peaks form. Transfer the hot peaches to individual serving plates and spoon any juices over the top. Serve the flavored cream in a separate bowl.

peach pie

Less famous than its cherry cousin but no less tasty, this American classic with a lattice top is a splendid summer dessert. Choose perfectly ripe peaches full of juice.

 40–45 MINS PLUS CHILLING 40–45 MINS

SPECIAL EQUIPMENT ▪ 9in (23cm) pie dish

SERVES 8

1⅔ cup all-purpose flour

salt

9 tbsp lard or white vegetable fat, chilled

5 tbsp unsalted butter, chilled

4–5 ripe peaches

⅔ cup granulated sugar

1–2 tbsp lemon juice, to taste

1 large egg

1 Sift 1⅓ cup of the flour and ½ tsp salt into a bowl. Cube the lard and butter, and rub into the flour with your fingers until crumbs form. Sprinkle with 3 tbsp water and mix until the dough turns into a ball. Wrap in plastic wrap and chill for 30 minutes.

2 Preheat the oven to 400°F (200°C) and put in a baking sheet. On a floured surface, roll out two-thirds of the dough and use to line the dish with some overhang. Press the dough into the dish and chill for 15 minutes.

2 Immerse the peaches in boiling water for 10 seconds, then plunge into ice water. Halve the peaches, remove the pits, and peel off the skins. Cut into ½in (1cm) slices and put in a large bowl. Sprinkle with the remaining flour, sugar, salt, and lemon juice. Stir, then transfer to the pie crust with their juices.

3 Roll out the remaining dough into a rectangle. Cut out 8 strips, each ½in (1cm) wide, and arrange them in a latticelike pattern on top of the pie; trim the pie dough. Beat the egg with ½ tsp salt and use this to glaze the lattice and secure the strips to the edge of the pie. Bake for 40–45 minutes until the crust is golden brown. Serve at room temperature or chilled, with a dollop of cream.

creamy rice pudding with peaches

Both the rice and the peaches can be prepared one day ahead and kept covered in the fridge. Let the rice come to room temperature, or warm it in a low oven, before serving.

 15–20 MINS PLUS MACERATING AND STANDING · 3 HRS

SERVES 4–6

4 ripe peaches

¼ cup granulated sugar, plus more if needed

1 cup dry red wine, plus more if needed

For the rice pudding

2¼oz (65g) short-grain rice

3½ cups milk, plus more if needed

2in (5cm) cinnamon stick

¼ cup granulated sugar

salt

1 To prepare the peaches, put them in a nonmetallic bowl and sprinkle with the sugar; they may need more or less sugar than specified, depending on their sweetness. Pour in enough red wine to cover the fruit completely. Set a plate on top and let macerate in the fridge for at least 2 hours and up to 24 hours.

2 Strain the liquid into a saucepan, bring to a boil, and simmer for 2 minutes until syrupy. Stir it back into the peaches.

3 Preheat the oven to 300°F (150°C). Put the rice, milk, cinnamon stick, sugar, and a pinch of salt into an ovenproof dish, and stir. Transfer to the oven and bake for 3 hours, uncovered, stirring gently every 30 minutes until the pudding is thick and creamy. Cover the dish with foil if it starts to brown too much.

4 Remove the pudding from the oven. Carefully slip a spoon down the side and stir from the bottom. Let it stand for 1 hour. Discard the cinnamon stick, ladle into serving bowls, and serve with the peaches and wine syrup, which can be either warmed or cold.

peach and nectarine puff pastry tart

If you don't have time to make puff pastry at home, store-bought versions are just as good. You can buy it in a block or ready-rolled, as suggested for this recipe.

 20 MINS PLUS CHILLING · 20 MINS · FREEZABLE

SPECIAL EQUIPMENT ▪ electric hand mixer

SERVES 8

1 large egg, plus 1 large egg yolk

¼ cup granulated sugar

3 tbsp all-purpose flour

1¼ cup milk

juice of 1 lemon

14oz package store-bought puff pastry

1 large egg yolk, beaten, to glaze

4 ripe peaches, halved and pitted

4 ripe nectarines, halved and pitted

confectioners' sugar, for dusting

1 Put the egg, egg yolk, sugar, and flour in a mixing bowl and whisk with an electric hand mixer until well combined. Heat the milk in a pan until almost boiling, then slowly whisk into the egg mixture with the lemon juice. Return the mixture to the pan and slowly bring to a boil, stirring continuously. Cook for a couple of minutes, then transfer to a bowl. Place a piece of wax paper on the surface so the custard doesn't form a skin, then let cool.

2 Meanwhile, on a lightly floured work surface, roll the pastry out into a 9 x 12in (23 x 30cm) rectangle and place on a lightly oiled baking sheet. With a knife, score a rectangle on it, leaving a ¾in (2cm) border all around the edge. Press the back of the knife into the border to make horizontal lines—these will ensure the pastry rises. Prick the base of the rectangle with a fork and place in the fridge for 20 minutes. Preheat the oven to 400°F (200°C).

3 Once the pastry has chilled, brush the border with the beaten egg yolk, then bake for 20 minutes, or until the pastry is cooked and golden. Push the inner rectangle down slightly, then let cool for 30 minutes.

4 Spoon in the custard, then top with the fruit, dust with confectioners' sugar, and serve.

Season's best **peaches and nectarines**

Peaches have a downy skin with a fragrant, sweet delicate flavor, whereas nectarines, which are close relatives, are smooth-skinned with a sweet but sharper, more intense flavor. They are the classic summer fruits and perfect partners with raspberries and strawberries, almonds, soft white cheeses, chile and sweet spices, brandy and amaretto, and also pair well with bacon, pork, and chicken.

Peach and nectarine trees are grown in hot and temperate climates. They can be trained on south-facing walls to protect them from the wind and for maximum sunlight, which ripens and sweetens the fruit.

The downy skin of peaches is best removed before eating.

Red Baron Large and richly colored, this freestone peach has firm yet juicy yellow flesh. Its fine flavor makes it an all-around winner, to be enjoyed both fresh and cooked.

Donut So named because it is shaped like a doughnut with a sunken middle, this peach has mildly sweet flavor with a hint of almonds. Eat fresh, use in salsas, or halve and grill.

The flesh of this variety does not adhere to the pit, hence the term "freestone."

Snow Pearl Round in shape with warmly colored skin, this nectarine has firm, white flesh that clings around the pit. It is a good choice for pies and baking.

Flavortop This is an excellent firm, sweet nectarine with yellow flesh. It is ideal for both eating and cooking.

Yellow-fleshed fruit has more robust flavor suited to baking, grilling, sautéing, or poaching.

Babcock A small- to medium-sized peach, this has fuzz-free, blushed skin. The white flesh is tender, juicy, and tangy sweet. Eat fresh or use to make perfect Bellini.

White-flesh peaches and nectarines have fragrant, low-acid flesh that is best eaten raw.

how to peel peaches

Peaches need to be peeled before use as their downy skin can be tough and unpalatable. Nectarines have smooth skin but can be treated the same way.

1 Starting at the base, with a sharp-pointed knife, make a cut crosswise around the middle, just through the skin. Then repeat the cut in the other direction.

2 Place in a heatproof bowl and pour in boiling water. Let stand for 30 seconds. Remove with a slotted spoon. Plunge in cold water. Drain and remove the skin.

essentials
varieties available

Numerous varieties of peaches and nectarines with either yellow or white flesh. Varieties depend on local conditions.

buy Select by touch, but handle carefully: when ripe, the fruit should yield to gentle pressure and have a sweet fragrance. Look for fruit with unblemished skin.

store Keep at room temperature for a couple of days, or in an open paper bag at the bottom of the fridge for up to a week. Both peaches and nectarines are suitable for freezing.

cook Eat raw; slice and sauté; or halve, stuff, and bake for hot desserts. Halve and grill to serve with savory dishes.

preserve Bottle in syrup or alcohol; make jams and jellies; or use underripe fruit for chutney; dry.

recipe ideas

Peach Melba ice cream p221

Peach pie p214

Peach tarte tatin p219

Sweet and sour nectarine and cherry relish p242

peaches with meringue and raspberry sauce

A lighter take on the classic English dessert known as "Eton mess." Instead of heavy cream mixed with broken meringue, here is a variation that uses half-and-half.

 15 MINS

SPECIAL EQUIPMENT ▪ handheld blender

SERVES 4

12oz (350g) raspberries

4 meringue shells

4 ripe peaches, pitted and coarsely chopped or sliced

zest of 1 lime, to decorate

half-and-half, to serve

1 Put the raspberries in a bowl, then puree with a handheld blender. Pass them through a sieve so you have a smooth puree.

2 Break the meringues up with your hands, then scatter the pieces in one large shallow serving dish or 4 individual ones. Top with the peaches, spoon over the raspberry puree, and decorate with lime zest. Serve with a drizzle of half-and-half.

variation

nectarine meringue melba

Make the raspberry sauce. Halve and pit 2 nectarines. Peel if liked. Sit each half in a meringue nest in a glass dessert dish. Top each half with a scoop of vanilla ice cream then drizzle the sauce on top.

berry friands

A friand is a small, light, and moist cake flavored with ground nuts, usually almond. They can be dressed up with berries or stone fruits, but make sure they are really ripe and juicy.

 15 MINS   35 MINS

SPECIAL EQUIPMENT ▪ electric hand mixer ▪ 6-cup muffin pan

MAKES 6

¾ cup confectioners' sugar

3 tbsp all-purpose flour

¾ cup ground almonds

3 large egg whites

5 tbsp unsalted butter, melted

5½oz (150g) mixed berries, such as blueberries and raspberries

1 Preheat the oven to 350°F (180°C). Line the muffin pan with paper liners. Sift the sugar and flour into a bowl, then stir in the ground almonds. In another bowl, beat the egg whites with an electric hand mixer until soft peaks form.

2 Gently fold the flour mixture and the melted butter into the egg whites to make a smooth batter.

Spoon the batter into the paper liners, then scatter over the berries, pressing them down slightly into the batter so they all fit in. Bake for 30–35 minutes, or until risen and golden. Let cool in the pan for 5 minutes, then serve warm or let cool.

variation

apricot friands

Prepare in the same way, but substitute the berries for 5½oz (150g) ripe apricots. Halve and pit the apricots, then chop into small pieces. Add the apricot pieces to the paper liners in step 2 and bake as in the recipe.

blueberry muffins

You can whip up a batch of muffins in next to no time, ready for serving as a dessert or to accompany a cup of coffee at a mid-morning break. Blueberries are the classic addition.

 15 MINS   20 MINS

SPECIAL EQUIPMENT ▪ 12-cup muffin pan

MAKES 12

1⅓ cup self-rising flour

1 tsp baking powder

¼ cup granulated sugar

grated zest of 1 lemon (optional)

salt

1 cup natural yogurt

2 large eggs, lightly beaten

4 tbsp butter, melted and cooled

9oz (250g) blueberries

1 Preheat the oven to 400°F (200°C). Line the muffin pan with paper liners. Sift the flour into a large bowl, mix in the baking powder, sugar, lemon zest, if using, and a pinch of salt, then make a well in the center with a spoon.

2 Mix the yogurt, eggs, and cooled, melted butter together in a large bowl, then pour into the well of the dry ingredients, along with the blueberries. Mix until just combined, but don't overmix or the muffins will be heavy. Don't worry if there are a few lumps left in the mixture.

3 Spoon evenly into the paper liners and bake for 20 minutes, or until risen and golden. Let cool in the pan for 5 minutes, then serve warm or let cool.

variation

raspberry muffins

Use raspberries in place of blueberries, and orange zest instead of the lemon.

peach tarte tatin

This is an unusual tarte tatin, since it is made with peaches rather than apples, which makes it a good choice for a high summer dessert when peaches are in season. Choose firm peaches to ensure that the fruit holds its shape as it cooks.

 40–45 MINS PLUS CHILLING   **35–40 MINS**

SPECIAL EQUIPMENT ▪ 10in (25cm) round baking dish

SERVES 6

3 large egg yolks

½ tsp pure vanilla extract

1⅓ cups all-purpose flour

¼ cup granulated sugar

salt

6 tbsp unsalted butter, cubed

For the filling

¾ cup granulated sugar

2¼lb (1kg) peaches

1 In a small bowl, mix the egg yolks with the vanilla extract. Mix together the flour, sugar, and ¼ tsp salt in a large bowl. Add the butter and, with your fingertips, mix to form crumbs. Add the egg mix and bring together to form a dough. Knead until smooth and chill for 30 minutes.

2 For the filling, place the sugar in a saucepan and heat gently until dissolved, stirring occasionally. Boil, without stirring, until the mixture starts to turn golden around the edge. Do not stir, or it may crystallize. Reduce the heat and continue cooking, swirling the saucepan once or twice so the syrup colors evenly, until the caramel is golden. Cook the caramel only until medium gold; if it gets too dark, it will become bitter.

3 Remove the saucepan from the heat and immediately plunge the base of the saucepan into a bowl of cold water, until cooking stops. Stand back in case of splashes; there are few things hotter than caramel. Pour the caramel into the bottom of the baking dish. Working quickly, tilt the dish so the bottom is coated with a thin, even layer. Let it cool.

4 Immerse the peaches in a pan of boiling water for 10 seconds, then plunge them into cold water. Cut them in half, remove the pits, and peel off the skin. Cut the peach halves lengthwise into two. Tightly pack the peach wedges on top of the caramel, rounded-side down, in concentric circles.

5 On a lightly floured work surface, roll out the dough to an 11in (28cm) round. Wrap it around the rolling pin and drape over the dish. Tuck the edge of the dough down around the peaches. Chill for 15 minutes. Preheat the oven to 400°F (200°C).

6 Bake for 30–35 minutes. Let the tart cool to tepid. To unmold, set a platter on top of the baking dish. Hold the dish and platter firmly together and invert them, then remove the baking dish. Serve at once, cut into wedges.

figs with cassis mascarpone

The sweet black currant flavor and dark red color of crème de cassis adds an unusual twist to the figs in this otherwise classically simple dessert. It's quick to make, too!

 15 MINS

SERVES 4

12 plump figs

drizzle of crème de cassis

7oz (200g) contianer mascarpone

1 Make a cross at the top of each fig (but don't cut all the way to the bottom), then gently prize them open. Place 3 figs in each of 4 dessert dishes and drizzle with crème de cassis.

2 Mix the mascarpone with a drizzle of cassis and stir gently until lightly marbled. Add a spoonful of mascarpone to each dish and serve.

variation

figs and raspberries with framboise

Prepare in the same way but use raspberry liqueur to drizzle over the figs and to flavor the mascarpone instead of cassis. Add a handful of crushed raspberries to the mascarpone with the liqueur and scatter a few on each plate with the figs.

boozy berries with mint and elderflower cream

Mint leaves add such a great fresh taste to a dessert and combine especially well with the summer berries. If you don't have crème de cassis, use a sweet dessert wine instead.

 10 MINS PLUS CHILLING

SPECIAL EQUIPMENT ■ electric hand mixer

SERVES 4–6

1lb (450g) mixed summer berries, such as strawberries, blackberries, raspberries, and red currants

⅔ cup crème de cassis

¾ cup heavy cream or whipping cream

1 tbsp finely chopped mint leaves

1–2 tbsp elderflower cordial, depending on taste

1 Put the berries in a shallow serving dish, pour over the cassis, then chill for 30 minutes, or overnight, stirring now and again.

2 Put the cream in a mixing bowl and beat with an electric hand mixer until soft peaks form. Fold in the mint and elderflower cordial, and serve with the berries.

variation

boozy wild strawberries with elderflower cream

Use a mixture of wild and baby cultivated strawberries instead of the mixed berries. Use strawberry liqueur instead of cassis. Top with the elderflower cream as before.

minted melon with vodka

Using contrasting colors of melons makes for an attractive dessert. Honeydew and watermelon also taste quite different, the honeydew being the sweeter of the two.

 15 MINS PLUS MARINATING

SERVES 6-8

1 galia or honeydew melon, cut in quarters lengthwise, rind and seeds removed, and flesh sliced

1 small watermelon, cut in half, rind and seeds removed, and flesh sliced

1-2 tbsp vodka

1-2 tbsp orange juice without pulp

handful of mint leaves, coarsely torn

1 Arrange the melon slices in a large flat serving bowl or platter, drizzle with the vodka and orange juice, then let sit for 15 minutes while the fruit absorbs the juices.

2 Sprinkle with the mint and serve.

variation

triple melon cocktail

Use 1 galia, 1 cantaloupe, and ½ small watermelon. Cube or ball the flesh instead of slicing. Place in a bowl. Add 4 tbsp orange liqueur instead of vodka and orange juice. Let sit for at least 15 minutes then toss again. Spoon into glasses and top each with a scoop of orange or raspberry sorbet and sprinkle with the coarsely torn mint.

peach melba ice cream

The classic peach Melba is a delightful combination of vanilla ice cream, fresh peaches, and a raspberry sauce. The three flavors marry to make a deliciously fragrant ice cream.

 30 MINS PLUS FREEZING **15 MINS**

SPECIAL EQUIPMENT ▪ handheld blender ▪ ice cream maker

SERVES 4-6

1¼ cup heavy cream

1¼ cup whole milk

3 large egg yolks

1 tsp pure vanilla extract

⅔ cup granulated sugar

3½oz (100g) raspberries

4 ripe peaches, pitted, peeled, and cubed

1 Heat the cream and milk gently in a saucepan until it almost boils, then take off the heat. In a bowl, beat together the egg yolks, vanilla extract, and ½ cup of the sugar until fluffy. Pour the cream and milk over the egg mixture, beating continuously. Return the mixture to the cleaned pan. Bring to a boil, reduce the heat, and simmer for 6–8 minutes, stirring continuously, until the custard thickens. Transfer the mixture to a bowl and leave it to cool, stirring occasionally to prevent skin from forming.

2 Put the raspberries and 2 tbsp of the sugar in a bowl. Puree with a handheld blender, pass through a sieve, and pour into a bowl. Puree the peaches and the remaining sugar and pour into another bowl.

3 When cold, process the custard in an ice cream maker for 20–30 minutes until nearly frozen. Transfer to a plastic container. Alternatively, pour in a plastic container with a lid and freeze for about 2 hours until half-frozen. Whisk with a fork to break up the ice crystals and freeze until nearly firm. Drizzle the raspberry puree over. Use a skewer to draw the puree through the ice cream to make a ripple effect. Freeze for a few hours before serving.

Season's best **melons**

Sweet and succulent, melons can be round, oblong, or ovoid. Smaller summer ones have a smooth or netted rind with orange, green, or yellow flesh. Large dark green-skinned watermelons have pink-red flesh dotted with black seeds. Imported all year but some are homegrown; both are best in summer and autumn, when yellow or green ridged-skinned honeydews are also good. Enjoy them with raspberries and other fruits, seafood, prosciutto, ginger, and mint.

Members of the gourd family, melons used to be cultivated only in hot, sunny regions (both tropical and subtropical), but are now grown in temperate climates too, such as the UK.

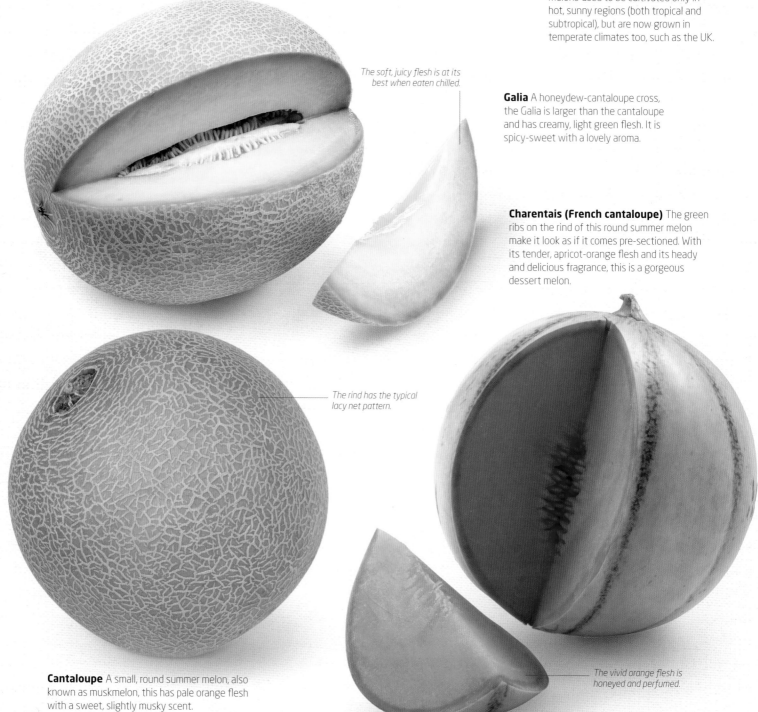

The soft, juicy flesh is at its best when eaten chilled.

Galia A honeydew-cantaloupe cross, the Galia is larger than the cantaloupe and has creamy, light green flesh. It is spicy-sweet with a lovely aroma.

Charentais (French cantaloupe) The green ribs on the rind of this round summer melon make it look as if it comes pre-sectioned. With its tender, apricot-orange flesh and its heady and delicious fragrance, this is a gorgeous dessert melon.

The rind has the typical lacy net pattern.

Cantaloupe A small, round summer melon, also known as muskmelon, this has pale orange flesh with a sweet, slightly musky scent.

The vivid orange flesh is honeyed and perfumed.

Watermelon It is round or oblong with dark green skin and super-sweet red flesh. The "icebox" variety (Sugar Baby pictured here) makes a fabulous sorbet.

The vivid, slightly granular flesh is scattered with black seeds.

essentials
varieties available
Many varieties of summer melons, watermelons, and honeydews.

buy Summer melons should feel heavy for their size and give off a pleasant aroma through the skin. Watermelons should be firm and evenly colored, and feel heavy. They should not sound empty when tapped, but give out a ringing sound.

store Whole melons are best kept in a cool, airy place, but when cut should be stored in the fridge.

cook Eat halved, or in balls, chunks, or wedges; purée for soups and sorbets; or briefly sauté in savory dishes.

preserve Make into jams. Chunks of watermelons can be pickled. Roast and salt seeds.

recipe ideas
Chilled melon and ginger soup p143

Melon and tomato salad p194

Watermelon and lime sorbet p224

Watermelon salad with feta and pumpkin seeds p159

how to seed and cut melons
Halve and seed melons before serving. Fill halves with seafood, berries, or some ginger wine for an appetizer, or further prepare in wedges or chunks as required.

1 Halve the melon and hold it over a bowl. With a spoon, scoop out the seeds into the bowl and discard.

2 Cut each half in wedges, then firmly holding a wedge with one hand, cut the flesh away from the rind in one piece with a chef's knife.

3 Serve in wedges with proscuitto or shrimp for an appetizer, or cut into chunks of desired size to add to fruit salads or fruit kebabs.

apricot clafoutis

A clafoutis is a baked French dessert with a flanlike batter covering fresh fruit. Usually black cherries, here apricots are used. It can be enjoyed warm or at room temperature.

 10 MINS　 **35 MINS**

SPECIAL EQUIPMENT ■ 1-quart shallow ovenproof dish

SERVES 4

9oz (250g) ripe apricots, halved and pitted

1 large egg, plus 1 egg yolk

3 tbsp all-purpose flour

¼ cup granulated sugar

⅔ cup heavy cream

¼ tsp pure vanilla extract

thick cream or crème fraîche, to serve (optional)

1 Preheat the oven to 400°F (200°C). Lightly butter the ovenproof dish. Place the apricots cut-side down in a single layer in the dish; there should be a small amount of space between them.

2 In a bowl, whisk together the egg, egg yolk, and the flour. Whisk in the sugar. Finally, add the cream and vanilla extract, and whisk thoroughly to form a smooth custardlike batter.

3 Pour the batter around the apricots, so the tops of a few are just visible. Bake on the top shelf of the oven for 35 minutes until puffed up and golden brown in places. Remove and let cool for at least 15 minutes. Serve warm, with thick cream or crème fraîche, if using.

watermelon and lime sorbet

This is very simple to prepare and is really refreshing on a hot summer's day. The little round watermelons often have very few black seeds, which saves time and effort.

 20 MINS PLUS FREEZING

SPECIAL EQUIPMENT ■ blender or food processor ■ ice cream maker (optional) ■ electric hand mixer (optional)

MAKES 4 CUPS

¾ cup granulated sugar

1 small watermelon, about 3¾lb (1.75kg) in weight

grated zest and juice of 1 lime

1 Put the sugar in a small heavy-bottomed pan with ½ cup water. Heat gently, stirring occasionally until the sugar dissolves, then bring to a boil and cook for 1 minute. Let cool.

2 Cut the melon into wedges, remove any black seeds then the rind and cut the flesh into chunks. Puree in a blender or food processor. Stir in the cold syrup and lime zest and juice.

3 Either freeze in an ice cream maker until set then transfer to a freezerproof container with a lid and freeze for up to 3 months, or place in the freezerproof container and freeze for about 2 hours until firm around the edges. Whisk with a fork or hand mixer to break up the ice crystals. Freeze and whisk twice more before freezing until firm. Transfer to the fridge 15 minutes before serving to soften slightly.

melon and raspberry baskets with ginger chantilly

These look prettiest with green-fleshed melon but you can use orange ones, too. You could serve this as a starter for 6 people (spooned in glasses) but without the topping.

 20 MINS PLUS CHILLING

SERVES 4

2 small, ripe Galia melons

2 tbsp orange liqueur

8oz (225g) raspberries

For the ginger Chantilly

1¼ cups heavy cream

3 tbsp ginger syrup from the jar

2 pieces of stem ginger in syrup, drained and finely chopped

1 Halve the melons and scoop out the seeds. Use a melon baller to scoop out the flesh, or score it in cubes using a sharp knife (taking care not to cut through the rind), then scoop out with a teaspoon. Reserve the shells.

2 Place the melon in a plastic container with a lid, add the orange liqueur, toss gently, cover, and chill in the fridge until ready to serve.

3 To make the Chantilly, whip the cream until softly peaking, then whisk in the ginger syrup until softly peaking again. Fold in the chopped ginger. Chill until ready to serve.

4 Just before serving, put the melon shells in small glass dishes (if they don't sit firmly upright, cut a thin slice off the base rind (but not right through to the flesh). Gently mix the raspberries with the macerated melon and spoon into the shells. Top each with a good dollop of the Chantilly cream and serve immediately.

bavarian plum tart

Bavaria is famous for its cakes and tarts. In this recipe, a quick version of brioche forms the base. Juice from the fruit mingles with the custard filling to bring about a deliciously moist result. Apricots are also delicious in this tart.

🥣 35-40 MINS PLUS RISING AND STANDING 🍲 50-55 MINS

SPECIAL EQUIPMENT ▪ 11in (28cm) round quiche dish

SERVES 8-10

1½ tsp dried yeast, or
⅓oz (9g) fresh yeast

2¼ cups flour, more if needed

2 tbsp granulated sugar

1 tsp salt

3 large eggs

8 tbsp unsalted butter, softened

For the filling

2 tbsp dried bread crumbs

1lb 15oz (875g) purple plums, pitted and quartered

2 large egg yolks

¼ cup heavy cream

½ cup granulated sugar

1 Sprinkle or crumble the yeast over 2fl oz (60ml) lukewarm water in a small bowl. Let stand for 5 minutes, until dissolved. Lightly oil a medium bowl. Sift the flour onto a work surface, make a well in the center, and add the sugar, salt, yeast mixture, and eggs.

2 With your fingertips, work the ingredients in the well until they are thoroughly mixed. Work in the flour to form a soft dough; adding more flour if it is very sticky. Knead on a floured work surface for 10 minutes, until very elastic. Work in more flour as needed, so that the dough is slightly sticky, but peels easily from the work surface.

3 Add the butter to the dough, pinch and squeeze to mix it in, then knead until smooth. Shape into a ball and put it into the oiled bowl. Cover, and let rise in the fridge for 1½–2 hours, until doubled in size.

4 Brush the quiche dish with melted butter. Knead the dough lightly to punch down the air. Flour a work surface; roll out the dough into a 13in (32cm) round. Wrap it around the rolling pin and drape it over the dish. Press it into the bottom and up the side of the dish. Trim off the excess and sprinkle the bread crumbs over the bottom. Preheat the oven to 425°F (220°C). Put a baking sheet in the oven to heat.

5 Arrange the plum wedges, cut-side up, in circles on the brioche shell. Let stand at room temperature for 30–45 minutes, until the edge of the dough is puffed. Put the egg yolks, heavy cream, and two-thirds of the sugar into a bowl. Whisk together. Sprinkle the plum wedges with the remaining sugar and bake the tart on the baking sheet for 5 minutes. Reduce the heat to 350°F (180°C).

6 Ladle the custard mixture over the fruit, return the tart to the oven, and continue baking for 45–50 minutes longer, until the dough is browned, the fruit is tender, and the custard is set. Let the tart cool on a wire rack. Serve warm or at room temperature.

blueberry-ripple cheesecake

In this classic baked cheesecake recipe, the blueberries are pureed and then swirled into the cheese mixture, before the whole dish is put in the oven to cook.

 20 MINS   45 MINS PLUS COOLING

SPECIAL EQUIPMENT ▪ 8in (20cm) round, deep springform cake pan ▪ blender or food processor

SERVES 8

4½oz (125g) vanilla wafers

4 tbsp butter

5½oz (150g) blueberries

⅔ cup granulated sugar, plus 3 tbsp

14oz (400g) cream cheese

7oz tub mascarpone

2 large eggs, plus 1 large egg yolk

½ tsp pure vanilla extract

2 tbsp all-purpose flour

1 Preheat the oven to 350°F (180°C). Grease the cake pan. Put the wafers in a large food bag and crush with a rolling pin. Melt the butter in a pan, then add the wafer crumbs and stir until well coated. Press the crumbs into the bottom of the pan.

2 Put the blueberries and the 3 tbsp of granulated sugar in a blender or food processor and pulse until smooth, then push the mixture

through a nylon sieve into a small pan. Bring to a boil, then allow to simmer for 3–5 minutes, or until thickened and jammy. Set aside. Rinse the goblet of the blender or food processor.

3 Put all the remaining ingredients into the blender or food processor and puree until well combined. Pour the mixture onto the wafer base and smooth the top. With a teaspoon, carefully drizzle the blueberry mixture over the cream cheese mixture in a swirly pattern.

4 Bake the cheesecake for 40 minutes, or until it has set, but still slightlt wobbly in the middle when you shake the pan. Let cool in the oven for an hour, then cool completely and serve.

mixed berries with white chocolate sauce

The chocolate sauce is made extra rich here through the addition of heavy cream. It is the perfect complement to the mixture of fresh summer berries.

 5 MINS   5 MINS

SERVES 4

14oz (400g) mixed berries, such as raspberries, strawberries, blackberries, and red currants

4½oz (125g) white chocolate, plus extra to grate (optional)

½ cup heavy cream

1 Divide the berries among 4 serving bowls. Break the chocolate into pieces and place in a pan with the cream. Slowly bring almost to a boil, stirring continuously until the chocolate has melted and is well combined.

2 Pour the chocolate mixture over the berries and serve topped with grated white chocolate, if you wish.

variation

mixed berry crepes with white chocolate sauce

Make a batch of crepes (see Swedish crepe stack opposite). Whisk ¾ cup each of heavy cream and plain yogurt. Roughly crush 10oz (300g) of the berries. Fold in and sweeten to taste. Add the grated zest of a small lemon. Make the chocolate sauce as before. Fold the crepes into cones and fill with the fruit mixture. Arrange on plates. Spoon the sauce over and scatter with the remaining berries.

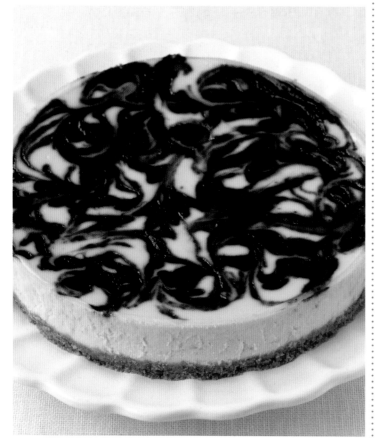

swedish crepe stack cake

Make sure you use only the thinnest of crepes for this sumptuous dessert. It makes a perfect summer birthday cake and is a children's favorite.

 10 MINS 15 MINS

SERVES 6-8

¾ cup heavy cream

1 cup crème fraîche

3 tbsp granulated sugar

¼ tsp pure vanilla extract

9oz (250g) raspberries

confectioners' sugar, for dusting

For the crepes

⅔ cup all-purpose flour, sifted

2 tsp granulated sugar

salt

2 eggs

¾ cup milk

1 For the crepes, mix the flour, sugar, and a pinch of salt in a mixing bowl. Make a well in the center. Crack the eggs into the well and add a little of the milk. Mix to a smooth batter using a wooden spoon or whisk. Gradually stir in the rest of the milk. Chill the batter in the fridge for 30 minutes, if you have time.

2 Heat a little oil in a small frying pan. Pour off the excess. Add 2–3 tbsp of batter and swirl around to coat the bottom of the pan. Cook for about 2 minutes until brown underneath. Flip over and quickly cook the other side. Slide onto a plate. Repeat to make 8 crepes. Let cool.

3 Whip the heavy cream, crème fraîche, granulated sugar, and vanilla extract until stiff peaks form. Reserve about 4 tbsp for decoration.

4 Set aside a handful of raspberries. Lightly crush the remaining fruit and roughly fold into the remaining cream mixture to create a ripple effect.

5 Layer the crepes with the raspberry cream on a platter. Decorate the top with the reserved cream mixture, scatter the remaining raspberries over the top, dust with confectioners' sugar, and serve.

chilled rice pudding with warm berry sauce

A creamy dessert that works so well with the sharpness of the warm berry sauce. Use whatever fresh berries you have available, but make sure they are well sweetened.

 10 MINS PLUS CHILLING 20 MINS

SPECIAL EQUIPMENT ▪ handheld blender

SERVES 4-6

2½ cups whole milk

5½oz (150g) long grain or basmati rice

½ cup granulated sugar

1 cup heavy cream

3oz (85g) blanched almonds, toasted and finely chopped

1 tbsp sweet sherry

1 tsp pure vanilla extract

10oz (300g) mixed berries, such as black currants, raspberries, and blackberries

1 Mix the milk, rice, and half the sugar in a large heavy-bottomed pan and bring to a boil, stirring frequently to prevent the rice from sticking. Reduce the heat and simmer for 15 minutes, or until the rice is soft, stirring frequently. Pour the rice into a bowl and let cool.

2 While the rice cools, whip the cream to form soft peaks, then fold it into the cooled rice.

3 Dry-fry the almonds in a frying pan over low heat until golden. Let cool, and then chop. Fold the chopped almonds, sherry, and vanilla extract into the rice and leave in the fridge for 3–4 hours or overnight to chill before serving.

4 To make the sauce, heat the berries gently with the remaining sugar and 1 tbsp water, and simmer on low heat for 3–4 minutes until they are cooked through. Puree the sauce with a handheld blender and pass through a sieve. To serve, pour the hot sauce over the chilled pudding.

knickerbocker glory

If you love ice cream with strawberries, this is the perfect dessert. It's best to serve it with extra long spoons so you can reach all the layered ingredients in the tall glasses.

 15 MINS

SPECIAL EQUIPMENT ▪ handheld blender or food processor
▪ electric hand mixer

SERVES 2

7oz (200g) strawberries, hulled

drizzle of strawberry liqueur, or other liqueur of your choice

⅔ cup heavy cream

2 slices plain sponge cake

6 scoops good-quality vanilla ice cream

1¾oz (50g) blanched almonds, coarsely chopped

1 Coarsely slice the strawberries, reserving 2 whole ones. Put the sliced berries in a bowl, drizzle with liqueur, then puree with a handheld blender. Alternatively, use a food processor and pulse to a puree. Pour the cream into a mixing bowl and beat it with an electric hand mixer until soft peaks form.

2 Sit the cake slices neatly in the bottom of two tall dessert glasses, then spoon over 1 tbsp of the strawberry sauce. Add a scoop of ice cream, followed by a spoonful of whipped cream. Add another drizzle of strawberry sauce, then continue building up in layers, finishing with ice cream at the top. Sprinkle with the almonds and top with the reserved strawberries.

mixed berry ice cream cake

This is a truly instant dessert, comprising a store-bought cake base filled with soft ice cream, juicy raspberries, strawberries, blackberries, and red currants.

 10 MINS

SERVES 6

3-4 scoops soft chocolate ice cream

3-4 scoops soft vanilla ice cream

8in (20cm) store-bought round plain cake base

1lb 2oz (500g) mixed summer berries, such as raspberries, blackberries, strawberries (hulled and quartered), and red currants

drizzle of crème de cassis, or other liqueur of your choice (optional)

1 Spoon the ice cream onto the cake base, arranging it in a small mound in the center of the base, if you like, then pile the fruit on top and around the edges of the base.

2 Drizzle over the crème de cassis, or other liqueur (if using), and serve immediately

gooseberry fool with elderflower

An all-time favorite way to serve gooseberries, this chilled, creamy dessert is the epitome of summer eating.

 20 MINUTES PLUS CHILLING **10 MINUTES**

SPECIAL EQUIPMENT ▪ blender or food processor

SERVES 4-6

12oz (350g) gooseberries, hulled

½ cup granulated sugar

1 tbsp elderflower cordial

9oz (250g) good-quality ready-made custard

¾ cup heavy cream

1 Put the gooseberries, sugar, and elderflower cordial into a pan and stir to dissolve the sugar. Cover and cook over low heat for 5 minutes until the gooseberries have given out some water and started to swell. Remove the lid and cook for another 5 minutes.

2 Mash the gooseberries lightly with a potato masher to break up a few of the bigger ones. Alternatively, if you prefer a smoother fool, puree the fruit in a blender or food processor. Leave the mixture to cool completely then chill in the fridge.

3 In a large bowl, whip the double cream until it forms fairly stiff peaks.

4 Once the puree is completely cold, fold it into the cream, and then fold in the custard to make a light, fluffy fool. Spoon into a serving dish or individual glasses and chill in the fridge for a few hours, or overnight, before serving.

variation

gooseberry and strawberry summer fool

Substitute half the gooseberries with ripe, hulled strawberries. Do not stew them. Stew 6oz (175g) gooseberries in ⅓ cup sugar and 2 tsp water. Puree with 6oz (175g) strawberries until smooth, then let cool and continue at step 3. Decorate the tops with a little grated dark chocolate before serving.

strawberry tart

Master the basics of this fresh fruit tart and you can adapt it easily by replacing the strawberries with other soft fruits.

 40 MINS PLUS CHILLING   **25 MINS**

SPECIAL EQUIPMENT ▪ 9in (23cm) round fluted tart pan with removable bottom ▪ ceramic baking beans

SERVES 6–8

1 cup all-purpose flour

7 tbsp unsalted butter, chilled and cubed

¼ cup granulated sugar

1 large egg yolk

¹/₂ tsp pure vanilla extract

6 tbsp red currant jelly, for glazing

10oz (300g) strawberries, hulled and thickly sliced

For the crème pâtissière

½ cup granulated sugar

½ cup cornstarch

2 large eggs

1 tsp pure vanilla extract

1¾ cups whole milk

1 Put the flour and butter in a mixing bowl and rub them together with your fingertips to form fine crumbs. Stir in the sugar. Beat together the egg yolk and vanilla extract, and add them to the flour mixture. Then combine all the ingredients together to form a dough, adding a little water if it seems dry. Wrap tightly in plastic wrap and chill in the fridge for 1 hour.

2 Preheat the oven to 350°F (180°C). Roll out the dough on a floured work surface to a large circle about ⅛in (3mm). If the dough starts to crumble, bring it together with your hands and gently knead. Use it to line the tart pan, pressing it into the corners and leaving an overlapping edge of ¾in (2cm). Use a pair of scissors to trim any excess dough that hangs down farther than this point.

3 Prick the bottom of the crust all over with a fork, to prevent air bubbles from forming as it bakes, then line the bottom with wax paper and fill with baking beans. Place on a baking sheet and bake in the oven for 20 minutes until the edges are golden. Remove the beans and paper, and bake for 5 more minutes. Remove from the oven and trim the excess dough. Melt the jelly with 1 tbsp water and brush a little over the crust. Leave to one side to cool, and reserve the melted jelly.

4 For the crème pâtissière, beat the sugar, cornstarch, eggs, and vanilla extract in a mixing bowl.

5 Pour the milk into a heavy-bottomed saucepan, bring it to a boil, and take it off the heat just as it begins to bubble. Pour the hot milk

onto the egg mixture, whisking all the time. Return the crème pâtissière to a pan and bring to a boil over medium heat, whisking constantly. When the crème pâtissière thickens, reduce the heat to low and continue to cook for 2–3 minutes. Transfer to a bowl, cover with plastic wrap, and let cool completely.

6 Beat the crème pâtissière once more and spread it over the crust. Top with the sliced strawberries arranged in a circular pattern. Heat the jelly glaze again and brush over the strawberries, then let set. When you are ready to serve the tart, remove it from the tart pan.

apricot crumble shortbread

This variation on classic shortbread has a buttery crumb topping and a chunky, lemony apricot layer beneath—a delicious, fruit-filled teatime treat.

 20 MINS PLUS CHILLING   1 HR 15 MINS

SPECIAL EQUIPMENT ▪ 9 x 13in (23 x 32cm) baking pan
▪ electric hand mixer or stand mixer

MAKES 10 BARS OR 20 SQUARES

14 tbsp butter, softened

½ cup granulated sugar

1½ cups all-purpose flour

1 cup cornstarch

9oz (250g) apricots, peeled, pitted, and coarsely chopped

grated zest of ½ lemon

For the crumble topping

5 tbsp butter, cubed

1 cup all-purpose flour

⅓ cup granulated sugar

1 Line the baking pan with parchment paper. Cream the butter and sugar together in a bowl with an electric hand mixer or stand mixer until pale and creamy. Sift in the flour and cornstarch and combine well so that the mixture comes together to form a dough. (You'll probably need to use your hands to bring it together at the end.) Knead the dough lightly until smooth, then push it evenly into the bottom of the pan and smooth the top. Chill in the fridge for at least 1 hour, or until firm.

2 Preheat the oven to 350°F (180°C). To make the crumble topping, put the butter and flour into a mixing bowl. Rub the butter into the flour with your fingertips until the mixture resembles bread crumbs. Add the sugar and stir it in. Scatter the apricots and lemon zest evenly over the chilled shortbread base, then top with the crumble mixture, pressing it down firmly.

3 Bake for 1¼ hours, or until a skewer inserted into the center comes out clean with no uncooked mixture on it (it might be a bit damp from the fruit, though). Leave to cool in the pan. When cold, remove from the pan and divide into either 10 bars or 20 squares.

variation

plum crumble shortbread

Replace the apricots with 10oz (300g) plums, pitted and coarsely chopped, and the lemon zest with the grated zest of 1 lime. In step 2, scatter the plums and lime zest over the chilled shortbread crust, top with the crumble mixture, and bake as instructed.

gratin of fresh berries with sabayon

Be sure to choose berries—such as strawberries, raspberries, blackberries or blueberries—that are plump and full of flavor to partner this fluffy sabayon sauce with lemon zest.

 15-20 MINS PLUS CHILLING   1-2 MINS

SPECIAL EQUIPMENT ▪ whisk or electric hand mixer
▪ blow torch (optional)

SERVES 4

13oz (375g) mixed berries, such as raspberries, strawberries, blackberries, or blueberries

1 lemon

3 egg yolks

¼ cup granulated sugar

⅓ cup Grand Marnier or Marsala

1 Pick over the berries, washing them only if they are dirty. Hull the strawberries. Cut any large berries into halves or quarters. Divide the berries evenly among 4 individual gratin dishes or heatproof dessert plates, and chill in the fridge.

2 Heat the broiler, or if you own a blow torch, have it on hand. Grate the zest from half the lemon. Put the egg yolks, sugar, and Grand Marnier or Marsala in a large heatproof bowl, and whisk them together with a whisk or electric hand mixer. Set the bowl over a saucepan half-filled with hot, but not simmering, water (the bottom of the bowl must not touch the water), and start to whisk the mixture again.

3 Continue whisking for 5–8 minutes, until the mixture is frothy and thick enough to leave a ribbon trail when the whisk is lifted and has almost doubled in size. Remove from the pan of hot water, whisk in the zest, and continue whisking for 1–2 minutes until slightly cooled.

4 Arrange the gratin dishes on a baking sheet and spoon the sabayon over and around the berries. Broil about 6in (15cm) from the heat for 1–2 minutes, or use a blow torch, until the sabayon is golden brown and the fruit is warm. Put each of the hot dishes onto small plates to keep from burning your or your guests' hands and serve immediately.

cherry cheesecake

Beautiful whole cherries in a sweet cherry sauce arranged on top of a lemony filling turn this unbaked cheesecake into a delightful fresh summer treat for a hot day.

 30 MINS PLUS CHILLING 5 MINS

SPECIAL EQUIPMENT ▪ 8in (20cm) round springform cake pan
▪ electric hand mixer

SERVES 6

5 tbsp unsalted butter

7oz (200g) vanilla wafers, crushed

2 x 7oz tubs ricotta cheese

⅓ cup granulated sugar

grated zest and juice of 4 lemons

½ cup heavy cream

6 gelatin leaves, cut into small pieces

12oz (350g) cherries, pitted

¾ cup apple juice

2 tbsp red currant jelly

1 Grease and line the cake pan. Melt the butter in a pan, add the crushed wafers, and stir until coated. Transfer the mixture to the pan, pressing it down firmly with the back of a spoon.

2 Mix together the ricotta, sugar, and zest. In a separate bowl, beat the cream with an electric hand mixer until it forms soft peaks.

Add the ricotta mixture to the whipped cream and beat with a wooden spoon until well combined.

3 In a pan, soak the gelatin in the lemon juice for 5 minutes to soften. Then gently heat, but do not boil, stirring to dissolve. Set aside. Add to the ricotta mixture and stir well. Then pour the mixture on top of the wafer crust, spreading it out evenly. Place in the fridge for at least 2 hours or until set and firm.

4 Put the cherries in a pan with the apple juice and stir for 2–3 minutes until the juices run. Carefully lift out the cherries with a slotted spoon. Stir in the red currant jelly until dissolved. Bring to a boil, then simmer until reduced by about three-quarters. Let cool, then arrange the cherries on top of the cheesecake, spoon the sauce over the top, and serve.

génoise cake with raspberries and cream

A sumptuous whisked cake with a delicate raspberry filling.

 30 MINS 25-30 MINS ❄ FREEZABLE

SPECIAL EQUIPMENT ▪ 8in (20cm) round springform cake pan
▪ electric hand mixer

SERVES 8-10

3 tbsp unsalted butter

4 large eggs

⅔ cups granulated sugar

1 cup all-purpose flour

1 tsp pure vanilla extract

grated zest of 1 lemon

2 cups heavy cream

11oz (325g) raspberries, plus extra to decorate

1 tbsp confectioners' sugar

1 Melt the butter in a saucepan and reserve. Preheat the oven to 350°F (180°C). Grease the baking pan and line the bottom with parchment paper.

2 Put the eggs and granulated sugar in a large heatproof bowl. Bring a pan of water to a boil, remove from the heat, then set the bowl over the top. Beat using an electric hand mixer for 5 minutes until the beaters leaves a trail when lifted; the mixture will expand up to 5 times its original volume. Remove the bowl from the pan and beat for 1 minute to cool. Sift in the flour and fold it in. Fold in the vanilla extract, lemon zest, and melted butter. Put the mixture into the pan. Bake for 25–30 minutes, or until the top is springy and light golden brown. A skewer inserted into the center should come out clean.

3 Leave the cake in its pan for a few minutes, then turn onto a wire rack. Remove the parchment paper. When cold, cut it horizontally into three equal pieces with a serrated knife.

4 In a large bowl, beat the cream until stiff peaks form. Lightly crush the raspberries with the confectioners' sugar and fold into the cream, leaving any juice behind. Place the bottom slice of cake on a serving plate and spread with half the cream mix. Top with the second slice, spread with the rest of the cream, and place the final slice on top. Decorate with raspberries, if using, dust with confectioners' sugar, and serve.

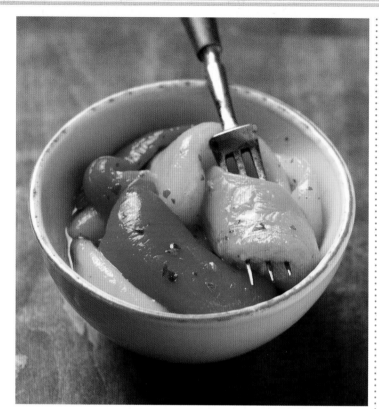

mixed bell peppers in oil

This is one of the best ways to enjoy ripe bell peppers. Roasting them amplifies their sweetness and concentrates their flavor, while the olive oil enhances their unctuous texture.

 10–15 MINS   25–30 MINS

MAKES ABOUT 2½ CUPS

3 red bell peppers

3 orange bell peppers

3 yellow bell peppers

1 tsp dried oregano

sea salt and freshly ground black pepper

2 tbsp extra virgin olive oil, plus extra to add as needed

2 tbsp cider vinegar

1 Preheat the oven to 400°F (200°C). Put the bell peppers in a roasting pan and cook for about 25–30 minutes until they begin to char slightly. Remove from the oven, put in a plastic bag (to make the skins easier to remove), and leave to cool.

2 Pull away the stalks, remove the skin, seed, and tear or slice the bell peppers into chunky strips. Put into a bowl with the oregano and season with sea salt and pepper. Mix the oil with the vinegar, then pour over the bell peppers and stir carefully.

3 Spoon the bell peppers into sterilized jars and add all the juices. Pour in oil to cover completely. Seal, label, and store in the fridge. Once opened, keep refrigerated, add oil if necessary so the bell peppers are always covered, and use within 1 month.

tomato and chile jam

Tomato jam is traditionally a sweet jam, but here it has been adapted slightly to give it a savory note. If you prefer a simple sweet tomato jam, omit the chile and mixed herbs.

 10–15 MINS   25–30 MINS

SPECIAL EQUIPMENT ▪ preserving pan ▪ sugar thermometer

MAKES 1½ CUPS

1lb 2oz (500g) tomatoes, peeled (p197) and coarsely chopped

1 tsp chile flakes

1 tsp dried mixed herbs

juice of 1 lemon

salt

1 cup granulated sugar

1 Put all the ingredients except the sugar into a preserving pan or a large heavy-bottomed saucepan. Bring to a boil and simmer gently for about 8 minutes, or until the tomatoes break down and soften.

2 Add the sugar and heat gently, stirring until it has all dissolved. Turn up the heat and bring to a boil. When the jam reaches a rolling boil, cook for 10–15 minutes, or until it starts to thicken and become glossy and reaches the setting point (stir occasionally to prevent the jam from sticking or burning). Remove the pan from the heat while you test for a set.

3 Test for a set with a sugar thermometer or using a wrinkle test (chill a plate in the fridge before cooking). If you use a thermometer, the temperature must reach 220°F (105°C); the mixture will also thicken around the sides of the pan, boil sluggishly, and the bubbles "plop" rather than froth. Or put 1 tsp jam on the chilled plate, allow to cool for a moment, then push it with a finger. If it leaves a trail and wrinkles slightly, the jam is set.

4 Ladle into a warm sterilized jar, cover with a disk of wax paper, seal, and label. Store in a cool, dark place and refrigerate after opening.

damson cheese

This glossy fruit cheese is packed with flavor. Serve sliced with cold meats and cheeses or as an after-dinner treat.

 25–45 MINS PLUS MATURING   1 HR 5 MINS–1 HR 45 MINS

SPECIAL EQUIPMENT ▪ preserving pan ▪ ramekins

MAKES 1¾ CUPS

2¼lb (1kg) damsons, pitted and chopped

granulated sugar (see method)

1–2 tbsp butter (optional)

1 Put the fruit in a preserving pan or a large heavy-bottomed saucepan with 1¼ cups of water. Bring to a boil and simmer for 30–40 minutes until the fruit is reduced to a thick, syrupy pulp. Crush the fruit occasionally with a potato masher or fork as it cooks.

2 Sieve the fruit in batches and collect the juices and fruit puree in a clean bowl. Measure the puree and add the sugar (for every 2 cups of damson puree, allow 2 cups of sugar. If the puree seems tart, use 2⅔ cups of sugar).

3 Return the puree to the pan and add the butter if you wish (it mellows the sharpness of the damsons). Stir over low heat to dissolve the sugar, then bring to a gentle boil.

4 Simmer gently for 35–45 minutes or longer, stirring often, until the pulp reduces to a black-purple glossy paste that "plops" and sticks to the wooden spoon, or leaves a clear trail if the spoon is drawn across the bottom of the pan.

5 Lightly oil warm sterilized jars, ramekins, or molds. Spoon in the cheese and level the top. Cover with disks of wax paper and seal with cellophane covers if leaving in their jars. Or cool, turn out using a palette knife, and wrap in wax paper or plastic wrap. Store in a cool, dark place for at least 6–8 weeks before eating.

tomato and roasted bell pepper chutney

This sweet, jammy, mild-flavored chutney is an ideal accompaniment to Brie, goat cheese, or other soft cheeses. Stir a teaspoon or two of chile flakes into the mixture at the end of cooking if you want to give it added spice.

 20 MINS PLUS MATURING   **1 HR 30 MINS–2 HRS**

SPECIAL EQUIPMENT ▪ food processor ▪ preserving pan

MAKES 3lb (1.35kg)

1 red bell pepper

1 orange bell pepper

1 yellow bell pepper

3lb (1.35kg) ripe tomatoes, peeled (p197)

2 onions, coarsely chopped

2 cups granulated sugar

2 cups white wine vinegar

1 Preheat the oven to 400°F (200°C). Put the bell peppers in a roasting pan and cook for about 25–30 minutes until they begin to char slightly. Remove from the oven, put in a plastic bag (to make the skins easier to remove), and let cool.

2 Pull away the stalks from the bell peppers, remove the skin, seed, and coarsely chop. Put the peeled tomatoes, roasted bell peppers, and onions in a food processor and pulse briefly until chopped but not mushy. Alternatively, chop by hand.

3 Pour the mixture into a preserving pan or a large heavy-bottomed, stainless-steel saucepan with the sugar and vinegar. Cook on low heat, stirring continuously, until the sugar has dissolved. Bring to a boil, then reduce to simmer and cook for about 1–1½ hours, stirring occasionally, until it starts to thicken and turn jammy. You may need to increase the heat a little toward the end of cooking. Stir continuously near the end so the chutney doesn't catch on the bottom of the pan.

4 Ladle into warm sterilized jars with nonmetallic or vinegar-proof lids, making sure there are no air gaps. Cover each jar with a wax-paper disk, seal, and label. Store in a cool, dark place. Allow the flavors to mature for 1 month, then refrigerate after opening.

plums in brandy

You can also use this method for preserving damson plums and greengages. If you like sweet spices, add a cinnamon stick or a star anise to the jar as you can the fruit.

 10 MINS PLUS MATURING

MAKES 3½ CUPS

about 1lb 2oz (500g) plums

about ⅔ cup granulated sugar

about 1½ cups brandy

1 Prick the fruits with a fork or darning needle. If the plums are quite large, halve them and pit them instead. Pack the fruits into sterilized jars, adding as many fruits as you can without squashing or bruising them.

2 Add enough sugar to fill about one-third of the jar. Pour in enough brandy to fill the jar completely. Tap the jars gently on a wooden board and turn them to and fro to release any air bubbles, then seal. Invert the jars a few times to mix the sugar around a bit.

3 The sugar will gradually dissolve. Shake the jars to help this process whenever you remember. Store in a cool, dark place for 2–3 months to allow the flavors to mature. Refrigerate after opening and eat within 2 weeks.

plum and rum jam

Rum enhances the flavor of plums superbly. Although most of the fruit will disintegrate as it cooks, the occasional piece of succulent plum may remain, adding welcome texture.

 30-35 MINS   **45-55 MINS**

SPECIAL EQUIPMENT ▪ preserving pan ▪ sugar thermometer

MAKES 3lb 3oz (1.5kg)

2¼lb (1kg) plums, washed, halved, and pitted

4½ cups granulated sugar

3 tbsp dark rum

1 Place the plums in a preserving pan or a large heavy-bottomed saucepan with 1¼ cups of water and bring to a boil.

2 Simmer for 30 minutes until the plums have softened, then add the sugar and heat gently, stirring until the sugar has all dissolved.

3 Bring to a boil. When it reaches a rolling boil, cook for 5–10 minutes, or until the setting point is reached. Remove the pan from the heat while you test for a set.

4 Test for a set with a sugar thermometer or using a wrinkle test (chill a plate in the fridge before cooking). If you use a thermometer, the temperature must reach 220°F (105°C); the mixture will also thicken around the sides of the pan, boil sluggishly, and the bubbles "plop" rather than froth. Or put 1 tsp jam on the chilled plate, let cool for a moment, then push it with a finger. If it leaves a trail and wrinkles slightly, the jam is set.

5 Add the rum and mix well, then ladle into warm sterilized jars, cover with disks of wax paper, seal, and label. Store in a cool, dark place and refrigerate after opening.

berry syrup

This homemade blackberry syrup tastes much fruitier than a store-bought version. Use it to flavor milkshakes and smoothies, as a sauce for ice cream, and stir into fruit salads.

 20 MINS   **5 MINS**   **FREEZABLE**

SPECIAL EQUIPMENT ▪ jelly bag or muslin

MAKES 2 CUPS

1lb (450g) ripe blackberries or loganberries, washed if needed

about 1½ cups granulated sugar

1 tsp citric acid

1 Place the fruit in a saucepan with a thin film of water at the bottom, and simmer very gently for the shortest time possible to extract the juice (3–5 minutes). Squash the fruit with a potato masher or the back of a wooden spoon as it cooks.

2 Strain the puree through a jelly bag or muslin-lined sieve into a clean bowl (to give a clearer syrup). Press the pulp in the sieve very gently to extract any remaining juice.

3 Pour the juice into a liquid measuring cup. Calculate and measure the amount of sugar needed (1½ cups sugar to 2 cups of juice), then add it to the juice with the citric acid. Stir until the sugar has dissolved.

4 Once the sugar has completely dissolved, immediately pour the fruit syrup into warm sterilized bottles using a sterilized funnel, then seal the bottles.

5 Store in the fridge if consuming immediately. Syrups can also be frozen in freezerproof containers, in which case, leave 1in (2.5cm) of space at the top of each container. Refrigerate after opening.

Season's best **plums**

One of the most versatile fruits, plums vary greatly in color, from green through yellow to red and purple; in size, large or small; and shape, round or tear-shaped. Some are sweet, others are tart, and they also differ in juiciness. Most of them ripen in high summer, and the rest in early autumn. Some are better eaten fresh, others are better cooked. All blend beautifully with other stone fruits, nuts, cheeses, rich meats, spirits, and wines.

Plums need plenty of sun and well-drained soil to grow. In cool climates, later-flowering varieties fare better when the risk of frost has passed.

essentials

varieties available

Many varieties, but essentially two types—the large, round Japanese and the European ones, which include all the gages and damsons. Also dried (often called prunes).

buy They should be firm, yet give slightly when pressed, and have a slight bloom. They should not feel squishy. Avoid hard, wrinkled, or shriveled plums, and ones with brown patches.

store Ripe plums can be kept for several days in an open paper bag in the fridge vegetable drawer. Soften fruit that is slightly underripe in a paper bag at room temperature.

cook Leave the skin on for dishes in which they need to keep their shape. Purée for soufflés, mousses, and sauces. Poach or bake in syrup. Use in pies, tarts, crumbles, dumplings, and cakes. Add to stews. Halve and grill. Enjoy raw.

preserve Bottle in syrup or brandy; dry; make into jam or chutney.

recipe ideas

Bavarian plum tart p225

Cinnamon and plum cobbler p337

Greengage wine p243

Plum and marzipan clafoutis p212

Plum and rum jam p234

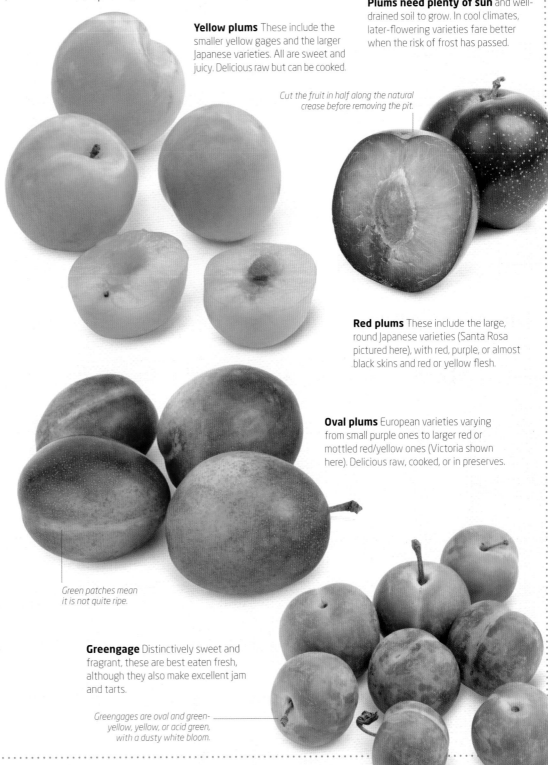

Yellow plums These include the smaller yellow gages and the larger Japanese varieties. All are sweet and juicy. Delicious raw but can be cooked.

Cut the fruit in half along the natural crease before removing the pit.

Red plums These include the large, round Japanese varieties (Santa Rosa pictured here), with red, purple, or almost black skins and red or yellow flesh.

Oval plums European varieties varying from small purple ones to larger red or mottled red/yellow ones (Victoria shown here). Delicious raw, cooked, or in preserves.

Green patches mean it is not quite ripe.

Greengage Distinctively sweet and fragrant, these are best eaten fresh, although they also make excellent jam and tarts.

Greengages are oval and green-yellow, yellow, or acid green, with a dusty white bloom.

pickled gherkins

Cold pickling is a simple process: vegetables are first salted to draw out moisture to avoid diluting the vinegar and thus keep them crisp, and then they are pickled in cold vinegar. Use pickling cucumbers or cornichons for this recipe.

 10 MINS PLUS SALTING AND MATURING   **1 HR 20 MINS–1 HR 30 MINS**

MAKES 2¼lb (1kg)

1lb 2oz (500g) small pickling cucumbers, 2–2½in (5–6cm) long

½ cup sea salt

3–4 peeled shallots

1–2 peeled garlic cloves (optional)

2–3 dried chiles (optional)

2–3 cloves (optional)

½ tsp coriander seeds, peppercorns, dill seeds, or 1 crumbled dried bay leaf

2 sprigs of tarragon, dill, or thyme

1 washed vine leaf (optional)

about 2½ cups white wine vinegar

1 Snip off the stalks and any dried blossom from the end of the cucumbers. Wash the skins thoroughly, then rub each with a cloth to dry and remove its fine down. If your jars are large enough, leave the cucumbers whole, otherwise cut them into quarters lengthwise, or into ⅛in (3mm) slices.

2 Put a layer of sea salt in a bowl, add a layer of cucumbers, then another layer of salt. Repeat the layers until all the cucumbers are used up, finishing with a layer of salt. Leave at room temperature for 24 hours.

3 Wash the cucumbers to remove all the salt and pack into clean, sterilized jars, leaving ½in (1cm) of head room. Add the shallots or garlic cloves, if using, spices, and herbs. Include fresh dill if you want a traditional flavor and a vine leaf to keep the pickles crisp and crunchy. Fill the jars with enough vinegar to cover the cucumbers completely.

4 Seal the jars with nonmetallic or vinegar-proof lids and label. Store in a cool, dark place for 3–4 weeks to mature before eating (remove the pickles with wooden tongs). Refrigerate after opening.

variation

pickled gherkins with spring onions

Use 10oz (300g) pickling cucumbers and 2 bunches of spring onions, bulbs only, trimmed and peeled, instead of all cucumbers. Salt in the same way. Omit the shallots. Flavor with 2 large bay leaves instead of the tarragon, dill, or thyme.

apricot and champagne conserve

The addition of a little Champagne transforms this classic apricot conserve into a premium preserve.

 15 MINS PLUS STANDING 25–30 MINS

SPECIAL EQUIPMENT ▪ preserving pan ▪ sugar thermometer

MAKES 1½lb (675g)

1lb 2oz (500g) ripe apricots, pitted and chopped

1¼ cups granulated sugar

juice of 1 lemon

¾ cup Champagne or dry sparkling wine

1 Layer the fruit and sugar in a bowl, cover, and leave for several hours or overnight at room temperature.

2 Put the fruit, sugar, lemon juice, and champagne in a preserving pan or a large heavy-bottomed saucepan and simmer gently for 10–12 minutes, or until the apricots become soft.

3 Turn up the heat and bring to a rolling boil, cook for about 10 minutes, or until it reaches the setting point. It will begin to set very quickly, so test frequently. Remove the pan from the heat and test for a set with a sugar thermometer or using a wrinkle test (chill a plate in the fridge before cooking). If you use a thermometer, the temperature must reach 220°F (105°C); the mixture will also thicken around the sides of the pan, boil sluggishly, and the bubbles "plop" rather than froth. Or put 1 tsp jam on the chilled plate, allow to cool for a moment, then push it with a finger. If it leaves a trail and wrinkles slightly, the jam is set.

4 Ladle into warm sterilized jars, cover with disks of wax paper, seal, and label. Store in a cool, dark place and refrigerate after opening.

mixed vegetable pickle

This crunchy, sharp cold pickle requires no cooking and could not be simpler to make. Try it with cheese sandwiches, as part of a mixed hors d'oeuvres, or with vegetarian dishes.

 30 MINS PLUS STANDING AND MATURING

MAKES 1lb 2oz (500g)

¼ cup sea salt

1 small cauliflower, chopped into florets

1 large onion, roughly chopped

2 carrots, sliced

10 cherry tomatoes

5 jalapeño peppers, left whole (optional)

2 cups ready-spiced pickling vinegar

1 tsp coriander seeds

1 tsp mustard seeds

1 Put the sea salt in a large bowl, add 2 cups water, and mix thoroughly. Add all the vegetables, cover the bowl, and let stand overnight. If you find that your prepared vegetables weigh more than 1lb 2oz (500g), you may need to make up more brine: always use a ratio of ¼ cup salt per 2 cups water.

2 Mix the vinegar in a bowl with the coriander and mustard seeds and set aside.

3 Rinse the vegetables under cold water, drain, and dry well with a clean kitchen towel or paper towels. Layer and pack them into a sterilized jar with a nonmetallic or vinegar-proof lid and pour over the spiced vinegar to cover them completely. Add more of the vinegar mix if needed, then seal and label. Keep at room temperature for 2 days, then put in the fridge and leave for at least 1 week before eating. Refrigerate after opening.

apricots and almonds in amaretto

Apricots seeped in almond liqueur taste heavenly. If you want to preserve them whole, prick them with a darning needle and poach in a single layer in the syrup for 1–2 minutes.

 10–15 MINS PLUS MATURING 20 MINS

MAKES 4 CUPS

⅓ cup granulated sugar

1lb (450g) apricots, halved and pitted

2oz (60g) blanched almonds

1 cup almond liqueur

1 Put the sugar and ⅔ cup cold water in a large saucepan. Heat gently, stirring continuously until the sugar has dissolved.

2 Remove half the apricots and reserve, then place the remaining apricots in a single layer in the pan. Bring the syrup and fruit to a boil and boil for 1 minute until the fruit has softened slightly, but still holds its shape well. Remove with a slotted spoon and place in a warm sterilized jar. Add half the almonds. Repeat with the remaining apricots and nuts.

3 Bring the syrup back to a boil, then pour it over the fruit. Add liqueur to cover completely. Leave to cool, cover tightly, and invert gently a few times to mix the syrup and liqueur. Store in a cool, dark place for 4 weeks for the flavors to develop. Refrigerate after opening.

apricot conserve

Conserves differ from jams in that they contain large pieces of fruit or whole fruits, which are steeped in sugar first to firm them up, and boiled more gently than jam.

 10–15 MINS PLUS STANDING   12–15 MINS

SPECIAL EQUIPMENT ▪ preserving pan ▪ sugar thermometer

MAKES 1½lb (675g)

1lb 2oz (500g) ripe apricots, halved and pitted

1½ cups granulated sugar

juice of 1 lemon

1 Layer the fruit and sugar in a bowl, cover, and leave for several hours or overnight at room temperature.

2 Put the fruit and sugar in a preserving pan with the lemon juice. Heat gently, stirring to dissolve the sugar. Raise the heat and bring to a steady—rather than a fast—boil for 7–10 minutes until the setting point is reached. Don't stir unless necessary. Remove the pan from the heat to test for a set with a sugar thermometer or using a wrinkle test

(chill a plate in the fridge before cooking). If you use a thermometer, the temperature must reach 220°F (105°C); the mixture will also thicken around the sides of the pan, boil sluggishly, and the bubbles "plop" rather than froth. Or put 1 tsp conserve on the chilled plate, let cool for a moment, then push it with a finger. If it leaves a trail and wrinkles slightly, it is set.

3 Leave the conserve to cool slightly so a thin skin forms and the fruit is evenly distributed throughout, then ladle into warm sterilized jars. Cover with disks of wax paper, seal, and label. Store in a cool, dark place and refrigerate after opening.

peaches in syrup

Bottled peaches in a light syrup have a charm and appeal of their own, and are a wonderful way to capture the flavors of summer. They also make excellent gifts.

 10 MINS   2 MINS PLUS HEAT-PROCESSING

MAKES 2 CUPS

about ½ cup granulated sugar

4–5 just-ripe peaches, peeled (p217)

cracked peach kernels (optional)

1 Preheat the oven to 300°F (150°C). Put the sugar and 2 cups water into a pan, bring gently to a boil, and boil for 1–2 minutes.

2 Place some warm sterilized jars in a deep roasting pan lined with newspaper. Pack the peaches into the jars, leaving ½in (1cm) of head room at the top. Add the peach kernels, if using, and fill the jars to the brim with the hot syrup. Bang the jars lightly and swivel them to remove air bubbles. Add more syrup, then fit the rubber-sealed or screw lids (loosen the screw lids by a quarter of a turn).

3 Put the roasting pan of filled jars in the center of the oven for 50–60 minutes to heat-process (remove the remaining air in the jars). Then remove from the oven and tighten the clips or lids (or screw on plastic screw-band lids) immediately. Leave for 24 hours, then unscrew or unclip and test the lids are firmly sealed, before refastening and storing. (If using preserving jars with metal lids, you will know if you have a seal as the lid becomes slightly concave and is firm with no "give" once pressed.) Store the jars in a cool, dark place and refrigerate after opening.

raspberry jam

Jams are the simplest of preserves: fruit cooked with sugar over high heat until set. This method, suitable for all soft-peeled berries, such as raspberries, produces a soft-set jam.

🥣 5 MINS   🍲 10-15 MINS

SPECIAL EQUIPMENT ▪ preserving pan ▪ sugar thermometer

MAKES 1lb (450g)

1½lb (650g) raspberries

juice of ½ lemon

2¼ cups granulated sugar

1 Wash the fruit only if needed and put in a preserving pan or a large saucepan. Add the lemon juice and pour in ⅔ cup water.

2 Simmer gently for 3–5 minutes to soften and release the juices from the fruit. Add the sugar, stir it in over low heat until it has dissolved, then turn up the heat.

3 Bring the jam to a rolling boil. Boil for 5–10 minutes or until a setting point is reached. Remove the pan from the heat while you test for a set with a sugar thermometer or using a wrinkle test (chill a plate in the fridge before cooking). If you use a thermometer, the temperature must reach 220°F (105°C); the mixture will also thicken around the sides of the pan, boil sluggishly, and the bubbles "plop" rather than froth. Or put 1 tsp jam on the chilled plate, let cool for a moment, then push it with a finger. If it leaves a trail and wrinkles slightly, the jam is set.

4 Ladle the jam into warm sterilized jars using a sterilized jam funnel, filling the jars almost to the brim. Cover with disks of wax paper, seal with cellophane covers and elastic bands, or metal lids, and label. Store the jam in a cool, dark place and refrigerate after opening.

mixed berry jam

Sometimes called jumbleberry jam, this can be made with any summer fruits, so choose what is plentiful. Blackberries, black currants, red currants, or cherries are also good.

🥣 5 MINS   🍲 10-15 MINS

SPECIAL EQUIPMENT ▪ preserving pan ▪ sugar thermometer ▪ skimmer

MAKES 1½ CUPS

1lb (450g) mix of strawberries, raspberries, and blueberries, hulled if needed

2 cups granulated sugar

juice of 2 lemons

1 Put the fruits in a preserving pan or a large heavy-bottomed saucepan and lightly crush them with the back of a wooden spoon.

2 Add the sugar and heat gently, stirring until the sugar has all dissolved. Turn up the heat and bring to a boil. When the jam reaches a rolling boil, cook for 5–10 minutes or until it reaches the setting point. Remove the pan from the heat while you test for a set with a sugar thermometer or using a wrinkle test (chill a plate in the fridge before cooking). If you use a thermometer, the temperature must reach 220°F (105°C); the mixture will also thicken around the sides of the pan, boil sluggishly, and the bubbles "plop" rather than froth. Or put 1 tsp jam on the chilled plate, let cool for a moment, then push it with a finger. If it leaves a trail and wrinkles slightly, the jam is set.

3 Use a skimmer to skim off any surface scum. Leave the jam to cool slightly so that a thin skin forms and the berries are evenly distributed throughout the jam. Ladle into warm sterilized jars, cover with wax paper disks, seal, and label. Store the jam in a cool, dark place and refrigerate after opening.

Season's best **summer berries**

The pleasant sight of colorful soft berries and currants ripening on the bushes marks the beginning of summer for most people. Abundant in high summer, berries picked and eaten fresh have an intense, sweet flavor, usually found missing from the supermarket varieties. They team incredibly well with rich meats, such as duck, pork, and game, are great combined in many desserts, and are also delicious juiced.

Easy to grow and quick to bear fruit, even in cool climates, berries (such as blueberries pictured here) are tolerant to most soil types and will even grow in the shade.

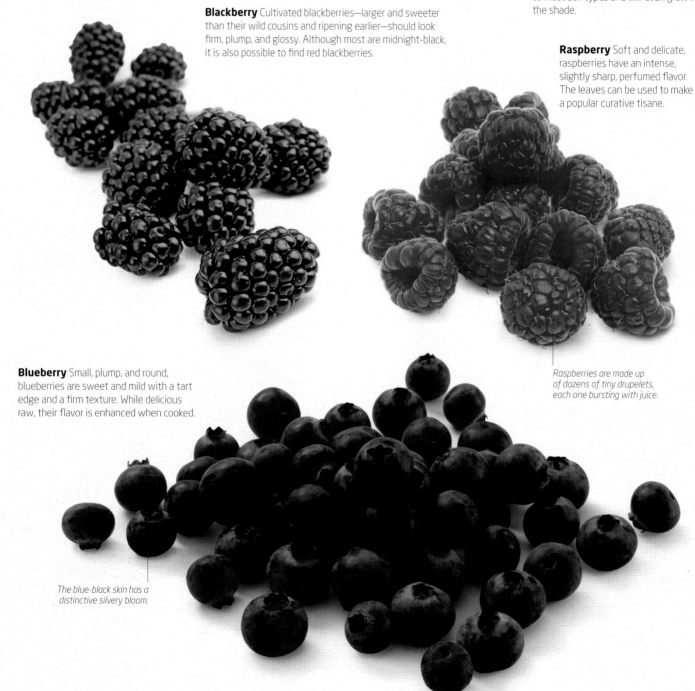

Blackberry Cultivated blackberries—larger and sweeter than their wild cousins and ripening earlier—should look firm, plump, and glossy. Although most are midnight-black, it is also possible to find red blackberries.

Raspberry Soft and delicate, raspberries have an intense, slightly sharp, perfumed flavor. The leaves can be used to make a popular curative tisane.

Raspberries are made up of dozens of tiny drupelets, each one bursting with juice.

Blueberry Small, plump, and round, blueberries are sweet and mild with a tart edge and a firm texture. While delicious raw, their flavor is enhanced when cooked.

The blue-black skin has a distinctive silvery bloom.

Redcurrant The shiny crimson berries are slightly smaller and more fragile than blackcurrants and have a tangy kick. They make good jellies, syrups, and decorations for cakes and desserts. Also good with lamb.

Whitecurrant These translucent, delicate berries have a pearl-like, pinkish blush. They are a bit smaller and sweeter than redcurrants, and can be served fresh or used for preserves. They can also be frosted with egg white and sugar.

These small, round, purple-black berries are full of juice.

Blackcurrant These have an intense, tart flavor, and are a classic choice for pies, sauces, and jam. The fragrant leaves are used to flavor ice cream.

essentials
varieties available

Many varieties of early-, mid-season-, and late-cropping fruits. Blueberries are also sold dried.

buy Avoid any with brown patches. They should all be bright, shiny, and have a rich uniform color. Running juices indicate they are overripe.

store Enjoy raw, on their own, or to decorate gâteaux, flans, pavlovas, and trifles. Purée for sauces, fools, and creams, or stew for compôtes.

cook Ideally eat or cook freshly picked, or store in the fridge for several days (depending on ripeness).

preserve Freeze; make into jam, jelly, cordials, wine, or fruit vinegar; bottle in syrup.

recipe ideas

Blueberry pancakes p211

Berry friands p218

Black currant and rosemary cheesecake p212

Cold raspberry soufflés p210

how to freeze soft fruits

Freezing preserves the flavor and nutritional content of fruit, but breaks down the cell walls so the fruit is soft when thawed—but the flavor will be just as delicious as fresh. The thawed fruit is particularly good puréed.

1 Discard any berries that are overripe or blemished. Spread out in a single layer on baking sheets. Sprinkle liberally with granulated sugar.

2 Freeze the sheets for about 1 hour until the berries are frozen. Once hard, scrape them off and put them into portion-sized freezer bags.

3 Label and date the freezer bags and return the berries to the freezer for up to 12 months, until they are needed.

raspberry and mint conserve

The addition of a little mint adds a subtle hint of flavor to this deep-red raspberry conserve.

 10 MINS PLUS STANDING 10–15 MINS

SPECIAL EQUIPMENT ▪ preserving pan ▪ sugar thermometer

MAKES 2lb (900g)

1½lb (675g) raspberries

2¼ cups granulated sugar

handful of mint, very finely chopped

juice of 1 lemon

1 Layer the fruit and sugar in a bowl, cover, and leave for several hours or overnight at room temperature.

2 Put the fruit and sugar, mint, and lemon juice in a preserving pan or a large heavy-bottomed saucepan and cook gently for 5–8 minutes. Increase the heat until the jam reaches a rolling boil and cook for 5–10 minutes, or until it reaches the setting point. Keep a close eye on it, as it will set very quickly. Remove the pan from the heat while you test for a set with a sugar thermometer or using a wrinkle test (chill a plate in the fridge before cooking). If you use a thermometer, the temperature must reach 220°F (105°C); the mixture will also thicken around the sides of the pan, boil sluggishly, and the bubbles "plop" rather than froth. Or put 1 tsp conserve on the chilled plate, allow to cool for a moment, then push it with a finger. If it leaves a trail and wrinkles slightly, it is set.

3 Ladle into warm sterilized jars, cover with disks of wax paper, seal, and label. Store in a cool, dark place and refrigerate after opening.

cherries in brandy

Juicy cherries preserved in alcohol taste deliciously boozy. Serve with coffee, or with the fragrant liquor on ice cream.

 10 MINS PLUS MATURING

SPECIAL EQUIPMENT ▪ sterilized preserving jars

MAKES 2½ CUPS

1lb 2oz (500g) just-ripe cherries (sweet or Morello) in perfect condition, washed and stemmed

⅔ cup granulated sugar

1½ cups brandy

1 Carefully place the cherries in some wide-necked, sterilized preserving jars, packing them in tightly. Take care not to squash or bruise them.

2 Add enough sugar to fill one-third of the jar and add alcohol. (As a general guide, use ¼–⅓ sugar and ¾–⅔ alcohol to fruit.)

3 Tap the jar gently on a board, turn it to and fro to release any air bubbles, and seal. The sugar will gradually dissolve—give the jar an occasional shake or turn it upside down to help it dissolve. Store in a cool, dark place for 2–3 months to mature before opening.

variation

rumtopf

Use a rumtopf jar or a sterilized earthenware jar with a lid. Instead of only cherries, choose a selection of fresh soft, ripe fruits, such as halved and pitted apricots, peaches, plums, and cherries, and whole strawberries, raspberries, grapes, and currants. Weigh the fruits and measure out half their weight in granulated sugar. Put the fruit and sugar in the jar and mix well. Leave to stand for 1 hour. Instead of brandy, pour in just enough rum to cover the fruit. Use a small, sterilized plate, or similar, to weigh down the fruit and keep it submerged. Cover the jar opening with plastic wrap, replace the lid, and store in a cool, dark place for at least 1 month to mature. It tastes best after 3 months of maturing.

sweet and sour nectarine and cherry relish

This tangy relish is full of fresh, fruity flavors and warm aromatic spices. The cherries provide texture, the nectarines give a soft base, and the onion delivers crunch.

 20 MINS PLUS MATURING 50 MINS–1 HR 10 MINS

SPECIAL EQUIPMENT ▪ preserving pan

MAKES APPROX 1¾lb (800g)

1 tbsp olive oil

2 red onions, finely chopped

sea salt

1 tsp chile flakes

1lb (450g) nectarines, pitted and chopped

4½oz (125g) dried sour cherries or cranberries

1 tsp coriander seeds

pinch of ground cinnamon

pinch of allspice

1½ cups light brown sugar

⅔ cup white wine vinegar

1 Heat the oil in a preserving pan or a large heavy-bottomed, stainless-steel saucepan. Add the onions and a little sea salt and cook until soft.

2 Stir in the chile flakes. Add the nectarines and cherries, spices, sugar, and vinegar, and stir until the sugar has dissolved. Bring to a boil, stirring occasionally, then reduce to simmer and cook on low heat for 40 minutes to 1 hour, until the mixture begins to thicken. Stir frequently toward the end of the cooking time so the mixture doesn't stick to the bottom of the pan. Add a little hot water if it becomes too dry.

3 Ladle into warm sterilized jars with nonmetallic or vinegar-proof lids, seal, and label. Store in a cool, dark place. Allow the flavors to mature for at least 1 month and refrigerate after opening.

greengage wine

An excellent pale yellow dessert wine.

 2 HRS PLUS FREEZING, BREWING, AND STORING

SPECIAL EQUIPMENT ▪ fermenting bin ▪ muslin cloth ▪ sterilized siphon ▪ sterilized demijohn ▪ sterilized airlock

MAKES 1 GALLON (4.5 LITERS)

4½lb (2kg) greengage plums, washed

juice of 1 lemon

1 tsp pectolase

1 tsp wine yeast

6 cups unrefined cane sugar

1 Put the fruit in the freezer overnight, then defrost (to destroy the pectin that turns wine cloudy).

2 Stone and mash the defrosted fruit and add the lemon juice. Place in a sterilized fermenting bin or other suitable container and cover with 12 cups boiling water. When cool, add the pectolase. Leave for 24 hours at room temperature (59–77°F/15–25°C).

3 Add the yeast to the fruit mash, cover, and leave for 4–5 days at room temperature (59–77°F/15–25°C) in a dark place.

4 Strain the pulp through a muslin cloth into a sterilized container to remove the skins. Put the sugar into a large bowl and add hot water to cover, stirring until it has dissolved. Stir it into the mash, mixing well.

5 Using the siphon, transfer the liquid into the demijohn and fit the airlock. Pour a little water into the airlock and let the liquid ferment at room temperature for 2 months.

6 When there are no air bubbles in the airlock, use the siphon to transfer the wine into sterilized bottles, leaving ¾in (2cm) space at the top. Seal and store in a cool, dark place for 6 months before opening and drinking.

variation

plum wine

Replace the greengage plums with 4½lb (2kg) red or purple plums to make a fruity red wine.

peach and raspberry conserve

Ripe peaches and raspberries produce a beautifully red-orange-colored, soft-set conserve. Its relatively low sugar content produces a lovely fresh flavor.

 10 MINS PLUS STANDING   25 MINS

SPECIAL EQUIPMENT ▪ preserving pan ▪ sugar thermometer

MAKES 2lb (900g)

1½lb (675g) just-ripe peaches, pitted and cubed

6oz (175g) raspberries

1¾ cups granulated sugar

juice of 1 lemon

1 Layer the fruit and sugar in a bowl, cover, and leave for several hours or overnight at room temperature.

2 Put the fruit, sugar, and lemon juice in a preserving pan or a large heavy-bottomed saucepan and cook at simmer for 15 minutes until the fruit softens.

3 Turn up the heat and bring to a boil. When the jam reaches a rolling boil, cook for about 10 minutes or

until it reaches the setting point. Remove the pan from the heat while you test for a set with a sugar thermometer or using a wrinkle test (chill a plate in the fridge before cooking). If you use a thermometer, the temperature must reach 220°F (105°C); the mixture will also thicken around the sides of the pan, boil sluggishly, and the bubbles "plop" rather than froth. Or put 1 tsp conserve on the chilled plate, allow to cool for a moment, then push it with a finger. If it leaves a trail and wrinkles slightly, it is set.

4 Ladle into warm sterilized jars, cover with disks of wax paper, seal, and label. Store in a cool, dark place and refrigerate after opening.

blueberry and raspberry freezer jam

This deliciously tangy combination of berries makes a healthy instant dessert served with natural yogurt and granola or on top of sliced, perfectly ripe peaches.

 6–8 MINS PLUS STANDING   7–9 MINS   ❊ FREEZABLE

SPECIAL EQUIPMENT ▪ freezer-safe container

MAKES 1lb 2oz (500g)

8oz (225g) blueberries

8oz (225g) raspberries

2 tsp lemon juice

1 tbsp agar flakes or 1 tsp agar powder

½ cup granulated sugar

1 Make sure the fruit is at room temperature. Put it in a bowl with the lemon juice and coarsely crush with a potato masher or fork; you want to leave some texture, not reduce the berries to a smooth pulp.

2 Put ¾ cup water in a small saucepan, sprinkle the agar flakes or powder over it, and leave to soften for 2–3 minutes. Give the pan a gentle swirl, then bring the water slowly to a boil over low heat without stirring it. Simmer gently for 3–5 minutes, stirring occasionally to make sure all the agar has dissolved. Add the sugar and stir for 2–3 minutes, until dissolved over low heat. Remove the pan from the heat.

3 Pour the hot agar syrup over the fruit in the bowl, constantly stirring the fruit gently until the ingredients are well mixed.

4 Pour into clean freezer containers, leaving ½in (1cm) of space at the top. Let cool, then seal and label. Leave overnight in the fridge to thicken fully, then freeze. To use, thaw in the fridge, then keep refrigerated and use within 2 weeks.

fresh figs in honey syrup

Although figs lose their vibrant color and turn greener when bottled, being macerated in honey syrup with lemon zest enhances their flavor.

 10 MINS   **5 MINS PLUS HEAT-PROCESSING**

MAKES 4 CUPS

1 cup honey

2 thinly pared strips of washed lemon zest about ½in(1cm) wide

juice of 1 lemon

about 16 small ripe figs (or 12 larger ones), washed and dried

1 Put the honey, 2 cups cold water, and the lemon zest and juice in a saucepan. Heat gently, stirring until the honey has dissolved. Bring to a boil and cook for 3 minutes. Then add the figs to the syrup and boil for 2 minutes.

2 Place some warm sterilized jars in a deep roasting pan lined with newspaper. Using a slotted spoon, pack the fruit tightly into jars without squashing them in too much. Lift the zest from the syrup and discard. Pour the hot syrup over the figs to cover them completely.

Tap each jar gently on a wooden board or work surface to remove any air bubbles.

3 Fit the rubber band or metal lid seal and clamp on the lid. If using screw-band jars, loosen by a quarter of a turn.

4 Put the roasting pan of filled jars in the center of the oven for 50–60 minutes to heat-process (remove the remaining air in the jars). Then remove from the oven and tighten the clips or lids (or screw on plastic screw-band lids) immediately. Leave for 24 hours, then unscrew or unclip and test the lids are firmly sealed before refastening and storing. (If using preserving jars with metal lids, you will know if you have a seal as the lid becomes slightly concave and is firm with no "give" once pressed.) Store the jars in a cool, dark place and refrigerate after opening.

cucumber pickle

This sweet cucumber pickle is an all-time American favorite. The cucumbers are pickled in hot vinegar, which makes them soft rather than crunchy.

 10 MINS PLUS STANDING AND MATURING   **10 MINS**

SPECIAL EQUIPMENT ▪ preserving pan

MAKES 2¾lb (1.25kg)

1 large cucumber, cubed or sliced

1 large onion (white), peeled and chopped or sliced

1 small green bell pepper, finely sliced

1 tsp sea salt

1¼ cups cider vinegar

1¼ cups light brown sugar

¼ tsp celery seeds

¼ tsp mustard seeds

¼ tsp ground cloves

¼ tsp dill

1 Put the cucumber, onion, and pepper in a large bowl, add the sea salt and mix thoroughly. Cover the bowl and let stand for 2 hours.

2 Rinse the vegetables under cold water, drain, and put into a preserving pan or a large heavy-bottomed, stainless-steel saucepan. Add the vinegar and bring to a boil. Turn off the heat.

3 Add the remaining ingredients and stir to dissolve the sugar. Let cool. Ladle into warm sterilized jars with nonmetallic or vinegar-proof lids, seal, and label. Store in a cool, dark place. Allow the flavors to mature for at least 1 month and refrigerate after opening.

hot-spiced eggplant chutney

Tender eggplant pieces, onion seeds, and a gingery mix gives this chutney an authentic flavor. Serve with lamb or Indian food such as curries or snacks.

 10 MINS PLUS MATURING   **1 HR 20 MINS – 1 HR 30 MINS**

SPECIAL EQUIPMENT ▪ preserving pan

MAKES 3lb 3oz (1.5kg)

2lb (900g) eggplants, cut into cubes

2 red onions, roughly chopped

sea salt

1 tbsp tomato paste

2 cups cider vinegar

2¼ cups light brown sugar

6oz (175g) golden raisins

pinch of dried chile flakes

1 cinnamon stick

2 tsp onion seeds (nigella seeds)

2in (5cm) piece of fresh ginger, peeled and finely chopped or grated

1 Put the eggplant in a preserving pan or a large heavy-bottomed, stainless-steel saucepan. Add the red onions and a little sea salt. Stir to combine, then stir in the tomato paste.

2 Pour in the vinegar and sugar and stir, then add the golden raisins, chile flakes, cinnamon stick, onion seeds, and ginger. Heat the ingredients gently, stirring occasionally until the sugar has dissolved. Turn the heat up and bring the mixture to a boil.

3 Reduce the heat to simmer and cook on low heat for about 1 hour, stirring occasionally so it doesn't burn. Stir continuously near the end of the cooking time so it doesn't catch on the bottom of the pan. The chutney is ready when it is thick and sticky and the vinegar has been absorbed. Remove the cinnamon stick from the pan.

4 Ladle into warm sterilized jars with nonmetallic or vinegar-proof lids, making sure there are no air gaps. Cover each pot with a wax paper disk, seal, and label. Store in a cool, dark place. Allow the flavors to mature for at least 1 month and refrigerate after opening.

quick salted herrings

Whether just cured or also marinated for added richness and flavor, these salted herrings can be served in salads with beets, radicchio, and sour cream or horseradish sauce.

 30 MINS PLUS CURING AND MARINATING

SPECIAL EQUIPMENT ▪ crock or sterilized jar

SERVES 2-4

2 boned, very fresh, herring fillets with heads removed and any excess skin and fins trimmed off

small slivers of lemon peel (optional)

olive oil, to cover

For the cure mix

2 tsp fine sea salt

2 tsp granulated sugar

1 tsp brandy

freshly ground black pepper

2 tsp chopped dill

1 Place one fillet, skin-side down, on a clean plate. Mix all the ingredients for the cure mix and spread them evenly over the fillet. Lay the second fillet on top, skin-side up, to make a sandwich. Cover the fillets with plastic wrap, put a heavy weight on top, and leave in the fridge for 24 hours to cure. Turn them after 12 hours (the cure will turn to liquid, which can be drained off) and return to the fridge.

2 The herrings can be eaten at this point, if you wish. Transfer them to a clean dry plate, cover with plastic wrap, and store in the fridge.

3 To marinate the herrings for extra flavor, slice the fillets into slivers, removing any surplus skin (or all the skin, if you prefer). Pack into a small sterilized jar or crock, add the lemon peel (if using), cover completely with oil, and return to the fridge. Leave for 48 hours before eating.

spiced beet pickle

This pickle has a lovely deep purple color, and the fragrance of the star anise and cinnamon blend beautifully with the earthy taste of the beets. It is great with Cheddar cheese.

 15 MINS PLUS MATURING   1-2 HOURS

SPECIAL EQUIPMENT ▪ preserving pan

MAKES 2¼lb (1kg)

2¼lb (1kg) raw beets, unpeeled, of similar size

3½ cups red wine vinegar

1 cup granulated sugar

1 small bay leaf

1 cinnamon stick

1 star anise

4 black peppercorns

1 tsp sea salt

1 Trim off any beet tops, taking care not to cut into the beets (or they will "bleed" when cooked) and leaving the roots intact.

2 Put the remaining ingredients in a preserving pan or a large heavy-bottomed, stainless-steel pan. Heat gently, stirring until the sugar has dissolved, then bring to a boil.

Add the beets, bring back to a boil, reduce the heat, cover tightly, and simmer gently for 1–2 hours, or until the beets are really tender when pierced with a skewer. Let cool in the liquid.

3 Lift out the beets with a slotted spoon. When cool enough to handle, cut off the roots and tops, peel, and cube. Wear rubber gloves to peel the beets, or your hands will stain. Pack into warm sterilized jars with nonmetallic or vinegar-proof lids.

4 Strain the liquid and return it to the pan. Bring back to a boil and pour over the beets to cover them completely. Seal, let cool, label, and store in a cool, dark place to allow the flavors to mature for 1 month. Refrigerate after opening.

green bean and zucchini chutney

With its mixture of sweet and tangy flavors, this chutney is perfect served with oily fish, but it is also delicious served with a salad and really perks up bread and cheese.

 15 MINS PLUS MATURING   1 HR 45 MINS

SPECIAL EQUIPMENT ▪ preserving pan

MAKES 2¼lb (1kg)

(1lb 5oz (600g) green or runner beans, thinly sliced

4 zucchinis, thinly sliced

12oz (350g) cooking apples, peeled, cored, and chopped

2 onions, finely chopped

2¼ cups light brown sugar

1 tsp mustard powder

1 tsp turmeric

1 tsp coriander seeds

2 cups cider vinegar

1 Put the beans, zucchini, apples, and onions in a preserving pan or a large heavy-bottomed, stainless-steel saucepan. Add the sugar, mustard powder, turmeric, and coriander seeds. Pour in the vinegar and stir.

2 Cook over low heat, stirring until all the sugar has dissolved, then bring to a rolling boil and cook, stirring occasionally, for about 10 minutes. Reduce to simmer and cook for about 1½ hours, stirring from time to time, until the mixture thickens. Stir continuously near the end of the cooking time so the chutney doesn't catch on the bottom of the pan.

3 Ladle into warm sterilized jars with nonmetallic or vinegar-proof lids, making sure there are no air gaps. Cover each pot with a wax paper disk, seal, and label. Store in a cool, dark place. Allow the flavors to mature for 1 month, then refrigerate after opening.

fall

at their best

vegetables artichokes ▪ beets ▪ bok choy ▪ Brussels sprouts ▪ cardoons ▪ carrots ▪ cavolo nero ▪ celery ▪ celery root ▪ chayote ▪ chiles ▪ eggplant ▪ fennel ▪ horseradish ▪ kale ▪ leeks ▪ parsnips ▪ peppers ▪ potatoes ▪ pumpkin ▪ squash (acorn, butternut, delicata, summer) ▪ sweet corn ▪ sweet potatoes ▪ swiss chard ▪ tomatoes ▪ wild mushrooms ▪ zucchini

fruit apples ▪ blackberries ▪ cranberries ▪ damson plums ▪ dates ▪ figs ▪ gooseberries ▪ grapes ▪ huckelberries ▪ melons ▪ pears ▪ persimmons ▪ plums ▪ pomegranantes ▪ quinces ▪ rosehips ▪ watermelon

seafood Albacore tuna ▪ bay scallops ▪ brown trout ▪ cod ▪ crawfish ▪ flounder ▪ haddock ▪ hake ▪ King crab ▪ ling cod ▪ mackerel ▪ mussels ▪ ocean perch ▪ octopus ▪ oysters ▪ Pacific bay shrimp ▪ pollock ▪ rainbow trout ▪ rockfish ▪ salmon (chum, coho, King) ▪ sea scallops ▪ shark (blue, bonito, mako, thresher) ▪ sole ▪ snapper ▪ squid ▪ swordfish ▪ whiting

meat, poultry, game chukar partridge ▪ duck (wild and farmed) ▪ goose (wild and farmed) ▪ grouse ▪ lamb ▪ pheasant ▪ quail ▪ rabbit (wild and farmed) ▪ turkey (wild and farmed) ▪ venison (wild and farmed) ▪ wild boar (wild and farmed)

also available

fruit lemons ▪ raspberries ▪ strawberries **vegetables** broccoli ▪ cabbages ▪ cauliflower ▪ cucumbers ▪ garlic ▪ Jerusalem artichokes ▪ lettuce ▪ mushrooms cultivated) ▪ onions ▪ pearl onions ▪ rutabaga ▪ shallots ▪ snowpeas ▪ sugarsnap peas ▪ spinach ▪ turnips ▪ watercress **seafood** clams ▪ mahi mahi ▪ tilapia **meat, poultry, game** beef ▪ buffalo ▪ chicken ▪ Cornish game hens ▪ pork ▪ veal

fall recipe planner

Pistou soup p267

Ground lamb and squash with green chiles p294

Vegetables

Acorn squash
Acorn squash and cumin soup p275 ⓥ
Butter bean and winter squash goulash p317 ⓥ
Roast squash and blue cheese crostini p260 ⓥ

Artichoke
Artichoke, green olive, and feta tart p310 ⓥ
Artichoke risotto p306 ⓥ
Baby artichokes in oil p349 ⓥ
Globe artichoke soup p266
Provençal stuffed artichokes p324
Tomato tagliatelle with artichokes p307 ⓥ
White fish, green beans, and artichoke paella p306

Beets
Beef with beets and spinach p252
Beet and apple soup p254 ⓥ
Beet relish p328 ⓥ
Beet risotto p298 ⓥ
Beet-topped mini rye breads p264 ⓥ
Borscht p254 ⓥ
Braised pheasant with beets and pears p305
Butterflied mackerel with sweet potato and beet pickle p312
Duck breasts with beets, blackberries, and spinach p252
Little Gem lettuce with blue cheese and beets p252 ⓥ
Little Gem lettuce with goat cheese, walnuts, and crispy bacon p252
Pastrami and beets on rye p264
Peppered beef with roasted beets p305
Spiced beets and carrot soup p254 ⓥ

Bok choy
Quick stir-fried fish with bok choy p291
Salmon with mushrooms and bok choy p291
Spicy garlic and green vegetable medley p327 ⓥ
Spicy mixed vegetable medley p327 ⓥ
Stir-fried Thai vegetables p280

Broccoli
Broccoli and blue cheese soup p278 ⓥ
Broccoli and mushroom quiche p318 ⓥ
Broccoli, tomato, and basil pie p253 ⓥ
Marinated lamb chops with crushed lemon and chile broccoli p318

Butternut squash
Brazilian black bean and pumpkin stew p314 ⓥ
Butternut squash stuffed with ground beef p286
Butternut squash tagine p286 ⓥ
Ground lamb and squash with green chiles p294
Lamb chops with butternut squash, beans, and mint p280
Pasta with butternut squash, cream, and sage p287 ⓥ
Plum and squash chutney p351 ⓥ
Pumpkin and ginger soup p275 ⓥ
Pumpkin stew p282 ⓥ
Quick pumpkin bread p330 ⓥ
Squash, thyme, and goat cheese tart p283 ⓥ
Sweet and sour pumpkin stew p282 ⓥ

Cabbage
Borscht p254 ⓥ
Chicken doner kebab p299
Cornish game hens with plums and cabbage p289
Grilled lamb chops and eggplant with red cabbage slaw p290

Carrot
Acorn squash and cumin soup p275 ⓥ
Braised pheasant with vegetables p311
Braised turkey with vegetables p311
French country soup p262 ⓥ
Genoese minestrone with red pesto p272 ⓥ
German potato soup p279
Mackerel roasted with carrots, chickpeas, and harissa p302
Piccalilli p348 ⓥ
Provençal vegetable soup p270 ⓥ
Spiced beet and carrot soup p254 ⓥ
Spicy, saucy fish p286
Yam pla fu p278

Cauliflower
Piccalilli p348 ⓥ
Stir-fried Thai vegetables p280

Celery
Apple, celery, and pecan salad p276 ⓥ
Beef with celery and mustard p288
Fennel and apple soup p276 ⓥ
Grilled lamb chops and eggplant with red cabbage slaw p290
Provençal vegetable soup p270 ⓥ
Quail's eggs with celery salt p268 ⓥ

Roast pumpkin, chile, and ginger dip p264

Sausage and chicken gumbo p295
Spicy, saucy fish p286
Stuffed mushrooms with basil and pine nuts p257 ⓥ
Waldorf chicken salad p260

Celery root
German potato soup p279 ⓥ
Pumpkin stew p282 ⓥ

Chile
Balinese spicy mackerel p324
Beef chile mole p298
Chicken doner kebab p299
Chilean pork and beans p314
Duck curry p295
Grilled squid salad p262
Ground lamb and squash with green chiles p294
Hot spiced pear pickle p349 ⓥ
Jamaican corn casserole p320 ⓥ
Jerk fish p322
Karahi chicken p315
Karahi rabbit p315
Kenyan fish curry p322
Paprika rice and eggplant p300 ⓥ
Roasted baby leeks with chile and crispy bacon p326
Roasted monkfish with chile, tomatoes, anchovies, and capers p281
Roast pumpkin, chile, and ginger dip p264
Spicy garlic and green vegetable medley p327 ⓥ
Spicy mixed vegetable medley p327 ⓥ
Thai dipping sauce p328
Vegetable tempura with chile dipping sauce p261 ⓥ

Eggplant massaman curry p289

Cucumber
Cucumber, almond, and dill soup p270 ⓥ
Cucumber and walnut soup p270 ⓥ
Cucumber gratin with toasted olive ciabatta p272 ⓥ
Yam pla fu p278

Eggplant
Eggplant massaman curry p289
Chunky ratatouille p305 ⓥ
Grilled lamb chops and eggplant with red cabbage slaw p290
Italian-style vegetables p353 ⓥ
Melanzane alla parmigiana p304 ⓥ
Paprika rice and eggplant p300 ⓥ
Smoky eggplant and lamb stew p306
Thai red vegetable curry p318 ⓥ
Vegetable tempura with chile dipping sauce p261 ⓥ

Fennel
Beef, fennel, and mushroom hotpot p320
Braised pheasant with vegetables p311
Braised turkey with vegetables p311
Fennel and apple soup p276 ⓥ
Fennel gratin p330 ⓥ
Fennel soup with beans, thyme, and chorizo p279
Greek-style vegetables p329 ⓥ
Italian-style vegetables p353 ⓥ
Mussels in fennel broth p276
Pear, fennel, and walnut salad p276 ⓥ
Pork with fennel and mustard p288
Pot roast chicken with turnips and fennel p298
Risotto with mussels p300

Pumpkin and ginger soup p275

Vegetarian leek and mushroom lasagna p313

Mushroom and ricotta pies with red bell pepper pesto p256

Tomato tagliatelle with artichokes p307

fall recipe planner continued

ⓥ suitable for vegetarians

Baked polenta with wild mushrooms p311

Filo pie with Swiss chard, ricotta cheese, and tomatoes p253

Broccoli and mushroom quiche p318

Apple and blackberry Brown Betty p332

Fig and vanilla jam p350

Pears

Plums

Quinces

Rosehips

Walnuts

Seafood

Cod

Grey mullet

Haddock

Halibut

Herring

Mackerel

Monkfish

Mussels

Oysters

Red snapper

Rockfish

Salmon

Sea bass

Sea bream

Sole

Squid

Striped mullet

Broiled bell pepper-stuffed mussels p265

Meat

Duck

Lamb

Pheasant

Rabbit

Venison

Pear and cinnamon strudel p344

Balinese spicy mackerel p324

Cornish game hens with plums and cabbage p289

Fried calamari p273

beef with beets and spinach

The dark, earthy colors and flavors of this dish suit the season. For even stronger shades, try using one of the vividly colored chards in place of the spinach.

 15 MINS

SERVES 4

12oz (350g) leftover roast beef, sliced

9oz (250g) spinach leaves

1lb (450g) beets, cooked, peeled (p255), and quartered

3 tbsp extra virgin olive oil

1 tbsp balsamic vinegar

juice of ½ clementine or satsuma

salt and freshly ground black pepper

handful of thyme, leaves picked

1 In a large bowl, gently toss together the roast beef, spinach, and beets. In a small bowl, whisk together the oil, balsamic vinegar, and citrus juice. Season with salt and pepper.

2 When ready to serve, drizzle the dressing over the beef and beets salad, and scatter the thyme leaves over the top.

variation

duck breasts with beets, blackberries, and spinach

Fry 2 well-seasoned, large duck breasts skin-side down for 5 minutes until well browned and the fat has run. Turn the breasts over and fry the other side for about 5 minutes until tender, but still pink in the middle. Wrap in foil and leave to rest for 10 minutes. Cut in diagonal slices then proceed as in the recipe, but add a handful of ripe blackberries with the spinach and beets.

little gem lettuce with blue cheese and beets

For a milder flavor, use Dolcelatte rather than Gorgonzola. It is made in a similar way and is sometimes called Dolcelatte Gorgonzola—but note that the fat content is higher.

 15 MINS

SPECIAL EQUIPMENT ▪ food processor

SERVES 4

5½oz (150g) blue cheese, such as Roquefort or Gorgonzola

1 tsp paprika

3 tbsp natural yogurt

1 tbsp chopped mint leaves

salt and freshly ground black pepper

1 Little Gem lettuce

3 beets, cooked, peeled (p255), and sliced

1 Put half the cheese, the paprika, yogurt, and mint in a food processor and pulse to a creamy paste. Crumble in the rest of the cheese and season with salt and pepper.

2 Separate the lettuce leaves, creating at least eight "boats." Place a couple of slices of beets in each one, then add a heaping teaspoon of the cheese mixture. Serve with fresh crusty bread and dry Spanish-style chorizo.

variation

little gem lettuce with goat cheese, walnuts, and crispy bacon

Prepare in the same way, but use 5½oz (150g) soft goat cheese instead of the blue cheese and simply beat with the paprika and yogurt, then beat in 1 tbsp finely chopped walnuts instead of the mint. Broil or dry-fry 4 smoked slices of bacon until crisp. Drain on paper towels, then snip with scissors, or crumble into small pieces. Assemble the dish with the beets as before, then sprinkle the crumbled bacon over the top.

seared halloumi cheese with figs

Halloumi is a traditional Cypriot cheese made from a mixture of goat and sheep milk. It combines perfectly with figs, which are at their sweetest in the fall.

 10 MINS   20 MINS

SERVES 4

10oz (300g) halloumi cheese, cut into ¼in(5mm) slices

8 large ripe figs, cut into quarters lengthwise

large handful of mixed salad leaves

¼ cup red wine vinegar

small handful of cilantro, finely chopped

1 red chile, deseeded and finely chopped

1 garlic clove, crushed

drizzle of olive oil, to serve

1 Put the halloumi and figs in a large, nonstick frying pan over medium heat and cook for 2–3 minutes on each side until they start to brown. Once cooked, place on a platter with the salad leaves.

2 Pour the red wine vinegar into the same pan and increase the heat slightly. Add the cilantro, chile, and garlic and simmer over medium-high heat until the sauce has reduced in volume by three-quarters. Pour sparingly over the figs and cheese. Splash the salad with the oil and serve immediately.

variation

seared pancetta with figs and crumbled feta

Put 12 thin slices of pancetta in a hot frying pan and dry-fry until crisp. Remove from the pan and drain on paper towels. Add the figs to the pan and fry for 2–3 minutes as before. Assemble the salad in exactly the same way, then scatter 3½oz (100g) crumbled feta cheese, instead of the halloumi, over before drizzling with olive oil.

filo pie with swiss chard, ricotta cheese, and tomatoes

Swiss chard is a relative of the beet, but its glossy, crinkled leaves and fleshy stems are eaten rather than its roots.

 15 MINS   30 MINS

SPECIAL EQUIPMENT ▪ 8in (20cm) round, loose-bottomed cake pan

SERVES 4–6

7oz (200g) ricotta cheese

1¼lb (550g) Swiss chard, chopped

4–6 sun-dried tomatoes in oil, drained and chopped

4 tomatoes, sliced

1 large egg

salt and freshly ground black pepper

4 tbsp butter, melted

8 sheets filo pastry

1 Preheat the oven to 350°F (180°C). In a bowl, mix together the ricotta, Swiss chard, sun-dried and fresh tomatoes, and egg. Season well with salt and pepper.

2 Brush the pan with melted butter. Lay 1 sheet of filo pastry in the pan, letting it hang over the edge on two sides. Lay another sheet at a right angle to the first. Brush with melted butter again. Continue in this way until you have 4 sheets for the crust of the pie.

3 Spoon the ricotta mixture into the pie. Fold in the edges of the pastry and top the pie with the remaining 4 sheets of filo pastry, brushing each with a little butter between layers and tucking them in neatly. Brush the top with the remaining butter and bake in the oven for 20–30 minutes until golden and crisp. Serve hot with a salad.

variation

broccoli, tomato, and basil pie

Cook 12oz (350g) broccoli, cut into tiny florets, in boiling salted water for 2–3 minutes until just tender. Drain, rinse in cold water, and drain again. Omit the Swiss chard. Mix with the ricotta and sun-dried and fresh tomatoes as before, then add 2 tbsp chopped basil, 12 halved and pitted green olives, the egg, and seasoning. Make the pie in the same way and bake for 25 minutes.

beet and apple soup

Here beet soup is given a different twist with plenty of herbs and the sweetness of apples and sugar, set against the sharpness of lemon and sour cream.

 20 MINS 1 HR ❄ FREEZABLE

SPECIAL EQUIPMENT ▪ blender or food processor

SERVES 6–8

3 tbsp olive oil

1 onion, grated or finely chopped

2 garlic cloves, grated or finely chopped

salt and freshly ground black pepper

12oz (350g) raw beets, peeled (p255) and grated or finely chopped

1 potato, peeled, and grated or finely chopped

4 apples, peeled, cored, and grated or finely chopped

5½ cups hot vegetable or chicken stock

1–2 tbsp dark brown sugar

juice of 1 lemon

2 tbsp finely chopped parsley, chives, dill, or cilantro, or a mixture

1 cup crème fraîche, sour cream, or thick, creamy yogurt

1 Heat the oil in a large pan over low heat and add the onion, garlic, and a pinch of salt. Cook gently, stirring once or twice, for 5 minutes until soft but not browned.

2 Add the beets, potato, and apples to the pan and stew gently for 10 minutes, stirring occasionally.

Pour in the stock, bring to a boil, then cover with a lid and simmer gently for 45 minutes, or until the beets are cooked through.

3 Transfer the mixture to a blender or food processor and pulse in batches until smooth. Season with the sugar, lemon juice, salt, and pepper.

4 Stir the herbs into the cream or yogurt. Ladle the soup into warmed bowls and drop a spoonful of sour cream into the middle.

variation

spiced beets and carrot soup

Make the soup in exactly the same way but substitute 2 large grated carrots or finely chopped for the apples and add 1 star anise, a piece of cinnamon stick, and the finely grated zest and juice of a small orange with the stock. Remove the cinnamon stick and star anise before pulsing the soup.

borscht

During a spell of cold weather, there is little that can be more cheering on the dinner table than a bowl of this startlingly bright, deep pink soup from Eastern Europe.

 50–55 MINS 🍲 1 HR 15 MINS

SERVES 4

3 raw beets, trimmed

2 tbsp butter

1 small carrot, chopped

1 small onion, chopped

½ small white cabbage, cored and shredded

14oz (400g) can chopped tomatoes

3½ cups chicken stock or water, plus more if needed

salt and freshly ground black pepper

½ tsp sugar, or to taste

2–3 sprigs of dill, leaves picked and finely chopped

2–3 sprigs of parsley, leaves picked and finely chopped

juice of ½ lemon

1–2 tbsp red wine vinegar

sour cream, to garnish

1 Bring the beets to a boil in a pan of salted water. Cook for about 30 minutes until tender.

2 Drain the beets. When cool enough to handle, peel off the skin and grate the flesh coarsely.

3 Melt the butter in a large saucepan. Add the carrot and onion and cook, stirring, for 3–5 minutes, until soft but not brown. Add the cabbage, beets, tomatoes, stock, salt, pepper, and sugar, and bring to a boil. Simmer for 45–60 minutes. Add more stock if the soup is too thick.

4 Just before serving, stir in the herbs, lemon juice, and vinegar and taste for seasoning. Pour into warmed bowls and top with a spoonful of sour cream.

pheasant and apple soup

This spicy soup is equally delicious made with other game birds, but if they are small, such as pigeon or partridge, use the whole bird, including the breasts.

 20 MINS 🍲 1 HR 15 MINS PLUS REHEATING ❄ FREEZABLE

SPECIAL EQUIPMENT ▪ blender or food processor

SERVES 4–6

1 small pheasant

1 tbsp butter

1 onion, coarsely chopped

1 small sweet potato, peeled and coarsely chopped

1 small apple, peeled and cubed

2 cups medium-sweet cider or apple juice

1¾ cups chicken stock

2in (5cm) piece of cinnamon stick

1 bay leaf

salt and freshly ground black pepper

⅔ cup half-and-half

4 small sprigs of parsley, to garnish

1 Cut the breasts off the pheasant and reserve to cook for a separate dish. Cut the rest of the bird into pieces using a large, sharp knife or poultry shears.

2 Melt the butter in a saucepan. Add the onion and cook gently, stirring, for 2 minutes until softened but not browned. Add the pheasant and the remaining ingredients, except the half-and-half. Bring to a boil, reduce the heat, cover, and simmer for 1 hour.

3 Remove the pheasant and leave to cool slightly. Discard the bay leaf and cinnamon, then pour the soup into a blender or food processor and pulse until smooth. Return to the pan and stir in the cream. Taste and adjust the seasoning if necessary.

4 Take the pheasant meat off the bones, discarding the skin, and shred it. Add half to the soup. Reheat the soup but do not boil. Ladle into shallow soup plates, place a small pile of the remaining pheasant in the center, and garnish with parsley.

Season's best **beets**

Beets vary in color, shape, and flavor, but the most common are globe-shaped and red, with an intensely colored juice. Available from early summer, but best in autumn. They also bring a luscious color to any dish, like in borscht, a classic Eastern European soup. Their sweetness works well with the aniseed flavors of dill and caraway, with cheeses, nuts, seeds, and carrots.

Beets evolved from wild seabeets in India. Their bulb size varies enormously, depending on the fertility of the soil, the time of sowing, and weather conditions.

Burpee's golden beets An exceptionally tasty beet, this has fine-textured, yellow flesh. It is best when no bigger than a golf ball. Great as a contrast in a red and yellow beet salad.

essentials

varieties available

Various varieties of red, golden, and striped beets.

buy Glossy and fresh leaves; roots should feel hard, with no mold, cuts, or abrasions.

store For up to 2 weeks in a paper bag in the vegetable drawer of the fridge. Remove leafy tops before storing.

cook Grate or thinly slice raw, bake, roast, or boil.

preserve Pickle, make into chutney or wine.

recipe ideas

Beef with beets and spinach p252

Beet relish p328

Beet risotto p298

Borscht p254

Striped beet Grown for looks rather than flavor, this variety is much milder than red beets. The colorful striped flesh looks great in salads. When cooked, the stripes fade and the flesh becomes a uniform pink.

how to cook and peel beets

Raw, peeled beets are delicious grated in salads (particularly when combined with grated carrots). If cooking, do not peel it beforehand or it will "bleed."

1 Cut off the green leaves, leaving short stalks. Don't cut the skin or roots, or the beet will bleed when cooked. Wash well.

2 Boil in lightly salted water until tender, for 30 minutes to 1½ hours, depending on size. Drain, cool, then trim and peel off the skin.

Red beets The firm, juicy flesh of red beets has a uniquely earthy, sweet flavor. Their stalks and leaves can be cooked like spinach, but use fresh as they don't keep as well as the roots.

mushroom and ricotta pies with red bell pepper pesto

For a slightly sweeter taste and a paler color, you can use orange or yellow bell peppers for the pesto.

 25 MINS   45 MINS   ❄ FREEZABLE

SPECIAL EQUIPMENT ▪ blender or food processor

SERVES 4

3 tbsp olive oil

5½oz (150g) button mushrooms, halved

5½oz (150g) mixed wild mushrooms

1 leek, white part only, finely sliced

2 sheets store-bought puff pastry

7oz (200g) ricotta cheese

1 large egg yolk, lightly beaten

For the red bell pepper pesto

2 tbsp olive oil

1 onion, sliced

2 red bell peppers, sliced

2 garlic cloves, crushed

zest and juice of 1 small lemon

salt and freshly ground black pepper

1 Preheat the oven to 400°F (200°C) and line a baking sheet with parchment paper. To make the red pepper pesto, heat the oil in a frying pan over low heat. Add the onion and sweat for a few minutes until translucent. Add the peppers and sweat for another 10–15 minutes until soft. Transfer the mixture to a blender or food processor. Add the garlic and lemon zest and juice, and pulse to a chunky purée. Season and set aside.

2 Heat the 3 tbsp oil in a large heavy-bottomed frying pan over medium heat. Add the mushrooms and leek, and sauté, stirring, for 5 minutes until the mushrooms have browned. Season with salt and pepper and set aside.

3 Cut each pastry sheet into quarters. Using a sharp knife, cut diagonal slashes across the surface of half the pastry squares, taking care not to slice all the way through. Spread the ricotta over the surface of the uncut squares, leaving a ½in (1cm) border of pastry round the edges. Spoon the mushroom and leek mixture evenly over the ricotta, then lay the slit pastry squares evenly over the top of the mushrooms. Pinch and twist together the corners of the pies and brush the tops with the egg yolk.

4 Place the pies on the baking sheet and bake in the oven for 25 minutes until golden brown. Serve with the red pepper pesto and a leafy green salad.

mixed mushroom and walnut tart

Fall is the time when fresh wild mushrooms are in abundance and you will have a choice of varieties such as porcini and meadow mushrooms, and golden chanterelles.

 15 MINS   1 HR   ❄ FREEZABLE

SPECIAL EQUIPMENT ▪ 5 x 14in (12 x 35cm) rectangular fluted tart pan with removable bottom ▪ ceramic baking beans

SERVES 6

9oz (250g) store-bought pie dough

2 large eggs, plus 1 lightly beaten

3–4 tbsp olive oil

5oz (140g) mixed wild mushrooms, coarsely chopped

7oz (200g) crimini mushrooms, coarsely chopped

3 garlic cloves, grated or finely chopped

1¾oz (50g) walnuts, coarsely chopped

salt and freshly ground black pepper

2 handfuls of spinach leaves, coarsely chopped

¾ cup heavy cream

1 Preheat the oven to 400°F (200°C). Roll out the dough on a floured work surface and use to line the tart pan. Trim away the excess, line the tart dough with wax paper, and fill with ceramic baking beans. Bake in the oven for 15–20 minutes until the edges are golden. Remove the beans and paper, brush the bottom of the crust with a little of the beaten egg, and return to the oven for 2–3 minutes to crisp. Remove from the oven and set aside. Reduce the oven temperature to 350°F (180°C).

2 Heat the oil in a large, deep frying pan over low heat. Add the mushrooms, garlic, and walnuts, and season well with salt and pepper. Cook, stirring occasionally, for about 10 minutes until the mushrooms release their juices. Add the spinach and cook, stirring, for another 5 minutes until just wilted. Spoon the mixture into the tart crust.

3 Mix together the cream and eggs and season well. Carefully pour the cream mixture over the mushroom filling. Sprinkle with a pinch of black pepper and bake in the oven for 15–20 minutes until set. Let cool for 10 minutes before releasing from the pan. Serve hot or cold.

stuffed mushrooms with herbs

For those who love the earthy, meaty taste of mushrooms, fall's bountiful selection is showcased in this recipe. Filled with mixed wild mushrooms and walnuts and perfumed with garlic and plenty of herbs, these stuffed mushrooms are unbeatable.

 25–30 MINS   15–20 MINS

SPECIAL EQUIPMENT ■ food processor

SERVES 4

12 large portabello mushrooms, total weight about 1lb 2oz (500g)

3oz (85g) mixed wild mushrooms

12–14 sprigs of tarragon, leaves picked and chopped, plus a few sprigs for garnish

10–12 sprigs of chervil, leaves picked and chopped, plus a few sprigs for garnish

7–10 sprigs of thyme, leaves picked and chopped, plus a few sprigs for garnish

3–4 tbsp grated Parmesan cheese

4 tbsp olive oil

3 garlic cloves, finely chopped

juice of ½ lemon

salt and freshly ground black pepper

⅓ cup heavy cream

3½oz (100g) walnuts, coarsely chopped

1 Pull out the stems from the large mushrooms, leaving the caps whole for stuffing. Wipe the caps with damp paper towels and trim the separated stems (p259). Wipe the fresh wild mushrooms and trim the stems. If using dried mushrooms, soak them in hot water for about 30 minutes until plump. Drain and cut into pieces.

2 Finely chop the wild mushrooms and the large mushroom stems with a sharp knife, or use a food processor, taking care to retain their texture and not to overwork them to a purée. Combine a quarter of the chopped herbs with the Parmesan and set aside.

3 Heat half the oil in a frying pan. Add the chopped mushrooms and garlic with the lemon juice, salt, and pepper. Cook, stirring, for 3–5 minutes, or until all the liquid has

evaporated. Stir in the cream and cook for 1–2 minutes, until slightly thickened. Add the walnuts and the remaining herbs and stir to mix. Remove from the heat and taste for seasoning.

4 Preheat the oven to 350°F (180°C). Lightly oil a baking dish. Season the mushroom caps and place 1–2 spoonfuls of stuffing in each, mounding it well. Place in the baking dish.

5 Sprinkle about 1 tsp Parmesan and herb topping on each mushroom, along with the remaining oil. Bake for 15–20 minutes, or until the mushrooms are tender when pierced with a knife and the filling is very hot. Serve garnished with the reserved herbs.

variation

stuffed mushrooms with basil and pine nuts

Prepare in exactly the same way, but substitute a handful of fresh basil for the tarragon and chervil, and a small handful of flat-leaf parsley for the thyme. Add 1 finely chopped celery stick and 2oz (60g) toasted pine nuts to the mixture at step 3 instead of the walnuts.

Season's best **wild mushrooms**

Mushrooms add varying levels of earthiness and savory flavor, as well as texture, to dishes. Foraging for them should be done only with sound knowledge, as there are also some very poisonous varieties. Most wild mushrooms grow in autumn through to early winter, but a few, such as morels, are spring fungi; many are available commercially. They pair well with garlic and herbs and enhance everything from meat to vegetables.

Mushrooms are the fruiting bodies of soil-borne fungi that live off the nutrients they take from living and dead plants. They flourish throughout the world's temperate zones.

Oyster mushroom Young oyster mushrooms are tender and mildly flavored, with a hint of anise, becoming acrid and tough as they age. Use in stir-frys and Asian-style soups.

Wood blewit It is a white mushroom with blue-tinged, fat stalk and cap, a faint aniseed smell, and a good flavor. Must eat cooked.

They have delicate flesh that needs gentle handling.

how to clean delicate mushrooms

As delicate mushrooms, such as oyster and chanterelle (and morel), damage easily, always use a soft brush rather than a cloth to clean off the dirt.

1 Clean carefully with a soft pastry brush. Any firmly embedded dirt, leaves, or pine needles can be removed with the point of a small knife.

Chanterelle (Girolle) Highly prized chanterelles have smooth, tender flesh and a noticeably nutty, fruity flavor that complements egg dishes, chicken, veal, and pork. They are best sautéed.

They have a slight scent of apricots.

Porcini Also known as Penny Bun, this is one of the most revered of all mushrooms, valued for its smooth, creamy flesh, rich, savory flavor and distinguished shape. Delicious sautéed or added to risotto and pasta dishes.

Horse mushroom White with a domed cap and pink gills, or black when flat, this variety is often found in "fairy rings" in meadows. It has an excellent flavor.

Field mushroom Recognizable by its thick, white flesh and pleasant earthy aroma, the field mushroom has pink or brown gills—never white, as you find in the deadly Amanita. Ideal for grilling and frying.

essentials
varieties available

Many varieties of edible fungi, the most common being oyster, porcini, chanterelle, horse, field, and wood blewit. Morels are also highly prized in spring.

buy To forage, go with a guide. To purchase, avoid if shriveled or wet. Choose firm, fresh-looking ones that smell earthy and "mushroomy."

store Fresh mushrooms can be kept in the fridge in a closed paper bag for up to 1 week.

cook Mushrooms suit just about any type of cooking. Fry, bake, broil, barbecue, sauté, or steam. They are also delicious in soups, stews, casseroles, dips, and in pasta and rice dishes.

preserve Preserve in oil; pickle; make into ketchup; dry.

recipe ideas

Dried mushrooms p352

Mixed mushroom and walnut tart p256

Mixed mushroom soup p270

how to clean hardy mushrooms

Carefully clean but do not wash hardy mushrooms, such as porcini, blewits, and field mushrooms, because this makes them waterlogged, reducing their flavor. Most do not need peeling unless large and open, like large field mushrooms.

1 Wipe off any mud or dry earth with a damp cloth or paper towels. The pores of old porcinis are best removed.

2 Gently scrape or peel the stem with a knife, if necessary, to remove any remaining dirt, and trim the end.

roast pumpkin and ricotta crostini

No vegetable is more closely linked with fall than the pumpkin, with its mellow golden flesh. Here its sweetness is set against the sharper flavor of ricotta cheese.

 20 MINS   50 MINS

MAKES 16

1lb 2oz (500g) pumpkin, peeled, seeded, and cut into chunks

2 tbsp olive oil

2 garlic cloves, crushed

grated zest and juice of 1 lemon

2 sprigs of rosemary, leaves picked and chopped

7oz (200g) ricotta cheese

4 sprigs of lemon-scented thyme, leaves picked

For the crostini

2 tbsp olive oil

16 slices of crusty baguette

salt and freshly ground black pepper

1 garlic clove, peeled but left whole

1 Preheat the oven to 400°F (200°C). To make the crostini, pour the oil over the bottom of a baking sheet, then gently press the bread into the oil on both sides. Season with salt and pepper. Bake for 13–15 minutes until golden brown. Remove from the oven and lightly rub each slice with the garlic. Set the crostini aside on a wire rack to cool, but do not turn off the oven.

2 Put the pumpkin on a baking sheet and toss with the oil, garlic, lemon zest, and rosemary. Season with salt and pepper, then roast for about 35 minutes until tender and golden. Let cool slightly.

3 In a bowl, combine the ricotta, thyme, and a little lemon juice. Spoon a little of the ricotta mixture onto each of the crostini and top with roasted pumpkin, squeezing it a little with your fingers as you go. Arrange on a large serving dish or platter and serve.

variation

roast squash and blue cheese crostini

Prepare in the same way, but use an acorn squash instead of pumpkin and flavor with 6 large chopped sage leaves instead of the rosemary before roasting. At step 3, use 3½oz (100g) each of ricotta and soft blue cheese, instead of all ricotta, and 2 tbsp chopped parsley instead of thyme.

waldorf chicken salad

A contemporary take on a classic, with yogurt in the dressing for added lightness. This salad is a great way to use up leftover roast chicken.

 25–30 MINS PLUS CHILLING   25–35 MINS

SERVES 6

4 celery stalks, with leaves if possible

1 onion, quartered

1 carrot, quartered

10–12 black peppercorns

1 bouquet garni, made with 5–6 sprigs of parsley, 2–3 sprigs of thyme, and 1 bay leaf

salt and freshly ground black pepper

4 skinless, boneless chicken breasts, total weight about 1lb 10oz (750g)

4½oz (125g) walnuts

1lb 2oz (500g) tart, crisp apples

juice of 1 lemon

⅔ cup natural yogurt

⅔ cup mayonnaise

1 Trim the tops from the celery and put the trimmings in a wide pan with the onion, carrot, peppercorns, bouquet garni, and salt. Bring to a boil and simmer for 10–15 minutes. Add the chicken and simmer for 10–12 minutes, turning once, until the juices run clear when the meat is pierced at its thickest point.

2 Remove the pan from the heat and cool the chicken in the poaching liquid for 10–15 minutes, then transfer to paper towels to drain. With your fingers, pull the chicken into slivers about 2in (5cm) long—the meat will be juicier this way than it would be if you cut it.

3 Preheat the oven to 350°F (180°C). Spread the walnut pieces on a baking sheet and bake for 5–8 minutes until crisp, stirring occasionally so that they toast evenly. Meanwhile, slice the celery stalks.

4 Cut the top and bottom ends from the apples. Halve and core them, then cube the flesh. Put in a large bowl, pour the lemon juice over, and toss to coat. Add the chicken, celery, yogurt, mayonnaise, and two-thirds of the walnuts to the apple. Season and stir until combined, then chill for 1 hour.

5 Coarsely chop the remaining walnuts. Spoon the salad into individual plates and sprinkle with the chopped nuts.

vegetable tempura with chile dipping sauce

This dish typifies the clean, fresh flavors of Japanese food. The secret to successful tempura is to make the batter at the last minute and to ensure that the water is really cold.

 15 MINS 15 MINS

SERVES 4

2 eggplants, slice into thin rounds

2–3 zucchini, cut into batons

2 red bell peppers, seeded and coarsely chopped

2 cups vegetable oil or sunflower oil, for frying

¾ cup all-purpose flour

1 tbsp cornstarch

¾ cup ice water

For the chile dipping sauce

2 tbsp rice wine vinegar

2 tbsp light soy sauce

1 tbsp olive oil

1 tbsp granulated sugar

1 garlic clove, grated or finely chopped

2 hot red chiles, seeded and finely chopped

salt and freshly ground black pepper

1 First, make the chile dipping sauce. Whisk together all the ingredients, seasoning generously with salt and pepper.

2 Once you have all the vegetables prepared, pour the oil into a wok and heat until very hot.

3 Meanwhile, make the batter. Whisk together the flour, cornstarch, and ice water. Don't overbeat; it doesn't matter if the batter is a little lumpy.

4 Drop a little of the batter into the oil to test whether it is hot enough— the batter should sizzle right away and become crisp. Dip the vegetable pieces one by one into the batter and shake away the excess. Carefully add to the oil, a few at a time, and fry for 2–3 minutes until golden and crispy. Remove with a slotted spoon and keep warm on a plate lined with paper towels until all the vegetable pieces are cooked. Serve immediately with the chile dipping sauce.

crisp sweet potato with zucchini and chive mascarpone

For this recipe, buy an orange-fleshed variety of sweet potato, both for the attractive color and because the flesh is moister and creamier than that of the white-fleshed type.

 15 MINS 25 MINS

SERVES 4

1lb 5oz (600g) sweet potato, peeled and slice into 8 even disks

2 tbsp olive oil, plus extra for drizzling

salt and freshly ground black pepper

1 zucchini, about 5½oz (150g)

juice of ½ lemon

5½oz (150g) mascarpone

1 tbsp snipped chives, plus extra to garnish

1 Preheat the oven to 400°F (200°C). Put the sweet potato in a bowl. Add the oil and season with salt and pepper. Toss until the sweet potato is well coated. Transfer to a baking sheet and roast for about 25 minutes until golden brown and tender when pierced with a skewer. Set aside to cool.

2 Trim both ends off the zucchini, then shave lengthwise into thin ribbons using a vegetable peeler or a mandoline. Put in a bowl with the lemon juice and season with salt and pepper. Toss gently to coat thoroughly.

3 Put the mascarpone in a separate bowl, add the snipped chives, and stir in.

4 To serve, put a disk of sweet potato in the center of each of 4 serving plates. Divide the zucchini evenly between each serving, placing it on top of the sweet potato disks. Arrange another disk on the zucchini, then spoon on some chive mascarpone. Garnish each serving with 2 chive leaves and drizzle with a little olive oil. Serve immediately.

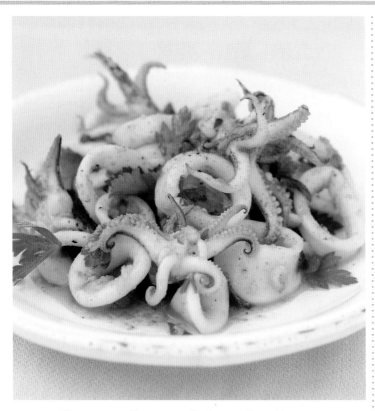

grilled squid salad

For this delicious and quick recipe, make sure you heat the grill pan until it is searingly hot. The squid is dressed with lemon, garlic, and chile to give this salad lots of impact.

 15 MINS　　 **2 MINS**

SERVES 4

1lb 5oz (600g) small squid, gutted and cleaned (opposite)

¼ cup olive oil

2 small hot red chiles, seeded and finely chopped

1 garlic clove, crushed

grated zest and juice of 1 lemon

salt and freshly ground black pepper

For the arugula salad

3½oz (100g) arugula leaves

large handful of flat-leaf parsley, coarsely chopped

2 tbsp olive oil

juice of ½ lemon

lemon wedges, to serve

1 Put the tentacles and bodies (tubes and wings attached) in a bowl with the oil, chiles, garlic, and lemon zest and juice. Season with salt and pepper.

2 Heat a ridged grill pan until hot. Grill the squid bodies and tentacles over high heat for 1–2 minutes, turning halfway through cooking, until lightly charred on all sides. Remove to a cutting board. Cut the tentacle clusters in half crosswise and put in a bowl. Slice the tubes into ⅛in (3mm) rings, slicing through the wings as you go, and put in the bowl with the tentacles.

3 Add the salad ingredients to the bowl and toss gently. Serve immediately with lemon wedges.

marinated squid salad

Squid is delicious and tender if cooked very briefly—too long and it becomes leathery. Marinating it in a garlic dressing enhances its sweet, slightly fishy flavor.

 15 MINS PLUS MARINATING　　 **5 MINS**

SERVES 4

10oz (300g) small squid, gutted and cleaned (opposite)

7 tbsp olive oil

salt and freshly ground black pepper

2 tbsp white wine vinegar

3 garlic cloves, crushed

1 tsp paprika

handful of flat-leaf parsley, finely chopped

1 Trim the squid tentacles but leave whole. Cut the bodies into rings. Brush the squid with a little of the oil and season well with salt and pepper.

2 Heat 1 tbsp of the oil in a frying pan, add the squid, and cook over medium heat, stirring constantly, for 2–3 minutes, or until it is cooked. Remove from the heat and transfer to a serving bowl.

3 Mix the remaining oil with the vinegar, garlic, paprika, and parsley, then season with salt and pepper. Pour over the squid, combine well, and leave to marinate for at least 30 minutes. Serve with fresh crusty bread and a green salad.

variation

marinated mushroom salad

Prepare in the same way, but use 10oz (300g) mixed wild mushrooms, trimmed and cleaned but left whole unless very large, instead of squid. No need to brush with oil, just season, then sauté in 3 tbsp olive oil for 2–3 minutes until tender. Pour the contents of the pan into a salad bowl. Mix the dressing in the same way but use 2 tbsp white balsamic vinegar instead of white wine vinegar, 2 crushed garlic cloves instead of 3, and 1 tsp smoked paprika instead of sweet paprika. Add the parsley and seasoning as before and leave to marinate for at least 30 minutes before serving.

french country soup

A mixed vegetable potage (soup) like this is traditional French family fare. It is ladled out of a tureen into wide shallow bowls as a starter all over the country.

 15 MINS　　 **45 MINS**

SPECIAL EQUIPMENT ▪ blender

SERVES 4

1 tbsp sunflower or peanut oil

2 tbsp butter

3 large leeks, cleaned and chopped

1 large floury potato, peeled and coarsely cubed

2 large carrots, chopped

2½ cups vegetable or chicken stock

2 bay leaves

sea salt and freshly ground black pepper

1 Put the oil and half the butter in a large sauté pan over very moderate heat. Add the leeks, potato, and carrots and cook, stirring frequently, for 5 minutes. Reduce the heat a little, add the stock and bay leaves, then season lightly with sea salt and pepper. Cover and cook gently, stirring occasionally, for 30 minutes, or until the vegetables are very soft.

2 Let cool for several minutes, then remove the bay leaves. Transfer the soup to a blender and pulse until smooth. Strain back into the pan through a sieve, using the back of a wooden spoon to push through as much as possible. Pour ½ cup hot water through the sieve to extract as much as you can from the vegetables.

3 Reheat gently, stirring frequently. Taste and adjust the seasoning, then stir in the remaining butter and serve very hot.

Season's best **squid**

The common squid, nicknamed "ink fish," is the best known. It is particularly good in autumn, although you will find it through summer and into winter. Its size ranges from ³⁄₄in (2cm) to the much larger 31–35in (80–90cm) and this determines the cooking method. The larger the squid, the more time it will need in the pot. Ideal flavor pairings include chile, olive oil, lemon juice, garlic, spring onions, and mayonnaise.

The mottled skin is best peeled off and reserved for stock, as it toughens and shrinks around the flesh when cooked.

The tough, wing-like fins are best either finely sliced and stir-fried, or reserved to flavor stock.

Common squid The "ink fish" has gained a reputation for being tough and chewy, but is only ever so if it is overcooked. In a hot pan, the meat takes no time at all. At its best, it tastes tender and mellow, with a subtle, distinctive flavor.

essentials
varieties available

Baby squid and larger specimens. Available cleaned and frozen.

buy If buying whole, they should be sweet-smelling and slippery. Sometimes sold neatly cleaned and also sliced in rings.

store Wrap in a sealable plastic bag in the fridge. Eat on the day of purchase.

cook Fry, braise, grill, poach, or casserole whole, cut in rectangles or rings. Whole tubes, flattened out into a sheet and scored, taste excellent barbecued. The tube can also be stuffed with a savory bread crumb mix, couscous, quinoa, or rice.

recipe ideas

Grilled squid salad p262

Marinated squid salad p262

Roasted squid and potato with spiced cilantro pesto p288

Spiced seafood salad p106

Squid stew p292

how to clean and prepare squid

The edible parts of squid are the tube, tentacles, and wings, and they are eaten all over the world. Over high heat, they cook in a minute or two, becoming translucent; overcooked, they become rubbery.

1 Hold the mantle (body) in one hand and gently pull the tentacles away from it to separate them. The eyes, some viscera, and beak (mouthpiece) will come away with the head.

2 Cut the tentacles with a small knife just below the eyes to separate the viscera. Trim the two long arms level with the remaining tentacles. Discard the head, beak, eyes, and viscera.

3 Locate the hard quill attached to the inside of the mantle and pull it away. Pinch the two fins (wings) together and pull away, with the purple membrane. Pull the membrane from the wings and discard.

roast pumpkin, chile, and ginger dip

In addition to pumpkin, there is a wide variety of squash at this time of year. Acorn, buttercup, and turban squashes would be equally good here.

 20 MINS 45 MINS

SPECIAL EQUIPMENT ▪ blender or food processor

SERVES 4

1lb 2oz (500g) pumpkin or butternut squash, peeled, and cut into chunks

2 tbsp olive oil

2 garlic cloves, crushed whole with the back of a knife

2 tsp grated or finely chopped fresh ginger

salt and freshly ground black pepper

½ long red chile, seeded and thinly sliced

2 sprigs of flat-leaf parsley, leaves only, plus extra for garnish

grated zest and juice of ½ lemon

¼ cup Greek-style yogurt

drizzle of extra virgin olive oil (optional)

pinch of paprika

slices of broiled sourdough bread, to serve

broiled pancetta or prosciutto, to serve

1 Preheat the oven to 400°F (200°C). Put the pumpkin on a baking sheet and toss with the olive oil, garlic, and ginger. Season with salt and pepper. Roast for about 30 minutes until tender and golden. Set aside.

2 Transfer the cooled pumpkin to a blender or food processor and add the chile, parsley, and lemon zest and juice. Pulse to a chunky purée and season to taste.

3 Put the pumpkin purée and the yogurt in a bowl and mix thoroughly. Season if needed, then spoon into a serving bowl. Top with a drizzle of extra virgin olive oil (if desired). Garnish with extra parsley and a sprinkle of paprika, and serve on broiled sourdough bread, with broiled pancetta or prosciutto over the top.

beet-topped mini rye breads

The combination of dark rye bread and beet gives an East European flavor here. Feta or goat cheese would make good substitutes for the Dolcelatte, if you prefer.

 15 MINS

SERVES 8-10

8 thin slices rye bread or pumpernickel

4½oz (125g) Dolcelatte cheese, cubed

10oz (300g) beet, cooked, peeled (p255), and finely cubed

2-3 tbsp creamed horseradish

1 Cut the rye bread into small squares—about 6 squares per slice, depending on how big the slices are.

2 Top each bread square with a fine slice of Dolcelatte cheese, a teaspoonful of cubed beet, and a tiny amount of creamed horseradish. Arrange on platters and serve.

variation

pastrami and beets on rye

Prepare the bread in the same way. Purée the beet in a blender or food processor and beat in ½ cup ricotta cheese. Season and beat in 2 tbsp chopped fresh dill (or 1 tsp dried) and 1 tsp white wine vinegar. Cut 4 slices of pastrami or salt beef into 12 neat pieces. Put a small dollop of the creamed beets on each of the bread squares and top with a piece of beef. Add a small dollop of horseradish cream and a tiny sprinkling of dill to finish.

smoked mackerel pâté

Sometimes the simplest dishes are among the most delicious. Smoked mackerel pâté belongs in this category—pair it with really good brown bread and you can't go wrong.

 5 MINS

SPECIAL EQUIPMENT ■ blender or food processor ■ ramekins

SERVES 4

3-4 smoked mackerel fillets, about 10oz (300g) total weight, skinned

10oz (300g) cream cheese

juice of 1-2 lemons, plus 1 lemon, cut into wedges

freshly ground black pepper

1-2 tbsp Greek-style yogurt

thinly sliced and toasted brown bread

1 Using your hands, break up the mackerel into chunks and add to a blender or food processor. Pulse until broken up completely.

2 Spoon in the cream cheese and pulse again until a smooth paste forms. Add the lemon juice a little at a time, pulsing between each addition. Taste as you go, adding more lemon as required. Season with plenty of black pepper and pulse again.

3 Add the yogurt and pulse again until the pâté is completely smooth. Spoon into a serving dish or 4 individual ramekins. Serve with thinly sliced and toasted brown bread and the lemon wedges.

variation

potted fresh mackerel

Broil 4 mackerel fillets, skin-side up, for 5 minutes until cooked. Skin, then flake the fish. Melt 8 tbsp unsalted butter. Pulse the mackerel with 1 crushed garlic clove, 5½oz (150g) of cream cheese, half the melted butter, and ¼ tsp each of ground mace and cayenne pepper. Flavor with lemon juice and seasoning to taste. Pack in 4 small ramekins or one slightly larger pot and pour the rest of the melted butter over. Chill until firm. Serve as before.

broiled bell pepper-stuffed mussels

This light dish is perfect for a special romantic meal, but so delicious that you'll want to make it everyday food. To make it even quicker to prepare, use roasted bell peppers from a jar.

 25-30 MINS 1-2 MINS

SPECIAL EQUIPMENT ■ blender or food processor

SERVES 4

small bunch of flat-leaf parsley

1 large red bell pepper

2 slices of white bread

2 garlic cloves, peeled

2 tbsp olive oil

salt and freshly ground black pepper

1 cup dry white wine

24 large mussels, about 1lb 10oz (750g), cleaned (discard any that do not close when tapped) (p364)

lemon wedges, to serve

1 Strip the parsley leaves from the stems and set them aside separately from each other.

2 Heat the broiler. Set the red bell pepper on a rack about 4in (10cm) from the heat and broil, turning, for 10-12 minutes, until black all over. Seal in a plastic bag and let cool, then remove the skin, scrape out the seeds and ribs, and cut the flesh into strips.

3 Trim the crusts from the bread and discard them. Cut the bread into cubes and pulse them in a blender or food processor to form crumbs. Add the parsley leaves, reserving a few for garnishing, and the garlic, oil, and red bell pepper. Pulse to a purée and season with salt and pepper.

4 Put the wine and parsley stems into a large saucepan. Bring to a boil and simmer for 2 minutes, then add the mussels.

5 Cover and cook over high heat, stirring once, for 2-3 minutes until the mussels open. Transfer to a large bowl with a slotted spoon. Discard any that have not opened.

6 Heat the broiler. Remove the top shell from each mussel and discard the rubbery ring surrounding the meat.

7 Spoon a little topping onto each mussel. Place the mussels in their bottom shells in a baking dish. Broil for 1-2 minutes until very hot and the topping is heated through. Serve with lemon wedges and a sprinkling of parsley leaves.

rich fish soup

The subtle combinations of meaty monkfish, delicate haddock, aniseed fennel, and the light scent of saffron marry well. You could add some mussels, if you like.

 15 MINS   1 HR   ❄ FREEZABLE

SPECIAL EQUIPMENT ▪ blender or food processor

SERVES 4-6

1 tbsp olive oil

1 onion, finely chopped

salt and freshly ground black pepper

sprig of thyme

3 garlic cloves, finely chopped

1 fennel bulb, trimmed and finely chopped, the fronds reserved to garnish (optional)

1 red chile, seeded and finely chopped

1 cup dry white wine

2 x 14oz (400g) cans chopped tomatoes

3 cups hot light vegetable stock

pinch of saffron threads

7oz (200g) monkfish, cut into bite-sized pieces

7oz (200g) haddock loin, cut into bite-sized pieces

1 Heat the oil in a large heavy-bottomed pan over medium heat, add the onion, and cook for 3–4 minutes until soft. Season with salt and pepper and toss in the thyme. Add the garlic and fennel, and cook on low heat for another 5 minutes until the fennel begins to soften.

2 Stir in the chile and cook for 1 minute, then increase the heat, add the wine, let it bubble for a minute, then pour in the canned tomatoes and stock. Add the saffron, bring to a boil, then reduce to simmer and cook gently, partially covered with a lid, for about 45 minutes. Make sure that the sauce doesn't dry out, adding a little hot water if needed.

3 Pour the soup into a blender or food processor and pulse until smooth, then pour into a clean pan. Add a little hot water (you will probably need about 1¼ cups in total) and simmer gently. Taste and season as needed, add the fish, put the lid back on, and cook on low heat for 6–10 minutes, or until the fish is opaque and cooked through. Ladle into warmed bowls and serve with white crusty bread. Garnish with chopped fennel fronds, if desired.

cajun sweet potato and bean soup

This soup makes a substantial meal on its own. It is important to rinse canned beans before cooking with them.

 10 MINS   1 HR–1 HR 30 MINS   ❄ FREEZABLE

SPECIAL EQUIPMENT ▪ blender or food processor

SERVES 4-6

1 tbsp olive oil

1 onion, finely chopped

salt and freshly ground black pepper

3 garlic cloves, finely chopped

2 celery stalks, finely chopped

7oz (200g) Spanish-style chorizo, cubed

pinch of dried chile flakes

a few sprigs of thyme

2 sweet potatoes, peeled and cubed

2 yellow bell peppers, seeded and coarsely chopped

2 x 14oz cans adzuki or black beans, drained

14oz can kidney beans, drained

3 cups hot vegetable stock

1 Heat the oil in a large heavy-bottomed pan over medium heat, add the onion, and cook for 3–4 minutes until soft. Season with salt and pepper, stir in the garlic and celery, and cook for another 10 minutes until the celery is soft. Stir in the chorizo, chile, and thyme, and cook for 1 minute. Add the sweet potatoes and cook for a few minutes, then add the peppers and cook gently for about 5 minutes.

2 Add the adzuki and kidney beans, add a little of the stock, increase the heat, and let the mixture simmer. Add the remaining stock, bring to a boil, then reduce to simmer, partially cover with a lid, and cook for 45–60 minutes. Check occasionally that it's not drying out, adding a little hot water if needed.

3 Pour the soup into a blender or food processor and pulse until it is well combined but still retains some texture, then pour back into the pan. Add a ladleful of hot water if it is too thick. Heat through, taste and season as needed, then ladle into warmed bowls and serve with tortilla bread.

globe artichoke soup

Nutmeg and saffron bring out the delicate, nutty taste of the artichoke, while the bacon adds a smoky flavor.

 20 MINS   20 MINS

SPECIAL EQUIPMENT ▪ blender or food processor

SERVES 4

1 tbsp olive oil

2 tbsp butter

½ Spanish onion, finely chopped

1 shallot, finely chopped

1 garlic clove, crushed

¼ tsp grated nutmeg

a few saffron strands

1¾lb (800g) artichoke hearts, chopped

salt and freshly ground black pepper

½ cup half-and-half

4 thin smoked slices of bacon

handful of spinach leaves, chopped

1 Heat the oil and butter in a pan over medium heat, add the onion, shallot, garlic, nutmeg, and saffron, and stir for 3 minutes. Add the artichoke hearts and season. Cook, stirring, for 3 minutes. Pour 3½ cups hot water into the pan and stir to mix. Bring to simmer, reduce the heat, cover, and simmer for about 10 minutes, or until the vegetables are tender. Let cool.

2 Pour the soup into a blender or food processor and pulse until smooth, then pour back into the pan. Reheat gently. Heat the cream until simmering in a separate pan.

3 Fry the bacon in a pan over medium heat until crisp, then drain on paper towels. Wilt the spinach in the same pan. Stir the cream into the soup, adjust seasoning, then ladle into bowls, stir in the spinach, and float a strip of bacon in the middle of each bowl. Serve immediately.

pistou soup

Pistou sauce is the Provençal version of Italian pesto but does not contain any pine nuts. It is used in this famous, rustic soup with beans and zucchini, but can also be tossed with pasta or smeared on slices of bread.

 30 MINS 1 HR 30 MINS

SERVES 4

1 small ham hock, or a thick piece of smoked bacon, about 2½oz (75g)

14oz can white beans, such as cannellini, drained and rinsed

6oz can borlotti or pinto beans, drained and rinsed

4½oz (125g) green beans, sliced

1 floury potato, peeled and cubed

1 large tomato, skinned, seeded (p197), and chopped

2 zucchini, chopped

salt and freshly ground black pepper

1¾oz (50g) small macaroni

For the pistou

1 large garlic clove, peeled

coarse sea salt and freshly ground black pepper

small handful of basil leaves

1 small tomato, skinned, seeded (p197), and chopped

½oz(15g) mimolette cheese or mature Cheddar cheese, grated

1½ tbsp olive oil

1 To make the pistou, pound the garlic in a mortar with a pestle, then add a little sea salt and the basil and pound to a paste. Add the tomato and continue pounding and mixing until you have a thick sauce. Add the pepper, cheese, and oil, mix well, and adjust the seasoning.

2 For the soup, put 7 cups cold water in a large pan. Add the ham hock. Bring to simmer, then partly cover with a lid and let bubble gently for 30 minutes, skimming occasionally.

3 Add the canned beans and all the vegetables to the ham hock pan. Season lightly. Return to simmer, then partly cover and let it bubble gently for 1 hour, skimming occasionally.

4 Remove the ham hock and shred the meat. Lift half of the ingredients out of the pan, mash with a fork, then return to the soup with the ham. Add the macaroni and cook until just tender. Stir in the pistou and serve.

quail's eggs with celery salt

This is a classic pairing of ingredients and they are very tasty, too. Quail's eggs have a higher proportion of yolk to white than hen's eggs and are slightly stronger in flavor.

 10 MINS   **15 MINS**

SPECIAL EQUIPMENT ▪ food processor

SERVES 4

2 celery stalks, finely chopped

salt

12 fresh quail's eggs or buy ready-
prepared ones

1 Preheat the oven to 400°F (200°C). To make the celery salt, spread out the celery over a baking sheet and sprinkle a couple of pinches of salt over it. Stir around a little, then roast in the oven for 5–8 minutes until crisp and dry. Put the celery into a food processor and pulse until fine.

2 To boil the eggs (if they are not ready-prepared), place them in a pan of gently boiling water, then simmer for 2½ minutes. Drain, then rinse in cold water until cool. Carefully peel away the egg shells. Sit the quail's eggs on a serving plate, and sprinkle with a little salt. Transfer the celery salt to a small bowl or plate and serve alongside the eggs for dipping.

mulligatawny

An Anglo-Indian soup from colonial days, mulligatawny has many variations. For extra heat, pop a split red chile (with or without its seeds) in the pan when you pour over the stock.

 20 MINS   **45 MINS** ❄ **FREEZABLE**

SPECIAL EQUIPMENT ▪ blender or food processor

SERVES 4

2 tbsp butter

1 large onion, chopped

2in (5cm) fresh ginger, peeled
and finely chopped

2 garlic cloves, finely chopped

1 tart apple, peeled and cubed

1 carrot, sliced

1 celery stalk, sliced

1 heaped tbsp mild curry powder

1 tbsp gram flour or all-purpose flour

4 tomatoes, coarsely chopped

2 tsp tomato paste

2 cups hot chicken stock

2 bay leaves

salt and freshly ground black pepper

¾ cup coconut milk or
half-and-half

6oz (175g) cooked chicken
meat, shredded

juice of ½ lime

2 tbsp chopped cilantro

1 Melt the butter in a large pan over low heat, add the onion, ginger, and garlic and cook for 10 minutes until soft but not colored. Add the apple, carrot, and celery, cover with a lid, and continue cooking for 5 minutes.

2 Stir in the curry powder and fry for 1 minute, stirring all the time. Sprinkle in the gram or all-purpose flour and cook for another 20 seconds.

3 Add the tomatoes and tomato paste, followed by the chicken stock. Add the bay leaves and season with salt and pepper. Bring to a boil, stirring, then reduce the heat and simmer, half-covered, for 20 minutes.

4 Remove the bay leaves, then pour the soup into a blender or food processor and pulse until smooth. Sieve the soup to remove any fibers and skin. Reheat, stir in the coconut milk or half-and-half, and add the shredded chicken. Sharpen with a squeeze of lime and add the chopped cilantro.

rosehip soup

Rosehip soup is very popular in Scandinavia, where it is served both chilled and hot. Fresh rosehips are best, but you can also make it with presoaked dried rosehips.

 30 MINS PLUS CHILLING   **1 HR**

SERVES 4

1lb 2oz (500g) ripe rosehips

1 vanilla bean, split lengthwise

granulated sugar, to taste

½ cup heavy cream

3 tbsp natural yogurt

2 tbsp lemon juice

1¾oz (50g) slivered almonds, toasted
and sprinkled with sugar

amaretti cookies, to serve (optional)

1 Put the rosehips in a large saucepan and pour in boiling water to cover generously. Add the vanilla bean. Simmer over low heat for 20–30 minutes until soft. Strain over a bowl, but reserve and set aside the cooking liquid as well as the vanilla bean.

2 Place the sieve with the rosehips over a second bowl. Press out the rosehips to extract a puree and set aside. Pour what's left in the sieve into the saucepan. Add the reserved cooking liquid and the vanilla bean. Return to simmer and cook for 20 minutes. Strain enough of the mixture into the reserved puree to produce a smooth soup. Stir in sugar to taste. Chill for 1 hour, or until ready to serve.

3 Just before serving, whisk the cream and yogurt together and sweeten to taste. Stir the lemon juice into the chilled soup and pour or spoon into glass bowls. Add a sprinkling of almonds and a dollop of whisked cream, and serve chilled with some amaretti cookies alongside, if desired.

Season's best **celery**

From a wild, bitter plant grown in marshy areas on the seashore to a widely cultivated mild, sweet, crunchy vegetable, the humble celery has certainly come a long way. At its best in autumn through winter, its texture and distinctive flavor make it a popular choice for many dishes. It pairs well with all cheeses, nuts, apples, oranges, lentils, seafood, cabbages, and roots.

Celery can be grown in all but extreme climates. It may be green or pale with yellow leaves (if a self-blanching variety, or if it has been earthed up to tenderize the stalks).

essentials

varieties available

Green celery and white, blanched celery; also sold as the trimmed hearts only.

buy The stalks should be stiff, and the leaves fresh looking.

store Celery can be kept for up to 10 days in a perforated plastic bag in the vegetable drawer of the fridge. Wrap in damp paper towels, if necessary, to keep it from drying out.

cook Enjoy raw, or steam, braise, bake in a gratin, sauté, stir-fry, or add to stuffings.

preserve Add to chutneys, pickles, and relishes; can be preserved in oil.

recipe ideas

Celery and apple salad with blue cheese dressing p471

Celery and celery root soup p428

Provençal vegetable soup p270

Quail's eggs with celery salt p268

Roasted celery with orange and walnuts p470

Green celery A kitchen staple, green celery is delicious both raw and cooked. With a strong flavor, firm, crisp stalks, and a creamy, nutty heart, it is now the most favored celery.

The stalks are virtually stringless, which makes them particularly palatable.

Giant Pascal This is another popular variety, sold green or blanched. It has noticeably thick, fleshy, succulent stalks with a nutty flavor.

how to prepare celery

When preparing celery stalks for eating raw with cheese at the end of a meal, simply prepare to step 2 and then place in a glass to serve at table. When preparing to cook, they need trimming, strings removing, then either cutting in julienne or chopping.

1 Place the head of celery on a board and cut off the green leaves in one go. Cut off the root end too. Use the leaves for garnish or in stock.

2 Separate into stalks and wash well, then dry. Peel off the strings using a vegetable peeler or a sharp paring knife.

3 Using a chef's knife, cut the sticks into short lengths, then into fine strips (julienne), or chop across the sticks into slices.

provençal vegetable soup

If you have any fresh tomatoes left over early in the fall use them instead of the canned variety. For added flavor, stir in some basil pesto just before serving.

 15 MINS 1 HR ❄ FREEZABLE

SERVES 4-6

1 tbsp olive oil

1 onion, finely chopped

salt and freshly ground black pepper

3 garlic cloves, finely chopped

2 celery stalks, finely chopped

2 carrots, coarsely chopped

sprig of tarragon, leaves finely chopped

2 sprigs of rosemary

14oz (400g) can tomatoes, blended until smooth

3 cups hot vegetable stock

3 potatoes, peeled and chopped into bite-sized pieces

11oz (325g) haricot vert or thin green beans, trimmed and chopped into bite-sized pieces

1oz (30g) Parmesan cheese, grated (optional)

1 Heat the oil in a large heavy-bottomed pan over medium heat, add the onion, and cook for 3–4 minutes until soft. Season with salt and pepper, then stir in the garlic and celery and cook for another 5 minutes, or until the celery is soft.

2 Stir in the carrots, tarragon, and rosemary and cook for a minute, then add in the pureed tomatoes and a little stock, and bring to a boil. Add the remaining stock and return to a boil, then reduce to simmer, partially cover with a lid, and cook gently for about 45 minutes. If more liquid is needed, add a little hot water. Add the potatoes for the last 15 minutes of cooking.

3 When the potatoes are soft, add the beans and cook for another 10 minutes, or until they are cooked but firm to the bite. Taste and season, remove the rosemary, and ladle into warmed large shallow bowls. Sprinkle on the Parmesan, if desired, and serve with some crusty French bread.

mixed mushroom soup

This simple soup recipe with onion, garlic, and parsley brings out the flavor of mixed wild mushrooms beautifully. It is even more delicious when served with sour cream.

 15 MINS 1 HR ❄ FREEZABLE

SERVES 4

5 tbsp unsalted butter

3½oz (100g) onion, finely chopped

1 garlic clove, finely chopped

2 tbsp chopped flat-leaf parsley

8oz (225g) mixed wild mushrooms, cubed

¼ cup milk

salt and freshly ground black pepper

pinch of grated nutmeg

¼ cup all-purpose flour

4 cups hot vegetable or chicken stock

¼ cup sour cream (optional)

1 Heat half the butter in a heavy-bottomed pan over medium heat, add the onion, garlic, and parsley, and cook for 3–4 minutes unil soft. Add the mushrooms and cook for another 3 minutes. Pour in the milk and season with salt and nutmeg. Cook for a few more minutes and set aside.

2 In another pan, melt the remaining butter. Remove the pan from the heat and beat in the flour. Return the pan to low heat and cook until the mixture deepens in color. Remove the pan from the heat once more and add the stock gradually by the ladleful. Stir constantly to prevent lumps from forming and return the pan to low heat.

3 When all the stock has been combined with the flour, add the mushroom mixture and the juices. Bring to a boil and simmer for 15–20 minutes. Season with salt and pepper to taste. Spoon 1 tbsp of sour cream into each bowl, if desired, and serve.

cucumber and walnut soup

This is delicious in the fall, when it will use up any particularly mature cucumbers, although you may need to remove any hard seeds and bitter skin.

 10–15 MINS PLUS CHILLING

SERVES 4-6

2 cucumbers, about 1lb 9oz (700g) in total

2¼ cups Greek-style or thick and creamy yogurt

1 garlic clove

coarse sea salt and freshly ground black pepper

1¾oz (50g) walnuts, plus more chopped walnuts for garnish

handful of mint, leaves finely chopped

2 tbsp fresh lemon juice

extra virgin olive oil, to serve

1 Trim the ends from the cucumbers, peel, cut in half lengthwise, scoop out the seeds with a teaspoon, and finely cube the flesh.

2 In a medium bowl, or large liquid measuring cup, mix together the yogurt and 1 cup cold water until combined. Pound the garlic with a large pinch of coarse sea salt in a mortar until smooth. Scrape it into the yogurt. Pound the walnuts in the garlicky mortar to a coarse paste; but do not crush them too fine. Add to the yogurt mixture with the cucumber, mint, lemon juice, and a good grinding of black pepper, and stir well. Taste for seasoning.

3 Cover and chill in the fridge for at least 30 minutes. Pour into bowls and garnish with a drizzle of oil and a few chopped walnuts.

variation

cucumber, almond, and dill soup

Prepare in the same way, but mix the cucumber with the yogurt blended with 1 cup milk instead of water. Substitute ½ cup ground almond and a handful of fresh chopped dill (or 2 tsp dried dill) for the walnuts and mint. Continue as before, but garnish with a few toasted sliced almonds.

moroccan harira soup

This is a substantial meal-in-one that is made from lentils and lamb and is full of complex flavors. It's also a dish that tastes better when reheated, so if you have the time, make it a day ahead and reheat to eat.

 25 MINS 2 HRS FREEZABLE

SERVES 4–6

1 tbsp olive oil

1 red onion, finely chopped

salt and freshly ground black pepper

3 garlic cloves, finely chopped

1 celery stalk, chopped

1½lb (675g) shoulder or shank of lamb, cut into bite-sized pieces

1 tsp ground turmeric

1 tsp ground cinnamon

2in (5cm) piece of fresh ginger, peeled and finely chopped

5 cups hot vegetable stock

4½oz (125g) green or brown lentils, rinsed well, and picked over for any stones

14oz can chickpeas, drained and rinsed

1 tsp harissa paste

a few sprigs of cilantro, leaves only, to serve

1 Heat the oil in a large flameproof casserole dish over medium heat, add the onion, and cook for 3–4 minutes until soft. Season with salt and pepper, then stir in the garlic and celery, and cook for another 6–10 minutes until the celery is soft.

2 Add the lamb, turmeric, cinnamon, and ginger. Increase the heat a little, stir until the lamb is coated, and cook for 6–10 minutes until the lamb is no longer pink. Add a ladleful of stock and bring to a boil. Stir in the lentils and chickpeas, turning them to coat evenly, add the remaining stock, and bring back to a boil.

3 Reduce to simmer and cook for 1–1½ hours until the lamb is meltingly tender. Check occasionally that it's not drying out, adding a little hot water if needed. Stir in the harissa paste and cook for a few more minutes. Ladle into warmed bowls, top with cilantro leaves, and serve with lemon wedges on the side.

variation

chicken harira soup

Prepare in the same way, but use 1¼lb (550g) cubed boneless, skinless chicken thighs instead of lamb. Use red lentils instead of green or brown ones and add 1lb (450g) pumpkin, seeded, peeled, and cubed, and 4 peeled and chopped tomatoes to the mixture at the end of step 2. Up the harissa paste to 1 tbsp.

red pepper and walnut dip

While you can buy roasted walnuts, it's easy to do yourself: spread them on a baking sheet and place under a hot broiler for 2 minutes. Keep an eye on them; they can burn easily.

 20 MINS   30 MINS

SPECIAL EQUIPMENT ▪ blender or food processor

SERVES 8

⅓ cup olive oil

1 onion, sliced

4 red bell peppers, seeded and sliced

2 garlic cloves, crushed

4½oz (125g) roasted walnuts, chopped

grated zest and juice of 1 lemon

1 Heat the oil in a heavy-bottomed pan over medium heat, add the onion, and cook for 3–4 minutes until soft and translucent. Reduce the heat.

2 Add in the peppers and cook for about 30 minutes until soft, stirring regularly. Stir in the garlic and cook for another 30 seconds, or until the garlic has turned white.

3 Transfer the pepper mixture to a blender or food processor. Add the walnuts and lemon zest and juice, and pulse to a chunky puree. Serve with warm pita bread or crudités, such as carrot or cucumber sticks, for dipping.

variation

red pepper and macadamia nut dip

Use macadamia nuts instead of walnuts. You may also like to add about ½ cup Greek-style yogurt and chopped cilantro leaves, stirring them into the mixture at the end.

genoese minestrone with red pesto

A pesto made from fresh tomatoes is a perfect addition here.

 45–50 MINS   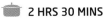 2 HRS 30 MINS

SPECIAL EQUIPMENT ▪ blender or food processor

SERVES 4

3oz (85g) elbow macaroni

14oz (400g) can red kidney beans, drained and rinsed

14oz (400g) can white beans, such as cannellini, drained and rinsed

4oz (115g) thin green beans, trimmed and cut into ½in (1cm) pieces

2 carrots, cubed

2 potatoes, peeled and cubed

1 small zucchini, cubed

4oz (115g) shelled fresh peas or defrosted frozen peas

salt and freshly ground black pepper

large bunch of basil

1 large tomato, peeled, seeded (p197), and chopped

2 garlic cloves, peeled

½ cup olive oil

3oz (85g) Parmesan cheese, grated

1 Cook the pasta in a pan of boiling salted water for about 12 minutes, or until it is tender but still firm to the bite. Drain, rinse with hot water, and set aside.

2 Put the canned beans in a large saucepan and add the green beans, carrots, potatoes, zucchini, peas, and a little salt and pepper. Add 7 cups water and bring to a boil, then reduce the heat and simmer for 1 hour, until the vegetables are very tender.

3 For the pesto, strip the leaves from the basil stems, reserving 6 sprigs. Put the basil, tomato, garlic, and some salt and pepper in a blender or food processor and pulse until smooth. With the blades turning, gradually add the oil. Scrape down the sides of the bowl from time to time with a rubber spatula. Taste for seasoning.

4 Add the macaroni to the soup and season to taste. Gently reheat to boiling, but do not cook or the pasta and vegetables will overcook rather than staying firm. Remove from the heat and stir in the tomato pesto. Ladle the soup into warmed bowls, top each serving with basil leaves, and serve the Parmesan separately.

cucumber gratin with toasted olive ciabatta

A clever idea for cooking cucumber to enhance its flavor.

 10 MINS   20 MINS

SERVES 4

1 large cucumber, trimmed, peeled, and cut into ½in (1cm) thick slices

1 tbsp chopped thyme

3 tbsp butter

1¼ cups vegetable stock

¼ cup all-purpose flour

⅔ cup half-and-half

4oz (115g) Cheddar cheese, grated

½ tsp English or other spicy mustard

salt and freshly ground black pepper

For the olive ciabatta

3 tbsp butter, softened

2 tbsp finely chopped, pitted black olives

2 tbsp chopped parsley

8 slices ciabatta bread

1 Place the cucumber in a pan with the thyme, 1 tbsp butter, and the stock. Bring to a boil, reduce the heat, cover, and simmer for 6–8 minutes until tender. Drain thoroughly, reserving the liquid. Place the cucumber in 4 buttered gratin dishes. Melt the

remaining butter in the pan, stir in the flour, and cook, stirring, for 1 minute. Remove from the heat and whisk in the reserved cucumber cooking liquid. Bring to a boil and cook for 2 minutes, stirring. Stir in the half-and-half, 3oz (85g) of the cheese, and the mustard. Stir and season to taste.

2 Preheat the broiler. Pour the sauce over the cucumber to cover completely. Sprinkle with the remaining cheese. Set aside while you make the olive butter.

3 For the ciabatta, mash the butter with the olives and parsley and season with plenty of pepper. Toast the ciabatta on one side. Place the gratin under the broiler and cook for 5 minutes until the cheese melts, bubbles, and turns golden. Cover with foil and place in the base of the broiler compartment. Spread the olive butter over the untoasted sides of the ciabatta. Broil until the butter melts and the edges turn brown. Serve slices of the ciabatta hot with the gratin.

fried calamari

This is a popular Mediterranean dish. Avoid overcooking the squid since it will become tough. Serve with a mixed salad and potato wedges for a more filling dish.

 15 MINS 10 MINS

SERVES 4

2 eggs

2 tbsp cold sparkling water

1 cup all-purpose flour

1 tsp dried chile flakes

salt

1lb 2oz (500g) small squid, gutted and cleaned (p263), and cut into ½in (1cm) rings

1 cup vegetable oil or sunflower oil

lemon wedges, to serve

1 Break the eggs into a bowl, add the sparkling water, and beat well with a hand whisk. Put the flour, chile flakes, and 1 tsp salt on a plate, and mix well. Dip each piece of squid into the egg mixture and then into the flour, making sure they are evenly coated, then set aside.

2 Heat the oil in a deep frying pan over high heat until hot, then carefully add the squid, one piece at a time. Do not overfill the pan. Cook in batches for 2–3 minutes, or until golden brown. Remove with a slotted spoon and place on paper towels to remove any excess oil. Serve with a squeeze of lemon.

variation

fritto misto

Make the batter in the same way, but instead of using all squid, use 7oz (200g) squid, prepared as before, 1 haddock fillet, about 6oz (175g), skinned and cut into chunks, and 8 shucked oysters. Dry the fish well before coating. Add ½ tsp coarse, crushed black peppercorns to the flour mixture. Serve the mixed fish just with wedges of lemon and some crusty bread as a starter or, for a main course for 2 people, serve it with a large mixed salad.

roasted red bell pepper, fennel, and tomato soup

Make this soup early in the fall when tomatoes and peppers are plentiful. It freezes well and is also a cheering stalwart for winter meals. Serve it with a warm roll.

 25 MINS 2 HRS ❄ FREEZABLE

SPECIAL EQUIPMENT ▪ blender or food processor

SERVES 4–6

1lb 2oz (500g) tomatoes

1 large fennel bulb, peeled and cut into wedges

1 red onion, cut into wedges

2 red bell peppers, halved and seeded

4 garlic cloves, in their skins

1½ tsp sugar

2 tbsp olive oil

large sprig of rosemary, leaves only

1–2 tbsp vegetable oil

1½ tsp fennel seeds

½ tsp nigella seeds

14fl oz (400ml) tomato sauce

3½ cups hot vegetable stock

1 red chile, seeded and chopped

salt and freshly ground black pepper

handful of fennel fronds

1 Preheat the oven to 400°F (200°C). Slice a cross into the base of each tomato and squeeze the juice and seeds into a bowl. Strain the juice and set aside.

2 Line a roasting pan with parchment paper and add the fennel, onion, peppers, garlic cloves, and squeezed tomatoes. Sprinkle in the sugar, drizzle with the olive oil, and scatter the rosemary on top. Roast the vegetables for about 1 hour, until the tomatoes are soft. Let the vegetables cool before peeling the blackened skin from the peppers. Peel the garlic and discard the skins.

3 Heat the vegetable oil in a large pan and toss in the fennel and nigella seeds, swirling them around for a few seconds. Add the tomato sauce, the stock, and the reserved tomato juice, and bring to a boil. Add the roasted vegetables and the chile, and season. Half cover with a lid and simmer for about 45 minutes.

4 Pour the soup into a blender or food processor and pulse until smooth. Strain back into the pan. Reheat, reseason, and sprinkle over fennel fronds. Serve in warmed bowls.

cream of tomato soup

This extra-special version of a classic takes the humble tomato to new heights by using fresh, sun-dried, and roasted varieties.

 30 MINS 40 MINS

SPECIAL EQUIPMENT ▪ blender or food processor

SERVES 4-6

20 plum tomatoes, about 3½lb (1.6kg)

2 tbsp olive oil

4 tbsp butter

2 onions, finely chopped

2 celery stalks, finely chopped

2 carrots, finely cubed

2 garlic cloves, crushed

6 sun-dried tomatoes, finely chopped

3½ cups hot vegetable stock

2-3 tbsp heavy cream

salt and freshly ground black pepper

1 To roast the tomatoes, preheat the oven to 400°F (200°C). Place 12 of the tomatoes in a roasting pan and toss with 1 tbsp of the oil. Roast in the oven for 12–15 minutes until slightly charred. Peel the remaining tomatoes (p197) and finely chop.

2 Heat the butter and remaining oil in a heavy-bottomed pan over low heat. Add the onions and cook for 8–10 minutes, stirring frequently, until very soft but not colored. Next, add the celery and carrots, and continue cooking gently for 10 minutes, stirring occasionally. Add the garlic and sauté for another 2 minutes.

3 Mix together the roasted plum tomatoes, peeled tomatoes, and sun-dried tomatoes. Add to the pan with any juices and cook for 5 minutes, stirring occasionally, to allow the flavors to combine. If the sauce looks too thick or starts catching on the bottom of the pan, add a little of the hot vegetable stock. Pour in the remaining vegetable stock and let the soup simmer for 15–20 minutes.

4 Pour the soup into a blender or food processor and pulse until smooth, then strain into a clean pan. Add the heavy cream, a teaspoon at a time, until you are happy with the taste and texture. Season with salt and pepper, reheat very gently if needed, and serve.

beef and green bean soup

Choose firm, waxy potatoes that will keep their shape and texture in this deliciously savory soup.

 20 MINS 1 HR FREEZABLE

SERVES 6

2 tbsp sunflower or vegetable oil

1lb 2oz (500g) beef stew meat, cut into ¾in(2cm) cubes

salt and freshly ground black pepper

1 onion, chopped

2-3 sprigs of thyme

3½ cups hot vegetable stock

1 large potato, peeled and cut into cubes

9oz (250g) green beans, trimmed and cut into small pieces

1-2 tbsp chopped parsley (optional)

1 Heat the oil in a pan over medium heat, season the meat with salt and pepper, and add half the meat to the hot oil. Brown the meat until golden all over. Remove from the pan and repeat with the rest of the beef. Remove it from the pan, add the onion, and fry until softened.

2 Return the browned meat to the pan, tie the thyme sprigs together with kitchen twine, and add them to the pan with the stock. Bring to a boil, cover, and cook over medium heat for about 40 minutes.

3 Add the potato, bring back to a boil, cover once again, and cook for 10–15 minutes, or until just tender. Add the chopped beans and cook for 4–5 minutes, or until the beans are tender but still firm to the bite.

4 Remove the thyme. Season with salt and pepper, break up the meat pieces slightly, and sprinkle with parsley, if desired, before serving.

black-eyed pea soup

If you can, make this soup in advance and let it stand for a while before reheating—it will taste even better. It's also good made with overgrown runner beans, shelled.

 15 MINS 40 MINS FREEZABLE

SPECIAL EQUIPMENT ▪ blender or food processor

SERVES 4-6

1 tbsp virgin rapeseed oil or sunflower oil

3 leeks, trimmed and sliced

1 small red bell pepper, seeded and chopped

1 small yellow bell pepper, seeded and chopped

3 garlic cloves

2in (5cm) piece fresh ginger, peeled and grated or coarsely chopped

1 small red or jalapeño chile, seeded

1 tsp cumin seeds

sea salt and freshly ground black pepper

2 x 14oz cans black-eyed peas, drained, rinsed, and drained again

1¾ cups coconut milk

2 cups hot vegetable stock

1 tsp brown sugar

cilantro leaves, to garnish

lime wedges, to serve

1 Heat the oil in a pan over medium heat, add the leeks and bell peppers, cover with a lid, and cook, stirring frequently, for 5–7 minutes, or until soft. Meanwhile, put the garlic, ginger, chile, cumin seeds, and 1 tsp sea salt in a blender or food puree until completely smooth. Add to the pan, using a little more water to rinse out every last bit. Cook, stirring, for 2–3 minutes, or until most of the liquid has evaporated.

2 Add the beans, coconut milk, stock, sugar, and a generous grinding of black pepper and bring to a boil. Reduce the heat and simmer gently for 30 minutes, stirring frequently. Taste for seasoning, then serve each bowlful garnished with fresh cilantro and a lime wedge.

pumpkin and ginger soup

This velvety smooth soup can be made using pumpkin or butternut squash, depending on what is in season. The dried chile flakes and finely chopped ginger give it just the right kick to cut through the richness.

 15 MINS   1 HR   ❄ FREEZABLE

SPECIAL EQUIPMENT ▪ blender or food processor

SERVES 4-6

1 tbsp olive oil

1 onion, finely chopped

salt and freshly ground black pepper

3 garlic cloves, finely chopped

2in (5cm) piece of fresh ginger, peeled and finely chopped

pinch of dried chile flakes

1 small cinnamon stick

2lb (900g) pumpkin or butternut squash, halved, seeded, peeled, and cut into cubes

3 cups hot vegetable stock

1 Heat the oil in a large heavy-bottomed pan over medium heat, add the onion, and cook for 3–4 minutes until soft. Season with salt and pepper, then add the garlic, ginger, chile flakes, and cinnamon stick. Cook for a few seconds before adding the pumpkin or squash (and a little more oil if needed), stirring to coat.

2 Pour in a little of the stock, increase the heat, and scrape up the bits from the bottom of the pan. Add the remaining stock, boil for 1 minute, then reduce the heat to very low, cover with a lid, and cook for about 45 minutes until the pumpkin is soft and the flavors have developed. Remove the cinnamon stick.

3 Pour the soup into a blender or food processor and puree until smooth, then pour back into a clean pan. Add a ladleful of hot water if it is too thick. Heat through, taste, and season as required. Serve with some chunky whole-wheat or rye bread.

variation

acorn squash and cumin soup

Prepare in exactly the same way, but add 1 tsp ground cumin instead of the grated ginger, use 1½lb (675g) acorn squash, prepared as the pumpkin, and add 2 large carrots, peeled and coarsely chopped at the end of step 1.

pear, fennel, and walnut salad

The Gorgonzola cheese dressing for this salad contrasts well with the sweet pears and aniseed flavor of the fennel.

 30-35 MINS   5-8 MINS

SERVES 6

2oz (60g) walnuts

1 large fennel bulb

3 ripe pears

1 lemon

For the cheese dressing

4½oz (125g) Gorgonzola cheese

¼ cup red wine vinegar

salt and freshly ground black pepper

¼ cup olive oil

1 Preheat the oven to 350°F (180°C). Spread the walnuts on a baking sheet and roast them in the heated oven for 5–8 minutes until crisp, stirring occasionally so they roast evenly.

2 To make the cheese dressing, cut the rind from the Gorgonzola and crumble with your fingers or crush with the tines of a fork. Put two-thirds into a bowl, add the red wine vinegar and salt and pepper, and whisk together. Gradually whisk in the oil so the dressing emulsifies and thickens slightly. Stir in the remaining cheese so a few larger pieces are left intact, and taste for seasoning. Cover and put in the fridge to chill.

3 Meanwhile, trim the stalks, root end, and any tough outer pieces from the fennel. Reserve any fronds for decoration. Cut the fennel bulb in half lengthwise. Set each fennel half flat-side down on the cutting board and slice it lengthwise.

4 Peel the pears, halve lengthwise, and remove the core. Set each half cut-side down and cut lengthwise into thin slices. Cut the lemon in half and squeeze lemon juice over the pear slices, tossing to coat.

5 On individual plates, arrange the pear and fennel slices and spoon on the cheese dressing. Scatter some roasted walnuts over each serving and decorate with fennel fronds.

variation

apple, celery, and pecan salad
Prepare in exactly the same way, but substitute 2oz (60g) pecan halves for walnuts and sprinkle them with 1 tsp mixed spice before roasting. Use 4 crisp apples (such as Fujis) instead of the pears and 4 tender celery stalks instead of the fennel bulb.

fennel and apple soup

Fennel will store better in the fridge if you remove the feathery fronds beforehand, but be sure to save a handful of the fronds for this soup as an attractive garnish.

 10 MINS   30 MINS

SPECIAL EQUIPMENT ▪ blender or food processor

SERVES 4

2 tbsp virgin vegetable oil or olive oil

1 onion, chopped

2 garlic cloves, chopped

1lb 5oz (600g) fennel bulbs, trimmed and coarsely chopped, the fronds reserved to garnish

1 celery heart with leaves, or 3 celery stalks, chopped

1 apple, peeled, cored, and coarsely chopped

sea salt

2½ cups hot vegetable stock

1 Heat the oil in a large pan over medium heat, add the onion, and cook for 3–4 minutes until soft. Add the garlic and cook for 1–2 minutes until fragrant, then stir in the fennel, celery, and apple with a little sea salt. Stir, cover with a lid, and sweat for 10 minutes, stirring frequently.

2 Pour in the stock and bring to a boil. Simmer for 15 minutes until the fennel is tender. Pour the soup into a blender or food processor and puree until smooth, then pour back into the pan and season. Serve hot or cold in bowls garnished with torn fennel fronds.

mussels in fennel broth

To clean mussels, scrub them under cold running water with a small stiff brush, then scrape with a knife to remove any barnacles, weeds, or "beards" from each one.

 10 MINS   20 MINS

SERVES 4

1 tbsp olive oil

1 onion, finely chopped

1 fennel bulb, trimmed and finely chopped

salt and freshly ground black pepper

2 garlic cloves, grated or finely chopped

2 Yukon Gold potatoes, peeled and finely cubed

1¼ cups hot vegetable or light fish stock

14oz (400ml) can coconut milk

3lb (1.35kg) mussels, scrubbed and cleaned (discard any that do not close when tapped) (p364)

handful of basil leaves, torn

1 Heat the oil in a large pan over low heat, add the onion, fennel, and a pinch of salt, and cook for about 5 minutes until softened. Add the garlic and potatoes and cook for a few more minutes, being careful not to allow the mixture to brown.

2 Pour in the stock and bring to a boil. Add the coconut milk, reduce the heat slightly, and simmer gently for about 10 minutes, or until the potatoes are cooked. Bring back to a boil, add the mussels, and put a lid on the pan. Cook for about 5 minutes, until all the mussels open (discard any that do not).

3 To serve, stir in the basil, taste the broth, and season if needed. Serve immediately.

variation

mussels in fennel and pernod broth
Prepare the mussels as before. Soften the onion with the fennel and 1 finely chopped carrot. Add the garlic but omit the potatoes. Add ⅔ cup each of water and dry white wine instead of the stock and a generous splash of Pernod. Omit the coconut milk. When the mussels are cooked, garnish with a handful of chopped fresh parsley instead of basil.

Season's best **fennel**

Florence fennel looks like a short, fat celery, but is the swollen base of the stem of the fennel plant, best in late summer and autumn. It has a crisp, crunchy texture and sweet, aniseed flavor. It pairs well with seafood, particularly mussels (with a splash of Pernod or other pastis) and is good with cheeses, citrus (roasted with sliced preserved lemons), chicken, lamb, and lentils. The herb fennel and fennel seed do not come from the same plant but taste similar.

Fennel originated in the Mediterranean regions, but is now grown in other mild, temperate climates around the world as well.

Baby fennel More tender than the large bulbs of Florence fennel, these can be eaten whole. They are delicious brushed with oil and grilled.

Use finely chopped fronds to give a subtle aniseed flavor to soups, salads, and fish dishes.

Florence fennel With its sweet, warm, aniseed flavor and crisp texture, fennel makes a tasty salad ingredient. The flavor is subtler when cooked, but the texture remains crunchy.

essentials

varieties available

Varying sizes of mature heads, and baby fennel.

buy Look for clean, freshly cut bulbs with the long stems and fronds attached. Old fennel will look dull with brown patches and the fronds will be limp.

store Bulbs can be kept in a plastic bag in the vegetable drawer of the fridge for a week.

cook Boil or steam whole or in wedges; braise, roast, or sauté; boil thick slices until tender, then grill.

preserve Blanch and freeze, make into pickles or relishes, or preserve in oil.

recipe ideas

Beef, fennel, and mushroom hotpot p320

Fennel soup with beans, thyme, and chorizo p279

Pot roast chicken with turnips and fennel p298

how to prepare fennel

This technique shows how to slice fennel for a salad. To prepare fennel for roasting or braising, simply trim as in Step 1, then cut in quarters lengthwise or leave baby fennel whole.

1 Trim the stalks, root end, and any tough outer pieces from the fennel. Reserve any fronds for decoration. Cut the fennel bulb in half lengthwise.

2 Set each fennel half flat-side down on the cutting board and slice it lengthwise into strips and separate the layers.

african sweet potato soup

This recipe is based on a classic African soup that is hot, spicy, and full of flavor. A dollop of peanut butter stirred through lends a rich, satisfying earthiness.

 20 MINS   20-25 MINS   ❄ FREEZABLE

SPECIAL EQUIPMENT ▪ blender or food processor

SERVES 4

2 tbsp olive oil

1 onion, chopped

2 garlic cloves, finely chopped

2 tsp grated fresh ginger

¼ tsp dried crushed chiles

1lb (450g) sweet potatoes, peeled and cut into small chunks

1 red bell pepper, seeded and chopped

7oz (230g) can chopped tomatoes

1 tsp cumin seeds, dry-roasted and crushed

1 tsp coriander seeds, dry-roasted and crushed

3 cups hot vegetable stock

2-3 tbsp smooth or crunchy peanut butter

splash of Tabasco sauce (optional)

drizzle of chile oil, to serve

1 Heat the olive oil in a large pan, add the onion, and cook for 3 minutes. Stir in the garlic, ginger, and chiles, and cook for 1 minute. Then stir in the sweet potatoes, pepper, tomatoes, and crushed spices, and cook for 2 minutes. Pour in the stock, bring to a boil, then simmer for 12–15 minutes, or until the sweet potatoes are tender.

2 Remove from the heat and pulse in a blender or food processor until smooth. You may need to do this in batches. Pass the soup through a sieve to remove the pepper skin and then return to the pan. Stir in the peanut butter, tasting to decide the amount you like. If you want to add more heat, add some Tabasco sauce. Reheat gently, then drizzle a little chile oil over each bowl to serve.

yam pla fu

These classic Thai fish balls are best made with good-flavored fish, such as red snapper. Great with a squeeze of lime.

 15 MINS   20-25 MINS

SPECIAL EQUIPMENT ▪ food processor

SERVES 4

1 large red snapper or grey mullet, filleted and scaled

1 tsp oil, plus extra for deep-frying

salt

2½oz (75g) dry-roasted peanuts, to serve

nam prik (hot chile dipping sauce) or sweet chile sauce, to serve

For the mango salad

2 green mangoes or papayas, shredded

1 carrot, shredded

2 scallions, trimmed and finely sliced

½ cucumber, peeled, seeded, and shredded

2oz (60g) bean sprouts

For the dressing

1 tbsp palm sugar or dark brown sugar

zest and juice of 1 large lime

1 garlic clove, grated or finely chopped

1 tbsp grated fresh ginger

splash of fish sauce (nam pla), to taste

1-2 bird's eye chiles, finely chopped

large handful of cilantro, chopped

large handful of mint, chopped

1 Preheat the oven to 400°F (200°C). Rub the fish with 1 tsp of oil and 2 tbsp salt and arrange on a baking sheet. Roast in the oven for 12–15 minutes until the skin crisps. Cool.

2 Put the fish in a food processor and pulse until finely chopped. Shape into golf balls. Heat the remaining oil to 350°F (180°C) in a large pan. Drop each fish ball into the oil and deep-fry in small batches for about 3 minutes, until brown and crispy. Drain on paper towels and keep warm.

4 Toss the salad ingredients in a bowl until evenly mixed. Whisk the dressing ingredients together and toss into the salad with the peanuts. Serve with the fish balls and nam prik.

broccoli and blue cheese soup

Blue cheese and broccoli make a tasty soup, hearty enough for a light meal, but also delicious as a starter.

 15 MINS   20 MINS

SPECIAL EQUIPMENT ▪ blender or food processor

SERVES 4

12oz (350g) broccoli

pat of butter

1 onion, chopped

1 potato, peeled and cubed

2½ cups chicken or vegetable stock

1 bay leaf

4oz (115g) blue cheese, cubed

4 tbsp heavy cream, plus extra to garnish

salt and freshly ground black pepper

1 Cut the stalk off the broccoli, peel, then coarsely chop. Separate the head into small florets.

2 Melt the butter in a large saucepan. Add the onion and cook gently, stirring for 3 minutes until softened, but not browned. Add the broccoli florets and chopped stalk, potato, stock, and bay leaf. Bring to a boil, reduce the heat, cover, and simmer for 20 minutes until the vegetables are really tender. Discard the bay leaf.

3 Puree the soup in a blender or food processor with the cheese. Return to the saucepan, stir in the cream, and season to taste. Reheat, but do not boil. Ladle into warmed soup bowls and garnish each with a small swirl of cream.

fennel soup with beans, thyme, and chorizo

The last-minute addition of paprika-flavored chorizo gives a spicy flavor to this substantial, filling soup.

 15 MINS PLUS SOAKING **1 HR**

SPECIAL EQUIPMENT ▪ blender or food processor

SERVES 4

9oz (250g) dried white beans

1 tbsp sunflower or mild olive oil

1 Spanish onion, finely chopped

2 garlic cloves, crushed

1 fennel bulb, cored and finely chopped

2 tsp dried fennel seeds

1 tbsp finely chopped flat-leaf parsley

2 tsp thyme leaves

salt and freshly ground black pepper

3½oz (100g) Spanish-style chorizo, cubed

1 Soak the beans overnight in cold water, then drain and rinse. Heat the oil in a heavy pan over medium heat, add the onion, and stir for 2 minutes. Add the garlic, fennel and seeds, parsley, and half the thyme, and cook for 3–5 minutes until softened. Add the beans. Stir in 7 cups water and season lightly.

2 Simmer for 40 minutes, or until the beans are tender, skimming from time to time. Cool a little, then pour into a blender or food processor and pulse briefly. Return to the pan, taste, and adjust the seasoning if necessary.

3 Gently reheat the soup. Meanwhile, place a nonstick pan over medium-high heat and fry the chorizo for 2–3 minutes until crisp, stirring frequently. Drain on paper towels. Ladle the soup into bowls, add a little chorizo to each, and finish with a scattering of thyme. Serve immediately.

german potato soup

If you can't obtain fresh chanterelle mushrooms for this, they are also sold in jars or cans. Drain and rinse them before cooking.

 25 MINS **45 MINS**

SPECIAL EQUIPMENT ▪ blender or food processor

SERVES 6

5 tbsp butter

¼ celery root, cubed

9oz (250g) carrots, cubed

1½lb (675g) Russet potatoes, peeled and cubed

1 onion, studded with a bay leaf and a clove

5½ cups hot vegetable stock

7oz (200g) leeks, sliced

1 onion, cubed

7oz (200g) chanterelles, large ones halved

½ cup heavy cream, or ⅔ cup crème fraîche

salt and freshly ground black pepper

pinch of dried marjoram

pinch of grated nutmeg

2 tbsp chopped flat-leaf parsley, chervil, or chives

1 Melt two-thirds of the butter in a large pan, add the celery root and carrots, and cook, stirring often, for 6–8 minutes or until light brown. Add the potatoes, clove-studded onion, and stock, and bring to a boil. Lower the heat, cover, and simmer for 20 minutes, or until tender. Add the leeks, cover, and cook for 10 more minutes.

2 Meanwhile, melt the remaining butter in a pan, add the cubed onion, and cook, stirring, for 4–5 minutes, until soft but not brown. Add the chanterelles and cook, stirring, for 5 minutes.

3 Remove the clove-studded onion from the soup and discard. Pour about one-third of the soup into a blender or food processor and pulse until smooth. Stir in the cream and return to the pan. Season, then add the marjoram, nutmeg, cooked onion, and chanterelles, and reheat gently. Serve sprinkled with the herbs.

sweet corn chowder

If you have grown your own sweet corn, wait until the very last minute to harvest it—the quicker you get it from the garden to the pan, the sweeter it will be.

 10 MINS **30 MINS**

SPECIAL EQUIPMENT ▪ blender or food processor

SERVES 4–6

4 sweet corncobs (about 1lb/450g kernels)

salt and freshly ground black pepper

2 bay leaves

2 tbsp olive oil

1 large onion, chopped

4 fresh sage leaves, chopped, or ½ tsp dried sage, crushed

1 tsp fresh thyme leaves, or ½ tsp dried thyme

1 carrot, chopped

2 celery stalks, chopped

1 large potato, peeled and chopped

7oz (200g) cream cheese

½ cup milk

half-and-half, to serve

pinch of paprika, to serve

1 Stand each corncob upright in a large bowl and strip the kernels by cutting downward with a sharp knife. Set the kernels aside. Place the cobs in a large saucepan and add 2 cups water, a generous sprinkling of salt, and bay leaves. Bring to a boil and simmer, covered, for 15 minutes. Remove and discard the corncobs and bay leaves.

2 Heat the oil in a saucepan and cook the onions until translucent. Add the herbs and remaining vegetables, except the corn kernels. Cook for about 5 minutes until softened. Add the corncob stock and simmer until the potato is collapsing. Meanwhile, place the kernels in a pan and barely cover with cold water. Bring to a boil and cook for 2 minutes. Set aside.

3 Add the cheese and milk to the soup and puree until smooth. Stir in the corn kernels with their cooking liquid. Pulse the chowder once more pulse if desired, to break up the corn kernels slightly. Reheat, adjust the seasoning and ladle into bowls. Drizzle with single cream and dust with paprika.

stir-fried thai vegetables

Almost any crisp vegetable is excellent stir-fried.

 30–35 MINS   15–20 MINS

SERVES 4

10oz (300g) long-grain rice

salt

1oz (30g) dried Oriental mushrooms, or other dried wild mushrooms

2oz (60g) skinned unsalted peanuts

3 tbsp fish sauce (nam pla)

2 tbsp oyster sauce

1 tsp cornstarch

1 tsp sugar

1 lemongrass stalk, trimmed, sliced in half lengthwise, and chopped

3 tbsp vegetable oil

2 garlic cloves, finely chopped

2 dried red chiles, left whole

1 cauliflower, cut into florets

1 red bell pepper, seeded and cut into strips

6oz (175g) bean sprouts, rinsed

1lb 2oz (500g) bok choy, trimmed and shredded

6oz (175g) snow peas, trimmed

3–5 sprigs of basil, leaves picked

1 Cook the rice in boiling salted water for 10–12 minutes, until barely tender. Drain, rinse in cold water, drain again, and set aside.

2 Preheat the oven to 375°F (190°C). Butter a baking dish and enough foil to cover the dish. Put the mushrooms in a bowl, pour in warm water to cover, set aside for 30 minutes to soften, then drain and slice. Meanwhile, scatter the peanuts on a baking sheet and roast in the oven until brown, 5–7 minutes, then chop coarsely. Then turn the oven to its lowest setting. Spread the rice in the baking dish, gently fluff up the grains with a fork, cover with the buttered foil, and put in the oven.

3 Put the fish sauce, oyster sauce, cornstarch, sugar, and lemongrass in a small bowl and whisk together. Heat the oil in a wok. Add the garlic and chiles, stir-fry for 30 seconds, then add the cauliflower, red bell pepper, bean sprouts, and bok choy and cook for 3 minutes, stirring constantly. Add the mushrooms and snow peas and stir-fry for 3 minutes more. Add the basil leaves and fish sauce mix to the wok and stir-fry for 2 minutes more. Remove the chiles and discard. Pile the rice on warmed plates. Spoon the vegetables and sauce over it, sprinkle with peanuts, and serve.

lamb chops with butternut squash, beans, and mint

The sweet, dense orange flesh of butternut squash marries well with tender lamb in this easy fall dish. The bigger the butternut squash, the more developed its flavor will be.

 15 MINS   30 MINS

SERVES 4

2 tbsp olive oil

pinch of five-spice powder

pinch of cayenne pepper

salt and freshly ground black pepper

8 lamb chops

1 butternut squash, halved, seeded, peeled, and coarsely chopped

10 cherry tomatoes

4½oz (125g) thin green beans, trimmed

handful of mint leaves, coarsely chopped

1 Preheat the oven to 400°F (200°C). Put half the oil with the five-spice powder and cayenne pepper in a small bowl, season with some salt and pepper, and mix together well. Brush half of it over the lamb chops and place them in a roasting pan. Mix the remainder with the squash and add to the pan. Cook in the oven for 20–30 minutes, or until the lamb is cooked to your liking and the squash is golden.

2 Meanwhile, put the tomatoes and green beans in a bowl and toss with the remaining oil. Add to the roasting pan for the last 10 minutes of cooking so they just char slightly. Sprinkle with the chopped mint leaves and serve.

variation

pork chops with sweet potatoes, beans, and thyme

Prepare as before, but use 4 lean pork chops instead of the 8 lamb chops and use 1 tsp Cajun spices instead of the five-spice powder and cayenne pepper. Substitute 1 fairly large sweet potato, peeled and cut into chunks instead of the butternut squash. Cook for 30–40 minutes until tender, adding the cherry tomatoes and beans for the last 10 minutes of cooking as before. Sprinkle with a handful of thyme leaves instead of chopped mint.

rabbit provençal

A wonderful dish of rabbit and dried herbes de Provence with semi-dried tomatoes that are first baked slowly in the oven.

 35–40 MINS PLUS MARINATING 3 HRS–3 HRS 30 MINS

SERVES 4

1 rabbit, about 3lb (1.35kg) total weight, cut into 8 pieces

2 shallots, chopped

1 cup dry white wine

¼ cup olive oil

2 tbsp herbes de Provence

1 tbsp all-purpose flour

1 cup chicken stock

5-7 sprigs of thyme

For the tomatoes

6 plum tomatoes, about 1lb 2oz (500g) total weight

1 tbsp olive oil

salt and freshly ground black pepper

1 Combine the rabbit, shallots, white wine, half the oil, and the herbes de Provence in a shallow, nonmetallic dish that is wide enough to hold the rabbit pieces in a single layer. Turn each of the rabbit pieces until completely coated in the other ingredients. Then cover and chill in the fridge for 2–3 hours to marinate.

2 Preheat the oven to 250°F (130°C). Brush a broiler rack with oil. Core the tomatoes and cut each lengthwise into 3 slices. Put them in a bowl with the oil, salt, and pepper, and toss to coat. Arrange the tomato slices on the broiler rack and bake for 2–2½ hours, until slightly shriveled. Transfer to a plate and increase the oven temperature to 375°F (190°C).

3 Remove the rabbit from the marinade and reserve the marinade. Season the rabbit with salt and pepper. Heat half the remaining oil in a casserole dish. Add half the rabbit pieces and cook for 5 minutes, until browned. Transfer to a plate, add the remaining oil, and brown the remaining pieces of rabbit.

4 Return all the rabbit pieces to the casserole dish and sprinkle in the flour. Cook for 2–3 minutes, then stir in the marinade and stock. Cover and bake in the oven for 50–55 minutes, stirring occasionally, until very tender. Return the tomatoes to the oven for the last 10 minutes to heat through. Strip the thyme leaves from the stems. Serve the rabbit and tomatoes sprinkled with the thyme.

roasted monkfish with chile, tomatoes, anchovies, and capers

Monkfish is a firm-textured fish that is succulent and meaty enough to take on the robust flavors of a chile, anchovy, and caper paste, which is applied just before the fish is roasted.

 20 MINS 30 MINS

SERVES 4

2¼lb (1kg) monkfish tail fillets

drizzle of olive oil

salt and freshly ground black pepper

2 red chiles, seeded and finely chopped

6-8 salted anchovies, finely chopped

2-3 tsp capers, rinsed, gently squeezed dry, and chopped

12 cherry tomatoes

1 Preheat the oven to 400°F (200°C). Place the monkfish fillets in a roasting pan and drizzle a little oil over them. Season well with salt and pepper and set aside.

2 Using a mortar and pestle, pound together the chiles, anchovies, and capers until they become a paste. Alternatively, squash into a paste with a fork. Then, using your hands, smother the monkfish with the paste.

3 Put the fish back into the roasting pan and cook in the oven for about 10 minutes. Add the tomatoes and roast for another 5–10 minutes until the fish is cooked through.

4 Leave to rest for 5 minutes, then serve immediately with a green salad or baby roast potatoes.

variation

whole stuffed fish

Make the paste in the same way. Use it to stuff 4 small, boned black rockfish or sea bream (about 14oz/400g each) instead of the monkfish. Place side by side in a large, oiled roasting pan and drizzle with olive oil. Bake as before.

pumpkin stew

This stew is delicious with Cheddar cheese grated on top.

 25 MINS   1 HR 10 MINS

SPECIAL EQUIPMENT ▪ food processor

SERVES 4

1 small celery root, peeled and cubed into 1in (2.5cm) pieces

1 tsp lemon juice

1 small pumpkin, halved, seeded, peeled and cubed into 1in (2.5cm) pieces

2 ripe tomatoes

4 tbsp butter

2 small leeks, cut into 1in (2.5cm) slices

1 garlic clove, finely chopped

2 tbsp all-purpose flour

1 cup vegetable or chicken stock, plus more if needed

salt and freshly ground black pepper

cayenne pepper

1 celery stalk, cut into ½in (1cm) slices

1 large turnip, peeled and cut into 1in (2.5cm) cube

1 small butternut squash, halved, seeded, peeled, and cubed into 1in (2.5cm)pieces

1 zucchini, cubed into 1in (2.5cm) pieces

2–3 sprigs of thyme, leaves picked

1 Put the cubes of celery root in a large bowl of water along with the lemon juice, to prevent discoloration. Cook the pumpkin in a pan of boiling water for about 10 minutes until tender. Drain, then pulse to a puree in a food processor. Cut the cores from the tomatoes and score an "x" on the bottom of each. Immerse them in a bowl of boiling water until the skin starts to split, then plunge into a bowl of cold water. Peel off the skin. Cut in half and squeeze out the seeds, then cut each half into quarters.

2 Heat the butter in a casserole dish, add the leeks and garlic, and soften over low heat, stirring occasionally, for 3–5 minutes. Add the flour and cook, stirring, for 1–2 minutes, until foaming, then stir in the stock and pumpkin puree. Drain the celery root and add it to the pot along with some salt, pepper, and cayenne to taste. Bring to a boil and simmer for 20 minutes. Add the celery and turnip and simmer for 20 minutes more, until the vegetables are beginning to soften.

3 Add the butternut squash, zucchini, tomatoes, and thyme leaves and simmer for 10 minutes longer. Taste and season, if needed. Ladle into warmed bowls and serve.

sweet and sour pumpkin stew

Puy lentils add texture to this dish, since they hold their shape well when cooked. Add a little chile for heat, if you wish.

 15 MINS   1 HR   ❄ FREEZABLE

SERVES 4

2 tbsp olive oil

1 onion, finely chopped

salt and freshly ground black pepper

3 garlic cloves, finely chopped

1 carrot, finely cubed

2 celery stalks, finely cubed

2 bay leaves

¼ cup red wine vinegar

pinch of brown sugar

1 pumpkin or large butternut squash, peeled and chopped into chunky pieces (about 1lb 2oz/500g prepared weight)

900ml (1½ pints) hot vegetable stock

3 cups Puy lentils, rinsed and picked over for any stones

bunch of mint leaves, coarsely chopped

pumpkin seeds, to serve

1 Heat the oil in a large flameproof casserole dish over medium heat, add the onion, and cook for 3–4 minutes until soft. Season well with salt and pepper, add the garlic, carrot, celery, and bay leaves, and cook for another 5 minutes until soft. Increase the heat, add the vinegar, let it simmer for a minute, then stir in the sugar and pumpkin. Turn to coat well, add a little stock, and cook on high for a minute. Stir in the lentils, add the remaining stock, and bring to a boil.

2 Partially cover with the lid, reduce the heat, and simmer for 45 minutes, or until the lentils are soft. Add water if the stew becomes too dry. Taste and season, and remove the bay leaves. Stir in the mint, then serve on a bed of rice with some pumpkin seeds scattered on top.

venison wellingtons

Wild mushrooms and venison in pastry make a special meal.

 40 MINS   45 MINS

SERVES 4

2 tbsp olive oil

sea salt and freshly ground black pepper

4 venison loin steaks, each 4¼–5½oz (120–150g)

2 tbsp unsalted butter

2 shallots, finely chopped

1 garlic clove, finely chopped

7oz (200g) mixed mushrooms, including wild mushrooms, chopped

1 tbsp chopped thyme leaves

1 tbsp brandy or Madeira

¼oz(10g) dried wild mushrooms (optional), rehydrated (see package)

1lb 2oz (500g) store-bought puff pastry

1 large egg, beaten, for glazing

1 Preheat the oven to 400°F (200°C). Heat the oil in a frying pan. Season the venison and fry them, two at a time, for 2 minutes each side, until browned all over. Remove from the pan and set aside to cool. Melt the butter in the pan over medium heat, add the shallots, and cook for 5 minutes until soft. Add the garlic, cook for 1–2 minutes, then add the mushrooms and thyme and cook for 5 minutes until soft and any juices evaporate. Add the brandy and cook over high heat for 1 minute. Season, remove from the heat and let cool. If using dried mushrooms, drain, chop, and add to the mushroom mixture.

2 Cut the pastry into 4 equal pieces and roll out rectangles ¼in(5mm) thick and large enough to wrap around each steak. Pat each steak dry with paper towels. Place a quarter of the mushroom filling at one end of the pastry rectangle, leaving an edge of ¾in(2cm). Place a steak on top, brush the edges of the pastry with beaten egg, fold the pastry over, press the edges down, and crimp them in. Repeat with the remaining steaks and pastry. Cut small slits in the tops of the pastry wellingtons and brush with more beaten egg. Place on a heavy baking sheet, bake for 20–25 minutes, or until puffed and golden, remove from the oven, let cool for 5 minutes, and then serve.

squash, thyme, and goat cheese tart

If you are planning a relaxed weekend lunch with friends, or want a dish to last for a couple of meals, try this tart, which relies on the creamy, buttery flavors of autumnal squash to balance the tang of soft goat cheese.

 15 MINS 1 HR 15 MINS ❄ FREEZABLE

SPECIAL EQUIPMENT ▪ 8in (20cm) round fluted tart pan with removable bottom ▪ ceramic baking beans

SERVES 4-6

10oz (300g) store-bought pie dough

2 large eggs, lightly beaten

1-2 tbsp olive oil

1 onion, finely chopped

salt and freshly ground black pepper

2 garlic cloves, grated or finely chopped

2¼lb (1kg) butternut squash, peeled, seeded, and chopped into small cubes

a few sprigs of thyme, leaves picked

4½oz (125g) soft goat cheese

¾ cup heavy cream

1 Preheat the oven to 400°F (200°C). Roll out the pie dough on a floured work surface to a large circle about ⅛in (3mm) thick and use to line the tart pan, pressing it into the corners. Trim away the excess and prick the bottom all over with a fork. Line the pie crust with wax paper and fill the bottom with ceramic baking beans. Bake the pie crust in the oven for about 15–20 minutes until the edges of the crust are golden. Remove the tart pan from the oven, remove the beans and paper, brush the bottom of the pie crust with a little of the beaten egg, and return to the oven

for 2–3 minutes to crisp. Remove from the oven once again and set aside. Reduce the oven temperature to 350°F (180°C).

2 Meanwhile, heat 1 tbsp of the oil in a large frying pan over low heat. Add the onion and a little salt, and cook gently for about 5 minutes until soft and translucent. Add the garlic, squash, and half of the thyme leaves, and continue cooking over low heat for 10–15 minutes until the squash softens and begins to turn golden. You may have to add a little more oil.

3 Spoon the squash and onion mixture into the pie crust, then crumble over the goat cheese. Mix the cream with the remaining beaten egg and season well with salt and pepper. Pour the cream mixture in the tart filling, then sprinkle with the remaining thyme leaves. Bake in the oven for 20–25 minutes until the tart is puffed and set. Let cool for at least 10 minutes before releasing it from the pan. Serve the tart while still warm with a arugula salad.

Season's best **winter squashes**

Winter squashes have a hard skin, large seeds, and can have a rich, robust sweetness that intensifies as they ripen. They are at their best when harvested, but can be stored, too. They have denser flesh than the summer varieties and add depth of flavor to many dishes. They taste great with cheeses, particularly blue ones, and are complemented by garlic, spices, tomatoes, nuts, and seeds.

Native to Mexico and Central America, squashes are now grown in tropical and warm, temperate regions around the world. They come in many different colors, shapes, and sizes.

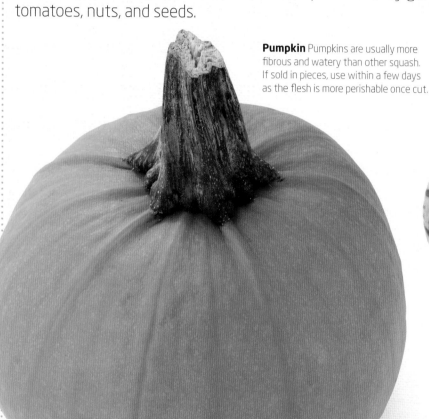

Pumpkin Pumpkins are usually more fibrous and watery than other squash. If sold in pieces, use within a few days as the flesh is more perishable once cut.

One of the few squash that doesn't need peeling. You can eat its thin skin.

Delicata Also known as sweet potato squash, this variety is renowned for its exceptionally smooth, moist, honey-flavored flesh. Ideal for pumpkin pie and cakes.

how to peel butternut squash

All winter squashes must be halved and seeded before use. Unless the squash will be stuffed, the hard skin should be removed as well. The flesh can then be cut into chunks before cooking.

1 Holding the squash firmly on a board, use a chef's knife to halve lengthwise, working from the stalk end to the core end.

2 Using a spoon, firmly scrape out the seeds and fibers from each half and discard (or keep the seeds to roast, then use for salads or snacks).

3 If stuffing, there is no need to peel; otherwise use a vegetable peeler or small sharp knife to cut off the skin. Cut into pieces or chunks to cook.

Butternut squash One of the more common varieties of winter squash, butternut has smooth, dense flesh that becomes sweet and nutty when baked or steamed. The cavity can be stuffed.

Harlequin squash Cream and green, this dumpling-shaped variety has high sugar content. It is excellent when roasted.

The seeds can be washed, dried, tossed in oil, and roasted in the oven, then tossed in salt and kept in an airtight jar.

Spaghetti squash A mellow-tasting squash, this has flesh that separates into long spaghetti-like strands as it cooks. Use as spaghetti, with or without sauce, or in salads, soups, and casseroles.

Turban squash Also known as Turk's turban, this is a distinctively shaped variety with bland, slightly dry, yellow-orange flesh. The internal cavity is larger than most winter squashes, so there is correspondingly less flesh.

The bottom half can be cut off and hollowed out for stuffing, or used as a striking bowl for soup.

essentials
varieties available

Types include butternut, acorn, turban, harlequin, crown prince, and onion squashes, spaghetti squash, and pumpkin.

buy Avoid any with damaged skin. Some younger varieties may be tender-skinned but for most, if ripe, your nail should not be able to pierce it.

store Whole ones can be kept for several weeks in a cool dark place on newspapers; keep cut ones in the fridge for a few days.

cook Steam, boil, fry, bake, roast, stew, or purée for soups and desserts.

preserve Make jam and chutney; roast and salt the seeds; candy pumpkin for dessert.

recipe ideas

Butternut squash stuffed with ground beef p286

Butternut squash tagine p286

Pumpkin pie p345

Roast pumpkin, chile, and ginger dip p264

Squash, thyme, and goat cheese tart p283

butternut squash tagine

Most squashes ripen as summer draws to a close and thoughts turn toward fall fare. A spicy tagine with flavorsome butternut squash suits this transition perfectly.

 20 MINS　 1 HR

SERVES 4

¼ cup light olive oil

2 red onions, finely chopped

1 large red bell pepper, seeded and cubed

4 garlic cloves, chopped

1 thumb-sized piece fresh ginger, finely chopped

1 tsp chile powder

1 tsp cinnamon

2 tsp smoked paprika

2 tsp ground coriander

1 tbsp ground cumin

2 x 14oz (400g) cans chopped tomatoes

2 cups vegetable stock

2 tbsp honey

sea salt and freshly ground black pepper

14oz (400g) butternut squash, halved, seeded, peeled, and cubed

7oz (200g) cooked chickpeas

3½oz (100g) dried apricots, chopped

bunch of cilantro leaves, chopped

1 Pour the oil into a large saucepan. Add the onions, red bell pepper, garlic, and ginger, and fry over low heat for 2 minutes until they are softened, but not browned.

2 Add the chile, cinnamon, smoked paprika, ground coriander, and cumin, and continue to cook for another 2 minutes over low heat to release the flavor of the spices. Add the tomatoes, stock, and honey and season well. Bring the sauce to a boil, then turn down the heat. Simmer slowly, uncovered, for 30 minutes.

3 Add the butternut squash, chickpeas, and chopped dried apricots, and continue to cook for 10–15 minutes until the squash is soft, but not falling apart. Add more water if it is beginning to look a little dry. Season to taste and stir in the chopped cilantro before serving with some herb couscous.

spicy, saucy fish

Serve this halibut with poppadums and aromatic basmati rice.

 30-35 MINS　 30-35 MINS

SPECIAL EQUIPMENT ▪ blender

SERVES 6

2 tbsp butter

1 apple, peeled, cored, and cubed into ½in (1cm) pieces

3 onions, 1 finely chopped and 2 thinly sliced

1 tsp ground cumin

1 tsp ground coriander

½ tsp ground ginger

½ tsp ground cloves

¼ tsp cayenne pepper, or ½ tsp crushed chiles

1½ tbsp cornstarch

¾ cup coconut milk

1¾ cup fish stock

salt and freshly ground black pepper

2¼lb (1kg) halibut fillets, skinned

¼ cup vegetable oil

2 tbsp paprika

2 x 14oz (400g) cans tomatoes

6 garlic cloves, finely chopped

4 bay leaves

2 celery stalks, peeled and thinly sliced

2 carrots, thinly sliced

1 To make the spicy sauce, melt the butter in a saucepan. Add the apple and chopped onion and cook for 3–5 minutes until soft. Add the cumin, coriander, ginger, cloves, and cayenne. Stir over low heat for 2–3 minutes. Put the cornstarch and 2–3 tbsp of the coconut milk in a small bowl and blend to a smooth paste. Add the remaining coconut milk and ⅔ cup of stock to the saucepan and bring to a boil. Stir in the cornstarch paste; the sauce will thicken at once. Remove from the heat, season to taste, and set aside.

2 Rinse the fish, pat dry with paper towels, and cut into 1in (2.5cm) cubes. Heat the oil in a casserole dish. Add the sliced onions and cook for 3–5 minutes until soft. Add the paprika and cook for about 1 minute, stirring to combine it evenly with the onions. Add the remaining stock, tomatoes, garlic, bay leaves, celery, and carrots. Season and bring to a boil. Reduce the heat and simmer until the liquid is reduced by a third; it should take 15–20 minutes.

3 Add the spicy sauce, stir well, and bring back to a boil. Add the fish, cover with a lid, and simmer, stirring occasionally, for 12–15 minutes, until the fish flakes easily. Discard the bay leaves and taste for seasoning, then serve in warmed bowls.

butternut squash stuffed with ground beef

A simple all-in-one dish that uses a halved squash as "bowls."

 15 MINS　 1 HR

SERVES 4

1 butternut squash, halved and seeded

2 tbsp olive oil

1 onion, finely chopped

1½lb (675g) ground beef

salt and freshly ground black pepper

handful of flat-leaf parsley, finely chopped

Gruyère cheese, grated, to serve

1 Preheat the oven to 400°F (200°C). Put the squash halves in a roasting pan, drizzle half the oil over the top, and roast in the oven for about 10–15 minutes until softened.

2 Meanwhile, heat the remaining oil in a frying pan over medium heat, add the chopped onion, and cook for 3–4 minutes until soft. Add the beef and cook, stirring frequently, for about 5 minutes until the meat starts to color. Season with salt and pepper, and stir in the parsley.

3 Remove the squash from the oven and spoon the ground beef into the hollows. Cover with foil and roast for 30 minutes. Then remove the foil, sprinkle the Gruyère cheese over the top, and return to the oven for about 5 minutes, or until the Gruyère cheese has melted.

yellow squash gratin

Although less sweet than zucchini, yellow squash becomes more concentrated in flavor when baked and makes a good base for other ingredients. This gratin tastes great with chicken.

 20 MINS 50 MINS

SERVES 4

2 tbsp olive oil

1 onion, finely chopped

2lb (900g) yellow squash, halved, seeded, peeled, and cut into cubes

1lb (450g) tomatoes, finely chopped

3 garlic cloves, grated or finely chopped

handful of flat-leaf parsley, finely chopped

salt and freshly ground black pepper

3 tbsp fresh bread crumbs

1¾oz (50g) Parmesan cheese, grated

1 Preheat the oven to 400°F (200°C). Heat the oil in a large pan, add the onion, and cook over low heat for 5 minutes, or until soft and translucent. Add the yellow squash and cook for another 5 minutes, then add the tomatoes and garlic and cook over low heat for 10 minutes, or until the tomatoes start to break down. Stir in the parsley and season well with salt and pepper.

2 Spoon the mixture into one large gratin dish or four small ones. Sprinkle on the bread crumbs and Parmesan cheese and bake in the oven for 20–30 minutes, or until the top is crisp and golden, then serve.

pasta with butternut squash, cream, and sage

This filling dish is so easy to make—the butternut squash needs just a little initial cooking in the oven. This meal is hard to beat as the days get shorter and the weather turns colder.

 15 MINS 20 MINS

SERVES 4

1 butternut squash, halved, seeded, peeled, and cubed

pinch of chile flakes

2 tbsp olive oil

1 red onion, finely chopped

2 garlic cloves, grated or finely chopped

6 sage leaves, coarsely chopped

⅔ cup heavy cream

salt and freshly ground black pepper

12oz (350g) conchiglie

Parmesan cheese, grated, to serve

1 Preheat the oven to 400°F (200°C). Place the squash in a large roasting pan, sprinkle with chile flakes, and drizzle with 1 tbsp of the oil. Combine well and roast in the oven for 10–15 minutes, or until the squash starts to soften.

2 Heat the remaining oil in a large frying pan, add the onion, and cook over low heat for 5 minutes, or until soft and translucent. Add the almost-cooked squash, garlic, and sage leaves, and stir together. Pour in the cream and simmer gently for 5 minutes. Season well with salt and lots of pepper.

3 Meanwhile, cook the pasta in a large pan of boiling salted water for 10 minutes, or until it is tender but still firm to the bite. Drain, keeping back a tiny amount of the cooking water. Return the pasta to the pan and toss it with the reserved cooking water. Then toss the pasta with the sauce, sprinkle with Parmesan, and serve.

roasted squid and potato with spiced cilantro pesto

Squid is sweet and tender when cooked quickly (or very slowly). Choose baby squid for the most succulent option.

  10 MINS   20 MINS

SPECIAL EQUIPMENT ▪ food processor

SERVES 4

large handful of cilantro

large handful of basil leaves

2 garlic cloves, chopped

large handful of pine nuts

pinch of chile flakes, plus extra (optional)

2oz (60g) Parmesan cheese, grated

⅔ cup extra virgin olive oil (use more or less as required)

salt and freshly ground black pepper

2½lb (1.1kg) Yukon Gold potatoes, peeled and cubed

2 tbsp olive oil

12oz (350g) squid, gutted, cleaned, and scored (p263, or you can have this done at the fish counter)

1 Preheat the oven to 400°F (200°C). To make the pesto, put the cilantro, basil, garlic, and pine nuts in a food processor and pulse until the nuts are ground. Add the chile flakes and most of the Parmesan cheese and pulse again. Now slowly add the extra virgin olive oil in a gradual stream and pulse until the pesto forms a smooth paste and reaches the right consistency. Stir in the remaining Parmesan, taste, and season with salt and pepper if it needs it. Set aside.

2 Put the potatoes in a roasting pan. Drizzle over 1 tbsp of the olive oil and toss. Season with salt and pepper. Roast in the oven for 15–20 minutes until golden.

3 Meanwhile, mix the squid with the chile flakes (if using) and remaining olive oil in a bowl. Add to the potatoes for the last 10 minutes or so of cooking and cook until the squid is slightly charred. Toss everything together, then serve hot with the cilantro pesto.

pork with fennel and mustard

Bulbous fennel has a light, aromatic aniseed taste. Eaten raw it is distinctive, crisp, and refreshing, but once cooked its flavors soften and sweeten, and marry well with pork.

 20 MINS   45 MINS   FREEZABLE

SERVES 4

3 tbsp olive oil

1 large onion, sliced

2 small fennel bulbs, sliced

1¼lb (550g) lean pork, cut into bite-sized pieces

4 garlic cloves, finely chopped

5 tbsp dry white wine

1 tbsp whole-grain mustard

½ tsp paprika

small handful of flat-leaf parsley, chopped

½ tbsp chopped sage leaves

½ tbsp chopped rosemary leaves

1 tbsp all-purpose flour

1¾ cups milk

salt and freshly ground black pepper

1 Preheat the oven to 350°F (180°C). Heat the oil in a large heavy-bottomed pan, add the onion and fennel, and cook for 5 minutes, or until the vegetables begin to soften. Add the pork and cook, stirring occasionally, for 5 minutes, or until it is no longer pink. Add the garlic and cook for 1 minute, then stir in the wine and mustard, raise the heat, and allow to boil for 3 minutes while the alcohol evaporates. Stir in the paprika, parsley, sage, and rosemary, then add the flour and mix well. Add a little of the milk, mix to a smooth paste, then stir in the rest of the milk. Season well with salt and pepper and cook for 5 minutes, adding a little more milk if the mixture looks dry.

2 Transfer to a casserole dish, cover, cook in the oven for 25 minutes or until piping hot, and serve.

variation

beef with celery and mustard

Prepare in exactly the same way, but use 2 celery hearts, sliced, instead of the fennel and 1lb 2oz (500g) beef sirloin steak, cut in thin strips, instead of the pork. Substitute 2 tsp chopped fresh thyme for the sage.

eggplant massaman curry

This is a spicy Thai curry with the distinctively sweet flavors of cinnamon and cardamom. The peanuts add a contrasting texture to the potatoes and eggplant.

 15 MINS   1 HR

SPECIAL EQUIPMENT ▪ food processor

SERVES 4–6

2 red chiles, seeded

1 lemongrass stalk, tough outer leaves removed

2in (5cm) piece of fresh ginger, peeled and coarsely chopped

5 cardamom pods, crushed

1 tbsp sunflower or vegetable oil

1 onion, finely chopped

salt and freshly ground black pepper

2 cups hot vegetable stock

14oz (400ml) can coconut milk

1 cinnamon stick, broken

splash of dark soy sauce

splash of fish sauce (nam pla)

4 potatoes, peeled and chopped into bite-sized pieces

6 baby eggplants, halved lengthwise, or use 2 large ones, coarsely chopped

3oz (85g) roasted unsalted peanuts, coarsely chopped

1 tbsp palm sugar or brown sugar (optional)

1 Put the chiles, lemongrass, ginger, and cardamom in a food processor and pulse with a drop of the oil to make a paste.

2 Heat the remaining oil in a large heavy-bottomed pan over medium heat, add the onion, and cook for 3–4 minutes until soft. Then add the paste and some seasoning and cook for a few minutes more. Stir in the stock and coconut milk, bring to a boil, then add the cinnamon stick, soy sauce, and fish sauce, and cook on low heat for about 20 minutes. Stir in the potatoes and eggplants and cook the curry for another 20 minutes.

3 Stir in half the peanuts, taste, and adjust the flavor by adding the sugar, if desired, and more salt or fish sauce, as needed. Ladle into warmed bowls and sprinkle with the remaining peanuts. Serve with rice and lime wedges.

cornish game hens with plums and cabbage

If you prefer, this recipe is equally good made with a chicken. Much of this dish can be made ahead and kept, covered, in the fridge; simply reheat and make the plum sauce before serving.

 15 MINS   1 HR 45 MINS

SERVES 4

2–3 Cornish game hens, each about 1lb 2oz (500g) in weight, trussed with twine

salt and freshly ground black pepper

½ Savoy cabbage, cored and coarsely shredded

2 tbsp vegetable oil

9oz (250g) thick-cut bacon, sliced

14oz (400g) purple plums, halved and pitted

1 onion, peeled and studded with 1 clove

1 bouquet garni (4 sprigs parsley, 4 sprigs thyme, and 1 bay leaf)

1 cup dry white wine

2 cups hot chicken stock

1 Preheat the oven to 350°F (180°C). Season the hens and set aside. Cook the cabbage in a pan of salted boiling water for 2 minutes until it begins to soften. Drain and set aside. Heat the oil in a large flameproof casserole dish, add the birds, one or two at a time, and cook for 5–10 minutes until browned all over. Remove and set aside. Reduce the heat and cook the bacon, stirring, for 3–5 minutes until the fat has rendered. Spoon off all but 2 tbsp of fat and spread half the cabbage across the bottom of the casserole dish. Add the hens, two-thirds of the plums, the onion, and bouquet garni. Cover with the remaining cabbage and pour in the wine and stock. Cover and cook in the oven for 45–55 minutes, until the birds are cooked and the juices run clear if the thighs are pierced with a sharp knife.

2 Discard the onion and bouquet garni. Transfer the cabbage to a serving dish. Set the birds on top (with twine removed), cover with foil, and keep warm. Add the last of the plums to the cooking liquid and simmer for 5–8 minutes until tender, then remove and transfer to the serving dish. Boil the plum sauce for 10–15 minutes until reduced by about half, season if needed, then serve with the hens and cabbage.

grilled lamb chops and eggplant with red cabbage slaw

Red cabbage coleslaw gives this dish of lamb and grilled eggplant a refreshingly different twist.

 25 MINS 10 MINS

SERVES 4

12 lamb chops, trimmed of any fat

2 tbsp olive oil

salt and freshly ground black pepper

1 eggplant, about 10oz (300g), thinly sliced lengthwise

½ small red cabbage

3½oz (100g) thin green beans, trimmed, blanched, and thinly sliced diagonally

1 small cucumber, thinly sliced or shaved lengthwise

1 small red onion, thinly sliced in rounds

2 celery stalks, peeled and thinly sliced diagonally

2oz (60g) hazelnuts, chopped

small handful of chives, snipped

2 tbsp extra virgin olive oil

1 tsp balsamic vinegar

1 Heat the grill to medium. Brush the lamb chops with olive oil and season with salt and pepper. Grill the lamb over medium heat for 3–5 minutes on each side until cooked to your liking. Remove the lamb to a plate and set aside to rest in a warm place. Turn the grill to high and brush the eggplant slices with a little olive oil and season with black pepper. Grill the eggplant over high heat for about 3 minutes on each side until golden. Remove the eggplant and transfer to the plate of lamb.

2 Finely slice or shred the red cabbage and place in a mixing bowl. Add the remaining ingredients, season with salt and pepper, toss gently, and serve with the lamb chops and eggplant slices.

hungarian beef goulash

Make the most of the season's glossy bell peppers and tomatoes with this traditional beef stew.

 25-30 MINS 2 HRS 45 MINS

SERVES 4

1 tbsp vegetable oil

2oz (60g) smoked bacon, cubed

6 onions, about 1lb 10oz (750g) total weight, chopped

2 tbsp paprika

1lb 10oz (750g) beef stew meat, cut into 1½in (4cm) cubes

2 garlic cloves, finely chopped

½ tsp caraway seeds

2 tomatoes, cored, seeded, and chopped

2 green bell peppers, sliced

salt and freshly ground black pepper

1 large egg

¼ cup all-purpose flour

½ cup sour cream (optional)

1 Heat the oil in a casserole dish, add the bacon, and stir for 3–5 minutes until it is lightly browned and the fat has rendered. Stir in the onions. Cut a piece of foil to fit the casserole dish, then cover the mixture and put on the lid. Cook over low heat, stirring occasionally, for 20–25 minutes until the onions are soft and translucent.

2 Preheat the oven to 350°F (180°C). Stir the paprika into the onions and bacon and cook for 2 minutes; don't let the paprika scorch. Add the beef, garlic, caraway seeds, and 2 cups water and stir. Bring to a boil, stirring, then cover and cook in the oven for 1–1½ hours until the beef is almost tender.

3 Stir the tomatoes and peppers into the goulash. Season to taste. Cover and cook for 30–45 minutes more until the meat is very soft and the stew rich and thick. Taste for seasoning.

4 Lightly beat the egg in a small bowl. Put the flour and a little salt in another bowl, then stir in the egg. Transfer the goulash to the stovetop and heat to boiling. Using 2 teaspoons, drop spoonfuls of the dumpling mix into the goulash and simmer for 5–7 minutes until cooked.

5 Ladle the goulash and dumplings into warmed soup bowls. Top each serving with a spoon of sour cream, if desired.

crispy duck char sui

Char sui is a Chinese barbecue sauce traditionally used with pork, chicken, or duck. It has a lovely spicy sweet-sour flavor that cuts through the richness of the duck meat.

 15 MINS   45 MINS

SERVES 4

4 duck thighs and legs, with small incisions made all over with a knife

3 garlic cloves, grated or finely chopped

3 tbsp light soy sauce

3 tbsp rice wine

1 tbsp hoisin sauce

2 tbsp honey

2 tsp five-spice powder

salt and freshly ground black pepper

1 Preheat the oven to 400°F (200°C). Put all the ingredients in a large bowl and season with salt and pepper. Mix everything together so that the duck is well coated. Wrap the coated duck pieces in foil and roast in the oven for 30 minutes.

2 Preheat the broiler until hot. Carefully unwrap the foil and sit the duck on the hot broiler, skin-side up.

Broil under high heat, turning frequently, for 10–15 minutes until the skin is golden and crisp. Remove to a plate and leave to rest in a warm place for about 10 minutes. Then cut the crispy duck into slices and serve with a crisp green salad.

variation

crispy wild duck with plums

Prepare in the same way but use 2 small wild ducks, halved, instead of the leg portions. Roast in the oven for 30–40 minutes. Brush 8 halved and pitted just-ripe plums with a mixture of 2 tbsp honey and ¼ soy sauce in a shallow, flameproof dish. Broil alongside the duck or, pan-fry in 1 tbsp sunflower or vegetable oil for 1–2 minutes on each side until softening but still holding their shape. Serve with the duck and salad.

salmon with mushrooms and bok choy

Crimini mushrooms have a lovely meaty taste and give depth to the mild flavors of salmon and bok choy in this dish.

 15 MINS   25 MINS

SERVES 4

1 tbsp olive oil

1 tbsp dark soy sauce

½ tbsp mirin

2in (5cm) piece of fresh ginger, peeled and finely chopped

2 garlic cloves, grated or finely chopped

salt and freshly ground black pepper

4 salmon fillets, approx 5½oz (150g) in weight

2 heads of bok choy, quartered lengthwise

7oz (200g) crimini mushrooms, large ones halved

1 Preheat the oven to 400°F (200°C). Put the oil, soy sauce, mirin, ginger, and garlic in a bowl and mix together well. Season with salt and pepper.

2 Put the salmon fillets, bok choy, and mushrooms in a roasting pan, then drizzle in the oil mixture and combine well. Put into the oven to roast for 20–25 minutes, or until the salmon is cooked through, and serve with plain rice.

variation

quick stir-fried fish with bok choy

Cube 1lb 5oz (600g) salmon steak or chunky white fish, such as cod or halibut. Slice the 7oz (200g) mushrooms and thickly shred the 2 heads of bok choy. Heat 1 tbsp olive oil or sunflower oil in a wok or large saucepan over medium heat. Stir-fry the fish and mushrooms for 2 minutes. Add the bok choy and stir-fry for another 1–2 minutes until slightly wilted. Add the flavorings as in the original recipe but add ½ tsp Chinese five-spice powder as well. Stir-fry briefly to combine. Moisten with a splash of water or chicken stock, then serve spooned onto egg noodles or rice.

broiled fish with spice rub

The firm flesh of rockfish is wonderful with the strong flavors in this recipe. Make the spice rub up to 6 hours ahead and store in an airtight container at room temperature.

 15 MINS 6–8 MINS ✳ FREEZABLE

SERVES 4

4 black rockfish or sea bream fillets, about 5½oz (150g) each, scaled and pinboned

1 tbsp walnuts

4 plum tomatoes, chopped

1 tbsp chopped cilantro leaves

1½ tsp walnut or olive oil

salt and freshly ground black pepper

lemon wedges, to serve

For the spice rub

3 tbsp walnut or olive oil

4 tbsp chopped cilantro leaves

2 garlic cloves, crushed

1 tsp crushed coriander seeds

1 tsp lemon juice

1 small jalapeño chile, seeded and finely chopped

salt

1 Mix all the ingredients for the spice rub together in a bowl and season with salt. Preheat the broiler.

2 Line a baking sheet with foil and place the fish fillets on it, skin-side down. Brush the spice rub over the fish. Place under the broiler for 6–8 minutes, until cooked through and lightly golden. Remove from the heat and keep warm.

3 Meanwhile, for the tomato salad, roast the walnuts by stirring them in a dry frying pan over medium heat for 2–3 minutes, then remove and lightly crush. Mix with the tomatoes, cilantro, and walnut or olive oil, and season with salt and pepper. Serve the fish with the salad and lemon wedges on the side.

whole fish with tomato sauce

Make sure you use flavorful tomatoes, since they make all the difference to the finished dish. You can make the tomato sauce 2–3 days in advance, cover, and store in the fridge.

 10 MINS 25 MINS

SERVES 4

4 small sea bream or black rockfish, about 12oz (350g) in total, scaled, gutted, and trimmed

1 tbsp all-purpose flour

salt and freshly ground black pepper

5 tbsp extra virgin olive oil

1 onion, finely chopped

2 celery stalks, finely sliced

2 garlic cloves, chopped

8 plum tomatoes, coarsely chopped

5 tbsp dry white wine

pinch of sugar

2 tbsp chopped flat-leaf parsley

1 Preheat the oven to 375°F (190°C). Slash the rockfish 3–4 times on each side with a sharp knife. Mix the flour with some salt and pepper and dust it over the fish. Arrange on a baking sheet.

2 Heat the oil in a pan over low heat, add the onion, celery, and garlic, and cook for 2–3 minutes, until the vegetables soften. Add the tomatoes and wine, and cook for 3–4 minutes, until the juices run. Season with salt and pepper and add the sugar.

3 Spoon the tomato sauce over the fish and bake in the oven for 15–20 minutes, or until cooked. The flesh will be white and opaque.

4 Slide the fish onto a large, warmed serving dish, sprinkle with parsley, and serve immediately.

squid stew

Squid transforms when it is cooked slowly. It defies all rubbery associations and becomes wonderfully tender.

 30 MINS 1 HR 15 MINS–1 HR 45 MINS ✳ FREEZABLE

SERVES 4–6

1 tbsp olive oil

1 onion, finely chopped

salt and freshly ground black pepper

1 bay leaf

a few sprigs of thyme

3 garlic cloves, sliced

2 red chiles, seeded and sliced into thin strips

7oz (200g) dry, Spanish-style chorizo, sliced

2½lb (1.1kg) squid, gutted, cleaned and cut into rings (and tentacles, if you wish) (p263)

1 cup red wine

14oz (400g) can chopped tomatoes

2¼ cups vegetable stock

14oz (400g) can butter beans, drained

handful of curly parsley, finely chopped

1 Preheat the oven to 325°F (170°C). Heat the oil in a large flameproof casserole dish over medium heat, add the onion, and season with salt and pepper. Add the bay leaf and thyme, and cook gently for about 6 minutes until the onions are soft.

2 Stir in the garlic, chiles, and chorizo, and cook for a few minutes. Then add the squid (in batches, if necessary) and cook for a few more minutes, until the squid starts to color slightly. Increase the heat and pour in the wine. Let it simmer for 1–2 minutes, then add the tomatoes and stock, and bring to a boil.

3 Add in the butter beans and stir, then add some seasoning, cover with a lid, and put in the oven for 1–1½ hours. Check occasionally that it is not drying out and add a little hot water if required. Taste and season if needed, remove the bay leaf and thyme, and stir in the parsley. Ladle into warmed bowls and serve with crusty bread.

Season's best **sea bream**

There are several species of sea bream, best in winter, but farmed all year. All have a round, flattish body with a long, single, spiny dorsal fin. They have a good flavor with firm, dense flesh. Sea bream is excellent cooked simply with a few herbs, some butter, and garlic, but can be served in numerous dishes. They go particularly well with sweet spices and chile, tomatoes, celery root, and olives.

Sea bream fillet The white, well-textured flesh tastes its best when simply pan-fried.

It is easily recognized by its long, spiny dorsal fin and large scales.

Sea bream This is a well-flavored fish. It is one of the most versatile, and one many people haven't heard of or tried.

essentials
varieties available

Whole or fillets, farmed and wild black bream, white bream, and red bream.

buy Choose line- or net-caught fish with firm bodies, bright eyes, and red gills. Fillets should smell fresh and be moist.

store Best eaten on the day of purchase.

cook Pan-fry, grill, stuff, and bake.

recipe ideas

Broiled fish with spice rub
p292

Whole fish with tomato sauce
p292

Whole stuffed fish
p281

how to cook sea bream *en papillote*

Cooking any small whole fish in a parcel retains all its flavor and natural juices. Open the parcel at the table for maximum mouthwatering aroma.

1 Lay the prepared fish on a sheet of parchment paper placed on a baking sheet. Top with lemon slices, fresh herbs, seasoning, and a pat of butter.

2 Fold the paper over the fish and envelop it completely, leaving enough paper to seal.

3 Twist and fold the edge all around to seal the fish. Bake at 375°F (190°C) for about 20 minutes.

ground lamb and squash with green chiles

Lamb with sweet squash is the perfect combination and the ground meat benefits from long, slow cooking. Stirring mint and oregano leaves into the dish adds a distinct freshness.

 25 MINS   **1 HR 30 MINS–2 HRS**   **FREEZABLE**

SERVES 4–6

2 tbsp olive oil

1 butternut squash, peeled, seeded, and chopped into bite-sized pieces

salt and freshly ground black pepper

1 onion, finely chopped

handful of fresh oregano, leaves only, or 1 tsp dried oregano

handful of thyme, leaves only

3 garlic cloves, finely chopped

1 green jalapeño chile, seeded and finely chopped

1lb (450g) ground lamb

3 cups hot vegetable stock

14oz (400g) can chopped tomatoes

2oz (60g) golden raisins

bunch of mint leaves, finely chopped

1–2 tsp harissa paste

1 Preheat the oven to 350°F (180°C). Heat half the oil in a large flameproof casserole dish over medium heat and add the squash. Season with salt and pepper, and cook for 5–8 minutes, stirring, until it starts to turn golden. Remove the squash from the casserole dish and set aside.

2 Heat the remaining oil in the casserole dish, add the onion, and cook for 3–4 minutes until soft. Stir in the oregano, thyme, garlic, and chile, and cook for a few more minutes. Add the ground lamb, increase the heat a little, and cook, stirring, for 5–8 minutes until it is no longer pink. Reduce the heat, return the squash to the casserole dish, add the stock and tomatoes, and bring to a boil. Reduce to simmer, stir in the golden raisins, cover with the lid, and put in the oven for 1–1½ hours. Check occasionally that it is not drying out, adding a little hot water if needed.

3 Taste and season, if necessary, then stir in the mint and harissa paste to taste. Serve with rice or warmed pita bread and a lightly dressed, crisp green salad.

variation

spicy ground beef with sweet potato and eggs

Prepare as for the ground lamb, but use a fairly large sweet potato instead of the butternut squash and add a cubed green bell pepper. Use 1lb (450g) extra-lean ground beef instead of the ground lamb. Add 1 tbsp sambal olek instead of the harissa paste to add extra fire and flavor. Spoon onto 4 plates and top each with a fried egg. Serve with rolled-up flour tortillas instead of pita breads or rice.

french-style duck legs

In this simplified version of duck confit, duck legs are steeped in a fragrant marinade and served with the traditional lentils.

 15 MINS PLUS MARINATING   3 HRS 45 MINS

SERVES 4

4 duck legs

1lb 2oz (500g) duck or goose fat

a few sprigs of rosemary

1 tbsp olive oil

1 onion, finely chopped

salt and freshly ground black pepper

2 garlic cloves, finely chopped

a few sprigs of thyme, leaves only

2 carrots, finely cubed

1 bay leaf

1 tbsp dry sherry

9oz (250g) Puy lentils, rinsed and picked over for any stones

1¾ cups hot chicken stock

For the marinade

3 tbsp brandy

1 tbsp black peppercorns, crushed

3 garlic cloves, finely chopped

pinch of ground cinnamon

a few sprigs of thyme

1 tbsp sea salt

1 Put the duck legs in a dish and add the marinade ingredients. Cover with plastic wrap, sit a weight on top, and refrigerate overnight. Preheat the oven to 300°F (150°C) and melt the duck fat in a large flameproof casserole dish. Add the legs (discard the liquid), ensuring they are covered in the fat. Add the rosemary, cover, and put in the oven for 3 hours, or until the meat is fork tender and the skin crispy. Let the casserole dish cool, remove the legs, and drain off the excess fat.

2 Meanwhile, heat the oil in a pan over medium heat, add the onion, and cook for 3–4 minutes until soft. Season, then stir in the garlic, thyme, carrots, and bay leaf. Stir over a low heat for 6–10 minutes, then increase the heat, add the sherry, and cook for 2 minutes. Stir in the lentils and then the stock. Bring to a boil, reduce to a simmer, and cook for 40 minutes, or until the lentils are tender. Add hot water if they start to dry out. Adjust the seasoning, remove the bay leaf and thyme, and serve with the duck.

duck curry

Duck curry is extremely rich and has a great depth of flavor. If you like your curry hot, use two red chiles rather than the one specified and leave the seeds in for an even greater kick.

 15 MINS   2 HRS

SERVES 4

2 duck breasts

1 tbsp sunflower oil

1 onion, finely chopped

2 celery stalks, finely chopped

salt and freshly ground black pepper

3 garlic cloves, finely chopped

1 red or jalapeño chile, seeded and finely chopped

2in (5cm) piece of fresh ginger, peeled and finely chopped

2 carrots, finely chopped

1 tbsp garam masala

1 tsp ground turmeric

1 tsp paprika

1 tbsp tomato paste

2 x 14oz (400g) cans chopped tomatoes

3 cups hot vegetable stock

1 Preheat the oven to 350°F (180°C). Heat a large flameproof casserole dish over medium-high heat and add the duck breasts, skin-side down. Cook each side for 3–6 minutes, or until golden. Remove and set aside. Heat the oil in the casserole dish over medium heat, add the onion and celery, and cook for 5 minutes until soft. Season with salt and pepper, stir in the garlic, chile, and ginger, and cook for 2 more minutes.

2 Add the carrots, turn to coat, and cook for 5 minutes, stirring from time to time. Stir in the spices and tomato paste and cook for 1–2 minutes, then add in the tomatoes and stock. Bring to a boil, reduce to simmer, and return the duck breasts to the casserole dish. Cover with the lid and put in the oven for 1½ hours. Check that it is not drying out, adding hot water if needed.

3 Remove from the oven and spoon out the duck breasts. Peel off the skin and shred the meat. Put the meat back into the casserole dish and return to the oven for another 30 minutes, uncovered if the sauce is too thin. Adjust the seasoning if necessary. Serve with rice and chapatis.

sausage and chicken gumbo

Cajun gumbo is related to paella and often contains seafood. If you wish to add some, do it at the end of the cooking time.

🥣 20 MINS   🍲 2 HRS

SERVES 4–6

1 tbsp olive oil

1 onion, finely chopped

salt and freshly ground black pepper

3 celery stalks, finely cubed

2 red bell peppers, seeded and finely chopped

2 garlic cloves, finely chopped

14oz (400g) pork sausages, each sliced into 3 pieces

2 tbsp all-purpose flour

2–3 tsp Cajun seasoning

14oz (400g) boneless, skinless chicken breast, cut into bite-sized pieces

3 cups hot chicken stock

1 Preheat the oven to 325°F (170°C). Heat the oil in a large flameproof casserole dish over medium heat, add the onion, and cook for

3–4 minutes until soft. Season, stir in the celery, peppers, and garlic, and cook for another 5–8 minutes until very soft. Add the sausages to the casserole dish and cook for 5–8 minutes until they are no longer pink.

2 Mix the flour and Cajun seasoning on a plate and coat the chicken in it. Add to the casserole dish and cook, stirring, for 5–8 minutes, then add a little stock and bring it to a boil. Pour in the remaining stock and continue boiling for a minute. Reduce to a simmer and check the seasoning.

3 Cover the casserole dish with the lid and put in the oven for 1½ hours. Check occasionally that it is not drying out and add a little hot water, if needed. Taste and season, then ladle out over warmed bowls of rice.

Season's best **duck**

Versatile and easy to cook, ducks are delicious and fairly rich. Those bred from the wild mallard have dark, rich meat with a thick layer of fat under the skin, while the ones from the Muscovy duck are larger and leaner. Wild ducks are leaner with a more gamey flavor. Farmed ducks are available all year; wild ones, in autumn and early winter. They taste phenomenal with the sharp and fruity flavors of garlic, scallions, ginger, apples, cherries, plums, oranges, olives, and wine.

Duck The ratio of meat to bone is low in a duck, but since it is rich, portions can be small. An average duck will serve 4 people. After roasting, store the drained-off duck fat in the fridge and use for roasting potatoes.

The breast meat remains succulent under the layer of fat.

Put an onion or herbs inside for flavor when roasting.

Leg Duck legs have superb flavor. They take longer to cook than breast meat and have a little more sinew, but can be grilled, roasted, or used to make confit. Prick or slash the skin and fat layer beneath before cooking.

Breast Duck breasts have dense, rich meat. If cooking whole, score or prick through the skin and fat, then cook skin-side down, or grill skin-side up, to melt and release excess fat. Or remove all skin and fat before cooking whole or in pieces.

The small inner fillets are sometimes sold separately as aiguillettes.

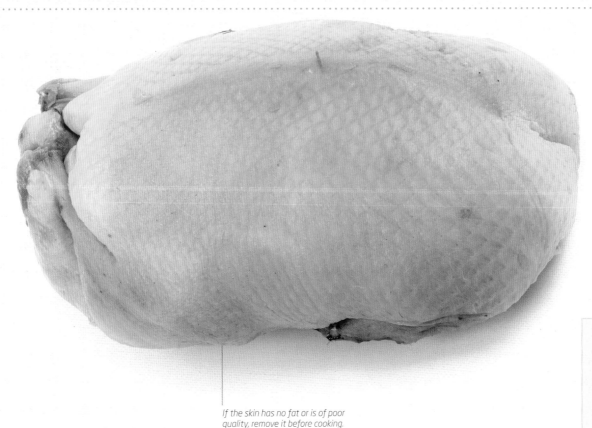

Mallard Many mallard are lured into ponds with grain, and eating this can make their fat quite yellow. Whiter fat usually indicates a more varied diet.

If the skin has no fat or is of poor quality, remove it before cooking.

how to joint a duck

For braising or casseroling, cut the bird into pieces. To roast, leave the bird whole. This technique gives you eight small portions, which is ample for four people. Use the cut-away rib bones and backbone for stock to braise or casserole the duck in, or for soup.

1 Trim the excess fat and skin. Using a sharp knife, cut down between a leg and the body. Twist to break the joint. Cut the whole leg. Repeat with the other.

2 Cut each leg in half at the joint between the thigh and the drumstick, using the line of white fat on the underside as a guide.

3 Slit closely along both sides of the breastbone to loosen the skin and meat from the bone. With poultry shears or a sharp knife, cut along the breastbone, to split it lengthwise in half.

4 Turn the bird over. Cut away the rib bones and backbone. Leave the breast pieces with the wing joints attached. Cut each breast piece diagonally in half. Remove any sharp bones.

essentials
varieties available

Several popular breeds including wild mallard, Aylesbury, Pekin, and Muscovy (Barbary).

buy Look for birds with plump breasts and firm skin. Rich duck meat is filling, so a large breast will stretch for 2 people if cut in pieces. Allow at least 1lb 2oz (500g) per person with whole birds.

store Keep whole birds and pieces well wrapped, at the bottom of the fridge, for up to 3 days.

cook Roast whole duck. Broil, fry, or barbecue duck breasts to serve pink; score or prick skin to release the fat and start cooking them fat-side to the heat. Or slice into the flesh into strips for stir-fry. Broil or barbecue legs, or use them for stews and confit.

preserve Freeze, with giblets separate. Duck can be smoked or the legs confited (salted, then slowly cooked in oil, and stored in it).

recipe ideas

Chinese roast duck p369

Duck curry p295

Duck in orange sauce p450

French-style duck legs p295

beet risotto

This colorful risotto is best when cooked with freshly harvested beets. The earthy flavor of the beet and the sharp tang of goat cheese combine beautifully.

 30 MINS   1 HR

SPECIAL EQUIPMENT ▪ food processor

SERVES 4

1lb 2oz (500g) raw beets, peeled and cubed

2 tbsp extra virgin olive oil, plus extra for tossing

sea salt and freshly ground black pepper

6 tbsp sunflower or vegetable oil

20 sage leaves

2 onions, finely cubed

2 garlic cloves, crushed

12oz (350g) risotto rice

3½ cups hot vegetable or chicken stock

2oz (60g) Parmesan cheese, grated

7oz (200g) firm goat cheese, cubed into ½in (1cm) pieces

1 Preheat the oven to 400°F (200°C). Toss the beets in a little olive oil, sea salt, and pepper. Wrap in foil and cook in the oven for 30–40 minutes until soft.

2 In a small pan, heat the sunflower oil over high heat until smoking. Drop in most of the sage leaves, a few at a time, and deep-fry for

5 seconds, or until they stop fizzing. Remove and drain.

3 Remove the beets from the oven and pulse in a food processor with 4 tbsp water, the remaining sage leaves, and some sea salt and pepper. Set aside.

4 Fry the onions in the olive oil over moderate heat for 3 minutes, until soft. Add the garlic and cook for 1 minute. Pour in the rice and stir, so that the grains are coated in oil.

5 Keeping the stock on low simmer, add a ladleful at a time to the rice, stirring continuously until each ladleful is absorbed, for about 15 minutes, until the rice is almost cooked. Add the beet puree to the risotto and cook, stirring, for another 5–10 minutes until the rice is still firm to the bite and creamy.

6 Remove the rice from the heat, season, then stir in two-thirds of the Parmesan and fold in the goat cheese. Garnish with the fried sage leaves and remaining Parmesan.

pot roast chicken with turnips and fennel

This slow-cooked whole chicken is simplicity itself and yields meltingly tender results. Use the bones for stock afterward.

 15 MINS   2 HRS–2 HRS 30 MINS

SERVES 4–6

2 tbsp olive oil

1 whole chicken, weighing about 3lb (1.35kg)

salt and freshly ground black pepper

6 pork sausages, coarsely chopped

1 fennel bulb, coarsely chopped

1 bay leaf

2 sprigs of rosemary

1 cup white wine

9oz (250g) turnips, peeled and coarsely chopped

3 cups hot chicken stock

1 Preheat the oven to 350°F (180°C). Heat half the oil in a large flameproof casserole dish, season the chicken with salt and pepper, then add it to the casserole, breast-side down. Cook for about 10 minutes, then turn and cook the other side for about the same time. Remove and set aside.

2 Heat the remaining oil in the casserole dish on high heat, add the sausages, and cook for 6–8 minutes until browned. Then reduce the heat, add the fennel, bay leaf, and rosemary, and cook for another 5 minutes. Increase the heat, add the wine, and let it bubble for a minute, then add the turnips.

3 Return the chicken to the casserole dish, breast-side down, and arrange the vegetables around it. Add the stock, bring to a boil, then cover and put in the oven for 1½–2 hours. Check occasionally that it is not drying out and add a little hot water, if needed. Carefully remove the chicken from the casserole dish, together with the bay leaf and rosemary, peel off the skin, and shred the meat back into the casserole. Serve immediately with steamed Savoy cabbage.

beef chile mole

This is a Mexican-inspired dish with lots of chile heat.

 15 MINS   2 HRS 30 MINS   FREEZABLE

SPECIAL EQUIPMENT ▪ food processor

SERVES 4

1lb 8oz (700g) beef stew meat, cut into bite-sized pieces

1 tbsp chipotle sauce or salsa

3 tbsp olive oil

1oz (30g) sesame seeds, roasted

2oz (60g) almonds, skin on, roasted

1 red bell pepper, seeded and coarsely chopped

4 tomatoes, coarsely chopped

2 flour tortillas, coarsely torn

2 cups hot vegetable stock

3 garlic cloves, finely chopped

1 red chile, seeded and finely chopped

1 jalapeño chile, seeded and finely chopped

salt and freshly ground black pepper

small bunch of cilantro, leaves chopped

1 red onion, finely chopped

1 Preheat the oven to 325°F (170°C). Toss the beef in the sauce. Heat 1 tbsp of the oil in a flameproof casserole dish and cook the beef for 5–8 minutes until browned. Remove and set aside.

2 Grind the sesame and almonds in a food processor, then leave them in it. Heat 1 tbsp of the oil in the casserole dish, add the bell pepper and tomatoes, and cook for 2–3 minutes until soft. Add to the food processor and pulse to a paste. Add the tortillas and 2 ladles of stock. Pulse to a sauce consistency.

3 In the remaining oil, cook the garlic and chiles for 1 minute. Add the sauce, the remaining stock, and seasoning. Bring to a boil, reduce to simmer, and add the beef. Cover and put in the oven for 2 hours. Add hot water occasionally if needed. Stir in the coriander and serve with the onion scattered on top.

chicken doner kebab

While doner kebab is often associated with too many calories, this fresh-tasting version with zingy flavors is a healthy and delicious take on a traditional favorite.

 15 MINS PLUS MARINATING   15 MINS

SERVES 4

1 tsp cayenne pepper

1 tbsp olive oil

juice of 1 lemon

4 boneless, skinless chicken breasts, cut into fine strips

4 pita breads

1 crispy lettuce, such as Romaine or Little Gem, shredded

2 onions, sliced

¼ red cabbage, shredded

hot chile sauce, to taste

garlic mayonnaise, to taste

1 ripe tomato, sliced

¼ cucumber, sliced

4 whole pickled green chiles

1 In a bowl, mix together the cayenne pepper, oil, and a quarter of the lemon juice. Add the chicken strips and marinate in the fridge for 1 hour.

2 Preheat the broiler until hot. Arrange the chicken strips in a shallow baking pan and cook under the hot broiler for about 10 minutes, turning occasionally.

3 Lightly roast the pita breads and cut open along one edge to form a pocket.

4 Stuff each pita pocket with a handful of lettuce, onion, and red cabbage, then the chicken pieces. Dress with the remaining lemon juice and some chile sauce and garlic mayonnaise to taste. Garnish with the tomato slices, cucumber, and a pickled chile. Serve immediately.

variation

chicken shish kebabs

Cut the chicken breasts into bite-sized pieces. Mix with the cayenne, olive oil, and lemon juice, but add 1 tsp dried oregano and a crushed garlic clove to the marinade. When ready to cook, thread alternately on 8 soaked wooden skewers with cubes of red and green bell pepper. Broil for 8–10 minutes, turning occasionally, until cooked through.

warm salad of wild mushrooms

To make expensive wild mushrooms go further, you can replace half the amount with button mushrooms for this salad.

 25-30 MINS   8-10 MINS

SERVES 4

13oz (375g) mixed wild mushrooms, such as chanterelles, oyster mushrooms, and porcini

2-3 tbsp butter

2 shallots, finely cubed

1 small bunch of parsley, leaves picked and chopped

1 small head of frisée, leaves picked

1 small head of radicchio, leaves picked

2½oz (75g) arugula leaves

For the vinaigrette

2 tbsp red wine vinegar

½ tsp Dijon mustard

salt and freshly ground black pepper

3 tbsp vegetable oil

3 tbsp walnut oil

1 First, make the vinaigrette. In a bowl, whisk together the vinegar, mustard, salt, and pepper. Gradually whisk in the vegetable and walnut oils, so that the vinaigrette emulsifies and thickens slightly. Taste for seasoning.

2 Wipe the mushrooms with damp paper towels. Trim the stalks and remove any woody portions. Place the mushrooms on a cutting board and cut them into medium-sized pieces.

3 Heat the butter in a frying pan until foaming. Add the shallots and cook, stirring occasionally, for 2–3 minutes, until soft. Add the mushrooms, salt, and pepper. Cook, stirring, for 5–7 minutes, until the mushrooms are tender and all the liquid has evaporated. Stir in the parsley and taste for seasoning, adjusting if necessary.

4 Briskly whisk the vinaigrette to reemulsify it, then pour it over the salad leaves in a bowl and toss them well until all are coated. Taste for seasoning. Divide the salad leaves between 4 plates and spoon the mushrooms from the pan over the top. Serve at once while the salad remains crisp and the mushrooms are still warm from the stove.

mackerel with garlic and tomatoes

When buying fresh mackerel, they should feel firm and rigid, and their bodies shiny and eyes bright. They are best eaten on the day of purchase or within 24 hours if kept chilled.

 10 MINS   **25 MINS**

SERVES 4

24 cherry tomatoes on the vine, snipped with a little of the stem left

4 garlic cloves, peeled

a few sprigs of thyme

grated zest of 1 lemon

pinch of dried chile flakes

1–2 tbsp olive oil

salt and freshly ground black pepper

4 mackerel fillets, each 4–5½oz (115–150g)

1 Preheat the oven to 400°F (200°C). Put the tomatoes, garlic, and thyme sprigs in a roasting pan. Sprinkle the lemon zest and chile flakes over the top. Drizzle with the oil and season with salt and pepper. Roast in the oven for about 10 minutes until the tomatoes begin to soften.

2 Remove from the oven, place the mackerel on top of the tomatoes, then cover the roasting pan with foil. Return to the oven and cook for another 10–15 minutes, until the fish is cooked through. Remove the sprigs of thyme and discard. Serve hot with salad and fresh crusty bread.

variation

mackerel with zucchini, tomato, and basil

Prepare in the same way, but add 2 large sliced zucchini to the roasting pan with the tomatoes. Add a small handful of chopped basil instead of the thyme. Drizzle the fish with a little chile oil before cooking in the oven and garnish when cooked, with torn basil leaves.

risotto with mussels

Mussels make a lovely, rich risotto, with the fennel adding a subtle aniseed flavor to the creamy rice.

 20 MINS   **45–55 MINS**

SERVES 4–6

1 tbsp olive oil

1oz (25g) butter

1 onion, finely chopped

salt and freshly ground black pepper

3 garlic cloves, finely chopped

pinch of dried chile flakes

1 fennel bulb, trimmed and finely chopped

10oz (300g) arborio rice or carnaroli rice

½ cup white wine

3 cups hot vegetable stock

2lb (900g) mussels, scrubbed and cleaned (discard any that do not close when tapped) (p364)

bunch of flat-leaf parsley, finely chopped

a few sprigs of dill, finely chopped

juice of 1 lemon, to serve (optional)

1 Heat the oil and butter in a heavy-bottomed pan over medium heat, add the onion, and cook for 3–4 minutes until soft. Season with salt and pepper, stir in the garlic and chile flakes, and cook for 1 minute.

2 Add the fennel and cook for about 5 minutes until soft, then stir in the rice. Increase the heat, add the wine, and let it simmer for 1–2 minutes until it has been absorbed. In a separate saucepan, simmer the stock. Add a ladleful to the rice and stir, until it has been absorbed. Continue doing this for 30–40 minutes, or until the rice is firm to the bite and is creamy. You may not need all the stock or you may need a little more.

3 Stir in the mussels, cover, and leave for a few minutes until the mussels have opened (discard any that do not open). Stir in the parsley and dill, and add a squeeze of lemon juice, if using. Taste and season with some pepper if needed. Serve immediately.

paprika rice and eggplant

Eggplant and paprika work together really well, since the eggplant absorbs the flavor of this pungent spice. The chickpeas make this a substantial supper dish.

 20 MINS   **45–55 MINS**

SERVES 4–6

3–4 tbsp olive oil

2 eggplants, chopped into bite-sized pieces

1 tbsp paprika

1 onion, finely chopped

1 tsp dried mint

salt and freshly ground black pepper

3 garlic cloves, finely chopped

2 green chiles, seeded and finely chopped

grated zest of 1 lemon and juice of 2 lemons

12oz (350g) basmati rice

14oz can chickpeas, drained and rinsed

3 cups hot vegetable stock

small bunch of cilantro leaves, coarsely chopped

small bunch of flat-leaf parsley, coarsely chopped

1 Heat half the oil in a heavy-bottomed pan over medium heat. Toss the eggplants in the paprika, add to the pan, and cook for 6–8 minutes, adding more oil if needed. Remove and set aside. Heat the remaining oil, if necessary, and reduce the heat to low. Add the onion and mint, season, and cook for 3–4 minutes until soft. Stir in the garlic, chiles, and lemon zest and cook for 2 minutes.

2 Stir in the rice. Add the lemon juice and chickpeas and return the eggplants to the pan. Pour in the stock and season again. Partially cover with a lid and cook for 30–40 minutes, adding a little hot water if needed, and stirring occasionally. Stir in the herbs. Serve with a lightly dressed leaf and tomato salad and some lamb chops.

Season's best **mackerel**

Mackerel is inexpensive and versatile and, being an oily fish, is great for your heart. It is in season from late summer through winter but is superb in autumn. All species (including bonito, chub, and king) have moist, brownish gray flesh and rich flavor. They are great grilled or fried whole, but can be boned and stuffed or filleted. They pair well with sharp fruits, such as rhubarb, citrus, or cranberry and are excellent with mustard, horseradish, chile, and tomatoes.

Atlantic mackerel This commercially important pelagic species is the most northerly member of the family. It is found extensively in the North Atlantic, with smaller pockets in the Mediterranean. It can grow up to 2ft (60cm) long. Grilling, broiling, and roasting make the most of the creamy-textured flakes.

The Atlantic mackerel is easily recognized by the bar or scribble markings along its back.

The skin should be shiny and slippery.

how to remove the gills

Remove the gills as soon as possible, as they contain bacteria, which cause the fish to decompose. However, the bones, head, and tail may be removed once the fish is cooked, if you prefer.

1 Firmly lift the gill flap with your thumb and forefinger and cut the throat with the tip of a sharp filleting knife. Lifting the gill makes it easier to get a clean cut through the fish.

2 Insert a thumb and index finger around the gills, and pull. They should come out fairly easily. If not, cut through the gills where they attach to the head, then pull them out.

how to gut through the stomach

Remove the guts (the internal organs) of the fish, as they quickly decompose. Once you have removed the guts, loosen and extract the dark bloodline running along the spine near the head and thoroughly rinse the belly cavity to remove any remaining traces of blood or viscera.

1 Insert a slim filleting knife into the vent (you will see a small hole), and with a single stroke cut along the belly to the chin.

2 With the back of the knife, release the bloodline, then scrape it away with the guts. Rinse, then firmly wipe the belly cavity clean.

essentials
varieties available

Atlantic mackerel, also available smoked, canned, dried, salted, and as frozen fillets.

buy Look for line-caught mackerel that are still stiff with rigor mortis.

store Wrap well and store in the coldest part of the fridge, as it doesn't keep well. Best eaten within 24 hours of purchase.

cook Grill, bake, broil, and roast. Also, cured and used in sushi and sashimi.

preserve Smoke, freeze.

recipe ideas

Butterflied mackerel with sweet potato and beet pickle p312

Mackerel roasted with harissa and potatoes p302

Mackerel with garlic and tomatoes p300

mackerel roasted with harissa and potatoes

Ask to have the fish gutted at the fish counter if you would rather not do it yourself. To check if the mackerel is cooked, slit the fish at the thickest part; the flesh should be opaque.

 10 MINS   30 MINS

SERVES 4

4 (or 8, if small) mackerel, gutted (p301) and washed

3–4 tsp harissa paste

1½ tbsp olive oil

2 limes, quartered

2½lb (1.1kg) small potatoes, scrubbed and halved

handful of cilantro, finely chopped

1 Preheat the oven to 400°F (200°C). Lay the mackerel in a roasting pan, then mix the harissa paste and half the oil together. Drizzle the harissa mixture over the fish, making sure they are covered inside and out. Add the limes to the pan, then toss the potatoes with the remaining oil and add them to the pan, too.

2 Roast in the oven for 20–30 minutes, or until the potatoes are cooked through—the fish will be cooked by then as well. Scatter with the cilantro leaves and serve with a crisp green salad.

variation

mackerel roasted with carrots, chickpeas, and harissa

Use 1lb 2oz (500g) baby chantenay carrots, trimmed, instead of the potatoes. Blanch them in lightly salted water for 3 minutes. Drain. Place in the roasting pan, toss in 2 tbsp olive oil, cover with foil, and roast for 45 minutes. Add a drained 14oz can of chickpeas and sprinkle with 1 tbsp chopped fresh thyme and 1 tbsp black mustard seeds. Lay the fish on top. Smear with the harissa mix as before and add the limes. Roast, uncovered, as before.

smoked mussels in fresh tomato sauce

This is a great starter or sauce for pasta. When smoking the mussels, turn on the ventilation fan and open a window.

 20 MINS 25 MINS

SPECIAL EQUIPMENT ▪ wok with a lid and rack

SERVES 4

1 level tbsp beech or alder wood chips

1lb 10oz (750g) mussels, scrubbed and cleaned (discard any that do not close when tapped) (p364)

1–2 tbsp olive oil

2 large shallots, finely diced

2 garlic cloves, finely diced

14oz can chopped tomatoes or tomato sauce

6 ripe tomatoes (about 1lb/450g), peeled (p197), seeded, and cut into bite-sized pieces

salt and freshly ground black pepper

a few sprigs of parsley, chopped

1 Wrap the wood chips in foil to form a flat package. Pierce several holes in the top of the package to allow the smoke to escape. Place in the bottom of the wok, then insert the wire rack. Spread the mussels out evenly on the rack, put the lid on tightly, and seal the join with a strip of foil. If there are too many mussels to fit in 1 layer on the rack, cook them in 2 batches.

2 Smoke over a high heat for 5 minutes until the mussels have opened. Turn off the heat, wait for the smoke to subside, and remove the mussels, setting them aside (discard and throw away any that haven't opened). Remove the package of wood chips and reserve any juices.

3 Wash and dry the wok. Set it over low heat, add the oil, and fry the shallots and garlic for about 5 minutes, until soft. Add the mussels and toss for 2–3 minutes, then add the canned tomatoes, bring to a boil, and simmer for 5–10 minutes. Add the fresh tomatoes and the reserved juices, to taste. Toss, season, and serve with the parsley.

striped mullet with middle eastern spices

A sprinkling of the pretty purple spice that is sumac adds a tangy, lemony flavor to this fish dish.

 20 MINS   1 HR 20 MINS

SERVES 4–6

1 tbsp olive oil

6 shallots, finely chopped

1 fennel bulb, trimmed and finely chopped

1 carrot, finely chopped

½ tsp ground cumin

1 tsp sumac or use a preserved lemon, flesh discarded and rind finely chopped (optional)

3 cups hot vegetable stock

4 plum tomatoes, coarsely chopped

salt and freshly ground black pepper

8 black olives, pitted

about 3½lb (1.6kg) striped mullet, filleted and cut into chunky pieces

handful of cilantro, finely chopped

handful of mint, finely chopped

1 Heat the oil in a heavy-bottomed pan or tagine, add the shallots, fennel, and carrot, and cook for 5 minutes until soft. Stir in the cumin and sumac or preserved lemon, and cook for another minute. Add the stock, tomatoes, and seasoning, and bring to a boil, then reduce to simmer.

2 Add the olives, partially cover with a lid, and simmer for about 1 hour, stirring and adding hot water, if needed. Place the fish on top of the tomato mixture, cover with the lid, and cook for another 10 minutes, or until the fish is cooked through.

3 Stir in most of the cilantro and mint, and add seasoning, if needed. Serve with couscous and scatter the remaining fresh herbs over the top.

pan-fried mackerel in rolled oats

A traditional Scottish recipe. For true authenticity (and lots of added flavor), use lard or bacon drippings instead of oil.

 15–20 MINS 8–12 MINS

SERVES 6

2 large eggs

¼ cup all-purpose flour, plus 2 tbsp

2 cups rolled oats

salt and freshly ground black pepper

6 large mackerel fillets

4 tbsp butter

juice of ½ lemon

1 tbsp Dijon mustard, or to taste

¼ cup vegetable oil, plus more if needed, for frying

lemon wedges, to serve

a few sprigs of watercress, to serve

1 Beat the eggs in a dish. Sift ¼ cup flour onto a sheet of parchment paper. With your fingers, combine the rolled oats and some salt and pepper on a second sheet of parchment paper. Turn each mackerel fillet in the flour to coat evenly. Then dip the mackerel in the egg and finally coat in the seasoned oats. Set aside on a plate.

2 Melt a third of the butter. Add 2 tbsp flour and whisk to a paste until foaming. Remove from the heat. Whisk in 1¼ cups boiling water. The sauce will thicken.

Return to the heat and whisk for 1 minute. Remove from the heat, add the remaining butter, and whisk. Add the lemon juice and mustard and season.

3 Line a baking sheet with paper towels. Heat the oil in a large frying pan. Add half the fish and cook for 2–3 minutes on each side, until crisp and golden. Transfer to the baking sheet and keep warm while you cook the remaining fish. Drain off any water and add extra oil between batches when frying, if necessary. Serve with lemon wedges, watercress, and the sauce.

variation

herrings in oatmeal with sweet mustard sauce

Prepare in exactly the same way but use 6 large herring fillets (pin-boned thoroughly) instead of mackerel and use 1 cup steel-cut oats instead of the rolled oats. For the mustard sauce, use English or spicy mustard instead of Dijon, sweeten with 1 tbsp brown sugar, and sharpen with a dash of white wine vinegar.

monkfish and white wine stew

The delicate flavor of monkfish here is highlighted by white wine. If you can find small meadow mushrooms, they taste wonderful with the monkfish and zucchini.

 45–50 MINS 25–30 MINS

SERVES 6

5 tbsp butter

2 shallots, diced

2 garlic cloves, finely chopped

2 leeks, trimmed and cut diagonally

1lb 2oz (500g) small zucchini, cut into bite-sized pieces

salt and freshly ground black pepper

9oz (250g) mushrooms, trimmed

3–5 sprigs of thyme, leaves picked

1 bay leaf

1 cup dry white wine

2 cups hot fish stock

1lb 10oz (750g) monkfish fillets, peeled and cut into ½in (1cm) slices

3 tbsp all-purpose flour

small bunch of parsley, leaves chopped

1 Melt 2 tbsp of the butter in a large pan over medium heat, add the shallots, garlic, leeks, and zucchini, and cook for 3–5 minutes, until soft. Season, then add the mushrooms, thyme, bay leaf, wine, and stock, cover, and simmer gently for 25–30 minutes.

2 Add the monkfish and stir very gently to combine. Do not stir too vigorously or the fish may fall apart. Cover the pan, bring back to a boil, and simmer for 3–5 minutes until the fish is opaque and cooked through.

3 Fork together the remaining butter with the flour to a paste. Add to the pan and simmer for 2 minutes. Discard the bay leaf, stir in half the parsley, and add seasoning, if needed. Serve sprinkled with the remaining parsley.

variation

monkfish and red wine stew

Cook the shallots in butter for 1 minute. Add 2 cups red wine and reduce by half. Peel 9oz (250g) pearl onions. Melt 2 tbsp butter in a pan, add the onions, and cook for 5–8 minutes until golden. Add the mushrooms and cook for 3–5 minutes, until the liquid evaporates. Add the stock and monkfish to the wine, cover, and simmer for 3–5 minutes. Stir in the onions and mushrooms, and thicken as directed.

melanzane alla parmigiana

This is a classic Italian recipe that makes perfect use of eggplants baked in a tomato sauce layered with Parmesan.

 20 MINS   20 MINS   ❄ FREEZABLE

SERVES 4

3 tbsp olive oil

4 garlic cloves, finely sliced

2 x 14oz cans chopped tomatoes

1 tbsp tomato paste

1 tsp dried oregano

1 tsp thyme leaves

salt and freshly ground black pepper

2 eggplants, cut into ½in (1cm) slices

5½oz (150g) Parmesan cheese, grated

7oz (200g) mozzarella, torn into pieces

1 Preheat the oven to 350°F (180°C). Heat 2 tbsp of the oil in a large heavy-bottomed pan over a low heat, add the garlic, and cook for 30 seconds. Add the chopped tomatoes, tomato paste, oregano, and thyme and bring to a boil. Season with salt and pepper, then remove the pan from the heat.

2 Put the eggplant slices in a bowl and brush with the rest of the oil. Heat a nonstick frying pan over medium heat, add the eggplants (in batches, if necessary) and cook on each side for 3 minutes, or until golden brown. When each piece is done, remove with a slotted spoon and place on a plate.

3 Pour a ½in(1cm) layer of tomato sauce in the bottom of an ovenproof dish and cover with eggplant slices. Sprinkle with a handful of Parmesan cheese, then repeat the process until all of the ingredients are used up (you should get 3–4 layers), making sure there is a ½in (1cm) layer of tomato sauce at the top. Cover with the mozzarella and cook for 25–30 minutes until browned on top and piping hot. Serve with a green salad.

lamb with roasted peppers

Such a great way to use up a glut of bell peppers, which are so abundant at this time of year. Don't feel that you have to limit yourself to red and green ones—yellow is just as good.

 15 MINS   30 MINS

SERVES 4

4 large lamb loin chops, or 8 small lamb loin chops

2 red bell peppers, seeded and coarsely chopped

2 green bell peppers, seeded and coarsely chopped

1 tbsp olive oil

salt and freshly ground black pepper

pat of butter

1 onion, finely chopped

4½oz (125g) crimini mushrooms, finely chopped

small handful of flat-leaf parsley, finely chopped

1 Preheat the oven to 400°F (200°C). Place the chops in a roasting pan and cut a pocket in each one. Toss the peppers with the oil, season well with salt and pepper, then add to the pan.

2 Melt the butter in a pan over medium heat, add the onion, and cook for 3–4 minutes, or until soft and translucent. Add the mushrooms and cook for another 5 minutes, or until the mushrooms have broken down. Stir in the parsley, season with salt and pepper, then spoon the mixture into the pocket of each lamb chop. If there's some left over, scatter it over the top.

3 Put the roasting pan in the oven to cook for 20–30 minutes, or longer if you like your meat well-done. Toss with the peppers and serve with small cubed roasted potatoes and a spoonful of chile or mint jelly.

chunky ratatouille

Ratatouille is a vegetarian evergreen; eggplants mixed with zucchini and tomatoes result in a juicy and flavorful dish.

 15 MINS 30 MINS

SERVES 4

1 tbsp olive oil

1 onion, finely chopped

salt and freshly ground black pepper

1 bay leaf

2 garlic cloves, thinly sliced

1-2 tsp dried oregano

pinch of fennel seeds

1 eggplant, cut into chunky pieces

¼ cup red wine

⅔ cup tomato juice

2 small zucchini, cut into chunky pieces

3 tomatoes, coarsely chopped

large handful of Swiss chard leaves

chopped flat-leaf parsley, to garnish

1 Heat the oil in a large pan over medium heat, add the onion, a pinch of salt, and the bay leaf, and cook for 3–4 minutes until the onion is soft and translucent.

2 Add the garlic, oregano, fennel seeds, eggplant, and wine. Let it simmer for a minute, then add the tomato juice. Cook for about 10 minutes, until the eggplant is soft.

3 Add the zucchini and tomatoes, and cook for another 5–10 minutes. Stir in the Swiss chard, and cook for another 1–2 minutes until all the vegetables are tender. Taste, and season if needed. Garnish with the chopped parsley, and serve hot with fluffy rice or some fresh crusty bread.

braised pheasant with beets and pears

The rich gamey flavor of pheasant goes very well with the sweet earthiness of beets and the muted fragrance of pears. Braising upside down keeps the flesh of the bird moist.

 25 MINS 1 HR

SERVES 4

1 tbsp butter

12 pearl onions, peeled and left whole

2½oz (75g) pancetta, diced

2 slightly underripe pears, quartered and cored

1 cock pheasant, quartered (or 2 small hens, halved)

4 beets, cooked, peeled (p255), and cut into chunks

1¼ cups medium-sweet cider

1¼ cups chicken stock

salt and freshly ground black pepper

a good pinch of granulated sugar

1 bay leaf

chopped parsley, to garnish

1 Preheat the oven to 350°F (180°C). Heat the butter in a large flameproof casserole dish. Add the onions, pancetta, and pear quarters and cook, stirring, for 5 minutes, or until lightly golden. Remove from the pan with a slotted spoon.

2 Add the pheasant and brown all over. Remove from the casserole dish. Return the onions, pancetta, and pears to the casserole dish. Place the pheasant on top, flesh-side down. Put the beets around the edge. Blend the cider and stock together and pour into the casserole dish. Bring to a boil, season well with salt and pepper, and tuck in the bay leaf. Cover with a lid and cook in the oven for 50–60 minutes until tender.

3 Discard the bay leaf. Taste and season again, if necessary. Remove the pheasant, vegetables, and pears with a slotted spoon and keep warm. Boil the liquid rapidly for a few minutes until reduced and thickened slightly. Put the pheasant and vegetables on warmed plates. Spoon the sauce over and sprinkle with a little chopped parsley. Serve hot with baked potatoes and green beans.

peppered beef with roasted beets

Beets are a wonder vegetable that can be cooked in many ways. Wear kitchen gloves when peeling them, though, to avoid staining your hands with the vivid juice.

 15 MINS 1 HR

SERVES 4

2½lb (1.1kg) beef tenderloin

1-2 tbsp cracked black pepper

2-3 tbsp olive oil

1lb 2oz (500g) beets, cooked and peeled (p255)

1 tbsp balsamic vinegar

6 sweet potatoes, peeled and quartered

salt

handful of thyme sprigs

creamed horseradish, to serve

1 Preheat the oven to 375°F (190°C). Roll the beef in the black pepper, covering it all over. Put 1 tbsp of the oil in a roasting pan and set the pan over high heat. When very hot, add the beef and cook for 5–6 minutes, or until lightly browned on all sides.

2 Toss the beets with the balsamic vinegar and add to the pan. Toss the sweet potatoes with the remaining oil and add to the pan. Season with a pinch of salt, sprinkle with the thyme, and put in the oven to cook for about 20 minutes if you like your beef rare; 40 minutes, for medium; and 50 minutes, for well-done.

3 Remove the beef and keep it warm while it rests. If the sweet potatoes are not ready, continue cooking until they are golden and beginning to char around the edges. Slice the beef and serve with the beets, sweet potatoes, and a little creamed horseradish on the side.

white fish, green beans, and artichoke paella

Haddock or cod are the best fish to use in this dish because they won't break up too easily, nor will their robust flavor be overwhelmed by the rest of the ingredients.

 15 MINS 30 MINS

SERVES 4–6

1 tbsp olive oil

1 onion, finely chopped

salt and freshly ground black pepper

pinch of ground turmeric

2 garlic cloves, grated or finely chopped

7oz (200g) green beans, trimmed

3 cooked artichoke hearts (p309), quartered

4 tomatoes, peeled (p197) and chopped

pinch of hot or regular paprika

14oz (400g) basmati rice

5 cups hot vegetable stock

1½lb (675g) white fish, such as haddock or sustainable cod, peeled and cut into chunky pieces

handful of dill or flat-leaf parsley, finely chopped

juice of 1 lemon

1 Heat the oil in a large heavy-bottomed pan over medium heat, add the onion and a pinch of salt, and cook for 3–4 minutes until soft and translucent. Stir in the turmeric, then add the garlic, beans, and artichokes. Cook gently for about 5 minutes until the beans begin to wilt, adding a little more oil if needed.

2 Add the tomatoes and paprika, and cook for 5 minutes. Add the rice and stir in. Pour in half of the hot stock. Bring to a boil, then reduce the heat slightly and simmer for about 15 minutes. Add the remaining stock and the fish, cover, and cook over low heat until the rice and fish are cooked through.

3 Keep the lid on the pan until ready to serve, then stir in the herbs and lemon juice. Season with salt and pepper and serve immediately.

artichoke risotto

This is a perfect light supper for vegetarians, although you could stir in pancetta to add a salty twist.

 20 MINS 45–50 MINS

SERVES 4

1 tbsp olive oil

4 tbsp butter

1 onion, finely chopped

salt and freshly ground black pepper

3 garlic cloves, finely chopped

10oz (300g) arborio rice or carnaroli rice

1 cup white wine

3½ cups hot vegetable stock or chicken stock

6 cooked artichoke hearts (p309), halved

1oz (25g) Parmesan cheese, grated, plus extra to serve

1 Heat the oil and half the butter in a large heavy-bottomed pan over medium heat, add the onion, and cook for 3–4 minutes until soft. Season with salt and pepper, stir in the garlic, and cook for about 1 minute.

2 Stir in the rice and turn it in the oily butter so all the grains are coated, and cook for a few seconds. Increase the heat, add the wine, and let it bubble for 1–2 minutes, or until it has been absorbed. In a separate saucepan, simmer the stock. Add a ladleful to the rice and stir, until it has been absorbed. Continue doing this for 30–35 minutes until the rice is cooked but still firm to the bite and is creamy. You may not need all the stock or you may need a little more.

3 Add the artichokes to the risotto for the last 10 minutes of cooking and carefully stir them in. Dot with the remaining butter and stir it in together with the Parmesan cheese. Taste and season, if needed. Serve with more Parmesan and some lightly dressed wild arugula and tomato salad on the side.

smoky eggplant and lamb stew

Eggplant and lamb are a classic combination from the Middle East, and the paprika adds a fine smoky flavor.

 15 MINS 1 HR 45 MINS

SERVES 4

2 tbsp olive oil

1 large eggplant, cubed

1 tsp smoked paprika

1lb 2oz (500g) middle neck of lamb, chopped into large chunks

1 small onion, coarsely chopped

5oz (140g) dried, Spanish-style chorizo, diced

2 tsp sherry vinegar

2 garlic cloves, finely chopped

pinch of ground cumin

10oz canned chickpeas, drained and rinsed

a few sprigs of thyme, leaves picked

2 cups hot vegetable stock

1 Heat 1 tbsp of the oil in a flameproof casserole dish over medium heat, add the eggplant and smoked paprika, and toss to coat. Cook, stirring and adding more oil as needed, for 6–8 minutes until the eggplant begins to color. Remove with a slotted spoon and set aside.

2 Add a drizzle of oil and cook the lamb (in batches, if necessary) for 4–6 minutes until brown on all sides. Remove and set aside. Add the onion and chorizo (again, with a little oil, if needed), and cook for 2 minutes, then add the vinegar. Increase the heat and cook for 2 minutes until it has evaporated. Stir to scrape up the bits from the bottom of the casserole dish, then add the garlic and cumin.

3 Return the lamb, add the chickpeas and thyme, and pour in the stock. Bring to a boil, then partially cover and cook for 1 hour, checking the liquid level and adding hot water if needed. Add the eggplant and cook for 30 minutes more. Serve with couscous.

tomato tagliatelle with artichokes

This flavorful pasta can be made, dried, and stored, loosely wrapped, in the refrigerator for up to 48 hours. Use a good extra virgin olive oil so the flavor of the finished dish is intense. Walnuts complement the artichokes in the sauce perfectly.

 50-60 MINS PLUS DRYING   3-4 MINS

SPECIAL EQUIPMENT ▪ pasta machine

SERVES 4-6

5 tbsp extra virgin olive oil

2 shallots, finely chopped

4 garlic cloves, finely chopped

6 large cooked artichoke hearts (p309), thickly sliced

3 tbsp dry white wine

salt and freshly ground black pepper

small bunch of parsley, leaves chopped

1½oz (45g) walnuts, coarsely chopped

1oz (30g) Parmesan cheese, grated

For the tagliatelle

1⅔ cup all-purpose flour, plus more if needed

3 large eggs

1 tbsp vegetable oil

salt

2½ tbsp tomato paste

1 To make the tagliatelle, sift the flour onto a work surface. With your fingers, make a well in the center. Add the eggs, oil, 1 tsp salt, and the tomato paste. Gradually mix in the flour to make a firm dough and press into a ball. Knead for 5–10 minutes, until elastic.

2 Cut the dough into 3 or 4 pieces and roll through a pasta machine, ending at the second narrowest setting and the wider of the machine's cutters. Toss the tagliatelle gently in a little flour, coil in bundles and leave for 1–2 hours on a floured kitchen towel.

3 Heat the oil in a pan over low heat, add the shallots and garlic, and cook for 1–2 minutes, until soft but not brown. Add the artichokes and white wine and simmer for 2–3 minutes. Season to taste with salt and pepper. Stir only very gently, to keep from breaking up the artichokes.

4 Fill a large pan with water, bring to a boil, and add 1 tbsp salt. Add the tagliatelle and simmer for 2–3 minutes, or until it is tender but still firm to the bite, stirring to prevent sticking. Drain and add the tagliatelle to the pan of artichoke mixture and toss over medium heat until the pasta is hot and evenly coated with olive oil.

5 Pile the pasta onto a warmed serving dish and sprinkle evenly with the parsley and walnuts. Finish by sprinkling with most of the Parmesan cheese, offering the remainder on the side.

Season's best **globe artichokes**

A globe artichoke resembles an unopened flower bud and has an earthy, nutty flavor with slight astringency. The peak season for artichokes is in the spring with another peak again in autumn. It is delicious simply served with melted butter or vinaigrette, stuffed whole, or the hearts only, served in a variety of dishes such as pasta, pies, and salads. Good flavor pairings include sausages, prosciutto, pancetta, anchovies, tomatoes, Parmesan cheese, and white wine.

Ranging in size from tiny buds to huge purple or green heads, globe artichokes need plenty of space and water. They are grown across Europe, Africa, and in North America, mainly coastal California.

Baby purple artichokes These are fully mature, but picked from the lower part of the plant where they don't develop as much. They taste similar to the large ones, but with a mildly smoky flavor.

Trim the stalks and about ½in (1cm) off the tops before eating whole, or in halves or quarters, raw or cooked.

how to prepare artichokes to serve whole

This is an elegant way to serve artichokes, and is also necessary if you are stuffing them. When not needing to impress, you can trim the stalk and boil whole. The hairy choke inside is inedible, so either remove it or leave for your diners to discard when eating.

1 Holding the stalk to steady the artichoke, cut the tough tips off the leaves with strong kitchen scissors.

2 Use a chef's knife to cut the stalk from the base as close as possible to the leaves, so the heads will sit upright when served on a plate.

3 Cut off the pointed tip, pull away the small inner leaves, scrape out the hairy choke, and brush with lemon.

how to prepare artichoke hearts

If you are planning to serve just the hearts, you will need to remove all the leaves and the choke. Rub all cut surfaces of the artichoke with lemon as soon as it is prepared, or drop it into water acidulated with lemon juice until ready to cook. This is important as the artichoke flesh discolors quickly when exposed to air. Wash your hands well, as the juice is very bitter (like dandelions).

1 Cut or pull away all the leaves from the artichoke, then cut the stalk from the base.

2 With a sharp knife, cut off the soft middle cone of leaves just above the hairy choke, or pull them away firmly with the hands.

3 Trim away the bottom leaves with a paring knife. Rub the exposed flesh with lemon juice to reduce browning.

4 Scoop out the hairy choke with a teaspoon and discard. Rub the heart with lemon juice, or put in a bowl of acidulated water until ready to cook.

essentials
varieties available

Green globe, baby purple, and green artichokes.

buy Choose firm tight heads that feel heavy.

store Best eaten fresh, or store in the vegetable drawer in the fridge for up to 5 days.

cook Steam or boil large globes; steam, boil, braise, or roast hearts; halve or quarter baby ones and grill or eat raw.

preserve Freeze hearts and baby ones, or preserve them in oil.

recipe ideas

Artichoke, green olive, and feta tart p310

Artichoke risotto p306

Baby artichokes in oil p349

Globe artichoke soup p266

Provençal stuffed artichokes p324

Green globe Widely available, this popular large-headed variety has succulent fleshy leaves with an earthy flavor.

The large leaves are pulled off and the fleshy bases eaten before enjoying the prize—the creamy-textured heart.

Draw the leaves through your teeth to eat their juicy flesh.

artichoke, green olive, and feta tart

There is a nice Mediterranean touch to this tart with salty olives and feta cheese counterbalancing the sweet artichoke.

  15 MINS **1 HR**

SPECIAL EQUIPMENT ■ 14 x 5in (35 x 12cm) fluted tart pan with removable bottom ■ ceramic baking beans

SERVES 6

9oz (250g) store-bought pie dough

3 large eggs, 1 lightly beaten, for egg wash

1 tbsp olive oil

1 onion, finely chopped

2 garlic cloves, grated or finely chopped

5 large cooked artichoke hearts (p309)

12 green olives, pitted

6oz (175g) feta cheese, cubed

a few sprigs of thyme, leaves picked

¾ cup heavy cream

salt and freshly ground black pepper

1 Preheat the oven to 400°F (200°C). Roll out the dough on a floured work surface and use it to line the tart pan. Trim away the excess, then line the tart dough with wax paper and fill with ceramic baking beans. Bake in the oven for 15–20 minutes until the edges are golden. Remove the beans and paper, brush the bottom of the crust with a little of the egg wash, and return to the oven for 2–3 minutes to crisp. Remove from the oven and set aside. Reduce the oven temperature to 350°F (180°C).

2 Heat the oil in a pan over low heat, add the onion, and cook for about 5 minutes until soft. Add the garlic and cook for a few more seconds. Spoon the onion mixture evenly over the bottom of the tart shell. Arrange the artichokes and olives over the top and sprinkle with the feta and thyme leaves.

3 Mix together the cream, 2 eggs, and seasoning. Pour over the tart filling. Bake in the oven for 25–35 minutes until set, puffed, and golden. Let cool for about 10 minutes before releasing from the pan. Serve warm, or at room temperature, with an arugula and tomato salad.

wild mushroom and gruyère pasta bake

The wild and domestic mushrooms make this a sophisticated take on an old favorite. Serve with a tomato salad.

 30-35 MINS   **25-30 MINS**

SPECIAL EQUIPMENT ■ 2-quart baking dish

SERVES 6

3 tbsp butter

3 shallots, finely chopped

3 garlic cloves, finely chopped

4½oz (125g) mixed wild mushrooms, sliced

4½oz (125g) button mushrooms, sliced

salt and freshly ground black pepper

2 tbsp white bread crumbs

small bunch of chives, snipped

1oz (30g) Parmesan cheese, grated

3½ cups milk

1 slice of onion

6 black peppercorns

1 bay leaf

2 tbsp all-purpose flour

pinch of grated nutmeg

8oz (225g) Gruyère cheese, grated

13oz (375g) penne

1 Preheat the oven to 350°F (180°C) and butter the baking dish. Melt 1 tbsp butter in a pan over a low heat, add the shallots, and cook for about 1 minute until soft. Add the garlic, mushrooms, and seasoning. Cook, stirring, for 3–5 minutes, until the liquid has evaporated. For the topping, combine the bread crumbs in a bowl with a quarter of the chives and the Parmesan cheese. Set aside.

2 Scald the milk in a pan with the onion, peppercorns, and bay leaf. Remove from the heat. Melt the remaining butter in another pan and whisk in the flour. Remove from the heat and strain in two-thirds of the milk. Return to the heat and whisk until it boils. Add the nutmeg and seasoning and simmer for 2 minutes. Remove from the heat, add the Gruyère, and whisk in the remaining milk.

3 Cook the pasta in a pan of boiling water for about 12 minutes, or until it is tender but still firm to the bite. Drain and mix with the mushrooms, sauce, and remaining chives. Spoon into the dish and sprinkle on the topping. Bake for 25–30 minutes, or until golden.

braised turkey with vegetables

The beauty of this dish is that you can cook it in just the one pot. This saves on clean-up and the end result is succulent, too. Serve the casserole with baked or mashed potatoes.

  20 MINS 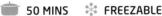 50 MINS ❄ FREEZABLE

SERVES 4

1 tbsp olive oil

pat of butter

2 skinless, boneless turkey breasts

salt and freshly ground black pepper

1 onion, sliced

1 carrot, sliced

½ fennel bulb, sliced

a few tarragon leaves, coarsely chopped

1¼ cups hot chicken stock

small handful of flat-leaf parsley, finely chopped, to serve

grated zest of 1 lemon, to serve

1 Preheat the oven to 350°F (180°C). Heat the oil and butter in a flameproof casserole dish, season the turkey with salt and pepper, then cook on medium heat, turning occasionally, for 10 minutes, or until lightly golden all over.

2 Add the vegetables and tarragon and season well with salt and pepper. Pour in enough stock so that it comes almost to the top of the dish but doesn't cover the ingredients. Cover with a lid and cook in the oven for 40 minutes, or until the turkey and vegetables are tender.

3 Let cool slightly, then remove the turkey with a slotted spoon and slice the meat. Return the meat to the casserole dish and reheat gently until piping hot. Top with the parsley and lemon zest, and serve with a pinch of black pepper.

variation

braised pheasant with vegetables

Prepare in the same way, but use 1 cock pheasant, cut in quarters, instead of the turkey breasts. Fry 2oz (60g) smoked, chopped bacon in the oil and remove before browning the pheasant. Add to the casserole dish with the vegetables and 1 tbsp brandy with the stock. Roast for 1 hour, not 40 minutes.

baked polenta with wild mushrooms

This is a hugely comforting dish, with its sweet polenta and meltingly unctuous cheese and mushrooms.

 40–45 MINS PLUS CHILLING 20–25 MINS

SPECIAL EQUIPMENT ▪ 9 x 13in (23 x 33cm) baking dish

SERVES 6

13oz (375g) fine polenta

9oz (250g) mixed wild mushrooms

13oz (375g) button mushrooms

3 tbsp olive oil

3 garlic cloves, finely chopped

5–7 sprigs of thyme or rosemary, leaves picked

½ cup dry white wine

1 cup hot vegetable stock or water

¼ cup heavy cream

salt and freshly ground black pepper

9oz (250g) fontina cheese, sliced

1 Sprinkle 2 baking sheets with water. Bring 5½ cups water to a boil in a pan and add 1 tbsp salt. Over medium heat, slowly whisk in the polenta in a thin, steady stream. Cook, stirring, for 10–15 minutes, until thick enough to pull away from the pan, yet soft and smooth. Spread on the baking sheets in a layer about 12in (30cm) square. Cool, then chill for 1 hour until firm.

2 Trim all the mushroom stems. Cut the wild mushrooms into slices and the button mushrooms into halves, or quarters if large. Heat the oil in the frying pan. Add all the mushrooms, the garlic, and thyme or rosemary and cook, stirring, for 5–7 minutes, until the mushrooms are tender and the liquid has evaporated. Add the wine, simmer for 2–3 minutes, then add the stock and cook until reduced by half. Pour in the cream, cook until the liquid thickens, and season.

3 Preheat the oven to 425°F (220°C). Brush the baking dish with oil. Cut the chilled polenta into 6 x 4in (10cm) squares; reserve the trimmings. Arrange half the squares in the dish in a single layer.

4 Spoon half the mushroom stew on top, then half the fontina. Repeat with another layer of polenta and mushrooms. Top with the remaining fontina. Bake for 20–25 minutes, until the cheese has melted, and serve very hot.

butterflied mackerel with sweet potato and beet pickle

To butterfly a fish means to remove its head, open the body, and debone it. It takes a bit of time, but it's well worth it for the delicate pieces of fish that you are left with.

 15 MINS 15 MINS

SERVES 4

2 sweet potatoes, peeled and cubed

4 mackerel, about 3½oz (100g) each, butterflied

4 medium-to-large beetss, cooked, peeled (p255), and cubed

1 small onion, finely chopped

1-2 tsp onion seeds

juice of 1 orange

1 Cook the sweet potato in a pan of boiling salted water for 3–5 minutes until just beginning to soften; do not overcook. Drain and allow to cool.

2 Preheat the broiler to high. Place the mackerel on an oiled baking sheet and broil for 3–4 minutes on each side until cooked through.

3 Meanwhile, to make the pickle, gently mix together the sweet potato and beets, then stir in the onion and onion seeds. Pour in the orange juice and stir until everything is coated.

4 Serve the mackerel hot, with a little of the sweet potato and beet pickle, or serve the pickle separately in a dish for diners to help themselves. Accompany with sautéed potatoes or a crisp, green salad.

sweet potato and butter bean stew

Gently spiced and flavored with maple syrup, this is a pleasingly chunky stew with a silky texture from the sweet potatoes. Wilt the chard or spinach only slightly to retain its bite.

 10 MINS 30 MINS

SERVES 4

1lb (450g) sweet potatoes, peeled and cut into thick slices

2 tbsp maple syrup

1 tbsp olive oil

1 red onion, finely chopped

1 tsp cumin seeds

salt and freshly ground black pepper

14oz (400g) can whole plum tomatoes, chopped

dash of balsamic vinegar

14oz (400g) can butter beans, drained and rinsed

handful of Swiss chard or spinach leaves

⅔ cup Greek-style yogurt

handful of mint leaves, to garnish

1 Cook the sweet potatoes and maple syrup in a large wide pan of boiling salted water for 10 minutes until tender, but not too soft. Drain well and set aside to keep warm.

2 Meanwhile, heat the oil in a large heavy-bottomed pan over low heat, add the onion, cumin seeds, and a pinch of salt and cook for about 5 minutes until the onion is soft and translucent. Pour in the tomatoes, including any juices, add the balsamic vinegar, and cook for about 10 minutes. Taste and season with salt and pepper.

3 Add the butter beans and simmer for another 5 minutes, then stir in the Swiss chard or spinach. Cook for a couple of minutes more until the leaves just wilt. Remove from the heat and top with the sweet potatoes.

4 Preheat the broiler. Transfer vegetables to an ovenproof dish, top with yogurt, and broil until golden. Garnish with mint leaves.

roast monkfish with peppers

Monkfish is a firm, meaty white fish and, as such, is great teamed with the robust flavor of bacon or pancetta. Sweet red bell peppers counterbalance the salty bacon.

 15 MINS   30 MINS

SERVES 4

1½lb (675g) monkfish (one or two pieces), membrane removed

4 red bell peppers, seeded and cut into strips

1 tbsp olive oil

½ tsp mild paprika

12 strips of bacon or pancetta

arugula leaves, to serve

1 Preheat the oven to 400°F (200°C). Toss the monkfish and bell peppers with the olive oil, then sprinkle the paprika over the top. Wrap the fish with the bacon or pancetta until entirely covered, then place in a roasting pan with the bell peppers.

2 Cook for 20–30 minutes, or until the bacon is crispy and the fish is opaque and cooked through. Remove from the oven and keep warm while the fish rests for 10 minutes. Slice the fish and serve with the bell peppers and an arugula salad.

vegetarian leek and mushroom lasagna

A lasagna doesn't have to be made with ground beef; a meat-free version is just as tasty, filling, and satisfying.

 25 MINS   45-50 MINS   ❄ FREEZABLE

SERVES 4

3 tbsp olive oil

2 large leeks, trimmed and sliced

7oz (200g) crimini mushrooms, sliced

7oz (200g) wild mushrooms, chopped

1 large red chile, seeded and finely chopped

3 garlic cloves, chopped

¼ cup dry white wine

small handful of thyme leaves

1 tbsp all-purpose flour

1¾ cup milk

6oz (175g) Cheddar cheese, grated

4 tomatoes, 3 coarsely chopped and the remaining 1 sliced, to serve

salt and freshly ground black pepper

8oz (225g) lasagna sheets

1 Preheat the oven to 350°F (180°C). Heat the oil in a large pan over low heat, add the leeks, and cook, stirring frequently, for 5 minutes, or until starting to soften. Add the mushrooms and cook for 5 minutes, then add the chiles and garlic, and cook for 1 minute. Pour in the wine, raise the heat, and boil for 3 minutes while the alcohol evaporates. Stir in the thyme.

2 Add the flour and mix well. Add a little of the milk, mix, then add the rest of the milk and cook for 5 minutes, stirring frequently. Add almost all the cheese, remove from the heat, and combine well. Stir in the chopped tomatoes and season well.

3 Put a ½in(1cm) layer of the mixture in the bottom of an ovenproof dish, then cover with a layer of the lasagna sheets. Pour in another layer of sauce and cover with lasagna. Repeat until all the sauce is used up, finishing with a layer of sauce. Top with the remaining cheese and the sliced tomatoes. Cook in the oven for 25–30 minutes until brown on top and piping hot.

brazilian black bean and pumpkin stew

If you prefer a meaty meal, you could add some spicy sausage or chorizo to this colorful and gutsy dish. Black beans are also called turtle beans and need to be soaked overnight.

 25 MINS PLUS SOAKING   2 HRS 30 MINS–3 HRS

❄ FREEZABLE

SERVES 4–6

11oz (325g) dried black beans, soaked in cold water overnight and drained

1 tbsp olive oil

1 onion, finely chopped

salt and freshly ground black pepper

3 garlic cloves, finely chopped

1 small pumpkin or butternut squash, peeled, seeded, and cubed

2 red bell peppers, seeded and cubed

2 x 14oz (400g) cans chopped tomatoes

1 small jalapeño chile, seeded and cubed

3 cups hot vegetable stock

1 mango, peeled, pit removed, and cubed

bunch of cilantro, chopped

1 Preheat the oven to 325°F (170°C). Put the beans in a large heavy-bottomed pan and cover with water. Bring to a boil, then reduce to simmer, partially cover with the lid, and cook on low heat for 1 hour. Drain and set aside.

2 Heat the oil in a large heavy-bottomed pan over medium heat, add the onion, and cook for 3–4 minutes until soft. Season with salt and pepper, stir in the garlic, and cook for 1–2 minutes until soft. Stir in the pumpkin or butternut squash, red peppers, tomatoes, and chile.

3 Add the beans, pour in the stock, and bring to a boil. Then reduce to simmer, cover with the lid, and put in the oven for 1½–2 hours. Taste and adjust the seasoning, if necessary, then stir in the mango and cilantro. Serve with some sour cream and rice on the side.

viltgryta

This venison stew with chanterelles is a Swedish favorite. Serve with boiled potatoes and lingonberry jelly.

 10 MINS PLUS MARINATING   2 HRS 15 MINS–2 HRS 30 MINS

SERVES 6

2¼lb (1kg) boned venison haunch, cubed

oil or butter, for frying

1¼ cups venison or beef stock

2 onions, chopped

12oz (350g) chanterelle mushrooms

1 tbsp wine vinegar

2 tsp sugar

salt and freshly ground black pepper

⅔ cup heavy cream

2 tbsp all-purpose flour

For the marinade

1¼ cups red wine

2 tbsp olive oil

¼ tsp cracked black pepper

¼ tsp ground cloves

2 tsp juniper berries, crushed

½ tsp dried thyme

2 bay leaves

1 Mix together all the marinade ingredients in a deep bowl. Add the venison, cover, and let marinate for 24 hours, turning once or twice.

2 Strain the marinade and reserve. Pat the meat dry. Heat the oil or butter in a large pan over medium heat and cook the meat until browned on all sides. Add the marinade and enough stock to cover the meat. Bring to a boil, then cover and simmer for 1½ hours.

3 In another pan, heat more butter and cook the onions until soft. Add the chanterelles and fry until the moisture is driven off. Stir in the vinegar and sugar, then add this mixture to the stew.

4 Simmer for another 30–45 minutes, or until the meat is almost cooked. Season with salt and pepper. Whisk the cream and flour together and mix into the stew. Simmer for 20 more minutes, adding more stock or water if too thick.

chilean pork and beans

Swap the sweet potatoes for squash in this recipe, if you wish. Serve with rice or flour tortillas.

 20 MINS PLUS SOAKING   3 HRS–3 HRS 30 MINS

SERVES 6

7oz (200g) dried red kidney beans, soaked in cold water overnight, drained, and rinsed

2 tbsp olive oil

2lb (900g) boned loin of pork, cut into bite-sized pieces

1 large onion, finely sliced

2 garlic cloves, finely chopped

salt and freshly ground black pepper

14oz (400g) can chopped tomatoes

1 tbsp tomato paste

a few sprigs each of parsley, cilantro, and oregano, leaves picked and chopped

1 jalapeño chile, seeded and cubed

2 green bell peppers, seeded and cubed

1lb 2oz (500g) sweet potatoes, peeled and cut into 1in (2.5cm) cubes

2 tbsp red wine vinegar

1 Boil the beans in fresh water for 10 minutes. Cover the pan and simmer for 1 hour until almost tender. Drain.

2 Preheat the oven to 350°F (180°C). Heat the oil in a casserole dish over medium heat and cook the pork for about 10 minutes until browned. Remove and set aside. Add the onion, garlic, and seasoning, and cook gently, covered, for 15 minutes until the onion is soft and brown. Add the pork, tomatoes, tomato paste, herbs, and 2 cups hot water. Cover with a lid and cook in the oven for 1¼–1½ hours until the pork is just tender.

3 Add the beans and vegetables and water to cover. Return to the oven and cook for 45–60 minutes, then transfer to the stovetop. Stir in the vinegar and simmer, uncovered, for 5 minutes. Check the seasoning and serve.

karahi chicken

Ripe, late-season tomatoes are the stars in this simple recipe. This is a relatively dry curry, although if you prefer more sauce, you can add water to the stock during cooking. Fresh ginger and bird's eye chiles make the dish more fragrant.

 15 MINS   1 HR

SPECIAL EQUIPMENT ▪ blender or food processor

SERVES 4

1 tsp coriander seeds

2 jalapeño chiles, seeded

3 garlic cloves

1 tsp ground turmeric

2 tbsp sunflower or vegetable oil

8 chicken thighs, with skin on, slashed a few times across each thigh

salt and freshly ground black pepper

1 onion, coarsely chopped

6 tomatoes, coarsely chopped

3 cups hot vegetable stock

2in (5cm) piece of fresh ginger, peeled and finely chopped

3–4 green bird's eye chiles, left whole

bunch of cilantro, finely chopped

1 Put the cilantro seeds, jalapeño chiles, garlic, turmeric, and half the oil into a blender or food processor and pulse to a paste. Season the chicken with salt and pepper and smother with the paste, using your hands and pushing it into all the cuts. Heat half the remaining oil in a large flameproof casserole dish over medium-high heat and add the chicken pieces. Cook for 5–6 minutes on each side or until beginning to color, then remove and set aside.

2 Heat the remaining oil in the casserole dish over medium heat, add the onion, and cook for 3–4 minutes until soft. Then add the tomatoes

and cook for another 5–10 minutes until they too are soft. Pour in the stock and bring to a boil. Reduce to simmer, stir in the ginger and bird's eye chiles, and return the chicken to the casserole dish. Cover with the lid and cook gently for 30–40 minutes, keeping an eye on the sauce. You want it to be fairly dry, but if it is sticking, add a little hot water.

3 Remove the bird's eye chiles, then taste and season, as necessary, stirring in the cilantro. Serve with rice, chapatis, and some minted yogurt on the side.

variation

karahi rabbit

Prepare in the same way, but use a rabbit, cut into 8 pieces, instead of the chicken thighs. For the spice paste, toast 1 tsp cumin seeds in a dry frying pan for 30 seconds and add with ¼ tsp ground cloves to the other spices in the food processor. Add 2 cubed red bell peppers with the tomatoes at step 2, then continue as before.

lamb, spinach, and chickpea hotpot

This hearty and nutritious hotpot will be equally good served with potatoes, rice, couscous, or quinoa. If you prefer to use fresh chickpeas, soak them overnight before cooking.

 25 MINS   20 MINS   FREEZABLE

SERVES 4

12oz (350g) lean lamb, diced into ¾in (2cm) pieces

1 tbsp all-purpose flour

½ tsp paprika

3 tbsp olive oil

1 large red onion, diced

3 garlic cloves, chopped

1 x 14oz (400g) can chickpeas, drained and rinsed

¼ cup dry white wine

1 x 14oz (400g) can chopped tomatoes

salt and freshly ground black pepper

10oz (300g) baby leaf spinach

1 Put the lamb, flour, and paprika in a mixing bowl and combine well. Heat the oil in a large heavy-bottomed pan over medium heat, add the onion, and cook, stirring frequently, for 5 minutes, or until softened and translucent.

2 Add the diced lamb and cook, stirring occasionally, for 5 minutes, or until it is evenly browned. Stir in the garlic and chickpeas, and cook for 1 minute.

3 Pour in the wine and allow to boil for 3 minutes while the alcohol evaporates. Add the tomatoes, bring to a boil, then reduce the heat and simmer for 15 minutes. Season well with salt and pepper, stir in the spinach, and cook for 3 minutes. Serve piping hot.

baby zucchini with fish and couscous

While couscous can be made from a variety of grains, including barley, it is usually manufactured from durum wheat semolina. It is also available as whole-wheat..

 20 MINS   25 MINS

SERVES 4

¼ cup olive oil

10oz (300g) baby zucchini, halved lengthwise

zest and juice of 1 lime

1½ tbsp tomato paste

½ tsp five-spice powder

½ tsp cayenne pepper

1 tsp paprika

½ tsp freshly ground black pepper

handful of flat-leaf parsley, finely chopped

2 garlic cloves, grated or finely chopped

10oz (300g) white fish, such as grey mullet, halibut, or cod, skinned and cut into chunky bite-sized pieces

1 cup hot vegetable stock

8oz (225g) couscous

1 Preheat the oven to 300°F (150°C). Put 1 tbsp of the oil in a bowl, add the zucchini, and mix well until evenly coated. Cook in a hot grill pan for 2 minutes on each side, then set aside. You may need to do this in batches.

2 Add the rest of the oil to the bowl, together with the lime juice and zest, tomato paste, five-spice powder, cayenne, paprika, black pepper, parsley, and garlic. Mix well, then add the fish, stock, couscous, and zucchini and combine carefully.

3 Transfer to a flameproof dish and cover with foil. Cook in the oven for 20 minutes, then stir well and serve.

tomato, bean, and zucchini stew

A colorful stew that delivers on flavor, while also being hearty and nutritious. The beans add bite, and the tomato sauce makes it a perfect, warming meal.

 10 MINS   **20 MINS**

SERVES 4

3 tbsp olive oil

1 large onion, finely chopped

2 zucchini, chopped into chunky pieces

3 garlic cloves, finely sliced

1 x 14oz (400g) can borlotti beans, drained and rinsed

3 tomatoes, diced

1 tsp paprika

1 tsp dried oregano

salt and freshly ground black pepper

drizzle of chili oil, to serve (optional)

1 Heat the oil in a deep frying pan, add the onion, and cook over medium heat for 3 minutes. Add the zucchini and cook for another 5 minutes, stirring constantly.

2 Add the garlic and beans, cook for 1 minute, then add the tomatoes, paprika, and oregano. Cook for 10 minutes, stirring occasionally, then season with salt and pepper. Drizzle with chili oil (if using) and serve with some fresh crusty bread.

variation

butter bean and winter squash goulash

Prepare in the same way but add a small diced acorn squash with the zucchini. Stir in 1 tbsp sweet paprika instead of 1 tsp, and add 1 tsp smoked paprika, too. Use 1 or 2 drained 14oz (400g) cans of butter beans instead of borlotti beans (depending on appetites) and a pinch of granulated sugar. When cooked, serve each bowl topped with a dollop of sour cream, sprinkled with a few caraway seeds.

sweet and sour stir-fried fish with ginger

You can use any white fish to make this Asian-style dish as long as it is firm-fleshed enough to withstand stir-frying.

 10 MINS   **20 MINS**

SERVES 4

1–2 tbsp cornstarch

salt and freshly ground black pepper

1½lb (675g) thick white fish fillets, such as haddock, cut into strips

1–2 tbsp vegetable oil or sunflower oil

1 onion, coarsely chopped

2 garlic cloves, grated or finely chopped

1in (2.5cm) piece of fresh ginger, peeled and finely sliced

large handful of snow peas or sugarsnap peas, sliced into strips

For the sauce

1 tbsp white wine vinegar

1 tbsp tomato paste

1 tbsp sugar

1 tsp cornstarch

2 tsp light soy sauce

2 tbsp pineapple juice

1 First, make the sauce. Mix together the vinegar, tomato paste, sugar, cornstarch, soy sauce, and pineapple juice in a jug, and set aside.

2 To prepare the fish, put the cornstarch on a plate and season with salt and pepper. Toss the fish in the seasoned flour to coat.

3 In a wok, heat about half of the oil until hot, then add the fish. Stir-fry for about 5 minutes until golden. Remove the fish with a slotted spoon and set aside to keep warm.

4 Carefully wipe out the wok with paper towels and add a little more oil. When hot, add the onion and stir-fry until it begins to soften, then add the garlic and ginger and stir-fry for a few more minutes.

5 Pour the sweet and sour sauce into the wok and allow it to boil for a few minutes, stirring constantly. Reduce the heat to medium, add the snow peas or sugarsnap peas, and stir-fry for 1 minute. Return the fish to the wok, quickly toss together to combine, and serve hot with sticky or steamed rice.

broccoli and mushroom quiche

Both broccoli stalks and florets earn a starring role in this lovely autumnal quiche flavored with garlic, Parmesan, and nutmeg.

 20 MINS 30–35 MINS

SPECIAL EQUIPMENT ▪ 10in (25cm) round loose-bottomed fluted flan pan ▪ ceramic baking beans

SERVES 6–8

10oz (300g) store-bought pie dough

1–2 heads of broccoli, total weight about 1lb 2oz (500g)

salt and freshly ground black pepper

2 tbsp butter

6oz (175g) mushrooms, sliced

2 garlic cloves, finely chopped

3 large eggs, plus 2 large egg yolks

1⅓ cups milk

1 cup heavy cream

2oz (60g) Parmesan cheese, grated

grated nutmeg

1 Preheat the oven to 425°F (220°C). Lightly flour a work surface and roll out the pastry to a 12in (30cm) round. Use to line the pan, pressing it into the corners. Trim away the excess and prick the bottom all over with a fork. Line the tart crust with wax paper and fill with ceramic baking beans. Bake in the oven for 12–15 minutes until the edges are golden. Remove the beans and paper and return to the oven for 2–3 minutes to crisp. Remove from the oven and set aside. Reduce the oven temperature to 375°F (190°C).

2 Cut the florets from the broccoli stalk, then slice the stalk lengthwise into sticks. Half-fill a saucepan with water and bring to a boil. Add salt, then the broccoli. Cook until just tender; it should take only about 3–5 minutes. Drain and set aside.

3 Melt the butter in a frying pan, add the mushrooms and garlic, and sauté until the mushrooms have first given out all their liquid, and then all that liquid has evaporated.

4 Whisk together the eggs, egg yolks, milk, cream, grated cheese, salt, pepper, and a pinch of nutmeg. Spread the mushrooms in the tart crust. Arrange the broccoli on top. Ladle in the cheese custard to fill almost to the rim. Bake for 30–35 minutes, until browned and the custard has a slight wobble in the center when shaken. Serve hot or at room temperature.

thai red vegetable curry

This versatile curry can be easily adapted to embrace the best seasonal produce. Eggplant and peppers are featured here but squash would also be delicious.

 15 MINS 20 MINS

SERVES 4

1–2 tbsp Thai red curry paste

1 x 14oz (400ml) can coconut milk

2 eggplants, cut into chunks

6 kaffir lime leaves, torn in half lengthwise

1¼ cups hot vegetable stock

1 tbsp palm sugar or brown sugar

splash of dark soy sauce

pinch of salt

1 red bell pepper, seeded and cut into strips

1 green bell pepper, seeded and cut into strips

juice of 1 lime

handful of cilantro

1 Heat the curry paste in a large frying pan or wok over medium-high heat for a few seconds, stirring around the pan. Shake the can of coconut milk, then pour into the pan or wok. Bring to a gentle boil, stirring occasionally, and cook for 2–3 minutes until the sauce releases its aroma.

2 Add the eggplant, lime leaves, stock, sugar, and soy sauce. Season with salt and bring to a boil again. Reduce the heat slightly and simmer gently for about 15 minutes until the eggplants are soft.

3 Now add the peppers and lime juice and stir well. Taste and adjust the seasoning accordingly, adding more sugar (sweetness), lime juice (sourness), or salt as needed. Stir in the cilantro and serve immediately with some jasmine or sticky rice.

marinated lamb chops with crushed lemon and chile broccoli

This traditional Western dish is given an international twist with the addition of some chile flakes and soy sauce.

 5 MINS PLUS MARINATING 30 MINS

SERVES 4

2 tbsp sherry vinegar, cider vinegar, or white wine vinegar

pinch of sugar

splash of dark soy sauce

4 lean lamb loin chops, fat removed

salt and freshly ground black pepper

handful of rosemary sprigs

1 head or about 10oz (300g) broccoli, florets and stalks chopped fairly small

juice of 1 lemon

pinch of chile flakes

mint jelly, to serve

1 Preheat the oven to 400°F (200°C). First, prepare the marinade. Mix together the vinegar, sugar, and soy sauce, then pour it over the lamb. Let marinate for 5 minutes, or longer if time permits.

2 Sit the lamb chops in a roasting pan, season well with salt and pepper, and throw in the rosemary sprigs. Roast in the oven for 20–30 minutes until cooked to your liking.

3 While the lamb is cooking, put the broccoli in a pan of boiling salted water and cook for about 10 minutes until just soft. Drain, keeping the broccoli in the pan, then mash very gently with a fork. Squeeze in the lemon juice and add the chile, a pinch of salt, and some pepper. Put a lid on the pan and give it a shake. Serve immediately with the roasted lamb chops and a dollop of mint jelly.

Season's best **broccoli**

Broccoli is made up of the unopened flower heads of the plant, much like cauliflower. The popular calabrese variety has a fine texture and a light, sweet, cabbage-like flavor. Best January through April, it works well with bacon, cheese, pesto, Hollandaise sauce, lemon, garlic, pine nuts, and olive oil. Other varieties such as sprouting broccoli and broccoli rabe (rapini) are available in late winter and spring, but may be used in the same way.

Calabrese (Italian sprouting broccoli) is widely grown in temperate climates, particularly in the cooler regions around the world. The buds are tightly packed in large, pebbly heads on thick stalks.

Dark green, closed buds are a sign of freshness.

The stalk can be peeled and cooked too.

Broccoli (Calabrese) The most common variety of broccoli, this is a rich green color with a meaty flavor and, if not overcooked, a crunchy texture. It is packed with nutrients that are best retained by steaming.

essentials
varieties available

Several popular varieties, all with the characteristic tight, dark green heads.

buy Select dark green, firm heads, with stalks that can be snapped off. Avoid if pliable or if even one tiny yellow flower is showing: it is past its best.

store Keeps well in a plastic bag in the vegetable drawer of the fridge for 3–4 days.

preserve Blanch the florets and freeze in sealable bags.

recipe ideas

Broccoli and mushroom quiche p318

Marinated lamb chops with crushed lemon and chile broccoli p318

Spaghetti with chile flakes, broccoli, and spring onion p50

how to prepare broccoli

Broccoli is trimmed and separated into florets before using raw, blanched, or cooked. When cut off, the thick stalk can be peeled, cut into matchsticks, and cooked with the florets.

1 Lay the broccoli stalk flat on a clean cutting board and cut off the thick portion of the stalk.

2 To remove the florets, slide the knife between the smaller stalks through the head and cut down the stalk. Cut into smaller florets, if required.

jamaican corn casserole

There is plenty of vibrant color and a lot of heat in this vegetable dish. Look for corn cobs with tightly packed, plump kernels and glossy, firm peppers for the best flavor.

 20 MINS　　 1 HR 30 MINS - 2 HRS

SERVES 4-6

2 tbsp olive oil

2 onions, finely chopped

salt and freshly ground black pepper

3 garlic cloves, finely chopped

1 tsp cayenne pepper

3 sweet corn cobs, cut into slices about ½in (1cm) thick

2 red bell peppers, seeded and coarsely chopped

3 sweet potatoes, peeled and diced

6oz (175g) yellow split peas

1¼ cups hot vegetable stock

1 x 14oz (400ml) can coconut milk

small handful of thyme

1 Scotch bonnet chile, left whole

lime wedges, to serve (optional)

1 Preheat the oven to 325°F (170°C). Heat the oil in a large flameproof casserole over medium heat, add the onions, and cook for 3–4 minutes until soft. Season with salt and pepper, then stir in the garlic and cayenne pepper and cook for 1 minute. Add the sweet corn, peppers, and sweet potatoes and turn them so they are all evenly coated. Then stir in the split peas and a little of the stock.

2 Bring to a boil, then add the remaining stock and coconut milk. Bring back to a boil, reduce to a simmer, season, and add the thyme and the Scotch bonnet. Cover with a lid and put in the oven to cook for 1½–2 hours. Check occasionally that it is not drying out, adding a little hot water if needed.

3 Remove the Scotch bonnet, taste, and season again if necessary. Ladle into warmed bowls and serve with the lime wedges, if using, and some plain rice.

beef, fennel, and mushroom hotpot

Fennel and mushrooms gently infuse this warming dish.

 40 MINS　　 1 HR 45 MINS　　 FREEZABLE

SERVES 4

1¼lb (550g) beef stew meat, cut into bite-sized pieces

salt and freshly ground black pepper

½ tbsp all-purpose flour

1 tsp mild paprika

1½ tbsp olive oil

1 onion, finely sliced

1 large fennel bulb, trimmed and cut into eighths

5 tbsp dry white wine

2 cups hot beef stock or vegetable stock

pat of butter

8oz (225g) crimini mushrooms, quartered

pinch of dried oregano

1 Preheat the oven to 350°F (180°C). Season the meat well, then place the pieces in a mixing bowl and toss with the flour and paprika until the pieces are all evenly coated.

2 Heat half the oil in a cast-iron pan, add the meat, and cook over medium heat, stirring frequently, for 8–10 minutes or until evenly browned. Remove with a slotted spoon and set aside.

3 Add the remaining oil, add the onion, and cook for 6–8 minutes or until soft. Season well, then add the fennel and cook, stirring occasionally, for 6 minutes, or until beginning to soften slightly. Add the wine, increase the heat, and simmer for 1–2 minutes until the alcohol evaporates. Return the meat to the pan, pour in the stock, and bring to a boil. Cover with the lid and cook in the oven for 1 hour.

4 Melt the butter in a frying pan, add the mushrooms and oregano, and cook, stirring occasionally, for 5 minutes or until soft. Stir into the beef and fennel, cook for another 30 minutes, then serve.

lamb tagine with walnuts and figs

Fig adds a sweet stickiness to this tagine and works well with lamb. You could use dried figs for a sweeter finish.

 20 MINS　　 1 HRS 45 MINS - 2 HRS 15 MINS

SERVES 4-6

1-2 tbsp olive oil

2lb (900g) lean lamb, cut into cubes

salt and freshly ground black pepper

2 onions, sliced

3 garlic cloves, finely chopped

grated zest and juice of 1 lemon

1 tsp ground cinnamon

½ tsp ground coriander

½ tsp ground ginger

2 tsp paprika

1 tbsp tomato paste

2 tbsp honey

2 x 14oz (400g) cans chickpeas, drained

3 cups hot vegetable stock

2½oz (75g) walnuts, chopped

large handful of flat-leaf parsley, coarsely chopped

4 figs, quartered

1 Preheat the oven to 300°F (150°C). Heat 1 tbsp of the oil in a large flameproof casserole or tagine over medium-high heat, season the lamb, and cook (in batches, if needed) for 6–8 minutes until browned all over. Remove and set aside.

2 Cook the onions, garlic, and lemon zest and juice in the casserole over medium heat for 2 minutes. Add seasoning, then stir though the spices and tomato paste.

3 Add the honey, chickpeas, and stock. Bring to a boil, then reduce the heat to a simmer, return the meat, and add the walnuts and half the parsley. Cover with the lid and cook in the oven for 1½ hours. Add hot water if it starts to dry out. Stir in the figs, re-cover, and cook in the oven for another 30 minutes. Garnish with the remaining parsley.

middle eastern lentils and peppers

Late-season red peppers are teamed with typical Middle Eastern ingredients, such as lentils and chickpeas in this lightly spiced rice dish. It is traditionally cooked in a tagine, a special earthenware pot with a conical lid, but any heavy-bottomed pan will do.

 15 MINS 45 MINS

SERVES 4–6

3½oz (100g) brown or green lentils, rinsed

salt and freshly ground black pepper

1 tbsp olive oil

1 onion, finely chopped

3 garlic cloves, finely chopped

pinch of dried oregano

grated zest and juice of 1 lemon

½ tsp ground allspice

pinch of grated nutmeg

½ tsp ground cumin

2 red bell peppers, seeded and sliced into strips

7oz (200g) rice

3 cups hot vegetable stock

14oz can chickpeas, drained and rinsed

bunch of parsley, finely chopped

1 Put the lentils in a large heavy-bottomed pan or tagine, season with salt and pepper, and cover with water. Bring to a boil, then simmer for about 30 minutes until the lentils are beginning to soften, but don't let them turn mushy. Drain and set aside.

2 Meanwhile, heat the oil in another heavy-bottomed pan over medium heat, add the onion, and cook for 3–4 minutes until soft. Season, then stir in the garlic, oregano, lemon zest, allspice, nutmeg, and cumin and cook for a minute.

3 Add the peppers and cook for about 5 minutes, stirring to coat with spices. Cook for 2–3 minutes until soft, then stir in the rice and a little stock. Bring to a boil, add most of the stock, and boil for 1 minute.

Reduce to a simmer, add the canned chickpeas, and cook over very low heat for 15–20 minutes. Check occasionally that it is not drying out, adding a little hot stock if needed. Then stir in the cooked lentils, taste and season, and add the parsley and lemon juice. Serve with yogurt and pita bread.

jerk fish

This style of cooking comes from the Caribbean, where jerk seasoning is used to flavor and tenderize meat and fish.

 10 MINS PLUS MARINATING   5 MINS

SPECIAL EQUIPMENT ▪ blender or food processor

SERVES 4

1½lb (675g) meaty white fish fillets, such as haddock, mahi mahi, monkfish, halibut, or cod

lime wedges, to serve

For the jerk seasoning

6 garlic cloves

4 fresh Scotch Bonnet chiles

2 small onions, quartered

2 tbsp fresh thyme leaves

3 tbsp brown sugar

2 tsp ground allspice

1 tsp ground cinnamon

½ tsp grated nutmeg

1 tsp freshly ground black pepper

½ tsp salt

1 Pulse all the ingredients for the jerk seasoning to a smooth, wet paste. Put the fish in a plastic freezer bag, pour in the jerk seasoning, coating the fish well, and seal. Marinate in the fridge for at least 2 hours, or preferably overnight.

2 Heat the broiler until hot. Broil the fish for 3–5 minutes on each side until nicely browned and just cooked through; be careful not to overcook.

3 Cut the fish fillets into chunky slices and serve immediately with lime wedges, fresh crusty bread, and a crunchy salad. Alternatively, serve with rice and some West Indian hot pepper sauce on the side.

fish with herb crust

This recipe works well with fish that have a slightly earthy taste, such as rockfish. Soaking the rockfish in a little acidulated water before cooking improves its flavor.

 15 MINS   12-15 MINS

SERVES 4

4 rockfish or grey mullet fillets, about 6oz (175g) each, peeled

3 tbsp butter

1 tbsp chopped flat-leaf parsley

juice of ½ lemon

salt and freshly ground black pepper

a few sprigs of sage, to garnish

lemon wedges, to garnish

For the crust

8 tbsp fresh bread crumbs

2 tbsp melted butter

1 tbsp chopped sage

1 tbsp snipped chives

grated zest of ½ lemon

1 Preheat the oven to 400°F (200°C). Arrange the fish on a baking sheet. Mix the butter, parsley, and lemon juice, and season with salt and plenty of pepper. Spread a thin layer of butter over each fish.

2 To make the crust, mix together the bread crumbs, melted butter, sage, chives, and lemon zest. Season lightly and sprinkle over the fish, pressing to stick to the butter.

3 Roast in the oven for 12–15 minutes, or until the fish is cooked—it will be firm, white, and opaque.

4 Transfer to a warmed serving dish, garnish with the sage and lemon wedges, and serve with green beans.

kenyan fish curry

Fiery, brothlike curries, enriched with coconut milk, are typical of the dishes from East Africa.

 20 MINS   45 MINS

SPECIAL EQUIPMENT ▪ coffee grinder

SERVES 4–6

juice of 1 lime

1 tsp black peppercorns, crushed

1lb 5oz (600g) haddock fillet, peeled and cut into 2in (5cm) pieces

6 tbsp vegetable oil

1 red onion, finely chopped

1 red bell pepper, seeded and finely chopped

1 red chile, finely chopped

4 garlic cloves, finely chopped

9oz (250g) plum tomatoes, peeled (p197) and finely chopped

¾ cup coconut milk

1 tbsp tamarind paste

For the spice mixture

2 dried chiles

¾ tsp coriander seeds

¾ tsp cumin seeds

1 tsp mustard seeds

¼ tsp ground turmeric

1 To make the spice mixture, dry-roast the chiles and seeds, then grind to a powder using a mortar and pestle or coffee grinder. Combine with the turmeric and set aside.

2 Combine the lime juice with the peppercorns and pour the mixture over the fish. Heat the oil in a heavy pan over medium heat. Cook the fish for 1 minute on each side until lightly colored, but not quite cooked through. Remove and set aside.

3 Add the onion to the pan, cover, and cook for 5 minutes until soft. Add in the red pepper, chile, and garlic, and cook, uncovered, for 10 minutes. Stir in the spice mixture and fry briskly for 1 minute, then stir in the tomatoes, and bring to a boil. Pour in ¾ cup water and simmer for 20 minutes until thickened. Stir in the coconut milk and tamarind paste and simmer for another 15 minutes. Add the fish and simmer for 5–10 minutes. Serve hot with rice.

Season's best **grey mullet**

The dashingly sleek silver-grey mullet is similar to sea bass, but with larger scales and a delicious, moist flesh—particularly if caught out at sea. Those caught near land taste a little muddy. At its best in autumn, its unique flavor can take on robust spices, fragrant herbs, and other strong flavorings, such as anchovy, tomatoes, citrus, and garlic.

Common grey mullet Its numerous names include black true, flathead, or striped mullet; it is not related to the red mullet. Long-living and slow-growing, grey mullet stocks are not subject to quota restrictions.

The grey mullet's olive-green back has silver shading at the sides.

Grey mullet fillet Mullet fillet is tender and slightly oily with a firm, meaty flesh. The flesh is pink in color, cooking to an off-white. The fillet does have a few fine bones, though, so needs careful pin-boning before cooking.

The flesh is pink in color, cooking to an off-white, and it is firm and meaty.

essentials
cuts available

Common grey mullet. Sold whole or in fillets; also available dried and salted. Roe fresh, dried, or salted.

buy Line-caught. Whole fish should be firm with bright eyes. Fillets should smell fresh and be moist.

store Best eaten on the day of purchase, or keep wrapped, in the coldest part of the fridge, for up to 24 hours.

cook Pan-fry, roast, steam, or bake. The salted roe is used to make taramasalata.

recipe ideas

Baby zucchini with fish and couscous p316

Fish with herb crust p322

Yam pla fu p278

how to descale a grey mullet

Visible scales on all fish from sardines to grey mullet need to be removed before cooking as they are inedible. Work in a clear space and lay down newspaper or parchment paper, as the scales can fly around.

1 Dip your fingers in salt to grip the tail without it slipping. Place the fish on paper to catch the scales. Hold the fish firmly by the tail.

2 Scrape away the scales with the back of a knife working from tail to head end. Rinse the fish under cold water and pat dry.

balinese spicy mackerel

Typical of the cuisine of Indonesia, this recipe uses kecap menis, soy sauce, and molasses. Lime wedges and fresh cilantro make an attractive garnish.

 10 MINS PLUS CHILLING   **15 MINS**

SPECIAL EQUIPMENT ▪ blender or food processor

SERVES 4

4 small mackerel, skin on, filleted, pinboned, and cut in half lengthwise

juice of 2 limes

½ tsp ground turmeric or 2 tsp freshly grated turmeric

salt

3 tbsp vegetable oil

1 lemongrass stalk, split into 4

3 tbsp kecap manis

For the chile paste

3 red or jalapeño chiles, seeded (optional) and finely chopped

6 shallots, chopped

2 garlic cloves, crushed

5 roasted candlenuts or macadamia nuts

1 tbsp grated fresh ginger

1 tbsp tamarind paste

½ tsp granulated sugar

salt and freshly ground black pepper

1 Sprinkle the mackerel with the lime juice, turmeric, and ½ tsp salt. Cover and refrigerate for 15–30 minutes.

2 Put the chiles, shallots, garlic, nuts, ginger, tamarind paste, and sugar into a blender or food processor and pulse to chop very finely. Season lightly.

3 Pat the mackerel dry with paper towels. Heat the oil in a large frying pan or wok. Fry the mackerel skin-side down, a few pieces at a time, until firm, opaque, and brown. Avoid stirring to prevent the fish from breaking up. Remove from the pan.

4 Add the chile paste to the pan and fry over medium heat until fragrant. Add ⅔ cup water and the lemongrass, bring to a boil, and simmer for 2–3 minutes. Return the fish, add the kecap manis, and stir over gentle heat until the ingredients are combined and the sauce reduced and bubbling. Serve with rice.

provençal stuffed artichokes

Artichokes braised in wine, served with rich red pepper sauce.

 50-55 MINS **40-45 MINS**

SPECIAL EQUIPMENT ▪ food processor

SERVES 4

4 globe artichokes, total weight about 3lb (1.35kg), prepared to serve whole with choke removed (p308)

½ lemon

salt and freshly ground black pepper

3 tbsp butter

3 small onions, finely chopped

6 garlic cloves, finely chopped

9oz (250g) mushrooms, finely chopped

9oz (250g) prosciutto, cut into strips

2 anchovy fillets, finely chopped

6oz (175g) pitted black olives, finely chopped

4 slices of white bread, made into crumbs

2-3 sprigs of thyme, leaves picked

large pinch of ground allspice

1 cup white wine

2 tbsp olive oil

1lb 10oz (750g) red bell peppers, roasted, peeled (p171), and chopped

14oz (400g) can chopped tomatoes

1 garlic clove, chopped

2 scallions, trimmed and chopped

bunch of basil, leaves chopped

1 Rub all cut surfaces of the prepared artichokes with the lemon half to prevent discoloration. Boil in salted water for 25–30 minutes until almost tender and a leaf can be pulled out with a slight tug. Remove

with a slotted spoon and set them upside down on a wire rack to drain.

2 Melt the butter in a frying pan, add the onions and garlic, and cook, stirring, until soft but not brown. Stir in the mushrooms, prosciutto, anchovies, and olives, then remove from the heat. Add the bread crumbs, thyme leaves, and allspice and mix thoroughly. Season with pepper.

3 Preheat the oven to 350°F (180°C). Fill the artichokes with the stuffing and tie with string to hold the leaves together. Put the artichokes in a flameproof casserole dish. Add the wine and boil for 5 minutes, or until reduced by half. Half-cover the artichokes with water; season. Bring back to a boil and cover.

4 Bake in the oven for 40–50 minutes, basting occasionally with the wine and juices, until tender and a central leaf can be pulled out easily.

5 Heat the olive oil in a frying pan. Add the remaining ingredients and cook, stirring occasionally, for 15–20 minutes, until thickened. Pulse to a coarse puree in a food processor. Season to taste. Discard the strings from the artichokes. Serve on plates with the sauce spooned around the bases. Pass extra sauce separately.

beef and leek couscous

Subtle, sweet leeks and paprika enhance this tasty beef dish.

 25 MINS   **30 MINS**

SERVES 4

¼ cup olive oil

3 leeks, finely sliced

12oz (350g) lean ground beef

1 red or jalapeño chile, seeded and finely chopped

1 tsp sweet paprika

3 garlic cloves, sliced

5 tbsp dry white wine

1 cup hot beef stock

small handful of flat-leaf parsley, finely chopped

8oz (225g) couscous

1 Preheat the oven to 300°F (150°C). Heat the oil in a heavy-bottomed pan, add the leeks, and cook over medium heat for 5 minutes. Add the ground beef and cook, stirring, for 10 minutes, or until it is no longer pink.

2 Stir in the chiles, paprika, and garlic, season again with salt and pepper, and cook for 2 minutes. Pour in the wine and cook for 3 minutes until the alcohol evaporates, then add the stock and parsley and combine well. Stir in the couscous, cover with a lid, and cook in the oven for 15 minutes. Remove from the oven, stir well, and serve.

sole veronique

This dish of sole poached with white grapes is part of the classic French repertoire. You can use other flatfish in season, such as flounder.

 30 MINS   20 MINS

SERVES 4

4 lemon sole, skinned and filleted

½ onion, thinly sliced

6 black peppercorns

1 bay leaf

½ cup dry white wine

6oz (175g) seedless white grapes, peeled

For the sauce

3 tbsp butter

1 heaping tbsp all-purpose flour

5 tbsp warm milk

5 tbsp heavy cream

salt and freshly ground white pepper

1 Preheat the oven to 350°F (180°C). Fold the sole fillets into 3, skin-side in. Arrange them in an ovenproof dish and scatter the onion, peppercorns, and bay leaf around them. Mix the wine with ½ cup water, pour it over the fish and onion, and cover with buttered wax paper.

2 Poach the fish in the oven for 10–12 minutes or until it is cooked; it will be white and opaque. Remove the fish and keep warm. Strain the cooking liquor into a saucepan and boil rapidly to reduce to ⅔ cup.

3 For the sauce, in another saucepan, melt half the butter, remove from the heat, and stir in the flour. Cook over low to medium heat for 30 seconds. Remove from the heat and blend in the milk, then the fish liquor. Return to low heat and bring to a boil, stirring. Stir in the cream, remove from the heat, and whisk in the remaining butter. Season, add the grapes, and heat through.

4 Lift the fish carefully onto warmed plates. Spoon the sauce over the fish to serve.

sea bass with black bean sauce

This is a wonderful combination—the well-flavored sea bass works beautifully with the saltiness of the sauce.

 25 MINS   30 MINS

SPECIAL EQUIPMENT ▪ bamboo steamer

SERVES 4

3 tbsp fermented black beans (available at Asian supermarkets)

2 tbsp sunflower oil

2 scallions, trimmed and chopped

2in (5cm) piece of fresh ginger, cut into matchsticks

1 garlic clove, very finely sliced

3 tbsp dark soy sauce

2 tbsp Chinese rice wine or dry sherry

1 tsp granulated sugar

1¼ cups fish stock

1 tsp cornstarch

4 sea bass fillets, about 6oz (175g) each, scaled and pinboned

a few sprigs of cilantro, to garnish

drizzle of sesame oil

1 Rinse the black beans very thoroughly under cold running water. Heat the sunflower oil in a large frying pan over low heat. Add the scallions and ginger and fry until aromatic. Add the garlic and stir-fry for another minute.

2 Remove the pan from the heat and add the soy sauce, rice wine, sugar, and three-quarters of the stock. Return to the heat, bring to a boil, and simmer for a couple of minutes. Mix the cornstarch with the remaining stock in a small bowl.

3 Arrange the fish on a bamboo steamer and cook for 7–8 minutes, covered, over a large saucepan of simmering water.

4 Meanwhile, stir the cornstarch mixture into the hot stock with the beans, bring to a boil, then reduce the heat and simmer for 2–3 minutes until thickened slightly.

5 Arrange the fish on a platter with the cilantro. Spoon the sauce over the top and drizzle with sesame oil. Serve with rice.

roasted baby leeks with tomato dressing

Leeks are rarely used as a main ingredient, but they sometimes deserve to be given a starring role. Served like this, baby leeks make a delicious appetizer or side dish.

 10 MINS   **12 MINS**

SERVES 4

1 tbsp finely chopped sun-dried tomatoes in oil

3 tbsp extra virgin olive oil, plus extra for tossing

1 tbsp red wine vinegar

1 tbsp very finely chopped black and green olives

1 tbsp finely chopped basil

sea salt and freshly ground black pepper

8 baby leeks, washed and trimmed

1 Preheat the oven to 400°F (200°C). Put the tomatoes with a little of their oil, the olive oil, vinegar, olives, and basil in a mixing bowl and combine. Season with sea salt and pepper to taste.

2 Put the leeks in a pan of boiling water and cook over high heat for 2 minutes, then drain well.

3 Toss a little olive oil in a roasting pan and place the leeks in the pan. Roast in the oven for 10 minutes until golden and tender. Spoon the dressing over to serve.

variation

roasted baby leeks with chile and crispy bacon

Blanch 8–12 baby leeks as in step 2. Place in the roasting pan and toss with the 3 tbsp olive oil, 1 tbsp white balsamic vinegar, and plenty of freshly ground black pepper. Scatter with 1 red chile, seeded and finely chopped, and 1 tbsp fresh thyme leaves. Roast as before. Transfer to a warm serving dish. Meanwhile dry-fry 2oz (60g) diced pancetta until crisp. Scatter with the leeks before serving.

chinese-style plum sauce

Use this authentic-tasting plum sauce as a dip, as a baste for grilled or roasted duck, chicken, or pork, or to replace hoisin sauce to smear on Chinese pancakes with crispy duck.

 20 MINS   **45-50 MINS**

SPECIAL EQUIPMENT ▪ blender or food processor

MAKES APPROX 2 CUPS

½ tsp wasabi paste or English mustard

⅔ cup rice (or white) wine vinegar

1lb 2oz (500g) ripe dark red or blue plums, halved and pitted

1 onion, chopped

1 garlic clove, crushed

⅓ cup dark brown sugar

5 tbsp honey

2 tbsp dark soy sauce

1 tsp Chinese five-spice powder

2 tbsp sake or dry sherry

1 Mix the wasabi paste or mustard and vinegar in a large saucepan until blended. Add the plums, onion, and garlic. Bring to a boil, reduce the heat, partly cover the pan with the lid, and simmer gently for 10–15 minutes until the plums are pulpy.

2 Put the mixture in a blender or food processor and pulse to a purée. Return the purée to the pan and stir in the remaining ingredients. Bring back to a boil, stirring continuously, then reduce the heat and simmer, uncovered, for 25 minutes, stirring occasionally, until thick and rich.

3 Spoon into warm sterilized jars, top with wax paper discs, allow to cool, seal, and label. Store in a cool, dark place for up to 3 months. Once opened, store in the fridge and use within 2 weeks.

tomato ketchup

Homemade tomato ketchup is full of goodness and free from chemical additives. This authentic-tasting recipe has the right balance of sweetness, acidity, and spice.

 15 MINS   **45 MINS - 1 HOUR 5 MINS**

SPECIAL EQUIPMENT ▪ blender or food processor
▪ preserving pan ▪ nylon sieve

MAKES APPROX 2½ CUPS)

2¼lb (1kg) ripe tomatoes, coarsely chopped

1 carrot, chopped

1 small onion, chopped

1 celery stalk, chopped

good pinch of ground cloves

1 large bay leaf

2 mace blades

1 tsp sea salt

⅔ cup red wine vinegar

⅓ cup light brown sugar

1 Put all the ingredients except the brown sugar in a preserving pan or a large heavy-bottomed, stainless steel saucepan. Bring to a boil, reduce the heat, cover with a lid, and simmer for 30 minutes. Then remove the lid and cook for another 15 minutes, stirring occasionally.

2 Discard the mace and bay leaf. Put the mixture in a blender or food processor, pulse to a purée, then rub it through a nylon sieve back into the rinsed-out pan.

3 Stir in the sugar over low heat, then bring back to a boil. Continue boiling, stirring all the time, for 5 minutes until the sauce becomes the consistency of thick cream.

4 Pour into warm sterilized screw-topped jars with non-metallic or vinegar-proof lids. Cover with wax paper discs, cool, seal, and label. Store in a cool, dark place for up to 3 months. Once opened, store in the fridge and use within 2 weeks. Shake before use.

spicy garlic and green vegetable medley

Vibrant autumn leafy greens, such as spinach and Swiss chard, and bok choy with its soft leaves and fleshy ends are all best served lightly stir-fried to retain their mild yet distinctive flavors.

 15 MINS   15 MINS

SERVES 4

handful of hazelnuts

1 tbsp sesame oil or vegetable oil

2 jalapeño chiles, seeded and finely chopped

3 garlic cloves, thinly sliced

1 tbsp dark soy sauce

1 tbsp Chinese rice wine

1–2 heads of bok choy, quartered lengthwise

handful of spinach or Swiss chard

2 handfuls of sugarsnap peas or snow peas, sliced into strips

salt and freshly ground black pepper

1 Spread the hazelnuts over a baking sheet and toast under a preheated broiler until golden brown, turning them frequently. While the hazelnuts are still hot, put them in a clean kitchen towel and rub off the skins. Coarsely chop and set aside.

2 Heat the oil in a wok over medium-high heat and swirl it around to coat the surface. Add the chiles and garlic and cook for 10 seconds, then add the soy sauce and Chinese rice wine, and cook for a few more seconds.

3 Throw in the bok choy and spinach or Swiss chard and stir-fry for a minute. Add the sugarsnap peas or snow peas and stir-fry for a minute more. Toss, then season with salt and pepper. Serve immediately with the hazelnuts scattered over the top and some fluffy rice.

variation

spicy mixed vegetable medley

Prepare in the same way but omit the spinach or Swiss chard and add 3½oz (100g) baby corn cobs, cut in thick diagonal slices, a handful of oyster mushrooms, cut in pieces if large, and red or yellow bell peppers, seeded and cut in strips at step 3. Add a splash more of rice wine and soy sauce to taste.

chunky potato wedges

Potatoes are incredibly versatile, but it is often the most basic of preparation and cooking methods that brings out their true flavor. This dish couldn't be simpler and tastes delicious.

 10 MINS **40 MINS**

SERVES 4-6

2lb (900g) all-purpose potatoes, such as russets, skins on, washed, quartered lengthwise, and if large, sliced again lengthwise

2 tbsp olive oil

sea salt

1 Preheat the oven to 400°F (200°C). Put the potatoes in a large roasting pan, add the oil, and combine well with your hands.

2 Sprinkle with plenty of sea salt and put in the oven to roast for 40 minutes, or until the wedges are crispy and golden.

variation

cajun vegetable fries
Use 1 small sweet potato and 1 large potato, both scrubbed but not peeled, and cut into thick slices, and 1 wedge of pumpkin, peeled, seeded, and cut into thick slices. Place them all in a large roasting pan and toss with 2–3 tbsp olive oil. Sprinkle with 1 tbsp Cajun spice mix instead of the z then sprinkle with a few grains of coarse sea salt before serving.

beet relish

This is a sweet relish with a hint of spice—perfect to serve with cheeses or beef. If you want to save time making the relish, pre-cook the beets the night before.

 10 MINS **2 HOURS 5 MINS**

SPECIAL EQUIPMENT ▪ muslin ▪ preserving pan

MAKES APPROX 2¼lb (1kg)

3lb (1.35kg) raw beets

1 tsp granulated sugar

1lb (450g) shallots, finely chopped

2 cups cider or white wine vinegar

1 tbsp pickling spices, placed in muslin with the ends brought together and tied firmly to make a spice bag

2 cups granulated sugar

1 Put the beets in a preserving pan or a large heavy-bottomed, stainless steel saucepan, pour in enough water to cover them, and add the granulated sugar. Bring to a boil and simmer for 1 hour, or until the beet is soft and cooked. Drain and let cool. When cool enough to handle, peel and dice each into small, neat pieces.

2 Put the shallots and vinegar in the rinsed-out preserving pan or saucepan and cook for 10 minutes over low heat. Add the chopped beets and the muslin bag of pickling spices. Give the mixture a stir, add the 2 cups granulated sugar, and heat gently until the sugar has all dissolved. Bring to a boil and cook at a rolling boil for 5 minutes, then reduce the heat to a simmer and cook the relish for about 40 minutes, or until the mixture thickens.

3 Remove the spice bag and ladle into warm sterilized jars with non-metallic or vinegar-proof lids, making sure there are no air gaps. Seal, label, and store in a cool, dark place. Allow to mature for 1 month and refrigerate after opening.

thai dipping sauce

A staple in Thailand, this hot sauce is good served with most things. It will improve in flavor after standing for a few days.

 10 MINS

SPECIAL EQUIPMENT ▪ food processor

SERVES 4

1 tsp palm sugar or brown sugar, plus extra if needed

3 garlic cloves, crushed

3-4 red or jalapeño chiles, seeded and finely chopped (leave in the seeds if you want a fiery-hot sauce)

2 tbsp fish sauce (nam pla)

1 tbsp light soy sauce

juice of 1 lime, plus extra if needed

2 tbsp chopped cilantro

salt

1 This can be made with a pestle and mortar, or in a small food processor. If using a pestle and mortar, pound the sugar, garlic, and chiles to a smooth paste, then stir in the rest of the ingredients. Check the seasoning and add a little salt to taste, adding more sugar or lime juice, if needed. If using a processor, pulse together all the ingredients except the lime juice, cilantro, and salt. Add the lime juice and salt to taste, then stir in the chopped cilantro.

2 Allow the sauce to sit for a few minutes to enable the flavors to mingle, then taste again and add more lime juice, salt, or sugar as needed. Spoon into a jar, seal, keep in the fridge, and use within a week.

green beans with toasted hazelnuts

Let the flavor of in-season green beans shine with this simple recipe—all that's needed are nuts to add crunch.

 5 MINS   5 MINS

SERVES 4

9oz (250g) thin green beans, trimmed

pinch of salt

2 tbsp butter

2½oz (75g) hazelnuts, coarsely chopped and toasted

1 Put the beans in a pan of salted water and boil for 5–6 minutes, or until they are cooked until al dente. Drain, then refresh under cold water so they stop cooking and retain their color.

2 Transfer to a serving dish, top with the butter and toasted hazelnuts, and serve with roast chicken or lamb.

greek-style vegetables

This piquant dish is great on the side of a rich main course, or as an appetizer. You can make it up to two days in advance and allow the flavors to mellow while it chills in the fridge.

 25-30 MINS   25-30 MINS

SPECIAL EQUIPMENT ▪ muslin ▪ food processor

SERVES 4

¼oz (10g) coriander seeds

½ tbsp black peppercorns

2 bay leaves

2-3 sprigs of thyme

1-2 sprigs of parsley

1 tbsp tomato paste

1⅓ cups vegetable stock or water, plus more if needed

juice of ½ lemon

2 tbsp dry white wine

12 baby onions

2 tbsp vegetable oil

2 tbsp olive oil

9oz (250g) button mushrooms, trimmed

7oz (200g) can chopped tomatoes

salt and freshly ground black pepper

9oz (250g) fennel bulbs, sliced

¾oz (20g) raisins

1 Combine the coriander seeds, black peppercorns, bay leaves, and thyme and parsley sprigs in a small bowl. Place the mixture on a small piece of muslin, bring the ends together, and tie firmly with string to make a bag.

2 To make the cooking liquid, whisk the tomato paste, half the vegetable stock or water, the lemon juice, and white wine in a bowl.

3 Put the baby onions in a bowl, cover with hot water, and let stand for 2 minutes. Drain and peel, leaving a little of the root attached.

4 Heat the vegetable oil and olive oil in a sauté pan. Add the baby onions and sauté for 3 minutes or so until lightly browned. Add the mushrooms, spice bag, and tomatoes. Pour in the cooking liquid so it just covers the vegetables, add some salt and the fennel, and bring to a rapid boil over high heat. Add the raisins and stir occasionally, adding a little stock or water as the liquid evaporates. Cook the vegetables for 25–30 minutes until tender when pierced with the tip of a knife. Remove the spice bag, taste for seasoning, and serve.

sweet corn and pepper relish

As its name implies, this diced sweet corn and pepper relish packs a tangy punch of flavor. It is part pickle, part chutney, but cooked for a shorter time than a chutney.

 10 MINS   25-30 MINS

MAKES APPROX 2¼lb (1kg)

4 sweet corn cobs, kernels removed (about 1lb/450g kernels, p155)

2 red bell peppers, or 1 green and 1 red bell pepper, seeded and finely diced

2 celery stalks, finely sliced

1 red or jalapeño chile, seeded and finely sliced (optional)

1 onion, peeled and finely sliced

1¾ cups white wine vinegar

1 cup sugar

2 tsp sea salt

2 tsp mustard powder

½ tsp ground turmeric

1 Blanch the kernels in a saucepan of boiling water for 2 minutes, then drain well. Put the sweet corn and the other ingredients in a large saucepan and cook over medium heat, stirring until the sugar has dissolved. Then bring to a boil. Turn the heat down and simmer gently, stirring frequently, for 15–20 minutes or until the mixture has thickened slightly and has only a little liquid left in the bottom of the pan when you draw a wooden spoon across it. The relish should be a spoonable consistency and wetter than a chutney.

3 Check the seasoning is right, then pour into warm sterilized jars. Seal with non-metallic or vinegar-proof lids, let cool, and label. Store in a cool, dark place. Like all relishes, this can be eaten immediately or stored. Once opened, store in the fridge.

quick pumpkin bread

The grated pumpkin in this quick bread ensures that it keeps moist for days. It's a perfect accompaniment for soup.

 20 MINS 50 MINS ❄ FREEZABLE

MAKES 1

1¾ cups all-purpose flour

¾ cup whole wheat flour, plus 1 tsp baking powder

1 tsp baking soda

½ tsp fine salt

4¼oz (120g) pumpkin or butternut squash, halved, seeded, peeled, and coarsely grated

1oz (30g) pumpkin seeds

1¼ cups buttermilk

1 Preheat the oven to 425°F (220°C). Put the flours, baking soda, and salt in a mixing bowl and mix well. Add the grated pumpkin and seeds and stir the ingredients well to combine so that no clumps remain. Make a well in the center and pour in the buttermilk. Stir together to form a dough.

2 Using your hands, bring the mixture together into a ball, then turn it onto a floured work surface. Knead the dough for 2 minutes until it forms a smooth mass. You may need to add a little more flour if it feels too sticky.

3 Shape the dough into a round 6in (15cm) in diameter and place on a lined baking sheet. Use a sharp knife to slash a cross into the top to help the bread to rise when baking.

4 Cook for 30 minutes in the center of the oven until risen. Then reduce the oven to 400°F (200°C) and cook for 20 minutes more until the base sounds hollow when tapped.

5 Transfer the bread to a wire rack and allow it to cool for at least 20 minutes before serving.

mushroom ketchup

Thin ketchups such as this can be used as a concentrated flavoring in soups, sauces, gravies, and savory dishes.

 1 HR 30 MINS PLUS STANDING 1 HR

SPECIAL EQUIPMENT ■ fine nylon sieve ■ muslin

MAKES APPROX 1¼ CUPS

4½lb (2kg) field or large open cultivated mushrooms, wiped and finely chopped

2 tbsp sea salt

1 tsp black peppercorns

1 tsp allspice berries

½ tsp cloves

½ cinnamon stick

1 small shallot

1¼ cups red or white wine vinegar

a few pieces of dried porcini

6 salted anchovies, rinsed (or 2 tbsp dark soy sauce)

2 mace blades

2 tsp brandy (optional)

1 Put the chopped mushrooms in a large bowl. Sprinkle with the sea salt, toss together with your hands to mix well, cover, and set aside for 24 hours, squashing the mushrooms down occasionally.

2 Grind the peppercorns, allspice, cloves, and cinnamon in a pestle and mortar. Peel and finely chop the shallot, measure the vinegar, and select a few dried porcinis.

Check the chopped mushrooms; they should have now reduced to a third of their original volume.

3 Put the mushrooms, their juice, the ground spices, and the shallot in a saucepan with the vinegar, dried porcinis, anchovies, and mace. Bring to a boil, cover with a lid, and simmer very gently for 1 hour.

4 Strain the cooked ingredients through a fine nylon sieve set over a clean bowl. Press the mixture hard against the sides of the sieve to extract as much liquor as possible.

5 Pour the contents of the sieve onto a square of muslin, gather up the corners, and squeeze the muslin ball tightly to extract the last of the liquor. Check the quantity of the liquor; if it is more than 1¼–1½ cups, return to the pan and cook until its volume reduces to about 1¼ cups. Pour the liquor into a warm sterilized bottle, add the brandy (if using), seal, and store in a cool, dark place. Once opened, keep refrigerated for 4–6 months.

fennel gratin

The rich, creamy gratin topping on this Italian dish works perfectly with the subtle aniseed flavor of fennel.

 5 MINS 40 MINS

SERVES 4

2 fennel bulbs, trimmed and cut lengthwise into 6 slices or wedges

salt and freshly ground black pepper

small sprig of rosemary, leaves picked and finely chopped (optional)

⅔ cup heavy cream

scant 1oz (25g) Parmesan cheese, grated

1 Preheat the oven to 350°F (180°C). Add the fennel to a pan of boiling salted water and simmer gently for about 5 minutes, or until starting to soften. Drain well.

2 Arrange the fennel in a shallow baking dish. Sprinkle with the rosemary, if using, and season with salt and pepper. Pour in the cream and sprinkle with half the Parmesan cheese. Cover the dish with foil and bake in the oven for 30 minutes.

3 Remove the foil. Sprinkle with the remaining Parmesan and put back into the oven, uncovered, to bake for another 5 minutes, or until the top turns lightly golden. Serve hot.

black olive and pepper ciabatta

A good ciabatta should be well risen and crusty, with large air pockets. Using black olives and roasted red bell peppers in this easy-to-master recipe makes for an unusual, tasty loaf studded with black and red.

 40 MINS PLUS RISING AND PROVING 30 MINS ❄ FREEZABLE

MAKES 2

2 tsp dried yeast

2 tbsp olive oil

2½ cups bread flour

1 tsp sea salt

1¾oz (50g) pitted black olives, drained, coarsely chopped, and dried with paper towels

1 red bell pepper, roasted, peeled (p171), and coarsely chopped

1 Dissolve the yeast with 1½ cups warm water in a bowl, then add the oil. Put the flour and salt in a separate mixing bowl. Make a well in the center of the flour, pour in the yeast mixture, and stir together to form a soft dough.

2 Knead the dough for 10 minutes on a floured work surface, then stretch it out thinly and scatter with the olives and pepper. Bring the sides of the dough together to cover the olives and pepper. Knead the dough briefly until the olives and pepper are fully incorporated. Put the dough in an oiled bowl, cover loosely with plastic wrap, and let rise in a warm place for up to 2 hours until doubled in size.

3 Turn the dough onto a floured work surface and knock it back. Divide it into 2 pieces, then knead and mold each piece into a 12 x 4in (30 x 10cm) traditional slipper shape. Place the loaves on a lined baking sheet, cover with plastic wrap and a kitchen towel, and leave for 1 hour until they have doubled in size.

4 Preheat the oven to 450°F (230°C). Spray the loaves with a mist of water and bake in the center of the oven for 30 minutes until golden brown; spray the loaves with water every 10 minutes. The bread is cooked when the base sounds hollow when tapped. Cool for 30 minutes before cutting.

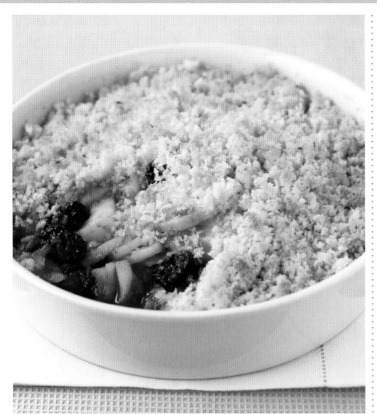

apple and blackberry brown betty

This classic combination of tart apples and juicy blackberries is topped by a layer of zesty lemon bread crumbs.

 15 MINS   **40 MINS**   **FREEZABLE**

SPECIAL EQUIPMENT ▪ 1-quart ovenproof dish

SERVES 4

1 cup fine white bread crumbs

generous pat of butter, softened

zest of 1 lemon

3 tart apples, peeled, cored, and sliced

5½oz (150g) blackberries

⅔ cup fresh orange juice

2-3 tbsp granulated sugar (depending on the tartness of the fruit)

1 Preheat the oven to 375°F (190°C). Put the bread crumbs, butter, and lemon zest in a mixing bowl, combine well, and set aside.

2 Place the apples in a greased ovenproof dish, then stir in the blackberries, orange juice, and enough of the granulated sugar to sweeten. Sprinkle the bread crumbs on top and bake for 35–40 minutes or until golden and piping hot. Serve while hot with ice cream.

variation

pear and raspberry brown betty

Prepare in exactly the same way but use whole wheat bread crumbs instead of white ones. Substitute 4 ripe pears for 2 of the cooking apples. Use 5½oz (150g) raspberries instead of blackberries and ⅔ cup apple juice instead of orange juice. 1–2 tbsp sugar will be sufficient to sweeten. Serve with scoops of vanilla ice cream.

apple jalousie

In this pastry, the top layer of dough is slashed before baking to look like a *jalousie*, French for louvred shutter.

 1 HR 15 MINS - 1 HR 30 MINS PLUS CHILLING   **30-40 MINS**

SERVES 6-8

1 tbsp unsalted butter

2¼lb (1kg) tart apples, peeled, cored, and diced

1in (2.5cm) piece of fresh ginger, peeled and finely chopped

½ cup granulated sugar

1lb 2oz (500g) store-bought puff pastry

1 large egg white

1 Melt the butter in a large frying pan. Add the apples, ginger, and all but 2 tbsp of the sugar. Sauté briskly, stirring often, for 15–20 minutes until the apples are tender and caramelized. Taste, adding more sugar if needed. Set aside to cool.

2 Sprinkle a baking sheet evenly with cold water. Roll out the puff pastry on a floured work surface and trim into a 11 x 12½in (28 x 32cm) rectangle. Cut in half lengthwise, then fold one of the halves in half lengthwise and cut across the fold at ¼in (5mm) intervals to form the shutter effect, leaving an uncut border at the edges. Use a very sharp knife so you don't press down hard, or the pastry will be hard to unfold. Transfer the uncut rectangle to the baking sheet and press it down lightly. Spoon the apple filling down the center, leaving a ¾in (2cm) border. Moisten the border with cold water using a pastry brush. Top with the slashed dough rectangle, then press the edges together with your fingertips and trim the edges. Scallop the edges at close intervals with the back of a small knife. Let chill in the fridge for 15 minutes. Preheat the oven to 425°F (220°C).

3 Bake for 20–25 minutes until puffed and light brown. Meanwhile, whisk the egg white just until frothy. Brush the hot jalousie with the egg white and sprinkle the remaining sugar on top. Return to the oven and continue baking for 10–15 minutes until the sugar glaze is crisp and the pastry is deep golden. Transfer to a wire rack and let cool, then cut the jalousie across into 6–8 slices and serve warm or at room temperature.

blackberry focaccia

The addition of blackberries turns this classic bread into a lovely sweet dessert, afternoon snack, or as part of a meal on the go.

 30-35 MINS PLUS RISING AND PROVING 15-20 MINS

SPECIAL EQUIPMENT ▪ 15 x 9in (38 x 23cm) Swiss roll pan

SERVES 6-8

1 tbsp dried yeast

2½ cups bread flour, plus extra
for dusting

1 tsp salt

3 tbsp granulated sugar

⅓ cup extra virgin olive oil

10oz (300g) blackberries

1 Sprinkle the yeast over ¼ cup lukewarm water in a small bowl. Let stand for 5 minutes until dissolved, stirring once.

2 Put the flour, salt, and 2 tbsp of the sugar in a mixing bowl and mix together. Make a well in the center of the mix and add the dissolved yeast, ¼ cup of the oil, and 1 cup lukewarm water. Draw in the flour and mix to form a smooth dough. The dough should be soft and sticky; avoid adding more flour to dry it out.

3 Flour your hands and the dough, and turn it onto a floured surface. Knead for 5-7 minutes until smooth and elastic. Transfer to an oiled bowl and cover with a damp kitchen towel. Let rise in a warm place for about 1-1½ hours until doubled in bulk.

4 Generously brush the pan with oil. Turn out the dough and knock out the air. Cover with a dry kitchen towel and let rest for 5 minutes. Transfer to the pan, flattening it with your hands so it fills the pan. Scatter the

blackberries over the surface of the dough, cover with the kitchen towel, and let rise in a warm place for 35-45 minutes until puffed.

5 Preheat the oven to 400°F (200°C). Brush the dough with the remaining oil and sprinkle with the rest of the sugar. Bake at the top of the oven for 15-20 minutes, until lightly browned. Cool slightly on a wire rack, then serve warm.

Season's best **apples**

In green, red, yellow, or russet; tasting sour, sharp, or sweet; some crisp, some soft, apples ripen in late summer or autumn and many can be stored over the winter. Most, except sour cooking apples or the bland red ones, can be eaten raw or cooked. Apples pair well with cheeses, rich meats such as pork, ham, duck, and game, and with nuts, other fruits, sweet spices, and chocolate.

Apples grown in cooler climates have the best flavor. There are numerous eating and cooking apple varieties, but only the bright, round, perfect ones are commercially cultivated.

Cox's Orange Pippin This scented, mottled yellow-green apple with an orange-red flush has a crisp and juicy flesh. Its superb flavor has made it one of the favorite dessert apples.

Fiesta Also known as Red Pippin, this variety is a Cox's offspring. It has a sweet flavor with slight acidity, and is greatly preferred for juicing.

Pink Lady (Cripps Pink) One of the best-looking apple varieties available, this eating apple has a strong pink blush, tender skin, crisp and firm flesh, and a well-balanced flavor.

how to core, peel, and chop apples

Apples can be cored, then stuffed and baked with their skin on; or peeled and cut into rings or slices; or after coring and peeling, chopped into neat pieces, depending on the recipe.

1 To core, push a corer straight into the stem of the apple and through to the bottom. Twist and loosen the core, then pull it out with the corer.

2 Using a peeler or a sharp paring knife, gently remove the skin of the apple by making a circular path around the body from top to bottom.

3 Place the cored apple on its side and slice down to make rings. To chop, stack the rings. Slice through at regular intervals to cut into small, even pieces.

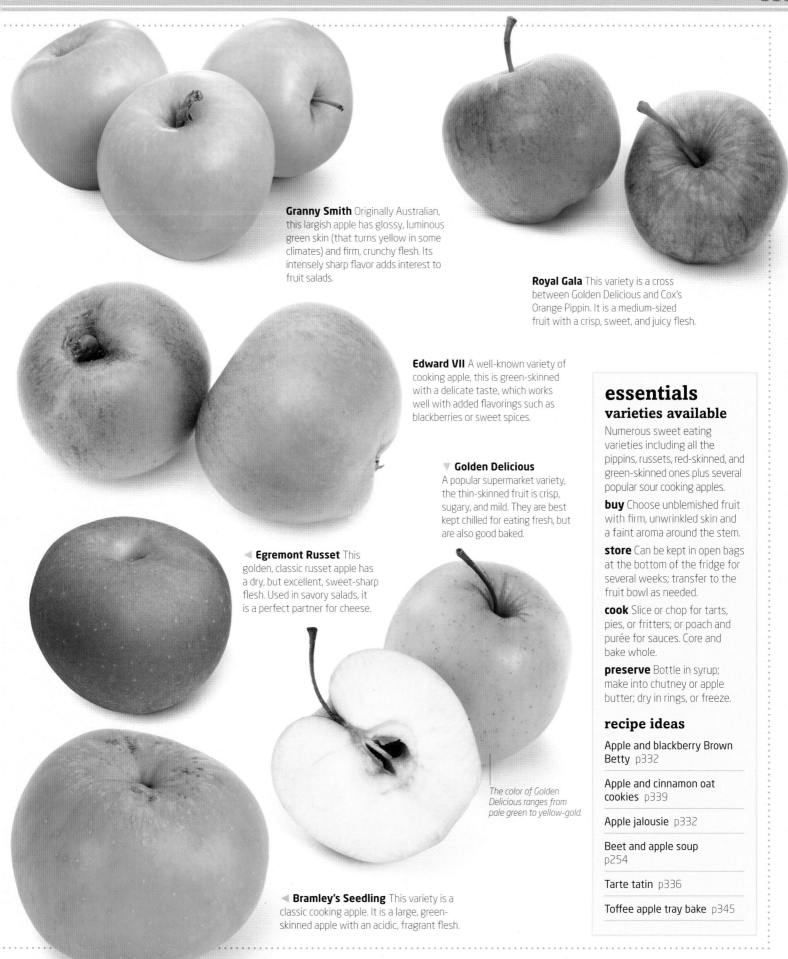

Granny Smith Originally Australian, this largish apple has glossy, luminous green skin (that turns yellow in some climates) and firm, crunchy flesh. Its intensely sharp flavor adds interest to fruit salads.

Royal Gala This variety is a cross between Golden Delicious and Cox's Orange Pippin. It is a medium-sized fruit with a crisp, sweet, and juicy flesh.

Edward VII A well-known variety of cooking apple, this is green-skinned with a delicate taste, which works well with added flavorings such as blackberries or sweet spices.

▽ **Golden Delicious** A popular supermarket variety, the thin-skinned fruit is crisp, sugary, and mild. They are best kept chilled for eating fresh, but are also good baked.

◀ **Egremont Russet** This golden, classic russet apple has a dry, but excellent, sweet-sharp flesh. Used in savory salads, it is a perfect partner for cheese.

The color of Golden Delicious ranges from pale green to yellow-gold.

◀ **Bramley's Seedling** This variety is a classic cooking apple. It is a large, green-skinned apple with an acidic, fragrant flesh.

essentials
varieties available

Numerous sweet eating varieties including all the pippins, russets, red-skinned, and green-skinned ones plus several popular sour cooking apples.

buy Choose unblemished fruit with firm, unwrinkled skin and a faint aroma around the stem.

store Can be kept in open bags at the bottom of the fridge for several weeks; transfer to the fruit bowl as needed.

cook Slice or chop for tarts, pies, or fritters; or poach and purée for sauces. Core and bake whole.

preserve Bottle in syrup; make into chutney or apple butter; dry in rings, or freeze.

recipe ideas

Apple and blackberry Brown Betty p332

Apple and cinnamon oat cookies p339

Apple jalousie p332

Beet and apple soup p254

Tarte tatin p336

Toffee apple tray bake p345

flaky pear tartlets

These are a party favorite, a spectacular contrast of hot and cold, and need very little last-minute preparation.

 35-40 MINS PLUS CHILLING   30-40 MINS

SERVES 8

1lb (450g) store-bought all-butter puff pastry

1 large egg beaten with ½ tsp salt, to glaze

¾ cup granulated sugar

½ cup heavy cream

4 pears

juice of 1 lemon

For the Chantilly cream

½ cup heavy cream

1-2 tsp confectioners' sugar

½ tsp pure vanilla extract

1 Sprinkle 2 baking sheets with cold water. Roll out the puff pastry dough, cut in half lengthwise, then cut diagonally at 4in (10cm) intervals along the length of each piece, to make 8 diamond shapes. Transfer to the baking sheets and brush with the glaze. With the tip of a knife, score a border around each. Chill for 15 minutes.

2 Preheat the oven to 425°F (220°C). Bake the pastries for about 15 minutes, until they start to brown, then reduce the temperature to 375°F

(190°C) and bake for 20-25 minutes more, until golden and crisp. Transfer to wire racks to cool, then cut out the lid from each pastry and scoop out any undercooked pastry from inside.

3 Put ½ cup water in a saucepan and dissolve ⅔ cup of the sugar. Boil, without stirring, until golden. Reduce the heat. Remove from the heat, stand back, and add the cream. Heat gently until the caramel dissolves. Cool.

4 Whip the cream for the Chantilly cream until soft peaks form. Add the confectioners' sugar and vanilla, and continue whipping until stiff peaks form. Chill.

5 Butter a baking sheet. Heat the broiler. Peel and core the pears. Thinly slice lengthwise, keeping attached at the stalk end. Flatten with your fingers, transfer to the sheet, brush with lemon, and sprinkle with the remaining sugar. Broil until caramelized.

6 Transfer the puff pastry to plates and place Chantilly cream and a pear fan in each. Pour a little cold caramel sauce over each fan and partially cover with the pastry lids.

tarte tatin

The special deliciousness of this upside-down tart comes from cooking the apples in the caramel itself.

 45-50 MINS PLUS CHILLING 20-25 MINS

SERVES 8

14-16 apples, about 5lb 6oz (2.4kg)

1 lemon, halved

8 tbsp unsalted butter

¾ cup granulated sugar

9oz (250g) store-bought pie dough

crème fraîche, to serve

1 With a vegetable peeler, carefully peel the apples, then halve and core them. Rub the apples all over with the cut lemon to prevent discoloration.

2 Melt the butter in a heavy, ovenproof frying pan. Add the sugar. Cook over medium heat, stirring occasionally, for 3-5 minutes, until caramelized to a deep golden brown. Remove from the heat and allow to cool to tepid. Arrange the apple halves over in concentric circles to fill the pan, packing them tightly.

3 Cook the apples over high heat for 15-25 minutes, until caramelized. Turn once to caramelize on both sides. Remove from the heat and leave to cool for 10-15 minutes.

4 Meanwhile, preheat the oven to 375°F (190°C). Roll out the pastry to a circle about 1in (2.5cm) larger than the pan. Roll up the dough around the rolling pin, then drape it over the pan. Tuck the edges around the apples. Bake for 20-25 minutes, until golden brown. Let cool, then set a plate on top, hold firmly together, and invert. If any apples stick to the pan, replace on the tart. Spoon some caramel over the apples. Serve with crème fraîche.

variation

pear tarte tatin

Substitute the apples for 12-14 flavorful, firm pears (about 5lb 6oz/2.4kg total weight). Peel, halve, and core the pears and rub them with lemon. Caramelize the pears as directed in the main recipe, arranging them with the tapered ends pointing inward. Cook until the liquid completely evaporates; this may take longer than the apples. Top with the dough and bake as before.

apple tart

When Gravenstein apples are in season, it is the classic apple tart that comes to mind. Slice the apples thinly for nice effect.

 10 MINS   25 MINS   ❄ FREEZABLE

SPECIAL EQUIPMENT ▪ 8in (20cm) round fluted tart pan ▪ ceramic baking beans

SERVES 6

8oz (225g) store-bought pie dough

1 large egg, beaten

4 Gravenstein or other sweet apples, peeled, cored, and thinly sliced

2–3 tbsp granulated sugar

pat of butter

1 Preheat the oven to 425°F (220°C). On a lightly floured surface, roll the pastry out as thinly as you can. Use to line the tart pan, pressing it into the corners. Trim away the excess and prick the bottom all over with a fork. Line the tart crust with wax paper and fill with ceramic baking beans. Bake in the oven for 10 minutes, or until the edges are golden. Remove the beans and paper, brush the bottom of the crust with a little of the egg wash, and return to the oven for 2–3 minutes to crisp. Remove from the oven and set aside. Allow the tart crust to cool, but leave the oven on.

2 Arrange the apple slices in the tart crust in a neat, overlapping design. Sprinkle with the sugar and dot with the butter. Bake in the oven for 10–15 minutes, or until the apples begin to caramelize and the pastry is golden. Let cool. Remove from the pan and place on a plate to serve.

variation

apple and custard tart

Make and bake the tart crust as before. Make a custard by whisking 1½ tbsp each of all-purpose flour and cornstarch with 3 tbsp granulated sugar, ¾ cup milk, and 1 large egg together in a saucepan until smooth. Bring to a boil, whisking, and cook for 2 minutes. Add a few drops of pure vanilla extract. Transfer to the tart crust and spread evenly. Top with the sliced cooking apples, then glaze and bake as before.

cinnamon and plum cobbler

Use really ripe plums for this recipe. The brown sugar and cinnamon will add a sweet, dark, spicy flavor to them.

 20 MINS   30 MINS

SPECIAL EQUIPMENT ▪ 2-quart ovenproof dish

SERVES 6–8

2¼lb (1kg) plums, pitted and halved

⅓ cup light brown sugar

1 tsp cinnamon

2 tbsp unsalted butter, chilled and cubed

For the cobbler

2 cups self-rising flour

2 tsp baking powder

¼ cup granulated sugar

½–¾ tsp ground cinnamon, to taste

salt

5 tbsp unsalted butter

1 large egg

⅓ cup buttermilk

1 tbsp light brown sugar

ice cream, custard, or cream, to serve (optional)

1 Preheat the oven to 375°F (190°C). Toss the plum halves with the sugar and cinnamon. Put them in the dish and dot with the butter.

2 To make the cobbler, sift the flour, baking powder, sugar, cinnamon, and a pinch of salt into a bowl. Rub in the butter until the mixture resembles fine crumbs. Whisk together the egg and the buttermilk. Add the liquid to the dry ingredients and bring together to form a soft, sticky dough.

3 Drop heaping tablespoonfuls of the dough over the surface of the fruit, leaving a little space between them. Sprinkle with the brown sugar.

4 Bake in the center of the preheated oven for 30 minutes, or until golden and bubbling. The cobbler is ready when a skewer inserted into the center of the topping comes out clean. Let cool for at least 5 minutes before serving with ice cream, custard, or cream.

Season's best **figs**

These delicate, almost sensual fruits are known for their honeyed, succulent flesh and tiny, crunchy seeds, which bring a unique taste and texture to many dishes. They ripen late summer through autumn and taste phenomenal with cheeses, cream, fruits, and nuts, poached in wine or syrup, or served with rich meats such as game, duck, proscuitto, or liver pâtés.

Native to the Middle East, figs grow widely on deciduous trees or large shrubs in Mediterranean climates, but also thrive in sunny, sheltered positions in cooler regions.

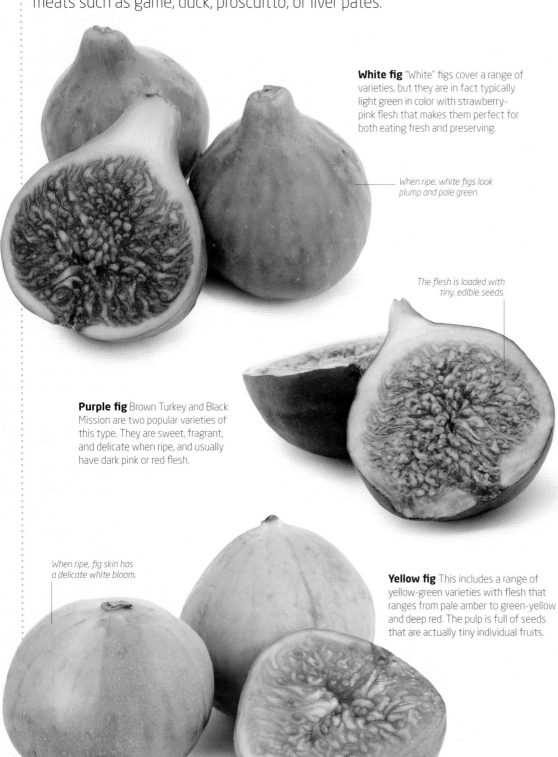

White fig "White" figs cover a range of varieties, but they are in fact typically light green in color with strawberry-pink flesh that makes them perfect for both eating fresh and preserving.

When ripe, white figs look plump and pale green.

The flesh is loaded with tiny, edible seeds.

Purple fig Brown Turkey and Black Mission are two popular varieties of this type. They are sweet, fragrant, and delicate when ripe, and usually have dark pink or red flesh.

When ripe, fig skin has a delicate white bloom.

Yellow fig This includes a range of yellow-green varieties with flesh that ranges from pale amber to green-yellow and deep red. The pulp is full of seeds that are actually tiny individual fruits.

essentials
varieties available

Numerous varieties of white, yellow, or purple-skinned figs, which range in color inside from gold to deep red.

buy Ripe figs damage easily. They should be unblemished, feel heavy in the hand, and just yield with a little pressure. A few beads of sugar juice around the stem is a good indication of ripeness.

store Eat as soon as possible, but they can be stored in the fridge for a day; serve at room temperature. Keep underripe figs at room temperature until the skin softens.

cook Enjoy fresh; poach in syrup; bake or stew for sauces and sweet or savory dishes.

preserve Bottle or make into jam; dry.

recipe ideas

Fig and mulled wine tart p339

Fig and vanilla jam p350

Fresh figs in honey syrup p244

Figs with cassis mascarpone p220

Lamb tagine with walnuts and figs p320

Seared halloumi cheese with figs p253

honey-broiled figs with zabaglione

The figs in this dish are lightly caramelized when broiled, smothered in lime-scented honey, and are then set on a sweet sherry foam for a truly decadent dessert.

 10 MINS   5 MINS

SPECIAL EQUIPMENT ▪ electric hand mixer

SERVES 4

4 large figs

grated zest and juice of 1 lime

2 tbsp honey

2 large eggs

2 tbsp granulated sugar

3 tbsp sweet sherry

1 Cut the figs in half not quite all the way through so they are "butterflied." Place in a shallow bowl, add the lime juice, and gently toss.

2 Half-fill a pan with water and set over medium heat to bring to simmer. Preheat the broiler. Warm the honey in a small heatproof bowl (under the broiler or in the pan of heating water)

and mix with the grated lime zest. Place the figs on oiled foil in a shallow flameproof dish. Drizzle all over with the honey. Broil for 4–5 minutes until caramelized at the edges.

3 Meanwhile, put the eggs, sugar, and sherry in a heatproof bowl over the pan of simmering water. Beat with an electric hand mixer until voluminous, pale, thick, and foamy.

4 Spoon the zabaglione into shallow glass serving dishes and carefully place a caramelized fig in the center of each. Drizzle the honey juices from the foil around each fig and serve immediately.

apple and cinnamon oat cookies

Adding grated apple to the cookie dough makes these cookies deliciously soft and chewy.

 20 MINS   10–15 MINS   ❄ FREEZABLE

SPECIAL EQUIPMENT ▪ electric hand mixer

MAKES 24

7 tbsp unsalted butter, softened

1 cup light brown sugar

1 large egg

1 tsp pure vanilla extract

1 tbsp honey

1 cup self-rising flour, sifted

1½ oats

2 tsp cinnamon

salt

2 apples, peeled, cored, and finely grated

a little milk, if needed

1 Preheat the oven to 375°F (190°C). Line 2 or 3 baking sheets with parchment paper. Put the butter and sugar in a bowl and cream together

with an electric hand mixer until pale and creamy. Add the egg, vanilla extract, and honey, and beat well until smooth.

2 With a wooden spoon, stir the flour, oats, and cinnamon, together with a pinch of salt, into the creamed mixture to combine. Mix in the apples. If the mixture seems too stiff, add a little milk. Take walnut-sized pieces of dough and roll them into a ball between your palms. Place on the prepared baking sheets and flatten slightly, leaving space for the cookies to spread.

3 Bake for 10–15 minutes until golden brown. Leave to cool slightly and then transfer to a wire rack to cool completely.

fig and mulled wine tart

With their delicate flavor, figs call for the simplest treatment.

 25–30 MINS PLUS CHILLING   15–20 MINS

SPECIAL EQUIPMENT ▪ 10in (25cm) round fluted tart pan with removable bottom

SERVES 6–8

13oz (375g) store-bought pie dough

1 cup milk

½ vanilla bean, split lengthwise

3 large egg yolks

3 tbsp granulated sugar

2 tbsp all-purpose flour

1 tbsp unsalted butter

⅓ cup heavy cream, whipped

peeled zest of 1 orange

peeled zest of 1 lemon

1 nutmeg, crushed

½ cup granulated sugar

2in (5cm) piece of cinnamon stick

2 whole cloves

2 cups dry red wine

1lb 2oz (500g) figs, skins pricked

1 Preheat the oven to 375°F (190°C). Butter the tart pan. Roll out the dough on a floured surface and use to line the pan. Chill for 15 minutes, then bake for 15–20 minutes until golden. Put on a wire rack, loosen the pan, and let the crust cool.

2 For the pastry cream, bring the milk and vanilla to a boil in a pan. Remove from the heat. In a bowl, whisk the egg yolks and sugar until thick. Stir in the flour and then the hot milk. Return to the pan. Bring to a boil, whisking, until thickened. Reduce the heat and cook, whisking, for about 2 minutes, until it softens. Remove from the heat, discard the vanilla bean, and transfer to a bowl. Rub the butter over and chill for 30 minutes. Fold in the whipped cream.

3 Put the zest and nutmeg into a pan with the sugar, spices, and wine. Heat, stirring, to dissolve the sugar. Bring to a boil, then add the figs. Poach for 3–5 minutes, until the figs are tender. Remove the figs and set aside. Simmer the syrup until reduced to about ½ cup. Strain and cool. Halve the figs, then cut them nearly through into quarters. Spread the pastry cream over the chilled pie crust and arrange the figs on top. Spoon 1–2 tbsp syrup over the figs. Just before serving, spoon over the rest.

blackberry brioche with mascarpone

This is the ultimate in fast desserts, yet it looks impressive and is incredibly tasty. It is pleasing to think that an afternoon's blackberry picking can give such rewarding results.

 5 MINS   10 MINS

SERVES 4

4 tbsp butter

¼ cup granulated sugar

14oz (400g) blackberries

4–8 slices of brioche

7oz (200g) mascarpone cheese

1 Melt the butter in a frying pan. Add the sugar and allow it to melt and start to turn golden brown, shaking the pan to dissolve the sugar.

2 Add the blackberries to the pan and allow them to cook over high heat for 2–3 minutes, until they are heated through and softened, but have not broken up. Leave the berries to cool slightly while you toast the slices of brioche.

3 Thickly spread the mascarpone cheese over the slices of toasted brioche and top with the sugary, fried berries. Spoon over any excess juice that is left in the pan and serve.

variation

spiced blackberry and pear toasties with mascarpone

Prepare in the same way, but use 7oz (200g) blackberries and 2 ripe pears, peeled, cored, and cubed, and add to the pan at step 2 with ½ tsp apple pie spice. Toast 8 slices of fruit bread instead of the brioche, and spread with the mascarpone in the same way as before. For a low-fat alternative, use quark instead of mascarpone.

blackberry and apple cake

There are many different ways to use blackberries and with the onset of shorter, cooler days, combining them with apples beneath a steaming layer of cake is truly comforting.

 20 MINS   50 MINS   ❄ FREEZABLE

SPECIAL EQUIPMENT ▪ electric hand mixer ▪ 1-quart ovenproof dish

SERVES 6

8 tbsp butter, softened

½ cup granulated sugar

2 large eggs

1½ cups self-rising flour, sifted

2 tart apples, peeled, cored, and coarsely chopped

9oz (250g) blackberries

2 tbsp granulated sugar

confectioners', to dust (optional)

1 Preheat the oven to 350°F (180°C). Put the butter and sugar in a bowl and cream together with an electric hand mixer until pale and creamy. Beat in the eggs, one at a time, adding 1 tbsp of the flour after each egg. Mix in the remaining flour and set aside. Put the apples and blackberries in the ovenproof dish, then stir in the granulated sugar along with 2 tbsp cold water. Spoon the cake mixture over the top and smooth the surface.

2 Bake for 50 minutes, or until golden brown and firm to the touch; a skewer should come out clean when inserted in the center. Dust with confectioners', if using, and serve while steaming hot.

variation

poached pears with chocolate cake

Poach 4 peeled, cored, and halved pears in light syrup. Drain and place in the ovenproof dish. Add 2 tbsp of the syrup. Make the cake in the same way, but replace ¼ cup of the all-purpose flour with cocoa powder. Spoon over and bake as before. Serve the pear syrup separately.

trio of sorbets

What better way to enjoy the essence of fresh fruit? This trio of blackberry, pear, and mango sorbets makes a pretty picture in a bowl. If you prefer, choose your favorite fruit and increase the quantities to make just one of the sorbets.

 40–50 MINS PLUS FREEZING   **15–20 MINS**   ❄ **FREEZABLE**

SPECIAL EQUIPMENT ▪ food processor ▪ ice cream maker

SERVES 8

1¼ cups sugar, plus more if needed

14oz (400g) blackberries, plus more if needed

3 lemons, plus more if needed

1lb 10oz (750g) ripe pears

about 2 tbsp Poire Williams liqueur

1lb 6oz (625g) ripe mangoes, peeled, pit removed, and coarsely chopped

1 Put the sugar and 1⅓ cups water in a pan and heat until the sugar has dissolved. Bring to a boil and cook without stirring for 2–3 minutes, until the syrup is clear. Pour into a liquid measuring cup and let it cool.

2 Put the blackberries in a food processor and pulse to a puree. Work it through a sieve held over a bowl, to remove the seeds. There should be ⅔ cup puree. If necessary, pulse a few more berries.

3 Squeeze the lemons; there should be just over ¼ cup juice. Keep the lemon halves. Add ¼ cup water, 2 tbsp of the lemon juice, and one-third of the sugar syrup to the blackberry puree. Taste and stir in more lemon or sugar if needed. Chill, then taste again. Pour the mixture into an ice-cream maker and churn until firm. Meanwhile, chill a bowl in the freezer. Transfer the sorbet to

the chilled bowl. Cover and freeze for at least 4 hours, to allow the flavor to mellow. Wash the food processor.

4 For the pear sorbet, pour half the remaining syrup into a small pan. Add 2 tbsp of the lemon juice. Peel, core, and quarter the pears, and rub with the reserved lemon halves. Cut the pear into chunks and drop them into the pan of syrup. Bring to a boil, then reduce the heat and simmer the pears for 5–10 minutes, until soft and translucent. Puree with their syrup in the food processor. Work through a sieve held over a bowl. There should be nearly 2 cups pear puree. Stir in the liqueur and taste, adding more

liqueur, lemon juice, or sugar if needed. Freeze the sorbet, as for the blackberry sorbet.

5 For the mango sorbet, clean the food processor once again and put the mango flesh into it. Add the remaining sugar syrup and lemon juice. Puree until smooth. There should be nearly 2 cups puree. Taste and add more lemon juice or sugar, if needed. Freeze as for the blackberry sorbet.

6 Soften all the sorbets in the fridge for 30 minutes before serving, so the true flavors emerge. Scoop the sorbets into bowls, and serve with fresh fruit, if desired.

Season's best **pears**

These delectable fruits are harvested in fall and stored for the winter. Their fine, granular, white flesh is soft, juicy, and perfumed. Pears ripen from the inside out and pass from rock-hard to woolly very quickly, so they should be eaten as soon as possible, once ripe. They are great with cheeses, pork, game and cured meats, walnuts, and sweet spices, such as star anise, ginger, cinnamon, and cloves. Their marriage partner is chocolate.

Pears are often picked when not quite ripe, to prevent them from deteriorating too quickly. They are related to the apple but, generally, have a shorter season.

Concorde This variety looks like a more regular, pear-shaped Conference pear, pictured right. It has an exceptionally good flavor.

Beurré Bosc Recognized by its long, tapered neck, lengthy stem, and dark green-yellow russeted skin, this variety has an aromatic, crisp, and sweetly spicy flesh. It holds its shape well when poached or baked.

Doyenné du Comice Considered to be the best-flavored dessert pear, the creamy-pink flesh of this variety is juicy, with a melting texture and spicy flavor. Serve fresh as a special dessert.

how to core and peel pears for poaching

Peeled fruit can absorb the poaching flavors better. It is more pleasant not to have to fiddle with the core when eating the poached fruit, although removing the core first is not essential.

1 Use a melon baller or a small spoon to scoop out the small core through the base of the pear.

2 Use a vegetable peeler or a small, sharp knife to peel off the skin thinly and evenly, leaving the stem in place.

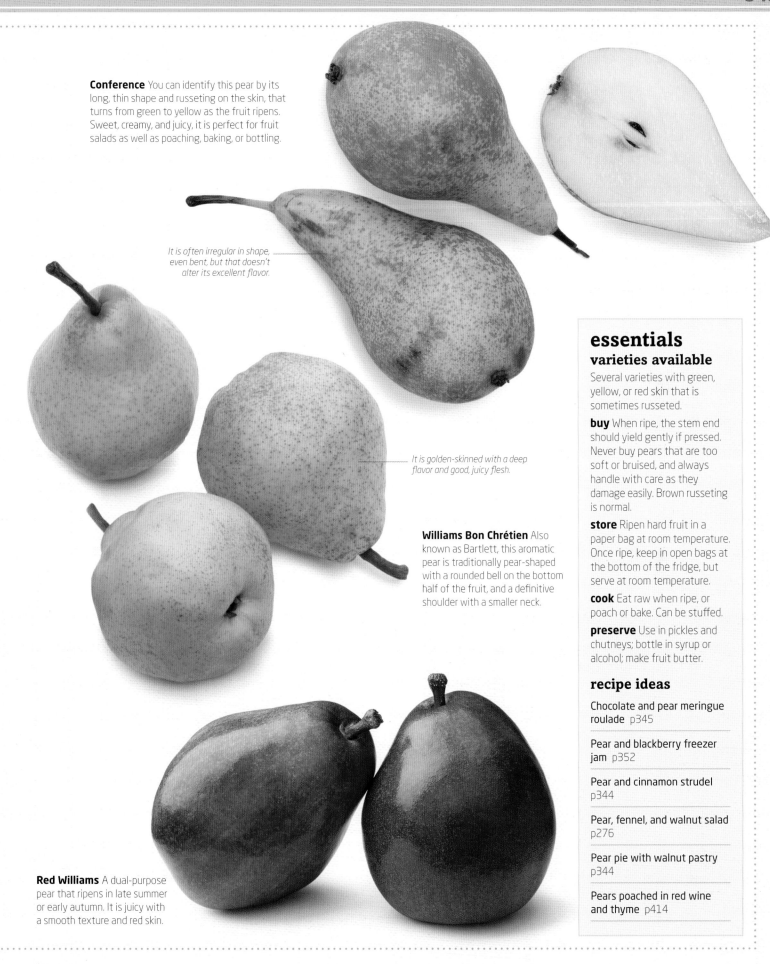

Conference You can identify this pear by its long, thin shape and russeting on the skin, that turns from green to yellow as the fruit ripens. Sweet, creamy, and juicy, it is perfect for fruit salads as well as poaching, baking, or bottling.

It is often irregular in shape, even bent, but that doesn't alter its excellent flavor.

It is golden-skinned with a deep flavor and good, juicy flesh.

Williams Bon Chrétien Also known as Bartlett, this aromatic pear is traditionally pear-shaped with a rounded bell on the bottom half of the fruit, and a definitive shoulder with a smaller neck.

Red Williams A dual-purpose pear that ripens in late summer or early autumn. It is juicy with a smooth texture and red skin.

essentials
varieties available
Several varieties with green, yellow, or red skin that is sometimes russeted.

buy When ripe, the stem end should yield gently if pressed. Never buy pears that are too soft or bruised, and always handle with care as they damage easily. Brown russeting is normal.

store Ripen hard fruit in a paper bag at room temperature. Once ripe, keep in open bags at the bottom of the fridge, but serve at room temperature.

cook Eat raw when ripe, or poach or bake. Can be stuffed.

preserve Use in pickles and chutneys; bottle in syrup or alcohol; make fruit butter.

recipe ideas

Chocolate and pear meringue roulade p345

Pear and blackberry freezer jam p352

Pear and cinnamon strudel p344

Pear, fennel, and walnut salad p276

Pear pie with walnut pastry p344

Pears poached in red wine and thyme p414

pear pie with walnut pastry

In this specialty from central France, wedges of pear are sandwiched between a double crust of walnut pastry. Serve the pie warm, with crème fraîche or whipped cream.

 35–40 MINS PLUS CHILLING　 35–40 MINS

SPECIAL EQUIPMENT ▪ 9in (23cm) round fluted tart pan with removable bottom

SERVES 6-8

2½oz (75g) walnuts, very finely chopped

1lb 2oz (500g) store-bought pie dough

1lb 15oz (875g) pears

½ tsp freshly ground black pepper

juice of 1 lemon

1 tbsp granulated sugar

1 Preheat the oven to 375°F (190°C) and brush the tart pan with melted butter. Lightly flour the work surface and knead the walnuts into the pastry. Roll out two-thirds of the dough into an 11in (28cm) round and line the pan, trimming the edges. Rewrap all excess dough and return to the fridge. Chill the pie crust for about 1 hour, until very firm.

2 Peel, core, and quarter the pears, then put in a bowl and toss with the pepper and lemon juice. Arrange the pear wedges in a cartwheel pattern on the bottom of the pie crust. Roll out the remaining dough into a 10in (25cm) round; stamp out a 2in (5cm) round from the center. Place the 10in (25cm) round over the pears, trim, and press the edges together firmly to seal.

3 Brush the top of the pie with water and sprinkle with the sugar. Chill the pie for about 15 minutes until firm. Meanwhile, heat a baking sheet in the oven. Put the pie on the baking sheet so the heat starts to cook the pie dough immediately, and bake the pie for 35–40 minutes until the crust is browned and the pears are tender when pierced with a metal skewer. If the top crust threatens to scorch before the pie is ready, cover it loosely with foil and continue to bake until the fruit is tender.

pear and cinnamon strudel

Here you have a favorite dessert from Austria, but filled with a variation on the usual: in place of tart apples, there are sweet pears, which complement cinnamon just as happily.

 10 MINS　 35–40 MINS　❄ FREEZABLE

SERVES 6

4 ripe pears, peeled, cored, and cubed

2 tsp ground cinnamon

handful of raisins

1-2 tbsp granulated sugar

4 sheets of filo pastry

4 tbsp butter, melted

confectioners' sugar, for dusting

1 Preheat the oven to 400°F (200°C). For the filling, place the pear, cinnamon, raisins, and sugar in a bowl and mix well. Set aside.

2 Lay a sheet of filo pastry on a large piece of parchment paper. Brush the filo sheet with some of the melted butter and lay a second sheet on top. Repeat to form 4 layers of filo. Spoon the pear filling down the middle of the layered filo sheets leaving a 2in (5cm) gap at each end.

3 Using the parchment paper, carefully lift one side of the filo over the filling. Brush this edge with melted butter (to help the second side stick).

Again, use the parchment paper to help lift the second side of the filo over the filling, overlapping the filo and enveloping the filling. Lightly seal. Seal the ends with melted butter and trim any excess pastry from the ends.

4 Line a large baking sheet with parchment paper. Lift the strudel onto the sheet and, using the paper to help, roll the strudel over so the seam is on the bottom. Brush the strudel all over with melted butter and bake in the oven for 35–40 minutes, or until golden brown on top. Dust with confectioners' sugar and serve with ice cream or a dollop of crème fraîche.

variation

apple and cinnamon strudel

For a more classic strudel, use the same quantity of apples in place of the pears. Make the dessert in exactly the same way.

pumpkin pie

This delicate version of the classic American dessert has seasonally warm tones of cinnamon and pumpkin pie spice. Serve it with thick cream or vanilla ice cream, if you like.

 30 MINS 1 HR – 1 HR 15 MINS

SPECIAL EQUIPMENT ▪ 9in (22cm) round tart pan with removable bottom ▪ food processor ▪ ceramic baking beans

SERVES 6–8

11oz (325g) store-bought pie dough

3 large eggs

½ cup light brown sugar

1 tsp ground cinnamon

1 tsp pumpkin pie spice

¾ cup heavy cream

14oz (400g) roasted and pureed pumpkin, or 14oz (425g) can processed pumpkin

1 Preheat the oven to 350°F (180°C). Roll out the dough on a floured surface to a thickness of ⅛in (3mm) and line the pan, leaving an overlapping edge of at least ¾in (2cm). Prick the bottom all over with a fork. Line the pie crust with parchment paper and weigh it down with ceramic baking beans. Place the crust on a baking sheet and blind bake for 20 minutes. Remove the beans and the paper and return to the oven for 5 minutes if the center is uncooked.

2 In a large bowl, beat together the eggs, sugar, spices, and cream. Then beat in the pumpkin until smooth. Partially pull out an oven rack from the oven and place the pie crust on it. Pour the filling into the crust and slide the rack back into the oven.

3 Bake for 45–50 minutes until the filling is set, but before it begins to bubble up at the edges. Trim the crust edge while still warm, then leave the pie to cool in its pan for at least 15 minutes before turning out.

toffee apple tray bake

Smothered in toffee sauce, this apple sponge cake is sure to please. Serve warm or cold with a spoonful of crème fraîche.

 20 MINS 45 MINS

SPECIAL EQUIPMENT ▪ electric hand mixer ▪ 8¾ x 12in (22 x 30cm) baking pan

MAKES 18

12oz (350g) tart apples, peeled, cored, and thinly sliced

squeeze of lemon juice

2 cups self-rising flour

2 tsp baking powder

1¾ cups light brown sugar

4 large eggs, lightly beaten

16 tbsp butter, melted

1 tbsp granulated sugar

For the toffee sauce

7 tbsp butter

½ cup light brown sugar

1 tbsp lemon juice

salt

1 Preheat the oven to 350°F (180°C). Line the bottom and sides of the pan with parchment paper. Toss the apple slices in a bowl with the lemon juice to prevent discoloration.

2 Sift the flour into a large mixing bowl, add the baking powder and brown sugar, and stir well. Mix in the eggs and melted butter to make a smooth batter. Pour into the pan and smooth the top. Arrange the apple slices in three or four long lines along the top of the mixture and sprinkle with the granulated sugar. Bake for 45 minutes, or until the cake is firm to the touch and a skewer comes out clean when inserted in the center.

3 Meanwhile, make the sauce by melting the butter, sugar, and lemon juice in a pan with a pinch of salt, beating with an electric hand mixer until the mixture is thick and smooth. Let cool slightly. Pour the sauce over the cake while it is still in the pan, brushing the sauce over the top. Cut into squares and serve.

chocolate and pear meringue roulade

To help you roll the meringue into the roulade, use the parchment paper, pulling it back from the meringue as you roll.

 25 MINS 15 MINS FREEZABLE

SPECIAL EQUIPMENT ▪ electric hand mixer ▪ 10 x 14in (25 x 35cm) jelly roll pan

SERVES 8

5 large egg whites, room temperature

1 cup granulated sugar

½ tsp white wine vinegar

1 tsp cornstarch

½ tsp pure vanilla extract

¼ cup cocoa powder, sifted

confectioners' sugar, for dusting

1 cup heavy cream, whipped

3 small pears, peeled, cored, and cubed

1 Preheat the oven to 350°F (180°C) and line the pan with parchment paper. Beat the egg whites with an electric hand mixer until stiff peaks form. Continuing to beat, add the granulated sugar, a little at a time. Gently fold in the vinegar, cornstarch, vanilla extract, and cocoa powder. Pour the mixture into the pan, smooth the surface, and bake in the center of the oven for 15 minutes. Remove from the oven and let it cool.

2 Carefully turn the meringue out of the pan onto another piece of parchment paper dusted with confectioners' sugar. Spread the cream over the underside of the roulade with a palette knife. Sprinkle the pears over it. Roll the meringue up around the cream filling. Place seam-side down on a serving plate, cover, and chill. Sift over confectioners' sugar to serve.

variation

chocolate, fig, and lime roulade

Prepare the roulade in the same way. For the filling, poach 6 ripe figs in syrup (½ cup sugar and 1¼ cups water) with the juice of 1 lime for 10 minutes. Cool, drain, chop, discarding the stems, and mix with the finely grated zest of the lime. Use instead of the pears in the filling.

red grape and cinnamon cake

Eat this delightful cake warm as a dessert with cream, yogurt, or custard, or cold with a cup of coffee. The grapes turn into a layer of sticky fruit on top of the cake and keep it moist.

 30 MINS   50 MINS

SPECIAL EQUIPMENT ▪ 8in (20cm) round springform cake pan ▪ blender or food processor

SERVES 6–8

10oz (300g) red grapes, halved lengthwise

2 tbsp light brown sugar

⅔ cup granulated sugar

11 tbsp butter, softened

3 large eggs

½ tsp pure vanilla extract

1 cup self-rising flour

1 tsp ground cinnamon

1 heaping tsp baking powder

1 Preheat the oven to 350°F (180°C). Line the cake pan with wax paper. Spread the grapes evenly, skin-side down, on the bottom of the cake pan and scatter the brown sugar over the top.

2 Put the granulated sugar and butter in a blender or food processor and pulse. When the mixture is smooth, add the eggs and vanilla extract and pulse to mix well. Add the flour, cinnamon, and baking powder and pulse the mixture again briefly until it is blended.

3 Spread the cake mixture over the grapes. Place the cake pan on a baking sheet and bake in the center of the oven for approximately 50 minutes until risen and golden brown and a skewer through the middle comes out clean. Turn the cake onto a serving plate, carefully peeling off the wax paper to reveal the grape topping. Serve warm or cold.

variation

green grape, spice, and orange cake

Prepare in the same way, but use 10½oz (300g) green grapes instead of red. Flavor the cake with the finely grated zest of 1 orange and 1 tsp apple pie spice, instead of the cinnamon.

schiacciata di uva

This sweet Italian "squashed" bread is similar to a sweetened focaccia, and can be served either warm or cold.

 25 MINS PLUS RISING AND PROVING   20-25 MINS

SPECIAL EQUIPMENT ▪ 8 x 12in (20 x 30cm) jelly roll pan

MAKES 1

4 cups bread flour

1 tsp fine salt

2 tbsp granulated sugar

1½ tsp dried yeast

1 tbsp olive oil

1lb 2oz (500g) small red seedless grapes, washed

3 tbsp granulated sugar

1 tbsp finely chopped rosemary (optional)

1 Put the flour, salt, and sugar into a large bowl. Dissolve the yeast in 2 cups warm water, then add the oil. Gradually pour the yeast mixture into the flour mixture, stirring to form a soft dough. Knead for 10 minutes on a floured work surface until smooth, glossy, and elastic. The dough should remain soft. Put the dough in a lightly oiled bowl and cover it loosely with plastic wrap. Let rise in a warm place for up to 2 hours until doubled in size.

2 Turn the dough onto a floured work surface and gently punch it down. Knead it briefly and divide it into 2 portions, with roughly one-third of the dough in one and two-thirds in the other. Lightly oil the jelly roll pan.

3 Take the largest piece of dough and roll it out roughly to the size of the pan. Place it in the pan and stretch it out to fill the pan, using your fingers to mold it to the sides. Scatter two-thirds of the grapes over the surface and sprinkle with 2 tbsp granulated sugar.

4 Roll out the smaller piece of dough to fit on top of the grapes, stretching it out with your hands if necessary. Scatter the remaining grapes, and the chopped rosemary (if using) on the surface. Place the dough on a large baking sheet and cover it loosely with lightly oiled plastic wrap and a clean kitchen towel. Let it prove in a warm place for up to 1 hour until well risen and almost doubled in size. Preheat the oven to 400°F (200°C).

5 Scatter the remaining tbsp of granulated sugar on top of the risen dough. Bake for 20–25 minutes until well risen and golden brown. Remove from the oven and allow to cool for at least 10 minutes before serving.

grapes marinated in port

Juicy grapes steeped in port—a sweet dessert wine made of red grapes—have a lovely deep flavor, and are a clever twist on grapes and cheese at the end of a meal.

 10 MINS PLUS MARINATING

SERVES 4

bunch of seedless red grapes

bunch of seedless green grapes

drizzle of port

vanilla ice cream, to serve

1 Prick the grapes with a knife, then place them in a large shallow serving dish and drizzle with port. Let marinate in the fridge for several hours or overnight.

2 To serve, bring the grapes back to room temperature, then spoon into glass dishes and top with a scoop of vanilla ice cream.

variation

grapes marinated in port with goat cheese croûtes

Cut each bunch of grapes into 4 small bunches. Prick and marinate as before, turning a few times. Toast 4 diagonal slices of baguette. Top each with slices of goat cheese and broil until just melted. Serve each croûte with a bunch each of red and green grapes on the side, with the port juices spooned over them.

Season's best **grapes**

These sun-loving fruit are harvested in autumn after the long days of summer. Seeded and seedless varieties in green, red, or black are produced—some for eating, some for wine. Grapes are popularly used in savory and fruit salads, sauces, poultry stuffings, tarts, and desserts. Good flavor pairings include chicken, fish, cheeses, and nuts. The leaves from the grapevines are also used in the kitchen, and are delicious stuffed.

All grapes need sunshine to ripen but many varieties thrive in temperate climates as well as the hotter countries, which are more famous for wine-making.

Italia This well-known seeded variety of the muscat type of grape has a delicious flowery flavor, juicy flesh, and thin skin. Halve and seed for fruit salads.

Muscat Rosada Also called Moscatel Rosada and Muscat Rosa, this is a gourmet grape with a rich, musky flavor. It has crisp skin and juicy flesh that contains seeds. Reserve for a special fruit dessert or to eat fresh.

Grapes that have been carefully transported retain their dusty "bloom."

Concord The oldest North American grape variety, this has medium to large, blue-black fruit. Eat fresh or use for making deeply colored jam, jelly, and juice, as well as wine.

Ribier A popular large, seeded variety, this has crisp, jet-black skin and juicy flesh with a mild flavor. A bunch of these is a perfect complement to a cheese plate.

Choose triangular bunches laden with plump grapes of equal size.

essentials
varieties available

Numerous varieties: green (white), red, or black, seeded or seedless. Also available dried as currants, golden raisins, and raisins; wine and juice.

buy Avoid wrinkled grapes or those with brown spots.

store Store unwashed bunches carefully on several layers of paper towel or in an open paper bag in the fridge for up to 5 days.

cook Peel or seed, if necessary; sauté for cream and wine sauces; add to poultry stuffings; use in tarts and other desserts.

preserve Make into juice or wine.

recipe ideas

Grapes marinated in port
p346

Red grape and cinnamon cake
p346

Simple grape wine p352

spiced port and plum jam

The addition of some port and cinnamon turns this into a rather special plum jam. Enjoy it dolloped onto hot steamed desserts, or spread onto dark fruit tea breads.

 10 MINS   30-35 MINS

SPECIAL EQUIPMENT ▪ preserving pan ▪ sugar thermometer

MAKES APPROX 4½lb (2kg)

4lb (1.8kg) dark plums, halved and pitted

1 cinnamon stick, snapped in half

juice of 1 lime

6 cups sugar

2-3 tbsp port (depending on your taste preference)

1 Put the plums, cinnamon stick, and lime juice into a preserving pan or a large heavy-bottomed saucepan, then pour in 2 cups water.

2 Simmer gently over low heat for 15–20 minutes, or until the plums begin to break down and soften.

3 Add the sugar, stir until it has all dissolved, then bring to a boil and keep at a rolling boil for 5–8 minutes, or until the jam begins to thicken and reaches the setting point. Remove the pan from the heat and test for a set with a sugar thermometer or

a wrinkle test (chill a plate in the fridge before cooking). If you use a thermometer, the temperature must reach 220°F (105°C); the mixture will also thicken around the sides of the pan, boil sluggishly, and the bubbles "plop" rather than froth. Or put 1 tsp jam on the chilled plate, allow to cool for a moment, then push it with a finger. If it leaves a trail and wrinkles slightly, the jam is set.

4 Remove the cinnamon stick and discard, stir in the port, then ladle into warm sterilized jars, cover with wax paper discs, seal, and label. Store in a cool, dark place and refrigerate after opening.

variation

spiced kirsch and plum jam

Make in exactly the same way but flavor the jam with 2 star anise instead of the cinnamon stick and add 2–3 tbsp kirsch instead of the port.

piccalilli

Originally known as "Indian pickle," this classic recipe contains cauliflower, zucchini, beans, and carrots. Its characteristic yellow color and flavor is due to a turmeric and mustard mix.

 15 MINS PLUS STANDING AND MATURING   20 MINS

SPECIAL EQUIPMENT ▪ preserving jar

MAKES 5lb (2.25kg)

1 large cauliflower, cut into florets

2 large onions, peeled, quartered, and sliced finely, or use pickling onions

2lb (900g) mixed vegetables such as zucchini, romano beans, carrots, and green beans, cut into bite-sized pieces

¼ cup sea salt

2 tbsp all-purpose flour

1 cup granulated sugar (increase this quantity slightly if you don't like the pickle too sharp)

1 tbsp turmeric

½ cup English mustard powder

3 cups pre-spiced pickling vinegar

1 Put all the vegetables in a large non-metallic bowl. Dissolve the sea salt in 4 cups of water and pour the brine over the vegetables. Put a plate on top of the vegetables to keep them submerged in the brine and leave for 24 hours.

2 Drain the vegetables and rinse in cold water. Bring a large pan of water to a boil, add the vegetables, and blanch for 2 minutes. Do not overcook—they should remain crunchy. Drain and refresh in cold water.

3 Put the flour, sugar, turmeric, and mustard powder in a small bowl and mix in a little of the vinegar to make a paste. Put the paste in a large stainless steel saucepan along with the remaining vinegar, bring to a boil, and stir continuously so no lumps appear. Reduce the heat and simmer for about 15 minutes.

4 Add the vegetables to the sauce and stir well so they are all coated. Ladle into warm sterilized jars with non-metallic or vinegar-proof lids, making sure there are no air gaps, seal, and label. Store in a cool, dark place to allow the flavors to mature for at least 1 month and refrigerate after opening.

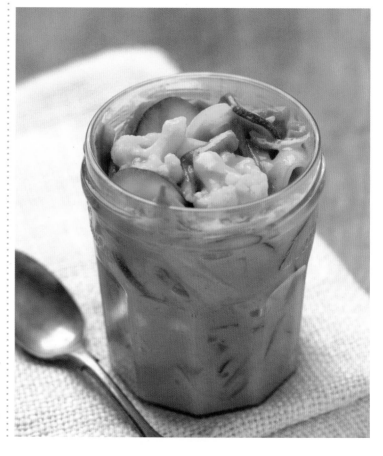

baby artichokes in oil

Baby artichokes are a delicacy, and the whole inner choke can be used. Serve as an antipasti or add to fresh pasta.

 10 MINS PLUS MARINATING   10 MINS

SPECIAL EQUIPMENT ▪ preserving pan

MAKES APPROX 1lb 2oz (500g)

10 baby artichokes

1¼ cups white wine vinegar

1 tbsp salt

1¾ cups extra virgin olive oil

¼ cup white wine vinegar

handful of black peppercorns

1 Trim the artichoke stalks and snap off the hard outside leaves (about 5–6 layers) until you reach the paler, more tender leaves. Cut off about 1in (2.5cm) from the top of each artichoke and discard. Leave whole or cut in half.

2 Put the vinegar, salt, and 1¼ cups water in a preserving pan or heavy-bottomed, stainless steel saucepan and bring to a boil. Add the prepared artichokes and blanch for 3–5 minutes in the simmering vinegar mix; they should still retain plenty of bite. Drain and let cool, then cut lengthwise into quarters.

3 For the oil marinade, put the oil, vinegar, and peppercorns into a saucepan and bring to a boil. Add the artichokes and bring back to a boil, then turn the heat off and let cool with the artichokes still sitting in the marinade.

4 Using a slotted spoon, remove the cooled artichokes and put them into a sterilized jar with a non-metallic or vinegar-proof lid. Pour the marinade over the top until the artichokes are completely covered (or you can strain the oil mixture first if you prefer). Seal, label, and store in the fridge. Once opened, keep refrigerated, add oil if necessary so the artichokes are always covered, and use within 2 months.

yellow squash and tomato chutney

Colorful and creamy textured, yellow squash are ideal for this chutney—or use any other squash.

 10 MINS PLUS MATURING   2 HRS 35 MINS

SPECIAL EQUIPMENT ▪ preserving pan

MAKES APPROX 2¼lb (1kg)

1lb (450g) yellow squash, trimmed and diced

9oz (250g) onions, coarsely chopped

12oz (350g) ripe tomatoes, coarsely chopped

1½ cups granulated sugar

1¼ cups white wine vinegar

1 garlic clove, finely chopped

1cm (½in) piece of fresh ginger, peeled and finely chopped

¼ tsp dried chile flakes

large pinch of sweet paprika

large pinch of ground white pepper

½ tsp sea salt

1 Put all the ingredients in a preserving pan or a large heavy-bottomed, stainless steel saucepan.

2 Bring slowly to a boil, stirring to dissolve the sugar. Reduce the heat and simmer for 2½ hours until a wooden spoon drawn across the base of the pan leaves a trail. Stir frequently toward the end so the chutney doesn't stick and burn on the base of the pan. If necessary, turn up the heat toward the end of cooking and boil rapidly until it is thick and glossy.

3 Ladle into warm sterilized jars with non-metallic or vinegar-proof lids, making sure there are no air gaps. Cover each pot with a wax paper disc, seal, and label. Store in a cool, dark place. Allow the flavors to mature for at least 1 month and refrigerate after opening.

spiced pear pickle

Serve this hot-pickled, sweet-sour pear condiment with cold meats, hamburgers, and cheese, or with rice or spiced dishes.

 10 MINS PLUS MATURING   25–30 MINS

SPECIAL EQUIPMENT ▪ preserving pan

MAKES APPROX 3 CUPS

For the syrup

1½ cups granulated sugar

⅔ cup cider vinegar

zest of ½ lemon

1in (2.5cm) piece of fresh ginger, peeled and chopped

seeds from 6 cardamom pods

2¼lb (1kg) firm, shapely pears such as Williams or Bosc, peeled, cored, and cut into quarters

1 For the syrup, put all the syrup ingredients into a preserving pan or a large heavy-bottomed, stainless steel saucepan and bring gently to a boil, stirring to dissolve the sugar. Simmer for 5 minutes, then remove from the heat.

2 Put the quartered pears into the syrup so they are completely covered, and poach gently for about 5–10 minutes until just soft. They are ready when a skewer can be inserted into the flesh. Remove each pear with a slotted spoon as soon as it is ready.

3 Pack the pears into warm sterilized jars. Return the pan of syrup and spices to the heat, bring back to a boil, and cook for 5 more minutes or so. When the boiling syrup has reduced by about a third, pour it over the pears, filling the jars to the brim so it completely covers the pears.

4 To keep the pears submerged, cover with a wax paper disc. Seal with vinegar-proof lids, label, and store in a cool, dark place for 1 month before using. Refrigerate after opening.

variation

hot spiced pear pickle

Prepare in the same way, but add 2 dried chipotle chiles and 2 small bay leaves to the spice syrup. Tuck them into the jars with the syrup if you like a stronger flavor.

fig and vanilla jam

This rich, densely fruity jam goes well with both sweet and savory foods—it's delicious with cold ham or cheese. Add a splash of ginger wine at the end for a hint of spice, if you like.

 5 MINS   45-50 MINS

SPECIAL EQUIPMENT ▪ preserving pan ▪ sugar thermometer

MAKES APPROX 2½lb (1.1kg)

1½lb (675g) ripe figs with soft skins, trimmed and cut into quarters

zest and juice of 1 lemon

1 small apple, peeled, cored, and coarsely chopped

1 vanilla bean, sliced lengthwise

3 cups granulated sugar

1 Put the figs in a preserving pan or a large heavy-bottomed saucepan with the lemon zest and juice, chopped apple, and vanilla bean. Cook over low heat for about 20 minutes or so, stirring occasionally, until the figs have softened and broken down.

2 Add the sugar and cook over low heat, stirring continuously, until the sugar has all dissolved. Then bring to a boil and cook at a rolling boil, stirring occasionally, for about

15–20 minutes or until it reaches the setting point. Skim away any foam as it cooks. Remove the pan from the heat and test for a set with a sugar thermometer or a wrinkle test (chill a plate in the fridge before cooking). If you use a thermometer, the temperature must reach 220°F (105°C); the mixture will also thicken around the sides of the pan, boil sluggishly, and the bubbles "plop" rather than froth. Or put 1 tsp jam on the chilled plate, allow to cool for a moment, then push it with a finger. If it leaves a trail and wrinkles slightly, the jam is set.

3 Carefully remove the vanilla bean, then ladle into warm sterilized jars, cover with discs of wax paper, seal, and label. Store in a cool, dark place and refrigerate after opening.

apple, golden raisin, and date chutney

This substantial, adaptable chutney gets better with age. Dried cranberries, figs, or dried apricots also complement apples well and can be used instead of the dried dates.

 30 MINS PLUS MATURING   1 HR 45 MINS

SPECIAL EQUIPMENT ▪ preserving pan

MAKES APPROX 4lb (1.8kg)

4½lb (2kg) apples (approx 8-10), peeled, cored, and chopped

3 onions, peeled and finely chopped

1in (2.5cm) piece of fresh ginger, peeled and finely chopped

4oz (115g) golden raisins

4½oz (125g) pitted dates, chopped

1 tsp mustard seeds

2¼ cups cider vinegar

1lb 2oz (500g) granulated sugar

1 Put the apples, onions, ginger, golden raisins, dates, and mustard seeds in a preserving pan or a large heavy-bottomed saucepan. Stir everything together, then pour in the cider vinegar and add the sugar.

2 Cook over low heat, stirring until the sugar has dissolved, then bring to a boil, reduce the heat, and cook gently for about 1½ hours. The mixture is ready when it is thick and sticky, and a wooden spoon drawn across the base of the pan leaves a trail. Stir continuously near the end of the cooking time so that the chutney doesn't stick and burn on the base of the pan.

3 Ladle into warm sterilized jars with non-metallic or vinegar-proof lids, making sure there are no air gaps. Cover with wax paper discs, seal, and label. Store in a cool, dark place to allow the flavors to mature for 1 month. Refrigerate after opening.

crab apple jelly

Make this jelly while autumn crab apples are in abundance.

 15 MINS PLUS STRAINING   45 MINS

SPECIAL EQUIPMENT ■ preserving pan ■ nylon sieve or jelly bag
■ sugar thermometer

MAKES APPROX 3lb (1.35kg)

2½lb (1.1kg) crab apples, washed and coarsely chopped with the seeds and stalks left intact

zest of 1 lemon, thinly pared

about 4-5 cups) granulated sugar (see method)

1 Put the crab apples in a preserving pan or a large heavy-bottomed pan, pour in 5 cups water, and add the lemon zest. Cook gently for 30 minutes, or until the apples become pulpy. Pour the pulp into a nylon sieve or jelly bag set over a large clean bowl and strain overnight.

2 Measure the juice and calculate 2 cups of sugar for every 2 cups of juice. Pour the juice back into the cleaned pan and bring to a simmer over medium heat. Add the sugar and stir until it has all dissolved. Bring to a boil and cook at a rolling boil for 10 minutes, or until the setting point is reached. Remove the pan from the heat and test for a set with a sugar thermometer or a wrinkle test (chill a plate in the fridge before cooking). If you use a thermometer, the temperature must reach 220°F (105°C); the mixture will also thicken around the sides of the pan, boil sluggishly, and the bubbles "plop" rather than froth. Or put 1 tsp jelly on the chilled plate, allow to cool for a moment, then push it with a finger. If it leaves a trail and wrinkles slightly, the jelly is set.

3 Skim off any surface foam, ladle into warm sterilized jars, cover with wax paper discs, seal, and label. Store in a cool, dark place and refrigerate after opening.

membrillo

Made from puréed quinces, membrillo is an intensely flavored fruit cheese that is solid enough to slice. It keeps for 12 months or longer and is excellent with cheeses.

 10 MINS PLUS COOLING AND MATURING   1 HR 20 MINS

SPECIAL EQUIPMENT ■ preserving pan ■ mouli food mill ■ ramekins

MAKES 1lb 10oz-2¼lb (750g-1kg)

2¼lb (1kg) quinces, scrubbed and coarsely chopped

juice of ½ lemon

about 2 cups granulated sugar (see method)

1 Put the quinces in a preserving pan or a large heavy-bottomed saucepan with 2 cups water. Add the lemon juice, bring to a boil, and simmer for 30 minutes or so. Once the fruit is soft enough, crush it with a potato masher or fork until it becomes a soft, syrupy pulp. Set the cooked pulp aside to cool.

2 Sieve the pulp in batches over a large, clean bowl, pressing the pulp hard against the sieve with a wooden spoon to extract as much of the purée as possible (or use a mouli food mill). Measure the purée: for every 1¾ cups of purée, calculate 2 cups of sugar.

3 Put the purée and sugar back in the pan and stir over low heat to dissolve the sugar. Then bring to a boil and simmer gently for 45-60 minutes or longer until the purée reduces down to a dark, very thick, glossy paste. It is ready when it makes a "plopping" noise, sticks to the wooden spoon, and leaves a trail if the spoon is scraped across the bottom of the pan. Stir frequently near the end of cooking so the paste doesn't stick and burn on the base of the pan.

4 Lightly grease some warm sterilized ramekin dishes or molds with a little oil. Spoon in the paste and level the top. Seal with wax paper discs and cellophane if leaving in the ramekin dishes, otherwise let cool. If you are turning the membrillos out of their ramekin dishes, loosen each with a palette knife, turn it out, wrap in wax paper, and tie with string. Leave to mature in a cool, dark place for 4-6 weeks. Serve thinly sliced with a cheeseboard or platter of cold meats, or as an after-dinner treat.

plum and squash chutney

This is a true autumnal chutney: an inspired combination of plums, apples, and squashes that harmonize beautifully.

 30 MINS PLUS MATURING   2 HRS 15 MINS - 2 HRS 45 MINS

SPECIAL EQUIPMENT ■ preserving pan ■ muslin

MAKES APPROX 3lb 3oz (1.5kg)

1lb 2oz (500g) squash, peeled and cut into cubes

1lb 2oz (500g) plums, pitted and coarsely chopped

1lb 2oz (500g) apples, peeled, cored, and diced

9oz (250g) onions, diced

9oz (250g) raisins or golden raisins

1¼ cups light brown sugar

1¾ cups cider or white wine vinegar

1½ tsp dried chile flakes

½ tsp sea salt

For the spice bag

2 mace blades

1 heaping tsp coriander seeds

12 black peppercorns

12 cloves

¾in (2cm) piece of fresh ginger, peeled and cut into cubes

1 Tie the spices in a piece of muslin and put the spice bag in a preserving pan or large heavy-bottomed saucepan. Add the other ingredients and heat gently, stirring occasionally, until all the sugar has dissolved.

2 Bring to a boil, turn the heat down, and simmer for 2-2½ hours, stirring occasionally until the mixture thickens and becomes sticky, and a wooden spoon drawn across the base of the pan leaves a trail. Stir frequently near the end of cooking.

3 Ladle into warm sterilized jars with non-metallic or vinegar-proof lids, cover with wax paper discs, seal, and label. Store in a cool, dark place to mature for 1-2 months and refrigerate after opening.

dried mushrooms

The sweet earthy flavor of mushrooms intensifies when dried and makes them an essential pantry ingredient. If dried properly, they will keep for 9–12 months.

 15 MINS PLUS DRYING   **4-6 HOURS**   ❊ **FREEZABLE**

SPECIAL EQUIPMENT ▪ wood-burning stove radiator, boiler, Aga, night storage heater, or warm airing cupboard

MAKES APPROX 2oz (60g)

1lb (450g) brown chestnut, shiitaki, and buna-shimeji mushrooms, or freshly picked wild mushrooms

1 Leave any small mushrooms whole and slice the large mushrooms into ¼–½in (5mm–1cm) thick slices. Arrange on trays lined with paper towels or wire racks, making sure they don't overlap. Place the trays in the oven on the lowest setting (120–140°F/50–60°C) for 4–6 hours. If you have an electric oven, leave the door slightly ajar using a skewer. To air-dry the mushrooms, leave the racks or trays 2–4in (5–10cm)

above a wood-burning stove radiator, boiler, Aga, night storage heater, or warm airing cupboard, overnight.

2 The mushrooms are ready when they have shrunk to at least half their original size, but are still pliable. Remove the trays from the oven and set aside until the mushrooms are completely cold.

3 Put in glass containers. Add a few grains of rice, if you like, as an extra precaution to help keep the mushrooms dry. Store in a cool, dark place until needed.

simple grape wine

Grapes contain the right amounts of sugar and acids to make wine. Use sterilized equipment to avoid problems like mold.

 2 HOURS PLUS FERMENTING AND STORING

SPECIAL EQUIPMENT ▪ hydrometer ▪ litmus paper ▪ muslin ▪ sterilized demijohn ▪ sterilized airlock ▪ sterilized siphon

MAKES 1 GALLON (4.5 LITERS)

11lb (5kg) ripe white grapes, washed, with stalks removed

1 Campden tablet

1 tsp pectolase

up to 4½ cups unrefined cane sugar

1 tsp tartaric acid or
  1 tsp potassium carbonate

1 package hock wine yeast

1 Put the grapes in a sterilized bucket or container. Using a sterilized plastic potato masher, mash the grapes well. Add the Campden tablet and pectolase and leave for 24 hours.

2 Dissolve ½ cup of the sugar in ¼ cup hot water, allow to cool, and add to the grapes. Repeat the process until a gravity of 1,090 can be read on your hydrometer. Use a litmus paper to test the acid level (the ideal level is 3–3.4 pH). If it is not acidic enough, add the tartaric acid; if it is too acidic, add the potassium carbonate instead. Pour some of

the grape mixture into a muslin cloth suspended over a sterilized bowl. Strain the grape mixture in batches to collect all the juice.

3 Pour the collected juice into a demijohn using a sterilized funnel. Add the yeast and attach the airlock. Let ferment at 70–75°F (21–24°C) for 3–4 months. Fermentation is complete when the bubbles have stopped and the water in the airlock is level. (To ensure fermentation is finished, move to a warm place for 24 hours to see if the bubbling has truly ceased.)

4 Being careful not to disturb the sediment (which spoils the flavor), draw off the clear liquid using a siphon, bottle into sterilized bottles, leaving ¾in (2cm) of space at the top, and seal. Store in a cool, dark place, ideally a cellar. The wine can be drunk immediately, but is better left for 6 months. Like commercial wine, its keeping qualities will vary, but it can last years.

pear and blackberry freezer jam

Freezing ripe pears and blackberries as a puréed autumn "jam" is a great way to preserve their fresh flavors and nutrients.

 10-12 MINS   **5-8 MINS**   ❊ **FREEZABLE**

MAKES APPROX 1lb 10oz (750g)

2 ripe pears, peeled, cored, and coarsely chopped

8oz (225g) ripe blackberries

2 tbsp lemon juice

1 tsp apple pie spice

1 tbsp agar flakes or 1 tsp agar powder

⅔ cup granulated sugar

1 Ensure the fruit is at room temperature, then put in a bowl with the lemon juice and spice. Coarsely crush with a potato masher or fork (don't reduce to a smooth pulp).

2 Put ¾ cup water in a small saucepan, sprinkle the agar flakes or powder over it, and set aside to

soften for 2–3 minutes. Give the pan a gentle swirl, then bring the water slowly to a boil over low heat without stirring. Simmer gently for 3–5 minutes, stirring occasionally, until the agar has dissolved. Add the sugar and stir over low heat until it has dissolved for 2–3 minutes. Remove from the heat and pour over the fruit, stirring the fruit gently until the ingredients are well mixed.

3 Pour into clean freezer containers, leaving ½in (1cm) of space at the top. Set aside to cool, then seal and label. Leave overnight in the fridge to thicken, then freeze. To use, thaw in the fridge, then keep refrigerated and use within 2 weeks.

squash and orange jam

A traditional preserve using overgrown yellow squash.

 5 MINS PLUS STANDING   35–40 MINS

SPECIAL EQUIPMENT ▪ preserving pan ▪ sugar thermometer

MAKES 3¼lb (1.5kg)

1 large yellow squash (approx 2lb/900g), peeled and cut into ½in (1cm) pieces

juice of 2 lemons

4 cups granulated sugar

juice of 1 orange and zest of 2 large oranges

1 Put the squash pieces and lemon juice in a preserving pan or a large heavy-bottomed saucepan. Bring to a boil and simmer for 15 minutes, or until the squash starts to soften. Add a little water if it starts to dry out and be sure it doesn't burn. This will all depend on the water content of your squash.

2 Add the sugar and orange juice and zest and heat gently, stirring until all the sugar has dissolved. Turn up the heat and bring to a boil. When the jam reaches a rolling boil, cook for about 20 minutes, or until it reaches the setting point. Remove the pan from the heat while you test for a set with a sugar thermometer or using a wrinkle test (chill a plate in the fridge before cooking). If you use a thermometer, the temperature must reach 220°F (105°C); the mixture will also thicken around the sides of the pan, boil sluggishly, and the bubbles "plop" rather than froth. Or put 1 tsp jam on the chilled plate, allow to cool for a moment, then push it with a finger. If it leaves a trail and wrinkles slightly, it is set.

3 Leave the jam for 5–10 minutes so the squash pieces are evenly distributed, then ladle into warm sterilized jars, cover with discs of wax paper, seal, and label. Store the jam in a cool, dark place and refrigerate after opening.

quinces in spiced syrup

Try these bottled quinces with ice cream or cream, or chopped or puréed and served with game, pork, or duck.

 5 MINS   25 MINS PLUS HEAT-PROCESSING

SPECIAL EQUIPMENT ▪ sterilized screw-band jars or kilner jars

MAKES 1 QUART (1 LITER)

2lb (900g) quinces, scrubbed

1 tbsp lemon juice

1¼ granulated sugar

2 star anise, 1 cinnamon stick, or 2 cloves

1 Put the quinces in a large pan, add 2 cups water, bring to a boil, and cook for 2 minutes. Remove and plunge into cold water. Reserve the pan of water. Peel, core, and quarter the quinces and put in a bowl of cold water with the lemon juice.

2 Add the sugar to the pan of water. Heat gently until it dissolves, then stir well. Drain the quinces and add them and the star anise to the pan. Bring to a boil, reduce the heat, cover, and poach the quinces for 12–15 minutes, or until just tender.

3 Pack the quinces tightly into the warm sterilized jars, leaving ½in (1cm) of space at the top. Bring the syrup back to a boil and pour over the fruit to cover it completely. Tap the jar gently on a wooden board to remove air bubbles. Fit the rubber band or metal lid seal and clamp on the lid. If using screw-band jars, loosen by a quarter turn. Place the filled jars in a deep roasting pan lined with newspaper to soak up spills.

4 Put the pan in the center of the oven for 40–50 minutes to heat-process (remove the remaining air in the jars). Remove from the oven and tighten the clips or lids (or screw on plastic screw-band lids). Leave for 24 hours, then unscrew or unclip and test the lids are firmly sealed before refastening and storing. (If using kilner jars with metal lids, you will know if you have a seal as the lid becomes slightly concave and is firm once pressed.) Store the jars in a cool, dark place and refrigerate once open.

italian-style vegetables

These vegetables are cooked first in vinegar before being stored in oil and refrigerated. Serve with a drizzle of fresh oil, torn basil leaves or chopped parsley, and good bread.

 20 MINS PLUS MATURING   10 MINS

MAKES APPROX 1½lb (675g)

1lb 5oz (600g) mixed vegetables (e.g. eggplant, fennel, romanesco broccoli florets, zucchini, small shallots, celery, carrots, peppers, button mushrooms)

about 2 cups white wine vinegar

2 tsp granulated sugar

2 tsp sea salt

about ⅔ cup extra virgin olive oil

seasonings – choose from

1 tsp fennel seeds

1 tsp dried oregano

1 fresh or dried bay leaf

1 sprig of rosemary

1 sprig of lemon thyme

pinch of chile flakes

1 Wash, peel as necessary, and dice or slice each vegetable into evenly sized pieces about ½in (1cm) thick. Leave small shallots and mushrooms whole. Put a batch of vegetables in a stainless steel saucepan and add enough vinegar to just cover them. Add the sugar and salt and bring to a boil. Boil the soft vegetables for 2–3 minutes and firmer vegetables for 5–10 minutes until al dente. Then remove from the pan, pat dry with paper towels, and allow to cool.

2 Loosely pack the vegetables into sterilized jars and add the seasonings. Cover with olive oil and press the vegetables down lightly to remove any air pockets. Add more oil, then seal and store in the fridge. Leave for at least 1 week before opening. Add extra oil once opened so the vegetables are always covered with ½in (1cm) of oil. They will keep for 1–2 months in the fridge.

early winter

at their best

vegetables beets . broccoli . Brussels sprouts . cabbages . cardoon . carrots (maincrop) . cauliflower . cavolo nero . celery . celery root . chicory . Hass avocados . horseradish . Jerusalem artichokes . kale . leeks . parsnips . potatoes (maincrop) . pumpkin . radicchio . rutabaga . salsify . spinach . sweet potatoes . Swiss chard . turnips . winter squashes

fruit apples . clementines . crabapples . cranberries . dates . grapes . kiwi fruit . oranges . pears . persimmons . pomegranate . quinces . raspberries . rosehips . satsumas . tangerines

seafood Albacore tuna . bay scallops . blue shark . brown trout (farmed) . clams . cod . crawfish (wild and farmed) . dab . Dover sole . flounder . haddock . hake . King crab . lemon sole . ling cod . mackerel . mussels . ocean perch . octopus . oysters . pollock . rockfish . salmon (chum, coho) . sardines . sea scallops . snapper . sole . squid . swordfish . whiting

meat, poultry, game chukar partridge (wild) . duck (wild and farmed) . goose (wild and farmed) . grouse (wild) . moose (wild) . pheasant (wild) . quail (wild and farmed) . rabbit (wild and farmed) . turkey (wild and farmed) . venison (wild and farmed) . wild boar (wild and farmed)

also available

vegetables garlic . mushrooms (cultivated and wild) . onions . radishes . spinach . watercress **seafood** monkfish . tilapia **meat, poultry, game** beef . buffalo . chicken . Cornish game hens (farmed) . lamb . pork . veal

early winter recipe planner

Ⓥ suitable for vegetarians

Butternut squash pasta in chile and Parmesan sauce p393

Roast sweet potato and chile tortilla p390

Pears poached in red wine and thyme p414

Vegetables

Baby onions
Beef and anchovy casserole p392
Pork chops with apple and baby onions p371

Beets
Carrot and beet salad with balsamic vinaigrette p404 Ⓥ
Goat cheese, pear, and beet salad p358 Ⓥ
Smoked trout with beets, apple, and dill relish p358

Brussels sprouts
Brussels sprouts with chestnuts and pancetta p395
Brussels sprouts with whole chestnuts and sausages p395
Potato, celery root, and sprout sauté p403

Butternut squash
Butternut squash pasta in chile and Parmesan sauce p393 Ⓥ
Kichidi p384 Ⓥ
Pork belly and squash p374
Roasted squash with sage and onion p407 Ⓥ
Spiced butternut squash soup p359 Ⓥ
Squash, sage, and blue cheese risotto p384 Ⓥ
Squash, spinach, and horseradish bake p370 Ⓥ
Squash with chestnuts and cranberries p407 Ⓥ

Cabbage
Cabbage stuffed with chestnut and pork p367
Carrot and shredded cabbage with peanuts p404
Creamy coleslaw p399 Ⓥ
Garbure p384
Ham hock with red cabbage p375
Ham hock with white cabbage and celery p375
Hot and spicy white cabbage p398 Ⓥ

Portuguese haddock soup p363
Red cabbage and bacon salad p398
Red cabbage pickle p421 Ⓥ
Sauerkraut p421 Ⓥ
Slow-cooked Swedish red cabbage p394 Ⓥ
Spicy pork with caraway seeds and cabbage p390
Sweet and sour cabbage p398 Ⓥ
Winter braised white cabbage and celery p394 Ⓥ

Cardoons
Baked cardoons with cheese p365 Ⓥ

Carrot
Beef and carrot casserole p387
Beef and parsnip casserole p388
Braised oxtail p368
Caramelized carrots p406 Ⓥ
Carrot and beet salad with balsamic vinaigrette p404 Ⓥ
Carrot and coriander relish p420 Ⓥ
Carrot and noodle salad p404
Carrot and shredded cabbage with peanuts p404
Celery root rémoulade with carrot salad p406 Ⓥ
Chicken salad with carrot and apple relish p391
Corned beef hash with horseradish p374
Cream of vegetable soup p362 Ⓥ
Creamy coleslaw p399 Ⓥ
Fragrant honeyed mixed roots p406 Ⓥ
Japanese-style fish broth p362
Mixed vegetable purée p395 Ⓥ
Ribollita p358 Ⓥ
Shepherd's pie p370
Turkey broth p362
Turkey, ham, and white bean soup p362

Cauliflower
Cauliflower curry p392 Ⓥ

Cavolo nero
Portuguese haddock soup p363
Ribollita p358 Ⓥ

Celery
Baked turkey rolls with celery, chestnuts, and chanterelles p383
Braised oxtail p368
Chestnut and celery stuffing p402 Ⓥ
Cream of vegetable soup p362 Ⓥ
Ham hock with white cabbage and celery p375
Potato, celery, and parsnip bake p400 Ⓥ
Roast pork with bacon and celery hearts p371
Smoked haddock, celery, and cheese chowder p363
Turkey broth p362
Winter braised white cabbage and celery p394 Ⓥ

Celery root
Beef and celery root casserole with stout and anchovies p387
Celery root rémoulade with carrot salad p406 Ⓥ
Celery root soufflé pie p374
Chicken with garlic and spiced celery root p387
Fragrant honeyed mixed roots p406 Ⓥ
Grilled sweet potato and celery root p395 Ⓥ
Mixed vegetable purée p395 Ⓥ
Pork belly and prunes p392
Potato, celery root, and sprout sauté p403
Roast celery root and leek tortilla p390 Ⓥ
Roasted sweet potato and celery root with garlic and herbs p407 Ⓥ
Turkey salad with celery root and orange relish p391

Chicory
Roast pork with bacon and chicory p371
Smoked trout with beets, apple, and dill relish p358

Horseradish
Corned beef hash with horseradish p374
Horseradish sauce p404 Ⓥ
Potato and horseradish mash p403
Salmon, horseradish, and kale bake p368
Squash, spinach, and horseradish bake p370 Ⓥ

Jerusalem artichoke
Venison and artichoke casserole p388

Kale
Portuguese haddock soup p363
Potato and horseradish mash p403
Ribollita p358 Ⓥ
Salmon, horseradish, and kale bake p368

Leek
Beef and anchovy casserole p392
Cheesy leeks on toast p360 Ⓥ
Cream of vegetable soup p362 Ⓥ
Leek and potato soup p360 Ⓥ
Leeks hollandaise p399 Ⓥ
Leeks vinaigrette p399 Ⓥ
Potato and leek croquettes p360 Ⓥ
Potato and leek gratin p402 Ⓥ
Roast celery root and leek tortilla p390 Ⓥ
Turkey broth p362
Turkey, ham, and white bean soup p362

Parsnip
Beef and parsnip casserole p388
Braised oxtail p368
Cream of vegetable soup p362 Ⓥ
Fragrant honeyed mixed roots p406 Ⓥ
Mustard chicken casserole p378
Parsnip and Parmesan bread p400 Ⓥ
Potato, celery, and parsnip bake p400 Ⓥ
Pumpkin and parsnip cassoulet p366 Ⓥ
Turkey broth p362

Potato
Beef and celery root casserole with stout and anchovies p387
Beef and herb potato pie p391
Cauliflower curry p392 Ⓥ
Chicken with garlic and spiced celery root p387
Corned beef hash with horseradish p374
Cream of vegetable soup p362 Ⓥ
Dauphinoise potatoes p402 Ⓥ
Leek and potato soup p360 Ⓥ
Patatas bravas p400 Ⓥ
Pork with potatoes and mushrooms in wine p389
Potato and horseradish mash p403
Potato and leek croquettes p360 Ⓥ
Potato and leek gratin p402 Ⓥ
Potato, celery, and parsnip bake p400 Ⓥ
Potato, celery root, and sprout sauté p403
Ribollita p358 Ⓥ
Shepherd's pie p370

Pumpkin

Chicken with garlic, preserved lemons, and pumpkin p387
Pumpkin and orange spiced jam p417 (V)
Pumpkin and parsnip cassoulet p366 (V)
Pumpkin farfalle with blue cheese sauce p393 (V)
Swiss chard and pumpkin bake p370 (V)

Rutabaga

Braised oxtail p368
Mixed vegetable purée p395 (V)
Turkey, ham, and white bean soup p362

Salsify

Salsify fritters p402 (V)

Shallots

Moroccan roasted sweet potato soup p363 (V)
Roast pork with bacon and chicory p371
Venison, shallot, and chestnut hotpot p388

Spinach

Chicken salad with carrot and apple relish p391
Clear soup with sea bass p368
Squash, spinach, and horseradish bake p370 (V)

Sweet potato

Curried sweet potato croquettes p360 (V)
Grilled sweet potato and celery root p395 (V)
Jamaican-style fish with sweet potatoes p376
Mixed vegetable purée p395 (V)
Moroccan roasted sweet potato soup p363 (V)
Roast sweet potato and chile tortilla p390 (V)
Roasted sweet potato and celery root with garlic and herbs p407 (V)
Soy and sesame-glazed sweet potatoes p394 (V)
Sweet potato and rosemary rolls p401 (V)
Sweet potato paratha p403 (V)

Swiss chard

Cheesy Swiss chard crêpes p377 (V)
Gratin of Swiss chard with white beans and pancetta p401
Swiss chard and pumpkin bake p370 (V)

Turnip

Cream of vegetable soup p362 (V)
Duck with turnips and apricots p389
Mixed vegetable purée p395 (V)
Turkey broth p362

Fruit and nuts

Apples

Apple butter p416 (V)
Apple, golden raisin, and pecan cake p410 (V)
Carrot and shredded cabbage with peanuts p404
Chicken salad with carrot and apple relish p391
Cider p420 (V)
Classic apple crumble p411 (V)
Cranberry and apricot chutney p418 (V)
Curried apple, peach, and walnut chutney p421 (V)
Dried apples p416 (V)
Pork chops with apple and baby onions p371

Slow-cooked Swedish red cabbage p394 (V)
Smoked trout with beets, apple, and dill relish p358
Sweet and sour cabbage p398 (V)
Winter braised white cabbage and celery p394 (V)

Chestnuts

Baked turkey rolls filled with chestnuts and mushrooms p383
Baked turkey rolls with celery, chestnuts, and chanterelles p383
Brussels sprouts with chestnuts and pancetta p395
Brussels sprouts with whole chestnuts and sausages p395
Cabbage stuffed with chestnut and pork p367
Chestnut and celery stuffing p402 (V)
Partridge soup p365
Pork scallops with tangerine, prunes, and chestnuts p383
Sausage and chestnut stuffing p402
Slow-cooked lamb with orange and chestnuts p366
Squash with chestnuts and cranberries p407 (V)
Venison, shallot, and chestnut hotpot p388

Cranberries

Cranberry and apricot chutney p418 (V)
Cranberry and orange butter p418 (V)
Cranberry jelly p416 (V)
Cranberry sauce with orange p418 (V)
Cranberry sauce with port p418 (V)
Festive wild rice salad p379
Squash with chestnuts and cranberries p407 (V)
Turkey and cranberry casserole p378
Winter braised white cabbage and celery p394 (V)

Dates

Middle Eastern date cakes with pomegranate drizzle p414 (V)

Grapefruit

Beef with soy sauce, lime, and grapefruit and ginger salsa p377
Grapefruit granita with almond cookies p413 (V)

Kiwi fruit

Prosciutto with kiwi on herb croûtes p359

Lemons

Cold lemon soufflé p413
Lemon sorbet p412 (V)
Lemon tart p412 (V)

Oranges and tangerines

Chicken and orange tagine p373
Chocolate orange truffle cake p409 (V)
Cranberry and orange butter p418 (V)
Cranberry sauce with orange p418 (V)
Hazelnut, chocolate, and orange tart p415 (V)
Orange and chocolate tiramisu p408 (V)
Orange and pistachio Swiss roll p408 (V)
Orange marmalade p417 (V)
Pears poached in red wine and thyme p414 (V)
Pistachio and orange biscotti p411 (V)
Pork scallops with tangerine, prunes, and chestnuts p383

Roast leg of pork with orange p376
Slow-cooked lamb with orange and chestnuts p366
Tangerine and almond biscotti p411 (V)
Turkey salad with celery root and orange relish p391

Pears

Chocolate mousse with cinnamon pears p414 (V)
Goat cheese, pear, and beet salad p358 (V)
Ham with pears p359
Hot and spicy white cabbage p398 (V)
Mulled pears p420 (V)
Normandy pear tart p410 (V)
Pear cake p408 (V)
Pear, coffee, and walnut tiramisu p408 (V)
Pears poached in red wine and thyme p414 (V)

Pomegranates

Middle Eastern date cakes with pomegranate drizzle p414 (V)
Shredded turkey, mint, and pomegranate salad p373
Turkish lamb and pomegranate pilaf p373

Quinces

Spiced quince dulce de leche pie p412 (V)

Seafood

Cod

Jamaican-style fish with sweet potatoes p376
Japanese-style fish broth p362

Haddock

Jamaican-style fish with sweet potatoes p376
Portuguese haddock soup p363
Smoked haddock, celery, and cheese chowder p363

Mussels

Mussels in a coconut and lemongrass broth p363
Pasta and mussel salad p385
Red curry mussels p363

Steamed mussels with saffron-cream sauce p365

Sea bass

Clear soup with sea bass p368

Meat

Duck

Chinese roast duck p369
Duck with turnips and apricots p389
Garbure p384

Goose

Stuffed roast goose p378

Partridge

Partridge soup p365

Turkey

Baked turkey rolls filled with chestnuts and mushrooms p383
Baked turkey rolls with celery, chestnuts, and chanterelles p383
Festive wild rice salad p379
Roast turkey with parsley and onion stuffing p382
Roast turkey with sage and bacon stuffing p382
Shredded turkey, mint, and pomegranate salad p373
Turkey and cranberry casserole p378
Turkey broth p362
Turkey scallops stuffed with prunes and pecans p383
Turkey, ham, and white bean soup p362
Turkey salad with celery root and orange relish p391
Warm turkey and chickpea salad p382
Warm white bean and turkey salad p382

Venison

Venison and artichoke casserole p388
Venison, shallot, and chestnut hotpot p388

Ham hock with red cabbage p375

ribollita

This hearty soup from Italy features the unusual combination of potatoes and bread: good and filling for the winter months.

 20 MINS   **50 MINS**   ❄ **FREEZABLE**

SERVES 4

1 tbsp olive oil, plus extra to serve

1 onion, finely chopped

salt and freshly ground black pepper

2 garlic cloves, grated or finely chopped

2 carrots, finely chopped

1 x 7oz (200g) can chopped tomatoes

1 x 14oz (400g) cannellini beans, drained and rinsed

8oz (225g) potatoes, peeled and cut into bite-sized pieces

6oz (175g) cavolo nero or curly kale, chopped

2½ cups hot vegetable stock

2 tsp finely chopped rosemary leaves

¼ ciabatta, cut into cubes, to serve

Parmesan cheese, grated, to serve

1 Heat the oil in a pan over low heat, add the onion, and cook for 6–8 minutes, or until soft and translucent. Season with salt and pepper, then add the garlic and carrots and cook for 5 minutes.

2 Stir in the tomatoes, beans, potatoes, and cavolo nero or kale and cook for 5 minutes. Pour in the stock, add the rosemary, and let simmer over low heat for 15–20 minutes, or until the potatoes are soft.

3 Meanwhile, preheat the oven to 400°F (200°C). Place the ciabatta cubes on a baking sheet, drizzle with oil, and bake for 10 minutes, or until golden. Taste the soup and season, if necessary. Serve topped with the ciabatta, a drizzle of oil, and a sprinkling of Parmesan cheese.

smoked trout with beets, apple, and dill relish

This is a wonderfully colorful and tasty light meal—dill and trout complement each other perfectly and the apples bring a sweet flavor to balance the bitterness of the chicory.

 15 MINS

SERVES 4

3-4 tsp creamed horseradish

½ red onion, finely diced

1-2 heads of chicory, leaves separated and rinsed

2 large cold-smoked trout fillets, about 8oz (225g) each, flaked

drizzle of olive oil

juice of ½ lemon

salt and freshly ground black pepper

2-3 apples

2 beets, cooked, peeled (p255), and diced

handful of dill, finely chopped

1 In a small bowl, mix together the horseradish and half of the red onion. Set aside.

2 Arrange the chicory and flaked trout on a serving plate and drizzle the oil and lemon juice over. Sprinkle with a pinch of salt and some pepper.

3 Peel, core, and chop the apple into bite-sized pieces. Put in a separate bowl with the beets and dill and mix together to make the relish.

4 To serve, spoon the relish over the chicory and fish. Sprinkle with the remaining red onion and serve with the creamed horseradish on the side.

variation

goat cheese, pear, and beet salad

Omit the horseradish. Arrange the leaves from 1–2 heads red chicory on serving plates with 7oz (200g) diced goat cheese instead of the trout. Mix ½ small finely diced red onion with 2 peeled, cored, and chopped pears instead of apple, the 2 diced beets, and a handful of fresh thyme, leaves only, instead of dill. Dress as before.

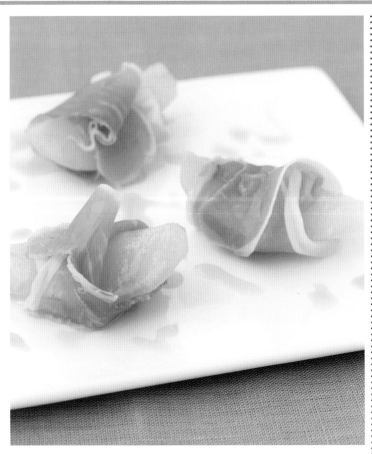

spiced butternut squash soup

Butternut squash is a type of winter squash and has a deliciously sweet, dense, and buttery flavor. It is also very versatile, so makes a fine pantry ingredient.

 20 MINS 40 MINS ❄ FREEZABLE

SPECIAL EQUIPMENT ▪ blender or food processor

SERVES 4

1 tbsp olive oil

1 onion, finely chopped

salt and freshly ground black pepper

2 garlic cloves, grated or finely chopped

2 sage leaves, finely chopped

1 red chile, seeded and finely chopped

pinch of grated nutmeg

1 butternut squash, halved, seeded, peeled, and chopped into small pieces

1 potato, peeled and diced

3 cups hot vegetable stock

chili oil, to serve

Gruyère cheese, grated, to serve

1 Heat the oil in a pan over low heat, add the onion, and cook for 6–8 minutes, or until soft and translucent. Season, then stir in the garlic, sage, chile, and nutmeg, and cook for a few seconds.

2 Stir in the squash, add the potato and stock, and bring to a boil. Reduce to a simmer and cook for 20–30 minutes, or until the squash and potatoes are soft. Pour the soup into a blender or food processor and blend until smooth. Season again with salt and pepper. Pour the soup into a bowl and serve drizzled with chili oil and a sprinkling of Gruyère cheese.

ham with pears

Thin slices of cured ham wrapped around fruit make tasty morsels at a party. The firm texture of Bosc pears makes them particularly good for this recipe.

 10 MINS PLUS COOLING 15 MINS

SERVES 4

½ cup dry sherry

½ cup granulated sugar

3 ripe pears, peeled and cut into quarters

5½oz (150g) thinly sliced Serrano or Parma ham

chili oil or mint yogurt, to serve

1 Put the sherry and sugar in a pan, add 1 cup water, and bring to a boil. Add the pears, return to a boil, and simmer gently for 15 minutes, or until they begin to soften. Turn off the heat and allow to cool for 30 minutes.

2 Wrap each quarter of pear in a piece of ham. Arrange on a serving plate and serve drizzled with chili oil or mint yogurt.

variation

prosciutto with kiwi on herb croûtes

Peel and quarter 2 kiwi fruit (no need to poach). Wrap each quarter in half a slice of raw cured ham. Mash 2 tbsp butter with ½ tsp dried mixed herbs, 1 crushed garlic clove, and a good grinding of black pepper. Toast 8 slices of ciabatta bread under a preheated broiler. Turn off the broiler. Spread each with a little of the herb butter and return to the cooling broiler until melted into the toast. Top each with a kiwi and ham roll.

cheesy leeks on toast

The leek is a versatile vegetable indeed. Here it is steamed to soften and then mixed with a cheese sauce. Spread over toast and broiled, the end result is perfect for a light lunch.

 10 MINS   10 MINS

SERVES 4

1 tbsp olive oil

1 leek, trimmed and chopped

2 tbsp butter

⅔ cup brown ale

6oz (175g) aged Cheddar cheese, grated

1 tbsp all-purpose flour

2 tsp English mustard

splash of Worcestershire sauce

salt and freshly ground black pepper

2 large egg yolks

4 slices of bread

1 Heat the oil in a pan over low heat. Add the leek and cook gently until soft. Remove from the pan with a slotted spoon and set aside.

2 Put the butter, brown ale, and cheese in the same pan and cook gently, stirring, until melted and smooth. Remove from the heat and stir in the flour until smooth. Return to the heat, stirring continuously, for 1–2 minutes.

3 Remove the pan from the heat once again and stir in the mustard, Worcestershire sauce, and the reserved leeks. Season with salt and pepper, then let cool and stir in the egg yolks until combined.

4 Preheat the broiler to hot. Toast the slices of bread on one side, then turn them over and smother with the cheesy leeks. Cook until the topping is simmering and golden, and then serve immediately.

potato and leek croquettes

These easy-to-make bites filled with savory flavor are the perfect appetizer for winter stews and roasts.

 20 MINS PLUS CHILLING   30 MINS   ❄ FREEZABLE

SERVES 4

1 tbsp olive oil

1 leek, white part only, trimmed and finely chopped

1 garlic clove, grated or finely chopped

1lb 2oz (500g) floury potatoes, such as russets, peeled and cut into chunks

3 large eggs

2oz (60g) Parmesan cheese, grated

2 tbsp chopped flat-leaf parsley

salt and freshly ground black pepper

½ cup all-purpose flour

1¾ cups fine bread crumbs

light olive oil, for deep-frying

1 Heat the olive oil in a frying pan over low heat, add the leek, and cook for 8–10 minutes until soft. Add the garlic and cook for 30 more seconds without coloring. Set aside to cool.

2 Cook the potatoes in a pan of boiling salted water for 15–20 minutes until tender. Drain, return to the pan, and mash until very smooth. Add the leek and garlic mixture, 1 of the eggs, Parmesan, and parsley. Season. Stir thoroughly and then chill for at least 1 hour to firm.

3 Spread the flour over a flat tray and lightly beat the remaining 2 eggs in a shallow bowl. Put the bread crumbs on a separate plate. Using wet hands, roll the chilled mixture into 12 balls, each about the size of a golf ball, then form into oblong shapes. Gently roll the croquettes in the flour until well coated, then dip each one in the beaten egg, and lastly coat in the bread crumbs.

4 Heat enough oil for deep-frying in a deep frying pan over medium-high heat. Cooking in batches, deep-fry the croquettes for 10–15 minutes until golden brown. Serve hot.

variation

curried sweet potato croquettes

Prepare in the same way but cook a small chopped onion instead of the leek and stir in 1 tbsp medium curry powder. Use 1 large potato and 1 large sweet potato instead of floury potatoes, then continue at step 2. Flavor with 2 tbsp fresh chopped cilantro instead of parsley.

leek and potato soup

An enduring classic, this warming soup can be blended to a smooth purée or left with a chunky texture. Either way, it is always satisfying, especially served with rustic bread.

 15 MINS   40 MINS

SPECIAL EQUIPMENT ▪ blender or food processor

SERVES 4

1 tbsp olive oil

1 onion, finely chopped

salt and freshly ground black pepper

2 garlic cloves, grated or finely chopped

3 sage leaves, finely chopped

1lb (450g) leeks, trimmed and finely sliced

4 cups hot vegetable stock

1lb (450g) potatoes, peeled and coarsely chopped

¼ cup heavy cream, to serve

1 Heat the oil in a pan, add the onion, and cook over low heat for 6–8 minutes, or until soft and translucent. Season with salt and pepper, then stir in the garlic and sage. Add the leeks and stir well, then cook over low heat for 8–10 minutes until soft.

2 Pour in the stock, bring to a boil, then add the potatoes and simmer for about 20 minutes until soft. Pour the soup into a blender or food processor and purée until smooth, then pour it back into the pan. Taste and season if needed. Stir in the cream and heat until piping hot. Serve immediately in warmed bowls.

Season's best **leeks**

Leeks are believed to be descendents of the wild onion found across Europe. They have long, cylindrical stems, with many layers of tightly wrapped leaves that are white where they have been earthed and green where exposed to light. When cooked, they have a mild flavor, but are pungent when raw. Although in season from autumn to late winter, they are at their best in early winter. They pair well with fish, cream, cheese, potatoes, lemon, and olive oil.

Cultivated in temperate zones, leeks can tolerate cold, making them a staple winter vegetable. The white part that grows underground stays tender, while the exposed green tops become coarse.

essentials
varieties available

Baby leeks to eat whole or thinly sliced, and large maincrop ones to slice or chop.

buy Choose those with a long run of white that "gives" slightly when bent. Avoid stiff leeks.

store Store unwashed and wrapped in a sealed plastic bag in the vegetable drawer for up to a week.

cook Boil, steam, sauté, or stir-fry slices; braise or grill whole or split. Use in soups, stews, and savory pie fillings.

preserve Blanch and freeze.

recipe ideas

Fish and leek pie p461

Leek and potato soup p360

Leek vinaigrette p399

Potato and leek croquettes p360

Baby leek These are tender enough to eat thinly sliced in a salad. They also make a tasty topping for pizzas and savory tarts, and are good grilled or roasted whole.

The coarse outer leaves need not be wasted. Chop them coarsely and add to the stockpot.

how to wash and cut leeks julienne

Leeks need thorough washing as dirt gets trapped between the layers. Cut them into julienne strips to cook or to use raw for salads or garnish. For use in purées, stews, and casseroles, simply slice or chop after washing.

1 Trim both ends of the leek. Cut in half lengthwise and gently spread the layers. Rinse under cold running water and shake off excess.

2 For julienne, cut off all the green part, then cut the white in desired lengths. Slice, cut-side down, into ⅛in (3mm) wide strips.

Leek Ranging in size from pencil thin to fat-shanked giants, leeks add texture and flavor to all kinds of dishes. Leeks should bend; if stiff, they will be tough and "woody" inside.

turkey broth

Make thrifty use of leftover turkey by creating your own stock, simmering the carcass after a roast dinner. This broth, however, is every bit as appealing when made with chicken.

 20 MINS 25 MINS

SERVES 6

3½ cups turkey stock or chicken stock

½ cup dry white wine

1 carrot, finely diced

1 parsnip, finely diced

2 celery stalks, finely diced

1 leek, white part only, trimmed and finely diced

1 small turnip, finely diced

salt and freshly ground black pepper

8oz (225g) cooked turkey meat, finely diced

½ cup half-and-half

2 tbsp chopped flat-leaf parsley

1 Bring the stock and wine to a boil in a large pan, then stir in the carrot, parsnip, celery, leek, and turnip. Season, partially cover with a lid, and simmer for 20 minutes.

2 Stir in the cooked turkey, half-and-half, and chopped parsley, and reheat gently. Serve the soup with plenty of crusty bread.

variation

turkey, ham, and white bean soup

Prepare in the same way but use 1 whole finely chopped leek (not just the white part), 2 finely diced carrots, and ¼ finely diced rutabaga instead of the original vegetables. Add a drained 14oz (400g) can of white beans and a mixture of 4oz (115g) finely diced ham and 4oz (115g) finely diced turkey instead of all turkey. Add 2 tbsp chopped thyme leaves instead of parsley.

japanese-style fish broth

The hot and fragrant broth in this recipe is a perfect foil for the delicate white fish. You could add some noodles to the soup, if you wish, or some soy beans for a little more bulk.

 15 MINS 1 HR

SERVES 4–6

scant 1oz (25g) dried shiitake mushrooms

3 carrots, finely sliced on the diagonal

1 tbsp dark soy sauce, plus extra to taste

2in (5cm) piece of fresh ginger, peeled and finely sliced

small bunch of cilantro

1 leek, trimmed and finely sliced on the diagonal

9oz (250g) white fish, such as cod, haddock, or pollack, skinned (p75)

For the broth

2 sheets of kombu (dried kelp), wiped clean and soaked for 30 minutes (optional)

scant 1oz (25g) dried bonito flakes (optional)

OR

5½ cups hot light vegetable stock

1 tsp fish sauce (nam pla)

1 tbsp rice vinegar

1 To make the broth, put 4 cups water in a large heavy-bottomed pan and add the kombu and bonito flakes, if using. Almost bring to a boil, drain through a sieve, and return the water to the pan (reserve the kombu and bonito flakes for another use). If not using kombu and bonito, put the vegetable stock into a heavy-bottomed pan, add the fish sauce and rice vinegar, and simmer very gently for 20 minutes.

2 Meanwhile, soak the shiitake mushrooms in warm water for 20 minutes. Drain and add to the broth along with the carrots, soy sauce, ginger, and cilantro. Partially cover with a lid and simmer gently for 20 minutes, or until the carrots are cooked, then stir in the leek and cook for another 10 minutes. Add the fish, cover with the lid, and cook for a few minutes until the fish is opaque and cooked through. Adjust the flavor with soy sauce and serve.

cream of vegetable soup

Soup is always a fantastic way to use up vegetables. Here, parsnips, leeks, and turnips combine into one delicious whole.

 15 MINS 40–55 MINS

SPECIAL EQUIPMENT ▪ blender or food processor

SERVES 6

3 tbsp butter

2 carrots, sliced

1 leek, white part only, trimmed and finely sliced

2 parsnips, sliced

1 onion, sliced

1 small turnip, sliced

3 celery stalks, sliced

1 potato, peeled and sliced

4 cups hot vegetable stock

2 tsp thyme leaves

1 bay leaf

pinch of grated nutmeg

salt and freshly ground black pepper

3 tbsp half-and-half

3 tbsp milk

bunch of chives, snipped, to garnish

1 Melt the butter in a large pan, add the carrots, leek, parsnips, onion, turnip, celery, and potato, and stir to coat well. Cover the pan with a lid and cook for 10–15 minutes, or until the vegetables have softened.

2 Add the stock, thyme, bay leaf, and nutmeg, then season. Bring to a boil and simmer uncovered for 30–40 minutes, or until the vegetables are meltingly soft. Scoop out the bay leaf and discard.

3 Pour the soup into a blender or food processor and process until smooth, then pour or strain back into the pan. Stir in the cream and milk, adding more milk if the consistency is still too thick. Season, then reheat gently. Garnish with the chives and serve.

moroccan roasted sweet potato soup

The vegetables for this soup are cooked in the oven, which brings out their naturally sweet flavor. This north African soup is made even more filling served with warm pita bread.

 20 MINS 50 MINS

SPECIAL EQUIPMENT ▪ blender or food processor

SERVES 4

1½lb (675g) sweet potatoes, peeled and cut into large chunks

6 large shallots, quartered

3 large garlic cloves, unpeeled

1 carrot, cut into large chunks

1 tbsp harissa paste, plus extra to serve

2 tbsp olive oil

salt and freshly ground black pepper

3 cups hot vegetable stock

1 tsp honey

generous squeeze of lemon juice

natural yogurt, to serve

warm pita bread, to serve

1 Preheat the oven to 400°F (200°C). Put the sweet potatoes, shallots, garlic, and carrot in a roasting pan. Mix the harissa paste with the oil, then pour over the vegetables and mix so they are well coated. Season with black pepper, then roast, turning occasionally, for 40 minutes, or until tender and turning golden. Remove from the oven.

2 Squeeze the garlic cloves out of their skins into the roasting pan. Stir in the stock and honey, then scrape up all the bits from the bottom of the pan. Pour the soup into a blender or food processor and purée until smooth, then pour back into the pan and reheat gently.

3 Add the lemon juice and season. Swirl the yogurt with a little harissa paste and top each bowl with a spoonful. Serve with warm pita bread.

mussels in a coconut and lemongrass broth

Ginger wine may be hard to get your hands on. To make your own, steep a 2in (5cm) knob of peeled ginger in sherry for a couple of days, then substitute the sherry for the wine. .

 20 MINS 30–35 MINS

SERVES 4

7 tbsp butter

2 onions, finely chopped

2 red chiles, finely chopped

2in (5cm) piece of fresh ginger, peeled and finely grated

5 large garlic cloves, finely chopped

2 lemongrass stalks, split lengthwise and lightly bruised

½ cup ginger wine

1¾ cups hot fish stock

3lb 3oz (1.5kg) mussels, cleaned (discard any that do not close when tapped) (p364)

⅔ cup coconut milk

3 tbsp coconut cream

salt and freshly ground black pepper

juice of 1–2 limes, to taste

3 tbsp chopped cilantro leaves

1 Melt the butter in a large pan over low heat and gently cook the onions, chiles, ginger, garlic, and lemongrass for 10 minutes until soft but not colored.

2 Increase the heat to high and add the ginger wine followed by the stock. Bring to a boil before adding in the mussels. Cover the pan and cook for 5–7 minutes, until the mussel shells have opened. Discard the lemongrass along with any mussels that remain closed.

3 Pour in the coconut milk and cream and bring to a boil. Season with salt and pepper, sharpen with lime juice, and stir in the cilantro leaves before serving.

variation

red curry mussels

Scrub and debeard the mussels. Cook the onions and 2 finely chopped celery stalks in 3 tbsp sunflower or vegetable oil instead of butter, and omit the other flavorings. Stir in ¼ cup Thai red curry paste, then a 14oz (400g) can of coconut milk and 1 tbsp fish sauce (nam pla) instead of the ginger wine, stock, coconut cream, and milk. Cook the mussels as in step 2. Sharpen with lime juice to taste and add the cilantro before serving.

portuguese haddock soup

The strong flavors of cavolo nero (or Savoy cabbage if you can't get ahold of cavolo nero) and smoked haddock develop in minutes, making this soup very satisfying.

 20 MINS 20 MINS

SERVES 4

10oz (300g) leaves of cavolo nero, kale, or Savoy cabbage

2 tbsp olive oil

1 Spanish onion, finely chopped

3 garlic cloves, crushed

1 large Yukon Gold potato, peeled and diced

1 cup whole or 2% milk

salt and freshly ground black pepper

10oz (300g) smoked haddock fillet, skinned and flaked

1 Rinse the greens, cut out the large ribs and discard, then finely shred the leaves. Heat the oil in a pan over medium heat, add the onion and garlic, and cook for 4–5 minutes until the onion and garlic are soft.

2 Add the potato and milk, then pour in enough water to cover everything by ¾–1¼ in (2–3cm). Season generously, bring to a simmer, and cook for 5 minutes. Add the greens and continue cooking for 10–15 minutes until the vegetables are tender.

3 Stir in the haddock and simmer for a minute, then remove from the heat and cover. Let stand for 5 minutes before serving.

variation

smoked haddock, celery, and cheese chowder

Omit the cavolo nero. Cook in the same way, but add 2 finely chopped celery stalks with the onion and omit the garlic. Cook for 15–20 minutes, then add the smoked haddock and simmer for a minute. Remove from the heat and stir in 2oz (60g) sharp Cheddar cheese, cover, and let stand as before.

Season's best **mussels**

Common mussels live in cool waters all over the world, unlike the larger, green-lipped mussel imported from New Zealand alone. At their best in winter, they are harvested from the wild by dredging and hand-gathering, but are also farmed, rope grown. One of the most sustainable seafoods, they taste great when cooked in wine, cider, or vermouth with shallots and garlic, and also with the aniseed flavors of pastis and fennel. Try, too, with chorizo, chile, and saffron.

Marine blue mussels grow in abundance in temperate and polar waters worldwide. Freshwater ones live in cool, clean lakes and rivers.

Common mussels Also known as the blue mussel, their shell varies from brown to a bluish-purple. The mussels attach themselves to rocks, or when farmed, to rope, by a strong thread called the byssus thread (or beard), a protein they secrete. They taste slightly salty, with an intense flavor of the sea.

Rope-grown mussels have little barnacle growth on the shell and are glossy. They require minimal preparation.

essentials
varieties available

The native variety is the blue mussel. Large green-lipped mussels are imported. Also available frozen, canned in brine or vinegar, smoked; often included in frozen seafood mix.

buy Shells should not be damaged and should shut or close quickly when tapped sharply. They should smell pleasantly of the sea.

store Eat on day of purchase.

cook Steam, usually in a pan with some stock, wine, or water with other flavorings. Cream may be added. Eat with the cooking liquid or add to rice, pasta, or fish sauces.

recipe ideas

Cod and mussel chowder
p460

Mussels in a coconut and lemongrass broth p363

Pasta and mussel salad p385

Risotto with mussels p300

Steamed mussels with saffron-cream sauce p365

how to prepare mussels

Mussels must be scrubbed and de-bearded before use. Before doing this, if there is time, place the mussels in a large bowl of cold water, sprinkle with oats, and leave for 2 hours to help them self-clean inside.

1 In the sink, scrub the mussels under cold, running water. Rinse away grit or sand and remove any barnacles with a small, sharp knife. Discard any mussels that are open.

2 To remove the "beard," pinch the dark stringy piece between your fingers, pull it away from the mussel, and discard.

baked cardoons with cheese

The delicate flavor of cardoons is particularly well enhanced when they are baked and topped with a delicious cheese sauce in this Italian classic.

 15 MINS 50 MINS - 1 HR 10 MINS

SERVES 4

2¼lb (1kg) cardoons, tough outer stalks discarded

salt and freshly ground black pepper

juice of 1 lemon

2 tbsp butter

1 heaping tbsp all-purpose flour

1¼ cups milk

2oz (60g) Parmesan cheese, grated

1 Trim the cardoons and remove any strings, then cut across into 3in (7.5cm) pieces. Put the cardoons into a pan of salted water and add the lemon juice. Bring to a boil, then reduce the heat and simmer for 30–45 minutes, or until softened. Drain well and arrange in a baking dish.

2 Preheat the oven to 350°F (180°C). Melt the butter in a small pan, then remove from the heat and stir in the flour. Gradually stir in the milk. Return to the heat and cook, stirring, until smooth and thickened. Remove from the heat, season with salt and pepper, and stir in half the Parmesan cheese. Pour evenly over the cardoons and sprinkle with the remaining Parmesan.

3 Bake for 20–25 minutes, or until golden and bubbling. Serve hot with some crusty bread.

partridge soup

This is a substantial soup that is a great way to make one partridge suffice for four people. You could use any other small game bird, such as quail, in exactly the same way.

 20 MINS 1 HR 20 MINS

SERVES 4

1 tbsp sunflower or vegetable oil

1 partridge, quartered

1 onion, unpeeled and quartered

3 cups hot chicken stock

1 bouquet garni

salt and freshly ground black pepper

1 potato, peeled and diced

1 carrot, diced

1 small turnip, diced

2 tbsp all-purpose flour

1 x 7oz (200g) can chestnuts, peeled and quartered

2 tbsp amontillado sherry

dash of soy sauce

a little chopped flat-leaf parsley, to garnish

1 Heat the oil in a saucepan over medium heat, add the partridge pieces, and cook until they are browned all over. Add the onion, stock, bouquet garni, and a little salt and pepper. Bring to a boil, reduce the heat, cover with a lid, and simmer gently for 1 hour.

2 Strain the stock and return to the pan. Add the potato, carrot, and turnip. Bring back to a boil, partially cover, and simmer gently for about 20 minutes until the vegetables are really tender. Meanwhile, take all the meat off the partridge, discarding the skin, and shred the meat.

3 Remove the bouquet garni from the soup and discard. Mix the flour with ¼ cup water and add to the soup. Bring to a boil, stirring, until lightly thickened, and simmer for 2 minutes.

4 Add the shredded meat, chestnuts, and sherry to the soup and simmer for 2 minutes. Add the soy sauce to taste. Ladle into warmed bowls, garnish with a little chopped parsley, and serve immediately.

steamed mussels with saffron-cream sauce

From the shores of Brittany comes this delectable dish. Just steam the mussels briefly so they are juicy and sumptuous.

 25-30 MINS 10-12 MINS

SERVES 4-6

3 shallots, very finely chopped

1 cup dry white wine

1 bouquet garni, made with 5-6 sprigs of parsley, 2-3 sprigs of thyme, and 1 bay leaf

large pinch of saffron threads

salt and freshly ground black pepper

6½lb (3kg) mussels, scrubbed and debearded (discard any that do not close when tapped) (p364)

½ cup heavy cream

5-7 sprigs of flat-leaf parsley, leaves picked and finely chopped

1 Put the shallots, wine, bouquet garni, saffron, and plenty of pepper in a large pot with a lid. Bring to a boil and simmer for 2 minutes. Add the mussels, cover, and cook over high heat, stirring occasionally, for 5-7 minutes. Discard any mussels that have not opened. With a slotted spoon, transfer the mussels to a large, warmed bowl.

2 Cover the mussels tightly with foil and keep in a warm place while making the sauce. You must work quickly now so they remain as plump and moist as possible and lose none of their fresh-cooked savor.

3 Discard the bouquet garni and bring the cooking liquid to a boil. Simmer until reduced by half. Pour in the cream, stirring, and bring back to a boil. Simmer for about 2-3 minutes, stirring, until slightly thickened. Lift out the spoon and run your finger across; it should leave a clear trail. Stir in the parsley and season to taste. Remove the foil, spoon the saffron-cream sauce over the mussels, and serve immediately.

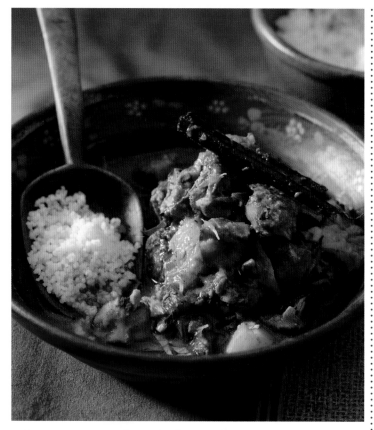

slow-cooked lamb with orange and chestnuts

Hearty chestnuts give substance to this classic combination of lamb and orange. The tagine tastes even better reheated the next day as the flavors will have melded together.

 15 MINS   **2 HRS 15 MINS**   **FREEZABLE**

SERVES 4–6

½ tsp ground cinnamon

½ tsp ground cumin

½ tsp ground coriander

salt and freshly ground black pepper

2lb (900g) lean leg of lamb, diced

2–3 tbsp olive oil

1 onion, chopped

1 cinnamon stick

6oz (175g) canned chestnuts

⅔ cup fresh orange juice

3 cups hot lamb stock

2 oranges, peeled and cut into thick slices

bunch of cilantro, coarsely chopped

1 Preheat the oven to 325°F (160°C). In a large bowl, mix together the ground spices and season with salt and pepper. Toss the meat in the mixture. Heat half the oil in a large flameproof casserole or tagine over medium-high heat, add the lamb in batches (with extra oil if necessary),

and cook for 6–8 minutes, or until the lamb is browned on all sides. Remove and set aside.

2 Heat the remaining oil in the casserole over medium heat. Add the onion and cinnamon stick and stir so the onion is coated in any residual lamb juices. Cook for 3–4 minutes until the onion is soft. Stir in the chestnuts and pour in the orange juice. Increase the heat and let it simmer for a minute, stirring. Reduce the heat and return the lamb to the casserole along with any juices from the lamb.

3 Pour in the stock, bring to a boil, then reduce to a simmer, cover with the lid, and put in the oven for 2 hours. Check occasionally that it's not drying out, and add a little hot water, if needed. Add the orange slices for the last 30 minutes of cooking. Check for seasoning, stir in the cilantro, and serve with couscous.

pumpkin and parsnip cassoulet

This light, vegetarian version of the traditional meaty cassoulet features creamy white beans with a crispy topping.

 15 MINS   **1 HR 45 MINS**   ✳ **FREEZABLE**

SERVES 4–6

2 tbsp olive oil

1 onion, finely chopped

salt and freshly ground black pepper

3 garlic cloves, finely chopped

1 tsp ground cloves

2 carrots, finely chopped

2 celery stalks, finely chopped

1 bay leaf

1lb (450g) pumpkin (prepared weight), chopped into bite-sized pieces

1lb (450g) small parsnips, sliced into rounds

1 cup white wine

a few sprigs of thyme

1 x 14oz (400g) can tomatoes

1 x 14oz (400g) can white beans, rinsed and drained

3 cups hot vegetable stock

For the topping

1 cup bread crumbs, lightly toasted

1oz (30g) Parmesan cheese, grated

1 tbsp chopped flat-leaf parsley

1 Preheat the oven to 350°F (180°C). Heat the oil in a large flameproof casserole over medium heat, add the onion, and cook for 3–4 minutes until soft. Season, add the garlic, cloves, carrots, celery, and bay leaf, and cook, stirring occasionally, over very low heat for 8–10 minutes until it is all soft. Stir in the pumpkin and parsnips and cook for a few minutes more, then pour in the wine. Increase the heat, stir, and let it bubble for a minute or two. Then add the thyme, tomatoes, beans, and stock and bring to a boil. Reduce to a simmer, season, cover with the lid, and put in the oven for 40 minutes.

2 Mix the topping ingredients together in a bowl, sprinkle it over the cassoulet, and put back in the oven for 30 minutes. Then remove the lid and cook for about 10 minutes until the topping is golden. Ladle into warmed bowls and serve with crusty bread.

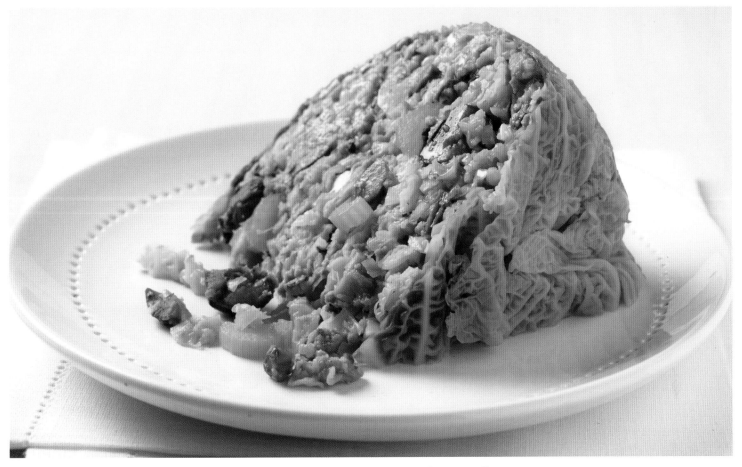

cabbage stuffed with chestnut and pork

An old favorite, ideal for a cold day, and easier than you might imagine to assemble. Everyone loves the rich, healthy stuffing.

 35–40 MINS   1 HR 30 MINS

SPECIAL EQUIPMENT ▪ food processor

SERVES 6

3lb (1.35kg) head of Savoy cabbage

salt and freshly ground black pepper

4½oz (125g) lean, boneless pork

2 onions, finely chopped

2 slices of white bread, crusts removed

4 tbsp butter

2 celery stalks, peeled and thinly sliced

1lb 2oz (500g) cooked, peeled chestnuts (approx 1½lb/675g unshelled weight), chopped

10 sprigs of parsley, leaves picked and chopped

10–12 sage leaves, finely chopped

grated zest of 1 lemon

2 large eggs, lightly beaten

2 tbsp vegetable oil

1 x 15oz (500g) can chopped tomatoes

1 tbsp tomato paste

1 garlic clove, finely chopped

1 bouquet garni

pinch of granulated sugar

4½oz (125g) mushrooms, sliced

1 Cut the outside leaf from the base of the cabbage stalk and peel off the leaf without tearing it. Repeat, removing 9 more cabbage leaves, and wash them all well in cold water to remove any dirt. Bring a large saucepan of water to a boil, add a little salt, and blanch the leaves for 1 minute. Transfer to a bowl of cold water. Trim and discard the stalk from the cabbage. Cook the cabbage head in the boiling water for 3–4 minutes. Transfer to a bowl of cold water, and when cool, drain, stalk-end down. Drain and pat dry the individual leaves with paper towels. Remove and discard the rib at the center of each leaf. Slice the cabbage head in half. Remove the core and discard, then shred the head reasonably fine.

2 Chop the pork in a food processor with one of the onions, and set aside. Put the bread slices in the food processor and pulse to crumbs.

3 Melt the butter in a frying pan, add the shredded cabbage, and cook, stirring, for 7–10 minutes until tender. Transfer to a large bowl. Put the pork and onion mixture into the frying pan with the celery. Cook, stirring, until the pork is crumbled and brown; it should take 5–7 minutes. Add the bread crumbs, chestnuts, herbs, zest, salt, pepper, and pork to the bowl of cabbage, stirring well. Stir the eggs into the stuffing.

4 Line another bowl with a damp kitchen towel. Arrange 9 cabbage leaves in a layer around the inside. Allow 2in (5cm) of the leaves to extend above the rim. Set the last leaf in the bottom of the bowl. Spoon in the stuffing, then fold the ends of the cabbage leaves over to enclose the stuffing completely. Gather the ends of the cloth together over the top and tie tightly with string. Bring a large pan of water to a boil. Lift up

the tied ends of the kitchen towel and transfer the stuffed cabbage to the pan, immersing it in the water. Set a heatproof plate on top to weigh it down and simmer for 50–60 minutes.

5 Heat half of the oil in a frying pan. Add the remaining onion and cook until soft. Stir in the tomatoes, tomato paste, garlic, bouquet garni, and sugar and cook, stirring occasionally, for 8–10 minutes until fairly thick. Remove from the heat and strain the tomato sauce into a bowl. Heat the remaining oil in the frying pan and sauté the mushrooms until tender. Stir in the tomato sauce and season well.

6 Lift the cabbage from the pan, drain, and allow to cool slightly. Unwrap the kitchen towel and set the stuffed cabbage, stalk down, on a warmed serving plate. Serve the sauce separately.

clear soup with sea bass

White radish or daikon adds some hot flavor to this broth.

 30–35 MINS   25 MINS

SPECIAL EQUIPMENT ▪ muslin

SERVES 4

4in (10cm) sheet of kombu (dried kelp)

¼oz (10g) dried bonito flakes

½ small carrot, sliced

salt

1in (2.5cm) piece of daikon, cut into 8 wedges

1 sea bass (about 13oz/375g), cleaned and cut into 4 steaks, head and tail discarded

1 tbsp Japanese rice wine

1 tbsp cornstarch

1 lemon

4½oz (125g) spinach leaves

1 tsp Japanese soy sauce, or to taste

1 Put 3½ cups cold water in a large saucepan and add the kombu. Bring to a boil over high heat, then immediately remove from the heat and discard the kombu. Sprinkle the dried bonito flakes evenly over the surface of the water. Let the stock stand for 3–5 minutes until the flakes settle to the bottom. Line a sieve with damp muslin, then strain the stock through the muslin.

2 Half-fill a saucepan with water and bring to a boil. Add the carrot and a pinch of salt and simmer for 3–5 minutes until tender. Drain and set aside. Repeat with the daikon wedges, simmering for 8–10 minutes until just tender. Drain and set aside.

3 Toss the fish with the rice wine. Put the cornstarch on a plate and press both sides of each sea bass into it, shaking off any excess. Bring a saucepan of water to a boil, add the steaks, and bring back to a gentle simmer. Cook for 2–3 minutes, until just firm, then drain and set aside.

4 With a vegetable peeler, peel 2–3 strips of zest from the lemon, being sure to leave behind any white pith. Cut the zest into 12 very thin strips. Trim and discard any tough stems from the spinach. Bring a pan of water to a boil, add the spinach, and simmer for 3 minutes or until tender. Drain, rinse with cold water, then gently squeeze. Chop, divide into 4 small piles, and keep warm.

5 Bring the soup stock to a very gentle boil with the soy sauce. Taste, adding more soy sauce if you like. Arrange the fish, carrot, and daikon in 4 warmed bowls. Ladle in the soup and garnish each bowl with 3 strips of lemon zest and a bundle of spinach. Serve immediately.

salmon, horseradish, and kale bake

This recipe is perfect for a mid-week meal with family or friends, as you can put all the ingredients together in next to no time and then put it in the oven to finish.

 10 MINS   35 MINS

SERVES 4

4 salmon fillets, above 5½oz (150g) each, skinned (p75)

4 cups milk, plus enough to cover the fish

11 tbsp butter

2 tbsp all-purpose flour

5½oz (150g) aged Cheddar cheese, grated

2 tsp Dijon mustard

salt and freshly ground black pepper

2 handfuls of kale

1–2 tbsp creamed horseradish

1 Preheat the oven to 400°F (200°C). Sit the salmon fillets in a frying pan and pour over enough milk to cover (leaving the 2 cups for the cheese sauce). Poach gently over low heat for about 10 minutes until opaque and cooked. Then transfer to an ovenproof dish using a slotted spoon or a fish spatula. Discard the poaching liquid.

2 To make a cheese sauce, melt the butter in a large pan, then remove it from the heat and stir in the flour to form a roux. Pour in a little milk taken from the 4 cups, then put the pan back on the heat and slowly add the rest of the milk, stirring all the time. Switch to a balloon whisk and whisk the sauce over low heat for about 5 minutes until it is smooth. Remove the pan from the heat once again and add the cheese and mustard. Stir thoroughly and season.

3 Meanwhile, trim the rough stems from the kale and coarsely chop the leaves. Place in a saucepan of boiling water and cook for about 5 minutes until nearly soft. Drain and add to the salmon. Combine gently.

4 Mix together the creamed horseradish and cheese sauce, pour over the salmon, and bake for about 15 minutes until golden.

braised oxtail

This traditional British dish is rich and hearty. For the best flavor, make it a day in advance and reheat to serve.

 25 MINS PLUS CHILLING   3 HRS PLUS REHEATING

SERVES 4

3lb 3oz (1.5kg) oxtails, in large pieces

all-purpose flour, to coat and toss

salt and freshly ground black pepper

3–4 tbsp beef drippings or vegetable oil

1 large onion, coarsely chopped

1 large carrot, cut into chunks

1 large celery stalk, cut into chunks

1 large parsnip, cut into chunks

3oz (85g) rutabaga, cut into chunks

2½ cups hot beef stock

⅔ cup red wine or port

1 bouquet garni, made with 1 bay leaf and 2–3 sprigs each of thyme, parsley, and rosemary

1 Preheat the oven to 325°F (160°C). Coat the oxtail in flour seasoned with pepper. Melt the dripping in a heavy flameproof casserole and brown the oxtail (fry in batches). Transfer to a dish.

2 Toss the vegetables in flour, then brown them too (adding more dripping, if needed). Pour in 1¼ cups of the stock and stir to scrape up the bits from the bottom of the pan. Return the oxtail to the casserole, pour in the wine, and add the bouquet garni. Cover the pan tightly. Bring to a boil, then transfer to the oven to cook for 2½–3 hours. Remove from the oven and allow to cool, then refrigerate overnight.

3 The next day, remove the excess fat from the surface and add the remaining stock. Reheat in the oven at 350°F (180°C) for 30 minutes. Serve with mashed potatoes.

chinese roast duck

It is the aromatic seasoning made from a range of Asian spices and other flavorings that gives the universally popular Chinese roast duck its particular flavor. The seasoning is spooned into the duck's body cavity and then the bird is roasted for several hours, during which time the seasoning imbues the duck with its flavor.

 45 MINS PLUS AIR-DRYING AND STANDING   **1 HR 45 MINS – 2 HRS**

SPECIAL EQUIPMENT ▪ bamboo skewer

SERVES 4

1 duck, total weight about 5lb (2.25kg)

1 tbsp honey

For the aromatic seasoning

1 tsp Szechuan peppercorns

2 tbsp ground bean sauce or black bean sauce

1 tbsp Chinese rice wine or dry sherry

2 tsp granulated sugar

½ tsp five-spice powder

2 tbsp light soy sauce

1 tsp sunflower or vegetable oil

3 garlic cloves, finely chopped

1in (2.5cm) piece of fresh ginger, peeled and finely chopped

4 scallions, trimmed and sliced, plus extra to serve

small bunch of cilantro, leaves chopped, plus extra sprigs for garnish (optional)

1 Rinse the duck inside and out with cold water and pat dry with paper towels. Pull away and discard any fat from the body cavity. Tie heavy string several times around the flap of skin at the neck opening. Half-fill a wok with water and bring to a boil. Immerse the duck in the water and use a ladle to pour water over the breast for 1 minute until the duck skin becomes taut. Remove the duck and pat dry with paper towels. Hang the duck by the string in a cool place for about 2 hours, until the skin is dry.

2 For the aromatic seasoning, heat a wok over medium heat. Add the peppercorns and cook, stirring, for 1–2 minutes, until they smoke slightly. Transfer to a mortar and pound to a coarse powder. Put the powder in a bowl with the bean sauce, rice wine or dry sherry, sugar, five-spice powder, and soy sauce. Stir together.

3 Reheat the wok over medium heat until very hot. Drizzle in the oil and heat until the oil is very hot. Add the garlic, ginger, and scallions, and stir-fry for about 30 seconds, until fragrant. Add the sauce mixture and the cilantro. Bring to a boil, then reduce the heat to low and simmer for about 1 minute. Transfer to a bowl and let it cool.

4 About 45 minutes before roasting the duck, put a bamboo skewer into a bowl of water and let it soak. Preheat the oven to 400°F (200°C). Spoon the seasoning into the body cavity. Overlap the skin to close the cavity and thread the skewer 2–3 times from the top of the cavity through both layers of skin, then through the tail. Tie string around the tail and the top of the skewer. Set the duck, breast-side up, on a rack in a roasting pan. Roast for 15 minutes.

5 Meanwhile, combine the honey and ¼ cup boiling water in a small bowl. Remove the duck from the oven and brush the honey all over the skin. Reduce the oven temperature to 350°F (180°C) and continue roasting for 1½–1¾ hours, brushing every 15 minutes with the honey mixture, until dark brown and the leg meat feels soft.

6 Transfer the duck to a cuting board and let it stand for about 15 minutes, then remove the string and skewer. Set a sieve over a bowl. Pour the seasoning from the duck cavity into the sieve. Skim off and discard the fat; reserve the liquid. Carve the duck and chop the meat into 1in (2.5cm) pieces. Arrange on a warmed platter, pour the seasoning over the top, and decorate with sliced scallions and cilantro sprigs, if using. Serve immediately.

squash, spinach, and horseradish bake

The ever-popular butternut squash has a starring role in this baked dish, ably assisted by colorful spinach leaves.

 10 MINS   **30 MINS**

SERVES 4

2 handfuls of spinach leaves, rinsed and drained

1 small to medium butternut squash, halved, seeded, peeled, and thinly sliced

2 garlic cloves, grated or finely chopped

1¼ cups heavy cream

2 tsp freshly grated horseradish (or 3–4 tsp creamed horseradish)

salt and freshly ground black pepper

1 Preheat the oven to 400°F (200°C). Put the spinach in a pan with a little water (the water clinging to the leaves should be enough) and cook for a few minutes until just wilted. Alternatively, put in a microwave-proof bowl, cover loosely, and wilt in the microwave. Drain and squeeze out the excess water. Set aside.

2 Put the squash and garlic in a wide pan, pour in the cream, and simmer gently over low heat for 10 minutes. Remove the squash with a slotted spoon and layer it in an ovenproof dish with the wilted spinach.

3 Stir the grated or creamed horseradish into the cream in the pan, then pour the mixture over the squash. Season with salt and lots of pepper. Cover with foil and roast in the oven for 20 minutes.

variation

swiss chard and pumpkin bake

Prepare in the same way, but use 7oz (200g) shredded Swiss chard instead of spinach and ½ small pumpkin for the butternut squash. Add a good grating of nutmeg instead of the horseradish in step 3.

shepherd's pie

A perennial favorite, shepherd's pie never fails to please, especially during winter. Perfect comfort food.

 30 MINS   **1 HR 30 MINS**   **FREEZABLE**

SERVES 4

1¼lb (550g) russet potatoes, peeled

large pat of butter

salt and freshly ground black pepper

3 tbsp olive oil

2 onions, diced

3 carrots, diced

1¼lb (550g) ground lamb

3 garlic cloves, chopped

1 tsp dried oregano

1 x 24oz (600g) can chopped tomatoes

4½oz (125g) frozen peas

1 Preheat the oven to 350°F (180°C). Cook the potatoes in a pan of boiling salted water for 15–20 minutes until tender. Drain, then mash well. Add the butter and mash again until creamy. Season with salt and pepper, then set aside.

2 Meanwhile, heat the oil in a heavy-bottomed pan over medium heat, add the onions and carrots, and cook for 5 minutes, or until the onions are starting to soften. Add the lamb and cook, stirring constantly, for 10 minutes, or until no longer pink. Add the garlic and oregano, cook for 1 minute, then stir in the tomatoes and bring to a boil.

3 Add the peas, season well, then bring to a boil before lowering the heat. Simmer for 20 minutes, stirring occasionally. Pour a layer of the lamb sauce into individual serving dishes and top with the mashed potato. Bake in the oven for 30–35 minutes until brown on top and piping hot.

roast pork with bacon and chicory

Chicory wrapped in bacon is a very satisfying foil to roast pork. This generous all-in-one recipe will give you plenty of leftovers—perfect for sandwiches the next day.

 10 MINS PLUS RESTING   2 HRS

SERVES 4

4lb (1.8kg) pork loin or boneless rolled shoulder

½ tbsp olive oil

1 tbsp salt

14oz (400g) shallots, large ones halved

⅔ cup dry or hard cider

4 heads of chicory, trimmed

12 strips thick-cut bacon

1 Preheat the oven to 475°F (240°C). Rub the pork all over with the oil, then smother with the salt. Put in the oven to cook for 15–20 minutes, or until the skin is crispy. Remove the pan from the oven and reduce the oven temperature to 350°F (180°C).

2 Lift the pork up, place the shallots underneath, then sit the pork down on top of them. Drizzle over the cider and return to the oven to cook for

1¾ hours. Meanwhile, wrap the chicory evenly in the bacon and add to the pan for the last 40 minutes of cooking.

3 Remove the pork and keep it warm while it rests for at least 20 minutes. Carve the roast and serve with the chicory and other accompaniments of your choice.

variation

roast pork with bacon and celery hearts
Prepare in the same way, but use 14oz (400g) pickling onions instead of shallots. Instead of chicory, blanch 2 halved celery hearts in boiling water for 2–3 minutes, drain, wrap in the bacon, and proceed as in the original recipe.

pork chops with apple and baby onions

A stuffing piled on top of pork chops before roasting them not only enhances their flavor, but also prevents the chops from drying out in the oven: a win-win situation.

 15 MINS   35 MINS

SPECIAL EQUIPMENT ▪ food processor

SERVES 4

2 slices of white bread

handful of sage leaves

1 small onion, coarsely chopped

salt and freshly ground black pepper

4 x pork loin chops, about ¾in (2cm) thick and about 4½oz (125g) each

12 baby onions or shallots, large ones halved

3 apples, peeled and coarsely chopped

2 tbsp brown sugar

drizzle of olive oil

handful of rosemary sprigs

1 Preheat the oven to 400°F (200°C). Put the bread, sage, and onion in a food processor and pulse until you have a crumb mixture. Spread out on

a baking sheet and put in the oven for 5 minutes, or until golden. Return to the food processor and pulse again until finely ground. Season well.

2 Sit the chops in a roasting pan and add the baby onions. Add the apples and sprinkle them with the sugar, then drizzle with a little oil. Add the rosemary and sprinkle over a pinch of salt, some pepper, and the golden bread crumb mixture.

3 Put in the oven to roast for 30–35 minutes, or until the meat is cooked through and the onions are beginning to brown. Turn the chops halfway through cooking. Serve with some creamy mashed potato.

Season's best **pomegranates**

Considered a superfood, the leathery skin of a pomegranate hides many "arils," each comprising a small, edible seed in a sac of ruby-red or white sweetly tart juice held by a bitter, white pith. Widely cultivated in many countries, it is at its best in early winter through to spring. Enjoy as a snack or scatter the arils over salads, or with chicken, duck, or pork. Try the juice in marinades and syrups.

Native to Iran, pomegranates are grown in Mediterranean-type climates around the world, mainly America, the Middle East, India, and Spain.

The calyx end is strikingly shaped like a crown.

Wonderful This is a leading Californian variety with a signature crimson color, abundant juice, a sweet flavor, and glowing red arils. It is a top choice for both eating and juicing.

Middle Eastern pomegranate
The Middle East is a major exporter of pomegranates, both whole fruit and processed seeds. They have been grown there for thousands of years.

Packs of ready-prepared arils are sold separately for use in salads, desserts, and for quick snacking.

essentials
varieties available

Available as whole fruit, fresh, ready-prepared seeds in packs, and as juice. Also look for pomegranate molasses and Grenadine syrup.

buy Choose glossy fruit that feels heavy for its size. Avoid any that look dry or damaged.

store Whole fruit can be kept in the fridge for a few weeks. Packs of ready-prepared arils can be refrigerated for a few days, or frozen to be used for juice.

cook Add the juice or arils to salads, desserts, soups, stews, and sauces.

recipe ideas

Middle Eastern oranges p475

Shredded turkey, mint, and pomegranate salad p373

Turkish lamb and pomegranate pilaf p373

how to cut and prepare pomegranate

This delicious fruit has a tough skin and requires patience when preparing; however, it is worth the effort. Make sure you remove all traces of the bitter white membrane.

1 Slice off the top of the pomegranate with a sharp knife. Slice into quarters, following the lines of arils.

2 The seeds are in clusters divided by a thin membrane. Pick out the seeds from each quarter.

chicken and orange tagine

The flavors in this tagine are a harmonious blend of citrus and spice. If you can't find the spice mix ras-el-hanout, use a pinch each of ground cinnamon and grated nutmeg instead.

 20 MINS 1 HR 45 MINS ❄ FREEZABLE

SERVES 4

8 chicken thighs, with skin on

1 tsp ras-el-hanout spice (optional)

salt and freshly ground black pepper

1–2 tbsp olive oil

1 red onion, finely chopped

2 tsp coriander seeds, half of them crushed

2 jalapeño chiles, seeded and finely chopped

3 garlic cloves, finely chopped

2 oranges, segmented and juice reserved

1 x 14oz (400g) chopped tomatoes

3 cups hot chicken or vegetable stock

handful of cilantro, coarsely chopped

1 Preheat the oven to 375°F (190°C). Smother the chicken with the ras-el-hanout spice mix, if using, and season well with salt and pepper. Heat half the oil in a large flameproof casserole or tagine over medium-high heat and cook the chicken (in batches, if necessary) for 6–8 minutes until golden. Remove and set aside.

2 Heat the remaining oil in the casserole over medium heat, add the onion, and cook for 3–4 minutes until soft. Season with salt and pepper, stir in the coriander seeds, chiles, and garlic, and cook for another minute. Add the orange juice, increase the heat, and let the sauce simmer for a minute, then return the chicken to the casserole together with its juices.

3 Add the tomatoes and a little of the stock and bring to a boil, then pour in the remaining stock and boil for 1–2 minutes. Reduce the heat, cover with the lid, and put in the oven for 1½ hours. Check occasionally that it's not drying out, and add a little hot water, if needed. Add the orange segments for the last 30 minutes of cooking. Stir in most of the cilantro and serve with couscous, with the remaining cilantro sprinkled over.

shredded turkey, mint, and pomegranate salad

Pomegranate molasses as well as seeds are used in this salad. The fragrant molasses has a tangy flavor and is essential in Middle Eastern cuisine. Find it in specialty food stores.

 15 MINS

SERVES 4

large handful of watercress

large handful of radicchio

10oz (300g) cooked turkey breast, sliced

1 red onion, finely sliced

handful of mint leaves

seeds from 1 pomegranate

For the dressing

3 tbsp extra virgin olive oil

1 tbsp lemon juice

1 tbsp pomegranate molasses

pinch of ground cinnamon

salt and freshly ground black pepper

pinch of sugar (optional)

1 Arrange the watercress and radicchio on a serving plate and top with the turkey. Scatter with the onion, mint leaves, and the pomegranate seeds.

2 In a bowl, whisk together the oil, lemon juice, pomegranate molasses, and cinnamon. Season to taste with salt and pepper, adding some sugar, if you like. Drizzle the dressing over the salad and serve.

turkish lamb and pomegranate pilaf

Fragrant and full of color, this pilaf has complex layers of flavor. Swap in different fruits and nuts for variety—dates, golden raisins, and almonds are often used in Turkish cuisine.

 15 MINS 1 HR

SERVES 4–6

2 tbsp olive oil, plus extra for drizzling

1½lb (675g) lamb leg, cut into bite-sized pieces

1 onion, finely chopped

salt and freshly ground black pepper

3 garlic cloves, finely chopped

1 jalapeño chile, seeded and finely sliced

1 tsp dried mint

1 tsp ground cinnamon

2oz (60g) golden raisins or use regular raisins

12oz (350g) easy-cook basmati rice

3 cups hot lamb stock

2oz (60g) hazelnuts, toasted and coarsely chopped

small handful of dill, finely chopped

seeds from 1 pomegranate

2½oz (75g) feta cheese, crumbled (optional)

1 Heat the oil in a large flameproof casserole over medium-high heat, add the lamb (in batches, if necessary), and cook for 6–8 minutes until browned on all sides. Remove and set aside.

2 Add the onion to the casserole and cook over medium heat for 3–4 minutes until soft. Season with salt and pepper, stir in the garlic, chile, mint, and cinnamon, and cook for another 2 minutes. Stir in the golden raisins.

3 Stir in the rice and turn it, so all the grains are coated and the juices soaked up. Return the lamb to the casserole, pour in the stock, and reduce to a simmer. Partially cover and cook for 30–40 minutes, adding a little more hot stock if it begins to dry out. Taste and season, then stir in the hazelnuts and dill and scatter with the pomegranate seeds. Top with crumbled feta, if using, and serve with warm pita bread and a lightly dressed, crisp green salad.

corned beef hash with horseradish

An economical classic that could evoke the winter dishes of childhood. Creamed horseradish adds a kick to this simple recipe.

 10 MINS **25 MINS** **FREEZABLE**

SERVES 4

1 tbsp olive oil

1 onion, finely chopped

pinch of salt

1 garlic clove, grated or finely chopped

1½lb (675g) potatoes, peeled and cut in chunks

3 large carrots, finely diced

2 cups hot beef stock

1 x 9oz (250g) can corned beef, coarsely chopped

2-3 tsp creamed horseradish

splash of Worcestershire sauce (optional)

pickled red cabbage, to serve

1 Heat the oil in a large frying pan over low heat. Add the onion and a pinch of salt and cook for about 5 minutes until soft and translucent. Next, add the garlic, potato, and carrot and cook for about 5 minutes. Pour in a little of the stock and bring to a boil. Stir in the corned beef and creamed horseradish and mix well.

2 Add the remaining stock, reduce the heat slightly, and simmer gently for about 15 minutes, until the potatoes and carrots are cooked, stirring occasionally so that it doesn't stick, and to break up the chunks of corned beef. Taste and season, if needed. Add the Worcestershire sauce and stir in (if using). Serve hot with pickled red cabbage.

celery root soufflé pie

A hearty, tasty warmer. Also try parsnips instead of celery root.

 40 MINS PLUS CHILLING **50 MINS**

SPECIAL EQUIPMENT ▪ 8in (20cm) flan pan ▪ ceramic baking beans

SERVES 4

1 cup whole wheat or spelt flour

salt and freshly ground black pepper

1 tbsp caraway seeds

5 tbsp cold butter, diced

3oz (85g) Cheddar cheese, grated

3 large eggs, separated

1 celery root, about 1lb (450g), peeled and cut into chunks

4 tbsp butter

¼ cup milk

4 strips thick-cut bacon, diced

2 tbsp snipped chives

1 Mix the flour, salt, and caraway seeds in a bowl. Rub in the butter until the mixture resembles bread crumbs. Stir in the cheese. Mix 3 tbsp cold water with 1 egg yolk and stir into the flour mixture to form a firm dough, adding more water if necessary. Knead gently on a lightly floured surface, then wrap with oiled plastic wrap and chill for at least 30 minutes.

2 Meanwhile, cook the celery root in boiling salted water until tender. Drain and return to the pan. Dry out briefly over low heat. Mash with the butter and milk. Dry-fry the bacon and add to the pan with fat. Beat in the remaining 2 egg yolks and chives. Season well.

3 Preheat the oven to 400°F (200°C). Roll out the dough and use to line the flan pan, pressing it into the corners. Trim away the excess and prick the bottom all over with a fork. Line the dough with wax paper and fill with ceramic baking beans. Bake for 10 minutes until the edges are golden. Remove the beans and paper and return to the oven for 5 minutes to crisp. Remove from the oven and set aside.

4 Whisk the 3 egg whites until stiff. Mix 1 tbsp into the celery root mixture. Fold in the remainder with a rubber spatula. Spoon into the pie dough and bake for 25 minutes until risen, just set, and golden. Serve hot.

belly pork and squash

No meat performs better when slow cooked than tender pork.

 30 MINS **2 HRS 15 MINS - 2 HRS 45 MINS**

SERVES 4-6

1 tbsp olive oil

1lb 9oz (700g) pork belly

salt and freshly ground black pepper

1 onion, finely chopped

3 garlic cloves, finely chopped

3 sage leaves, finely chopped

1 sprig of rosemary

1 butternut squash, peeled, seeded, and cut into cubes

½ cup dry sherry

4 cups hot vegetable stock

1 Preheat the oven to 325°F (160°C). Heat half the oil in a large flameproof casserole over medium-high heat. Season the pork belly with salt and pepper and add it, skin-side down, to the casserole. Cook for about 10 minutes, or until it begins to color and become crispy. Remove from the casserole and set aside.

2 Heat the remaining oil in the casserole over medium heat, add the onion, and cook for 3-4 minutes until soft. Stir in the garlic, sage, and rosemary, followed by the squash, and turn over the ingredients to coat. Pour in the sherry, increase the heat, and let it bubble for a minute.

3 Return the pork belly to the casserole, add the stock, and bring to a boil. Reduce to a simmer, cover with the lid, and put in the oven for 2-2½ hours. Check occasionally that it's not drying out, adding a little hot water if needed. Slice or cut the pork into bite-sized pieces and serve in warmed shallow bowls together with the squash and its juices. Serve with crusty bread.

ham hock with red cabbage

Slow-cooked sweet cabbage is the perfect complement to ham, and with the addition of spices and dried fruit, the humble piece of meat is transformed. Ham hocks are also known as knuckles.

 20 MINS   **3 HRS**

SERVES 4-6

2 ham hocks, about 3lb (1.35kg) each

1 small red cabbage, cored and finely shredded

2 onions, sliced

4 garlic cloves, finely chopped

a few sprigs of thyme

2oz (60g) raisins

pinch of grated nutmeg

pinch of ground cinnamon

1¼ cups white wine vinegar

2 cups hot vegetable stock

salt and freshly ground black pepper

1 Preheat the oven to 325°F (160°C). Sit the ham hocks in a large heavy-bottomed pan and cover with water. Bring to a boil, then reduce to a simmer, partially cover, and cook gently for 1 hour. Remove the hams and reserve the ham stock, if you wish to use it instead of the vegetable stock (it can be salty). When the hams are cool enough to handle, remove the skin and discard, then sit the hams in a large flameproof casserole.

2 Add all the other ingredients to the casserole, using either the stock or the cooking liquid, and tuck the hams in neatly. Season with salt and pepper, cover, and put in the oven for 2 hours. Check occasionally that it's not drying out, adding a little hot water if necessary.

3 Remove the hams, shred the meat, and stir it into the casserole. Serve with baked or roast potatoes.

variation

ham hock with white cabbage and celery

At step 2, add 1 small shredded white cabbage instead of red, and 2 chopped celery stalks along with the other onions, garlic, and thyme. Omit the raisins, nutmeg, and cinnamon and add 1 tbsp caraway seeds. Cook as before. Serve with plain boiled potatoes.

roast leg of pork with orange

This is easy to adapt for a cooked ham or fresh ham on the bone (bake for 1 hour only). It is also excellent cold, so it is worth cooking even if you don't have a crowd to feed.

 20-25 MINS   3 HRS 30 MINS - 4 HRS

SERVES 8-10

1 leg of pork or pork shoulder, total weight about 10lb (4.5kg)

8 oranges

1 tbsp Dijon mustard

1 cup dark brown sugar

20 cloves

small bunch of watercress

For the sauce

¼ cup Grand Marnier

½ tsp grated nutmeg

½ tsp ground cloves

1 Preheat the oven to 350°F (180°C). Wipe the pork with paper towels, then set it in a roasting pan. Halve 6 of the oranges and squeeze out the juice. There should be about 2 cups.

2 Pour some of the orange juice over the pork and roast in the oven for 3–3½ hours, pouring more orange juice over every 30 minutes or so to keep it moist. Slice the remaining oranges, discarding any seeds.

3 To test if the pork is cooked, insert a metal skewer for 30 seconds near the center of the leg; it should be warm to the touch when withdrawn. A meat thermometer should show 170°F (77°C).

4 Remove the pork from the oven and let it cool slightly. Increase the heat to 400°F (200°C). Cut through the skin around the bone end of the joint. With a knife, peel the skin from the fat, starting from the wider end of the joint.

5 Mix the mustard and sugar together. Spread and press over the pork. Overlap the orange slices over the joint and stud each one with a clove. Roast for 30–45 minutes, basting with the juices every 10 minutes. Transfer to a warmed serving platter. Remove the orange slices and arrange next to the pork. Cover with foil and keep warm.

6 Pour the Grand Marnier into the roasting pan. Bring to a boil and whisk to dissolve the juices. Add the nutmeg and cloves and mix them in. Transfer to a sauce boat.

7 Carve the pork and serve on warmed plates with the orange slices, adding a little watercress, if you like. Serve the sauce separately.

jamaican-style fish with sweet potatoes

In Jamaica, typical West Indian fish species such as snapper and tilapia would be used for this dish, but flounder, pollack, and sustainable cod are good seasonal choices.

 15 MINS   30 MINS

SERVES 4

1 tsp allspice

1 tsp paprika

2in (5cm) piece of fresh ginger, peeled and finely sliced

2 red or jalapeño chiles, seeded and finely chopped

1 tbsp olive oil

salt and freshly ground black pepper

4 x 7oz (200g) fillets of firm-fleshed white fish, such as haddock, hake, or sustainable cod

4 sweet potatoes, peeled and cut into bite-sized pieces

small handful of cilantro, finely chopped

1 Preheat the oven to 375°F (190°C). Mix the allspice, paprika, ginger, and chiles with the olive oil. Add a pinch of salt and lots of pepper. Smother the fish with most of the spice mixture and set aside. Toss the sweet potatoes with the remaining spice mixture and place in a roasting pan. Put in the oven to roast for 15 minutes.

2 Add the fish to the roasting pan and roast for 15 minutes, or until the potatoes are cooked—the fish will be cooked by then as well. Sprinkle with cilantro and serve.

cheesy swiss chard crepes

Most greens can be substituted for the chard in this recipe.

 1 HR PLUS STANDING   30-35 MINS

SERVES 6

1 quantity crepe batter (p147)

3-4 tbsp vegetable oil

For the filling

1lb 10oz (750g) Swiss chard

2 tbsp butter

2 garlic cloves, finely chopped

3 shallots, finely chopped

3oz (85g) soft goat cheese

4½oz (125g) feta cheese

salt and freshly ground black pepper

pinch of grated nutmeg

For the cream sauce

1 cup milk

2 tbsp butter

2 tbsp all-purpose flour

½ cup heavy cream

pinch of grated nutmeg

1oz (30g) Gruyère cheese, grated

1 First make the crepes as on p147 to make a total of 12. Pile them on a plate so they stay moist and warm.

2 Cut off the chard leaves and cut the stems into ½in (1cm) slices. Boil the leaves in salted water for 2-3 minutes until tender. Drain, then chop.

3 Heat the butter in a frying pan. Add the garlic and shallots and cook until soft but not browned. Add the chard stalks and sauté for 3-5 minutes, stirring. Add the leaves and sauté for 2-3 minutes, stirring, until all moisture has evaporated. Take the pan off the heat and crumble in the goat cheese, then the feta. Add salt, pepper, and a pinch of nutmeg. Stir to mix, then set aside.

4 Preheat the oven to 350°F (180°C). Butter a baking dish. To make the sauce, scald the milk in a pan. Melt the butter in another pan over medium heat. Whisk in the flour and cook for 30-60 seconds, until foaming.

5 Remove from the heat, cool slightly, then whisk in the milk. Return to the heat and whisk until it boils and thickens. Whisk in the cream. Season with salt, pepper, and nutmeg, and simmer for 2 minutes. Keep warm.

6 Put 2 spoonfuls of filling on one half of the paler side of a crepe. Fold the crêpe in half, then in half again, to form a triangle. Arrange in the dish, then continue. Spoon over the sauce. Sprinkle with the Gruyère. Bake for 20-25 minutes, until bubbling and brown. Serve hot from the dish.

beef with soy sauce, lime, and grapefruit and ginger salsa

The winter citrus salsa is spiced up with fiery chile to add a refreshing sweet-hot dimension to this dish.

 10 MINS   15 MINS

SERVES 4

1 tbsp peanut oil or sunflower oil

1 red onion, cut into 8 wedges

1½lb (675g) flank steak, cut into strips

1 red chile, seeded and finely sliced into strips

splash of dark soy sauce

juice of 1 lime

1 tbsp honey

7oz (200g) crimini mushrooms, cleaned and sliced

small handful of cilantro

For the grapefruit and ginger salsa

2 grapefruit, segmented and chopped

1in (2.5cm) piece of fresh ginger, grated

1 red or jalapeño chile, seeded and finely chopped

pinch of sugar (optional)

1 First, make the salsa. Put all the ingredients in a bowl, stir, and taste. Add a little sugar, if you wish. Set aside.

2 Heat the oil in a wok over high heat until hot. Add the onion and stir-fry for about 5 minutes until soft, before adding the beef strips and chile. Continue to stir-fry for another 5 minutes or so, keeping everything moving in the wok. Add the soy sauce, lime juice, and honey, and keep stir-frying.

3 Throw in the mushrooms and stir-fry for a few minutes until they are soft and begin to release their juices.

4 To serve, pile the cilantro on top of the beef and serve immediately with the grapefruit salsa and rice or noodles.

mustard chicken casserole

Chicken and mustard is a classic combination—and in this recipe, mustard is mixed with honey for a sweet marinade. If you have the time, let the chicken marinate for a few hours.

 10 MINS PLUS MARINATING   1 HR 45 MINS
❄ FREEZABLE

SERVES 4-6

2 tbsp whole-grain mustard

1 tbsp English or Dijon mustard

2 tbsp honey

8 chicken thighs, with skin on

salt and freshly ground black pepper

2 tbsp olive oil

2 onions, coarsely chopped

10oz (300g) parsnips, coarsely chopped

1 tbsp thyme leaves

3 cups hot vegetable or chicken stock

small bunch of flat-leaf parsley, finely chopped

1 Preheat the oven to 325°F (160°C). Mix together the mustards in a bowl and stir in the honey. Season the chicken thighs well with salt and pepper, then smother them with the mustard mixture. Cover and let marinate for at least 30 minutes and up to 2 hours.

2 Heat half the oil in a large flameproof casserole over medium-high heat and add the chicken thighs, a few at a time. Cook for 6–10 minutes until golden—be careful, as the honey may cause them to blacken quickly. Remove and set aside.

3 Heat the remaining oil in the casserole over medium heat, add the onions, and toss them around the casserole to coat in any juices. Stir to scrape up the sticky bits from the bottom, then add the parsnips and thyme. Pour in the stock, bring to a boil, then reduce to a simmer. Return the chicken to the casserole together with any juices, nestling them in between the parsnips and making sure they are covered in liquid. Season, cover, and put in the oven for 1½ hours. Check occasionally that it's not drying out, and add a little hot water, if needed. Add the parsley, taste, and season. Serve with steamed leeks or greens.

turkey and cranberry casserole

This festive stew is an excellent use for leftover turkey.

 15 MINS   1 HR 15 MINS - 1 HR 45 MINS   ❄ FREEZABLE

SERVES 4-6

2 large turkey breasts

salt and freshly ground black pepper

2-3 tbsp olive oil

4 sausages, sliced

1 red onion, finely chopped

3 garlic cloves, finely chopped

9oz (250g) crimini mushrooms, quartered

a few sprigs of rosemary

1 tbsp Dijon mustard

1 cup red wine

2 cups hot chicken stock

handful of fresh cranberries

9oz (250g) thin green beans, trimmed

1 Preheat the oven to 325°F (160°C). Season the turkey and heat half the oil in a flameproof casserole over medium-high heat. Cook the turkey in the casserole for 6–8 minutes; remove and set aside.

2 Heat the remaining oil in the casserole and cook the sausage for 3–4 minutes until it starts to color. Add the onion, and cook for 2–3 minutes until soft. Stir in the garlic, mushrooms, rosemary, and mustard, cook for a minute, then increase the heat and add the wine. Let the sauce bubble for a minute, add the stock, and bring to a boil.

3 Return the turkey to the casserole, add seasoning, and stir in the cranberries. Cover with the lid and put in the oven for 1–1½ hours. Check occasionally that it's not drying out, adding a little hot water, if needed. Add the beans for the last 15 minutes of cooking. Remove the rosemary and the turkey breasts and shred the meat with a fork. Return the meat to the casserole and stir. Serve with creamy mashed potatoes.

stuffed roast goose

A rich roasted goose is a traditional treat at Christmas time.

 40 MINS PLUS RESTING   3 HRS

SERVES 6-8

10lb (4.5kg) goose with giblets

4 onions, finely chopped

10 sage leaves, chopped

1¾oz (50g) butter

4oz (115g) fresh bread crumbs

salt and freshly ground black pepper

1 large egg yolk

2 tbsp all-purpose flour

tart apple sauce, to serve

1 Preheat the oven to 450°F (230°C). Remove excess fat from inside the goose. Prick the skin. Make a stock with the giblets, reserving the liver.

2 Boil the onions and chopped liver in a little water for 5 minutes, then drain. Mix with the sage, butter, and bread crumbs, and season. Bind with the egg. Stuff loosely into the neck end of the goose and sew or secure with a skewer. Any leftover stuffing can be cooked separately in a small roasting pan. Cover the wings and drumsticks with foil.

3 Place the goose upside down on a rack in a deep roasting pan. Roast for 1 hour, turning the goose over after 30 minutes. Drain and reserve the fat in the roasting pan. Cover the goose with foil, lower the heat to 375°F (190°C), and roast for 1½ hours. Drain the fat. Remove the foil and roast for a final 30 minutes. Transfer to a serving dish and let it rest for 30 minutes.

4 For the gravy, simmer the reserved giblet stock. Heat 3 tbsp of goose fat in a pan, stir in the flour, and cook for 5 minutes over low heat. Slowly whisk in the hot stock to thicken the gravy. Add the gravy to the roasting pan after removing the fat, stirring up the brown juices. Strain the gravy.

5 Carve the goose and serve with the gravy, stuffing, and a tart apple sauce.

festive wild rice salad

This tastes even better a few hours after cooking, so it is an ideal buffet party dish. You can prepare the wild rice salad a day ahead and keep it, covered, in the fridge. Let it come to room temperature before adding the turkey and serving.

 30–35 MINS PLUS STANDING   **45 MINS - 1 HR 15 MINS**

SERVES 4

salt and freshly ground black pepper

7oz (200g) wild rice

3oz (85g) fresh cranberries

2 tbsp sugar

1oz (30g) pecans

julienned zest and juice of 1 small
  orange

2 tbsp cider vinegar

1 shallot, very finely chopped

¼ cup vegetable oil

7oz (200g) sliced, smoked turkey breast

1 Put 2½ cups water in a saucepan with ½ tsp salt and bring to a boil. Stir in the rice, cover, and simmer for about 1 hour, or until tender. Drain, cool, then pour into a large bowl. Set aside.

2 Preheat the oven to 375°F (190°C). Spread the cranberries in a baking dish, sprinkle with the sugar, and bake in the heated oven for 10–15 minutes, until they start to pop. Let cool in the dish. Set aside.

3 Spread the pecans on a baking sheet and bake for 5–8 minutes, stirring occasionally, until toasted, then coarsely chop.

4 Bring a small saucepan of water to a boil and add the julienned orange zest. Simmer for 2 minutes, then drain and finely chop. Set aside.

5 Put the orange juice, vinegar, shallots, salt, and pepper into a bowl. Gradually whisk in the oil so the dressing emulsifies and thickens

slightly. Taste for seasoning. Add the cranberries, leaving their juice behind, and stir.

6 If necessary, remove the skin from the cooked turkey breast. Add the pecans, orange zest, and two-thirds of the dressing to the rice. Toss and let stand for 1 hour, to let the flavors combine. Taste for seasoning. To serve, transfer the rice salad to a platter, arrange the turkey on top, and spoon over the remaining cranberry dressing.

Season's best **turkey**

Mostly reared for Thanksgiving and Christmas in winter, with some in spring for Easter, turkey is a popular choice because of its unique flavor. It is a good, low-fat source of protein. Choose free-range birds, such as bronze turkeys, for ethical reasons and for better flavor. Cranberries are a favorite pairing, but it is also great with sweet spices, fragrant herbs, chestnuts, mushrooms, and citrus.

The breast has tender, white meat; good cooked any way.

Turkey (whole) Whole birds can be very large. It is best to start roasting them breast-down to ensure the white meat stays succulent and that the thicker bone areas cook through.

The leg and thigh have dark meat; roast, stew, or casserole.

The wing has high bone-to-meat ratio; good stewed or casseroled.

Diced turkey Leg meat is darker than breast meat, but when slowly cooked, is very succulent. It is best suited to stews and pies, or for grinding.

Breast is the whitest and most tender meat on a turkey.

Breast steak A slice of lean turkey breast is good for poaching, grilling, or frying. If skinless, it may be called a breast filet. When sliced or beaten out very thinly it is called an escalope. It can also be diced or sliced for stir-frying.

Leg One of the cheapest cuts, the leg comprises the thigh and the drumstick (or, from a very large bird, just the drumstick to serve several people). It can be roasted, but is often better stewed or braised.

Turkey drumstick has darker meat and includes some sinew.

Bard with bacon or baste with butter to prevent drying.

Boneless breast joint A tender joint for roasting. One breast makes a slim joint; both breasts together are plumper. The two boneless breasts sold joined, but untied, is called a butterfly, which you can stuff and tie yourself.

how to carve a turkey

This technique is suitable for turkey and other plump-breasted poultry, such as chicken or pheasant. Before carving, let the roasted bird rest a while in a warm place (on a plate to collect any juices). This relaxes the flesh, softens it, and makes it easier to carve. Use a sharp carving knife and fork to make the process of carving easier.

1 Cut through the leg joint, then cut it in half to separate the drumstick from the thigh. Repeat on the other side.

2 To remove the breast, slice down along a side of the breastbone, cut through the joint, repeat the other side.

3 Cut the breast portions in half on a slight diagonal, leaving a good piece of breast meat attached to the wings.

4 To carve the breast meat only, make a horizontal cut above the wing. Continue to slice along the same line.

essentials
cuts available

Whole birds, breast steak, boneless breast joint, crown, large turkey drumstick with or without thigh, wings, diced meat, ground, sausages. Also available smoked.

buy Sold both fresh and frozen, whole or in pieces. For roasting, select one with a plump breast.

store Remove giblets and store separately. Whole birds and pieces will keep well in the bottom of the fridge for several days, completely wrapped.

cook Grill, fry, or stir-fry breast cuts; these and legs can also be stewed. Diced turkey can be stewed or stir-fried, or grilled or cooked on skewers. Use as a lean substitute for beef in many dishes, or ground for burgers.

preserve Freeze fresh meat.

recipe ideas

Roast turkey with parsley and onion stuffing p382

Turkey and cranberry casserole p378

Turkey broth p362

Turkey scallops stuffed with prunes and pecans p383

roast turkey with parsley and onion stuffing

The classic dish at Christmas, this recipe is too good to save for only once in the season. Try stuffing the turkey cavity with 4 lemon halves to add a zesty flavor to the meat.

 15 MINS   3 HRS 20 MINS

SERVES 8

18 tbsp butter

3 onions (1 finely chopped, 2 quartered)

1 cup white bread crumbs

handful of flat-leaf parsley, finely chopped

salt and freshly ground black pepper

9lb (4kg) turkey

1 First, make the stuffing. Melt half the butter in a pan over low heat, add the chopped onion, and cook gently until soft. Remove from the heat, stir in the bread crumbs and parsley, season, and set aside to cool. Preheat the oven to 400°F (200°C). Sit the turkey in a large roasting pan and season, inside and out. Spread the remaining butter over the skin. Stuff the onion quarters into the body cavity and the stuffing into the neck end. Roast for 20 minutes, then reduce the oven temperature to 375°F (190°C).

2 Cover the turkey loosely with foil and roast for 20 minutes per 1lb (450g), plus 20 minutes. Baste every hour with juices from the pan. Pierce the bird with a skewer. If the juices run clear, it is ready; if not, cook for a little longer. Remove the foil for the last 10–15 minutes.

3 Remove the turkey from the pan and put on a large warmed plate. Cover with foil and let rest in a warm place for 15 minutes. Serve slices of turkey with gravy, roast potatoes, cranberry sauce, and seasonal vegetables.

variation

roast turkey with sage and bacon stuffing

For the stuffing, prepare in the same way, but add 2 slices thick-cut bacon, finely diced, with the onion. Use 4oz 1 cup whole wheat bread crumbs instead of white, and a handful of fresh sage instead of the parsley. Season and use as before.

warm turkey and chickpea salad

A creative alternative to cold turkey the day after Thanksgiving, this salad is light and healthy—great when you're feeling a bit guilty about the previous day's excesses!

 15 MINS   10 MINS

SERVES 4

1 x 14oz (400g) can chickpeas, drained and rinsed

1 tbsp olive oil

pinch of mild paprika

juice of 1 lemon

salt and freshly ground black pepper

12oz (350g) leftover roast turkey, sliced or coarsely shredded

handful of dill, finely chopped

1 Put the chickpeas in a pan, pour in the oil, add the paprika and lemon juice, and season well with salt and pepper. Simmer very gently over low heat for 5–8 minutes, until the chickpeas have softened slightly and warmed through.

2 To serve, toss the chickpeas with the leftover turkey, taste, and season again if needed. Scatter over the dill and serve warm with a fresh green salad or some wilted spinach.

variation

warm white bean and turkey salad

Make in the same way but use a 14oz (400g) can cannellini beans instead of chickpeas. Add 1 large crushed garlic clove to the beans when simmering, and add a small handful each of chopped fresh flat-leaf parsley and cilantro instead of the dill.

turkey scallops stuffed with prunes and pecans

Turkey scallops are very easy to make from the breasts. Serve these sweetened versions with sautéed potatoes and wilted spinach. .

 15 MINS   15–20 MINS

SERVES 4

2 boneless, skinless turkey breasts, about 14oz (400g) each

large handful of pitted prunes, chopped

handful of roasted pecans, finely chopped

handful of flat-leaf parsley, chopped

1 tbsp olive oil

1 Preheat the oven to 400°F (200°C). Cut each turkey breast in half and sandwich the 4 pieces between sheets of plastic wrap. Pound them with a meat hammer or the edge of a rolling pin until they are an even thickness of about ¼in (5mm). Remove the plastic wrap and slice the breasts in half so that you now have 8 scallops.

2 Mix the prunes and nuts with the parsley in a bowl, then spoon the mixture into the middle of each turkey scallop. Roll up from one narrow end and secure with a cocktail stick.

3 Sit the turkey rolls in a roasting pan, drizzle with the oil, and roast in the oven for 15–20 minutes, until cooked through. Serve with sautéed potatoes and wilted spinach.

variation

pork scallops with tangerine, prunes, and chestnuts
Prepare in exactly the same way, but use 4 small boneless pork chops instead of the turkey breasts. Beat out as before. For the stuffing, use the grated zest and chopped segments of 1 tangerine instead of half the prunes, and a handful of cooked, peeled chestnuts instead of the pecans. Add a good pinch of ground cinnamon with the chopped parsley.

baked turkey rolls filled with chestnuts and mushrooms

Catch fresh chestnuts at the end of their season by combining them with apricots, parsley, and delicate turkey breast in this impressive yet simple dish.

 20 MINS   40 MINS

SPECIAL EQUIPMENT ▪ blender or food processor

SERVES 4

1¼lb (550g) boneless, skinless turkey breasts, cut into 3in (7.5cm) strips

salt and freshly ground black pepper

3½oz (100g) cooked, peeled chestnuts

2 garlic cloves, grated or finely chopped

small handful of flat-leaf parsley, finely chopped

2½oz (75g) dried apricots

10oz (300g) crimini mushrooms

½ tsp dried thyme

¼ cup olive oil

1 Preheat the oven to 350°F (180°C). Season the turkey strips with a little salt and pepper and set aside. Meanwhile, put the chestnuts, garlic, and parsley in a blender or food processor and pulse for 10 seconds. Add the apricots and mushrooms and pulse for another 5 seconds. Add the thyme and 3 tbsp of the oil and pulse for 5 seconds, or until you have a chunky paste. Season well with salt and pepper.

2 Place 1 tbsp of the mixture on each turkey strip and carefully roll it up. Place the rolls join-down in a baking dish, making sure they are quite tightly packed. Drizzle with the remaining oil, cover with foil, and bake in the oven for 30 minutes. Remove the foil and cook for another 10 minutes, or until brown. Serve with a crisp green salad.

variation

baked turkey rolls with celery, chestnuts, and chanterelles
Prepare in the same way, but pulse a coarsely chopped celery stalk in the food processor with the chestnuts. Substitute 2 tbsp raisins for the apricots, and use 5oz (140g) each of chanterelle mushrooms or button mushrooms, instead of criminis.

squash, sage, and blue cheese risotto

Blue cheese and sage are a winning winter combination. Cut the squash into equal-sized pieces to help it cook evenly.

 15 MINS   30 MINS

SERVES 4

1 butternut squash, halved, seeded, peeled, and cut into bite-sized pieces

pinch of chile flakes

2 tbsp olive oil

4 cups light vegetable stock

pat of butter

1 onion, finely chopped

salt and freshly ground black pepper

2 garlic cloves, grated or finely chopped

4 sage leaves, torn

12oz (350g) risotto rice, such as Arborio

1 cup dry white wine

2½oz (75g) Gorgonzola or similar blue cheese

1 Preheat the oven to 400°F (200°C). Put the squash in a roasting pan, sprinkle with the chile flakes, and drizzle with 1 tbsp of the oil. Mix together, using your hands. Roast in the oven for about 15 minutes until golden and beginning to soften.

2 Meanwhile, pour the stock into a large pan and heat to a gentle simmer. Heat the remaining oil and

a pat of butter in a large non-stick frying pan over low heat. Add the onion and a pinch of salt and cook for 5 minutes until the onions are soft and translucent. Stir in the garlic and sage leaves and cook for a few seconds more.

3 Next, stir in the rice, making sure that the grains are completely coated. Increase the heat to medium-high, pour in the wine, and let it simmer for a couple of minutes until the alcohol has evaporated.

4 Reduce the heat slightly and add the simmering stock a ladleful at a time, stirring frequently with a wooden spoon; when each addition of stock has been absorbed, add some more. Continue like this for about 20 minutes until the rice is al dente and creamy. Use more or less stock as required. Stir in the roasted squash and the Gorgonzola cheese, season with salt and black pepper, and serve immediately.

garbure

This winter vegetable and pancetta one-pot recipe from southwest France is best made the day before and reheated.

 40 MINS   1 HR

SERVES 4–6

3½oz (100g) diced bacon or pancetta

1 Spanish onion, finely chopped

3 garlic cloves, grated or finely chopped

1 leg confit of duck

5½ cups chicken stock

1 small Savoy cabbage, core removed and leaves cut into 1 x 3in (2.5 x 7.5cm) strips

1 large carrot, sliced

1 celery stalk, diced

1 leek, cleaned and sliced

1 large russet potato, peeled and diced

salt and freshly ground black pepper

1 tsp pimentón picante or hot smoked paprika

½ tsp ground cumin

2–3 sprigs of thyme

2–3 sprigs of flat-leaf parsley, plus 1 tbsp finely chopped parsley, to garnish

9oz (250g) can white beans, drained, rinsed, and drained again

1 Put a large, deep, heavy-bottomed casserole pan over medium heat, add the bacon or pancetta, and cook,

stirring frequently, for 2–3 minutes or until crisp and cooked through. Remove with a slotted spoon and drain on paper towels. Add the onion and garlic to the pan, reduce the heat a little, and cook, stirring frequently, for 5–8 minutes or until softened.

2 Pick the meat from the duck leg, discarding the skin and bones but reserving the fat, and cut into shreds. Stir into the onion and garlic, then add the stock, cabbage, carrot, celery, leek, and potato. Season lightly with salt and more generously with pepper, then add the pimentón or paprika, cumin, thyme, and parsley. Bring to a simmer, cover, reduce the heat a little, and cook, stirring occasionally, for 30 minutes.

3 Removet the thyme and parsley. Lightly mash the beans in a bowl, then stir them into the soup and continue cooking until the vegetables are tender. Taste and season. To serve, stir in the reserved bacon or pancetta and 1 tbsp of the duck fat, then sprinkle with the parsley.

kichidi

A warming Indian lentil dish with spiced butternut squash.

 15 MINS   50 MINS   FREEZABLE

SERVES 4

1 butternut squash, about 1lb 9oz (700g), halved and seeded

½ tsp garam masala

salt and freshly ground black pepper

2 tbsp olive oil

3½oz (100g) basmati rice

3½oz (100g) pink or red lentils

2in (5cm) piece of fresh ginger, peeled and grated

2 tbsp ghee or clarified butter

2 tsp cumin seeds

½ tsp red chile flakes

juice of 1 lime

3 tbsp chopped cilantro

2 tbsp unsalted butter

1 Preheat the oven to 400°F (200°C). Put the squash halves in a roasting pan, cut side up, sprinkle with the

garam masala, season, and drizzle with the oil. Cover with foil and roast for 45 minutes, or until meltingly tender. Let cool, then scoop out the flesh, lightly crush it with a fork, and set aside.

2 Meanwhile, combine the rice and lentils in a large saucepan and cover with 7 cups water. Add the ginger, bring to a boil, then simmer for about 30 minutes until the grains have broken down. Add more water if needed. Stir in the squash.

3 Heat the ghee in a separate pan and cook the cumin and chile for about 30 seconds until darker in color. Add the spices and ghee into the rice and lentils and stir, seasoning well. Stir in the lime juice and cilantro. Serve with a generous dollop of butter in the center of each helping.

pasta and mussel salad

The spiral fusilli pasta absorbs this gorgeous, tart dressing wonderfully, although hollow shells or macaroni would be good too. The pasta perfectly complements the texture of the mussels. This can be made 1 day ahead, covered, and refrigerated. When juicing your lemons, if you first roll them on a hard surface, you will find that you are able to extract more juice.

 30–35 MINS   8–10 MINS

SERVES 4-6

juice of 2 lemons ¼ cup

4 shallots, finely chopped

3 garlic cloves, finely chopped

salt and freshly ground black pepper

¾ cup olive oil

bunch of tarragon, leaves picked and finely chopped

bunch of parsley, leaves picked and finely chopped

2¼lb (1kg) mussels, scrubbed and debearded (discard any that do not close when tapped)

⅔ cup dry white wine

9oz (250g) fusilli pasta

3 scallions, trimmed and sliced

1 Whisk together the lemon juice, half the shallots, garlic, salt, and pepper. Gradually whisk in the oil, so the dressing emulsifies and thickens slightly. Whisk in the herbs. Taste for seasoning and set aside.

2 Scrape each mussel with a small knife to remove any barnacles, then detach and discard any weed or "beard." Scrub under cold, running water; discard any with broken shells or those that do not close when gently tapped.

3 Put the wine, remaining shallots, and plenty of black pepper in a large saucepan. Bring to a boil and simmer for 2 minutes. Add the mussels, cover, and cook over high heat for 4–5 minutes, stirring occasionally, just until the mussels open.

4 Transfer the mussels to a large bowl, discarding the cooking liquid and any that have not opened. Leave until they are cool enough to handle.

5 With your fingers, remove the mussels from their shells, reserving 4–6 mussels in their shells. Pull off and discard the rubbery ring from around each shelled mussel and put them in a large bowl.

6 Briskly whisk the herb vinaigrette and pour it over the mussels.

7 Stir gently, so all the mussels are well coated with dressing. Cover and refrigerate while cooking the pasta.

8 Cook the pasta in a large pan of boiling salted water for about 8–10 minutes, or until it is tender but still al dente. Stir occasionally to keep from sticking. Drain, rinse with cold water, and drain again.

9 Pour the pasta into the bowl of mussels and dressing. Sprinkle the scallions over the pasta, add salt and pepper, toss well, and taste for seasoning. Arrange on 4–6 plates. Garnish each serving with a reserved mussel in its shell, adding a lemon wedge and tarragon sprig, if you like.

Season's best **celery root**

Also known as celeriac, the thick rough skin conceals white flesh that tastes more strongly of celery than celery itself. The peak season is late fall through winter. It has a creamy texture when cooked, which makes it perfect for puréeing. It also makes delicious low-carbohydrate chips. Try it with other roots, mayonnaise, citrus, or walnuts. It is also good with fish and seafood.

Celery root grows best in cool temperate regions but cannot stand harsh frosts. When harvested in early winter, if undamaged, it can be stored well right through to spring.

Celery root What it lacks in looks, celery root makes up with great flavor. It has a thick, gnarled skin that needs to be peeled before use.

The best celery root is firm and wrinkle-free. Old corms are tough and can be tasteless.

essentials
varieties available

Corms vary in size from a tennis ball to a saucer.

buy Choose roots that are at least the size of a small grapefruit. They should feel heavy and be firm to the touch, especially at the top where the leaves emerged.

store Keep for up to 2 weeks, unpeeled, in a paper bag in the vegetable drawer of the fridge, but is best used as fresh as possible.

cook Steam, boil, braise, roast, fry, or use in soups and stews. After boiling until tender, purée and mix with an equal amount of mashed potato. Add diced celery root with celery to poultry stuffings. Eat raw in salads.

preserve Pickle alone or with other vegetables.

recipe ideas

Beef and celery root casserole with stout and anchovies p387

Celery root rémoulade with carrot salad p406

Celery root soufflé pie p374

Chicken broth with celery root and orange p450

Chicken with garlic and spiced celery root p387

Grilled sweet potato and celery root p395

how to prepare celery root

Unlike some vegetables, it is important to peel thickly to remove all traces of dark skin from the celery root. Always place it in a bowl of acidulated water (water with 1 tbsp lemon juice added) after cutting until ready to use, as it discolors quickly.

1 Holding the celery root firmly, thickly peel the corm to remove all gnarled skin using a sharp chef's knife.

2 Cut the peeled celery root in slices, then cut into chunks, grate, dice, or julienne as required.

chicken with garlic and spiced celery root

Celery root is such a versatile root vegetable. Spiced with curry powder and served with tender chicken, this recipe allows its texture and flavor to come to the forefront.

 25 MINS 45 MINS

SERVES 4

8 chicken thighs, with skin on

salt and freshly ground black pepper

2 tbsp olive oil

4 whole bulbs of garlic, unpeeled, tops sliced off

4 large potatoes, peeled and chopped into bite-sized cubes

1 large celery root or 2 small celery root, peeled and chopped into bite-sized pieces

1-2 tsp mild curry powder

1 Preheat the oven to 400°F (200°C). Season the chicken well with salt and pepper. Put half the oil in a large roasting pan and heat on the stove top over high heat. When very hot, add the chicken pieces, skin-side down, and cook for 5–8 minutes, or until browned all over, then remove the pan from the heat.

2 Add the garlic and toss with the oil. Toss the potatoes and celery root with the remaining oil and curry powder, season well with salt and pepper, and add to the pan.

3 Put in the oven to roast for 45 minutes, or until the chicken and potatoes are cooked and golden. Give the potatoes and celery root a turn halfway through, then keep an eye on them to make sure they don't burn. Serve with wilted spinach.

variation

chicken with garlic, preserved lemons, and pumpkin

Prepare in the same way, but substitute ½ pumpkin (total weight about 1lb 10oz/750g), seeded, peeled, and cut into chunks for the celery root; add 2 preserved lemons, cut in slices, to the pan. Use 1–2 tsp ground cumin instead of curry powder.

beef and celery root casserole with stout and anchovies

A hearty stew, perfect for Sunday lunch. Stout helps to tenderize the beef and adds a malty flavor to the stock.

 30 MINS 2 HRS ❄ FREEZABLE

SERVES 4

1¼lb (550g) beef stew meat, cut into bite-sized pieces

salt and freshly ground black pepper

1½ tbsp olive oil

1 onion, finely chopped

handful of fresh thyme sprigs

4 salted anchovies

½ large celery root, peeled and cut into bite-sized pieces

1 cup bottle stout

2 cups hot vegetable stock

3 medium potatoes, peeled and cut into chunky pieces

1 Preheat the oven to 350°F (180°C). Season the meat with salt and pepper. Heat half the oil in a large cast-iron pan or flameproof casserole, add the meat, and cook over medium heat, stirring occasionally, for 10 minutes, or until browned all over. Remove with a slotted spoon and set aside. Heat the remaining oil in the pan, add the onion and thyme, and cook over low heat for 6–8 minutes, or until soft.

2 Stir in the anchovies, then stir in the celery root and cook for 5–8 minutes. Add a little of the stout and stir to scrape up all the sticky bits from the bottom of the pan. Add the remaining stout and the stock, season with salt and pepper, then return the meat to the pan, cover with a lid, and put in the oven for 1 hour.

3 Add the potatoes, together with a little hot water if the casserole looks dry. Cook for another 30 minutes. Serve immediately with chunks of crusty white bread.

variation

beef and carrot casserole

Prepare in the same way but substitute 4 coarsely chopped carrots for the celery root. Add the carrots to the casserole in step 2 after the anchovies, then continue as in the original recipe.

venison, shallot, and chestnut hotpot

Lean venison, sweet chestnuts, dried mushrooms, and shallots together make a rich, robust casserole full of flavor.

 30 MINS   2 HRS 15 MINS   FREEZABLE

SERVES 4

2 tbsp all-purpose flour

2 tbsp thyme leaves

salt and freshly ground black pepper

1¼lb (550g) boned leg or shoulder of venison, cut into bite-sized pieces

pat of butter

2 tbsp olive oil

4½oz (125g) sliced bacon or sliced pancetta

4½oz (125g) shallots, peeled and left whole

¾ cup red wine

1¾oz (50g) dried mushrooms, such as shiitake, oyster, or porcini, soaked in 1¼ cups warm water for 20 minutes

4½oz (125g) cooked and peeled chestnuts

2 cups hot vegetable stock

3 sprigs of rosemary

1 Preheat the oven to 300°F (150°C). Put the flour, thyme, and some salt and pepper in a mixing bowl, add the venison pieces, and toss well to coat them in the seasoned flour. Heat the butter with 1 tbsp of the oil in a cast-iron pan, add the venison, and cook over medium heat, stirring frequently, for 6–8 minutes, or until it begins to color a little. Remove with a slotted spoon and set aside. Add the bacon or pancetta to the pan and stir for 5 minutes, or until brown and crispy. Remove with a slotted spoon and set aside.

2 Add the remaining oil to the pan, then add the shallots and cook over medium-low heat for 8 minutes, or until they are soft and turning golden. Return all the meat to the pan, season with black pepper, then add the wine and boil for 2 minutes while you stir to scrape up the crispy bits from the bottom of the pan.

3 Drain the mushrooms (reserving the liquid) and stir into the pan. Strain the reserved liquid and add it to the pan, too. Stir in the chestnuts, pour in the stock, then add the rosemary. Cover with a lid and put in the oven to cook for 2 hours, or until the meat is tender, adding a little hot water if necessary.

beef and parsnip casserole

This is a warming dish with tender beef and sweet parsnips. Choose parsnips that are about the size of a large carrot with firm unblemished flesh for the best flavor.

 30 MINS   1 HR 45 MINS   ❄ FREEZABLE

SERVES 4

1½ tbsp olive oil

1 onion, finely chopped

2 tbsp chopped thyme

2 garlic cloves, grated or finely chopped

salt and freshly ground black pepper

1¼lb (550g) braising steak, cut into bite-sized pieces

2 large carrots, coarsely chopped

3 small parsnips, coarsely chopped

2½ cups hot beef stock

pat of butter

7oz (200g) button mushrooms, any large ones halved

1 Preheat the oven to 350°F (180°C). Heat the oil in a cast-iron pan or flameproof casserole, add the onions, and cook over low heat for 6–8 minutes, or until soft and translucent. Stir in the thyme and garlic and season well with salt and pepper. Add the steak and cook, stirring often, for 10 minutes, or until sealed. Add the carrots, parsnips, and stock. Bring to a boil, then reduce to a simmer, cover with a lid, and put in the oven to cook for 1 hour.

2 Just before the hour is up, melt the butter in a small frying pan, add the mushrooms, and cook, stirring, for 5–8 minutes, or until golden. Add the mushrooms to the casserole and cook for another 30 minutes, adding hot stock or water if it begins to look dry. Season and serve while piping hot.

variation

venison and artichoke casserole

Prepare in exactly the same way, but use 1¼lb (550g) diced venison haunch instead of beef, and substitute 12oz (350g) Jerusalem artichokes, scrubbed or peeled and cut in chunks, instead of the parsnips. Add 3 tbsp port to the casserole with the stock.

duck with turnips and apricots

Sweet Madeira wine adds a wonderful flavor to the sauce in this dish. The recipe is suitable for wild or domestic duck.

 20 MINS PLUS STANDING   **1 HR 30 MINS - 2 HRS**

SERVES 4

1 whole duck, quartered

salt and freshly ground black pepper

1 tbsp vegetable oil

1 tbsp butter

2 tbsp all-purpose flour

⅔ cup dry white wine

2 cups hot chicken stock, plus more if needed

1 bouquet garni (made with 5-6 sprigs of parsley, 2-3 sprigs of thyme, and 1 bay leaf)

2 shallots, finely chopped

12-16 pearl onions, peeled and left whole

1lb 2oz (500g) turnips, peeled and coarsely chopped

1 tsp granulated sugar

¼ cup Madeira wine

6oz (175g) dried apricots

1 Preheat the oven to 350°F (180°C). Season the duck. Heat the oil and butter in a large flameproof casserole over low heat and add the duck, skin-side down. Cook for 20-25 minutes until it has browned and the fat has rendered. Turn over and cook for only about 5 minutes until browned. Remove and set aside, draining and reserving the duck fat. Heat 2-3 tbsp of the duck fat in the casserole. Add the flour and cook, stirring constantly, for 1-2 minutes until lightly browned but not burnt. Stir in the white wine, hot stock, bouquet garni, shallots, and seasoning, and bring to a boil. Return the duck to the casserole, cover with the lid, and cook in the oven for 40-45 minutes.

2 Meanwhile, heat 1-2 tbsp of the duck fat in a heavy-bottomed pan over medium heat. Add the onions, turnips, sugar, and seasoning and cook, stirring occasionally, for 5-7 minutes until the vegetables begin to caramelize. Add to the casserole with the Madeira wine and apricots and add hot water if necessary. Cover with the lid and return to the oven to cook for another 20-25 minutes until the duck and vegetables are tender. Skim off any fat from the surface, remove the bouquet garni, taste, and add more seasoning, if needed. Serve on warmed plates with wide noodles.

pork with potatoes and mushrooms in wine

Pork skin becomes crackly and delicious when cooked, but a skinless pork shoulder will work just as nicely.

 20 MINS   **1 HR 45 MINS**

SERVES 6

3lb (1.35kg) boneless shoulder of pork, skin scored

sea salt

2¼lb (1kg) potatoes, peeled and halved, or large ones quartered

1 tbsp olive oil

a few sprigs of rosemary

1½ cups dry white wine

9oz (250g) button mushrooms

1¼ cups hot vegetable stock

1 Preheat the oven to 425°F (220°C). Sit the pork in a large roasting pan and rub the skin all over with sea salt, ensuring it gets into all the cuts. Toss the potatoes in the oil, season with sea salt, and add to the pan along with the rosemary. Roast in the oven for 20 minutes, or until the pork skin is crispy.

2 Meanwhile, heat the wine in a pan over low heat until warm, then spoon it over the meat. Add the mushrooms, pour in the stock, then turn the oven down to 350°F (180°C) and cook for 1 hour.

3 Reduce the oven temperature to 300°F (150°C) and cook for another 30 minutes, or until the potatoes are meltingly soft and the liquid has almost disappeared. Remove from the oven and discard the rosemary. Keep warm while the pork rests for 15 minutes. Then slice the pork and serve with the potatoes and mushrooms, and some fresh crusty bread on the side.

spicy pork with caraway seeds and cabbage

Pork can take the powerful flavors of spices and other strong ingredients well. Here, chile adds heat while caraway seeds give a sharp aromatic flavor with sweet undertones.

 10 MINS   2 HRS 30 MINS

SPECIAL EQUIPMENT ▪ food processor

SERVES 4

handful of thyme sprigs, leaves only

2 garlic cloves, finely chopped

1 tbsp olive oil

1 tsp chile flakes

2½lb (1.1kg) pork belly, skin scored

salt and freshly ground black pepper

1 cup dry hard cider

½ Savoy cabbage, halved, cored, and shredded

pat of butter

½ tsp caraway seeds

1 Preheat the oven to 425°F (220°C). Put the thyme, garlic, oil, and chile flakes in a food processor and purée to a paste, then rub the paste over the pork flesh (but not the skin). Sit the pork in a roasting pan, skin-side up, and rub the skin with salt, ensuring it gets into all the cracks. Cook in the oven for 30 minutes, or until the skin is golden.

2 Reduce the oven temperature to 350°F (180°C). Pour the cider around the pork, then cover with foil, securing it around the edges of the pan, and cook for 2 hours.

3 Just before the 2 hours are up, put the cabbage in a pan of boiling salted water, and cook for 4–6 minutes, or until soft. Drain, then toss with the butter, caraway seeds, and a pinch of black pepper. Transfer to a large shallow serving bowl.

4 Slice or cut the pork into bite-sized pieces and arrange on top of the cabbage along with the juices. Serve with a spoonful of chile jelly on the side and some fresh crusty bread.

roast sweet potato and chile tortilla

Their creamy texture and mild flavor make sweet potatoes versatile enough for savory dishes and desserts. A little chile helps to cut through their spicy-sweet flavor in this tortilla.

 15 MINS   45 MINS

SERVES 4-6

1¼lb (550g) sweet potatoes, peeled and cut into ¾in (2cm) cubes

1 tsp chile flakes

5 tbsp olive oil

2 onions, finely chopped

6 large eggs

salt and freshly ground black pepper

1 Preheat the oven to 400°F (200°C). Put the sweet potatoes on a non-stick baking sheet, add the chile flakes and 2 tbsp of the oil, and mix well. Roast in the oven for 30 minutes, or until they start to brown, turning occasionally.

2 Meanwhile, put the remaining oil in a deep frying pan, add the onions, and cook over medium heat for 5 minutes, or until soft and translucent. Add the sweet potato, combine well, and let cool.

3 Break the eggs into a mixing bowl, season with salt and pepper, and beat well with a fork. Pour onto the potato and onion mixture, combine well, then pour the mixture into an oven-proof frying pan and cook over low heat for 10 minutes, or until the egg is beginning to set. Transfer the pan to the oven and cook for another 10 minutes, or until the top is golden. Turn out onto a plate and serve with a mixed salad.

variation

roast celery root and leek tortilla

Make in the same way, but use 1¼lb (550g) celery root, peeled and cut in ¾in (2cm) cubes, instead of the sweet potatoes. Sprinkle with 1 tsp chopped fresh rosemary instead of the chile flakes before roasting. Substitute 1 chopped leek for one of the chopped onions, and cook in the same way at step 2, then continue the recipe as before.

beef and herb potato pie

This reliably good recipe is an update of a French classic.

45-50 MINS   1 HR 30 MINS

SPECIAL EQUIPMENT ▪ food processor

SERVES 6

¼ cup olive oil

1 large onion, diced

4 garlic cloves, 2 of the cloves finely chopped and 2 cloves left whole

2¼lb (1kg) ground beef

salt and freshly ground black pepper

1 x 14oz (400g) can chopped tomatoes

1 cup beef stock

½ cup dry white wine

2¼lb (1kg) potatoes, peeled and each cut into chunks

handful of basil leaves

handful of flat-leaf parsley leaves

1 cup milk, plus more if needed

1 Heat one-third of the oil in a sauté or frying pan. Add the onion and cook, stirring, for 3–5 minutes until soft but not brown. Add the chopped garlic, beef, salt, pepper, and tomatoes. Reduce the heat and simmer very gently for 10–12 minutes, stirring occasionally, until the meat is brown. Stir in the stock and wine. Simmer for 25–30 minutes until most of the liquid has evaporated and the meat is still moist.

2 Boil the potatoes in a saucepan until tender. Meanwhile, pulse the herbs, the 2 whole garlic cloves, and the remaining oil to a purée in a food processor. Drain the potatoes, return them to the pan, mash them, and add the herb purée. Scald the milk in a small pan and gradually beat it into the potatoes over medium heat. Stir for 2–3 minutes until the potatoes just hold a shape. Season to taste.

3 Preheat the oven to 375°F (190°C). Brush a large shallow baking dish with oil. Spoon the meat and any liquid into the dish and cover completely with an even layer of the herb potatoes. Smooth the top with the back of a spoon, then make a scalloped pattern with the tip of a dessert spoon or the tines of a fork. Dip the spoon or fork into a bowl of hot water, set nearby, once or twice during the process so the potato does not stick to it. Bake in the oven for 35–40 minutes until the top is golden brown and the edges are bubbling with gravy. Serve immediately on warmed plates.

chicken salad with carrot and apple relish

A delicious instant salad. If you cook the chicken fresh, poach 2 boneless, skinless chicken breasts with seasoning in a shallow pan with stock for 8 minutes or until tender, then drain.

15 MINS

SERVES 4

2 handfuls of spinach leaves, rinsed

12oz (350g) cooked chicken, any skin removed, cut into bite-sized pieces

1¾oz (50g) pine nuts, toasted

1 tbsp olive oil

juice of ½ lemon

For the carrot and apple relish

2 carrots

2 sweet red apples

2 preserved lemons, finely chopped

small handful of golden raisins

salt and freshly ground black pepper

1 For the carrot and apple relish, grate the carrots into a mixing bowl. Quarter and core the apples, then grate them into the bowl with the carrot. Add the preserved lemons and golden raisins and mix together. Season with salt and pepper.

2 Lay the spinach leaves in a large shallow salad bowl or plate and top with the chicken pieces and toasted pine nuts. When ready to serve, drizzle with the oil and lemon juice and sprinkle with a pinch of salt. Serve with the carrot and apple relish.

variation

turkey salad with celery root and orange relish

For the relish, grate ½ small celery root instead of the carrots and toss immediately in 1 tsp lemon juice. Add the segments from 2 oranges instead of the grated apple, 2 tsp capers instead of the preserved lemons, and a small handful raisins. Season. Use cooked turkey instead of chicken (either poached turkey breast or leftover roast). Sprinkle with 1¾oz (50g) coarsely chopped walnuts instead of the pine nuts. Dress as before.

pork belly and prunes

Dried fruit works well with a fatty meat such as pork belly; it creates a delicious, sweet sauce that cuts through the meaty richness. The earthiness of celery root is a great addition.

 15 MINS   3 HRS – 3 HRS 30 MINS

SERVES 4–6

1 tbsp olive oil

2½lb (1.1kg) pork belly, cut into bite-sized pieces

salt and freshly ground black pepper

1 onion, finely sliced

3 garlic cloves, finely chopped

1 tbsp sherry vinegar

½ cup white wine

3 cups hot vegetable stock

5oz (140g) soft prunes, finely chopped

6 sage leaves, finely shredded

1lb 5oz (600g) celery root, peeled and chopped into bite-sized pieces

1 Preheat the oven to 325°F (160°C). Heat half of the oil in a large flameproof casserole over high heat. Season the pork belly with salt and pepper, add it (in batches, if necessary), skin-side down, and cook until it turns golden and begins to crisp a little. Remove the pork and sit it on paper towels to drain.

2 Heat the remaining oil in the casserole over medium heat, add the onion, and cook for 3–4 minutes until soft. Then stir in the garlic and cook for 1 more minute. Increase the heat and add the sherry vinegar, letting it simmer for 2–3 minutes. Pour in the wine and continue to boil for a few more minutes until the alcohol evaporates.

3 Add the stock and stir to scrape up the bits from the bottom of the casserole. Return the pork to the casserole and stir in the prunes, sage, and celery root. Bring back to a boil, cover, and put in the oven for 2½–3 hours. Check occasionally that it's not drying out, adding a little hot water, if needed. Taste and season more, if needed, and serve with creamy mashed potatoes.

beef and anchovy casserole

Serve this deep-flavored stew on cold days. The anchovies will melt into it and the redcurrant jelly adds a distinctive sweetness. It is delicious over mashed or baked potatoes.

 20 MINS   2 HRS 15 MINS – 2 HRS 45 MINS

SERVES 4–6

¼ cup olive oil, plus extra if necessary

pat of butter

12 baby onions, peeled

a few sprigs of thyme

salt and freshly ground black pepper

2½lb (1.1kg) beef chuck, cut into chunky cubes

1 tbsp all-purpose flour, seasoned with salt and pepper

2 leeks, trimmed and sliced

pinch of ground allspice

1 cup red wine

6 anchovy fillets in oil, drained and chopped

1 tbsp small capers

3 cups hot beef stock

1–2 tbsp redcurrant jelly

1 Preheat the oven to 325°F (160°C). Heat 2 tbsp of the oil and the butter in a large flameproof casserole over medium heat, then add the onions, thyme, and salt and pepper. Cook for about 10 minutes until the onions start to soften and turn translucent. Remove with a slotted spoon and set aside.

2 Toss the beef in the seasoned flour. Add more oil to the casserole, increase the heat to medium-high, and cook the beef in batches for a few minutes on each side until browned all over. Remove and set aside. Add a little more oil, stir in the leeks and allspice, and cook for about 5 minutes. Also remove and set aside.

3 Add the wine and bring to a boil, stirring to scrape up the bits from the bottom of the casserole. Let it simmer for a few minutes, then stir in the anchovies, capers, stock, and redcurrant jelly. Bring to a boil, then reduce to a simmer, return the meat, leeks, and onions to the casserole, and season again if you wish. Cover with the lid and cook in the oven for 2–2½ hours until the beef is tender. Check occasionally that it's not drying out and add a little hot water, if needed. Serve while piping hot.

cauliflower curry

Potatoes and cauliflower are tossed in a tikka coconut sauce in this simple and economical dish.

 15 MINS   1 HR

SERVES 4–6

1 tbsp vegetable oil

1 onion, coarsely chopped

salt and freshly ground black pepper

2in (5cm) piece of fresh ginger, peeled and finely chopped

3 garlic cloves, finely chopped

2 jalapeño chiles, seeded and finely chopped

2 tbsp medium-hot tikka curry paste

14oz can chickpeas, drained and rinsed

14oz can coconut milk

2 cups hot vegetable stock

3 potatoes, peeled and cut into bite-sized pieces

1 cauliflower, cut into bite-sized florets

1 Heat the oil in a large heavy-bottomed pan over medium heat, add the onion, and cook for 6–8 minutes until soft. Season, stir in the ginger, garlic, and chiles, and cook for 2–3 minutes. Stir in the tikka paste, chickpeas, coconut milk, and stock, and bring to a boil. Reduce to a simmer and cook gently, partially covered with the lid, stirring occasionally, for 30 minutes.

2 Bring another large pan of salted water to a boil. Add the potatoes and cook for 15 minutes, or until just beginning to soften. Remove with a slotted spoon and set aside. Put the cauliflower in the boiling water and cook for about 5 minutes, then drain.

3 Add the potato and cauliflower to the sauce and turn so they are well coated, then simmer gently for another 15 minutes or so. Serve with some rice and naan bread.

butternut squash pasta in chile and parmesan sauce

Ripe pumpkins and winter squashes herald the onset of early winter. This pasta dish is perfect for these cooler days, as it has the comfort of cream and the warmth of red chiles. Slow-roasting the butternut squash enhances its sweetness.

 20 MINS 35 MINS

SPECIAL EQUIPMENT ▪ food processor or blender

SERVES 4

7oz (200g) butternut squash, peeled and diced (prepared weight)

1–2 tbsp extra virgin olive oil

salt and freshly ground black pepper

1 garlic clove, crushed

½ red chile, seeded and finely chopped

8 sage leaves

⅔ cup half-and-half

scant 1oz (25g) Parmesan cheese, grated, plus extra to finish

12oz (350g) conchiglie pasta

1 Preheat the oven to 400°F (200°C). Place the squash in a roasting pan, toss it in a little of the olive oil, season well with salt and pepper, and roast it in the oven for 30 minutes, or until soft. Remove and set aside to cool for a few minutes.

2 Meanwhile, gently cook the garlic, chile, and sage in a little oil in a small saucepan or frying pan for 2–3 minutes.

3 Once the butternut squash has cooled slightly, put it into a food processor or blender. Pour in the half-and-half and add the Parmesan cheese, garlic, chile, sage leaves, plenty of black pepper, and a little salt. Pulse to a fine purée, adding 1–2 tbsp water if it looks too thick.

4 Cook the pasta until tender, but still al dente, and drain. Reheat the sauce in the pasta pan, adding more water if it seems a little stiff. Put the pasta back in the pan and mix well, allowing the sauce to coat the pasta shells. Serve hot with plenty of fresh Parmesan cheese to finish.

variation

pumpkin farfalle with blue cheese sauce

Prepare in the same way, but use 7oz (200g) peeled and diced pumpkin instead of butternut squash. Omit the chile, use 2oz (60g) blue cheese instead of the Parmesan, and farfalle pasta instead of conchiglie.

slow-cooked swedish red cabbage

This traditional recipe, full of big fruity flavors, has become a classic requirement for a big Christmas dinner, whether you are serving roast turkey or ham, or a vegetarian dish.

 20 MINS 2 HRS

SERVES 8

4 tbsp butter

2 tbsp granulated sugar

1 tsp salt

6 tbsp rice wine vinegar, or white wine or cider vinegar

1 red cabbage, approx 2¼lb (1kg), finely shredded

2 apples, peeled, cored, and grated

2 heaping tbsp redcurrant jelly

1 Preheat the oven to 300°F (150°C). In a large, heavy flameproof casserole, heat together the butter, sugar, salt, 6 tbsp water, and the vinegar. Bring to a boil and simmer for 1 minute.

2 Fold the cabbage into the liquid and bring it back to a boil. Take the casserole off the heat and cover tightly with a double layer of foil. Fit the lid on snugly and cook in the oven for 1½ hours.

3 Remove from the oven and add the grated apples and redcurrant jelly, stirring well. Add a little more water if the cabbage looks dry. Replace the foil and the lid, and return the cabbage to the oven for another 30 minutes. Serve warm.

variation

winter braised white cabbage and celery

Prepare in the same way, but substitute 1 white cabbage (about 2¼lb/ 1kg) instead of the red cabbage. Add 2 chopped celery stalks, 2 thinly sliced onions, and ¼ cup dried cranberries with the cabbage, and tuck in a bay leaf. At step 3, add the grated apples as before. Discard the bay leaf before serving.

soy and sesame-glazed sweet potatoes

The inspiration for this dish comes from a classic Japanese dish known as *daigakuimo*. It is a wonderfully simple recipe that turns the humble sweet potato into something special.

 10 MINS 40 MINS

SERVES 4

2 tbsp soy sauce

2 tbsp light brown sugar

2 tbsp rice wine

1 tbsp sesame oil

2 garlic cloves, crushed

1lb 2oz (500g) sweet potatoes, peeled and cut into wedges

1 tbsp toasted sesame seeds

1 Preheat the oven to 400°F (200°C). Put all the ingredients except the sweet potatoes and sesame seeds in a small saucepan. Bring to a boil, reduce the heat, and simmer for 2 minutes.

2 Put the potato wedges on a baking sheet or ovenproof serving dish and pour the sauce mixture over them, tossing well. Scatter the sesame seeds over the top and cover the baking sheet or dish with foil.

3 Cook for 20 minutes, then turn the oven up to 425°F (220°C). Remove the foil and cook for another 20 minutes. Turn the potatoes several times while cooking until they have absorbed all the sauce and are soft, glazed, and sticky. They are superb eaten alongside a piece of grilled mackerel and some wilted greens.

grilled sweet potato and celery root

This simple combination of vegetables makes a lovely winter side dish and is a delicious accompaniment to both roast meats and casseroles.

 10 MINS PLUS COOLING 20 MINS ❄ FREEZABLE

MAKES APPROX 2¼lb (1kg)

2 small or 1 large celery root, cut in half if small, quarters if large, and then in slices, and brushed all over with vegetable oil to prevent browning

2–3 sweet potatoes, peeled and cut into ¼in (5mm) thick slices

freshly ground black pepper

a little sweet or smoked paprika (optional)

1 Season the celery root and sweet potato on both sides with salt and black pepper and dust lightly with paprika, if using. Preheat a grill pan or electric grill and brush the vegetables with oil on both sides.

2 When the grill is very hot, but not smoking, add a single layer of vegetables (don't overcrowd them).

Press them down firmly with a metal spatula until the undersides are nicely striped. Turn the vegetables over and cook for another 2–3 minutes until just cooked and striped. Don't overcook them, or they will become too soft. If using an electric grill, close the lid and cook the slices for about 3 minutes.

3 Once the batch of vegetables are cooked until striped and just tender, transfer to a warm place while you cook the rest of the slices, reheating the grill between each batch. Then serve all the slices piping hot.

mixed vegetable purée

This purée is a great topping for cottage pie or bobotie, a South African baked curried meat dish. It also makes a delicious accompaniment to meat or poultry.

 30 MINS 30–40 MINS FREEZABLE

SPECIAL EQUIPMENT ▪ food processor or hand-held blender

MAKES APPROX 4lb (1.8kg)

1 rutabaga

1lb (450g) carrots

2 sweet potatoes

2 large turnips or 1 celery root

salt and freshly ground black pepper

4 tbsp unsalted butter

1 Peel and chop all the vegetables into evenly sized chunks or thick slices. Place in a large saucepan of cold water with a little salt. Bring to a boil, reduce the heat slightly, cover partially, and simmer for 20–25 minutes, or until all the vegetables are really tender. Drain well.

2 Purée the vegetables in a food processor or with a hand-held blender. Alternatively, use a potato ricer or mash thoroughly by hand with a potato masher.

3 Return the purée to the pan and add the butter and a good grinding of pepper. Heat gently, beating well until the butter is absorbed. Then use to top a pie before baking.

brussels sprouts with chestnuts and pancetta

A perfect foil to a Christmas meal. Although some people dislike Brussels sprouts, it is hard to find someone who doesn't like them when treated in this manner.

 10 MINS 10 MINS

SERVES 4

14oz (400g) Brussels sprouts, washed and trimmed

pat of butter

3½oz (100g) pancetta, diced

3½oz (100g) chestnuts, cooked, peeled, and coarsely chopped

1 tsp grated lemon zest

sea salt and freshly ground black pepper

1 Boil the Brussels sprouts in plenty of salted water for 5–7 minutes, depending on their size, until they are just tender, but not overcooked. Then drain well.

2 Melt the butter in a large frying pan or wok and cook the pancetta for 3–4 minutes until crispy. Add the Brussels sprouts, chestnuts, and lemon zest, and cook for 2 minutes until everything is heated through.

3 Season well with pepper and a little sea salt, to taste (you may not need much, as the pancetta can be very salty) and serve hot.

variation

brussels sprouts with whole chestnuts and sausages

Cook 14oz (400g) Brussels sprouts as before. Drain. Meanwhile, cook 8oz (225g) cocktail sausages for 4–5 minutes until cooked through. Drain on paper towels. Wipe out the pan and melt 4 tbsp butter. Add 9oz (250g) cooked, peeled chestnuts and toss in the butter until heated through and lightly golden. Add 2 tsp chopped thyme. Toss again, add the sprouts and the sausages, and toss to heat through as before. Season to taste and serve.

Season's best **cabbages and brussels sprouts**

All cabbages and Brussels sprouts are delicious raw and cooked. Brussels are traditional for the festive season but are good through to early spring. Cabbages are best in winter but varieties are available all year. Red and white ones are good with fruits, nuts, and seeds; green ones and sprouts with nuts or curry pastes and are particularly good with pork products and celery.

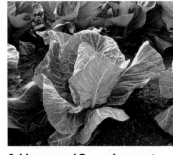

Cabbages and Brussels sprouts are hardy brassicas grown in temperate zones all over the world in different soils and are staples of the diets of many countries.

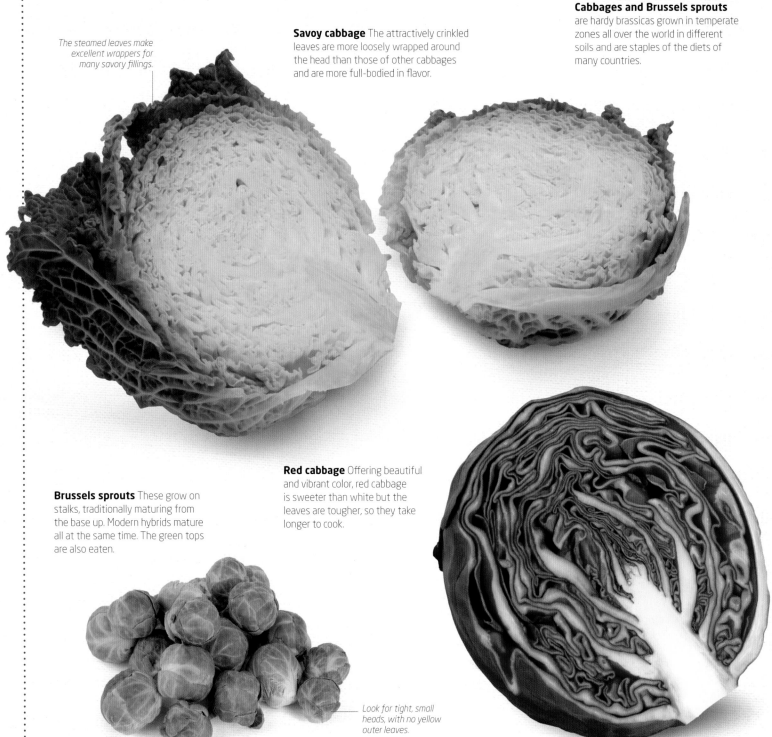

The steamed leaves make excellent wrappers for many savory fillings.

Savoy cabbage The attractively crinkled leaves are more loosely wrapped around the head than those of other cabbages and are more full-bodied in flavor.

Brussels sprouts These grow on stalks, traditionally maturing from the base up. Modern hybrids mature all at the same time. The green tops are also eaten.

Red cabbage Offering beautiful and vibrant color, red cabbage is sweeter than white but the leaves are tougher, so they take longer to cook.

Look for tight, small heads, with no yellow outer leaves.

The large outer leaves are excellent for blanching and stuffing; the heart is tender and sweet.

Round cabbage Also known as ball-head cabbage, this can be eaten raw and cooked, as most varieties of cabbage, but best suits stir-frying and braising.

White cabbage Also known as Dutch cabbage, this makes a firm head of tightly packed leaves with a solid core. It has a sweet taste and keeps particularly well.

Pointed cabbage This is also known as spring cabbage since it grows right through winter and spring into summer, when others are not available.

essentials
varieties available
Savoy, round green, pointed, red, white, and Brussels sprouts. Brussels tops are also sold as greens.

buy All heads should be tight and solid with no yellowing or damaged leaves. Choose sprouts of even size; the smaller ones are sweetest.

store Keep in a plastic bag in the vegetable drawer of the fridge; cabbages for several weeks, sprouts up to 5 days.

cook Shred or chop and eat raw in salads; or steam, boil, or braise. Add to soups, stews, and casseroles. Large leaves can be stuffed.

preserve Ferment white cabbage as sauerkraut, pickle red cabbage.

recipe ideas
Brussels sprouts with chestnuts and pancetta p395

Cabbage stuffed with chestnut and pork p367

Creamy coleslaw p399

Ham hock with red cabbage p375

Sauerkraut p421

Slow-cooked Swedish red cabbage p394

Spicy pork with caraway seeds and cabbage p390

how to core and shred cabbage
This technique applies to all varieties. For the most efficient control and action when shredding, anchor the point of the knife on the cutting board, raising and lowering the blade through the cabbage. Guide the blade with the knuckles of your other hand, keeping your fingers tucked away.

1 Hold the head of cabbage firmly on the cutting board and use a sharp knife to cut it in half, straight through the stalk end.

2 Cut the halves again through the stalk lengthwise and slice out the core from each quarter.

3 Working with each quarter at a time, place the wedge cut-side down. Cut across the cabbage, creating shreds.

red cabbage and bacon salad

A hearty salad for winter, the contrasts in taste, texture, and color are wonderful.

 20-25 MINS PLUS MARINATING   5 MINS

SERVES 6

½ head red cabbage (about 1lb 10oz/ 750g), cored and finely shredded

¼ cup red wine vinegar

9oz (250g) thick-cut bacon, sliced

leaves from 1 small romaine lettuce, chopped

3oz (85g) Roquefort cheese, crumbled

For the vinaigrette

¼ cup red wine vinegar, plus more if needed

1 tbsp Dijon mustard

salt and freshly ground black pepper

⅔ cup olive oil

1 For the vinaigrette, combine the vinegar, mustard, and a pinch of salt in a mixing bowl. Grind in the black pepper. Gradually whisk in the oil so the vinaigrette emulsifies and thickens. Then taste for seasoning.

2 Transfer the shredded cabbage to a large bowl. Boil the vinegar in a small saucepan, then pour over the cabbage and toss. Pour in 7 cups boiling water and let stand for 3–4 minutes, until slightly softened. Drain thoroughly, then return it to the large bowl. Toss the cabbage with enough vinaigrette to moisten it well. Taste for seasoning, adding more vinegar if necessary. Cover and marinate for 1–2 hours.

3 Right before serving, fry the bacon in a frying pan for 3-5 minutes or until crisp and the fat is rendered. Then spoon the hot bacon and its pan juices over the cabbage, reserving some bacon pieces for garnish, and toss them together.

4 Arrange a bed of lettuce on each of 6 plates. Spoon the remaining dressing over the lettuce. Mound the red cabbage and bacon mixture over the top. Top the salads with the crumbled blue cheese and reserved bacon and serve at once.

sweet and sour cabbage

This is a warming, slightly spicy alternative to the more traditional slow-cooked red cabbage. It is cooked on the stove (rather than baked in the oven) in just over 1 hour.

 15 MINS   1 HR 15 MINS

SERVES 8

1 tbsp olive oil

1 large red cabbage, outer leaves removed, halved, and finely shredded

2 apples, cut into bite-sized pieces

2in (5cm) piece of fresh ginger, peeled and finely sliced

¾ cup balsamic vinegar

2 tbsp brown sugar

salt and freshly ground black pepper

1 Put the oil in a large heavy-bottomed pan, add the cabbage, apple, and ginger, and cook over low heat for 10 minutes, or until the ingredients begin to soften and reduce down.

2 Add the balsamic vinegar and sugar, bring to a boil, then cover and simmer for 40–60 minutes, or until the cabbage is soft. Stir occasionally so it doesn't stick. Season well with salt and pepper and serve with roast pork or pork chops.

variation

hot and spicy white cabbage

Prepare in the same way, but use a white cabbage instead of red cabbage. Add 2 unripe pears instead of apples. Use ½ cup white distilled vinegar and 1¼ cup water instead of balsamic, and add 2–3 dried red chiles to the mix along with a large handful of golden raisins and a bouquet garni. When cooked, discard the chiles and bouquet garni before serving.

creamy coleslaw

This salad makes a generous quantity for a party, or the recipe can easily be halved. This version of the old favorite is pepped up with caraway seeds, sour cream, and mustard.

 15–20 MINS PLUS CHILLING

SPECIAL EQUIPMENT ▪ mandoline ▪ food processor

SERVES 8–10

1lb 2oz (500g) carrots, trimmed

1 white cabbage, about 3lb (1.35kg), trimmed and cut into quarters with the core removed

2 tbsp sugar

salt and freshly ground black pepper

1 cup sour cream

⅔ cup cider vinegar

2 tsp dry mustard powder

2 tsp caraway seeds

1 cup mayonnaise

1 onion, finely diced

1 Using the coarse side of a grater, grate the carrots and leave in a bowl of iced water for half an hour so they crisp up. Drain very well, then wrap in a clean kitchen towel and shake to remove all the excess water.

2 Shred the cabbage leaves into a large bowl using a mandoline, discarding any thick ribs.

Alternatively, shred the cabbage quarters in a food processor, using the slicing blade.

3 Put the sugar, salt, pepper, sour cream, and cider vinegar in a mixing bowl. Add the mustard powder and caraway seeds, then add the mayonnaise and whisk to combine. Taste for seasoning. Put the onion, carrot, and cabbage in a bowl and pour in the dressing. Stir until coated. Cover and refrigerate for at least 4 hours, so the flavors mellow.

4 Remove the coleslaw from the refrigerator and stir it once more to redistribute the dressing (you may find it has sunk to the bottom of the bowl in the refrigerator). Taste for seasoning, then serve chilled.

leeks vinaigrette

This simple, elegant dish should be prepared with the freshest leeks you can find. They can be left to marinate in the vinaigrette, covered and refrigerated, for up to 1 day.

 15–20 MINS PLUS MARINATING   15–25 MINS

SERVES 4–6

6 leeks, about 2¼lb (1kg) total weight

salt and freshly ground black pepper

3 tbsp white wine vinegar

1 tsp Dijon mustard

⅔ cup vegetable oil

2 shallots, finely chopped

1 large egg

5–7 sprigs of parsley, leaves picked and finely chopped

1 Trim the leeks, discarding the roots and green tops. Slit lengthwise, leaving the leeks attached at the root end. Wash thoroughly, fanning them out under cold, running water. Divide into 2 bundles and tie them together at each end with kitchen string. Fill a wide, shallow pan with salted water and bring to a boil. Add the leeks and simmer for about 10 minutes, or until just tender.

2 Meanwhile, whisk together the vinegar, mustard, salt, and pepper in a mixing bowl. Gradually whisk in the oil so the vinaigrette emulsifies and thickens slightly. Whisk in the shallots, then taste for seasoning.

3 Test whether the leeks are tender by piercing with the tip of a small knife. Drain in a colander, remove the

strings, pat dry with paper towels, and cut on the diagonal into 3in (7.5cm) lengths. Lay the leeks in a dish and pour in the vinaigrette. Cover and refrigerate for 1 hour or longer, if you have enough time. Then bring back to room temperature while you hard-boil and peel the egg.

4 Divide the leeks between plates. Cut the egg in half and separate the yolk from the white. Chop the white finely. Work the yolk through a sieve set over a small bowl with a spoon. Then sprinkle the leeks with parsley, the egg white, and yolk, and serve.

variation

leeks hollandaise

Cook the leeks in the same way, drain, and place in a serving dish. To make a quick Hollandaise, whisk 3 large eggs in a small saucepan with 3 tbsp lemon juice. Gradually whisk in 12 tbsp melted butter until blended. Whisk over low heat until thickened. Do not boil. Season and pour Hollandaise over the leeks. Garnish as before.

patatas bravas

This classic tapas dish features cubes of potatoes mixed with a spicy sauce. Be generous with the flat-leaf parsley as it looks great and adds contrasting taste and texture.

 15 MINS 1 HR

SERVES 4

6 tbsp olive oil

1lb 9oz (700g) white potatoes, peeled and cut into ¾in (2cm) cubes

2 onions, finely chopped

1 tsp dried chile flakes

2 tbsp dry sherry

grated zest of 1 lemon

4 garlic cloves, grated or finely chopped

1 x 7oz (200g) can chopped tomatoes

small handful of flat-leaf parsley, chopped

salt and freshly ground black pepper

1 Preheat the oven to 400°F (200°C). Heat half the oil in a non-stick frying pan, add the potatoes, and cook, turning frequently, over low heat for 20 minutes, or until starting to brown. Add the onions and cook for another 5 minutes.

2 Add the chile, sherry, lemon zest, and garlic, and allow to reduce for 2 minutes before adding the tomatoes and parsley. Season with salt and

pepper, combine well, and cook over medium heat for 10 minutes, stirring occasionally.

3 Add the remaining oil, place all the ingredients in a shallow baking dish, and cook in the oven for 30 minutes, or until cooked. Serve hot with a selection of tapas dishes.

variation

potato, celery, and parsnip bake
Prepare in the same way, but cook a combination of 12oz (350g) potatoes and 12oz (350g) parsnips, both peeled and cut into ¾in (2cm) cubes, instead of all potatoes, and add 2 thinly sliced celery stalks at the same time. Add the zest of an orange instead of lemon, and 2 tbsp chopped fresh thyme as well as the parsley.

parsnip and parmesan bread

A perfect combination of flavors to serve with a bowl of warming soup on a cold winter's day.

 20 MINS 50 MINS ❄ FREEZABLE

MAKES 1 LOAF

1¾ cups all-purpose flour

¾ cup whole wheat flour, plus 1 tsp baking powder

1 tsp baking soda

1¾oz (50g) Parmesan cheese, finely grated

salt and freshly ground black pepper

5½oz (150g) parsnip, coarsely grated

1¼ cups buttermilk

1 Preheat the oven to 425°F (220°C). Line a baking sheet with parchment paper. In a bowl, mix together the flours, baking soda, and Parmesan cheese together with some salt and pepper. coarsely chop the grated parsnip to reduce the size of the shreds. Add it to the bowl, mixing it in well.

2 Make a well in the center of the dry ingredients and gently stir in the buttermilk, bringing the mixture together to form a loose dough.

Use your hands to bring the mixture together into a ball, then turn it out onto a floured work surface and knead for 2 minutes until it forms a smooth dough. You may need to add a little extra flour at this stage.

3 Shape the dough into a round, about 6in (15cm) in diameter. Slash a cross in the top of the dough with a sharp knife to allow the bread to rise easily when baking.

4 Place the dough on the baking sheet and cook in the middle of the oven for 30 minutes to create a good crust. Reduce the temperature to 400°F (200°C) and bake for 20 minutes until well risen, golden brown, and a skewer inserted into the middle emerges clean. Transfer to a wire rack and allow it to cool for at least 20 minutes before serving.

sweet potato and rosemary rolls

The gentle scent of rosemary and chunks of sweet potato in the dough make these rolls something special.

 20 MINS **20-25 MINS** ❄ **FREEZABLE**

MAKES 8

1¾ cups all-purpose flour, plus extra if necessary

¾ cup whole wheat flour, plus 1 tsp baking powder

1 tsp baking soda

salt and freshly ground black pepper

5oz (140g) sweet potato, peeled and grated

1 tsp finely chopped rosemary

1 cup buttermilk

1 Preheat the oven to 425°F (220°C). Line a baking sheet with parchment paper. In a bowl, mix the flours and baking soda together with some salt and pepper. Coarsely chop the grated potato to reduce the size of the shreds. Add it to the bowl with the rosemary, mixing it in well.

2 Make a well in the center of the dry ingredients and gently stir in the buttermilk, bringing the mixture together to form a loose dough. Use your hands to bring the mixture together into a ball, then turn it onto a floured work surface and knead for 2 minutes until it forms a smooth dough. You may need to add a little extra flour at this stage.

3 Divide the dough into 8 equal pieces and shape them into tight rounds. Flatten the tops and cut a cross in the center of each roll with a sharp knife, to help the rolls to rise easily when baking.

4 Place the rolls onto the baking sheet and cook in the middle of the oven for 20–25 minutes until well risen and golden brown. Transfer to a wire rack and cool for at least 10 minutes before serving. These are particularly delicious eaten still warm.

gratin of swiss chard with white beans and pancetta

This rich, warming dish uses only the leaves of chard. Cut up the colorful stems, steam briefly, and serve alongside.

 10 MINS PLUS SOAKING **1 HR 20 MINS PLUS RESTING**

SPECIAL EQUIPMENT ▪ 1-quart gratin dish ▪ food processor

SERVES 4-6

14oz (400g) dried white navy or canellini beans, soaked overnight

7oz (200g) pancetta, diced

2 tbsp extra virgin olive oil

4 garlic cloves, crushed

14oz (400g) Swiss chard, stem removed and finely shredded

2 cups heavy cream

sea salt and freshly ground black pepper

3½oz (100g) white bread

2oz (60g) Parmesan cheese, grated

8 basil leaves

1 Preheat the oven to 400°F (200°C). Drain the soaked beans, put them in a large pan of water, and bring to a boil. Turn down to a strong simmer and skim off any foam that has collected on the surface. Continue to cook for around 40 minutes or until soft.

2 In another large, deep-sided pan, cook the pancetta in the oil for 3–4 minutes until it is golden brown. Add the garlic and continue to cook for up to 30 seconds, being careful not to burn the garlic. Remove the garlic and pancetta from the oil and set aside. Add the chard to the oil in the pan and cook, stirring, for about 1 minute until it has collapsed, but is still al dente.

3 Add the pancetta, garlic, and cooked beans to the chard. Mix well, stir in the cream, and season.

4 Pour everything into the gratin dish. Top with bread crumbs made by pulsing the white bread, Parmesan cheese, and basil in a food processor. Cook at the top of the oven for 30 minutes until golden brown. Let the gratin rest for 10 minutes before serving.

sausage and chestnut stuffing

You can buy cooked and peeled chestnuts in packages, or if you want to prepare your own, boil or roast them in a hot oven for 15–20 minutes, let them cool, and then peel them.

 10 MINS   **20 MINS**

SERVES 4

1 tbsp olive oil

1 onion, chopped

salt and freshly ground black pepper

6 pork sausages, casings removed

9oz (250g) cooked and peeled chestnuts, chopped

small handful of flat-leaf parsley

1 Heat the oil in a frying pan over medium heat, add the onion, and cook for 3–4 minutes until the onion is soft. Season with salt and pepper and set aside to cool.

2 Put the sausage in a bowl and add the chestnuts, parsley, and cooled onion. Mix together and season with salt and pepper.

3 Use the mixture to stuff the neck of a turkey, or spread it out under the skin of a whole chicken. Alternatively, roll the mixture into balls and roast in a preheated 400°F (200°C) oven for about 20 minutes, or cook in a little oil until cooked through and golden.

variation

chestnut and celery stuffing
Cook the onion in the same way, but add 1 finely chopped celery stalk at the same time. Stir in 1 cup fresh bread crumbs instead of the sausage, then add the chopped chestnuts, a handful of fresh chopped thyme, and the parsley as before. Add a beaten egg to bind and season well.

dauphinoise potatoes

Creamy and garlicky potatoes are an ideal accompaniment for any roast dish. If you have a mandoline, it is the perfect piece of equipment for cutting the potatoes into thin slices.

 20 MINS   **1 HR 45 MINS**

SPECIAL EQUIPMENT ▪ 2-quart shallow ovenproof dish

SERVES 4

2lb (900g) waxy potatoes, peeled and cut into slices ⅛in (3mm) thick

1¼ cups heavy cream

1¼ cups milk

salt and freshly ground black pepper

3 garlic cloves, grated or finely chopped

1 Preheat the oven to 350°F (180°C). Put the potatoes, cream, and milk in a large pan and season with salt and pepper. Bring to a boil, then cover and simmer for 10–15 minutes, or until the potatoes begin to soften.

2 Using a slotted spoon, transfer the potatoes to the ovenproof dish. Sprinkle with the garlic and season well with salt and pepper. Strain the cream and milk mixture, then pour over the potatoes. Cover the dish with foil, then put in the oven to cook for 1 hour. Remove the foil and cook for another 30 minutes, or until the top has begun to turn golden.

variation

potato and leek gratin
Follow step 1, but use 1lb 10oz (750g) potatoes. Meanwhile, sauté 2 sliced leeks in 2 tbsp butter for 4–5 minutes until soft. Transfer half the potatoes to the ovenproof dish at step 2, then cover with a layer of all the leeks. Sprinkle with a handful of grated Gruyère cheese and half the garlic. Add the remaining potatoes, then sprinkle with another handful of grated Gruyère and the remaining garlic and continue as before.

salsify fritters

Salsify is a root vegetable that looks a little like a carrot and is cooked in exactly the same way. Serve these tasty Mediterranean fritters as an easy side dish with meat or fish.

 10 MINS   **25 MINS**

MAKES 4

14oz (400g) salsify, peeled and cut into small, equal-sized pieces

4 tbsp butter

1 garlic clove, crushed

freshly ground black pepper

1 tbsp all-purpose flour

1 tbsp olive oil

1 Add the salsify to a pan of boiling salted water and cook for about 20 minutes, or until beginning to soften. Drain well.

2 Mash the salsify, then add half the butter, all the garlic, and some black pepper, and mash again. Divide into four and shape each portion into a cake.

3 Toss the cakes in the flour to coat lightly. Heat the oil with the remaining butter in a non-stick pan, add the cakes, and cook for about 2 minutes, or until the underside is golden. Flip over and cook the other side for about 2 minutes. Serve hot.

potato and horseradish mash

While potatoes are a fine addition to almost any main course, combining them with hearty kale, bacon, and spicy horseradish adds tons of flavor. Mashed potato also works well.

 15 MINS **30 MINS**

SERVES 4

1lb (450g) russet potatoes, peeled and coarsely chopped

1 tbsp olive oil

pat of butter

7oz (200g) bacon, chopped

3 tsp creamed horseradish

salt and freshly ground black pepper

9oz (250g) curly kale, cooked and chopped

1 Boil the potatoes in a pan of salted water for 15–20 minutes until soft. Drain, then cut into bite-sized pieces, or mash, if you like.

2 Heat the oil and butter in a large non-stick frying pan over medium heat. When the butter has melted, add the bacon. Cook for 5–6 minutes until golden and crispy.

3 Add in the potatoes and stir through. Add the horseradish cream and season with salt and pepper. Stir in the curly kale until everything is combined. Cook for a few minutes until lightly golden and a little crispy. Serve hot with some red cabbage on the side.

variation

potato, celery root, and sprout sauté

Prepare in the same way, but use 1 large potato and ½ small celery root, peeled and cut into chunks, instead of all potatoes. Strain then crush, don't mash. Cook the bacon as before. Omit the horseradish. Add the potato and celery root mix and 9oz (250g) cooked, sliced Brussels sprouts. Stir, season well, and cook as before.

sweet potato paratha

These flat breads are so quick to make, it's worth doubling up and freezing half layered between parchment paper.

 20 MINS PLUS RESTING **15-20 MINS** ❄ **FREEZABLE**

MAKES 4

2 cups chapatti flour

salt

4 tbsp unsalted butter, melted and cooled

For the stuffing

9oz (250g) sweet potato, peeled and diced

1 tbsp sunflower or vegetable oil, plus extra for brushing

½ red onion, finely chopped

2 garlic cloves, crushed

1 tbsp finely chopped red or jalapeño chile, or to taste

1 tbsp finely chopped fresh ginger

2 heaped tbsp chopped cilantro

½ tsp garam masala

1 To make the dough for the paratha, sift the flour and ½ tsp salt into a bowl. Add the butter and ⅔ cup water, and bring the mixture together to form a soft dough. Knead for 5 minutes, then let the dough rest, covered, for 1 hour.

2 To make the stuffing, boil or steam the sweet potato for about 7 minutes until tender. Drain it well. Heat the oil in a frying pan over medium heat, add the red onion, and cook for 3–4 minutes until soft. Add the garlic, chile, and ginger, and continue to cook for 1–2 minutes.

3 Add the cooked onion mixture to the sweet potato and mash well. Add the cilantro, garam masala, and a good seasoning of salt and beat until smooth. Set aside to cool.

4 When the dough has rested, divide it into 4 pieces. Knead each piece and roll it out into a circle, around 4in (10cm) in diameter. Put ¼ of the stuffing in the middle. Pull the edges up around it, forming a purse shape.

5 Pinch the edges together to seal in the stuffing, turn the dough over, and roll it out into a circle, about 7in (18cm) in diameter, taking care not to roll too hard. If the filling bursts out, wipe it off and pinch the dough together to reseal the paratha.

6 Heat a large cast-iron frying pan or grill pan over medium heat. Cook the parathas for 2 minutes on each side, turning occasionally to make sure they are well cooked and browning in places. Once they have cooked on each side once, brush the surface with a little oil before turning them again. Serve immediately alongside a curry, or as a light lunch dish with a green salad.

carrot and beet salad with balsamic vinaigrette

This richly-colored salad is not just pretty; it's also packed with beneficial antioxidants. Choose young, fresh vegetables for the best flavor for a raw salad such as this.

 30 MINS   **3–4 MINS**

SERVES 4–6

1lb 5oz (600g) carrots, trimmed and scrubbed

1 bunch of beets, about 1lb 5oz (600g), peeled and halved

1¾oz (50g) sunflower seeds or pumpkin seeds

1 tsp soy sauce (optional)

small bunch of flat-leaf parsley, chopped, or salad cress, snipped

salt and freshly ground black pepper

For the vinaigrette

6 tbsp extra virgin olive oil, plus 1 tsp for toasting the seeds

¼ cup balsamic vinegar

1 garlic clove, crushed (optional)

1 Coarsely grate the raw carrots and beets and combine in a large bowl. For the vinaigrette, put the 6 tbsp oil, vinegar, and garlic (if using) in a screw-top jar, put the lid on tightly, and shake.

2 Gently heat the remaining 1 tsp olive oil in a small frying pan and toast the seeds for 3–4 minutes over medium heat, stirring frequently to prevent sticking. Add the soy sauce at the end of cooking (if using). Most of the soy sauce will evaporate, leaving a salty taste and extra browning for the seeds.

3 Add the parsley or cress to the carrot and beets. Shake the vinaigrette again, pour over the vegetables, then season to taste. Toss the salad gently, scatter with the toasted seeds, and serve.

carrot and shredded cabbage with peanuts

This Thai-style salad proves that winter recipes can be fresh and light. With its salty-sweet flavors and zingy lime and chile dressing, it enlivens grilled chicken or fish.

 15 MINS

SERVES 4

2 apples

4 carrots, grated

1 small white cabbage, shredded

small handful of sunflower seeds

small handful of salted peanuts or dry-roasted peanuts

For the dressing

1 tbsp light soy sauce

1 tbsp fish sauce (nam pla)

1 jalapeño chile, seeded and finely chopped

1 garlic clove, grated or finely chopped

juice of 2 limes

1–2 tsp granulated sugar

small handful of cilantro, finely chopped

salt and freshly ground black pepper

1 To make the dressing, put all the dressing ingredients in a small bowl, except the salt and pepper, and mix thoroughly until the sugar has dissolved. Taste and season with salt and pepper as needed, then taste again. If it needs sweetening, add more sugar; if it needs saltiness, add a little more fish sauce (nam pla).

2 Quarter and core the apples, then chop into bite-sized pieces. Put in a bowl with the carrots, cabbage, and sunflower seeds. Toss well. Drizzle with the dressing and toss together so that everything is well mixed. Transfer to a serving dish and scatter with the peanuts.

variation

carrot and noodle salad

Cook 7oz (200g) thin rice noodles, drain, rinse with cold water, and drain again. Use these instead of the shredded cabbage. Continue as in the original recipe, but transfer to individual serving bowls instead of one large bowl and offer some sweet chili sauce to drizzle over.

horseradish sauce

Serve this hot sauce with beef, ox tongue, sausages, beets, and salted or smoked fish. The horseradish root should not be cooked or it will lose its pungency.

 5 MINS PLUS MATURING   **10–15 MINS**

MAKES ABOUT 1½ CUPS

1¼ cups white wine vinegar

1 bay leaf

12 peppercorns

2 tbsp granulated sugar

2 cloves

½ cup heavy cream at room temperature, plus extra for serving (optional)

5½oz (150g) horseradish, grated

salt

1 Put the vinegar, bay leaf, peppercorns, sugar, and cloves in a small saucepan. Bring to a boil, stirring until all the sugar has dissolved, and then boil rapidly for about 5 minutes until the volume has reduced by half. Stir in the cream and boil for 1 minute.

2 Strain the liquid through a sieve into a bowl. Allow it to cool, then stir in the grated horseradish and season with salt.

3 Spoon the sauce into sterilized jars with non-metallic or vinegar-proof lids, top with wax paper discs, seal, label, and store in a cool, dark place for up to 2 months. Thin with a little extra cream, if needed, when serving.

Season's best **carrots**

Their exceptional flavor, versatility, and the promise of good health make carrots extremely popular. As well as the familiar long, orange variety, they may be cylindrical, stubby, round, or finger-size, and purple, yellow, dark red, or white, with a sweet, refreshing taste and aroma. Maincrop are best in autumn and early winter; young finger and bunched ones in spring and summer. They are great with sweet spices and other roots, or glazed with orange juice and honey.

The sweet orange carrot was developed by the Dutch in the 16th century in honor of their king. Many varieties are now cultivated worldwide in countries with mild temperatures.

essentials

varieties available

Many varieties of young finger, bunched, maincrop, chantenay, purple, white, and round carrots.

buy The green tops should be fresh and bright; if trimmed, there should be no mold on the top. They should smell fresh and be firm. Avoid any sprouting thin white rootlets.

store Twist off any green tops and leave unwashed for up to 2 weeks in a cool, dark place. If washed and trimmed, store in the fridge for up to 1 week.

cook Eat raw, or roast, boil, braise, steam, sauté, or stir-fry. Use in soups, stews, casseroles, cakes, and breads.

preserve Pickle with other vegetables, or use to make a sweet jam or conserve.

recipe ideas

Caramelized carrots p406

Carrot and coriander relish p420

Carrot and shredded cabbage with peanuts p404

Purple carrot The original wild carrots of Afghanistan were purple. New strains have regained the color that supplies beneficial anthocyanin and lycopene along with rich carrot flavor.

These carrots are purple outside and orange in the center.

Leaves should be bright green and fresh.

Chantenay They are short and stubby when fully grown. Their flavor is extraordinarily rich and there is no need to peel them before use.

They have a classic cone shape.

how to make carrot batonnets

Batonnets are ideal for crudités, steaming, or stir-frying. They are about ¼in (5mm) wide and 2–2½in (5–6cm) long. Any straight vegetable can be cut to this shape.

1 Peel each carrot and cut in half crosswise. Cut into ¼in (5mm) thick slices with a mandolin or a large, sharp chef's knife.

2 Stack the slices in their natural order. Trim off the rounded sides to make a neat block. Slice lengthwise into strips of equal width.

Bunched carrot These delicious, sweet, fragrant carrots are perfect for scrubbing and grating raw, or for cooking lightly.

celery root rémoulade with carrot salad

Both salads can be prepared and tossed in their dressings up to 1 day ahead of eating them. Once made, cover them and store in the fridge. The flavors will mellow and deepen.

 25-30 MINS PLUS CHILLING 1-2 MINS

SERVES 6

For the carrot salad

3 tbsp cider vinegar

1 tsp sugar

salt and freshly ground black pepper

¼ cup light olive oil

1lb 2oz (500g) carrots, coarsely grated

3oz (90g) raisins

For the celery root salad

1 celery root, about 1lb 10oz (750g) in weight

⅔ cup mayonnaise

2 tbsp Dijon mustard, or to taste

1 For the carrot salad, whisk the vinegar with the sugar and some salt and pepper. Gradually whisk in the oil, so the vinaigrette emulsifies and thickens slightly. Taste for seasoning. Add the carrots and the raisins. Toss everything together and taste for seasoning. Cover and refrigerate for at least 1 hour.

2 For the celery root salad, place the celery root on a cutting board and slice away all the thick, knobbly peel. Cut into thin slices, then into fine, even strips. Put the celery root strips in a saucepan of cold, salted water and bring to a boil. Simmer for 1–2 minutes until tender, but still al dente, then drain.

3 Mix the mayonnaise and mustard with some salt and pepper in a bowl. Taste, adding more mustard if you like. Add the celery root, toss, then taste for seasoning. Cover and refrigerate for at least 1 hour. Arrange the celery root and carrot salads in individual bowls and serve.

caramelized carrots

Caramelizing carrots in a pan with butter and brown sugar results in a glorious glossy finish and a slightly nutty flavor. Steam cabbage leaves or leeks to serve alongside.

 10 MINS 25 MINS

SERVES 4

2½lb (1.1kg) carrots

4 tbsp butter

sprinkling of brown sugar

handful of flat-leaf parsley, finely chopped (optional)

1 Peel and trim the carrots. Cut them in half lengthwise and then in half again to make chunky batons. Cook them in a pan of lightly salted water for 10–15 minutes, or until nearly cooked, then drain.

2 Return the carrots to the pan with the butter, sugar, and parsley, and cook over medium heat, stirring occasionally, for 10 minutes or until the carrots start to caramelize. Sprinkle with parsley, if using. Serve with roast chicken or beef.

variation

fragrant honeyed mixed roots

Prepare in the same way, but use a mixture of 12oz (350g) carrots, 12oz (350g) parsnips, and 12oz (350g) celery root, all peeled and cut into batons, instead of all carrots. Cook in the same way at step 1. At step 2, add 1 tbsp honey instead of the sugar and cook as before, but sprinkle in the chopped leaves of 2 large sprigs of rosemary while cooking. Garnish with parsley as before (optional).

roasted squash with sage and onion

Roasting vegetables to serve alongside roast meat is one of the easiest ways for cooking a side dish. Add some whole cloves of garlic for an even greater flavor.

 15 MINS 40 MINS

SERVES 4

1 butternut squash, halved, seeded, peeled, and cut into wedges

2 red onions, cut into eighths

handful of sage leaves, finely chopped

pinch of dried chile flakes (optional)

salt and freshly ground black pepper

1–2 tbsp olive oil

1 Preheat the oven to 400°F (200°C). Put the squash, onions, sage, and chile flakes, if using, in a large roasting pan and season well with salt and pepper. Add the oil and combine all the ingredients with your hands.

2 Put the pan in the oven to roast for 30–40 minutes, or until the squash is cooked and golden. Serve with roast chicken or pork.

variation

roasted sweet potato and celery root with garlic and herbs

Prepare in the same way, but use 1 sweet potato and 1 small celery root, both peeled and cut into chunks, instead of the squash. Omit the onions and sprinkle the vegetables with 2 finely chopped garlic cloves and 2 tbsp each of chopped fresh thyme, sage, and parsley. Cook as before.

squash with chestnuts and cranberries

This is a great recipe for any festive occasion. Combining sweet squash and tart cranberries in an unusual and successful way, it's an eye-catchingly colorful seasonal dish.

 15 MINS 35 MINS

SERVES 4

1–2 tbsp olive oil

pat of butter

pinch of allspice

pinch of ground cinnamon

1 butternut squash, halved, seeded, peeled, and cut into bite-sized pieces

salt and freshly ground black pepper

7oz (200g) cooked and peeled chestnuts

1¾oz (50g) fresh cranberries

granulated sugar, to taste (optional)

1 Preheat the oven to 400°F (200°C). Heat the oil and butter in a large frying pan over medium heat. Add the allspice, cinnamon, and squash, season well with salt and pepper, and cook, stirring occasionally, for 15 minutes or until the squash begins to soften. Add a little more oil, if needed.

2 Add the chestnuts and stir so they are coated with the oil. Cook over low heat for 5–10 minutes, then add the cranberries and cook for 5 more minutes.

3 Taste and season again, if needed, adding a little sugar if the cranberries are too tart (cook until the sugar has dissolved). Serve with roast chicken or turkey.

orange and chocolate tiramisu

You'll love this clever, seasonal version of the classic tiramisu dessert. Here coffee is substituted by orange juice and an orange-based liqueur complements the flavor.

 20 MINS PLUS CHILLING

SPECIAL EQUIPMENT ■ 2-quart serving dish ■ electric hand mixer

SERVES 8

20-24 ladyfingers

¾ cup orange juice

2 tbsp Grand Marnier or Cointreau

2 large eggs, separated

3 tbsp confectioners' sugar, sifted

1lb 2oz (500g) mascarpone cheese

grated zest of 1 orange

2½oz (75g) orange-flavored chocolate, finely grated

1 Arrange the ladyfingers in the base of the serving dish. Drizzle with the orange juice and Grand Marnier or Cointreau and set aside while the cookies soak up the liquid.

2 Put the egg yolks and confectioners' sugar in a large bowl and beat with a wooden spoon until smooth and creamy. Beat in the mascarpone cheese until smooth. Put the egg whites in a mixing bowl and whisk with an electric hand mixer until soft peaks form. Fold into the mascarpone mixture along with the orange zest.

3 Pour the mixture over the ladyfingers and smooth the top. Cover and chill for at least 4 hours or overnight. To serve, decorate with the grated chocolate.

variation

pear, coffee, and walnut tiramisu

Drizzle the ladyfingers with ¾ cup strong black coffee and 2 tbsp brandy instead of the orange juice and orange liqueur. Make the mascarpone topping as in step 2, omitting the orange zest, then fold in 2 peeled, cored, and chopped ripe pears. Finish as in the recipe at step 3, but decorate with 3 tbsp finely chopped walnuts instead of the chocolate.

orange and pistachio swiss roll

The delicate flavors of pistachio nuts and orange flower water used here give a traditional recipe a modern twist.

 20 MINS **15 MINS**

SPECIAL EQUIPMENT ■ 13 x 9in (32.5 x 23cm) Swiss roll pan ■ electric hand mixer

SERVES 8

3 large eggs

½ cup granulated sugar, plus extra for sprinkling

salt

⅓ cup self-rising flour

grated zest of 2 oranges, and 3 tbsp juice

2 tsp orange flower water (optional)

¾ cup heavy cream

2½oz (75g) unsalted pistachio nuts, chopped

confectioners' sugar, for dusting

1 Preheat the oven to 400°F (200°C). Line the pan with parchment. Set a bowl over a pan of simmering water. Add the eggs, sugar, and a pinch of salt and whisk with an electric hand mixer for 5 minutes until thick and creamy. Remove the bowl from the pan and whisk for another 1–2 minutes until cool. Sift in the flour, then add half the orange zest, and 1 tbsp of juice. Fold together, pour into the pan, and bake for 12–15 minutes until firm to the touch.

2 Sprinkle a sheet of parchment paper with granulated sugar. Turn the cake onto the parchment. Let cool for 5 minutes, then peel off the parchment from the cake and discard. Sprinkle with the orange flower water if using.

3 Make an indent along one short side, about ¾in (2cm) from the edge, with the back of a knife. Using the indent to start it off, roll up the cake around the sugared parchment. Let cool.

4 Whip the cream and fold in the pistachios and the remaining orange zest and juice. Unroll the cake, discard the parchment, and spread the cream filling evenly over the surface. Roll up the cake again and place, joint downward, on a serving plate. Dust with confectioners' sugar just before serving.

pear cake

Fresh pear, yogurt, and almonds make this a very moist cake.

40 MINS **45–50 MINS** ❄ **FREEZABLE**

SPECIAL EQUIPMENT ■ 7in (18cm) round springform cake pan

SERVES 6–8

7 tbsp unsalted butter, softened

⅓ cup light brown sugar

1 large egg, lightly beaten

1 cup self-rising flour

1 tsp baking powder

½ tsp ground ginger

½ tsp cinnamon

grated zest and juice of ½ orange

¼ cup Greek-style yogurt

¼ cup ground almonds

1 large or 2 small pears, peeled, cored, and sliced

For the topping

2 tbsp sliced almonds, lightly toasted

2 tbsp brown sugar

1 Preheat the oven to 350°F (180°C). Grease the pan and line with parchment. Whisk together the butter and sugar until light and fluffy. Beat the egg into the creamed mixture.

2 Sift together the flour, baking powder, ginger, and cinnamon, and gently fold into the batter. Fold in the orange zest and juice, yogurt, and the ground almonds. Pour half the batter into the pan. Top with the pears and cover with rest of the batter.

3 In a small bowl, toss together the sliced almonds and brown sugar. Sprinkle over the top of the cake and bake for 45–50 minutes until a skewer comes out clean. Leave the cake for about 10 minutes, then turn it onto a wire rack to cool.

chocolate orange truffle cake

Beneath the rich chocolate ganache topping lies a layer of chocolate sponge cake flavored with Grand Marnier. Orange zest sprinkled over the top is the perfect finishing touch. Make sure you leave at least 6 hours' chilling time.

 35–40 MINS PLUS CHILLING   **40 MINS**

SPECIAL EQUIPMENT ▪ 10in (25cm) round cake pan ▪ electric hand mixer ▪ 9in (23cm) round springform cake pan

SERVES 10-12

1 cup all-purpose flour

¼ cup cocoa powder, plus 3 tbsp to decorate

salt

4 large eggs

⅔ cup granulated sugar

4 tbsp butter, melted and cooled

4–5 tbsp Grand Marnier

grated zest of 3 oranges

For the chocolate ganache

13oz (375g) semi-sweet chocolate, cut into large chunks

1⅔ cups heavy cream

3 tbsp Grand Marnier

1 Preheat the oven to 425°F (220°C). Butter the 10in (25cm) cake pan and line the bottom with parchment paper. Butter the parchment. Sprinkle in 2–3 tbsp flour, and turn the pan to coat the bottom and side; tap the pan upside down to remove excess flour.

2 Sift together the flour, cocoa powder, and a pinch of salt. Put the eggs in a large bowl and beat with an electric hand mixer for a few seconds. Add the sugar and continue beating for about 5 minutes, until the mixture leaves a ribbon trail when the beaters are lifted.

3 Sift about a third of the flour and cocoa mixture over the egg mixture and fold together. Add another third of the flour and cocoa mixture and fold together in the same way. Add the remaining flour and cocoa

mixture and the butter, and fold them in gently, but quickly.

4 Pour the mixture into the prepared pan, then gently tap the pan on the work surface to level the mixture and knock out any large air bubbles. Bake for about 40 minutes, until the cake has risen and is just firm to the touch. Turn the cake onto a wire rack. Peel off the paper and let cool.

5 Trim the cooled cake to fit the 9in (23cm) springform pan. Lightly butter the bottom and side. Transfer the trimmed cake to the pan. Sprinkle the Grand Marnier evenly over the top, cover, and set aside.

6 For the chocolate ganache, put the chocolate in a large bowl. Heat the cream until almost boiling, then pour it over the chocolate. Stir until the chocolate has melted. Allow to cool,

stirring occasionally. Add the Grand Marnier and gently stir until blended. Using the electric hand mixer, beat the chocolate ganache for 5–10 minutes, until fluffy. Do not overbeat, or it will be very stiff. With a rubber spatula or a wooden spoon, turn out the chocolate ganache on top of the cake and smooth the surface. Cover with plastic wrap and chill for at least 6 hours, until firm.

7 Just before serving, take the cake from the fridge. Stand it on top of a bowl, then release the side of the pan. Carefully remove the base of the pan, using a palette knife. Place the cake on a wire rack with a baking sheet beneath. Sift cocoa powder over the top, using a stencil if you like, then transfer to a serving plate and sprinkle with the orange zest.

apple, golden raisin, and pecan cake

If you like a healthier cake, this is an excellent choice. It uses little fat and is packed full of fruit and nuts, making it a wholesome yet delicious choice.

 25 MINS   30-35 MINS

SPECIAL EQUIPMENT ▪ 9in (23cm) round springform cake pan

SERVES 10-12

1¾oz (50g) shelled pecans

7oz (200g) apples, peeled, cored, and finely diced

¾ cup light brown sugar

2 cups self-rising flour

1 tsp baking powder

2 tsp cinnamon

salt

3½ tbsp sunflower or vegetable oil

3½ tbsp milk

2 large eggs

1 tsp vanilla extract

1¾oz (50g) golden raisins

whipped cream or confectioners' sugar, to serve (optional)

1 Preheat the oven to 350°F (180°C). Grease the cake pan with butter and line the base with parchment paper. Place the nuts on a baking sheet and toast them in the oven for 5 minutes until crisp. Allow to cool, then coarsely chop.

2 Mix the apples and sugar together in a large mixing bowl. Sift in the flour, baking powder, cinnamon, and a little salt, and fold in. Then whisk together the oil, milk, eggs, and vanilla extract in a separate bowl.

3 Pour the milk into the cake mixture and stir until well combined. Fold in the pecans and raisins and pour the mixture into the prepared pan.

4 Bake in the center of the oven for 30–35 minutes until a skewer comes out clean. Let cool for a few minutes in the pan, then turn onto a wire rack and remove the parchment paper. Serve warm with whipped cream as a dessert, or cooled and dusted with confectioners' sugar.

normandy pear tart

This frangipane-filled fruit tart is a signature dish of Normandy, France, where wonderful pears are grown.

 40-45 MINS PLUS CHILLING   37-45 MINS

SPECIAL EQUIPMENT ▪ 9-10in (23-25cm) round fluted tart pan with removable bottom ▪ food processor ▪ electric hand mixer

SERVES 6-8

13oz (375g) store-bought pie dough

4½oz (125g) whole blanched almonds

8 tbsp unsalted butter, softened

½ cup granulated sugar

1 large egg, plus 1 large egg yolk

3 tbsp kirsch

2 tbsp all-purpose flour, sifted

3-4 ripe pears, peeled, cored, and cut into wedges

juice of 1 lemon

⅔ cup apricot jam

1 Grease the tart pan with butter. Roll out the dough on a floured surface to a large circle, 2in (5cm) larger than the pan, and use to line the pan, pressing it into the corners. Trim away the excess and prick the bottom all over with a fork.

2 Preheat the oven to 400°F (200°C). Grind the almonds to a fine powder in a food processor.

3 To make the frangipane, put the butter and sugar in a mixing bowl and whisk with an electric hand mixer for 2–3 minutes until pale and creamy. Gradually add the egg and egg yolk, beating well after each addition. Add 1 tbsp kirsch, then gently stir in the almonds and flour until well blended.

4 Spoon the frangipane into the pie crust and spread it with a palette knife. Toss the pear wedges in the lemon juice, then place the pears in a spiral pattern on top of the frangipane. Set the pan on a baking sheet and bake in the oven for 12–15 minutes. Reduce the heat to 350°F (180°C) and bake for another 25–30 minutes, until the frangipane sets. Remove from the oven and let cool.

5 To make a glaze, melt the jam and 2 tbsp kirsch or water in a pan, then work it through a sieve set over a bowl. Unmold the tart, brush the glaze over the pears and frangipane, and serve.

classic apple crumble

This is one of the easiest and most satisfying of desserts. It makes the most of tart apples, which develop a beautifully fluffy texture and milder taste when baked.

 15 MINS 30 MINS ❄ FREEZABLE

SPECIAL EQUIPMENT ▪ 1-quart ovenproof dish

SERVES 4

3 large tart apples, peeled, cored, and coarsely chopped

¼–⅓ cup granulated sugar (depending on the tartness of the apples)

For the crumble topping

4 tbsp butter, diced

1 cup all-purpose flour

½ cup granulated sugar

1 Preheat the oven to 375°F (190°C). To make the crumble, place the apples and sugar in a pan with a tiny amount of water. Simmer gently until the apples begin to break down, but don't let them get too soft. Then transfer the apple mixture to an ovenproof dish.

2 To make the crumble topping, place the butter and flour in a mixing bowl. Using your fingertips, rub the butter into the flour until the mixture resembles bread crumbs. Add the sugar and rub it in using the same method. Sprinkle the crumble on top of the apple and bake for 30 minutes, or until the topping is golden brown. Serve while still hot.

pistachio and orange biscotti

These fragrant biscotti are delicious served either with coffee or dipped in a glass of sweet dessert wine.

 15 MINS 40–45 MINS ❄ FREEZABLE

MAKES 25–30

3½oz (100g) whole pistachios, shelled

2 cups self-rising flour

½ cup granulated sugar

grated zest of 1 orange

2 large eggs

1 tsp vanilla extract

4 tbsp unsalted butter, melted and cooled

1 Preheat the oven to 350°F (180°C). Spread the pistachios on an unlined baking sheet and bake in the oven for 5–10 minutes. Allow to cool, then rub in a clean kitchen towel to remove the skins and coarsely chop.

2 Mix the flour, sugar, zest, and nuts together in a mixing bowl. In a separate bowl, whisk the eggs and vanilla extract with the butter. Then mix the wet and dry ingredients together to form a dough.

3 Turn the dough onto a floured work surface and form into 2 logs, each 8in (20cm) x 3in (7.5cm). Place

them on a baking sheet lined with parchment paper and bake for 20 minutes in the center of the oven. Allow to cool slightly, then cut diagonally into 1¼–2in (3–5cm) thick slices with a serrated knife.

4 Return to the oven to bake for another 15 minutes, turning them after 10 minutes, until golden and hard to the touch. Then remove from the oven and allow to cool.

variation

tangerine and almond biscotti

Prepare in exactly the same way but use 3½oz (100g) coarsely chopped blanched almonds instead of pistachios and the finely grated zest of 2 tangerines instead of the orange. Add 1 tsp natural almond extract instead of vanilla.

lemon tart

With its zesty lemon filling and buttery pastry crust, this classic tart is always guaranteed to taste good.

 20 MINS PLUS CHILLING   55 MINS

SPECIAL EQUIPMENT ▪ 8in (20cm) round fluted tart pan with removable bottom ▪ ceramic baking beans ▪ food processor (optional)

SERVES 8

8 tbsp cold butter, diced

1¼ cups all-purpose flour

½ cup ground almonds

juice of 4 lemons, finely grated zest of 1 lemon

¼ cup granulated sugar

3 large large eggs

⅔ cup heavy cream

1 Preheat the oven to 400°F (200°C). Put the butter and flour in a mixing bowl. Using your fingertips, rub the butter into the flour until the mixture resembles bread crumbs. Alternatively, use a food processor. Stir in the almonds, then stir in enough ice-cold water (about 3 tbsp), so the mixture comes together to form a dough. Roll the dough out on a lightly floured work surface to a large circle about ⅛in (3mm) thick and use to line the tart pan, pressing it into the corners. Trim away any excess around the edges, prick the bottom all over with a fork, then chill in the fridge for 30 minutes.

2 Line the tart dough with parchment paper and fill with ceramic baking beans. Bake in the oven for 15 minutes, then remove the paper and beans and return to the oven for another 5 minutes, or until the crust is cooked through. Set aside while you make the filling and turn the oven down to 300°F (150°C).

3 Put the lemon juice and sugar in a mixing bowl and stir together until the sugar has dissolved. Then mix in the eggs and lemon zest. Stir in the cream and pour into the tart crust. Bake for 35 minutes, or until just set—the tart should wobble in the middle slightly when you shake the pan. Let cool, then chill until ready to serve. Serve with half-and-half.

lemon sorbet

Lemon sorbet is an international classic; light and refreshing at the end of a meal or between courses.

 20 MINS PLUS CHILLING AND FREEZING   ❄ FREEZABLE

SPECIAL EQUIPMENT ▪ ice cream maker

MAKES ABOUT 1¼ PINTS (750ml)

6 large lemons, preferably unwaxed

1 cup sugar

1 large egg white

1 Use a vegetable peeler to remove the peel thinly in strips from 3 of the lemons. Make sure you don't take any white pith or the sorbet will be bitter. Put the sugar, strips of lemon peel, and 1 cup water in a pan and bring to a boil. Boil for 5 minutes to make a syrup. Remove from the heat and allow to cool.

2 Squeeze the juice from all of the lemons and pour into a liquid measuring cup. Add enough water to make the liquid 1¾ cups. Mix with the cooled syrup, then cover and chill in the fridge overnight.

3 Strain the mixture into an ice cream maker and follow the instructions for freezing. When the sorbet mixture starts to look icy, lightly beat the egg white just to loosen it and add to the mixture. When the sorbet is firm, transfer to the freezer for storage. If not using an ice cream maker, pour the mixture into a container, cover, and still-freeze for 1–2 hours, or until about 1in (2.5cm) of the mixture is frozen around the sides. Whisk to break up the ice particles, then cover and return to the freezer. After about 30 minutes, whisk again until smooth, then fold in the egg white. Continue freezing the sorbet until firm.

4 Half an hour before serving, transfer the sorbet to the fridge to soften slightly, then serve.

spiced quince dulce de leche pie

You can use a can of store-bought dulce de leche instead of boiling your own if you prefer.

🥣 20 MINS   🍲 3 HOURS

SERVES 6

1 x 14oz (400g) sweetened condensed milk

2 large quinces (about 8oz/225g), scrubbed

1 tbsp lemon juice

¼ cup granulated sugar

1 star anise

grated zest of 1 lemon (optional)

1 store-bought pie crust

1¼ cups heavy cream, whipped

1 tsp ground cinnamon

1 Put the unopened can of condensed milk in a large saucepan and cover it with water. Bring to a boil, reduce the heat, cover, and simmer gently for 3 hours, adding more boiling water as necessary. Remove and let cool in the water.

2 While it is simmering, put the quinces in the pan too, and blanch for 2 minutes (it makes them easier to peel). Remove with a slotted spoon and place in a bowl of cold water. Drain, peel, quarter, and core. Place in a bowl of water with the lemon juice to prevent browning as you prepare.

3 Put the sugar and 1¼ cups water in a separate pan and heat gently until the sugar dissolves. Lift the quinces out of the water, place in the syrup with the star anise, cover, and poach gently for about 30 minutes until tender. Set aside to cool in the syrup, then drain, chop, and gently toss in the lemon zest, if using.

4 Put the pie crust on a serving plate. Spoon the dulce de leche in it and level the surface. Arrange the quinces in a single layer on top. Smother with the whipped cream and dust with a little ground cinnamon. Chill until ready to serve.

cold lemon soufflé

This sharp yet sweet dessert is cool, light, and fluffy.

 35–40 MINS PLUS CHILLING 15–20 MINS

SPECIAL EQUIPMENT ▪ 1-quart soufflé dish
▪ electric stand mixer or electric hand mixer

SERVES 8

¼oz (10g) powdered gelatin

4 large lemons

4 large eggs, separated, plus 2 large egg whites

1 cup granulated sugar

1 cup heavy cream

2 tbsp granulated sugar

1 Cut a piece of foil, 2in (5cm) longer than the circumference of the soufflé dish, fold in half lengthwise, and wrap around the dish so it stands well above the rim. Secure with tape.

2 Put 5 tsp water in a small bowl, add the gelatin, and leave for 2–3 minutes until spongy. Stand the bowl in a pan of gently simmering water and stir until the gelatin is dissolved. Do not allow to boil.

3 Meanwhile, grate the zest from 3 of the lemons, thinly peel strips of zest from the remaining lemon and reserve, then squeeze the juice from all 4 lemons. In a pan, mix the 4 egg yolks, lemon zest, and juice, and two-thirds of the sugar, and cook, stirring, just until the mix boils. Pour into a bowl and beat with an electric stand mixer for 5–7 minutes until light and thick. Whisk the dissolved gelatin into the lemon mix and continue whisking until cool.

4 In a bowl, whip the cream until soft peaks form, then chill in the fridge. Heat the remaining sugar with ½ cup water in a pan until dissolved. Boil without stirring until it reaches the hard-ball stage: to test, drop 1 tsp of the syrup into cold water. Take it between finger and thumb; it should form a firm, pliable ball.

5 While the syrup is boiling, put the 6 egg whites in a bowl and whisk until stiff peaks form. Gradually add the hot syrup, whisking constantly for 5 minutes until the meringue is cool and stiff. Set the bowl of lemon mix in a larger bowl of iced water and stir the mix gently until it thickens. Remove from the ice bath, gently fold in the chilled whipped cream, then fold in the meringue in 2 batches. Pour the soufflé into the dish and chill for at least 2 hours until firmly set.

6 Cut the reserved peeled lemon zest into very fine strips. Bring a small pan of water to a boil, add the zest, and simmer for 2 minutes. Drain in a sieve, rinse with cold water, drain again, and set aside for decoration. Remove the soufflé from the fridge and allow to stand at room temperature for 30 minutes. Then sprinkle with the peeled lemon zest, remove the foil collar, and serve with whipped cream.

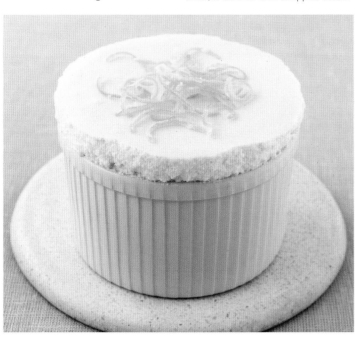

grapefruit granita with almond cookies

Unlike a smooth sorbet, the texture should resemble coarse snow. Whisk the granita while freezing to achieve this.

 15–20 MINS PLUS FREEZING 35–40 MINS

SERVES 4

3 grapefruit

juice of ½ lemon

¼ cup sugar, plus more to taste

¾ cup all-purpose flour

1 tbsp butter

grated zest of 1 lemon

1⅓ cups ground almonds

½ cup granulated sugar

1 tbsp brandy

1 large egg, beaten

12–15 whole, blanched almonds

1 Thinly peel the zest from half a grapefruit, leaving behind the white pith, and reserve. Squeeze the juice from all the grapefruits. Strain the juice into a non-metallic bowl with the lemon juice. Add 2 tbsp of the sugar and stir until dissolved. Freeze for 45–60 minutes until ice forms on top. Whisk to break the ice. Repeat every hour for 4–5 hours until the granita is slushy and slightly granular.

2 Preheat the oven to 350°F (180°C). Butter a baking sheet and sprinkle with flour. Sift the flour into a bowl. Add the butter, lemon zest, ground almonds, sugar, brandy, and egg and stir to form a dough. Wet your hands and roll the dough into 1in (2.5cm) balls. Place on a baking sheet, leaving 1in (2.5cm) between the cookies. Press a whole almond into each. Bake for 15–20 minutes, until light brown. Allow to cool on a wire rack.

3 With a very sharp knife, cut the peeled grapefruit zest into fine julienne. In a small pan, dissolve the remaining 2 tbsp of sugar in 2 tbsp water. Add the zest and simmer for 12–15 minutes until the water has evaporated and the zest is translucent. Spread on parchment paper and allow to cool.

4 Spoon the grapefruit granita into 4 chilled glasses or bowls. Pile the candied zest on top and serve at once with the cookies on the side.

pears poached in red wine and thyme

This impressive dinner party dessert is made with just a few simple ingredients. Prepare it a day in advance to allow the colors and flavors of the sauce to soak into the fruit.

 20-30 MINS PLUS CHILLING   50 MINS

SERVES 4

2½ cups red wine

¾ cup granulated sugar

2 sprigs of thyme

1 cinnamon stick

1 orange

4 firm dessert pears

1 Mix the wine, sugar, thyme, and cinnamon stick in a saucepan just big enough to hold the 4 pears. Bring to a boil and reduce to a simmer.

2 Using a peeler, remove the zest of the orange in large slivers and add to the pan. Cut the orange in half and squeeze the juice into the pan.

3 Peel the pears, leaving the stalks intact, but slicing off the base of each pear to leave a flat surface, so it can stand upright. Add the pears to the pan, adding water, if necessary, to cover them. Cover with a lid and simmer over low heat for 20 minutes, or until the fruit is soft. Set the fruit and liquid aside to cool, then remove the cinnamon stick and discard. Chill in the fridge overnight.

4 Before serving, remove the pears and return the liquid to the heat in a small saucepan. Bring to a boil and simmer until it reduces to a depth of ½in (1cm), or is thickened and slightly sticky. Taste the sauce to make sure the flavors are strong, but not burnt. Strain and pour the hot sauce over the cold pears and serve with cream or ice cream.

middle eastern date cakes with pomegranate drizzle

The sharp fruitiness of the pomegranate molasses contrasts beautifully with the sweetness of dates. You can serve them plain as a treat with coffee, too.

 25 MINS   4 MINS

SERVES 4

1½oz (45g) sesame seeds

6oz (175g) fresh dates, pitted and chopped

grated zest and juice of ½ orange

¾ cup all-purpose flour

sunflower or vegetable oil, for frying

⅔ cup crème fraîche, plus extra to serve

½ vanilla bean, scraped seeds only

1 tbsp confectioners' sugar, sifted

3-¼ cup pomegranate molasses

¼ cup pomegranate seeds

1 Heat a large frying pan and toast the sesame seeds, stirring until golden. Immediately transfer to a bowl. Add the dates, orange zest, and juice to the bowl and stir in the flour to form a firm dough.

2 Using wet hands, roll the mixture into 16 small ovals (date-shaped).

3 Heat about ¼in (5mm) oil in the frying pan over medium heat and fry the little cakes for about 2 minutes each side until golden brown. Drain on paper towels.

4 Mix the crème fraîche with the vanilla seeds and confectioners' sugar until well blended.

5 Arrange the little cakes on serving plates. Drizzle the pomegranate molasses over and around the cakes and scatter with the pomegranate seeds. Add a dollop of vanilla crème fraîche on the side and serve.

chocolate mousse with cinnamon pears

Pears and chocolate go extremely well together. You could use diced poached pears, but this is a quick way of making the dessert using fresh ones tossed in a little cinnamon sugar.

 25 MINUTES PLUS CHILLING

SERVES 6

3 ripe pears

1 tsp lemon juice

1 tbsp confectioners' sugar

1 tsp ground cinnamon

For the mousse

5½oz (150g) dark chocolate

3 large eggs, separated

⅔ cup heavy cream

½ cup granulated sugar

1 tbsp brandy

grated chocolate, to decorate

1 Peel, halve, and core the pears. Dice, then toss with the lemon juice, confectioners' sugar, and cinnamon. Divide between 6 wine goblets or small serving dishes.

2 Place the chocolate in a small heatproof bowl set over a pan of simmering water (the base of the bowl must not touch the water) and heat until mostly melted.

3 Meanwhile, in a clean mixing bowl, whisk the egg whites until peaking. Next, whip the cream in a separate bowl, then the egg yolks and sugar in a third bowl until thick and pale. Remove the chocolate from the heat, stir to melt completely, then stir in the brandy. Add this mixture to the egg yolks and sugar and gently fold in. Next, fold in the cream, and, finally, the egg whites.

4 Spoon the mousse over the pears and chill to firm. Decorate with a little grated chocolate before serving.

hazelnut, chocolate, and orange tart

With a base made of pasta frolla, an Italian sweet pastry, this is a most delicious recipe for a special occasion. The tart contains a richly flavored filling of ground hazelnuts, plain chocolate, and orange zest, all topped with a chocolate glaze.

 45–50 MINS PLUS CHILLING 35–40 MINS

SPECIAL EQUIPMENT ▪ 9in (23cm) round fluted springform pan ▪ food processor

SERVES 6–8

For the pasta frolla dough

1 cup all-purpose flour, plus more if needed

5 tbsp unsalted butter, softened

¼ cup granulated sugar

¼ tsp salt

grated zest of 1 orange

1 large egg

For the filling

pared zest of 2 oranges

4½oz (125g) hazelnuts

½ cup granulated sugar

11 tbsp unsalted butter

2 tsp all-purpose flour

2 large egg yolks, plus 1 large egg

2oz (60g) semi-sweet chocolate, grated

For the chocolate glaze

4½oz (125g) semi-sweet chocolate

5 tbsp unsalted butter, diced

2 tsp Grand Marnier

1 For the dough, sift the flour onto a work surface and make a well in the center. Put the rest of the ingredients into the well and work with your fingertips until thoroughly mixed. Work in the flour until coarse crumbs form, then press into a ball. If it is sticky, work in a little more flour. Lightly flour the work surface and knead the dough for 1–2 minutes until very smooth. Shape into a ball, wrap tightly, and chill for about 30 minutes until firm.

2 Brush the pan with melted butter. Lightly flour a work surface, roll the dough into an 11in (28cm) round and use it to line the pan, pressing it into the corners. Trim away the excess. With your thumbs, press the dough evenly up the sides of the pan to increase the height of the rim. Prick the bottom all over with a fork, then chill for 15 minutes until firm.

3 Meanwhile, bring a pan of water to a boil, add the peeled orange zest, and simmer for 2 minutes. Drain, rinse with cold water, drain again, and coarsely chop two-thirds of it.

4 Preheat the oven to 350°F (180°C). For the filling, spread the nuts on a baking sheet and toast in the oven for 6–15 minutes (watch them closely) until lightly browned. Rub in a kitchen towel to remove the skins and set aside to cool. Leave the oven on.

5 Once cool, grind the nuts with the sugar in a food processor. Beat the butter in a mixing bowl until creamy.

Add the flour and nut mix and beat until light and fluffy. Add the yolks and egg, one at a time, beating after each addition. Mix in the chocolate and chopped orange zest, then spread the filling over the tart crust. Bake on a baking sheet for 35–40 minutes, or until a knife inserted in the center comes out clean. Allow to cool on a wire rack.

6 For the glaze, break the chocolate into chunks and heat in a bowl set over a pan of hot water (the base of the bowl must not touch the water) until melted. Gently stir the butter into the chocolate in 2–3 batches. Add the Grand Marnier, then let cool to tepid. Unmold the tart and spread the glaze over the top. Slice the remaining cooked orange zest into fine julienne strips and use to decorate the top.

dried apples

Dried fruits make healthy, additive-free snacks and are an excellent addition to muesli, baked pies, and lamb, pork, or vegetarian dishes. Apples are ideal fruits to oven-dry.

 15–20 MINS PLUS DRYING AND COOLING   ❄ FREEZABLE

MAKES APPROX 4–8oz (115–225g)

2¼lb (1kg) ripe apples

2 tbsp lemon juice or ½ tsp citric acid

1 Briefly wash the apples in cold water, then core and slice them into ⅛–¼in (3–5mm) rings. If using windfalls, cut away any bruised, damaged, or soft parts first. Discard the outer rings that have the most skin on them.

2 Add the lemon juice or citric acid to 2 cups water in a bowl. Drop the apple slices into the bowl of acidulated water, drain on a kitchen towel, and place separately in a single layer on wire racks over baking sheets.

Dry in the oven on the lowest setting (120–140°F/50–60°C) for 8–24 hours, depending on the temperature (this can be done in stages if needed).

3 Turn the slices occasionally as they dry. They are ready when they look and feel like soft, pliable, chamois leather. (For a crunchier version, dry the slices until they are crisp). Remove from the oven, cover with paper towels, leave for 12–24 hours, and turn occasionally to ensure they contain as little moisture as possible (to reduce the risk of mold later on).

4 Pack into airtight jars and store in a cool, dry, dark place. Check regularly for any signs of deterioration.

cranberry jelly

This deep red, clear jelly has a tart, fruity flavor that goes perfectly with poultry, pork, sausages, and any cold meats.

 10 MINS PLUS STRAINING   35–45 MINS

SPECIAL EQUIPMENT ■ preserving pan ■ jelly bag ■ sugar thermometer

MAKES 14oz (400g)

1lb 2oz (500g) cranberries

1 tbsp lemon juice

approx 1lb 2oz (500g) granulated sugar (see method)

1 Put the berries, 2 cups water, and the lemon juice in a preserving pan or large heavy-bottomed saucepan and bring to a boil over medium heat. Turn the heat down, cover, and simmer for 25–30 minutes, or until the berries are tender. Remove from the heat and mash to a pulp with a potato masher.

2 Pour the pulp into a jelly bag or fine sieve set over a large, clean bowl and let strain overnight until all the juice has dripped through.

3 Measure the strained juice and calculate the quantity of sugar— allow 2 cups of sugar per 2 cups of juice. Pour the juice into the clean preserving pan, add the sugar, and stir gently until all the sugar has dissolved. Increase the heat, bring to a boil, and boil for 10–15 minutes. Remove the pan from the heat to test for a set with a sugar thermometer, or using a wrinkle test (chill a plate in the fridge before cooking). If using a thermometer, the temperature must reach 220°F (105°C); the mixture will also thicken around the sides of the pan, boil sluggishly, and the bubbles "plop" rather than froth. Or put 1 tsp jelly on the chilled plate, allow to cool for a moment, then push it with a finger. If it leaves a trail and wrinkles slightly, it is set.

4 Skim off any surface foam, then ladle into warm sterilized jars, cover with wax paper discs, seal, and label. Store in a cool, dark place and refrigerate after opening.

apple butter

This mild, soft spread, in which the subtle, sweet flavor of apples combines well with warm spices and citrus fruit, is best enjoyed on good, fresh bread or in desserts.

 15 MINS   2 HRS 10 MINS

SPECIAL EQUIPMENT ■ preserving pan

MAKES APPROX 2¼lb (1kg)

2lb (900g) apples, coarsely chopped

juice of 1 orange

pinch of ground allspice

pinch of ground cinnamon

3 cups granulated sugar

1 Put the apples in a preserving pan or a large heavy-bottomed saucepan and pour in 1 cup water. Bring to a boil and simmer the apples for about 10 minutes, or until soft.

2 Sieve the fruit in batches and collect the juice and purée in a clean bowl. Put this mixture back into the pan and add the orange juice, spices, and sugar. Cook over low heat, stirring until all the sugar has dissolved.

3 Bring the mixture back up to a boil and simmer gently for about 2 hours, or longer if needed, until the mixture thickens. Stir occasionally so that it doesn't stick to the bottom of the pan.

4 The butter is ready when it is thick enough to rest on the back of a spoon without running off, or a wooden spoon drawn across the bottom of the pan leaves a clear trail. It should now be a soft, moist, spreadable paste.

5 Ladle into warm sterilized jars. Cover with discs of wax paper, seal, and label. Store in a cool, dark place and refrigerate after opening.

pumpkin and orange spiced jam

This orange-scented jam with a subtle, spiced flavor is tasty on toast and also with savory foods like tangy blue cheese.

 20 MINS   30–40 MINS

SPECIAL EQUIPMENT ▪ preserving pan ▪ sugar thermometer

MAKES APPROX 4½lb (2kg)

3lb (1.35kg) pumpkin, peeled, seeded, and cut into small pieces

2 apples, peeled and chopped into small pieces

6 cups granulated sugar

juice of 1 lemon

juice of 1 orange

pinch of cinnamon

pinch of grated nutmeg

1 Put the pumpkin and apple in a preserving pan or a large heavy-bottomed saucepan. Pour in ¼ cup water (or enough to prevent the pumpkin from catching and burning), bring to a boil, then reduce to a simmer and cook for 10–20 minutes, or until the pumpkin is soft. Mash with a potato masher or fork, keeping a few chunks of pumpkin whole.

2 Add the sugar, lemon and orange juice, cinnamon, and nutmeg and stir until all the sugar has dissolved. Then bring to a boil and cook at a rolling boil for 15–20 minutes, or until the jam begins to thicken. Remove the pan from the heat to test for a set with a sugar thermometer, or using a wrinkle test (chill a plate in the fridge before cooking). If you use a thermometer, the temperature must reach 220°F (150°C); the mixture will also thicken around the sides of the pan, boil sluggishly, and the bubbles "plop" rather than froth. Or put 1 tsp jam on the chilled plate, allow to cool for a moment, then push it with a finger. If it leaves a trail and wrinkles slightly, it is set.

3 Ladle into warm sterilized jars, cover with wax paper discs, seal, and label. Store in a cool, dark place and refrigerate after opening.

orange marmalade

This marmalade has a sweeter finish than the classic Seville version. The oranges need long cooking to soften the peel.

 20 MINS   🍲 1 HR 25 MINS – 1 HR 40 MINS

SPECIAL EQUIPMENT ▪ muslin ▪ preserving pan ▪ sugar thermometer

MAKES APPROX 1LB (450g)

2¼lb (1kg) large sweet oranges, scrubbed, with stems removed

2 lemons

4½ cups granulated sugar

1 Halve the oranges and lemons, squeeze the fresh juice into a bowl, and reserve it in the fridge. Put the pith and seeds in the center of a muslin square and tie into a bundle with a length of string. Put the citrus shells and 4 cups water in a preserving pan. Add the bag of pith and seeds, bring to a boil, half cover, and simmer for 1 hour, or until soft.

2 Pour the ingredients into a large colander over a bowl to collect the liquid and scoop out the mush from the shells with a spoon. Using a sharp knife, slice the citrus peel into evenly sliced thick or thin strands depending on how you like it. Use as much or as little lemon peel as you wish.

3 Add the liquid, sliced peel, reserved fruit juice, and sugar to a preserving pan. Heat gently, stirring until the sugar has dissolved, turn up the heat, and boil rapidly for 5–20 minutes until a set is achieved. Remove the pan from the heat to test for a set with a sugar thermometer or using a wrinkle test (chill a plate in the fridge before cooking). If you use a thermometer, the temperature must reach 220°F (150°C); the mixture will also thicken around the sides of the pan, boil sluggishly, and the bubbles "plop" rather than froth. Or put 1 tsp marmalade on the chilled plate, allow to cool for a moment, then push it with a finger. If it leaves a trail and wrinkles slightly, it is set.

4 Skim off any surface foam, leave for 10–15 minutes, then stir and ladle into warm sterilized jars. Cover with wax paper discs, seal, and label. Store in a cool, dark place and refrigerate after opening.

cranberry sauce with port

A fruity cranberry sauce is a traditional—and essential—accompaniment to poultry. This quick and easy recipe includes port or wine for added depth of flavor.

 5 MINS 20 MINS

SERVES 4

8oz (225g) cranberries

¼ cup port wine or red wine

¼ cup sugar

1 Put the cranberries in a wide saucepan and pour in the port or red wine. Bring to a boil, then cover with a lid and simmer gently for 10–15 minutes, or until the berries start to soften and pop. Then squash them in the pan with the back of a spoon to your desired consistency.

2 Stir in the sugar a little at a time, tasting as you go, until it has dissolved and the sauce is the right flavor. Serve in a small dish with roast turkey or chicken.

variation

cranberry sauce with orange
For a fruitier flavor, add the finely grated zest and juice of 1 orange with the cranberries in step 1. Omit the alcohol and continue as in the original recipe.

cranberry and apricot chutney

This colorful chutney-cum-relish is a tangy alternative to cranberry sauce. It's quicker to make than other chutneys.

 10-15 MINS PLUS MATURING 40-45 MINS

SPECIAL EQUIPMENT ▪ food processor ▪ preserving pan

MAKES APPROX 2¾lb (1.25kg)

12oz (350g) cranberries

2 apples, about 12oz (350g), peeled, quartered, and cored

8oz (225g) dried apricots

1 onion, about 6oz (175g), coarsely chopped

½in (1cm) piece of fresh ginger, peeled and grated

1 cup light brown sugar

⅔ cup apple cider vinegar

zest and juice of 1 orange

1 cinnamon stick

¼ tsp ground coriander

¼ tsp ground cumin

¼ tsp dried chile flakes

sea salt

1 Put the cranberries, apples, and apricots in a food processor with the onion and ginger. Pulse lightly until finely chopped, then place in a preserving pan or a large heavy-bottomed, stainless steel saucepan and add the rest of the ingredients.

2 Bring slowly to a boil, stirring until the sugar has dissolved. Reduce the heat to a gentle simmer and cook gently, uncovered, for 30–35 minutes, or until the cranberries have softened and burst and are thick and pulpy. A wooden spoon drawn across the base of the pan should leave a clear trail. Stir frequently toward the end of cooking so the chutney doesn't burn.

3 Remove the cinnamon stick and spoon into warm sterilized jars with non-metallic or vinegar-proof lids, making sure there are no air gaps. Cover each pot with a wax paper disc, seal, and label. Let cool, then store in the fridge to mature for at least 2 weeks before opening. Once opened, keep refrigerated.

cranberry and orange butter

Use this fruit butter as a savory accompaniment or sweet spread, or eat with freshly shelled nuts.

 10 MINS 50 MINS ❄ FREEZABLE

SPECIAL EQUIPMENT ▪ preserving pan

MAKES APPROX 1¾lb (800g)

1lb (450g) cranberries

approx 1½–2 cups granulated sugar (see method)

approx 1 tbsp butter (see method)

juice and 1 tsp grated zest of 1 large sweet orange

1 Put the cranberries and 1¼ cups water into a preserving pan or a large heavy-bottomed saucepan, cover, and bring to a boil, keeping the lid on until the cranberries have all popped. Then remove the lid and simmer the berries for 10 minutes, or until they are soft. Then mash the berries to a pulp with a potato masher or fork.

2 Sieve the fruit in batches and collect the juice and purée in a clean bowl. Measure the purée and for every 2 cups of purée, allow 1½ cups of sugar and 1 tbsp butter; if the pulp seems very tart, allow 2 cups of sugar. Put the purée, sugar, butter, and orange juice and zest back in the preserving pan and cook over medium heat. Stir gently until the sugar has dissolved.

3 Bring the ingredients to a boil, then simmer gently, stirring often, for about 40 minutes, or until the mixture has reduced to a soft, moist, spreadable paste. A wooden spoon drawn across the bottom of the pan should leave a clear trail. Ladle the mixture into warm sterilized jars, cover with wax paper discs, seal, and label. Store in a cool, dark place and refrigerate after opening.

Season's best **cranberries**

Cranberries are harvested in September and October but available through winter and range alluringly in color from bright light red to dark crimson. The hard waxy berries have a mouth-puckering sour taste when raw so need plenty of sweetening, but they make delicious juice, as well as sauces and relishes for meat, poultry, and game. They are often teamed with the flavors of orange and port or red wine.

Cranberries are commercially cultivated in North America, Britain, and Northern Europe. They grow on dwarf shrubs or trailing vines. The fruit is initially white and turns red when ripe.

Cranberry The fruit is high in pectin so when cooked quickly with sugar, it sets like conserve. Rich in vitamin C, it tops the list of health-promoting antioxidant berries.

Look for firm, brightly colored cranberries of uniform size.

essentials
varieties available

Common cranberry, small cranberry, and large American Cranberry.

buy They are at their peak in autumn, when shiny and red. Avoid bags containing squishy or shriveled fruit.

store Keep in a closed plastic bag in the fridge for up to 2 weeks. Or freeze, and cook from frozen.

cook Stew for sauces and desserts. Add to tarts, pies, muffins, cakes, and parfaits, as well as pâtés and stuffings for poultry and meat.

preserve Make jelly, dry, or bottle in syrup.

recipe ideas

Cranberry and apricot chutney p418

Cranberry and orange butter p418

Cranberry jelly p416

Squash with chestnuts and cranberries p407

Turkey and cranberry casserole p378

how to make a simple cranberry sauce

Cranberry sauce is the traditional accompaniment to festive birds, particularly turkey for Thanksgiving and Christmas. It is also a favorite with baked ham and pork.

1 Put 8oz (225g) cranberries in a pan with 1¼ cups water or orange juice and ½ cup sugar.

2 Bring to a boil and simmer gently until the fruit "pops." Transfer to a bowl and leave to cool.

cider

Use any apples, including windfalls, to make cider. Generally, the sweeter the apple, the sweeter the cider.

 1 HR - 1 HR 30 MINS PLUS FREEZING, STRAINING, BREWING, AND MATURING

SPECIAL EQUIPMENT ▪ food processor or fruit juicer ▪ jelly bag or muslin ▪ sterilized funnel ▪ sterilized demijohn ▪ sterilized siphon ▪ hydrometer

MAKES APPROX 14 CUPS

7–8lb (3.5kg) apples, or 14 cups apple juice

½ cup unrefined cane sugar

⅛oz (5g) champagne yeast

1 Ensure that the fruit is in good condition and, if using windfalls, cut away any badly bruised parts. Put all the apples in the freezer overnight to soften them by breaking down their fibrous cell walls.

2 Allow the apples to thaw thoroughly and then grind to a pulp in small batches using a food processor. If you have an electric fruit juicer, simply juice the fresh apples instead.

3 Strain the pulp through a jelly bag or clean, muslin-lined sieve set over a large clean bowl. Let strain until you have 14 cups of juice. Measure the gravity of the strained juice with a hydrometer. If it is not in the range of 1,035–1,050, gradually dilute with water until it falls within this range. Add the sugar to the juice, stir well, and pour the juice into a demijohn using a funnel. Add the yeast and leave for 2 days at room temperature (59–77°F/15–25°C) with cotton wool in the top of the demijohn as a seal.

4 When the frothing has reduced, fit the airlock and pour water into it. The liquid should start to fizz. Leave the cider to ferment for 2 weeks or longer until the airlock has stopped bubbling.

5 Siphon the cider into sterilized bottles using a siphon, leaving ¾in (2cm) of space at the top. Seal the bottles and leave them for approximately 3 months in a dark place (a cupboard is fine) at room temperature before opening.

mulled pears

Use just-ripe, slightly firm pears for this recipe; overripe fruit will become unpalatably soft. Wine alone isn't strong enough to preserve the fruit, so the jars must be heat-processed too.

 5 MINS   1 HR 10 MINS PLUS HEAT-PROCESSING

MAKES 1 QUART (1 LITER)

½ cup granulated sugar

2 tsp lemon juice

2 cups red wine, plus extra if needed

1 cinnamon stick

2 star anise

2 cloves

6 pears, peeled, cored, and halved

1 Put the sugar in a large saucepan (large enough for the pears to sit in one layer) with the lemon juice, 1 cup of the wine, and the spices. Bring to a boil over medium heat, stirring until the sugar has dissolved, then boil for 2 minutes without stirring. Add the pears and cook gently for 2 minutes, turning them over once.

2 Place warm sterilized preserving jars on a cloth or wooden board. Lift the fruit out of the syrup with a slotted spoon and pack tightly into the jars without squashing it, leaving ½in (1cm) of space at the top.

3 Add the rest of the wine to the syrup. Bring back to a boil for a few seconds. Pour the syrup into a heat-proof bowl (discard the cinnamon stick) and pour over the fruit. Add a little extra wine if needed so the fruit is completely covered. Fit the rubber band or metal lid seal and clamp on the lid. If using screw-band jars, loosen by a quarter of a turn. Then place the filled jars in a deep roasting pan lined with newspaper.

4 Put the pan of jars in the center of the oven for 50–60 minutes to heat-process (remove the remaining air in the jars). Then remove from the oven and tighten the clips or lids (or screw on plastic screw-band lids) immediately. Leave for 24 hours, then unscrew or unclip and test the lids are firmly sealed before refastening and storing. (If using kilner jars with metal lids, you will know if you have a seal as the lid becomes slightly concave and is firm with no "give" once pressed.) Store the jars in a cool, dark place and refrigerate once open.

carrot and coriander relish

Sweet, sticky, and spicy, this relish, with its lovely hints of orange, is perfect served with a curry.

 10–15 MINS PLUS MATURING   40–45 MINS

SPECIAL EQUIPMENT ▪ preserving pan

MAKES APPROX 1LB (450g)

1lb 2oz (500g) carrots, grated

1 tsp mustard seeds

2 tsp coriander seeds, crushed

1 tsp cardamom seeds (taken from pods)

1in (2.5cm) piece of fresh ginger, peeled and grated

zest and juice of 1 orange

½ cup cider vinegar

½ cup granulated sugar or light brown sugar

1 Put the carrots in a preserving pan or a large heavy-bottomed, stainless steel saucepan, then add the mustard seeds, coriander seeds, and cardamom seeds and stir.

2 Add the ginger and orange juice and zest, then pour in the vinegar and sugar and stir. Slowly simmer, stirring until the sugar has dissolved, then cook for 10 minutes more, stirring occasionally, until the carrots have softened. Increase the heat a little and cook for 15–20 minutes, or until most of the liquid has disappeared. Stir frequently so the mixture doesn't burn or stick on the base of the pan.

3 Ladle the relish into warm sterilized jars with non-metallic or vinegar-proof lids, seal, and label. Allow to mature for at least 1 month and refrigerate after opening.

curried apple, peach, and walnut chutney

Apples combine well with dried peaches and walnuts, which provide extra texture and flavor. If you prefer a sweeter spiced chutney, substitute apple pie spice for the curry powder.

 15 MINS PLUS MATURING 1 HR 30 MINS

SPECIAL EQUIPMENT ▪ preserving pan

MAKES APPROX 4lb (1.8kg)

2 apples, about 12oz (350g), peeled, quartered, cored, and cut into bite-sized pieces

1 large onion, about 8oz (225g), peeled and cut into bite-sized pieces

12oz (350g) dried peaches, cut into bite-sized pieces

6oz (175g) walnuts, coarsely chopped

4½oz (125g) golden raisins

2 cups light brown sugar

2 tsp mild curry powder

sea salt

1¼ cups apple cider vinegar

1 Put all the ingredients in a preserving pan or large heavy-bottomed, stainless steel saucepan. Bring slowly to a boil, stirring until the sugar has dissolved. Reduce the heat to a gentle simmer and cook for 1½ hours, or until a wooden spoon drawn across the base of the pan leaves a trail. Stir frequently toward the end of cooking so the chutney doesn't burn or stick on the base of the pan.

2 Check the seasoning and add salt or more curry powder, if needed. Simmer gently for an extra minute, stirring, to cook out the spice.

3 Spoon into warm sterilized jars with non-metallic or vinegar-proof lids, making sure there are no air gaps. Cover each pot with a wax paper disc, seal, and label. Store in a cool, dark place for at least 1 month before using. Once opened, keep refrigerated.

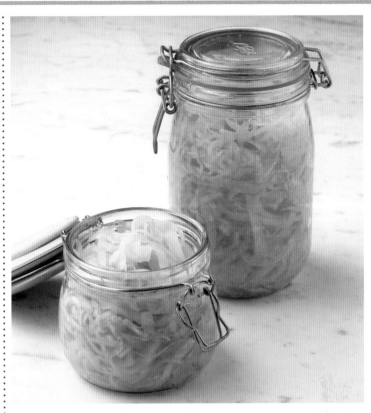

red cabbage pickle

This vibrant, slightly sweet pickle is crunchy and pleasantly spiced. A wide-necked kilner jar is best for this cold pickling method so that the vegetables can fit in easily.

 30 MINS PLUS STANDING AND MATURING

MAKES APPROX 2½lb (1.1kg)

1½lb (675g) red cabbage, cored and shredded

1 red onion, sliced

3 tbsp sea salt

2 cups white wine vinegar

½ cup granulated sugar

1 tsp mustard seeds

1 tsp coriander seeds

1 Put the cabbage and onion into a large glass or ceramic bowl. Sprinkle with the sea salt and mix the ingredients together so the vegetables are well coated. Put the mixture into a colander over a bowl, sit a plate on top of the cabbage, and leave overnight for it to drain—you want to lose as much liquid from the cabbage as possible. Pour the vinegar into a large bowl, add the sugar and spices, and whisk to dissolve the sugar. Cover and leave overnight too.

2 Rinse the cabbage and onion under cold water to remove the salt, then dry the vegetables thoroughly with a clean kitchen towel or paper towels.

3 Layer the vegetables in warm sterilized jars with non-metallic or vinegar-proof lids, packing them down. Stir the vinegar and pour it over the vegetables so that they are completely covered. Seal, label, and store in a cool, dark place for 1 week, then leave in the fridge for at least 1 month before using, to allow the flavors to develop and mellow. Keep refrigerated once opened.

sauerkraut

Preserving cabbage in salt relies on its natural lactic bacteria reacting with the salt and fermenting. Homemade sauerkraut has a much better flavor than bought versions.

 30-45 MINS PLUS FERMENTATION

SPECIAL EQUIPMENT ▪ food processor ▪ sterilized crock ▪ muslin

MAKES APPROX 3lb (1.35kg)

5½–6½lb (2.5-3kg) hard white or red cabbage, or half red and half white cabbage, outer leaves removed

approx ¼ cup coarse sea or rock salt (see method)

1 tbsp caraway seeds

1 Slice the cabbage in half, remove the core, quarter it, and finely shred it using a food processor or a sharp knife. Weigh the shredded cabbage and calculate the amount of salt you will need: approximately ¼ cup of salt per 5½lb (2.5kg) of cabbage.

2 Place the cabbage in a large clean bowl and sprinkle the salt evenly over it. Using your hands, work the salt thoroughly into the cabbage until it begins to feel wet. Leave for a few minutes for the salt to soften the cabbage and draw out its juices.

3 Pack into a very large sterilized crock or jar. Add 2in (5cm) of cabbage at a time and scatter with the caraway seeds. Pack each layer down with the end of a rolling pin, a large pestle, or a jam jar. Leave 3in (7.5cm) of space at the top. Add any juices from the bowl and cover with cold brine (1½ tbsp of salt to 3½ cups of boiled water) to cover the cabbage. Put the jar on a tray, cover with clean muslin, and put a snug-fitting plate on top. Place a large jar or sandwich bag filled with water on top of the plate.

4 Leave in a well-ventilated place at room temperature (68–72°F/20–22°C) for 3-4 weeks. (Fermentation will stop and the cabbage will spoil above 76°F/24°C; if it is cooler than room temperature, the sauerkraut will take up to 5-6 weeks.) Check daily that the cabbage is submerged. Remove any foam regularly and replace with clean muslin. If the cabbage develops a pinkish hue on the surface, goes dark, or turns soft and mushy, discard the whole batch; it shouldn't be eaten. Fermentation is complete when all the bubbling has ceased. Can into sterilized jars, seal, and store in the fridge for 1–2 months.

late winter

at their best

vegetables beet greens ▪ beets ▪ broccoli rabe ▪ Brussels sprouts ▪ cabbages ▪ carrots (maincrop) ▪ cauliflower ▪ cavolo nero ▪ celery root ▪ celery ▪ dandelion greens ▪ endive ▪ Hass avocados ▪ Jerusalem artichokes ▪ kale ▪ leeks ▪ mustard greens ▪ parsnips ▪ potatoes (maincrop) ▪ radicchio ▪ rutabaga ▪ Swiss chard ▪ turnips

fruit apples ▪ bananas ▪ clementines ▪ grapefruit ▪ kiwi fruit ▪ oranges ▪ pears ▪ pomegranate ▪ satsumas ▪ tangerines

seafood blue shark ▪ cod ▪ clams ▪ Columbia river smelt ▪ crawfish ▪ Dungeness crab ▪ flounder ▪ King crab ▪ ling cod ▪ octopus ▪ ocean perch ▪ oysters ▪ rockfish ▪ sea bass ▪ sea scallops ▪ snapper ▪ sole ▪ squid ▪ striper ▪ trout (farmed)

meat, poultry, game buffalo ▪ duck (wild and farmed) ▪ lamb ▪ pork ▪ veal ▪ venison (farmed)

also available

vegetables mushrooms (cultivated) ▪ onions ▪ spinach ▪ watercress
seafood mahi mahi ▪ tilapia **meat, poultry, game** beef ▪ chicken

late winter recipe planner

Split pea and bacon soup p435

Mini chicken, leek, and mushroom pies p430

Avocado, grapefruit, and Parma ham salad p432

Vegetables

Avocado
Avocado, grapefruit, and Parma ham salad p432
Beef and vegetable chili with guacamole p443
Crispy bacon and avocado wraps p432
Spicy chicken, avocado, and spinach wraps p432

Bok choy
Wasabi beef and bok choy p442

Cabbage
Bigos p456
Duck legs with cabbage, pine nuts, and raisins p454
French cabbage soup p438
Pancetta and potatoes with red cabbage p469
Red cabbage slaw p469 ⓥ
Red cabbage with cider p469 ⓥ

Carrot
Beef and ale cobbler p451
Beef with barley and mushrooms p447
Braised oxtail with Jerusalem artichokes p449
Carrot cream soup with onion and cumin p430 ⓥ
Carrot soup with coconut and lemongrass p438 ⓥ
Chicken and cornmeal cobbler p441
Creamy four root soup p432 ⓥ
Jerusalem artichoke soup with saffron and thyme p426 ⓥ
Lamb daube p456
Lamb shanks in red wine p447
Marsala chicken with pine nuts and golden raisins p441
Minestrone soup p434 ⓥ
Pot roast smoked ham p444
Poule au pot p463
Scotch broth p435
Spiced carrot and orange cake p479 ⓥ
Split pea and bacon soup p435
Smoky split pea soup p435
Turkey and mushroom casserole with dumplings p446
Vegetable casserole with dumplings p464 ⓥ

Cauliflower
Braised cauliflower with chile and cilantro p448 ⓥ
Cauliflower cheese soup p434 ⓥ
Cauliflower soup p434 ⓥ
White bean and cauliflower gratin p470 ⓥ

Cavolo nero
Pork with cavolo nero p445

Celery
Beef with barley and mushrooms p447
Celery and apple salad with blue cheese dressing p471 ⓥ
Celery and celery root soup p428 ⓥ
Celery, leek, and pear salad p471 ⓥ
Chicken and cornmeal cobbler p441
Marsala chicken with pine nuts and golden raisins p441
Minestrone soup p434 ⓥ
Osso buco with celery, leek, and almonds p466
Poached trout salad with red grapefruit, orange, and celery p438
Roasted celery with orange and walnuts p470 ⓥ
Scotch broth p435
Split pea and bacon soup p435
Smoky split pea soup p435
Turkey and mushroom casserole with dumplings p446
Vegetable casserole with dumplings p464 ⓥ

Celery root
Celery and celery root soup p428 ⓥ
Celery root and pear coleslaw p470 ⓥ
Celery root cream soup with orange and cinnamon p430 ⓥ
Chicken broth with celery root and orange p450
Creamed celery root soup p426 ⓥ
Fruity lamb shanks p448
Lamb shanks in red wine p447
Lamb with roasted winter vegetables p455
Pork belly with leeks and celery root p467

Chicory and endives
Bistro salad with egg and bacon p439
Duck with pink grapefruit and chicory salad p442
Hunter's chicken stew p467
Pheasant with pomegranate, frisée lettuce, and leek salad p442

Jerusalem artichoke
Jerusalem artichoke soup with saffron and thyme p426 ⓥ
Pot roast smoked ham p444

Kale
Beef and greens p445
Caldo verde p430 ⓥ
Filo pie with spicy kale and sausage p428

Leek
Beef and ale cobbler p451
Celery, leek, and pear salad p471 ⓥ
Creamy sweet potato and leek bake p469 ⓥ
Fish and leek pie p461
Leek and Cheddar cheese tart p431 ⓥ
Lentils with mushrooms and leeks p443 ⓥ
Mini chicken, leek, and mushroom pies p430
Osso buco with celery, leek, and almonds p466
Pheasant with pomegranate, frisée lettuce, and leek salad p442
Pork belly with leeks and celery root p467
Poule au pot p463
Sweet balsamic baby leeks p468 ⓥ
Vegetable casserole with dumplings p464 ⓥ

Onion
Lamb with red onions p455
Onion confit and Gorgonzola pizza p465 ⓥ
Onion tart p431 ⓥ
Red onion marmalade p482 ⓥ
Sautéed liver and onions p450
Sweet balsamic onions p468 ⓥ

Parsnip
Creamy four root soup p432 ⓥ

Potato
Caldo verde p430 ⓥ
Cornish pasties p463
Duck with apple and rosemary potatoes p440
Lamb chops champvallon p464
Lamb with red onions p455
Meat and potato pie p440
Pancetta and potatoes with red cabbage p469
Perfect fish and chips p457
Pork belly with onions and potatoes p467
Potato-chive monkey bread p471 ⓥ
Potatoes boulangère p469 ⓥ

Rutabaga
Beef and vegetable chili with guacamole p443
Cornish pasties p463
Creamy four root soup p432 ⓥ
Creamy rutabaga soup p432 ⓥ
Mixed vegetable caldo verde p430 ⓥ

Shallots
Caramelized shallot tart p427 ⓥ
Greek stifado p444
Lamb shanks in red wine p447

Sweet potato
Creamy sweet potato and leek bake p469 ⓥ
Lamb with roasted winter vegetables sweet potato and leek bake p469

Turnip
Creamy four root soup p432 ⓥ
Mixed vegetable caldo verde p430 ⓥ
Poule au pot p463
Seared duck with red miso, shredded turnip, and noodles p455
Turnip soup with pimento, chile, and noodles p439 ⓥ
Venison casserole with turnips and prunes p454

Fruit

Apples
Apple dumplings p480 ⓥ
Applesauce p468 ⓥ
Apple streusel cake p480 ⓥ
Celery and apple salad with blue cheese dressing p471 ⓥ
Chicken liver and apple pâté p427
Chile jelly p483 ⓥ
Cinnamon apple cake p479 ⓥ
Crêpes with caramelized apples and chocolate p480 ⓥ
Duck with apple and rosemary potatoes p440
Fruity lamb shanks p448
Pancetta and potatoes with red cabbage p469
Pork Normandy p448
Rosemary jelly p482 ⓥ
Toffee apple cake p481 ⓥ

Braised oxtail with clementine and star anise p449

Hunter's chicken stew p467

Apple dumplings p480

Spiced carrot and orange cake
p479

**Oysters with shallot and vinegar
dressing** p436

**Duck legs with cabbage, pine nuts,
and raisins** p454

soupe de poissons

This flavorful fish soup needs no accompaniment, but croûtes made from baguette slices rubbed with garlic, spread with rouille, or topped with Gruyère are a tasty addition.

 20 MINS 1 HR ❄ FREEZABLE

SERVES 6

5 tbsp olive oil

4 onions, chopped

2 leeks, trimmed and chopped

3lb 3oz–4½lb (1.5–2kg) mixed fish and seafood, such as cod, halibut, shrimp, sole, sea bass, and salmon

1 celery stalk, halved

14oz (400g) tomatoes, chopped

9 garlic cloves, crushed

5 sprigs of flat-leaf parsley

3 bay leaves

thinly pared zest of ½ orange

1 tbsp tomato paste

salt and freshly ground black pepper

pinch of saffron threads

6 croûtes, to serve

1 Heat the oil in a large heavy-bottomed pan over medium heat. Add the onions and leeks, and cook for about 5 minutes until just golden.

2 Scale and gut the fish. Rinse all the fish and seafood. Add to the pan and stir, then add the celery, tomatoes, garlic, parsley, bay leaves,

orange zest, and tomato paste. Stir and cook for 8–10 minutes until the fish is just beginning to flake when pierced with a fork. Pour in 9 cups hot water and season lightly with salt and pepper. Reduce the heat and simmer gently for 20 minutes.

3 Remove from the heat. Let cool a little, stirring and mashing down the soft fish pieces with the back of a large wooden spoon. Remove the celery, orange zest, and bay leaves. If you like, blend the soup to a coarse puree using a food processor or hand-held blender. Push the soup through a sieve into a clean saucepan. Return the soup to a simmer over medium heat.

4 Soften the saffron in a ladleful of the soup, then stir into the rest of the soup in the pan. Adjust the seasoning. Ladle the soup into warmed bowls and serve hot, with croûtes.

jerusalem artichoke soup with saffron and thyme

Use whatever proportion of carrots and Jerusalem artichokes you have, adding up to 1lb 9oz (700g) in total. The carrots enhance the color and sweetness of the soup.

 15 MINS 35–45 MINS ❄ FREEZABLE

SPECIAL EQUIPMENT ▪ food processor or hand-held blender

SERVES 4–6

2 tbsp virgin olive oil, plus extra to drizzle

2 onions, chopped

3 garlic cloves, chopped

12oz (350g) Jerusalem artichokes, scrubbed and coarsely chopped

12oz (350g) carrots, scrubbed and coarsely chopped

sea salt and freshly ground black pepper

4 cups hot vegetable stock

1 tbsp fresh thyme leaves or 1½ tsp dried thyme

large pinch (about 30 strands) of saffron

juice of ½ lemon

1 Heat the oil in a large pan over medium heat, add the onions, and cook for 3–4 minutes until soft and translucent. Add the garlic and cook for 30 seconds, or until fragrant. Stir in the Jerusalem artichokes, carrots, and a little sea salt, then cover with

a lid and cook, stirring frequently, for 10–15 minutes, or until the vegetables are softened.

2 Add the stock, thyme, and saffron, bring to a boil, then reduce the heat and simmer for 20 minutes, or until the vegetables are thoroughly soft.

3 Remove the soup from the heat and using a food processor or hand-held blender, purée until smooth. Stir in the lemon juice and season to taste. Serve with a drizzle of oil.

variation

creamed celery root soup with cumin

Prepare in exactly the same way, but substitute 1 small celery root, peeled and chopped, for the Jerusalem artichokes. Add 1 tsp ground cumin when cooking the vegetables, and omit the saffron. Use fresh thyme and stir in ¼ cup half-and-half just before serving.

caramelized shallot tart

The allium family is indispensible to most cooks, yet we rarely find ways of allowing onions and shallots to take center stage. This simple recipe gives shallots a starring role.

 20 MINS PLUS CHILLING   45 MINS

SPECIAL EQUIPMENT ▪ food processor

SERVES 4–6
2 tbsp butter

2 tbsp extra virgin olive oil

14oz (400g) shallots, split in half lengthwise

2 tbsp balsamic vinegar

a few sprigs of thyme

For the crust
1 cup all-purpose flour

sea salt

5 tbsp butter

1 For the crust, combine the flour, a pinch of sea salt, and the butter in a food processor and mix to form fine bread crumbs. With the motor running, add cold water, 1 tbsp at a time, until the dough starts to stick together. Form the dough into a ball, wrap it in plastic wrap, and leave it in the fridge to chill for 30 minutes.

2 Preheat the oven to 400°F (200°C). In a large, ovenproof frying pan, melt the butter with the oil over medium heat. Put the shallots in, cut-side down, and cook very gently for 10 minutes until they are browned. Turn them over and cook for another 5 minutes. Add the balsamic vinegar and 2 tbsp water, then remove from the heat. Tuck the sprigs of thyme between the shallots.

3 Roll out the dough into a circle a little larger than the frying pan. Lay the dough over the shallots, trim, and tuck it in. Transfer the pan to the oven and cook for 30 minutes until the crust is golden brown.

4 Remove the pan from the oven and bang it gently to loosen the shallots. Run a knife around the edges of the crust, then put a large plate over the pan and quickly turn it over. Serve warm with a green salad.

chicken liver and apple pâté

Topped with golden slices of caramelized apple, these individual pâtés make an elegant first course.

 30-35 MINS PLUS CHILLING   12-15 MINS

SPECIAL EQUIPMENT ▪ food processor ▪ 6 ramekins

SERVES 6
3 sweet apples

1.125 cups butter

salt and freshly ground black pepper

1lb 2oz (500g) chicken livers, trimmed

4 shallots, finely diced

2 garlic cloves, finely chopped

¼ cup Calvados or cognac

2 tbsp granulated sugar

6 slices of whole-grain bread

6 sprigs of mint, to serve (optional)

1 Core, peel, and dice 2 of the apples. Melt 2 tbsp of the butter in a frying pan. Add the diced apples, salt, and pepper. Sauté, stirring frequently, for 5–7 minutes until tender. Transfer to a bowl with a slotted spoon.

2 Melt another 2 tbsp of the butter in the pan. Add the chicken livers and season. Cook, stirring, for 2–3 minutes, until brown. Add in the shallots and garlic and cook for 1–2 minutes until slightly soft. Increase the heat to medium-high. Pour the Calvados into the pan and bring to a boil. Hold a lit match to the pan's side to set the alcohol alight. Baste the chicken livers for 20–30 seconds until the flames subside. Set aside to cool.

3 Pulse the mixture in a food processor until almost smooth. Wipe out the frying pan. Cream 1lb of the butter in a bowl until soft. Add the livers and the sautéed apples. Mix, season, and spoon into the ramekins. Smooth the tops, cover, and chill for 2–3 hours.

4 Core the remaining apple and slice into 6 rings. Melt the remaining butter in the pan. Add the apple, sprinkle with half the sugar, and cook for 2–3 minutes each side, until caramelized. Meanwhile, toast the slices of bread. Set a caramelized apple slice and a sprig of mint, if liked, on top of each pâté and serve with the toast.

filo pie with spicy kale and sausage

If you don't have kale on hand, other winter greens work well.

 35–40 MINS **45–55 MINS**

SPECIAL EQUIPMENT ▪ 11in (28cm) round springform cake pan

SERVES 6

14 tbsp unsalted butter

9oz (250g) loose sausage meat

3 onions, finely chopped

1lb 10oz (750g) kale, shredded

½ tsp ground allspice

salt and freshly ground black pepper

2 large eggs, beaten

1lb 2oz (500g) package of filo pastry

1 Heat 2 tbsp of the butter in a pan, add the sausage, and cook, stirring, until brown. Transfer to a bowl, leaving the fat behind. Add the onions to the pan and cook until soft. Add the kale, cover, and cook until wilted. Uncover and cook for 5 minutes, stirring so the moisture evaporates.

2 Return the sausage to the pan with the allspice and stir into the kale mixture. Season to taste. Remove from the heat and let cool completely. Stir in the eggs. Preheat the oven to 350°F (180°C). Melt the remaining

butter in a pan; brush the pan with a little butter. Lay a damp kitchen towel on the work surface. Unroll the filo onto the towel, then using the pan as a guide, cut through the pastry sheets with a 3in (7.5cm) border. Cover the sheets with a second damp towel.

3 Put 1 filo sheet on top of a third damp towel and brush with butter. Transfer to the cake pan, pressing it well into the side. Butter another filo sheet and put it in the pan at a right angle to the first. Continue buttering and layering until half the filo is used, alternating layers at right angles.

4 Spoon the filling into the crust. Butter another sheet of filo and cover the filling. Top with the rest of the filo, buttering each sheet. Fold the overhanging dough over the top and drizzle with the remaining butter. Bake the pie in the oven for 45–55 minutes until golden. Let cool slightly, then cut into wedges.

puff-crusted game soup

A delicious soup to showcase a variety of game meat—use diced venison, rabbit, or even wild boar.

 20 MINS **1 HR 20 MINS** ❄ **FREEZABLE**

SPECIAL EQUIPMENT ▪ 4 deep, ovenproof soup cups

SERVES 4

large pat of butter

6oz (175g) diced game meat, cut into small pieces

1 red onion, chopped

2 tbsp all-purpose flour

3 cups hot beef stock

1 tbsp redcurrant jelly

3 crimini mushrooms, halved and sliced

1 tbsp chopped sage

¼ cup ruby port

salt and freshly ground black pepper

1 sheet store-bought puff pastry, thawed if frozen

1 egg, beaten

1 Melt the butter in a saucepan over medium heat. Add the meat and onion and cook for about 5 minutes, stirring until browned.

2 Blend in the flour and cook for 1 minute. Remove from the heat, gradually stir in the stock, add the redcurrant jelly, and bring to a boil,

stirring. Add the mushrooms, sage, port, and season with salt and pepper. Return to a boil, reduce the heat, cover, and simmer very gently for 1 hour, stirring occasionally until rich and really tender. Taste and adjust the seasoning if necessary.

3 Meanwhile, preheat the oven to 425°F (220°C). Cut four circles from the pastry slightly larger than the soup cups, and brush with the beaten egg. Stand the soup cups on a baking sheet. Brush the edges with more beaten egg. Ladle in the soup. Top with the circles of pastry, pressing down lightly with a fork around the edge to secure. Make a small slit in the top of each pie lid with a sharp knife to allow the steam to escape. Bake in the oven for about 15 minutes, or until puffy, crisp, and golden brown. Allow to cool for 3–5 minutes before serving.

celery and celery root soup

This earthy soup combines mildly nutty celery root and the more assertive celery to create a satisfying winter warmer.

 15 MINS **20 MINS** ❄ **FREEZABLE**

SPECIAL EQUIPMENT ▪ blender or food processor

SERVES 4

1 tbsp sunflower, vegetable, or mild olive oil

4 tbsp butter, half diced and chilled

1lb 2oz (500g) celery root, peeled and chopped

1 large head of celery, cored and chopped

1 russet potato, peeled and chopped

sea salt and freshly ground black pepper

3½ cups hot light vegetable or chicken stock

4 slices walnut bread, lightly toasted, to serve

1 Put the oil and the unchilled butter in a large frying pan over medium heat. Add the celery root, celery, and potato. Stir well for 2–3 minutes, then

reduce the heat a little. Add 3–4 tbsp water and season lightly. Partly cover with a lid and let stew gently until very soft. Stir the vegetables occasionally and keep the heat low.

2 Pour the soup into a blender or food processor and purée until smooth. Return to the pan and add the stock. Season with sea salt and pepper, stir briskly to blend, and bring to a simmer over medium heat, stirring frequently. Reduce the heat a little and let simmer for 10–15 minutes, still stirring occasionally. Taste and adjust the seasoning.

3 Just before serving, whisk in the remaining chilled, diced butter. Serve hot with toasted walnut bread.

Season's best **winter leafy greens**

Asian greens is the catch-all name for a number of different brassicas, such as bok choy and the leafy mustard greens, all with varying degrees of pepperiness. Kale (both red and green) has descended from the wild cabbages of southern Europe; and dark green cavolo nero initially came from Italy. Both have a chewy texture and a slightly bitter, cabbagey flavor. Enjoy all with garlic, soy sauce, chile, ginger, and nuts.

Cavolo nero and kale, with their sturdy leaves, are popular crops thriving in cold to warm climates. Peppery Asian greens are originally from that continent, but today grow worldwide.

Curly kale Exceptionally nutritious, the leaves of curly kale have a rich, robust flavor and coarse texture. Boil or steam until tender and bright green. Overcooked, they turn gray.

essentials
varieties available

Red and dark green curly kale, dark green cavolo nero, and various Asian greens such as bok choy (pak choi), joy soy, mustard spinach, leaf mustard.

buy Look for firm stalks and fresh-looking leaves. Avoid any that are yellowing, limp, or have brown spots.

store Best eaten fresh, or store unwashed in a plastic bag in the fridge for 3–4 days. Kale becomes bitter if stored too long. Do not put near fruits that give off ethylene gas, such as apples, or the leaves will turn yellow.

cook Boil, steam, braise, stir-fry, or add to soups and stews.

preserve Blanch and freeze.

recipe ideas

Beef and greens p445

Filo pie with spicy kale and sausage p428

Wasabi beef and bok choy p442

Cavolo nero Also known as Tuscan black cabbage or Dinosaur kale, this member of the kale family is a popular gourmet vegetable. The puckered leaves have a rich, strong flavor. Lightly steam, or sauté.

Bok choy (pak choi) Also known as Chinese white cabbage, the crunchy, mild-flavored stalks are almost sweet, while the leaves taste slightly mustardy.

Small heads are delicious braised whole; larger ones shredded and stir-fried, or added to soups and stews.

mini chicken, leek, and mushroom pies

Small in size but big in taste, these delicious morsels contain a creamy filling of winter produce flavored with garlic and wine. Choose a small leek for a sweeter flavor.

 15 MINS **50 MINS** ❄ **FREEZABLE**

SPECIAL EQUIPMENT ▪ 2½in (6cm) and 2in (5cm) cookie cutters ▪ 12-hole mini muffin pan

MAKES 12

1 tbsp olive oil

2 tbsp butter

1 small carrot, finely chopped

1 small celery stalk, finely chopped

1 small leek, white part only, trimmed and finely chopped

1 small garlic clove, grated or finely chopped

3½oz (100g) crimini mushrooms, diced

9oz (250g) boneless, skinless chicken breasts, diced

1 tbsp chopped thyme leaves

grated zest of ½ lemon

3 tbsp dry white wine

½ cup heavy cream

salt and freshly ground black pepper

1½ sheets store-bought puff pastry

1 large egg, lightly beaten, for egg wash

mixed green leaves and herbs, to serve

1 Heat the oil and butter in a frying pan over low heat. Add the carrot and celery, and gently cook for about 5 minutes until soft. Add the leek and cook for a few more minutes until softened. Stir in the garlic and cook for 30 seconds, before adding the mushrooms. Cook, stirring occasionally, for another 5 minutes.

2 Increase the heat slightly and add the chicken, thyme, lemon zest, and white wine. Cook, stirring occasionally, for 15–20 minutes. Pour in the cream and season with salt and pepper. Continue to cook for about 5 minutes until thickened slightly. Let cool.

3 Preheat the oven to 400°F (200°C). Lightly oil the muffin pan. Using the larger cookie cutter, cut 12 circles from the puff pastry and line the holes in the prepared muffin pan. Spoon the chicken mixture into the pastry shells. With the small cookie cutter, cut 12 circles from the puff pastry and use them to cover each of the chicken pies. Gently press the edges together to seal. Brush the tops with the egg wash, and bake for 15–20 minutes, until golden brown. Serve hot with a mixed-leaf salad.

carrot cream soup with onion and cumin

Pushing this colorful, zingy soup through a sieve with a wooden spoon to make it super smooth may seem tedious, but it does wonders for the texture and is well worth the effort.

 20 MINS **30 MINS** ❄ **FREEZABLE**

SPECIAL EQUIPMENT ▪ blender or food processor

SERVES 6

2 tbsp sunflower, vegetable, or mild olive oil

2 large Spanish onions, coarsely chopped

1 tsp cumin seeds

1 tsp ground cumin

2¼lb (1kg) carrots, coarsely chopped

sea salt and freshly ground black pepper

grated zest and juice of 1 small unwaxed orange

½ cup half-and-half

1 tbsp finely chopped flat-leaf parsley

1 Heat the oil in a large frying pan over medium heat, add the onion, cumin seeds, and ground cumin, and cook for 3–4 minutes or until soft. Add the carrots and 5½ cups water, then season lightly with sea salt and pepper. Reduce the heat, cover, and simmer for 20 minutes, or until the carrots are very tender. Turn off the heat and allow to cool a little.

2 Pour the soup into a blender or food processor and process until smooth. Place a sieve over a saucepan (or the frying pan if possible) and pour the soup into it, pushing through with the back of a wooden spoon.

3 Taste and adjust the seasoning. Stir in the orange zest and juice. Reheat until piping hot and stir in the half-and-half and the parsley. Season with a little extra pepper and serve hot.

variation

celery root cream soup with orange and cinnamon

Prepare in the same way but substitute 1 large celery root for the carrots. Add the grated zest and juice of 1 large orange (instead of a small one). Omit all the cumin but add a cinnamon stick and a bay leaf when cooking. Discard before puréeing. Stir in finely chopped cilantro instead of parsley.

caldo verde

A traditional Portuguese soup, caldo verde—meaning "green soup"—is made from kale (in Portugal called "galega" cabbage) and potatoes. It is fabulous comfort food.

 10 MINS **20 MINS** ❄ **FREEZABLE**

SERVES 4

4 russet potatoes, peeled and cut into chunks

salt and freshly ground black pepper

1lb 2oz (500g) kale, leaves pulled from the core and very finely sliced

2 tbsp olive oil

1 Put the potatoes in a saucepan along with 8 cups water and add a little salt. Bring to a boil, then reduce the temperature and simmer for about 15 minutes, or until tender. Mash the potatoes lightly with a fork, leaving them in the water.

2 Cook the kale in a pan of boiling water for 3–4 minutes. Drain and stir into the potato broth with the oil. Simmer for 1–2 minutes. Season with salt and pepper and serve hot.

variation

mixed vegetable caldo verde

Make in the same way but use 2 potatoes, 1 turnip, and ½ rutabaga, peeled and cut in chunks instead of 4 potatoes. Serve sprinkled with grated Parmesan.

onion tart

An onion tart is very simple fare made with a minimal number of ingredients. Don't hold back on the seasoning, which helps to bring out the flavor of the onions even more. The addition of paprika in this version brings added color as well as flavor.

 15 MINS   **55 MINS**   **FREEZABLE**

SPECIAL EQUIPMENT ▪ 8in (20cm) round fluted tart pan ▪ ceramic baking beans

SERVES 6

1 tbsp olive oil

4 onions, sliced

1 tbsp all-purpose flour

1¼ cups milk

2 tsp mild paprika

salt and freshly ground black pepper

10oz (300g) store-bought pie dough

1 large egg, lightly beaten, for egg wash

1 Preheat the oven to 400°F (200°C). Heat the oil in a large, non-stick, heavy-bottomed pan over low heat. Add the onions and cook very gently for about 15 minutes until soft and translucent. Keep stirring throughout, so that the onions don't stick or brown.

2 Remove from the heat and stir in the flour with a wooden spoon. Add a little of the milk and stir until combined. Return the pan to the heat and keep adding the milk, slowly and gradually, stirring continuously as the mixture thickens. Add 1 tsp of the paprika and season well with salt and pepper. Remove from the heat and set aside.

3 Roll out the dough on a floured work surface and use to line the tart pan. Trim away any excess, line the pie dough with parchment paper, and fill with the ceramic baking beans. Bake in the oven for 15–20 minutes until the edges of the crust are golden. Remove the beans and paper, brush the bottom of the crust with a little of the egg wash, and return to the oven for a couple of minutes to crisp. Reduce the oven temperature to 350°F (180°C).

4 Carefully spoon the onion mixture into the pie crust and sprinkle with the remaining paprika. Return the pie to the oven and bake for 15–20 minutes until lightly golden. Serve warm with a green salad.

variation

leek and cheddar cheese tart

Prepare in exactly the same way, but use 3–4 leeks thinly sliced, instead of the onions, and add 2oz (60g) sharp Cheddar cheese to the leek mixture with the paprika, at the end of step 2.

avocado, grapefruit, and parma ham salad

Great flavor and texture contrasts with the sweet and silky Parma ham against the bitter arugula and sharp grapefruit.

 25–30 MINS

SERVES 4

½ small onion, grated

3 tbsp red wine vinegar

1 tbsp honey

½ tsp mustard powder

¼ tsp ground ginger

salt and freshly ground black pepper

⅔ cup vegetable oil

1 tbsp poppy seeds

4 grapefruit

2 avocados

juice of 1 lemon

6oz (175g) arugula leaves

4½oz (125g) Parma ham, cut into 1in (2.5cm) strips

1 For the vinaigrette, put the onion, vinegar, honey, mustard powder, ginger, salt, and pepper into a bowl and whisk. Gradually whisk in the oil, so the vinaigrette emulsifies and thickens. Stir in the poppy seeds and taste for seasoning.

2 With a vegetable peeler, peel half of the zest from 1 grapefruit, leaving behind the white pith. Cut into very fine julienne strips. Half-fill a small saucepan with water and bring to a boil. Add the grapefruit julienne, simmer for 2 minutes, drain, and set aside.

3 Slice off the top and base of the grapefruit. Cut away the zest, pith, and skin, following the curve of the fruit. Holding each grapefruit over a bowl, cut out the segments, cutting between the membranes. Release the segments into the bowl. Discard any seeds, cover, and refrigerate.

4 Halve the avocados and remove the pits, then peel the skin. Cut into slices lengthwise and place in a bowl. Pour in the lemon juice and toss the avocado to prevent it from browning. Briskly whisk the dressing. Toss the arugula with one-third of it, then divide between 4 plates. Arrange the grapefruit, Parma ham, and avocado on top. Spoon over the remaining vinaigrette and sprinkle with grapefruit julienne.

creamy rutabaga soup

As a strictly cold-season vegetable, rutabaga stores up a lot of starch in the edible root base. It is this, combined with honey and cream, that gives this rich, wintry soup its velvety texture.

 10 MINS 🍲 40–50 MINS ❄ FREEZABLE

SPECIAL EQUIPMENT ▪ blender or food processor

SERVES 4–6

2 tbsp butter

2 onions, chopped

1lb 10oz (750g) rutabaga (trimmed weight), cut into cubes

sea salt and freshly ground black pepper

3½ cups hot vegetable stock

1 tbsp honey

½ nutmeg

⅔ cup half-and-half, plus extra to garnish

1 Melt the butter in a large pan over medium heat, add the onions, and cook for 6–8 minutes or until lightly golden. Stir in the rutabaga and a pinch of sea salt, cover with a lid, and cook for 10 minutes, stirring frequently. Pour in the stock, add the honey, and bring to a boil. Grate the nutmeg over the soup as it boils, then lower the heat and simmer for 20–30 minutes, or until the rutabaga is completely soft.

2 Cool briefly, then process in a blender until smooth and velvety. You may need to do this in batches. Season with sea salt and pepper, then stir in the half-and-half. Serve each bowlful with a swirl of cream and a good grinding of black pepper.

variation

creamy four root soup

Prepare in exactly the same way but use 1 small rutabaga, 2 turnips, 1 parsnip, and 1 large carrot instead of all rutabaga.

crispy bacon and avocado wraps

Avocado flesh can turn an unattractive shade of brown very quickly, so it is always worth tossing the peeled flesh in lemon juice as quickly as possible to prevent this from happening.

 5 MINS 🍲 10 MINS

SERVES 4

8oz (225g) thick-cut bacon

1 avocado

juice of 1 lemon

freshly ground black pepper

3–4 tbsp mayonnaise

4 flour tortillas

handful of romaine lettuce leaves, shredded

1 Cook the bacon in a heavy-bottomed frying pan over medium-high heat until golden and crispy.

2 Halve the avocado and remove the pit, then peel the skin. Cut into slices and place in a bowl. Pour in the lemon juice and toss the avocado to prevent it from browning. Add plenty of black pepper and then stir in the mayonnaise.

3 Fill the tortillas with the bacon and shredded romaine and top with the avocado in mayonnaise. Then roll up the tortillas and serve immediately.

variation

spicy chicken, avocado, and spinach wraps

Prepare in the same way but substitute 8oz (225g) diced cooked chicken for the bacon. Use a handful of spinach leaves instead of romaine lettuce and sprinkle each wrap with a pinch of dried chile flakes before rolling up.

Season's best **avocado**

Also called avocado pears because of their shape, avocados are at their best in the winter months and into spring. They are loaded with potassium, fiber, and exceptional levels of monosaturated fat (the good kind). They have a mild, somewhat nutty, flavor and a smooth, oily texture. Good flavor pairings include Parma ham, shrimp, tomatoes, grapefruit, lime, pineapple, sugar, and balsamic vinegar.

Unlike most fruits, avocados ripen off the tree. Originally native to Central America and the Caribbean, there are over 500 cultivars planted worldwide.

essentials
varieties available

Hass, Fuerte, and Sharwill are the most popular varieties.

buy The shiny, green varieties, like Fuerte, should "give" slightly when gently squeezed. Others, like Hass, must be black and should "give" slightly at the stalk end but not feel too soft.

store Unripe at room temperature. If ripe, keep in the fridge and eat in a day or two.

cook Eat raw; cook, stuffed and baked, or in a soup.

preserve Mash the flesh with lemon juice, then freeze.

recipe ideas

Avocado and spinach soup p16

Avocado, grapefruit, and Parma ham salad p432

Crispy bacon and avocado wraps p432

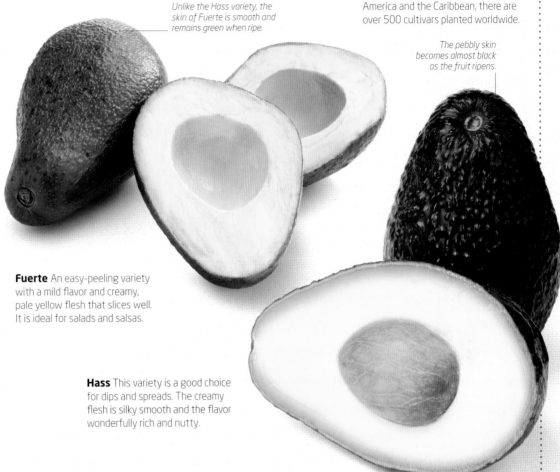

Unlike the Hass variety, the skin of Fuerte is smooth and remains green when ripe.

The pebbly skin becomes almost black as the fruit ripens.

Fuerte An easy-peeling variety with a mild flavor and creamy, pale yellow flesh that slices well. It is ideal for salads and salsas.

Hass This variety is a good choice for dips and spreads. The creamy flesh is silky smooth and the flavor wonderfully rich and nutty.

how to pit and peel avocado

Using a knife to remove the avocado pit is clean, quick, and surprisingly easy. The avocado must be just ripe to taste rich and luxurious. If underripe, the flesh is tough and slightly bitter. If overripe, it becomes black and "soapy." Rub the flesh with lemon afterward to prevent it from browning.

1 With a chef's knife, slice straight into the avocado, cutting all the way around the pit. Gently twist the halves in opposite directions and separate.

2 Strike the cutting edge of your knife into the pit and lift the knife (wiggling if necessary) to remove it from the avocado.

3 Use a spatula to remove the flesh cleanly from the skin if you want to keep it whole. Cut into slices or wedges, or mash for dips and spreads.

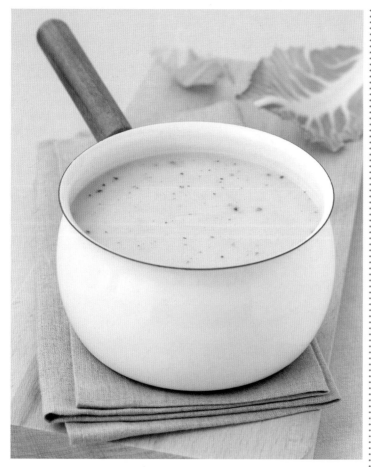

minestrone soup

This is a hearty cold-weather version of the Italian soup, using a base of sweet carrot and aromatic celery.

 10 MINS 40 MINS

SERVES 4

1 tbsp olive oil

1 onion, finely chopped

salt and freshly ground black pepper

1 tsp dried oregano

4 carrots, finely diced

4 celery stalks, finely diced

3 garlic cloves, grated or finely chopped

¼ cup red wine

1 tbsp tomato paste

1 x 14oz (400g) can whole plum tomatoes, chopped

2 cups hot vegetable stock

7oz (200g) pasta, such as macaroni or vermicelli

handful of flat-leaf parsley, finely chopped

Parmesan cheese, grated, to garnish

1 Heat the oil in a large pan over medium heat, add the onion, and cook for 3–4 minutes, or until soft and translucent. Add a pinch of salt, the oregano, and stir in the carrots and celery. Cook gently for about 10 minutes until softened.

2 Stir in the garlic and cook for a few seconds more. Pour in the wine, increase the heat, and let it boil for 1–2 minutes until the alcohol has evaporated. Stir in the tomato paste and season well with salt and pepper. Add the canned tomatoes and vegetable stock. Bring to a boil, reduce the heat slightly, and simmer for about 20 minutes, adding hot water if the minestrone gets too thick (but don't make it too thin).

3 Meanwhile, cook the pasta in a large pan of boiling salted water for about 12 minutes, or until it is tender but still al dente. Drain, and chop if large. Add the pasta to the soup. Sprinkle over the parsley and serve hot with a bowl of Parmesan cheese for sprinkling over the top.

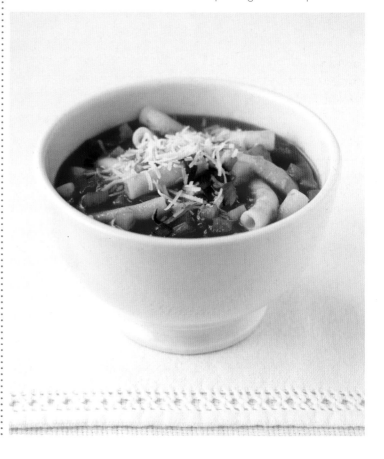

cauliflower soup

Be sure to cut off all the green leaves of the cauliflower because they can make this soup taste a little bitter.

 15 MINS   40 MINS   FREEZABLE

SPECIAL EQUIPMENT ▪ blender or food processor

SERVES 4

1 tbsp olive oil

1 onion, finely chopped

salt and freshly ground black pepper

1 large garlic clove, grated or finely chopped

2 celery stalks, finely chopped

1 bay leaf

2 potatoes, peeled and cut into bite-sized chunks

2½ cups hot vegetable stock

1 cauliflower, trimmed and cut into florets

drizzle of heavy cream, to serve (optional)

1 Heat the oil in a large pan, add the onion, and cook over low heat for 6–8 minutes, or until soft and translucent. Season well with salt and pepper, then add the garlic, celery, and bay leaf and cook for 5 minutes, or until the celery begins to soften. Stir in the potatoes and cook for

5 minutes, then pour in the stock, bring to a boil, and cook for 15 minutes, or until the potatoes are nearly soft.

2 Add the cauliflower and cook for 10 minutes, until soft but not watery. Remove the bay leaf and discard, then transfer the soup to a blender or food processor and blend until smooth. Add a little more hot stock if it seems too thick. Taste and season with salt and pepper if needed. To serve, drizzle with heavy cream, if using, and serve with fresh crusty bread.

variation

cauliflower cheese soup

Use only 2 cups stock in step 1. Purée with 1 cup milk and return to the pan. Stir in 2 large handfuls grated sharp Cheddar cheese. Thin with a little more milk if too thick. Reheat but do not boil.

scotch broth

The traditional ingredients of a Scotch broth are lamb and barley, both of which feature prominently in this recipe. Barley needs a good hour of cooking to become sufficiently tender.

 20 MINS 1 HR 45 MINS ❄ FREEZABLE

SERVES 4

8oz (225g) lamb neck

salt and freshly ground black pepper

1 tbsp olive oil

1 small onion, finely chopped

2 carrots, finely chopped

2 celery stalks, finely chopped

4 cups hot chicken stock

4oz (115g) pearl barley

handful of curly parsley, finely chopped

1 Put the lamb in a large pan, cover with cold water, and season with salt and pepper. Bring to a boil, then reduce the heat and simmer for 30 minutes, or until cooked. Remove with a slotted spoon, let cool slightly, then shred and set aside. Reserve the cooking liquid.

2 Heat the oil in a large pan, add the onion, and cook over medium heat for 3–4 minutes until soft and translucent. Add the carrots and celery, and cook over very low heat for 10 minutes. Strain the reserved liquid, then add to the pan and pour in the stock. Season with salt and pepper, then add the pearl barley and bring to a boil. Reduce the heat to low and simmer for 1 hour, or until the pearl barley is cooked. Add more hot water if it begins to dry out too much.

3 Stir in the parsley, then season again with salt and pepper if needed. Serve with fresh crusty bread.

split pea and bacon soup

Root vegetables from the cellar are invaluable during the cold winter months for heart-warming soups like this. Split peas take a long time to cook, so start early or use a slow cooker.

 15 MINS 2 HRS 15 MINS ❄ FREEZABLE

SPECIAL EQUIPMENT ▪ blender or food processor

SERVES 4

2 tbsp olive oil

7oz (200g) bacon or pancetta, chopped into bite-sized pieces

1 onion, finely chopped

salt and freshly ground black pepper

2 celery stalks, finely chopped

2 carrots, finely chopped

10oz (300g) yellow split peas

3 cups hot vegetable stock

1 Heat half the oil in a large heavy-bottomed pan over medium heat, add the bacon or pancetta, and cook, stirring occasionally, for 5 minutes, or until crispy and golden. Remove with a slotted spoon and set aside. Heat the remaining oil in the pan, add the onion, and cook over low heat for 6–8 minutes, or until soft and translucent. Season with salt and pepper, then add the celery and carrots, and cook over low heat for 5 minutes.

2 Add the split peas and stock and bring to a boil slowly. Cover with a lid, reduce to a simmer, and cook for 2 hours, or until the peas are tender. Check occasionally and add more hot water if the soup begins to look too thick. Transfer to a blender or food processor and purée until smooth. Return to the pan. Add the bacon or pancetta and season with salt and pepper. Reheat then serve with fresh crusty bread.

variation

smoky split pea soup

Omit the bacon. Cook the onions in the 2 tbsp olive oil and continue the recipe as before but add 1 tsp smoked paprika at step 2. Meanwhile, dry-fry 4oz (115g) finely diced Spanish-style chorizo. Ladle the soup in bowls and garnish with a small spoonful of the fried chorizo.

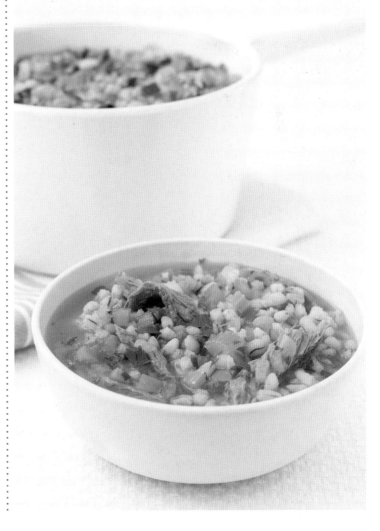

oysters with chile and lime mayonnaise

An oyster knife is essential when shucking these shell fish. It will have a sturdy handle and a point at the end of the blade.

 15 MINS

SPECIAL EQUIPMENT ▪ oyster knife

SERVES 4–6

2 small red or jalapeño chiles, seeded

1 garlic clove, grated or finely chopped

salt and freshly ground black pepper

1 large egg yolk

⅔ cup light olive oil

juice of 1 lime

24 oysters in their shells

rock salt, to serve

1 To make the chile and lime mayonnaise, pound the chiles, garlic, and a good pinch of salt to a paste with a pestle in a mortar. Spoon the paste into a large bowl, then add the egg yolk. Stir thoroughly with a wooden spoon or whisk until smooth.

2 Gradually add the oil, drop by drop, whisking continuously, ensuring it is absorbed completely before making the next addition. Once the mixture starts to thicken, add the oil in a slow, thin drizzle. When a third of the oil

has been combined, start adding the lime juice a little at a time. Keep adding and whisking until everything is well incorporated. Season with black pepper, cover with plastic wrap, and chill until needed.

3 To prepare the oysters, discard any that have opened or do not close immediately when tapped on the work surface. Use an oyster knife and hold the oysters over a bowl as you open them. Carefully shuck the oysters one by one (p437), catching any liquid in the bowl and transferring the opened oysters in their shells and their liquid to the fridge as you go.

4 Put a layer of rock salt on a platter to keep the oysters level. Arrange the open oysters in their shells on top of the salt and spoon over the chilled oyster liquid. Add a little chile and lime mayonnaise over the top of each oyster and serve immediately.

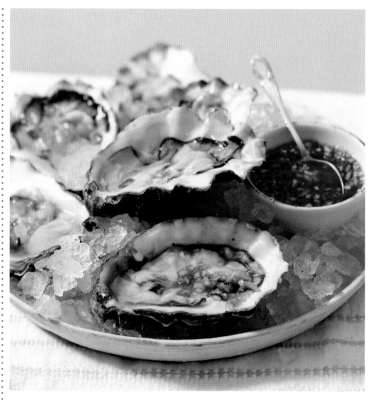

oysters with shallot and vinegar dressing

Take great care when shucking an oyster as the knife can slip all too easily. For safety's sake, wrap your knife-free hand in a thick kitchen towel to protect it, should the worst happen.

 15 MINS

SPECIAL EQUIPMENT ▪ oyster knife

SERVES 4–6

24 oysters in their shells

crushed ice

¼ cup red wine vinegar

1 large or 2 small shallots, very finely chopped

1 To prepare the oysters, discard any that have opened or do not close immediately, when tapped on the work surface. Use an oyster knife, and hold the oysters over a bowl as you open them. Carefully shuck the oysters one by one (p437), catching any liquid in the bowl and transferring the opened oysters in their shells and their liquid to the fridge as you go.

2 Arrange the oysters on an oyster plate with ice, or pack 4 serving dishes with lots of crushed ice and place the oysters on top.

3 Mix the vinegar and shallots together and put into a small dish. Place in the center of the oysters—or the middle of the table—and serve.

variation

oysters with lemon and tabasco

Shuck the oysters as directed and serve on crushed ice with lemon wedges and Tabasco sauce on the side. Allow your guests to choose their preferred dressing or to eat the oysters unadorned.

Season's best **oysters**

Oysters are a delicacy and differ in flavor and shell color, depending on their location. Mostly found in temperate coastal waters, they are harvested from the wild from autumn to spring, and farmed all year. Oyster tasting is an art, with many gourmet terms for its varied flavors. Pair raw oysters with shallots, red wine, vinegar, Tabasco, and lemon juice; cooked oysters go well with anchovy paste, butter, cream, and spinach.

Pacific oyster The taste of this widely cultured oyster varies enormously, depending on where it is grown. Flavors range from smoky, grassy, and acidic, through to milky and creamy. Usually graded by weight, a fair size would be 4oz (115g), or 4½in (11cm). Store the oysters cup-side down to prevent their natural juices from escaping.

Native oysters have an oval, scaly shell, intense taste, and firm texture.

Native oyster Also called the European flat oyster, it is often served raw on a bed of crushed ice, dressed with lemon juice, Tabasco, and shallot vinegar. Graded by size, from 1 to 4, the largest "royals" can reach 4in (10cm).

Pacific oysters are larger and less expensive than native ones and grow more quickly.

The meat of the Pacific oyster is a delicate beige in color, with a smooth, creamy texture.

essentials
varieties available

The two main varieties, wild and farmed, are Native and Pacific oysters.

buy They should be shut tight and undamaged and smell pleasantly of the sea.

store Keep in the fridge, rounded sides down. Eat on the day of purchase.

cook Usually eaten *au naturel*, or fry, poach, grill, or bake.

preserve Can be frozen in their half shells and juice, but only if very fresh.

recipe ideas

Broiled oysters with crème fraîche and Parmesan p439

Oysters with chile and lime mayonnaise p436

Oysters with shallot and vinegar dressing p436

how to shuck an oyster

Fresh oysters are tightly closed and hard to open without an oyster shucking knife. When shucking oysters, always protect the hand holding the oyster with a towel or oven mitt, in case the knife slips while applying pressure to pry off the top shell. Holding the oyster flat on a towel will help prevent the deliciously briny liquid from spilling out.

1 Insert the tip of an oyster knife into the hinge to open the shell. Keep the blade close to the top of the shell so the oyster is not damaged. Cut the muscle and lift off the top shell.

2 Detach the oyster from the bottom shell by carefully sliding the blade of the knife beneath the oyster. They can be served raw on the half shell (scrub the shells thoroughly before opening), or removed and cooked.

crab salad with grapefruit and cilantro

White crabmeat comes from the claws and legs of a crab. It has a delicate flavor and is low in fat, in contrast to brown crabmeat from the body, which has a higher fat content.

 10 MINS

SERVES 4

12oz (350g) cooked fresh or canned white crabmeat, drained

handful of baby salad leaves

handful of cilantro leaves

2 pink grapefruits, peeled, segmented, and any pith removed

For the dressing

3 tbsp olive oil

1 tbsp white wine vinegar

pinch of sugar

salt and freshly ground black pepper

1 In a small bowl, whisk together the dressing ingredients. Season with salt and pepper.

2 Mix the crabmeat with a drizzle of the dressing. Divide the salad leaves and half of the cilantro leaves among 4 serving plates and scatter the grapefruit segments over the top.

3 When ready to serve, drizzle the salad with the remaining dressing. Divide the crabmeat among the plates, spooning it neatly on top of the leaves. Scatter over the remaining cilantro and serve immediately.

variation

poached trout salad with red grapefruit, orange, and celery

Poach 4 trout fillets in water, in a shallow frying pan for about 5 minutes until cooked through. Drain, flake the fish, discarding the skin, and let cool. Prepare the salad in exactly the same way, but use 1 red grapefruit and 1 large orange instead of the 2 pink grapefruits. Scatter 2 chopped celery stalks over the salad leaves and omit the cilantro.

carrot soup with coconut and lemongrass

This spicy, exotically flavored carrot soup makes an elegant appetizer. Serve it with lime wedges on a plate alongside, so that the guests can adjust the flavor to their liking.

 15 MINS   **35 MINS**   **FREEZABLE**

SPECIAL EQUIPMENT ▪ blender or food processor

SERVES 4

2 tbsp vegetable oil or sunflower oil

1 onion, chopped

1 lemongrass stalk, trimmed and outer leaves removed

2 garlic cloves, chopped

2 tsp finely grated ginger

1 tbsp red Thai curry paste

1lb (450g) carrots, sliced

3 cups hot vegetable stock

3 kaffir lime leaves

¾ cup coconut milk

salt and freshly ground black pepper

lime wedges, to serve

1 Heat the oil in a large pan, add the onion, and cook for 3–4 minutes until the onion is soft. Meanwhile, finely chop the lemongrass, then add to the pan along with the garlic and ginger, and cook for 2 minutes. Add the curry paste and cook for 1 minute, stirring all the time, then add the carrots and cook for 2 minutes. Pour in the stock, add the lime leaves, and simmer for 20–25 minutes, or until the carrots are tender.

2 Remove from the heat and discard the lime leaves. Pour in the coconut milk, then pour the soup into a blender or food processor, and process until smooth. The soup shouldn't be too thick—dilute with more stock if it is. Season to taste, then serve with a grating of black pepper and lime wedges.

french cabbage soup

This chunky country soup takes only minutes to prepare and makes a good light supper or lunch dish. For a meat-free option, leave out the diced bacon.

 15 MINS   **30 MINS**   ❄ **FREEZABLE**

SERVES 4

1 tbsp olive oil

3½oz (100g) diced bacon

1 Spanish onion, finely chopped

1 garlic clove, crushed

1 large Savoy cabbage, halved, cored, and leaves cut into shreds

salt and freshly ground black pepper

3 sprigs of parsley

croutons, to garnish (optional)

1 Heat the oil in a large heavy-based casserole over medium heat. Add the bacon (setting aside 2 tbsp to finish), onion, and garlic. cook, stirring frequently, for 3–4 minutes or until the onion and garlic start to color. Add the cabbage shreds, reserving a handful to finish. Stir well and season lightly with salt and generously with black pepper. Continue cooking for 2–3 minutes, stirring occasionally.

2 Boil about 3 cups water in a teapot. Pour the boiling water over the vegetables and bacon, stir well, and add the parsley. Cover, reduce the heat a little, and simmer for about 20 minutes, stirring from time to time.

3 Meanwhile, place a non-stick frying pan over medium heat. Add the reserved bacon and cook until crisp and golden. Then add the reserved cabbage shreds and cook them until they have wilted, stirring frequently. Season with a little black pepper.

4 Taste the soup and adjust the seasoning. Lift out the parsley. Ladle into individual bowls and scatter over the cooked bacon and cabbage mixture. A few croutons, if using, scattered across the surface provide a nice finishing touch.

turnip soup with pimento, chile, and noodles

A light, colorful soup with quite a chile kick. Larger turnips have a stronger flavor, which is perfect for this dish. Don't use the delicate baby ones.

 10 MINS   30 MINS   FREEZABLE

SERVES 4–6

1 onion, finely chopped

2 good-sized turnips, peeled and diced

½ tsp crushed dried chiles

1 green jalapeño chile, seeded and cut into thin rings

2 star anise

2 tsp tomato paste

3 cups hot vegetable stock or light chicken stock

1 slab dried, thin Chinese egg noodles

1 preserved pimento or cherry pepper, drained and diced

soy sauce

freshly ground black pepper

small handful of cilantro leaves, torn

1 Put the onion, turnips, chiles, star anise, tomato paste, and stock in a saucepan and bring to a boil. Lower the heat, partially cover with the lid, and simmer gently for 30 minutes, or until the turnips are really tender. Discard the star anise.

2 Meanwhile, put the noodles in a bowl, cover with boiling water, and let stand for 5 minutes, stirring to loosen, then drain. Stir the noodles into the soup, along with the pimento. Season to taste with soy sauce and black pepper, then stir in half the cilantro. Ladle into warmed soup bowls, top with the remaining cilantro, and serve.

broiled oysters with crème fraîche and parmesan

These are deliciously rich, so you can get away with serving only 3 oysters per person. Serve immediately while still piping hot or the oysters will lose their succulence.

 20 MINS   1 MIN

SPECIAL EQUIPMENT ▪ oyster knife

SERVES 4

12 large oysters

Tabasco sauce

1¼ cups crème fraîche

3 tbsp snipped chives

½oz (15g) Parmesan cheese, grated

½oz (15g) fresh bread crumbs

1 To prepare the oysters, discard any that have opened or do not close immediately when tapped on the work surface. Use an oyster knife and hold the oysters over a bowl as you open them. Carefully shuck the oysters one by one (p437), catching any liquid in the bowl and transferring the opened oysters in their shells and their liquid to the broiler rack.

2 Preheat the broiler. Add a few drops of Tabasco sauce to each oyster. Mix the crème fraîche with the chives and spoon over. Mix the Parmesan and bread crumbs together and sprinkle over each oyster. Broil for about 1 minute until the cheese is bubbling. Serve at once.

variation

broiled oysters with tabasco

Prepare in the same way but add a few drops of Tabasco to each shucked oyster and sprinkle with a mixture of snipped chives and chopped cilantro. Top with the crème fraîche and Parmesan as before.

bistro salad with egg and bacon

Here the bitter taste of frisée lettuce is offset by the saltiness of bacon and the unctuous texture of a perfectly poached egg. Add other crunchy lettuce leaves for variety.

 5 MINS   10 MINS

SERVES 4

4 large eggs

1 tbsp lemon juice

6 tbsp extra virgin olive oil

2 thick slices of bread, crusts cut off and bread diced

1 garlic clove, halved

¼in slice fresh ginger, peeled (optional)

4oz (115g) thick-cut bacon, cut into ½in (1cm) strips

½–1 head frisée lettuce, torn

3 sprigs of thyme, leaves picked

small handful of flat-leaf parsley

small handful of cilantro leaves

1 small red onion, thinly sliced

For the dressing

2 tbsp red wine vinegar

¼ tsp dried chile flakes

2 tsp Worcestershire sauce

¼ tsp granulated sugar

sea salt and freshly ground black pepper

1 Poach the eggs in gently simmering water with the lemon juice for about 3 minutes. Scoop out and put straight into cold water.

2 Heat 1 tbsp of the oil in a frying pan. Add the bread, garlic, and ginger, if using, tossing and stirring until golden. Drain the croutons on paper towels. Discard the garlic and ginger.

3 In the same pan, dry-fry the bacon until crisp and golden. Drain on paper towels.

4 Put the lettuce in a salad bowl and tear in the herbs. Add the onion, separated into rings, bacon, and croutons. Add the remaining 5 tbsp of the oil to a pan with the dressing ingredients. Heat gently, stirring. Pour over the salad and toss. Arrange the salad into individual bowls and top each with a poached egg.

meat and potato pie

Cook this warming winter pie either in a large dish or as individual portions to be eaten with steamed cabbage.

 15 MINS 1 HR 30 MINS FREEZABLE

SPECIAL EQUIPMENT ▪ 1 quart (1.2-liter) pie dish or 4 small individual pie dishes

SERVES 4

3 potatoes, peeled and cut into bite-sized pieces

1½lb (675g) stew meat, chopped into bite-sized pieces

1 tbsp olive oil, plus extra for braising

1 onion, finely chopped

1 tbsp all-purpose flour

1 tbsp Worcestershire sauce

1¾ cups hot beef stock

salt and freshly ground black pepper

10oz (300g) store-bought puff pastry

1 large egg, lightly beaten, for egg wash

1 Cook the potatoes in a pan of boiling salted water for 15–20 minutes until soft. Drain and set aside. Put the meat in a large frying pan with a drop of oil and cook over high heat for 5–8 minutes until browned all over. Remove with a slotted spoon and set aside.

2 Using the same pan, heat the oil over low heat. Add the onion and cook gently for about 5 minutes until soft and translucent. Stir in the flour

and continue to cook for another 2 minutes. Increase the heat a little and add the Worcestershire sauce and stock. Bring to a boil, reduce the heat, and return the meat to the pan. Cover and simmer for about 30 minutes, stirring occasionally. Stir in the potato and season well.

3 Meanwhile, preheat the oven to 400°F (200°C). Spoon the meat into the pie dish or small dishes. On a floured work surface, roll out the pastry until 2in (5cm) larger all around than the top of the pie dish. Cut out a strip of pastry about 1in (2.5cm) in from the edge. Wet the edge of the pie dish with a little water; fit the pastry strip all the way around and press down firmly. Brush the pastry collar with a little of the egg wash, then top with the pastry lid. Trim the excess and pinch the edges to seal. Brush the top of the pie with the egg wash and make 2 slits with a sharp knife to allow steam to escape. Bake for about 30 minutes until puffed and golden. Serve hot.

duck with apple and rosemary potatoes

Potatoes roasted with sprigs of rosemary are a most flavorful combination. Make sure the sprigs are small, though, or they can become a little woody when cooked.

 20 MINS 40–60 MINS

SERVES 4

4 large duck legs

salt and freshly ground black pepper

1¼lb (550g) potatoes, peeled and cut into chunks

3 red-skinned apples, halved, cored, and coarsely chopped

a few sprigs of rosemary

drizzle of olive oil

1 Savoy cabbage, halved, cored, and leaves coarsely chopped

pinch of dried chile flakes (optional)

redcurrant jelly (optional)

1 Rub the duck legs generously with salt and pepper. Set aside for 30 minutes, if you have the time—it will help crispen up the skin. Otherwise, cook immediately.

2 Preheat the oven to 400°F (200°C). Heat a large frying pan, add the duck, and cook for 8–10 minutes, or until

golden all over. Using a slotted spoon, transfer the duck to a large roasting pan. Add the potatoes and apples, scatter over the rosemary, drizzle with the oil, season, then combine well using your hands. Place in the oven and cook for about 40–60 minutes until the duck is crispy and the potatoes are golden. You may need to turn the potatoes halfway through cooking.

3 Meanwhile, put the cabbage in a pan of boiling salted water and cook for 4–5 minutes, or until it is cooked but still al dente. Drain and keep warm. Add to the roasting pan for the last 10 minutes of cooking, tucking it in and around the duck. Sprinkle with chile flakes, if using. Transfer to a serving dish and serve with redcurrant jelly, also if using.

chicken and cornmeal cobbler

Cover the dish with foil if the top is browning too quickly.

 20 MINS   **1 HR 45 MINS**   ❄ **FREEZABLE**

SPECIAL EQUIPMENT ▪ 1½in (4cm) cookie cutter

SERVES 4

1 tbsp olive oil

3 boneless, skinless chicken breasts, cut into bite-sized pieces

salt and freshly ground black pepper

1 red onion, finely sliced

2 celery stalks, coarsely chopped

¾ cup red wine

2 large carrots, coarsely chopped

1¾ cups hot vegetable stock

½ cup all-purpose flour

1 cup cornmeal

2 tbsp butter

small handful of flat-leaf parsley, chopped

splash of milk

1 small egg yolk, lightly beaten

1 Heat half the oil in a large, shallow flameproof casserole over medium heat. Season the chicken, then cook for 10 minutes or until lightly golden, turning occasionally. Remove with a slotted spoon and set side.

2 Preheat the oven to 350°F (180°C). Heat the remaining oil in the pan over low heat, then add the onions and cook for 6–8 minutes until soft. Add the celery and cook for 5 minutes, or until soft. Pour in the wine, increase the heat, and boil for 2 minutes while the alcohol evaporates. Add the carrots, return the chicken to the pan, and season well. Pour in the stock and cook over low heat for 1 hour, uncovered, stirring occasionally, or until all the ingredients are tender. Add hot water if necessary.

3 Meanwhile, put the flour, cornmeal, and a pinch of salt in a large bowl. Rub in the butter with your fingertips until you have a bread crumb texture. Stir in the parsley, then add the milk a little at a time until the dough comes together. Form into a ball and rest it in the fridge for 20 minutes. Flatten on a floured work surface, then roll it out with a rolling pin. Cut out about 18 rounds using the cutter, and add to the casserole, brushing with egg yolk. Cook in the oven for 30 minutes until the cobblers are golden and the casserole hot.

marsala chicken with pine nuts and golden raisins

Marsala wine is a fortified wine similar to port or sherry. It adds body as well as flavor, complementing the raisins.

 15 MINS   **45 MINS**

SERVES 4

2 tbsp olive oil

8 chicken pieces, such as thighs and breasts with skin on

1 onion, finely chopped

2 carrots, finely chopped

2 celery stalks, finely chopped

1¼ cups Marsala wine

salt and freshly ground black pepper

1¾oz (50g) pine nuts, toasted

1¾oz (50g) golden raisins

handful of flat-leaf parsley, finely chopped

1 Heat the oil in a large cast-iron pan or casserole over medium heat. Add the chicken pieces and cook for about 8 minutes until golden all over. Remove from the pan and set aside.

2 Reduce the heat to low. Add the onion, carrots, and celery to the pan and cook gently for a few minutes until soft. Pour in the Marsala wine and season with salt and pepper.

Return the chicken to the pan and simmer gently for about 30 minutes, adding water a little at a time if it begins to dry out—but don't add too much, because it should be fairly dry and the water will only dilute the flavor.

3 Stir in the pine nuts and golden raisins and cook for a few minutes more. Just before serving, stir in the parsley. Serve with a dressed green salad and fresh crusty bread.

variation

chicken in sherry with pears
Prepare in the same way, but use ⅔ cup medium-dry sherry and ⅔ cup chicken stock instead of the Marsala. Omit the pine nuts and golden raisins. Melt a pat of butter and cook 2 unripe pears, peeled, cored, and diced, until lightly golden. Stir into the sauce just before serving.

duck with pink grapefruit and chicory salad

The flavors of a winter citrus salad with chicory and fennel give a refreshing sweet-sour edge to roasted duck breast.

 10 MINS   25 MINS

SERVES 4

pat of butter

4 duck breasts, about 5½oz (150g) each, skin on and scored in a crisscross pattern

handful of rosemary sprigs

2 tbsp balsamic vinegar

1 head of chicory, leaves separated

1 fennel bulb, trimmed and finely sliced

2 pink grapefruits, peeled and segmented

salt and freshly ground black pepper

1 Preheat the oven to 400°F (200°C). Melt the butter in a large non-stick frying pan over high heat, then add the duck breasts, skin-side down, and the rosemary. Sear the duck for 2–3 minutes on each side until golden all over. Increase the heat, add half of the balsamic vinegar, and let it simmer for a few minutes, scraping up any bits from the bottom of the pan with a wooden spoon.

2 Transfer the duck and its vinegar juices to a roasting pan and roast in the oven for 15–20 minutes, until the duck is cooked to your liking.

3 Meanwhile, prepare the salad. Mix together the chicory and fennel, add the grapefruit segments, and toss gently. Drizzle with the remaining balsamic vinegar and season with salt and pepper. Slice each duck breast into two and serve with the salad.

variation

pheasant with pomegranate, frisée lettuce, and leek salad

Prepare in exactly the same way, but use 4 pheasant breasts instead of duck. Use half a small head of frisée lettuce, torn into pieces, instead of the chicory and 2 chopped baby leeks instead of the fennel. Scatter with the seeds from 1 pomegranate instead of the grapefruit.

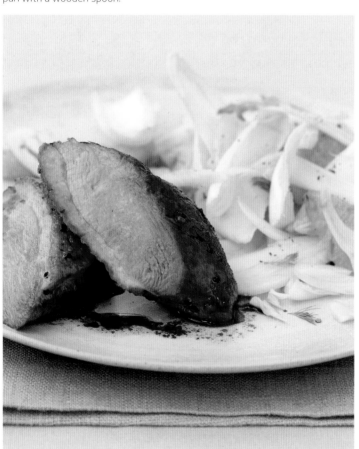

wasabi beef and bok choy

Japanese wasabi paste, a type of hot mustard, is extremely strong, so you only need a little of it to lift the flavor of the steak.

 10 MINS   10 MINS

SERVES 4

3 tbsp olive oil

2 tsp wasabi paste

4 sirloin steaks, about 7oz (200g) each

7oz (200g) bok choy, cut lengthwise into 8 pieces

5 garlic cloves, grated or finely chopped

1 tbsp dark soy sauce

salt and freshly ground black pepper

1 Mix 1 tbsp of the oil with the wasabi paste in a shallow bowl. Coat the sirloin steaks completely in the mix, ensuring a thin, even covering.

2 Heat half the remaining oil in a frying pan over medium-high heat, and cook the steaks for 2–3 minutes on each side for medium-rare, or 5 minutes on each side for well done. Transfer to a plate, then let rest in a warm place for 5 minutes.

3 Heat the last of the oil in the pan over low heat, add the bok choy and cook, turning once or twice, for 1–2 minutes. Add the garlic and soy sauce and cook for 1 minute, or until the bok choy has just wilted. Cut the steak into ½in (1cm) slices, season, and serve with the bok choy.

lentils with mushrooms and leeks

Lentils and mushrooms are both meaty, tasty ingredients that give this quick vegetarian dish depth and flavor. Use dried puy lentils instead of canned, for added texture.

 10 MINS 25 MINS FREEZABLE

SERVES 4

1 tbsp olive oil

1 onion, finely chopped

1 bay leaf

salt and freshly ground black pepper

2 garlic cloves, grated or finely chopped

3 leeks, trimmed and sliced

2 tsp Marmite or Vegemite, or a splash of light soy sauce

8oz (225g) crimini mushrooms, halved, or quartered if large

1 x 14oz (400g) can green lentils or puy lentils, drained and rinsed

1¼ cups hot vegetable stock

handful of curly-leaf parsley, leaves picked and finely chopped

1 Heat the oil in a large frying pan over low heat. Add the onion, bay leaf, and a little salt, and cook for 5 minutes until the onion is soft and translucent. Add the garlic and leek and stir in the Marmite, Vegemite, or soy sauce. Cook for another 5 minutes until the leeks begin to soften.

2 Add the mushrooms and cook until they release their juices—you may need to add a little more oil if necessary. Season well with salt and pepper, then stir in the lentils and hot stock. Bring to a boil, reduce the heat, and simmer gently for 15 minutes.

3 Remove from the heat and stir in the parsley. Taste and season again if needed. Serve with some roasted tomatoes and fresh crusty bread.

beef and chickpeas cooked with orange and cinnamon

In place of canned chickpeas, try dried ones for a fuller flavor. Soak them in cold water for 8–10 hours, then boil for 1–2 hours to soften them.

 10 MINS 20 MINS

SERVES 4

1 tbsp olive oil

1 red onion, finely chopped

2 garlic cloves, grated

1in (2.5cm) piece of ginger, peeled and grated

pinch of ground cinnamon

salt and freshly ground black pepper

1½lb (675g) ground beef

grated zest and juice of 1 orange

1 x 14oz (400g) can chickpeas, drained and rinsed

⅔ cup hot vegetable stock

1 Heat the oil in a large pan over medium heat, add the onion, and cook for about 5 minutes until the onion is soft and translucent. Add the garlic, ginger, and cinnamon and season with salt and pepper. Stir in the beef and cook for a few minutes until the meat is no longer pink.

2 Add the orange zest and juice together with the chickpeas and stock and bring to a boil. Reduce the heat, cover, and simmer gently for about 15 minutes, stirring occasionally. Serve on a bed of rice, or with boiled new potatoes and steamed green beans.

variation

beef and vegetable chili with guacamole

Prepare in exactly the same way, but add ¼ small rutabaga, finely diced, and 2 carrots, finely diced, with the onion. Use 1 tsp ground cumin instead of the ginger and 1 tsp dried oregano instead of the cinnamon. Substitute 2 tbsp tomato paste for the orange zest and juice, and a 14oz (400g) can drained red kidney beans for the chickpeas. Mash a ripe avocado with a squeeze of lime juice and spoon on top of the chili before serving.

pot roast smoked ham

Knuckle or ham hock is amazing value and tasty, too. The Jerusalem artichokes add a nutty, creamy texture, but if they're not available you can use parsnips instead.

 25 MINS   3 HRS 15 MINS   FREEZABLE

SERVES 4–6

2 smoked ham hocks (knuckles), about 3lb (1.35kg) each

1 bay leaf

1 tbsp olive oil

1 onion, finely chopped

salt and freshly ground black pepper

3 garlic cloves, finely chopped

a few sprigs of thyme

3 carrots, chopped

8oz (225g) Jerusalem artichokes, peeled and sliced

4½oz (125g) yellow split peas

½ cup dry hard cider

3 cups hot vegetable stock

1 Put the ham hocks and bay leaf in a large heavy-bottomed pan, cover with water, and cook for about 2 hours, skimming away any foam that comes to the top of the pan. Remove the hams and when cool enough to handle, peel away the skins and discard. Set the hams aside. (You can reserve the stock and use it if you wish, but it can be salty.)

2 Preheat the oven to 350°F (180°C). Heat the oil in a large flameproof casserole over medium heat, add the onion, and cook for 3–4 minutes until soft. Season with salt and pepper, stir in the garlic, thyme, carrots, and artichokes, and cook for a few more minutes. Stir in the split peas to coat. Increase the heat and pour in the cider, let it bubble for a minute, then add the stock and bring to a boil. Reduce to a simmer and add the hams to the casserole, tucking them down as much as possible.

3 Cover and put in the oven for about 1 hour, or until the split peas are soft. Check occasionally that it's not drying out too much, adding hot water if needed. By now the ham meat should slide easily off the bone, so remove it with a fork and stir it into the casserole. Taste and season if necessary, and serve with some fresh crusty bread.

greek stifado

Stifado is a rich mix of beef and onions in a red wine sauce.

 30 MINS   2 HRS 15 MINS   ✳ FREEZABLE

SERVES 4–6

3 tbsp olive oil

2½lb (1.1kg) chuck steak, cut into bite-sized pieces

salt and freshly ground black pepper

⅔ cup red wine

2 tbsp red wine vinegar

1 cinnamon stick

1 tsp ground cloves

½ tsp grated nutmeg

3 garlic cloves, finely chopped

4 tomatoes, coarsely chopped

1 tbsp tomato paste

2 cups hot vegetable stock

a few sprigs of thyme

pat of butter

1lb 2oz (500g) shallots, peeled and left whole

1 Preheat the oven to 350°F (180°C). Heat 2 tbsp of the oil in a large flameproof casserole over medium-high heat. Add the meat, season with salt and pepper, and cook for 6 minutes, or until lightly browned. Increase the heat and add the wine and vinegar. Cook for a couple of minutes, then stir in the cinnamon stick, cloves, nutmeg, and garlic and cook for another minute.

2 Add the tomatoes, tomato paste, and then the stock. Bring the sauce to a boil, then add the thyme, cover with the lid, and cook in the oven for about 1 hour. Check occasionally that it's not drying out, and add a little hot water if needed.

3 Heat the remaining oil with the butter in a heavy-bottomed pan over medium heat, add the shallots, and cook for 6–8 minutes until golden. Stir the onions into the stew, cover, and return to the oven. Reduce the temperature to 325°F (160°C) and cook for another hour, checking occasionally that it's not drying out. Remove the cinnamon and thyme and serve with mashed potatoes or baby roast potatoes with rosemary.

jugged hare

This traditional, rich, blood-thickened stew can also be made with venison. In France, it is called a *civet*.

 40 MINS PLUS MARINATING   2–3 HRS

SERVES 6

2 tbsp wine vinegar

1 hare, about 4½–6½lb (2–3kg) total weight, prepared and jointed (liver and blood reserved)

4 tbsp butter

9oz (250g) diced salt pork

15 baby onions or small shallots, peeled and left whole

2 tbsp all-purpose flour

1¼ cups red wine

2 cups chicken stock

salt and freshly ground black pepper

For the marinade

1 onion, sliced

bunch of fresh herbs

½ cup white wine

½ cup wine vinegar

½ cup olive oil

1 Stir the vinegar into the blood and set aside in a covered dish with the liver. Put the hare joints in a bowl. Mix the marinade ingredients and pour over the meat. Cover and leave in a cool place for 12–24 hours, turning the joints over once or twice.

2 Remove the joints and pat dry with paper towels; reserve the marinade. Melt the butter in a large pan and cook the salt pork and onions. Add the joints and brown gently all over. Blend in the flour. Pour in the wine and stock. Season, bring to a boil, reduce the heat, cover, and simmer for 2–3 hours until tender.

3 Mash the liver into the blood with 2–3 tbsp of the reserved marinade and pass through a fine sieve. Add to the stew and keep stirring as the sauce thickens. Do not allow it to boil. Taste, add more salt, pepper, and marinade if needed, and serve.

beef and greens

Tender beef with robust kale is a great combination. The chile hint is subtle, but there is just enough to add interest to the dish, while the anchovies are added to enrich the sauce.

 15 MINS **2 HRS 45 MINS** **FREEZABLE**

SERVES 6

3-4 tbsp olive oil

2¾lb (1.25kg) beef chuck, cut into bite-sized pieces

salt and freshly ground black pepper

1 tsp paprika

1 tbsp all-purpose flour

2 onions, coarsely chopped

3 garlic cloves, finely chopped

1 jalapeño chile, seeded and finely chopped

8 salted anchovies

4 large carrots, coarsely chopped

1 cup red wine

3 cups hot beef or vegetable stock

4 large potatoes, peeled and coarsely chopped

7oz (200g) curly kale, stems trimmed and leaves coarsely chopped

1 Preheat the oven to 325°F (160°C). Heat 1 tbsp of the oil in a large flameproof casserole over medium heat. Season the meat with salt, pepper, and paprika, and sprinkle over the flour. Add the beef pieces to the casserole (in batches and with extra oil, if necessary) and cook for 5–8 minutes until they are browned all over. Remove with a slotted spoon and set aside.

2 Add the remaining oil to the casserole, add the onions, and cook for 3–4 minutes until soft. Then stir in the garlic, chile, and anchovies, and cook for a minute. Add the carrots and cook for another 2–3 minutes.

3 Pour in the wine and bring to a boil, stirring and scraping up the bits from the bottom of the casserole. Pour in the stock and bring back to a boil. Add the meat and potatoes, cover, and cook in the oven for 1½ hours. Check occasionally that it's not drying out, adding a little hot water if needed. Add the kale and cook for another 1 hour, again checking that it doesn't dry out too much. Serve while piping hot with some crusty bread.

variation

pork with cavolo nero

Prepare in the same way, but use 2¼lb (1kg) diced pork shoulder instead of beef. Add 1 cup white wine instead of red, and use 7oz (200g) shredded cavolo nero instead of the kale.

beef and orange daube

Boef en daube is a classic beef stew in red wine from Provence in France. It is enhanced with the tang of orange zest and enriched with anchovies that "melt" into the sauce.

 30 MINS 2 HRS FREEZABLE

SERVES 4

2 tbsp olive oil

1lb 2oz (500g) beef stew meat, cut into bite-sized pieces

½ tbsp all-purpose flour

salt and freshly ground black pepper

1 bay leaf

2 tbsp butter

2 onions, finely sliced

zest and juice of 1 orange

6 salted anchovies, finely chopped

⅔ cup red wine

1¼lb (550g) crimini mushrooms, quartered

2 cups hot vegetable stock

small handful of thyme, finely chopped

1 Preheat the oven to 300°F (150°C). Heat 2 tbsp of the oil in a cast-iron pan over medium heat, toss the meat in the flour, season well with salt and pepper, then add to the pan with the bay leaf and stir. Cook, stirring occasionally, for 8–10 minutes, or until the meat is no longer pink. Add the butter and cook for 5 minutes, or until the meat is golden. Remove with a slotted spoon and set aside.

2 Add the remaining oil to the pan, then add the onions and cook over low heat for 6–8 minutes, or until soft. Add the orange zest, increase the heat a little, then add the orange juice and stir to loosen all the sticky bits from the bottom of the pan.

3 Stir in the anchovies, then add the wine and simmer over high heat for 2 minutes. Stir in the mushrooms, add the stock and thyme, and season with salt and pepper. Return the steak to the pan, cover with a lid, then put in the oven for 2 hours, or until the meat is meltingly tender.

turkey and mushroom casserole with dumplings

A filling stew with porcini mushrooms, celery, and carrots.

 30 MINS PLUS SOAKING 1 HR 30 MINS FREEZABLE

SERVES 4

scant 1oz (25g) dried porcini mushrooms

pat of butter

1 tbsp olive oil

1½lb (675g) turkey breast, cut into bite-sized pieces

1 onion, finely chopped

2 garlic cloves, grated or finely chopped

1 bay leaf

a few sprigs of rosemary, coarsely chopped

salt and freshly ground black pepper

3 carrots, cut into chunky pieces

3 celery stalks, cut into chunky pieces

1 tbsp all-purpose flour

½ cup dry sherry

2 cups hot chicken stock

small handful of flat-leaf parsley, finely chopped (optional)

For the dumplings

2 cups self-rising flour

8 tbsp frozen white vegetable fat or lard, grated through the large holes of a box grater

1 tbsp dried oregano

1 Put the porcini in a bowl, cover with 1¼ cups hot water, and let soak for 30 minutes. Preheat the oven to 400°F (200°C). Heat the butter and half the oil in a cast-iron pan, add the turkey, and cook over medium heat, turning the pieces frequently, for 5–8 minutes or until golden all over. Remove with a slotted spoon and set aside.

2 Heat the remaining oil in the pan, add the onions, and cook for 6–8 minutes, or until soft and translucent. Stir in the garlic, bay leaf, and rosemary and season with salt and pepper, then add the carrots and celery and cook for 5 minutes. Stir in the flour and cook for 2 minutes.

3 Increase the heat, add the sherry, and boil for a few minutes, stirring, until the alcohol evaporates, then pour in the stock. Drain the porcini (reserve the liquid) and add to the pan. Strain the soaking liquid, then add this as well. Return the turkey to the pan, cover, and put in the oven for 1 hour.

4 Meanwhile, make the dumplings. Put the flour, fat, and oregano in a mixing bowl with a pinch of salt, then add about ⅔ cup cold water a little at a time, until the mixture forms a dough. Flour your hands and shape the dough into 16 dumplings. Add these to the pan for the last 30 minutes of cooking. To serve, sprinkle over the parsley, if using.

beef with barley and mushrooms

Barley adds body and an earthy flavor to this dish. If you can find them, use wild mushrooms as a treat.

 30-35 MINS 2 HRS 15 MINS – 2 HRS 30 MINS

SERVES 6

1½ tbsp vegetable oil

1½lb (675g) beef stew meat, in 2in (5cm) dice

2 large onions, thinly sliced

salt and freshly ground black pepper

1 bouquet garni (5–6 sprigs of parsley, 2–3 sprigs of thyme, and 1 bay leaf)

3½ cups beef stock, plus more if needed

1 large carrot, sliced

2 celery stalks, peeled and sliced

3½oz (100g) pearl barley

9oz (250g) mushrooms, trimmed and sliced

2 sprigs of flat-leaf parsley, leaves picked and finely chopped (optional)

1 Preheat the oven to 350°F (180°C). Heat the oil in a flameproof casserole on top of the stove until hot. Add half the beef (it should sear when it hits the pan) and brown well. Transfer to a bowl. Brown the remaining beef in the same way.

2 Add the onions with a little salt and pepper. Cook over medium heat, stirring for 5–7 minutes, until lightly browned. Return the beef and add the bouquet garni, salt, and pepper. Pour in the stock and stir.

3 Cover the casserole and transfer to the heated oven. Cook, stirring occasionally, for about 1½ hours, then add the carrots, celery, and barley. Stir in more stock or water, if necessary, to keep the casserole moist.

4 Cover and continue cooking for 40–45 minutes longer, until the meat and vegetables are tender when pierced. The barley should be tender, but still slightly chewy. Stir in the mushrooms about 10 minutes before the end of the cooking time.

5 Discard the bouquet garni and taste the stew for seasoning. Serve in warmed individual bowls, sprinkled with the parsley, if using, and some fresh crusty bread.

lamb shanks in red wine

Perfect for a chilly day. You will need to start this dish at least 1 day ahead to have enough time to marinate the lamb.

 50 MINS PLUS MARINATING 2 HRS 45 MINS

SERVES 6

2 tsp black peppercorns, crushed

2 tsp juniper berries, crushed

4 shallots, coarsely chopped

2 garlic cloves, peeled

2 onions, quartered

2 carrots, roughly sliced

1 bouquet garni (5–6 sprigs of parsley, 2–3 sprigs of thyme, and 1 bay leaf)

2 tbsp red wine vinegar

2½ cups dry red wine

6 lamb shanks, total weight 4lb (1.8kg), trimmed of excess fat and sinew

3 tbsp vegetable oil

¼ cup all-purpose flour

2½ cups beef stock, plus more if needed

salt and freshly ground black pepper

2 tbsp butter

1 celery root, about 1lb 2oz (500g), diced

9oz (250g) mushrooms, quartered

3 tbsp redcurrant jelly

1 Put the peppercorns, juniper berries, shallots, garlic, onions, carrots, bouquet garni, and vinegar in a pan. Add the red wine, bring to a boil, and simmer for 2 minutes. Transfer to a shallow dish and set aside to cool completely. Once the marinade is cold, add the shanks and coat in the mix. Cover and refrigerate, turning occasionally, for 1–2 days.

2 Preheat the oven to 350°F (180°C). Dry the shanks on paper towels. Reserve the bouquet garni. Drain the vegetables in a sieve over a bowl. Reserve the vegetables and marinade separately. Heat half the oil in a flameproof casserole, add half the shanks, and brown well over high heat for 3–5 minutes. Repeat with the other shanks. Add the vegetables and cook for 5–7 minutes until they start to brown. Add the flour and stir for 3–5 minutes. Add the reserved marinade, then the lamb with any juices, bouquet garni, stock, salt, and pepper. Cover and cook in the oven for 2–2¼ hours, until tender. Add more stock if needed.

3 Melt the butter in a frying pan, add the celery root, season, and cook until tender. Transfer to a bowl. Add the mushrooms to the pan and repeat. Transfer the shanks to a plate and keep warm. Ladle the sauce into a sieve over a large pan, reserving some shallot and carrot. Press the rest with a ladle to extract the juices.

4 Whisk the redcurrant jelly into the sauce with plenty of black pepper. Bring to a boil and simmer for 20–30 minutes, until reduced by half. Add the celery root, mushrooms, reserved carrot and shallot, and shanks. Heat until very hot, about 5–10 minutes, and serve.

braised cauliflower with chile and cilantro

A few spices can turn the humble cauliflower into something far more interesting. This dish can be served simply with some buttery basmati rice or as part of an Indian meal.

 10 MINS   10 MINS

SERVES 4

14oz (400g) cauliflower, outer leaves removed, chopped into small florets

2 dried red chiles

1 tsp cumin seeds

2 tbsp sunflower or vegetable oil

1 tsp black mustard seeds

½ tsp turmeric

2 garlic cloves, crushed

pat of butter

sea salt

2 tbsp cilantro leaves, finely chopped

1 Blanch the cauliflower in salted boiling water for 1–2 minutes, drain, and rinse under cold water.

2 Grind together the chiles and cumin seeds in a mortar and pestle until coarsely crushed. Heat the oil in a large, deep frying pan or wok,

and add the chile and cumin seeds, mustard seeds, turmeric, and garlic. Cook gently for 1 minute until the mustard seeds start to pop.

3 Add the cauliflower and enough water so that it covers the bottom of the pan (about 6 tbsp). Bring the water to a boil and cover the pan or wok. Turn the heat down and simmer the cauliflower for 3–5 minutes, until almost cooked through.

4 Uncover the pan or wok and turn up the heat. Allow the water to cook off, turning the cauliflower all the time. When all the water has evaporated (about 5–6 minutes), add the butter and mix well until it melts. Season with sea salt and sprinkle with cilantro before serving.

fruity lamb shanks

Lamb works very well with fruit, and the prunes and apple in this recipe are no exception. They add a piquant flavor.

 15 MINS   3 HRS 15 MINS   FREEZABLE

SERVES 4

¼ cup olive oil

4 lamb shanks

1 tbsp all-purpose flour

1 cup white wine

1 large onion, sliced

salt and freshly ground black pepper

3 garlic cloves, finely chopped

1 tsp fennel seeds

a few sprigs of thyme

2 bay leaves

1 celery root, peeled and chopped into bite-sized pieces

1 apple, peeled, cored, and diced

7oz (200g) soft prunes, pitted and left whole

⅔ cups fresh orange juice

3 cups hot vegetable stock

1 Preheat the oven to 300°F (150°C). Heat half the oil in a large flameproof casserole over medium-high heat. Toss the shanks in the flour. Cook one or two at a time in the oil until

golden on all sides, then set aside in a bowl. Add the wine to the casserole, increase the heat, let it simmer, and pour over the lamb. Wipe the casserole with paper towels.

2 Heat a little more oil over medium heat, add the onion, and cook for 3–4 minutes until soft. Season with salt and pepper, then stir in the garlic, fennel seeds, thyme, bay leaves, and celery root, and cook for about 5 minutes, adding more oil as needed, until just turning golden. Add the apple and prunes, season, and cook for 1–2 minutes. Return the lamb shanks and sauce to the casserole, add the orange juice and stock, and bring to a boil.

3 Reduce to a simmer, cover, and cook in the oven for 3–3½ hours until the lamb falls off the bone, adding a little hot water if needed. Serve with creamy mashed potatoes.

pork normandy

This casserole of tart apples and creamy, mustardy pork makes a welcome change from heavy wintry stews.

 30 MINS   1 HR

SERVES 4

1 tbsp olive oil

pat of butter

1½lb (675g) lean pork, cut into bite-sized pieces

1 onion, finely chopped

1 tbsp Dijon mustard

2 garlic cloves, grated or finely chopped

3 celery stalks, finely chopped

3 carrots, finely chopped

½ tbsp rosemary leaves, finely chopped

1 large tart apple, peeled and coarsely chopped

⅔ cup dry hard cider

½ cup heavy cream

⅔ cup hot light chicken stock

½ tsp black peppercorns

1 Preheat the oven to 350°F (180°C). Heat the oil and butter in a cast-iron pan, add the pork, and cook over

medium heat for 6–8 minutes, or until golden brown on all sides. Remove with a slotted spoon and set aside.

2 Add the onions and cook over low heat for 5 minutes, or until soft and translucent. Stir in the mustard, add the garlic, celery, carrots, and rosemary, and cook over low heat, stirring often, for 10 minutes or until tender. Add the apple and cook for another 5 minutes.

3 Pour in the cider, then increase the heat and boil for 1–2 minutes while the alcohol evaporates. Return the pork to the pan and pour in the cream and stock. Stir in the peppercorns, bring to a boil, then cover with a lid and put in the oven to cook for 1 hour, or until the sauce has reduced and the pork is tender. Serve with fluffy rice or creamy mashed potatoes.

braised oxtail with clementine and star anise

Rich and robust, oxtail makes an interesting change to beef, and braising it very slowly tenderizes it to the full. Prunes and clementines are a tasty addition to this stew, as their fruity sweetness and texture complement the meat.

 20 MINS 3 HRS 15 MINS FREEZABLE

SERVES 4–6

2 oxtails, about 3lb (1.35kg) each, cut into bite-sized pieces

salt and freshly ground black pepper

2 tbsp olive oil

2 red onions, sliced

3 garlic clovse, finely chopped

pinch of dried chile flakes

1½ cups red wine

4 star anise

handful of black peppercorns

1 bay leaf

8 soft prunes, pitted and chopped

3 cups hot beef stock

4 clementines or 2 oranges, peeled and sliced into rings

small bunch of curly parsley leaves, finely chopped

1 Preheat the oven to 300°F (150°C). Season the oxtail with salt and pepper. Heat half the oil in a large flameproof casserole over medium heat, then add the meat in batches and cook for 8–10 minutes until browned on all sides. Remove with a slotted spoon and set aside.

2 Heat the remaining oil in the casserole over medium heat, add the onions, and cook for 3–4 minutes to soften. Stir in the garlic and chile flakes, then pour in the wine and let it simmer for about 5 minutes until slightly reduced. Return the meat to the casserole and add the star anise, peppercorns, bay leaf, and prunes, and pour over just enough stock to cover the meat.

3 Bring to a boil, then reduce to a simmer, add the remaining stock, cover, and put in the oven for about 3 hours. Check occasionally that it's not drying out, and add a little hot water if needed. Add the clementines or oranges for the last 30 minutes of cooking, and leave the casserole uncovered to allow the liquid to thicken slightly. Stir it occasionally to keep the oxtail moist and coated with the gravy. When ready, the meat will fall away from the bone. Remove the bone and discard it together with the bay leaf and star anise. Serve on a bed of pasta, sprinkled with the parsley.

variation

braised oxtail with jerusalem artichokes

Prepare in the same way, but add 9oz (250g) Jerusalem artichokes, scrubbed or peeled and cut into chunks, and 2 sliced carrots to the mixture before cooking. Omit the star anise, chile flakes, and clementines. Add 1 tbsp brandy with the red wine. Cook as before, but serve spooned over fluffy mashed potatoes instead of the pasta.

sautéed liver and onions

This delicious recipe is a classic Venetian meal. The sweet, caramelized onions are the star of this meal and can be cooked the night before if you want to get ahead.

 15-20 MINS 1 HR

SERVES 6

⅓ cup olive oil

2¼lb (1kg) large onions, sliced

salt and freshly ground black pepper

1lb 10oz (750g) calf's liver

For the mashed potatoes

1lb 6oz (635g) potatoes, peeled

¼ cup milk

4 tbsp butter

1 Heat two-thirds of the oil in a frying pan. Add the onions and a little salt and pepper and cover. Cook over low heat, stirring occasionally, for 25–30 minutes until very soft.

2 Uncover, increase the heat to medium-high, and cook, stirring constantly, for 5–7 minutes until caramelized and golden but not burned. Transfer to a bowl with a slotted spoon, leaving any excess oil in the pan.

3 Meanwhile, cut the potatoes into pieces. Put in a saucepan of salted water, cover, and bring to a boil. Simmer for 15–20 minutes until tender. Drain thoroughly and mash with a potato masher. Heat the milk in a small saucepan, add the butter, season, and mix. Gradually add the hot milk to the potatoes, beating until light and fluffy. Taste for seasoning and keep warm.

4 Slice the liver about ¼in (5mm) thick and season. Add the remaining oil to the frying pan and heat over high heat. Add half the liver and cook for 45–60 seconds on each side, until just browned; the liver should be pink in the center. Transfer to a plate and keep warm. Repeat with the rest of the liver. Return the onions to the pan with all the liver and stir quickly over high heat for 30–60 seconds until very hot. Season with salt and pepper and serve at once on warmed plates with the mashed potatoes.

duck in orange sauce

A superb French classic of rich wild duck with a bitter orange sauce. It also works well with domestic duck.

 10 MINS 2 HRS

SERVES 4

4 tbsp butter

½ cup all-purpose flour

3½ cups hot game stock

1 wild duck, about 2¼lb (1kg)

2 Seville (bitter) oranges

¼ cup sugar

3 tbsp red wine vinegar

1 Melt the butter in a saucepan. When it turns golden brown, stir in the flour. Gradually whisk in the stock until smooth. Bring to a boil, then reduce the heat and simmer for about 1 hour, or until reduced by half.

2 Meanwhile, preheat the oven to 400°F (200°C). Prick the skin of the duck with a fork and season with salt, place breast-side down on a rack in a roasting pan, and roast in the oven for 30 minutes. Turn the duck over and roast for another 30 minutes. Remove from the oven and, when cool enough to handle, remove the legs and breasts. Slice the breast meat and joint the legs, if desired. Then set aside in a warm place to rest.

3 Use a peeler to pare the zest off the oranges and cut it into fine strips. Blanch in boiling water for 5 minutes, then drain; reserve the zest. Squeeze the juice from the oranges.

4 Heat the sugar in a small saucepan until it melts and starts to caramelize. Add the vinegar (add with caution, as it can spit) and dissolve the caramel—this takes a few minutes. Add to the thickened game stock together with the orange juice and stir to mix. Add most of the strips of orange zest, reserving the rest as a garnish.

5 Warm the duck pieces gently in the orange sauce, being careful not to overcook them. Garnish with the remaining orange zest before serving.

chicken broth with celery root and orange

This main meal soup has a great balance of flavors of earthy celery root, chicken, and aromatic orange giving an extra tang.

 15 MINS 1 HR ❄ FREEZABLE

SERVES 4-6

1 tbsp olive oil

1 onion, finely chopped

1 bay leaf

salt and freshly ground black pepper

2 garlic cloves, finely chopped

zest of 1 orange and juice of ½ orange

a few sprigs of oregano, leaves picked

1 celery root, peeled and cut into small chunks

3½ cups hot chicken stock

4 boneless, skinless chicken breasts

4 sprigs of flat-leaf parsley, finely chopped, to serve

1 Heat the oil in a large heavy-bottomed pan over medium heat, add the onion and bay leaf, and cook for 3–4 minutes until the onion begins to soften. Season with salt and pepper, then add the garlic, orange zest, and oregano leaves, and cook for a few seconds. Stir in the celery root and orange juice, scraping up the bits from the bottom of the pan. Then pour in the stock, add the chicken breasts, and bring the broth to a boil.

2 Reduce to a simmer and cook gently for 20–30 minutes, or until the chicken breasts are cooked. Remove the chicken with a slotted spoon and set aside until cool enough to handle, then shred into chunky pieces using your hands or two forks.

3 Continue simmering the stock for another 15 minutes or so, adding a little hot water if needed. Taste and adjust the seasoning as needed and remove the bay leaf. Return the shredded chicken to the pan and stir. Serve in warmed bowls, garnished with parsley.

beef and ale cobbler

Making use of a host of winter vegetables, this hearty cobbler is great for feeding a crowd. The filling can be prepared days ahead and the whole dish needs no additional attention once it has gone into the oven.

 40 MINS   **2 HRS 30 MINS – 3 HRS 15 MINS**   **FREEZABLE**

SPECIAL EQUIPMENT ▪ 2in (5cm) pastry cutter

SERVES 4

¼ cup olive oil

2 onions, finely chopped

1 celery stalk, finely diced

1 leek, finely sliced

5½oz (150g) button mushrooms, wiped, halved or quartered, if needed

1lb 5oz (600g) beef stew meat, such as chuck, cut into 1¼in (3cm) chunks

2 tbsp all-purpose flour

sea salt and freshly ground black pepper

2 cups dark ale, such as stout or porter

1¼ cups beef stock

1 bouquet garni

1 tbsp sugar

2 large carrots, cut into ¾in (2cm) chunks

For the cobbler

1¾ cups self-rising flour

1 tsp baking powder

½ tsp salt

8 tbsp unsalted butter, chilled and diced

1 tbsp finely chopped flat-leaf parsley

3 tbsp horseradish sauce or horseradish cream

2–4 tbsp milk

1 large egg, beaten, for glazing

1 In a large flameproof casserole, heat 2 tbsp of the oil and cook the onion, celery, and leek for about 5 minutes until soft and translucent. Add the mushrooms and cook for 3–4 minutes until they begin to color in places. Remove the vegetables with a slotted spoon and set aside.

2 Toss the steak in 2 tbsp seasoned flour. Heat the remaining oil in the casserole and cook the meat, a few pieces at a time, until browned on all sides. Remove the meat as it cooks and add it to the vegetables. Return the meat to the casserole with the vegetables, cover with the ale, stock, the bouquet garni, sugar, and carrots, and bring to a boil. Reduce the heat to its lowest setting, cover, and cook for 2–2½ hours, until the meat is tender. Check it from time to time and add a little water if it is drying out.

3 Preheat the oven to 400°F (200°C). Sift together the flour, baking powder, and salt. Using your fingertips, rub in the butter until the mixture resembles fine crumbs. Add the parsley. Whisk the horseradish sauce and milk, and use it to bind the dry ingredients to form a soft dough.

4 Roll out the dough on a floured work surface to about ¾in (2cm) thick. Using a pastry cutter, cut out circles. Re-roll the offcuts and re-cut until the dough is used up. When the stew is cooked, remove the bouquet garni and top the stew with the disks of cobbler dough. Overlap them slightly so that there are very few gaps where the filling can be seen.

5 Brush the cobbler tops with beaten egg and bake in the middle of the oven for 30–40 minutes until the pastry is puffed up and golden brown. Remove the casserole dish from the oven and let the stew rest for 5 minutes before serving.

venison stew

This recipe uses fresh and dried mushrooms for added flavor.

 15 MINS PLUS MARINATING   **2 HRS 15 MINS**

SERVES 4–6

2 cups red wine

3 tbsp olive oil

1 tbsp crushed juniper berries

2 sprigs of rosemary

2½lb (1.1kg) venison, cut into bite-sized pieces

2 tbsp all-purpose flour, seasoned

1 onion, coarsely chopped

7oz (200g) pancetta, diced

1oz (30g) dried porcini mushrooms, soaked in warm water for 30 minutes

zest of 1 orange, coarsely chopped

3 cups hot vegetable stock

pat of butter

9oz (250g) crimini mushrooms, halved

salt and freshly ground black pepper

1 Mix the wine, 2 tbsp oil, the juniper berries, and 1 sprig of rosemary in a large bowl. Immerse the meat in the marinade, cover, and refrigerate for 1 hour or overnight. Drain the meat, reserving the liquid and rosemary. Heat the remaining oil in a large flameproof casserole over medium-high heat. Toss the venison in the flour and cook in batches until golden. Remove and set aside.

2 Reduce the heat, add the onion and pancetta, and cook for 5 minutes. Drain the porcini and strain the juice; add them and a little juice to the casserole with the orange zest, wine marinade, and rosemary. Add the stock and boil. Add the meat, reduce to a simmer, cover, and cook on a low heat for 1½–2 hours until tender. Add enough reserved porcini juice or hot water to keep the meat covered. Heat the butter in a frying pan, cook the crimini mushrooms until golden, then stir into the stew for the last 30 minutes. Taste and season, if needed. Serve with polenta.

game casserole

A highly flavored stew with mushrooms, celery, and carrots.

 30 MINS   **1 HR 15 MINS**   **FREEZABLE**

SERVES 4

1½lb (675g) (boned weight) mixed game, such as pheasant, venison, and duck, cut into bite-sized pieces

all-purpose flour, for dusting

salt and freshly ground black pepper

1 tbsp olive oil

1 tbsp brandy

1 onion, finely chopped

2 garlic cloves, grated or finely chopped

2 celery stalks, finely diced

2 carrots, finely diced

1 bouquet garni

9½oz (275g) crimini mushrooms, quartered

¾ cup dry white wine

2 tsp redcurrant jelly

2½ cups hot chicken stock

1 Preheat the oven to 350°F (180°C). Dust the meat lightly with a little flour, then season well with salt and pepper. Heat half the oil in a cast-iron pan, add the meat, and cook over medium heat, stirring occasionally, for 6–8 minutes, or until browned on all sides. Remove with a slotted spoon and set aside.

2 Add the brandy to the pan and stir to deglaze, then add the rest of the oil, if needed, and the onions, and cook over low heat for 6 minutes, or until soft. Stir in the garlic, celery, carrots, and bouquet garni and cook over low heat, stirring occasionally, for 8 minutes, or until tender.

3 Stir in the mushrooms, then increase the heat, add the wine, and allow to boil for 2 minutes while the alcohol evaporates. Stir in the redcurrant jelly, then pour in the stock. Cover with a lid and put in the oven to cook for 1 hour, or until the meat is tender. Add hot water during the cooking if needed. Serve with creamy mashed potatoes.

venison casserole with pears

Pear makes the perfect partner to venison. This stew is tasty served with steamed Savoy cabbage with butter.

 30 MINS PLUS MARINATING   **1 HR 45 MINS**

SERVES 6

2 tsp black peppercorns, crushed

2 tsp juniper berries, crushed

4 shallots, coarsely chopped

2 garlic cloves, peeled and left whole

2 onions, quartered

2 carrots, coarsely sliced

1 bouquet garni

2 tbsp red wine vinegar

2½ cups dry red wine

2¼lb (1kg) stewing venison (leg or shoulder), fat trimmed, cut into 1½in (4cm) cubes

3 tbsp vegetable oil

¼ cup all-purpose flour

2½ cups hot beef stock

salt and freshly ground black pepper

4 ripe pears, peeled, cored, and chopped

3 tbsp redcurrant jelly

1 Put the spices, vegetables, bouquet garni, vinegar, and wine in a pan and bring to a boil, then simmer for about 2 minutes. Transfer to a shallow dish and let cool. Add the venison, stir to coat evenly, cover, and refrigerate for 6–8 hours, turning the meat occasionally.

2 Preheat the oven to 350°F (180°C). Remove the venison and pat dry with paper towels. Strain the marinade, reserving the bouquet garni, vegetables, and marinade. Heat half the oil in a large flameproof casserole over high heat, add the venison, and cook in batches for 3–5 minutes until brown all over. Transfer to a bowl. Heat the remaining oil over medium heat, add the reserved vegetables, and cook for 5–7 minutes. Add the flour and cook, stirring, for 3–5 minutes until it has been absorbed. Stir in the marinade, venison, bouquet garni, stock, and seasoning. Cover and cook in the oven for 1¼–1½ hours until tender. Stir in the pears and redcurrant jelly, cook for 6–8 minutes until the pears are tender, and serve.

Season's best **venison**

Venison is the meat of all species of deer. They are hunted wild in season, which varies according to breed and gender, but most are available from autumn through to late winter. Deer are also responsibly farmed. Dark red, the meat is extremely lean, so much lower in saturated fat than most meat. Its coarse texture and mild, sweet flavor work well with cream, ginger, fennel, cabbage, pears, chocolate, and red wine for warming seasonal dishes.

Filet or tenderloin The boned-out saddle (back) yields the loin and filet muscles. These two prime cuts are often confused in recipes, with the loin erroneously called filet, but cooking times are very different, as loin is at least twice as thick as filet; also, the cuts from different species vary in size.

The filet muscle tapers at one end; the other end may have a thicker muscle attached. The loin muscle does not taper.

Diced venison Stir-fry, grill, or stew diced haunch. Diced shoulder and shin are best stewed, but should not be mixed together as they cook differently.

Rolled haunch (leg) The haunch from small species of deer may be roasted whole or boned, or sliced into steaks. Larger haunches can be cooked on the bone, but are usually parted into individual muscles or pavés. These may be rolled and tied for roasting, or sliced into steaks.

Venison haunch is as lean as skinless chicken. Roasts should be served pink or they will be dry.

essentials
cuts available

Cuts include haunch/back leg, saddle, loin (whole and steaks), filet/tenderloin, shoulder, shin, ground, sausages.

buy Avoid any excessively dark, bruised meat. Prime cuts come from the haunch and saddle. Allow about 6oz (175g) of boneless meat per portion.

store If pre-packaged, follow the storage instructions. If not, keep covered on a plate at the bottom of the fridge for up to 4 days.

cook Prime cuts can be eaten raw as carpaccio. Roast prime cuts and cook steaks, then rest them well to serve pink. Shoulder from young and small deer can also be roasted. Braise or stew venison from older deer and all forequarter cuts; cuts to be braised should be larded. Use ground venison for burgers and meatballs, pasta sauces, pies, and other made dishes.

preserve Smoke and freeze fresh meat.

recipe ideas

Venison, shallot, and chestnut hotpot p388

Venison stew p452

Venison Wellingtons p282

Viltgryta p314

duck legs with cabbage, pine nuts, and raisins

Duck legs are very succulent with lots of tasty meat on them. They can, however, be fatty so the addition of redcurrant jelly and raisins helps balance this. Pine nuts give an added twist.

 15 MINS   2 HRS 30 MINS

SERVES 4–6

6 duck legs

2 red onions, coarsely chopped

2 garlic cloves, finely chopped

a few sprigs of thyme

1 bay leaf

1 tbsp redcurrant jelly

2 cups hot chicken stock

salt and freshly ground black pepper

1oz (30g) raisins

1oz (30g) pine nuts, toasted

1 Savoy cabbage, cored and chopped into eighths

1 Preheat the oven to 350°F (180°C). Heat a large flameproof casserole over medium heat, add the duck legs, and cook for 15–20 minutes, turning them as you go, until they begin to turn golden. Remove them from the casserole, set aside, and pour off any fat.

2 Add the onions, garlic, thyme, and bay leaf and cook for 5 minutes, then add the redcurrant jelly and cook for a few more minutes. Return the duck legs to the casserole and nestle them into the onion mixture, skin-side up. Pour over the stock, bring to a boil, then reduce to a simmer. Season with salt and pepper, cover with the lid, and put in the oven for 2 hours. Check occasionally that it's not drying out, adding a little hot water if needed.

3 Add the raisins, pine nuts, and cabbage to the casserole for the last 30 minutes of cooking. Discard the bay leaf, taste, and adjust the seasoning. Serve with creamy mashed potatoes and some chile jelly on the side.

beef tagine with orange and bay leaves

Sweet, slightly acidic orange cuts through the richness of the beef in this robust Middle Eastern-style dish and blends beautifully with cinnamon and nutmeg spices.

 30 MINS   1 HR 30 MINS   ❄ FREEZABLE

SERVES 4

1½ tbsp olive oil

1½lb (675g) stew meat, cut into bite-sized pieces

salt and freshly ground black pepper

½ cup dry white wine

2 bay leaves

3 cups hot vegetable stock

2 sticks of cinnamon

pinch of grated nutmeg

1 x 14oz (400g) can chickpeas, drained and rinsed

1 orange, peeled and sliced into rings

2 tbsp chopped cilantro

1 Preheat the oven to 350°F (180°C). Heat the oil in a large cast-iron pan or flameproof casserole, add the meat, season with salt and pepper, and cook over medium heat, stirring occasionally, for 10 minutes, or until brown on all sides. Carefully add the wine—it will spit—then stir the meat around the pan and allow the liquid to boil for 1–2 minutes while the alcohol evaporates.

2 Add the bay leaves, then pour in the stock. Add the cinnamon and nutmeg and season again with salt and pepper. Bring to a boil, add the chickpeas, then cover with a lid and put in the oven to cook for 1 hour. Add the orange and cook for another 30 minutes, then stir in the chopped cilantro and serve with fresh crusty bread.

variation

venison casserole with turnips and prunes

Prepare in the same way, but use 1½lb (675g) diced venison haunch instead of beef, ½ cup of red wine instead of white, and add 2 diced turnips to the browned meat. Add 8 halved and pitted prunes instead of the orange rings.

lamb with red onions

Red onions have a distinctive red-purple skin and are sweeter and milder than white onions. Choose firm bulbs with even-colored skins and no signs of sprouting or dampness.

 20 MINS 2 HRS

SERVES 4

8 red onions, quartered

3 tbsp olive oil

2lb (900g) potatoes, peeled and quartered

salt and freshly ground black pepper

2 tbsp mint sauce

2lb (900g) lamb loin

1 tbsp balsamic vinegar

1 Preheat the oven to 350°F (180°C). Put the onions in a large roasting pan and toss with 1 tbsp of the oil. Add the potatoes, toss with the onions, then season well with salt and pepper.

2 Mix the remaining oil with the mint sauce and use to coat the lamb. Add the lamb to the roasting pan, drizzle over the balsamic vinegar, and put in the oven to roast for 1½–2 hours.

3 Remove the lamb and keep warm while it rests for 15 minutes. Slice and serve with the red onion and potato mixture.

variation

lamb with roasted winter vegetables

Prepare in the same way, but use 2 red onions, quartered, 1 small celery root, 1 small sweet potato and 2 potatoes, peeled and cut in bite-sized chunks instead of all potatoes. Use 2 tbsp redcurrant jelly instead of mint sauce to coat the lamb.

seared duck with five-spice and noodles

Duck breasts make a quick mid-week dinner. This dish of rich, spicy duck and noodles is sharpened by fresh orange juice.

 10 MINS 20 MINS

SERVES 4

4 duck breasts, about 5½oz (150g) each, skin on and scored in a crisscross pattern

2-3 tsp five-spice paste or 1 tsp five-spice powder mixed with 2 tsp vegetable oil

pat of butter

2 tbsp freshly squeezed orange juice

1 tsp light brown sugar

10oz (250g) fresh Chinese egg noodles

handful of cilantro, finely chopped

1 Rub the duck breasts in the five-spice paste. Melt the butter in a frying pan over medium-high heat. Add the duck breasts, skin-side down, and cook for 10 minutes until the skin is golden and crisp. Pour out the fat, turn the breasts over, and cook on the other side for 8 minutes.

2 Remove the meat, cut into slices, and arrange on a warm plate. Pour away any remaining fat, then add the orange juice to the pan along with the sugar. Simmer for a minute or two, stirring to scrape up the bits from the bottom of the pan.

3 Add the noodles and toss them in the sauce for a couple of minutes. Remove from the heat and stir in the cilantro. Serve at once with the duck.

variation

seared duck with red miso, shredded turnip, and noodles

Mix 2 tsp red miso paste with 2 tsp honey and a small, crushed garlic clove. Melt a pat of butter over medium-high heat and cook the duck breasts, skin-side down, for 8–9 minutes. Turn over and cook for another 7–8 minutes. Brush the miso glaze all over the duck breasts and brown each side for a minute or two. Add a splash of water with the orange juice at step 2 and add a finely shredded turnip with the noodles.

fish fingers with chunky tartar sauce

This familiar family favorite is fresh, simple, and tasty. The fish stays moist and succulent inside its crispy coating, while the tartar sauce adds a little bit of crunchy tang.

  15 MINS   10 MINS   ❄ FREEZABLE

SERVES 4

1½lb (675g) thick white fish fillets (loin works best), such as haddock, sustainable cod, or pollack, skinned

1–2 tbsp all-purpose flour

1 large egg, lightly beaten

1 cup bread crumbs, toasted

2oz (60g) Parmesan cheese, finely grated

salt and freshly ground black pepper

3 tbsp tartar sauce

1 tsp capers, rinsed, drained, and chopped

3 gherkins, drained and finely chopped

1 Preheat the oven to 400°F (200°C). Cut the fish fillets into thick, even strips about 1in (2.5cm) wide; you should end up with about 20 fingers of fish.

2 Pour the flour and egg onto separate plates. Mix the bread crumbs with the Parmesan cheese and season with salt and pepper. Dredge the fish in the flour, then dip in the egg to coat. Use the bread crumb mixture to coat each of the fish fingers. Make sure that you coat them well, as it protects the fish while it's cooking.

3 Sit the fish fingers on a lightly oiled baking sheet and bake in the oven for 5–8 minutes on each side until golden and cooked through. (Alternatively, you can shallow-fry them in a little sunflower or vegetable oil if you prefer.)

4 Pour the tartar sauce into a bowl and stir in the capers and gherkins. Serve immediately with the hot fish fingers.

lamb daube

Choose a robust wine that you would happily drink for this lamb daube, and serve the dish with mashed potatoes.

 45–50 MINS PLUS MARINATING   4 HRS

SERVES 4–6

2lb (900g) boned lamb shoulder, cut into large cubes

10oz (300g) piece of thick-cut bacon, cut into ¼in (5mm) lardons

1 x 14oz (400g) can chopped tomatoes

2 onions, sliced

2 carrots, sliced

6oz (175g) mushrooms, trimmed and sliced

5oz (140g) pitted green olives

1 cup hot beef stock

For the marinade

1 orange, zest peeled in wide strips

2 garlic cloves, finely chopped

2 cups red wine

2 bay leaves

10 peppercorns

3–4 sprigs each of rosemary, thyme, and parsley

2 tbsp olive oil

salt and freshly ground black pepper

1 Combine the marinade ingredients, except the oil, in a bowl. Add the lamb and mix well. Pour the oil on top and season. Cover and chill in the fridge for 2 hours, or 12 hours if time permits.

2 Preheat the oven to 300°F (150°C). In a large pan of boiling water, blanch the bacon for 5 minutes. Drain and rinse with cold water. Remove the lamb and dry on paper towels. Strain the marinade, reserving the bay leaves and zest. Put the bacon in a flameproof casserole, add the lamb, layer the tomatoes and onions on top, and add the carrots, mushrooms, and olives. Pour in the marinade and stock, season with black pepper, and add the bay leaves and zest. Bring to a boil, cover, and cook in the oven for 3½–4 hours. Add a little hot water if needed. Then remove the bay leaves and zest and serve.

bigos

A Polish dish that includes a variety of meats and cabbage.

 40 MINS   2 HRS   ❄ FREEZABLE

SERVES 4

1 small Savoy cabbage, cored, ribs removed, and leaves shredded

salt and freshly ground black pepper

1lb 2oz (500g) sauerkraut, drained

3½oz (100g) smoked bacon, diced

7oz (200g) smoked Polish sausage, sliced

7oz (200g) duck breast or lean venison, cubed

1 large red onion, diced

1 garlic clove, crushed

5½oz (150g) crimini mushrooms, sliced

½ tsp smoked paprika

1 bay leaf

½ tsp juniper berries

1 tsp dried marjoram

½ tsp caraway seeds, crushed using a pestle and mortar

¾ cup red wine

1 cup beef stock

1 Put the cabbage in a large flameproof casserole. Cover with boiling water, season, and simmer for 10 minutes. Drain and reserve. Repeat with the sauerkraut, simmering for 5 minutes only. Drain, reserving the sauerkraut and cooking liquid.

2 Cook the bacon in a frying pan over medium heat until crisp. Remove to a plate lined with paper towels. Repeat with the sausage and duck. Cook the onion, garlic, and mushrooms until soft; return the fried meats to the casserole. Stir in the paprika, bay leaf, juniper berries, marjoram, and caraway seeds. Pour in the wine and stock, cover, and simmer for 1 hour.

3 Add the cabbage, cover, and cook for 10 minutes. Stir in the sauerkraut and add some or all of the reserved cooking liquid (so the mixture is like a thick soup). Simmer for 15 minutes, then serve very hot.

perfect fish and chips

Cod in a light beer batter has an extra crispy and delicious crust. Double-fried french fries are fluffy within and crisp on the outside. The traditional accompaniment is tartar sauce and the recipe here beats anything you can buy in a jar.

 45-50 MINS PLUS STANDING   20-25 MINS

SPECIAL EQUIPMENT ▪ deep-fat fryer ▪ electric hand whisk or mixer

SERVES 4

6 potatoes, total weight about 1lb 10oz (750g), peeled

vegetable oil for deep-frying

¼ cup all-purpose flour

salt and freshly ground black pepper

4 skinned cod fillets, total weight 1lb 10oz (750g)

1 lemon, cut into wedges, to serve

For the tartar sauce

½ cup mayonnaise

1 hard-boiled egg, coarsely chopped

1 tsp drained capers, chopped

2 gherkins, coarsely chopped

1 small shallot, finely chopped

2-3 sprigs of parsley, leaves picked and chopped

2-3 sprigs of chervil or tarragon, leaves picked and chopped

For the batter

1½ tsp dried yeast (or ⅓oz/9g fresh yeast)

1 cup all-purpose flour

1 tbsp vegetable oil

¾ cup pale ale

1 egg white

1 For the tartar sauce, mix together the mayonnaise, egg, capers, gherkins, shallot, and herbs, and taste for seasoning. Cover and chill in the fridge until ready to serve.

2 Square off the sides and ends of the potatoes with a knife and cut lengthwise into ½in (1cm) sticks. Soak in a bowl of cold water for 30 minutes to remove the starch. Meanwhile, sprinkle the yeast over ¼ cup warm water and let stand for about 5 minutes until dissolved.

3 For the batter, sift the flour and a little salt into a large bowl and make a well in the center. Add the yeast

mixture, oil, and two-thirds of the beer; stir to form a smooth paste. Stir in the remaining beer, but don't overmix. Let the batter stand in a warm place for 30–35 minutes until thick and frothy.

4 While the batter is standing, heat the vegetable oil in a deep-fat fryer until it is at 350°F (180°C) on an oil thermometer. Drain the potatoes, transfer to paper towels, and pat dry. Dip the empty frying basket in the hot oil (to keep the potatoes from sticking). Lift the basket out of the oil, add the potatoes, and deep-fry for 5–7 minutes, until just tender when pierced with the tip of a knife and starting to brown. Lift out and let drain over the deep fryer, then place on a plate lined with paper towels.

5 Heat the oil to 375°F (190°C). Put the flour on a plate and season with salt and pepper. Coat the fish with the flour, patting them with your

hands so they are evenly coated. Whisk the egg white in a medium metal bowl with an electric hand mixer or stand mixer until stiff peaks form. Fold the whisked egg white into the batter with a wooden spoon. Using a 2-pronged fork, dip a piece of fish in the batter, coat it thoroughly, then hold it over the bowl briefly so excess batter can drip off. Deep-fry the fish until golden brown and crisp, about 6–8 minutes depending on the thickness of the fillets. Transfer to a baking sheet lined with paper towels, cover with foil, and keep warm. Repeat with the rest of the fish.

6 Put the partially cooked fries back in the frying basket and deep-fry for 1–2 minutes more until very hot and golden brown. Drain on paper towels. Serve with lemon wedges, accompanied by the tartar sauce.

Season's best **cod**

Caught throughout the cold waters of the Atlantic and Pacific, cod is an important commercial white fish. As it has been over-fished in some areas, choose line-caught ones from sustainable stocks (they will be clearly marked). Renowned for its succulent, chunky flakes with a sweet, seafood flavor, cod is famously fried in batter with french fries, but also tastes excellent with tomatoes, peppers, olives, garlic, sweet corn, cheese, and bacon.

Look out for the three-fin dorsal pattern that is typical of the Gadidae family.

Atlantic cod Also known as codling, sprag, or scrod, Atlantic cod is one of the largest members of the Gadidae family. It is identified by a white lateral line, green-yellow marbled skin that fades to white on the belly, and a square tail. Delicious grilled, fried, poached, baked, or cooked in soups, stews, and curries.

Atlantic cod has white flesh with a firm texture that chunks and flakes well.

Cod steak Cod steaks or cutlets are thick slices cut across the backbone, from the widest part of the fish. They can be stuffed, then poached, baked, or grilled.

how to make goujons

Goujons are small strips of fish, coated with egg and bread crumbs, then fried. Try a few as an appetizer with tartar sauce or serve as a main course instead of battered larger fillets.

1 Choose thick cod fillets (or other sustainable white fish). Skin them, if necessary, then cut into finger-length strips.

2 Put some seasoned flour in a bowl, beaten egg in another, and fresh bread crumbs in a third. Dip each strip in the flour, egg, and crumbs to coat.

3 Heat about ½in (1cm) sunflower, corn, or vegetable oil in a pan and fry the strips, a few at a time, until crisp and golden. Drain on paper towels.

The cheeks, considered a delicacy, are sold ready prepared and can be poached or fried.

Pacific cod Also known as Alaska cod, grey cod, true cod, or treska brown, it has dark mottled skin and a pale belly. It can grow to over 6 ½ft (2m) and is an excellent all-around fish.

Pacific cod fillet is firm, sweet, and well flavored.

essentials
varieties available

Atlantic and Pacific cods are usually sold in fillets or steaks (fresh and smoked). The head, cheeks, and roe (fresh and smoked) are also available.

buy Choose firm, moist flesh that smells of the ocean but not too "fishy." Avoid any that are slimy, discolored, or dying.

store Best eaten on the day of purchase but can be stored, wrapped in the fridge, for up to 24 hours.

cook Deep- or pan-fry fillets in batter or bread crumbs; poach in stock, wine, or milk; use chopped flesh for soup or chowder; stuff and bake, grill, or poach steaks.

recipe ideas

Cod and mussel chowder p460

Fish fingers with chunky tartar sauce p456

Perfect fish and chips p457

White fish with spinach and pine nuts p169

cod and mussel chowder

A hearty dish from New England laden with chunks of cod and potatoes, and mussels to add color and flavor. Traditionally, all this chowder needs with it is some oyster crackers, or serve it with crusty whole-wheat or rustic bread.

 45-50 MINS   55-60 MINS

SERVES 4

1 large potato, about 9oz (250g) total weight, peeled and diced

2½ cups fish stock

1 bay leaf

¼ cup white wine

3oz (85g) thick-cut bacon, diced

1 onion, finely chopped

1 celery stalk, peeled and finely chopped

1 small carrot, finely chopped

1 tsp dried thyme

¼ cup all-purpose flour

1lb 2oz (500g) mussels, scrubbed and debearded (discard any that do not close when tapped) (p364)

1lb 2oz (500g) skinned cod fillets, cut into 1in (2.5cm) pieces

½ cup heavy cream

salt and freshly ground black pepper

3 sprigs of dill, leaves picked and finely chopped

1 As soon as you have diced the potato, put it in a bowl of cold water so it doesn't discolor. Then put the fish stock and bay leaf into a large saucepan and pour in the wine. Bring to a boil and simmer for 10 minutes until very hot and all the flavors have combined.

2 Put the bacon in a flameproof casserole and cook, stirring occasionally, for 3–5 minutes until crisp and the fat is rendered. Add the onion, celery, carrot, and thyme. Cook, stirring, for 5–7 minutes until soft. Sprinkle the flour over the casserole and cook, stirring, for a minute. Add the hot fish stock mixture to the casserole and bring to a boil, stirring until the liquid thickens slightly.

3 Drain the potato and add it to the casserole. Simmer, stirring occasionally, for about 40 minutes until the potato is very tender. Remove the casserole from the heat.

With a fork, crush about a third of the potato against the side of the casserole, then stir to combine.

4 Return the casserole to the heat and add in the mussels. Simmer for 1–2 minutes until the shells start to open. Stir in the cod and simmer for another 2–3 minutes until the fish just flakes easily. Do not continue to cook or the fish will start to break apart. Pour in the cream and bring just to a boil. Taste for seasoning, adding salt and pepper to taste.

5 Discard the bay leaf and any mussels that have not opened, and warn your guests to do the same if they come across any firmly shut shellfish. Ladle the chowder into warmed soup bowls and sprinkle each with some dill. Serve very hot. Accompany with oyster crackers, crumbled into each bowl or fresh crusty bread.

variation

manhattan cod and mussel chowder

This adds tomatoes for a colorful finish. Peel, seed, and coarsely chop 1¼lb (550g) tomatoes, or use a 14oz (400g) can of tomatoes. If tomatoes are not ripe and in season, canned are usually the better choice. Also finely chop 2 garlic cloves. Make the chowder as directed in step 1, using double the amount of wine, 1½ tsp dried thyme, and half the all-purpose flour. Add the garlic and 1 tbsp tomato paste with the onion, celery, and carrots. Add the tomatoes together with the potatoes in step 3; do not crush any of the potatoes. Omit the heavy cream, sprinkle with chopped thyme, and serve with crusty whole-wheat bread.

fish and leek pie

The subtle, sweet flavor of leeks are a great match for fish.

 15 MINS 50 MINS ❄ FREEZABLE

SPECIAL EQUIPMENT ▪ 1-quart (1.2-liter) pie dish

SERVES 4

1 tbsp olive oil

1 onion, finely chopped

salt and freshly ground black pepper

4 leeks, finely sliced

1 tsp all-purpose flour

⅔ cup hard cider

handful of flat-leaf parsley,
  finely chopped

⅔ cup heavy cream

1½lb (675g) white fish, such as cod or
  pollack, cut into chunks

10oz (300g) store-bought puff pastry

1 large egg, lightly beaten, for egg wash

1 Preheat the oven to 400°F (200°C). Heat the oil in a large frying pan over low heat. Add the onion and a little salt, and cook gently for about 5 minutes until soft and translucent. Add the leeks and continue to cook gently for about 10 minutes until softened. Remove from the heat, stir in the flour, and add a little of the cider. Return to the heat, pour in the remaining cider, and cook for another 5–8 minutes until thickened. Stir in the parsley and cream, then spoon the mixture into a pie dish with the fish. Combine gently, and season well with salt and pepper.

2 Roll out the pastry on a floured work surface, so it is about 2in (5cm) larger all around than the top of the pie dish. Cut out a strip of pastry about 1in (2.5cm) in from the edge to make a collar. Wet the edge of the pie dish with a little water, fit the pastry strip all the way around the edge of the dish, and press down firmly. Brush the pastry collar with a little egg wash, then top with the pastry lid. Trim away the excess and pinch together the edges to seal. Using a sharp knife, make 2 slits in the top to allow steam to escape.

3 Brush the top of the pie with the egg wash and bake in the oven for 20–30 minutes until the pastry is puffed and golden. Serve the pie hot.

creole fish and corn stew

This chunky fish and vegetable winter stew has great texture. If you can't get find creamed sweet corn, use a can of regular sweet corn and blend it in the food processor.

  15 MINS 1 HR 15 MINS ❄ FREEZABLE

SERVES 4-6

2 tbsp olive oil

1 onion, finely chopped

3 garlic cloves, finely chopped

3 celery stalks, finely chopped

3 carrots, finely chopped

1 tsp dried oregano

a few sprigs of thyme, leaves picked

1 tsp cayenne pepper (use less if you
  don't like it too hot)

1 x 14oz (400g) can creamed sweet corn

1 x 14oz (400g) can sweet corn, drained

3 cups hot vegetable stock

salt and freshly ground black pepper

2 potatoes, peeled and diced into
  bite-sized pieces

7oz (200g) cooked, peeled shrimp,
  chopped

10oz (300g) coley, pollack, or cod,
  skinned and cut into chunky pieces

splash of Tabasco sauce (optional)

1 Heat the oil in a large heavy-bottomed pan over medium heat, add the onion, and cook for 3–4 minutes until soft. Then stir in the garlic, celery, and carrot, and cook over low heat for another 5 minutes, or until the carrot is soft.

2 Stir in the herbs and cayenne pepper, then add both cans of sweet corn and the stock. Season well with salt and pepper, bring to a boil, reduce to a simmer, and cook gently, partially covered, for 30–40 minutes. Add the potatoes and cook for another 15 minutes.

3 Add the shrimp and fish to the pan and simmer gently for 6–10 minutes, until the fish is opaque and cooked through. Taste and season further, if necessary, and stir in the Tabasco sauce, if using. Ladle into warmed bowls and serve with some crusty bread.

Season's best **rutabaga and turnip**

The large, hardy rutabaga has a deep, rich, earthy-sweet flavor, while turnips are smaller, white inside, and have a strong taste, faintly resembling mustard. In season throughout winter, they are excellent at the beginning of the year when other crops are scarce. They pair well with lamb, beef, game, offal, sausages, other root vegetables, cream, mushrooms, and sweet spices.

Root-like members of the cabbage family, rutabagas and turnips are widely grown staple crops in the cooler parts of temperate zones around the world.

Rutabaga A heavy vegetable with tough outer skin, it needs peeling thickly before use. Its color and flavor intensify when cooked, but it is also delicious grated raw for winter salads.

White turnip Pure white, round turnips, such as the Tokyo Cross (pictured here), have a mild flavor and a crunchy, juicy texture, much like a radish, so are particularly good grated in salads.

Purple turnip The familiar top-shaped turnip is usually purple fading to white at the root. When small in size the flavor is sweet and delicate.

Distinctive white and pinkish-purple skin.

essentials
varieties available

Large rutabaga with purple and white or yellow skin; purple and white turnips of varying sizes, including baby turnips—tiny specimens to cook whole.

buy Choose roots without any rot, pits, or scars.

store Uncut, they will keep well in the vegetable drawer of the fridge for 3–4 weeks; wrap a cut rutabaga in plastic wrap and store for up to 1 week.

cook Grate raw, boil, steam, bake, roast, deep-fry as chips, or add to soups and stews.

preserve Use diced small in pickles and chutneys.

recipe ideas

Creamy rutabaga soup p432

Poule au pot p463

Turnip soup with pimento, chile, and noodles p439

cornish pasties

Rutabaga lends sweetness and bulk to these traditional savory pasties. Worcestershire sauce adds depth of flavor.

 20 MINS PLUS CHILLING **40–45 MINS**

MAKES 4

7 tbsp lard, chilled and diced

4 tbsp unsalted butter, chilled and diced

1¾ cups all-purpose flour, plus extra for dusting

½ tsp salt

1 large egg, beaten, for glazing

For the filling

9oz (250g) skirt steak, trimmed, cut into ½in (1cm) cubes

2¾oz (80g) rutabaga, peeled, cut into ¼in (5mm) cubes

3½oz (100g) waxy potatoes, peeled, cut into ¼in (5mm) cubes

1 large onion, finely chopped

splash of Worcestershire sauce

1 tsp all-purpose flour

sea salt and freshly ground black pepper

1 In a mixing bowl, rub the lard and butter into the flour to resemble fine crumbs. Add the salt and enough cold water to bring the mixture together into a soft dough. Knead briefly on a lightly floured work surface, then wrap in plastic wrap and chill for 1 hour.

2 Preheat the oven to 375°F (190°C). Mix all the filling ingredients in a bowl and season well.

3 Roll the pastry out to a thickness of ¼in (5mm) on a floured work surface. Using a side plate or saucer, cut 4 circles from the dough. Fold the circles in half, then flatten them out again. Pile one-quarter of the filling into each circle, leaving a ¾in (2cm) border. Brush the border with a little beaten egg, pull both edges up over the filling, and press together to seal. Crimp the sealed edge with your fingers to form a decorative ridge. Brush beaten egg all over the pasties.

4 Bake in the center of the oven for 40–45 minutes until golden brown. Allow to cool for at least 15 minutes before eating warm or cold.

poule au pot

This classic French dish is a complete meal in itself.

 1 HR **1 HR 15 MINS – 1 HR 30 MINS**

SPECIAL EQUIPMENT ▪ trussing string ▪ muslin

SERVES 4–6

1 onion, trimmed and peeled

1 clove

1 large chicken, about 4½lb (2kg)

salt and freshly ground black pepper

1 bouquet garni

14 cups chicken stock, plus more if needed

2¼lb (1kg) leeks, trimmed, cut lengthwise, and sliced

13oz (375g) carrots, sliced

13oz (375g) turnips, diced

2 hard-boiled eggs, peeled

juice of ½ lemon

1 tsp Dijon mustard

2 tbsp dry white wine

1 cup vegetable oil

1 tbsp drained capers, finely chopped

3 gherkins, finely chopped

5–7 sprigs of parsley, finely chopped

1 small bunch of chives, finely snipped

2oz (60g) vermicelli

1 Stud the onion with the clove. Put the chicken in a flameproof casserole, season, and add the bouquet garni and onion. Cover three-quarters of the chicken with stock. Bring to a boil, cover, and simmer for 45 minutes.

2 Put the leeks on a piece of muslin and tie securely to make a bundle. Repeat with the carrots and turnips in separate muslin. Add to the chicken and pour in more stock to cover. Cover and simmer for 25–30 minutes.

3 To make the sauce gribiche, separate the hard-boiled yolks and whites by pulling them apart. Cut the whites into strips and finely chop. Sieve the yolks into a bowl using the back of a spoon. Add the lemon juice, mustard, salt, pepper, and wine, and whisk until combined. Gradually pour in the oil, whisking constantly. Add the egg whites, capers, gherkins, and herbs, and whisk to combine.

4 Carve the chicken, cover the pieces with foil, and keep warm. Remove the vegetables from the broth and keep warm. Strain the broth into a pan and simmer for 10–20 minutes. Skim off the fat and taste for seasoning. Add the vermicelli and cook according to package instructions.

5 Unwrap the vegetables, discarding the muslin, and add them and the chicken to the broth. Stir and remove from the heat. Serve in bowls with the sauce gribiche in a separate bowl.

lamb chops champvallon

This is a classic French recipe where lamb chops are cooked with potatoes and herbs: good winter warming fare.

 25–30 MINS 2 HRS – 2 HRS 15 MINS

SPECIAL EQUIPMENT ▪ 9 x 13in (23 x 32cm) baking dish

SERVES 6

6 lamb loin chops (about 2¼lb/1kg), each 1in (2.5cm) thick, trimmed

salt and freshly ground black pepper

1 tbsp vegetable oil

1lb 2oz (500g) onions, thinly sliced

2½lb (1.1kg) baking potatoes, peeled and cut into very thin slices

leaves from 1 small bunch of thyme, plus a few sprigs for garnish

3 garlic cloves, finely chopped

3½ cups hot chicken or beef stock, plus more if needed

1 Trim off any excess fat from the lamb chops and season both sides with salt and pepper. Heat the oil in a large frying pan over high heat, add the chops, and cook for 1–2 minutes on each side until well browned. Transfer to a plate and set aside.

2 Pour off all but about 1 tbsp of fat from the pan. Add the onions and cook over medium heat for 3–4 minutes, until soft and translucent. Remove the pan from the heat.

3 In a large bowl, gently stir the potato slices with the softened onions, thyme leaves, and season with salt and pepper.

4 Preheat the oven to 350°F (180°C) and brush the baking dish with oil. Spread half the potato mixture in the dish and sprinkle with the garlic.

5 Arrange the chops on top of the potatoes. Cover with the remaining potato mixture, placing the slices neatly in rows. Pour in enough stock to come just to the top of the potatoes. Bake, uncovered, for 2 hours, or until the lamb and potatoes are tender when pierced.

6 Divide the chops, potatoes, and onions among 6 warmed plates and spoon in a little cooking liquid. Decorate with a sprig of thyme and serve immediately.

vegetable casserole with dumplings

Dumplings are the perfect addition to a casserole or stew, as they make the dish a complete meal. For variety, add other herbs, such as thyme or tarragon to the parsley in the mixture.

 25 MINS 1 HR 15 MINS ❄ FREEZABLE

SERVES 4–6

1 tbsp olive oil

1 onion, coarsely chopped

salt and freshly ground black pepper

3 garlic cloves, finely chopped

pinch of dried chile flakes

2 leeks, trimmed and thickly sliced

3 carrots, coarsely chopped

2 celery stalks, coarsely chopped

1 tbsp all-purpose flour

3 cups hot vegetable stock

1 x 14oz (400g) can white navy beans, drained and rinsed

a few sprigs of rosemary

1⅓ cups self-rising flour

8 tbsp white vegetable fat

2 tbsp finely chopped flat-leaf parsley

1 Preheat the oven to 325°F (160°C). Heat the oil in a large flameproof casserole over medium heat, add the onion, and cook for 3–4 minutes until soft. Season with salt and pepper, then stir in the garlic and chile flakes. Add the leek, carrots, and celery, and continue cooking for another 10 minutes, stirring occasionally, until softened. Stir in the all-purpose flour, then gradually stir in the stock. Add the navy beans and rosemary. Bring to a boil, then reduce to a simmer, cover, and put in the oven for 1 hour, checking on the liquid level as it cooks and adding more hot stock if needed.

2 While this is cooking, prepare the dumplings. Mix together the self-rising flour, fat, and parsley, and season well. Add about ½ cup cold water to form a soft, slightly sticky dough, trickling in more water if it seems too dry. Form into 12 balls and drop them into the stew for the last 30 minutes of cooking. Push them down a little so they are just immersed and cover with the lid. Remove the lid for the final 10 minutes, or until the dumplings are browned. Remove the rosemary, ladle the casserole into warmed bowls, and serve with crusty bread.

onion confit and gorgonzola pizzas

Onions and Gorgonzola are delicious together, topping a crust made crunchy with fine yellow cornmeal or polenta.

 40–45 MINS PLUS RISING 35–40 MINS

MAKES 6

1⅓ cups bread flour, plus more
  if needed

1½ tsp quick-rise yeast

2 tbsp olive oil

½ cup fine yellow cornmeal
  or polenta

6oz (175g) Gorgonzola cheese,
  cut into slices

For the onion confit

2 tbsp olive oil

1lb 10oz (750g) red onions,
  thinly sliced

2 tsp sugar

salt and freshly ground black pepper

¼ cup red wine

5-7 sprigs of oregano, leaves picked
  and chopped, plus reserve some
  to serve

1 Sift the flour into a bowl and add the yeast. Stir in the oil and enough warm water (about ⅔ cup) to form a soft, but not sticky, dough. Knead gently on a lightly floured surface for several minutes until smooth and elastic. Return to the bowl, cover with oiled plastic wrap, and let rise in a warm place for about 40 minutes until the dough has doubled in size.

2 For the onion confit, heat the oil in a frying pan over medium heat. Add the onions and sugar, and season with salt and pepper. Cook for 5–7 minutes, stirring often, until the onions are soft and lightly brown. Add the wine and continue cooking until it has evaporated. Reduce the heat, press a piece of foil on top of

the onions, and cover with a lid. Cook, stirring occasionally, for 15–20 minutes, or until the onions are soft enough to cut with a spoon. Let cool. Stir in the chopped oregano leaves.

3 Preheat the oven to 450°F (230°C). Put 2 baking sheets on separate racks in the bottom half of the oven to heat. Cut 6 x 9in (23cm) squares of foil and sprinkle each generously with the cornmeal or polenta.

4 Turn out the dough onto a floured surface and punch it down by re-kneading briefly. With your hands, roll the dough into a cylinder about 2in (5cm) in diameter. Cut the cylinder in half, then cut each half into 3 equal pieces. Shape the pieces of dough into balls.

5 Roll out a ball of dough into a 7in (18cm) round. Transfer the round to one of the squares of foil. Repeat to shape the remaining dough. If you like, press up the edges of the rounds with your fingertips to form shallow rims. Spread the rounds with the onion confit.

6 Top the rounds with slices of the cheese and leave them in a warm place for about 15 minutes, until the dough is puffed. Bake the pizzas, on the foil, on the baking sheets, for 15–20 minutes until lightly browned and crisp. Switch the baking sheets after 7 minutes so the pizzas brown evenly. Serve the pizzas hot from the oven. Brush the crusts with oil and top them with the reserved oregano leaves.

osso buco

Winter citrus lends a delicious fragrance to this Italian classic, which is served with a zesty gremolata. A saffron and Parmesan risotto is the traditional accompaniment. Ask your butcher for a hindleg of veal as they are meatier than the front legs.

 30-35 MINS   1 HR 45 MINS – 2 HRS 15 MINS

SERVES 4-6

¼ cup all-purpose flour

salt and freshly ground black pepper

4-6 pieces of veal shank cut crosswise (about 4lb/1.8kg)

2 tbsp vegetable oil

2 tbsp butter

1 carrot, thinly sliced

2 onions, finely chopped

1 cup white wine

1 x 14oz can Italian plum tomatoes, drained and coarsely chopped

1 garlic clove, finely chopped

grated zest of 1 orange

½ cup hot chicken or veal stock

For the citrus gremolata

small bunch of flat-leaf parsley, leaves picked and finely chopped

grated zest of 1 lemon

1 garlic clove, finely chopped

1 Preheat the oven to 350°F (180°C). Put the flour on a large plate, season with salt and pepper, and stir to combine. Lightly coat the veal pieces with the seasoned flour.

2 Heat the oil and butter in a large flameproof casserole over medium heat, add the veal pieces (in batches and with extra oil, if necessary), and brown thoroughly on all sides. Transfer to a plate with a slotted spoon and set aside.

3 Add the carrot and onions to the casserole and cook, stirring occasionally, until soft. Add the wine and boil until reduced by half. Stir in the tomatoes, garlic, and orange zest and add seasoning. Lay the veal on top and pour in the stock. Cover and put in the oven for 1½–2 hours until very tender. Check occasionally that it's not drying out, adding a little hot water if needed.

4 For the gremolata, mix the parsley, lemon, and garlic in a small bowl. To serve, put the veal on warmed plates, spoon the sauce on top, and sprinkle with the gremolata.

variation

osso buco with celery, leek, and almonds

Prepare in the same way, but substitute 1 sliced leek for one of the onions, and add 2 chopped celery stalks to the mixture at the beginning of step 2. Use an Italian red wine, such as Chianti, instead of the white wine and add a pinch of sugar in step 3. Prepare the gremolata for garnish, but add a small handful of toasted, sliced almonds to the mix.

pork belly with onions and potatoes

The secret behind a crisp piece of crackling is rubbing plenty of salt and oil into the skin and then cooking the meat at a high temperature for its first 20 minutes in the oven.

🥣 25 MINS   🍲 2 HRS 10 MINS

SERVES 4

1lb 2oz (500g) piece of pork belly

sea salt and freshly ground black pepper

3 tbsp olive oil

2 onions, cut into eighths

2 large potatoes, peeled and cut into wedges

4½ oz (125g) button mushrooms, halved

⅔ cup white wine

2 garlic cloves, chopped

2 tsp chopped thyme

1¼ cups hot vegetable stock

1 Preheat the oven to 425°F (220°C). Score the skin of the pork belly deeply, then rub ½ tsp sea salt and 1 tbsp of the oil into it. Transfer to a baking sheet and place in the oven for 20 minutes, or until the skin has crisped up. Remove from the oven and reduce the temperature to 340°F (170°C).

2 Heat the remaining oil in a frying pan over medium heat, add the onions and potatoes, and cook for 10 minutes, stirring constantly. Add the mushrooms and cook for 5 more minutes. Then add the wine and cook for 2 more minutes. Transfer the mixture to a large baking dish, add the garlic, thyme, stock, and black pepper, and combine well. Nestle the pork in the mixture, ensuring the crackling is not covered, and roast in the oven for 1½ hours.

3 Allow to rest for 10 minutes, then cut the pork into 4 pieces with scissors and serve with steamed broccoli.

variation

pork belly with leeks and celery root

Prepare in exactly the same way, but use 3 leeks, cut in chunks, instead of the onions, and a large celery root, peeled and cut into chunks, instead of the potatoes. Cook for 5 minutes only at step 2.

hunter's chicken stew

In Italy, this dish is called *alla cacciatora*, meaning "hunter's style." Chicory, with its slight bitterness, makes a flavorful addition and must be added toward the end of cooking.

🥣 20-25 MINS   🍲 45-60 MINS   ❄ FREEZABLE

SERVES 4

3lb 3oz (1.5kg) chicken, cut into 8 pieces

salt and freshly ground black pepper

¼ cup olive oil

1 onion, chopped

4 garlic cloves, finely chopped

a sprig of rosemary

1 bay leaf

¼ cup dry white wine

½ cup hot chicken stock

2 heads of chicory, trimmed, leaves separated, and coarsely chopped

1 Season the chicken all over with salt and pepper. Heat half the oil in a large flameproof casserole over medium heat, add the thighs and drumsticks skin-side down, and cook for about 5 minutes until they begin to brown. Add the breast pieces and cook gently for 10-15 minutes until very brown. Turn and brown the other side. Reduce the heat.

2 Add the onion and garlic, stir, and continue cooking gently for 3-4 minutes until they are soft. Season with salt and pepper, then stir in the rosemary, bay leaf, wine, and stock. Cover and simmer for 15-20 minutes until tender.

3 Add the chicory for the last 5 minutes of cooking, return the lid, and cook gently until the chicory has just softened. Discard the bay leaf and rosemary from the sauce, taste, and add seasoning if needed. Spoon into warmed bowls and serve with crusty bread.

variation

hunter's rabbit stew

Prepare in exactly the same way, but use a rabbit cut into pieces instead of the chicken. Add a finely chopped carrot with the onion and garlic, use red wine instead of white, and 2 heads of either red chicory or radicchio instead of the chicory.

sweet balsamic onions

Baby onions are also known as button or pearl onions. They are really immature onions kept small by dense planting. Braising them in balsamic vinegar keeps them sweet and moist.

 10 MINS   35 MINS

SERVES 4

3 tbsp olive oil

14oz (400g) baby onions, peeled and left whole

3 garlic cloves, finely sliced

3 tbsp balsamic vinegar

salt and freshly ground black pepper

drizzle of olive oil or chili oil, to serve

1 Preheat the oven to 350°F (180°C). Heat the oil in a deep frying pan over low heat, add the onions, and cook, stirring frequently, for 15 minutes, or until evenly brown.

2 Transfer the onions to a small baking dish, packing them in tightly. Sprinkle with the garlic and spoon over the balsamic vinegar. Season well with salt and pepper, and bake for

20 minutes, stirring every 5 minutes. Serve hot or cold with a good drizzle of olive oil or chili oil and some fresh crusty bread and cheese.

variation

sweet balsamic baby leeks
Use 8oz (225g) baby leeks, trimmed but left whole, instead of the baby onions. Cook them in 3 tbsp butter instead of the oil for 2 minutes only, turning once or twice until lightly golden and softening. Transfer to a baking dish and add a small handful of chopped walnuts, a bay leaf, and 3 tbsp white balsamic vinegar instead of the balsamic vinegar. Season. Cook as before but no need to turn. Serve hot or cold.

applesauce

The perfect accompaniment to pork, no matter how the meat is cooked. While traditionally served with a roast, applesauce is just as good with cold meat or pork chops.

 10 MINS   10 MINS   ❄ FREEZABLE

SERVES 4

1lb (450g) apples, peeled, cored, and quartered

2-3 tbsp sugar (depending on the tartness of the apples)

1 Put the apples in a pan, sprinkle in 1 tbsp water, then add the sugar. Cover and cook on a low heat for 10 minutes, or until the apples have begun to break down.

2 Stir with a wooden spoon until the sauce reaches your preferred consistency—either a smooth purée or more chunky. Taste and add more sugar, if required. Serve warm or cold with roast pork.

pancetta and potatoes with red cabbage

Here is a speedy side dish that would happily accompany any casserole or stew—and as it includes potatoes, it is very filling as well. Even better, you can reheat it the next day.

 10 MINS 15 MINS

SERVES 4

pat of butter

1 tbsp olive oil

3 cooked potatoes, peeled and cut into cubes

salt and freshly ground black pepper

6oz (175g) pancetta, diced

7oz (200g) red cabbage, lightly cooked and shredded

2 apples, peeled, cored, and chopped

1 Heat the butter and oil in a large frying pan over medium-high heat. Add the potatoes and sauté for 5–10 minutes until golden and crispy, adding more oil if needed. Season with salt and pepper, then push the potatoes to one side of the pan.

2 Add the pancetta and cook until crispy, then stir in the cabbage and apples. Cook until well combined and the apple is golden. Season again, if needed, and serve while hot.

red cabbage with cider

Red cabbage is transformed when slow cooked, becoming sweet and tender. Add a handful of golden raisins, if you wish, for extra flavor, and serve with couscous or sausages.

 15 MINS 1 HR - 1 HR 30 MINS

SERVES 4

½ red onion, sliced

1 large red cabbage (about 2¼lb/1kg), cored and shredded

1 apple, cored (but not peeled) and finely chopped

1 tsp five-spice powder

salt and freshly ground black pepper

1¼ cups dry hard cider

1 Put the onion, cabbage, apple, and five-spice powder into a large heavy-bottomed pan and season well with salt and pepper. Turn to mix everything together.

2 Pour in the cider and stir, then cover with the lid and cook over low heat for 1–1½ hours, stirring occasionally. Taste and season as needed.

potatoes boulangère

Perfect for a cold winter's night, these garlicky and finely sliced potatoes are baked in the oven. The end result is a moist and tender side dish to accompany any main course.

 25 MINS 1 HR

SPECIAL EQUIPMENT ▪ 2-quart (2.3-liter) ovenproof dish

SERVES 4–6

4 tbsp butter

6 onions, sliced

2lb (900g) potatoes, peeled and cut into ¼in (5mm) slices

3 garlic cloves, sliced

2½ cups hot vegetable stock or chicken stock

salt and freshly ground black pepper

1 Preheat the oven to 400°F (200°C). Melt the butter in a large pan over low heat, add the onions, and cook, stirring often, for 10 minutes, or until soft and translucent. Add the potatoes, garlic, and stock and season with salt and pepper. Stir well, then cover with a lid and simmer for 5–6 minutes, or until the potatoes start to soften.

2 Transfer the mixture to the ovenproof dish and cook for 40–50 minutes, or until the potatoes are tender and most of the stock has been absorbed. Serve with roast beef.

variation

creamy sweet potato and leek bake

Prepare in the same way, but use the white part of 3 leeks, sliced, in place of 4 of the onions, 2lb (900g) sweet potatoes, peeled and sliced, instead of ordinary ones, and use 1¾ cups stock and 1¼ cups heavy cream instead of all stock.

roasted celery with orange and walnuts

An unusual way to cook celery. Here the heart is quartered and roasted with orange and walnuts. Delicious served with roast chicken, pork, or a piece of grilled halibut or monkfish.

 10 MINS   **55 MINS**

SERVES 4

4 celery hearts, trimmed and quartered

zest and juice of 1 orange

extra virgin olive oil, for drizzling

pat of butter, melted

1 tsp granulated sugar

a sprig of thyme, leaves picked and chopped

handful of walnuts, chopped

sea salt and freshly ground black pepper

1 Preheat the oven to 400°F (200°C). Put the celery hearts in a roasting pan and add the orange zest and juice. Drizzle with a little oil and the butter. Sprinkle in the sugar, thyme, and walnuts. Season with sea salt and pepper to taste.

2 Cover the roasting pan tightly with foil and cook in the oven for 40 minutes. Remove the foil and leave in the oven to brown for another 15 minutes until tender and glazed. Serve hot or warm.

red cabbage slaw

This crisp, crunchy, colorful salad goes particularly well with cold meats and baked potatoes, but is also delicious with cheeses and crusty bread for a light lunch.

 15 MINS

SERVES 6

½ small red cabbage, finely shredded

2 celery stalks, chopped

½ small red onion, thinly sliced

1 red and 1 green apple, cored and diced (leaving the skins on)

large handful of raisins

large handful of walnuts, coarsely chopped

For the dressing

6 tbsp heavy cream

2 tsp light brown sugar

½ tsp Dijon mustard

salt and freshly ground black pepper

2 tbsp red wine vinegar

1 Mix all the salad ingredients together in a salad bowl.

2 To make the dressing, lightly whip the cream with the sugar. Whisk in the mustard and a little salt and pepper. Whisk in the vinegar to form a thick pouring consistency.

3 Pour over the salad. Toss well. Any leftover salad will keep in the fridge for 2–3 days.

variation

celery root and pear coleslaw

Use ½ small white cabbage instead of red, ½ small celery root, grated instead of the celery stalks. And 2 large carrots, grated and 2 diced pears instead of the apples. Substitute peanuts for the walnuts. Make the dressing as before.

white bean and cauliflower gratin

This gratin is a complete meal in itself, although you may like to serve it with some lightly steamed leafy greens, such as cavolo nero, mustard greens, or kale.

 10 MINS   **30 MINS**

SERVES 4

pat of butter

1 tbsp all-purpose flour

1¼ cups milk

pinch of paprika

salt and freshly ground black pepper

4½oz (125g) sharp Cheddar cheese, grated

2 tsp Dijon mustard

1 head of cauliflower, broken into florets

1 x 14oz (400g) can white beans, drained and rinsed

1 Preheat the oven to 400°F (200°C). To make the cheese sauce, melt the butter in a pan over low heat. Remove from the heat and stir in the flour with a wooden spoon until smooth. Add a little of the milk and stir until smooth. Return to the heat and slowly add the remaining milk, stirring continuously. Keep stirring for 5–10 minutes until the sauce has thickened.

2 Remove from the heat, sprinkle in the paprika, and season well with salt and pepper. Add 2½oz (75g) of the cheese and the mustard and stir them into the sauce. Set aside.

3 Bring a pan of salted water to a boil, add the cauliflower, and cook for about 10 minutes until soft. Drain.

4 Put the cauliflower in an ovenproof dish with the white beans and toss together. Pour in the sauce and top with the remaining cheese. Cook in the oven for 10–15 minutes until golden and simmering. Serve hot.

potato-chive monkey bread

This bread made of mashed potato has a soft crust.

 50-55 MINS PLUS RISING 40-45 MINS

SPECIAL EQUIPMENT ▪ 6-cup ring mold

MAKES 1

9oz (250g) potatoes, cut into large pieces

2½ tsp dried yeast, or ½oz (15g) fresh yeast

8 tbsp unsalted butter, plus more for greasing

1 large bunch of chives, snipped

2 tbsp sugar

2 tsp salt

2½ cups flour, plus more if needed

1 Boil the potatoes, drain, reserving 1 cup of the cooking liquid, and mash well. Let the reserved liquid and potatoes cool. In a small bowl, sprinkle the yeast over ¼ cup lukewarm water. Let stand for 5 minutes until dissolved, stirring once.

2 Melt half the butter in a pan. Put the potatoes, cooking liquid, dissolved yeast, and melted butter into a large bowl. Add the chives, sugar, and salt, and mix. Add half the flour and mix well with your hands. Add the remaining flour, ½ cup at a time.

3 Knead the dough on a floured work surface until it is smooth and elastic and forms a ball. Wash out the bowl and brush with melted butter. Put the dough in the bowl and flip until lightly buttered. Cover with a damp kitchen towel and leave in a warm place for 1–1½ hours, or until doubled in size.

4 Brush the ring mold with melted butter. Melt the remaining 4 tbsp butter and pour it into a shallow dish. Turn the dough onto a lightly floured work surface and knead just to knock out the air. Cover and let it rest for about 5 minutes. Make 30 or so walnut-sized balls of dough, toss in melted butter, and transfer to the mold. Cover the mold with a dry kitchen towel and let rise in a warm place until the mold is full. Preheat the oven to 375°F (190°C).

5 Bake for 40–45 minutes, until golden brown and the bread starts to shrink from the side of the mold. Let it cool slightly on a wire rack, then carefully unmold.

celery and apple salad with blue cheese dressing

In this salad, the strong tastes of celery and bitter leaves more than hold their own against the pungency of a blue cheese dressing, with the walnuts adding crunch and texture.

 10 MINS 2 MINS

SPECIAL EQUIPMENT ▪ food processor

SERVES 4

8 tbsp or 2oz (60g) chopped walnuts

10½oz (300g) blue cheese, such as Dolcelatte or Gorgonzola

¼ cup cider vinegar

¼ cup hazelnut oil or walnut oil

freshly ground black pepper

4 celery stalks, trimmed and sliced diagonally into ½in (1cm) slices

2 green apples, cored and cut into thin wedges

4 large handfuls of watercress or arugula

sea salt

1 Dry-fry the walnuts for a couple of minutes in a frying pan or wok until they are golden and crispy. Set aside and let cool.

2 In a food processor, mix together 3½oz (100g) of the blue cheese, vinegar, oil, and a good grinding of black pepper. Blend to a smooth, creamy dressing, which should have thick pouring consistency. Add up to 1 tbsp cold water to thin the dressing a little if it is too thick.

3 Put the celery, apples, and watercress or arugula in a large bowl and mix well. Coat the salad with the dressing and check it for seasoning. Top with the walnut pieces and the rest of the blue cheese, crumbled or diced into bite-sized pieces.

variation

celery, leek, and pear salad

Use pecans instead of walnuts. Substitute 1 small leek, thinly sliced for 2 of the celery stalks and 2 firm pears for the apples. Dress as before.

lemon cheesecake

This cold-set cheesecake needs no baking and so produces a lighter, more delicate result.

 30 MINS PLUS CHILLING

SPECIAL EQUIPMENT ■ 9in (22cm) round springform cake pan

SERVES 8

9oz (250g) vanilla wafers

7 tbsp unsalted butter, diced

4 gelatin leaves, coarsely cut up

grated zest and juice of 2 lemons, plus thinly pared zest, to garnish

12oz (350g) cream cheese

¾ cup granulated sugar

1¼ cups heavy cream

1 Line the cake pan with parchment paper. Put the wafers in a bag and crush to crumbs with a rolling pin. Melt the butter in a pan, then add the crushed wafers, mixing well to combine. Press the wafer mixture firmly into the base of the pan using a wooden spoon. Transfer to the fridge to chill.

2 In a small heatproof bowl, soak the gelatin in the lemon juice for 5 minutes to soften. Place the bowl over a pan of hot water and stir until the gelatin melts. Set aside to cool.

3 Beat together the cream cheese, sugar, and lemon zest in a bowl until smooth. In a separate bowl, whisk the heavy cream to soft peaks.

4 Pour the gelatin mixture into the cream cheese mixture, stirring well to combine. Then gently fold the whisked cream into the cheese mixture. Be careful not to lose volume.

5 Pour the cheese mixture onto the chilled wafer base and spread evenly. Smooth the top with a damp palette knife or the back of a damp spoon. Chill for at least 4 hours or overnight.

6 To serve, run a sharp, thin knife around the inside of the pan. Gently transfer the cheesecake to a plate, making sure you remove the parchment paper. Garnish with the thinly pared lemon zest.

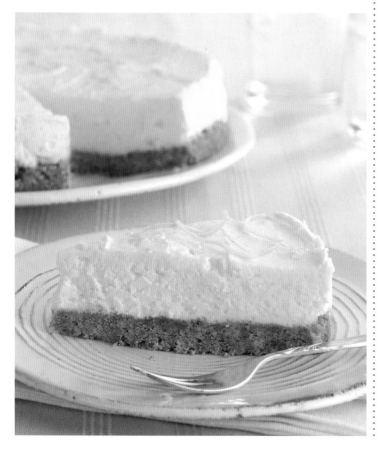

chocolate orange whoopie pies

A whoopie pie is two small cakes sandwiching a creamy filling. Rich, dark chocolate combined with the zesty tang of orange is a classic combination and used here to full advantage.

 40 MINS 12 MINS

MAKES 10

19 tbsp unsalted butter, softened

¾ cup light brown sugar

1 large egg

2 tsp vanilla extract

grated zest and juice of 1 orange

2 cups self-rising flour

⅔ cup cocoa powder

1 tsp baking powder

⅔ cup whole milk or buttermilk

2 tbsp Greek-style yogurt or thick natural yogurt

1⅔ cups confectioners' sugar

1 Preheat the oven to 350°F (180°C). Line several baking sheets with parchment paper. Cream 12 tbsp of the butter and the brown sugar until fluffy. Beat in the egg and 1 tsp of the vanilla extract and add the zest. In a bowl, sift the flour, cocoa powder, and baking powder. Mix the dry ingredients and the milk into the batter in alternate spoonfuls. Fold in the yogurt.

2 Place 20 heaping tablespoons of the mixture onto the baking sheets, leaving space between them. Dip a spoon in warm water and use the back to smooth the surface of the cake mounds. Bake for 12 minutes until risen. Let cool slightly, then transfer to a wire rack.

3 For the buttercream, blend the remaining butter and vanilla extract with the confectioners' sugar and orange juice, loosening with a little water. Spread 1 tbsp of the filling onto the flat side of each cake half and sandwich together with the remaining halves.

grapefruit crème de menthe jelly

Crème de menthe works fantastically with the bitter taste of grapefruit. This fruit jelly makes a really refreshing dessert with a dollop of crème fraîche.

 15 MINS PLUS STANDING AND SETTING

SERVES 4

2 white grapefruit

2 tbsp granulated sugar, plus extra for frosting

1 large egg white, lightly beaten

1 package powdered gelatin

1¼ cups apple juice

¼ cups crème de menthe

1 Peel and segment the grapefruit (p474). Put the fruit in a bowl and squeeze the membranes over the fruit to extract all the juice, then discard. Sprinkle the sugar over the grapefruit, stir, and let stand for an hour, if possible, to allow the juice to run.

2 Frost the rims of 4 wine goblets: dip them in the egg white, then in granulated sugar, and let set.

3 Meanwhile, put the gelatin in a small bowl with 2 tbsp water. Let soften for 5 minutes, then stand the bowl in a pan of gently simmering water and stir until the gelatin has completely dissolved. Stir into the apple juice. Add the crème de menthe.

4 Put the grapefruit slices in the wine goblets. Strain the remaining grapefruit juice into the apple juice mixture. Stir, then pour over the fruit and chill until set.

lemon meringue pie

With the sharpness of lemon combined with a smooth vanilla meringue topping, it is no wonder this pie is a family favorite.

 30 MINS PLUS CHILLING   **40-50 MINS**

SPECIAL EQUIPMENT ▪ 9in (23cm) round tart pan with removable bottom ▪ ceramic baking beans

SERVES 8

14oz (400g) store-bought pie dough

6 large eggs, at room temperature, separated

3 tbsp all-purpose flour

3 tbsp cornstarch

1¾ cups granulated sugar

1 tbsp grated zest and juice of 3 lemons

3 tbsp butter, diced

½ tsp cream of tartar

½ tsp vanilla extract

1 Preheat the oven to 400°F (200°C) and lightly butter the pan. Lightly flour a work surface and roll out the dough. Use it to line the pan.

2 Line the pie dough with parchment paper, then fill with ceramic baking beans. Place on a baking sheet and bake for 10–15 minutes, or until the crust looks pale golden. Lift off the paper and beans, return the crust to the oven, and bake for 3–5 minutes until golden. Reduce the temperature to 350°F (180°C). Let cool slightly in the pan.

3 Put the egg yolks in a bowl and lightly beat. Combine the flour, cornstarch, and 1 cup of the sugar in a saucepan. Slowly add 1½ cups water and heat gently, stirring, until the sugar dissolves and there are no lumps. Increase the heat slightly and cook, stirring, for

3–5 minutes, or until the mixture starts to thicken.

4 Beat several spoonfuls of the hot mixture into the egg yolks. Pour this mixture back into the pan and slowly bring to a boil, stirring constantly. Boil for 3 minutes, then stir in the lemon zest and juice together with the butter. Continue boiling for another 2 minutes, or until the mixture is thick and glossy, stirring constantly and scraping down the sides of the pan as necessary. Remove the pan from the heat; cover to keep warm.

5 Whisk the egg whites in a large clean bowl until foamy. Sprinkle in the cream of tartar and whisk. Continue whisking, adding the

remaining sugar, 1 tbsp at a time. Add the vanilla extract with the last tablespoon of the sugar, whisking until the meringue is thick and glossy.

6 Place the pie crust on a baking sheet, pour in the lemon filling, then top with the meringue, spreading it so it completely covers the filling right up to the crust's edge. Be careful not to spill it over the crust, or the tart will be difficult to remove from the pan after baking.

7 Place in the oven and bake for 12–15 minutes, or until the meringue is lightly golden. Transfer to a wire rack and let cool completely, before removing from the pan and serving.

tangerine macarons

Sharp, zesty tangerines are used here, rather than oranges, to counterbalance the sweetness of the meringues.

 30 MINS 18–20 MINS

SPECIAL EQUIPMENT ▪ blender or food processor ▪ piping bag fitted with a ½in (1cm) plain nozzle

MAKES 20

1⅔ cups confectioners' sugar

¾ cup ground almonds

2 tsp grated zest and 1 tbsp tangerine juice

2 large egg whites, at room temperature

¼ cup granulated sugar

3–4 drops orange food coloring

4 tbsp unsalted butter, softened

1 Preheat the oven to 300°F (150°C). Line 2 baking sheets with parchment paper. Draw 40 x 1¼in (3cm) circles on the parchment with a pencil, leaving a 1¼in (3cm) gap between each one. Pulse half the confectioners' sugar with the ground almonds in a blender or food processor until finely mixed. Add 1 tsp of the tangerine zest and pulse briefly once more.

2 In a bowl, whisk the egg whites to form stiff peaks. Add the granulated sugar, a little at a time,

whisking well with each addition. Whisk in the food coloring. Fold in the almond mixture, a spoonful at a time. Transfer to the piping bag and pipe meringue into the center of each circle.

3 Bake in the middle of the oven for 18–20 minutes until the surface is set firm. Leave the macarons to cool on the baking sheets for 15–20 minutes and then transfer to a wire rack to cool completely.

4 For the filling, cream together the remaining confectioners' sugar and tangerine zest with the butter and tangerine juice until smooth. Transfer into the (cleaned) piping bag, using the same nozzle. Pipe a blob of icing onto the flat side of half the macarons, and sandwich with the other half. Serve the same day, or the macarons will start to go soft.

orange and cinnamon crème brûlée

In this dessert, translated as "burnt cream," a rich custard is sprinkled with sugar and then broiled for a few minutes.

 15–20 MINS PLUS CHILLING 30–35 MINS

SPECIAL EQUIPMENT ▪ electric hand mixer ▪ 1-quart (1-liter) gratin dish

SERVES 8

1 cinnamon stick, snapped in half

3½ cups heavy cream

grated zest of 1 orange

8 large egg yolks

¾ cup granulated sugar

1 Preheat the oven to 375°F (190°C). Put the cinnamon in a pan. Warm over low heat for 40–60 seconds, until you can smell the spice. Let cool slightly, then add the cream and orange zest. Bring just to a boil. Remove from the heat, cover, and let the cream infuse for 10–15 minutes.

2 Put the yolks and a third of the sugar in a bowl. Mix with an electric hand mixer. Slowly pour the cream mixture into the egg yolks, whisking constantly. Ladle the mixture through a large sieve into the gratin dish. Fold an old, clean kitchen towel and put it on the bottom of a roasting pan. Then set the gratin dish on the towel.

3 Pour hot water into the roasting pan to come about halfway up the sides of the gratin dish. Bring the water to a boil on top of the stove, then move to the oven. Bake for 30–35 minutes, until a thin skin forms and the cream is almost firm when the dish is moved from side to side. Remove from the pan, let cool to room temperature, then chill for 3–8 hours.

4 Preheat the broiler. Sprinkle the remaining sugar over the surface of the cream. Half-fill a roasting pan with cold water and set the gratin dish in it. Add some ice cubes to the water to keep the custard cool. Broil for 3 minutes, until the sugar melts and caramelizes on top. Let cool a few minutes so the caramel becomes crisp, then serve.

lemon polenta cake

Polenta makes a rich, moist cake with a great lemon flavor. This recipe is also a good wheat-free option.

 30 MINS   **50–60 MINS**   **FREEZABLE**

SPECIAL EQUIPMENT ▪ 9in (22cm) round springform cake pan
▪ electric hand mixer

SERVES 6–8

12 tbsp unsalted butter, softened

¾ cup granulated sugar

3 large eggs, beaten

½ cup coarse yellow cornmeal or polenta

1½ cups ground almonds

grated zest and juice of 2 lemons

1 tsp baking powder

crème fraîche, to serve (optional)

1 Preheat the oven to 325°F (160°C). Grease the cake pan and line the base with parchment paper. Cream the butter and ⅔ cup of the sugar with an electric hand mixer until fluffy. Pour in the beaten eggs, a little at a time, beating after each addition. Gently stir in the cornmeal or polenta and the almonds using a rubber spatula. Fold in the lemon zest and baking powder.

2 Scrape the mixture into the prepared pan and smooth the surface with a palette knife. Bake for 50–60 minutes until springy to the touch and a skewer inserted in the center comes out clean. It will not rise much. Leave the cake in the pan for a few minutes until cool enough to handle.

3 Heat the lemon juice and the remaining sugar in a small pan over medium heat until the sugar has dissolved. Remove from the heat.

4 Turn the cake out onto a wire rack, baked side upward. Retain the parchment. Using a thin skewer or cocktail stick, poke holes in the top of the cake while still warm. Pour the hot lemon syrup, a little at a time, over the surface of the cake. Remove the parchment and serve at room temperature on its own or with crème fraîche.

middle eastern oranges

Slices of fresh orange are made more exotic with rosewater, pomegranate seeds, and pistachio nuts.

 15 MINS

SERVES 4

4 oranges

1–2 tbsp honey

2 tbsp rosewater

large pinch of ground cinnamon

seeds from 1 pomegranate

small handful of chopped pistachio nuts (optional)

handful of mint leaves, to decorate

1 Slice the top and bottom from each orange and place them on a cutting board. Carefully slice off the skin and pith, leaving as much flesh as possible, and following the sides of the orange so you keep the shape of the fruit. Slice the oranges horizontally into thin strips, discarding any seeds as you come across them, then arrange the orange slices on a serving platter. Pour in any juice that remains on the cutting board.

2 Drizzle with the honey and rosewater and sprinkle with the cinnamon. Scatter with the pomegranate seeds and pistachio nuts, if using, then decorate with the mint leaves and serve.

variation

caramelized oranges and passion fruit

Put ¼ cup sugar in a saucepan with 2 tbsp water. Stir, then heat gently without stirring, until the sugar melts. Boil rapidly until a rich golden brown. Remove from the heat and add 2 tbsp water. Stir over low heat until the caramel dissolves, then let cool. Prepare the dish in the same way, but drizzle with the caramel instead of honey, omit the rosewater, and scatter with passion fruit seeds instead of pomegranate.

Season's best **oranges, tangerines, clementines, and grapefruit**

Best in winter, these members of the citrus family are rich in vitamin C and help to detoxify the body. Oranges vary widely in size, thickness of skin, and taste; the smaller, sweeter mandarin is a popular variety, which also includes tangerines, satsumas, and clementines. Grapefruit are grown in clusters like oversized yellow grapes. They all team well with chocolate, rich meats, poultry and game, cheeses, and other fruits.

Oranges, grapefruit, and other citrus are grown in the Mediterranean and subtropical regions worldwide, especially Spain, the US, Brazil, China, Japan, South Africa, Israel, and Mexico.

Clementine This is among the smallest of the mandarin citrus family and looks like a bright orange golf ball, with thin, shiny skin, a delicate membrane, and hardly any seeds. The juice has a sweet, elusive fragrance with a tangy edge.

how to segment an orange

This technique is the quickest, easiest way to segment an orange, leaving the flesh pith-free.

1 With a sharp knife, slice away the top and bottom of the orange, then work around the fruit, slicing away the skin and pith.

2 Slice between each segment, leaving the thin layer of membrane behind until you have cut out all the segments.

Tangerine A classic small-seeded citrus with a good fragrance, sweet or sharp flavor, and a pebbly skin.

The Jaffa is a good winter orange with bright orange-colored flesh.

Jaffa The nearly seedless Jaffa has pale, thick skin that is easily removed. The flesh is sweet, crisp, and juicy with an intense orange flavor. It is excellent to eat and to use for candied peel dipped in chocolate.

Bitter orange Unlike sweet oranges, bitter varieties such as the Seville are unpleasant to eat raw. However, they are the classic marmalade orange because of their acidity, thick peel, and numerous seeds that help the preserve to set. The Seville has a very short, early season.

Their juice and zest can also be used to make tangy sauces for rich meats, game, and duck.

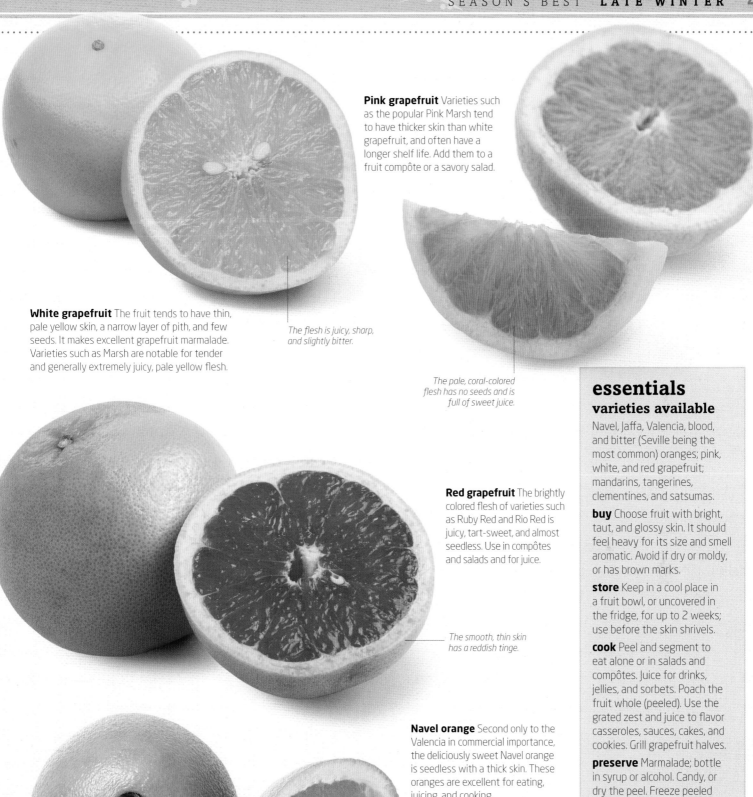

Pink grapefruit Varieties such as the popular Pink Marsh tend to have thicker skin than white grapefruit, and often have a longer shelf life. Add them to a fruit compôte or a savory salad.

The flesh is juicy, sharp, and slightly bitter.

White grapefruit The fruit tends to have thin, pale yellow skin, a narrow layer of pith, and few seeds. It makes excellent grapefruit marmalade. Varieties such as Marsh are notable for tender and generally extremely juicy, pale yellow flesh.

The pale, coral-colored flesh has no seeds and is full of sweet juice.

Red grapefruit The brightly colored flesh of varieties such as Ruby Red and Rio Red is juicy, tart-sweet, and almost seedless. Use in compôtes and salads and for juice.

The smooth, thin skin has a reddish tinge.

Navel orange Second only to the Valencia in commercial importance, the deliciously sweet Navel orange is seedless with a thick skin. These oranges are excellent for eating, juicing, and cooking.

essentials
varieties available

Navel, Jaffa, Valencia, blood, and bitter (Seville being the most common) oranges; pink, white, and red grapefruit; mandarins, tangerines, clementines, and satsumas.

buy Choose fruit with bright, taut, and glossy skin. It should feel heavy for its size and smell aromatic. Avoid if dry or moldy, or has brown marks.

store Keep in a cool place in a fruit bowl, or uncovered in the fridge, for up to 2 weeks; use before the skin shrivels.

cook Peel and segment to eat alone or in salads and compôtes. Juice for drinks, jellies, and sorbets. Poach the fruit whole (peeled). Use the grated zest and juice to flavor casseroles, sauces, cakes, and cookies. Grill grapefruit halves.

preserve Marmalade; bottle in syrup or alcohol. Candy, or dry the peel. Freeze peeled segments and slices, or whole.

recipe ideas

Beef tagine with orange and bay leaves p454

Seville marmalade p484

Tangerine macarons p474

chocolate orange pound cake

Candied orange peel adds great flavor to this loaf cake.

 2 HRS PLUS CANDYING PEEL　　 50-60 MINS

SPECIAL EQUIPMENT ▪ 2lb (900g) loaf pan ▪ electric hand mixer

SERVES 6-8

2 oranges, peel removed and juice of 1 orange

1 cup all-purpose flour

3 tbsp cocoa powder

1 tsp baking powder

salt

12 tbsp unsalted butter

¾ cup granulated sugar

3 large eggs

½ cup confectioners' sugar

1 Candy the peel as in the recipe on p484. Allow 24 hours or more for drying. Reserve several pieces for decoration and finely chop the rest.

2 Preheat the oven to 350°F (180°C). Butter, line, and flour the loaf pan. Sift the flour into a bowl with the cocoa powder, baking powder, and a pinch of salt. In another bowl, cream the butter and sugar with an electric hand mixer until light and fluffy. Add the eggs, one by one, beating thoroughly after each addition. Stir in the chopped candied orange peel.

3 Lightly stir in the flour and cocoa mixture. Transfer the mixture to the prepared loaf pan. Tap the pan on a work surface to level the surface, and bake for 50–60 minutes, until it shrinks slightly from the sides of the pan and a skewer inserted in the center comes out clean.

4 Run a knife around the sides of the pan to loosen the cake, invert the pan, and transfer the cake to a wire rack. Keep a baking sheet below the rack to catch any drips from the icing later. Remove the parchment paper. Leave the cake to cool completely.

5 Sift the confectioners' sugar into a small bowl and slowly stir in enough of the orange juice to make a soft paste. Place the bowl in a saucepan of hot (not simmering) water and heat until the icing is warm and pours easily from the spoon. Drizzle the icing over the cake. Finely slice the reserved candied peel and use to top the cake. Let stand for about 1 hour, until the icing has set. Serve in slices.

chocolate and pear tartlets

For the best result, ensure your pears are fully ripe and juicy.

 30-35 MINS　　 25-30 MINS

SPECIAL EQUIPMENT ▪ 8 x 4in (10cm) round fluted tartlet pans

MAKES 8

melted butter, for greasing

12oz (350g) store-bought pie dough

5½oz (150g) semi-sweet chocolate, finely chopped

1 large egg

½ cup half-and-half

2 large ripe pears

1-2 tbsp granulated sugar, to sprinkle

1 Brush the insides of the tartlet pans with melted butter. Group 4 of the tartlet pans together with their edges nearly touching. Sprinkle a work surface lightly with flour. Divide the dough in half and roll 1 piece out to ¹⁄₈in (3mm) thick. Roll the pastry loosely round the rolling pin and drape it over the 4 pans to cover them.

2 Tear off a small piece of dough from the edge, form it into a ball, dip it in flour, and use it to push the dough into the pans. Roll the rolling pin over the tops of the pans to cut off excess dough. Roll up the trimmings with the other piece of pastry and repeat with the remaining pans.

3 Preheat the oven to 400°F (200°C). Heat a baking sheet on a shelf near the bottom of the oven. Sprinkle the chocolate into each tartlet shell.

4 To make the custard, whisk the egg and cream until thoroughly mixed. For an extra-smooth custard, run the mixture through a sieve. Spoon 2–3 tbsp of the custard over the chocolate in each tartlet shell.

5 Peel the pears, cut them in half, and remove the cores. Cut each pear half into very thin slices widthwise. Arrange the slices on the custard so they overlap. Press them down very lightly into the custard, so it will bake up around the fruit, then sprinkle each tartlet evenly with the sugar.

6 Place the tartlet pans on the heated baking sheet. Bake for 10 minutes, then reduce the heat to 350°F (180°C) and continue baking for 15–20 minutes until the crust is golden and the custard has set.

7 Leave the tartlets to cool slightly. Once cool enough to handle, carefully unmold them and place the tartlets on individual plates to serve.

cinnamon apple cake

This recipe is rather like making a sweet toad-in-the-hole. It can be served warm as a dessert with custard or cream, or left to cool and sliced to serve with coffee.

 30 MINS 25-30 MINS

SPECIAL EQUIPMENT ▪ electric hand mixer ▪ 9½in (24cm) large square baking pan

SERVES 8-12

3-4 apples (depending on size)

1 tbsp lemon juice

3 large eggs

1 cup, plus 2 tbsp granulated sugar

8 tbsp butter, diced

6 tbsp milk

¼ cup half-and-half

1½ cups all-purpose flour

1 tbsp baking powder

2 tsp ground cinnamon

1 Preheat the oven to 400°F (200°C). Butter a large baking pan, about 9½in (24cm) square, and dust with flour.

2 Peel, core, quarter, and slice the apples, and put in a bowl of water with lemon juice to prevent browning.

3 Whisk the eggs and 1 cup of the sugar with an electric hand mixer until thick and pale, and leaves a trail when the beaters are lifted out of the mixture.

4 Put the butter, milk, and half-and-half in a pan and heat gently until the butter melts, then bring to a boil. Remove the pan from the heat and allow to cool briefly, then stir into the egg mixture. Sift the flour and baking powder over the surface and stir in with a rubber spatula. Pour into the prepared pan.

5 Drain the apples and arrange them attractively over the batter. Mix the remaining sugar with the cinnamon, and sprinkle over. Bake for 25–30 minutes until golden and cooked through. Let cool in the pan, then cut into squares.

spiced carrot and orange cake

Grated carrots really help keep this cake moist and add flavor, too. But it's the apple pie spice that makes this cake just a little bit different from standard carrot cake recipes.

 20 MINS 30 MINS ❄ FREEZABLE

SPECIAL EQUIPMENT ▪ 8in (20cm) square cake pan ▪ electric hand mixer

MAKES 16

1½ cups self-rising flour

1 tsp ground cinnamon

1 tsp apple pie spice

½ tsp baking soda

½ cup brown sugar

⅔ cup sunflower oil or light olive oil

2 large eggs

¼ cup corn syrup

4½oz (125g) carrots, coarsely grated

zest of 1 orange

For the icing

⅔ cup confectioners' sugar

3½oz (100g) cream cheese, at room temperature

1-2 tbsp orange juice

zest of 1 orange, plus extra to decorate (optional)

1 Preheat the oven to 350°F (180°C). Line the base and sides of a cake pan with parchment paper. In a large bowl, mix together the flour, spices, baking soda, and sugar. In another bowl, mix the oil, eggs, and syrup together, then combine with the dry ingredients. Stir in the carrots and orange zest, transfer to the pan, and level the top. Bake for 30 minutes, or until firm to the touch. Let cool in the pan for 5 minutes, then cool completely on a wire rack.

2 For the icing, sift the confectioners' sugar into a bowl, add the cream cheese, orange juice, and orange zest, and beat with an electric hand mixer until the mixture becomes thick. When the cake is cool, spread the icing over the top. Decorate with extra orange zest, if using, and cut into 16 squares, to serve.

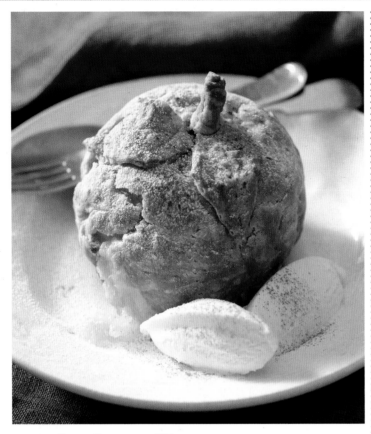

apple dumplings

Change the cinnamon in these apple dumplings for grated nutmeg or apple pie spice if you like, and use orange zest instead of lemon for a slightly sweeter finish.

 20 MINS   30–40 MINS

SERVES 4

2 cups self-rising flour, sifted

8 tbsp white vegetable fat

1 tsp ground cinnamon, plus extra to serve

grated zest of 1 lemon

4 apples, peeled and cored

1 tbsp brown sugar

2oz (60g) golden raisins

confectioners' sugar, to serve

1 Preheat the oven to 350°F (180°C) and lightly grease a baking sheet. To make the dough, put the flour, fat, cinnamon, and lemon zest into a bowl. Slowly trickle in about ½ cup cold water and mix together until it forms a dough.

2 Roll out the dough on a floured work surface and cut out 4 circles, large enough to cover each apple. Sit an apple on each round, sprinkle the brown sugar into the holes where the apples were cored, and add the golden raisins to each. Brush the edges of the pastry with water and bring them together at the top, pinching the dough firmly to secure it in place.

3 Turn the apples over so their sealed side is face down. If you have any dough left over, you could fashion leaves and stalks for the dumplings. Sit the dumplings on the baking sheet and cook in the oven for 30–40 minutes until golden. Sprinkle the dumplings with confectioners' sugar and ground cinnamon and serve with cream, custard, or ice cream.

variation

pear and walnut dumplings
Prepare in the same way, but use 4 slightly unripe pears instead of apples. Peel and cut out a ¾in deep hole in the core ends. Mix scant 1oz (25g) finely chopped walnuts with 1 tbsp corn syrup and use to stuff the pears, then wrap in pastry and bake.

crêpes with caramelized apples and chocolate

These thin French pancakes are surprisingly easy to make.

 15 MINS   20 MINS

SPECIAL EQUIPMENT ▪ electric hand mixer

SERVES 4–6

½ cup all-purpose flour

salt

1 large egg, lightly beaten

⅔ cup milk

½ cup heavy cream

pat of butter

2–3 tbsp granulated sugar, depending on the sweetness of the apples

4 pink-skinned apples, sliced

vegetable oil

4½oz (125g) dark chocolate, grated

1 Sift the flour into a mixing bowl with a little salt and make a well in the center. Put the egg and a little of the milk in the well. Using a wooden spoon, gradually stir the egg mixture, slowly incorporating the flour and the rest of the milk. Then whisk the mixture with a balloon whisk to remove any lumps. Chill in the fridge for 15 minutes, if you have time.

2 Put the cream in a bowl and whisk with an electric hand mixer until lightly whipped. Put the butter and sugar in a frying pan over low heat and stir until the sugar has dissolved. Add the apples and toss well. Cook for 5–10 minutes, or until caramelized, then set aside and keep warm.

3 In a small, flat frying pan or crêpe pan, heat a drizzle of oil over high heat, swirling it around the pan, then tipping it out. Stir the batter, then spoon 2 tbsp of it into the pan, swirling it around so it reaches the edges. Cook for a couple of minutes, then pull up the edges with a palette knife. Turn the crêpe over and cook the other side for 1 minute. Slide it out onto a warmed plate and repeat until all the batter is cooked.

4 To serve, pile some of the apple mixture and a dollop of cream onto each crêpe, fold, and top with plenty of dark chocolate shavings.

apple streusel cake

A delicious apple cake with a crunchy cinnamon topping.

 20 MINS   1 HR 15 MINS

SPECIAL EQUIPMENT ▪ 8in (20cm) springform cake pan
▪ electric hand mixer

SERVES 8

1 cup all-purpose flour

8 tbsp butter, softened

½ cup granulated sugar

1 tsp ground cinnamon

2 large eggs, lightly beaten

½ tsp vanilla extract

1 tart apple, peeled, cored, and cut into chunks

1¾oz (50g) golden raisins

For the streusel topping

5 tbsp butter, diced

1 cup all-purpose flour

¼ cup ground almonds

1 tsp ground cinnamon

¼ cup granulated or light brown sugar

1 Preheat the oven to 350°F (180°C). Lightly grease and line the base of the cake pan with parchment paper. Sift the flour into a bowl, add the butter, sugar, cinnamon, eggs, and vanilla, and mix with an electric hand mixer until pale and creamy. Spoon into the pan, level the top, and scatter with the apple and raisins.

2 For the topping, rub the diced butter and flour in a bowl with your fingertips to resemble bread crumbs. Add the almonds, cinnamon, and sugar. Scatter on top of the cake and level it, pressing down slightly. Bake for 1¼ hours, or until a skewer inserted into the cake comes out clean (it may be damp from the fruit). Let cool in the pan for 20 minutes. Serve warm, or cool completely.

banana, date, and walnut loaf

Rich dates lend extra decadence to the banana loaf—the medjool variety are truly flavorful. For added sweetness, use really ripe bananas with a brown speckled skin.

 20 MINS   **1 HR 15 MINS**   **FREEZABLE**

SPECIAL EQUIPMENT ▪ 5 x 9in (12 x 23cm) loaf pan ▪ electric hand mixer

SERVES 8-10

7 tbsp butter, softened

½ cup granulated sugar

2 large eggs

1⅓ cups self-rising flour, sifted

2 bananas, about 10oz (300g) in total, unpeeled

3½oz (100g) pitted dates (medjool are best), chopped

1¾oz (50g) walnuts, coarsely chopped

1 tsp baking powder

1 Preheat the oven to 350°F (180°C). Line the loaf pan with parchment paper. Put the butter and sugar in a mixing bowl and beat with an electric hand mixer until pale, light, and fluffy. Add the eggs one at a time, beating well as you do so, and add 1 tbsp of the flour after each one to stop the mixture from curdling.

2 Peel and mash the bananas in a small bowl with a fork, then stir into the loaf mixture along with the chopped dates and walnuts. Stir in the remaining flour and the baking powder, then spoon the mixture into the pan. Smooth the top, pressing well into the corners. Bake in the oven for 1–1¼ hours, or until risen and firm to the touch. If the top of the cake starts to brown too much before it is fully cooked, cover with foil. Let cool in the pan, then cut into slices.

toffee apple cake

Caramelizing the apples before baking them in the cake gives them a wonderful toffee apple taste.

 30 MINS   **50-55 MINS** ❄ **FREEZABLE**

SPECIAL EQUIPMENT ▪ 9in (23cm) round springform cake pan ▪ electric hand mixer

SERVES 8-10

14 tbsp unsalted butter, softened, plus extra for greasing

¼ cup granulated sugar

9oz (250g) apples, peeled, cored, and diced

¾ cup light brown sugar

3 large eggs

1 cup self-rising flour

1 heaping tsp baking powder

whipped cream or confectioners' sugar, to serve (optional)

1 Preheat the oven to 350°F (180°C). Grease the pan and line the base with parchment paper. Put 4 tbsp of the butter and the granulated sugar in a large frying pan and heat gently until melted and golden brown. Add the diced apple and cook gently for 7–8 minutes until it starts to soften and caramelize.

2 Put the rest of the butter and the brown sugar in a bowl and beat with an electric hand mixer until pale and creamy. Add the eggs one at a time, beating well after each addition. Sift the flour and baking powder together and gently fold into the mixture.

3 Remove the apples with a slotted spoon, reserving the pan with the juices. Scatter the apples over the base of the pan. Spoon the batter on top, place the pan on a baking sheet, and bake in the center of the oven for 40–45 minutes. Let cool for a few minutes, then turn out onto a wire rack.

4 Put the pan with the juices back over low heat, and heat gently. Put the cake on a plate, make holes in it with a fine skewer or a wooden cocktail stick, and pour over the apple syrup, letting it soak in. Serve warm with whipped cream, or cooled and dusted with confectioners' sugar, if using.

rosemary jelly

This aromatic, robust rosemary jelly is fantastic with lamb.

 10 MINS PLUS STRAINING   1 HR 20 MINS – 1 HR 50 MINS

SPECIAL EQUIPMENT ▪ preserving pan ▪ jelly bag or muslin
▪ sugar thermometer

MAKES APPROX 4½lb (2kg)

large handful of rosemary sprigs

2lb (900g) apples, coarsely chopped
    (reserve the cores and seeds)

approx 4 cups granulated sugar

juice of 1 lemon

1 Preheat the oven to 300°F (150°C).
Strip off the rosemary leaves (reserve
the stalks), scatter onto a baking
sheet, and bake in the oven for
30–40 minutes to dry out.

2 Put the apples, cores, and seeds in
a preserving pan or heavy-bottomed
saucepan. Pour in 4 cups water and
add the rosemary stalks. Simmer for
30–40 minutes until the apples are
mushy. Mash with a potato masher or
fork, spoon the pulp into a jelly bag
set or muslin-lined sieve over a large
bowl, and let strain overnight.
Measure the juice and calculate the
sugar: for every 2 cups juice use
2 cups sugar.

3 Put the juice, sugar, lemon juice,
and dried leaves back in the pan and
cook over medium heat, stirring until
the sugar has dissolved. Bring to a
boil and cook at a rolling boil for 20
minutes, or until the jelly reaches the
setting point. Remove the pan from
the heat to test for a set with a sugar
thermometer, or wrinkle test (chill
a plate in the fridge before cooking).
If you use a thermometer, the
temperature must reach 220°F
(105°C); the mixture will also thicken
around the sides of the pan, boil
sluggishly, and the bubbles "plop"
rather than froth. Or put 1 tsp jelly on
the chilled plate, allow to cool for a
moment, then push it with a finger. If
it leaves a trail and wrinkles slightly, it
is set. Let stand for 10 minutes.

4 Ladle into warm sterilized jars,
cover with wax paper discs, seal, and
label. Store in a cool, dark place and
refrigerate after opening.

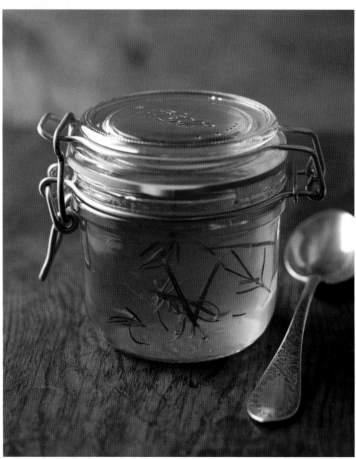

red onion marmalade

This delicious marmalade made with sweet, sticky onions
is perfect served with cold meats and cheese.

 20 MINS PLUS MATURING   1 HR 10 MINS

SPECIAL EQUIPMENT ▪ preserving pan

MAKES APPROX 1½lb (675g)

2 tbsp extra virgin olive oil

2¼lb (1kg) red onions (approx 6),
    peeled, halved, and sliced

sea salt and freshly ground
    black pepper

⅔ cup red wine

3 tbsp balsamic vinegar

3 tbsp white wine vinegar

6 tbsp light brown sugar

1 Heat the oil in a preserving pan or
a large heavy-bottomed stainless
steel saucepan. Add the onions, a little
sea salt, and some pepper. Cook over
low to medium heat for about 30
minutes until the onions soften and
turn translucent, stirring occasionally;
slow cooking is essential at this point.

2 Increase the heat a little, add
the wine and vinegars, and stir to
combine. Bring to a boil, then reduce
the heat, stir in the sugar, and cook
over low heat, stirring occasionally,
for another 30–40 minutes until most
of the liquid has evaporated.

3 Remove the pan from the heat.
Taste and adjust the seasoning as
necessary, although the flavors will
mature with time. Spoon into warm
sterilized jars with non-metallic or
vinegar-proof lids, making sure there
are no air gaps. Cover with wax paper
discs, seal, and label. Store in a cool,
dark place for at least 1 month to
allow the flavors to develop.
Refrigerate after opening.

three-fruit marmalade

Combining three fruits results in a lovely balance of flavors,
good color, and a good set.

 25 MINS   1 HR 50 MINS   ❄ FREEZABLE

SPECIAL EQUIPMENT ▪ preserving pan ▪ food processor ▪ muslin
▪ sugar thermometer

MAKES APPROX 5lb (2.25kg)

1 grapefruit, washed

1 orange, washed

2 lemons, washed

6 cups granulated sugar

1 Halve the fruit, squeeze to extract
the juice, and strain the juice into a
preserving pan or a large heavy-
bottomed saucepan, reserving the
seeds. Scrape any soft flesh from the
citrus shells and add to the pan. Scoop
out the membranes and white pith
from the shells and gather with the
seeds in the muslin. Pull up the ends
to make a bag and tie it with string.

2 Thinly shred the fruit peel and
cut into short lengths, or finely chop
in a food processor. Add to the pan
with 6 cups water and the muslin
bag. Bring to a boil, reduce the heat,
and simmer for 1½ hours, or until the
peel is really soft and the liquid has
reduced by half.

3 Squeeze the bag against the side
of the pan to extract the liquid, then
discard. Add the sugar and stir until
dissolved. Bring to a rapid boil and
cook for 15 minutes, or until the
setting point is reached. Remove the
pan from the heat to test for a set
with a sugar thermometer, or using
a wrinkle test (chill a plate in the
fridge before cooking). If you use a
thermometer, the temperature must
reach 220°F (105°C); the mixture will
also thicken around the sides of the
pan, boil sluggishly, and the bubbles
"plop" rather than froth. Or put 1 tsp
marmalade on the chilled plate, allow
to cool for a moment, then push it
with a finger. If it leaves a trail and
wrinkles slightly, it is set.

5 Skim off any foam. Let stand for
10 minutes, then stir well and ladle
into warm sterilized jars, cover with
wax paper discs, seal, and label. Store
in a cool, dark place and refrigerate
after opening.

chile jelly

This red-flecked, jewel-like jelly can be served with almost any savory dish from cheese to lamb to give it a fiery kick. Use sour apples (which have the most pectin) and add 1–2 tsp chile flakes depending on how hot you like it.

 30 MINS PLUS STRAINING   **50-60 MINS**

SPECIAL EQUIPMENT ▪ jelly bag or muslin ▪ preserving pan ▪ sugar thermometer

MAKES APPROX 1LB (450g)

1½lb (675g) apples, skin on, chopped (reserve the cores and seeds)

3 cups granulated sugar

juice of 1 lemon

1–2 tsp chile flakes

1 Put the apples, cores, and seeds in a preserving pan or large heavy-bottomed saucepan. Pour in 6 cups cold water, bring to a boil, and simmer for 30–40 minutes, or until the apples are mushy. Mash with a potato masher or a fork, spoon the pulp into a jelly bag or muslin-lined sieve set over a large bowl, and let strain overnight. Don't be tempted to squeeze the pulp mixture if you want a crystal-clear jelly.

2 Measure the juice and calculate the sugar: for every 2 cups juice use 2 cups sugar. Pour the juice into the pan, bring to a boil, then add the sugar and lemon juice. Stir until the sugar has dissolved, then bring to a rolling boil and cook for 20–30 minutes, or until the jelly reaches the setting point. Remove the pan from the heat to test for a set with a sugar thermometer, or using a wrinkle test (chill a plate in the fridge before cooking). If you use a thermometer, the temperature must reach 220°F (105°C); the mixture will also thicken around the sides of the pan, boil sluggishly, and the bubbles "plop" rather than froth. Or put 1 tsp jelly on the chilled plate, allow to cool for a moment, then push it with a finger. If it leaves a trail and wrinkles slightly, it is set. Let stand for 10 minutes.

4 Skim off any surface foam, then stir in the chile flakes. Ladle into warm sterilized jars, cover with discs of wax paper, seal, and label. Store in a cool, dark place and keep refrigerated after opening.

candied citrus peel

Homemade candied peel has much more flavor than bought varieties, is preservative-free, and is a delicious addition to cakes or desserts, or as a treat with coffee.

 15 MINS PLUS DRYING **1 HR 50 MINS**

MAKES APPROX 8OZ (225g)

1 large or 2 small grapefruit, plus 1 pink grapefruit or 1 pomelo (or a mixture of all three), washed

granulated sugar—for quantity, see method

granulated sugar, for coating

1 Score the surface of each piece of fruit into quarters with a sharp knife, then carefully remove the peel. Weigh the pieces of peel all together. Put the peel in a heavy-bottomed saucepan, cover with water, and cook gently for up to 1 hour until soft, changing the water 2 or 3 times.

2 Drain the peel and scrape out any ragged or inner pulp from the inside of the shells. Either leave the peel in quarters, or cut into thick strips.

3 Use the same weight of sugar to peel. Put the prepared peel and sugar into a snug-fitting pan, barely cover with water, set over low heat, and stir to dissolve the sugar. Bring to a boil and simmer very gently for 45 minutes, or until the peel is translucent and has absorbed nearly all the syrup.

4 Remove the peel from the pan and spread it out on baking sheets lined with parchment paper. Leave at room temperature for 24 hours or longer to dry out.

5 Dip each piece of dried peel in a bowl of granulated sugar until it is thoroughly coated. Place the sugared candied peel in a sterilized jar and seal. Store in a cool, dry place.

rhubarb, pear, and ginger jam

A great combination of flavors and textures makes this jam a little bit more special than most.

 15–20 MINS **25–30 MINS**

SPECIAL EQUIPMENT ▪ preserving pan ▪ sugar thermometer

MAKES APPROX 2¼lb (1kg)

1½lb (675g) rhubarb, rinsed and chopped into 1in (2.5cm) pieces

2 pears, peeled, cored, and chopped

3½ cups granulated sugar

juice of 1 lemon

juice of ½ orange

2 balls of stem ginger or 2 pieces crystallized ginger, finely chopped

1 Put the rhubarb, pears, and sugar in a preserving pan or a large heavy-bottomed saucepan. Stir, then add the lemon juice, orange juice, and ginger. Cook over low heat, stirring until all the sugar has dissolved.

2 Increase the heat, bring to a boil, and cook at a rolling boil for 15–20 minutes, or until the mixture reaches the setting point. Remove the pan from the heat to test for a set with a sugar thermometer, or using a wrinkle test (chill a plate in the fridge before cooking). If you use a thermometer, the temperature must reach 220°F (105°C); the mixture will also thicken around the sides of the pan, boil sluggishly, and the bubbles "plop" rather than froth. Or put 1 tsp jam on the chilled plate, allow to cool for a moment, then push it with a finger. If it leaves a trail and wrinkles slightly, it is set.

4 Ladle into warm sterilized jars, cover with discs of wax paper, seal, and label. Store in a cool, dark place, and refrigerate after opening.

seville marmalade

This makes an authentic, bitter-sweet marmalade.

 45 MINS ▪ **1 HR 20 MINS – 1 HR 30 MINS**

SPECIAL EQUIPMENT ▪ muslin ▪ preserving pan ▪ sugar thermometer

MAKES APPROX 2¼lb (1kg)

2¼lb (1kg) Seville oranges, scrubbed in hot water, with stem ends removed

1 large lemon, washed

5 cups granulated sugar

1 Cut the fruit in half, squeeze the juice into a bowl, and reserve in the fridge. Gather the pith and seeds in muslin, pull up the ends to make a bag, and tie it with string.

2 Put the citrus shells, bag of pith and seeds, and 6 cups water in a preserving pan or large heavy-bottomed saucepan. Bring to a boil, half-cover, and simmer for 1 hour, or until the shells are soft (not mushy). Pour into a large sieve or colander over a bowl and press lightly to extract the liquor. Scoop excess mush from inside the cooked shells with a spoon and discard. Slice the peel into thick or thin strands, or coarse or fine chunks.

3 Put the liquor, peel, and fruit juice back in the pan. Add the sugar, heat gently, stir until the sugar dissolves, and boil rapidly for 5–15 minutes, or until the setting point is reached. Remove the pan from the heat to test for a set with a sugar thermometer, or wrinkle test (chill a plate in the fridge before cooking). If you use a thermometer, the temperature must reach 220°F (105°C); the mixture will also thicken around the sides of the pan, boil sluggishly, and the bubbles "plop" rather than froth. Or put 1 tsp marmalade on the chilled plate, allow to cool for a moment, then push it with a finger. If it leaves a trail and wrinkles slightly, it is set. Let settle for a few minutes.

4 Skim off any foam, then stir and ladle into warm sterilized jars. Cover with wax paper discs, seal, and label. Store in a cool, dark place and refrigerate after opening.

clementines in caramel syrup

You can also use other soft citrus fruits for this recipe.

 10 MINS   15 MINS PLUS HEAT-PROCESSING

SPECIAL EQUIPMENT ▪ screw-band jar or kilner jar

MAKES 1 QUART (1 LITER)

⅔ cup granulated sugar

10 small clementines, peeled, with the white pith scraped off with a knife

1 Put the sugar and ½ cup cold water in a medium saucepan. Stir well, then heat without stirring or boiling until the sugar has dissolved. Bring to a rapid boil and cook for 5–10 minutes, or until a rich golden brown. Pour in ¾ cup hot water, stir until the caramel dissolves, then bring the syrup back to a boil.

2 Preheat the oven to 300°F (150°C). Stand a warm sterilized jar on a roasting pan lined with newspaper. Pack the fruit tightly into the jar without squashing it, leaving ½in (1cm) of space at the top. Fill to the brim with the hot syrup. Tap the jar down lightly on the work surface and swivel back and forth to remove any air pockets. Add extra syrup if needed so the fruit is completely covered. Fit the rubber band or metal lid, seal, and clamp on the lid. If using screw-band jars, loosen by a quarter of a turn.

3 Put the jars in the oven for 30–40 minutes to heat process (remove remaining air), then remove from the oven and tighten the clip or lid (or screw-on plastic screw-band lid) immediately. Leave for 24 hours, then unscrew or unclip and test the lid is firmly sealed before refastening and storing. (If using a kilner jar with metal lids, you will know if you have a seal as the lid becomes slightly concave and is firm with no "give" once pressed.) Store in a cool, dark place and refrigerate after opening.

clementine and whiskey marmalade

The flavor of whiskey in this marmalade greatly enhances those of the citrus fruits. Clementines aren't too high in pectin or acid, so lemon juice helps the set.

 10 MINS   55 MINS - 1 HR 5 MINS

SPECIAL EQUIPMENT ▪ food processor ▪ preserving pan ▪ sugar thermometer

MAKES APPROX 2¼lb (1kg)

2lb (900g) clementines, scrubbed, rinsed, and halved, with seeds removed

juice of 2 large lemons

4 cups granulated sugar

1-2 tbsp whiskey, or use brandy

1 Either put the clementines in a food processor and pulse until shredded but not turned to mush, or squeeze the juice by hand and finely shred the skins with a sharp knife. Put the chopped fruit in a preserving pan or za large heavy-bottomed saucepan. Pour in 3 cups water and bring to a boil, then simmer for 30 minutes or longer, until the rind has softened.

2 Add the lemon juice and sugar and cook over low heat, stirring until the sugar has dissolved. Bring to a boil, then keep at a rolling boil for 20–30 minutes, or until the setting point is reached. Remove the pan from the heat to test for a set with a sugar thermometer, or a wrinkle test (chill a plate in the fridge before cooking). If you use a thermometer, the temperature must reach 220°F (105°C); the mixture will also thicken around the sides of the pan, boil sluggishly, and the bubbles "plop" rather than froth. Or put 1 tsp marmalade on the chilled plate, allow to cool for a moment, then push it with a finger. If it leaves a trail and wrinkles slightly, it is set. Let settle for a few minutes.

4 Stir in the whiskey, then ladle into warm sterilized jars. Cover with wax paper discs, seal, and label. Store in a cool, dark place and refrigerate after opening.

index

acknowledgments

Dorling Kindersley would like to thank:

Ian O'Leary for new photography; Jane Bamforth, Claire Tennant-Scull, and Diana Vowles for additional copy editing; Jane Bamforth, Jan Stevens, Clare Greenstreet, and Ann Reynolds for recipe testing; Dorothy Kikon, Martha Burley, and Elizabeth Yeates for proofreading; Michele Clarke for the index; Steve Crozier and Tom Morse for image retouching; David Roberts and Rob Laidler for the recipe database; Allison Singer, Alison Shaw and Elizabeth Yeates for editorial assistance; Mandy Earey and Anne Fisher for design assistance; and Alicia Ingty and Neha Ahuja for their valuable input.